New Voices on Adam Smith

There is a general resurgence of interest in the writings and significance of Adam Smith. This volume includes fourteen original, commissioned and refereed papers by already established young scholars who have recently finished their PhD dissertations on Adam Smith or a closely related topic. The international and multidisciplinary character of all these contributions reflects the intellectual fertility of Smith's works. Issues ranging from analysis of Smith's sources, economics, philosophy, ethics, aesthetics, and politics to penetrating treatment of Smith's relevance in recent discussions of gender, cultural diversity, or environmental protection make this volume a must for all those interested in his legacy. The book is a useful first introduction to the state of the art in scholarship on Adam Smith as well as a provocative reorientation for those familiar with long-standing debates on Smith's continuing importance.

Leonidas Montes is Associate Professor of Economics at Universidad Adolfo Ibañez, Santiago, Chile. **Eric Schliesser** is Assistant Professor in the Department of Philosophy, Syracuse University, Syracuse, NY, Research Fellow, Netherlands Organization for Scientific Research, Department of Philosophy, Leiden University and Research Associate, Amsterdam Research Group in History and Methodology of Economics, University of Amsterdam.

Routledge studies in the history of economics

1 **Economics as Literature**
Willie Henderson

2 **Socialism and Marginalism in Economics 1870–1930**
Edited by Ian Steedman

3 **Hayek's Political Economy**
The socio-economics of order
Steve Fleetwood

4 **On the Origins of Classical Economics**
Distribution and value from William Petty to Adam Smith
Tony Aspromourgos

5 **The Economics of Joan Robinson**
Edited by Maria Cristina Marcuzzo, Luigi Pasinetti and Alesandro Roncaglia

6 **The Evolutionist Economics of Léon Walras**
Albert Jolink

7 **Keynes and the 'Classics'**
A study in language, epistemology and mistaken identities
Michel Verdon

8 **The History of Game Theory I**
From the beginnings to 1945
Robert W. Dimand and Mary Ann Dimand

9 **The Economics of W. S. Jevons**
Sandra Peart

10 **Gandhi's Economic Thought**
Ajit K. Dasgupta

11 **Equilibrium and Economic Theory**
Edited by Giovanni Caravale

12 **Austrian Economics in Debate**
Edited by Willem Keizer, Bert Tieben and Rudy van Zijp

13 **Ancient Economic Thought**
Edited by B. B. Price

14 **The Political economy of Social Credit and Guild Socialism**
Frances Hutchinson and Brian Burkitt

15 **Economic Careers**
Economics and economists in Britain 1930–1970
Keith Tribe

16 **Understanding 'Classical' Economics**
Studies in the long-period theory
Heinz Kurz and Neri Salvadori

17 **History of Environmental Economic Thought**
E. Kula

18 **Economic Thought in Communist and Post-Communist Europe**
Edited by Hans-Jürgen Wagener

19 **Studies in the History of French Political Economy**
From Bodin to Walras
Edited by Gilbert Faccarello

20 **The Economics of John Rae**
Edited by O. F. Hamouda, C. Lee and D. Mair

21 **Keynes and the Neoclassical Synthesis**
Einsteinian versus Newtonian macroeconomics
Teodoro Dario Togati

22 **Historical Perspectives on Macroeconomics**
Sixty years after the *General Theory*
Edited by Philippe Fontaine and Albert Jolink

23 **The Founding of Institutional Economics**
The leisure class and sovereignty
Edited by Warren J. Samuels

24 **Evolution of Austrian Economics**
From Menger to Lachmann
Sandye Gloria

25 **Marx's Concept of Money: the God of Commodities**
Anitra Nelson

26 **The Economics of James Steuart**
Edited by Ramón Tortajada

27 **The Development of Economics in Europe since 1945**
Edited by A. W. Bob Coats

28 **The Canon in the History of Economics**
Critical essays
Edited by Michalis Psalidopoulos

29 **Money and Growth**
Selected papers of Allyn Abbott Young
Edited by Perry G. Mehling and Roger J. Sandilands

30 **The Social Economics of Jean-Baptiste Say**
Markets and virtue
Evelyn L. Forget

31 **The Foundations of *Laissez-faire***
The economics of Pierre de Boisguilbert
Gilbert Faccarello

32 **John Ruskin's Political Economy**
Willie Henderson

33 **Contributions to the History of Economic Thought**
Essays in honour of R. D. C. Black
Edited by Antoin E. Murphy and Renee Prendergast

34 **Towards an Unknown Marx**
A commentary on the manuscripts of 1861–1863
Enrique Dussel

35 **Economics and Interdisciplinary Exchange**
Edited by Guido Erreygers

36 **Economics as the Art of Thought**
Essays in memory of G. L. S. Shackle
Edited by Stephen F. Frowen and Peter Earl

37 **The Decline of Ricardian Economics**
Politics and economics in post-Ricardian theory
Susan Paskoff

38 **Piero Sraffa**
His life, thought and cultural heritage
Alessandro Roncaglia

39 **Equilibrium and Disequilibrium in Economic Theory**
The Marshall–Walras divide
Michel de Vroey

40 **The German Historical School**
The historical and ethical approach to economics
Edited by Yuichi Shionoya

41 **Reflections on the Classical Canon in Economics**
Essays in honor of Samuel Hollander
Edited by Sandra Peart and Evelyn Forget

42 **Piero Sraffa's Political Economy**
A centenary estimate
Edited by Terenzio Cozzi and Roberto Marchionatti

43 **The Contribution of Joseph Schumpeter to Economics**
Economic development and institutional change
Richard Arena and Cecile Dangel

44 **On the Development of Long-run Neoclassical Theory**
Tom Kompas

45 **F.A. Hayek as a Political Economist**
Economic analysis and values
Edited by Jack Birner, Pierre Garrouste and Thierry Aimar

46 **Pareto, Economics and Society**
The mechanical analogy
Michael McLure

47 **The Cambridge Controversies in Capital Theory**
A study in the logic of theory development
Jack Birner

48 **Economics Broadly Considered**
Essays in honor of Warren J. Samuels
Edited by Steven G. Medema, Jeff Biddle and John B. Davis

49 **Physicians and Political Economy**
Six studies of the work of doctor-economists
Edited by Peter Groenewegen

50 **The Spread of Political Economy and the Professionalisation of Economists**
Economic societies in Europe, America and Japan in the nineteenth century
Massimo Augello and Marco Guidi

51 **Historians of Economics and Economic Thought**
The construction of disciplinary memory
Steven G. Medema and Warren J. Samuels

52 **Competing Economic Theories**
Essays in memory of Giovanni Caravale
Sergio Nisticò and Domenico Tosato

53 **Economic Thought and Policy in Less Developed Europe**
The nineteenth century
Edited by Michalis Psalidopoulos and Maria-Eugenia Almedia Mata

54 **Family Fictions and Family Facts**
Harriet Martineau, Adolphe Quetelet and the population question in England 1798–1859
Brian Cooper

55 **Eighteenth-Century Economics**
Peter Groenewegen

56 **The Rise of Political Economy in the Scottish Enlightenment**
Edited by Tatsuya Sakamoto and Hideo Tanaka

57 **Classics and Moderns in Economics I**
Essays on nineteenth and twentieth century economic thought
Peter Groenewegen

58 **Classics and Moderns in Economics II**
Essays on nineteenth and twentieth century economic thought
Peter Groenewegen

59 **Marshall's Evolutionary Economics**
Tiziano Raffaelli

60 **Money, Time and Rationality in Max Weber**
Austrian connections
Stephen D. Parsons

61 **Classical Macroeconomics**
Some modern variations and distortions
James C. W. Ahiakpor

62 **The Historical School of Economics in England and Japan**
Tamotsu Nishizawa

63 **Classical Economics and Modern Theory**
Studies in long-period analysis
Heinz D. Kurz and Neri Salvadori

64 **A Bibliography of Female Economic Thought to 1940**
Kirsten K. Madden, Janet A. Sietz and Michele Pujol

65 **Economics, Economists and Expectations**
From microfoundations to macroeconomics
Warren Young, Robert Leeson and William Darity Jnr

66 **The Political Economy of Public Finance in Britain 1767–1873**
Takuo Dome

67 **Essays in the History of Economics**
Warren J. Samuels, Willie Henderson, Kirk D. Johnson and Marianne Johnson

68 **History and Political Economy**
Essays in honour of P. D. Groenewegen
Edited by Tony Aspromourgos and John Lodewijks

69 **The Tradition of Free Trade**
Lars Magnusson

70 **Evolution of the Market Process**
Austrian and Swedish economics
Edited by Michel Bellet, Sandye Gloria-Palermo and Abdallah Zouache

71 **Consumption as an Investment**
The fear of goods from Hesiod to Adam Smith
Cosimo Perrotta

72 **Jean-Baptiste Say and the Classical Canon in Economics**
The British connection in French classicism
Samuel Hollander

73 **Knut Wicksell on Poverty**
No place is too exalted
Knut Wicksell

74 **Economists in Cambridge**
A study through their correspondence 1907–1946
Edited by M. C. Marcuzzo and A. Rosselli

75 **The Experiment in the History of Economics**
Edited by Philippe Fontaine and Robert Leonard

76 **At the Origins of Mathematical Economics**
The economics of A. N. Isnard (1748–1803)
Richard van den Berg

77 **Money and Exchange**
Folktales and reality
Sasan Fayazmanesh

78 **Economic Development and Social Change**
Historical roots and modern perspectives
George Stathakis and Gianni Vaggi

79 **Ethical Codes and Income Distribution**
A study of John Bates' Clark and Thorstein Veblen
Guglielmo Forges Davanzati

80 **Evaluating Adam Smith**
Creating *The Wealth of Nations*
Willie Henderson

81 **Civil Happiness**
Economics and human flourishing in historical perspective
Luigino Bruni

82 **New Voices on Adam Smith**
Edited by Leonidas Montes and Eric Schliesser

New Voices on Adam Smith

Edited by Leonidas Montes and Eric Schliesser

With a foreword by Knud Haakonssen

Routledge
Taylor & Francis Group
LONDON AND NEW YORK

First published 2006
by Routledge
2 Park Square, Milton Park, Abingdon, Oxon OX14 4RN

Simultaneously published in the USA and Canada
by Routledge
270 Madison Ave, New York, NY 10016

Routledge is an imprint of the Taylor & Francis Group, an informa business

Typeset in Baskerville by Wearset Ltd, Boldon, Tyne and Wear
Printed and bound in Great Britain by TJ Digital, Padstow, Cornwall

British Library Cataloguing in Publication Data
A catalogue record for this book is available from the British Library

Library of Congress Cataloging in Publication Data
A catalog record for this book has been requested

ISBN10: 0-415-35696-2 (hbk)
ISBN10: 0-203-00295-4 (ebk)

ISBN13: 978-0-415-35696-1 (hbk)
ISBN13: 978-0-203-00295-7 (ebk)

To Warren Samuels, whose invisible hand promotes the best kind of intellectual exchange

Contents

Contributors

Lauren Brubaker obtained his PhD at the Committee on Social Thought, University of Chicago, in 2002. His dissertation is entitled 'Religious Zeal, Political Faction, and the Corruption of Morals: Adam Smith and the Limits of Enlightenment'. Lauren is Tutor at St John's College, Santa Fe. He has published articles in the *Adam Smith Review* and *Eighteenth Century Scotland*, among others, and has contributed articles to several collections.

Chad Flanders obtained his PhD at the Philosophy Department, University of Chicago, in 2004. His PhD dissertation is entitled 'Responsibility and Objectivity'. Chad is studying at Yale Law School. He has published in *Ethics*, has co-edited (with Martha Nussbaum) an issue of *Philosophical Topics* on 'Global Inequalities', and is an editor at the *Yale Journal of Health Policy, Law, and Ethics.*

Fonna Forman-Barzilai obtained her PhD from the Department of Political Science, University of Chicago, in 2001. Her PhD dissertation is entitled 'Adam Smith and the Circles of Sympathy'. Fonna is Assistant Professor in Political Science at the University of California, San Diego. She is completing her book *Adam Smith and the Circles of Sympathy*, has published articles in *Political Theory*, the *Adam Smith Review*, *Critical Review*, and *History of Political Thought*, and is Book Review Editor of the *Adam Smith Review.*

Patrick Frierson obtained his PhD at the Philosophy Department, University of Notre Dame, in 2001. His PhD dissertation is entitled 'Anthropology and Freedom in Kant's Moral Philosophy: Saving Kant from Schleiermacher's Dilemma'. Patrick is Assistant Professor at the Department of Philosophy, Whitman College. He published *Freedom and Anthropology in Kant's Moral Philosophy* in 2003, and has contributed articles to *Kantian Review* and *Journal of the History of Philosophy*, among others.

Ryan Patrick Hanley obtained his PhD at the Committee on Social Thought, University of Chicago, in 2002. His PhD dissertation is entitled 'Magnanimity and Modernity: Self-love in the Scottish

Enlightenment'. Ryan is Assistant Professor of Political Science at Marquette University. He has published articles in *Studies on Voltaire and the Eighteenth Century*, *Studies on Eighteenth Century Culture*, *History of Political Thought*, and *Review of Politics*, among others.

Jimena Hurtado-Prieto obtained her PhD at the Department of Economics, Université Paris X Nanterre, in 2004. Her PhD dissertation is entitled 'La Philosophie économique de Jean-Jacques Rousseau, Adam Smith et Jeremy Bentham à la lumière de Bernard Mandeville'. Jimena is Assistant Professor at the Department of Economics, Universidad de los Andes, Bogotá, Colombia. She has published in the *European Journal of History of Economic Thought*, *Colombian Economic Journal*, and *Cuadernos de Economía.*

Edith Kuiper obtained her PhD in the Department of Economics and Econometrics, Universiteit van Amsterdam, in 2001. Her PhD dissertation is entitled '"The most Valuable of all Capital": A Gender Reading of Economic Texts'. Edith is Researcher in the Department of Economics and Econometrics, Universiteit van Amsterdam. She co-edited *Towards a Feminist Philosophy of Economics*, and has published chapters in several collections.

Robert Edward Mitchell obtained his PhD at the Department of Comparative Literature, University of Washington, in 2001. His PhD dissertation is entitled 'The Commerce of Identity: A Genealogy of "Identification" in the Romantic Era, 1740–1822'. Robert is Assistant Professor at the Department of English, Duke University. He has published in *Coleridge Bulletin* and *Ideas, Aesthetics and Inquiries in the Early Modern Era* and has contributed several chapters to collective volumes.

Leonidas Montes obtained his PhD at the Faculty of Economics and Politics, King's College, University of Cambridge, in 2002. His PhD dissertation is entitled 'Philosophical and Methodological Underpinnings of Adam Smith's Political Economy: A Critical Reconstruction of some Central Components of his Thought'. Leonidas is Associate Professor of Economics at the Universidad Adolfo Ibañez in Santiago, Chile. He published *Adam Smith in Context* in 2004 and has contributed articles to the *Journal of the History of Economic Thought*, *Cambridge Journal of Economics*, *Research in the History of Economic Thought and Methodology* and *Centro de Estudios Públicos*, among others.

Maria Pia Paganelli obtained her PhD at the Department of Economics, George Mason University, in 2002. Her PhD dissertation is entitled 'Topics on Eighteenth Century Money: Robust and Fragile Models of Money and Man'. Maria is Assistant Professor of Economics at Yeshiva University. She has published in *History of Political Economy*, the *Adam Smith Review*, *Annali di Storia Moderna e Contemporánea*, and *Studies on Voltaire and the Eighteenth Century*, among others.

Eric Schliesser obtained his PhD in the Department of Philosophy, University of Chicago, in 2002. His PhD dissertation is entitled 'Indispensable Hume: from Isaac Newton's Natural Philosophy to Adam Smith's "Science of Man"'. Eric is Assistant Professor, Department of Philosophy, Syracuse University, and a postdoctoral researcher funded by the Netherlands Organization for Scientific Research and a research associate, Amsterdam Research Group in History and Methodology of Economics, University of Amsterdam. He has published in the *British Journal for the History of Philosophy*, *Journal of the History of Philosophy*, *Adam Smith Review*, *Research in the History of Economic Thought and Methodology*, *Hume Studies*, and *Philosophy of the Social Sciences*, among others.

Craig Smith obtained his PhD at the Department of Politics, University of Glasgow, in 2003. His PhD dissertation is entitled 'The Idea of Spontaneous Order in Liberal Political Thought'. Craig is British Academy Postdoctoral Fellow at the Department of Politics, University of Glasgow. His book *Adam Smith's Political Philosophy: The Invisible Hand and Spontaneous Order* is in press, and he has published articles in the *Journal of Utopian Studies* and a collective volume on Hayekian Economics.

Estrella Trincado obtained her PhD at the Facultad de Ciencias Económicas y Empresariales, Universidad Complutense de Madrid, in 2003. Her PhD dissertation is entitled 'Crítica a la doctrina de la utilidad y revisión de las teorías de Hume, Smith y Bentham'. Estrella is Lecturer in the Department of Economic History and Institutions, Universidad Complutense de Madrid. She has published in *Storia del Pensiero Económico*, *History of Economic Ideas*, *Télos: Revista Iberoamericana de Estudios Utilitaristas*, and *Informacion Comercial Española*.

Carola von Villiez obtained her PhD at the Department of Philosophy, University of Bremen, in 2001. Her PhD dissertation is entitled 'Grenzen der Rechtfertigung? Internationale Gerechtigkeit durch transnationale Legitimation'. Carola is Wissenschaftliche Assistentin at the Department of Philosophy, University of Bremen. She has contributed chapters to several collections. In 2005 she published her book *Grenzen der Rechtfertigung? Internationale Gerechtigkeit durch transnationale Legitimation*.

Foreword

Knud Haakonssen

Newcomers to the study of Adam Smith can hardly avoid a sense of bewilderment at the sheer variety of angles of approach and topics of discussion offered by commentators. Not only is Smith more than the father of political economy, as scholars never tire of pointing out; he is a great deal more. The present collection of essays by young scholars from several cultural and academic backgrounds is a fine continuation of the sort of wide-ranging scholarship that has been brought to bear on Smith during the past generation. Smith is here related to ancient and early modern moral and social thinkers; he is considered as an aesthetician and a cultural theorist; a set of epistemological concerns are unearthed as inherent in his moral and political thought; Smith is seen as a historian of science with intriguing ideas on scientific methodology; his economic ideas, their critical edge against mercantilist predecessors, and their policy implications are not, it is argued, what orthodox scholarship has claimed and have to be reinterpreted; he may be said to foreshadow Romanticism; not least, he can be made an active participant in contemporary moral debates about issues from Rawls to environmentalism, from virtue ethics to moral luck theories. What is more, even the range and variety of the essays in this volume are far from exhaustive of the themes that have been employed in the reading of Smith, as the editors rightly emphasize.

While this pluralism in both scholarly and more popular interpretation is a relatively recent phenomenon, it presupposes a multiplicity of academic disciplines which can lay 'claim' to Smith. It may be appropriate, therefore, to point out here that Smith himself helped bring about this situation. While the formation of contemporary academic disciplines and sub-disciplines is a complicated and long-drawn-out process, Smith played a distinctive role. The academic landscape in which Smith found himself as a professor was still subject to a structure that derived from scholasticism. The basic academic education consisted in the four parts of philosophy – logic, metaphysics, and moral and natural philosophy (with assorted supporting subjects); on this basis were built the three vocational studies of theology, law, and medicine. Smith was a professor first of logic, then of moral philosophy, and transformed both subjects with considerable disciplinary implications. Before looking at this development, let me remark briefly upon Smith and the other academic disciplines mentioned. Traditional metaphysics is virtually certain to have been entirely ignored by Smith. It is true that the first very brief section of his lectures on moral philosophy was on natural theology, which traditionally had considered the proofs of God's existence and the nature of His attributes. We have no record of these lectures, but everything Smith says about the subject elsewhere concerns religion as a factor in the psychology of moral motivation and as a cultural phenomenon. As for natural philosophy (physical sciences), we know that it greatly interested Smith, and in his wider pedagogical role as mentor and tutor he put great emphasis on the full variety of scientific subjects, as we see for example in his remarkable correspondence with Lord Shelburne about the education of Shelburne's son. Smith had nothing to say about theology and medicine as academic subjects but offered interesting social and economic considerations of the two professions. Finally, the study of law was substantially influenced by Smith's teaching in moral theory, which laid the foundations for a combined historical and systematic approach that was later employed by his most important immediate disciple, John Millar.

Smith's own two subjects were considerably changed by his teaching. While making sure that students had an understanding of the basics of traditional logic, he obviously thought the subject of little importance. Instead he lectured on rhetoric and belles-lettres. Rejecting traditional rhetoric as firmly as he did formal logic (and, in ethics, casuistry), Smith studied stylistics and literature. This was directly instrumental in the formation of English literature as an academic discipline through Hugh Blair, who with full acknowledgment to Smith developed the latter's ideas in the newly created professorship in rhetoric and belles-lettres at Edinburgh. However, Smith's notion of this new subject was more ambitious. He saw the study of language and literature as closely allied with moral theory – and both of them as part of his grand scheme to replace traditional metaphysics of the soul with the empirical study of the social manifestations of the life of the mind. Since we have no access to the minds of other people, all study of humanity must be concerned with the public, interpersonal expressions of mental life. Smith's moral philosophy is, hence, at core a theory of intersubjective communication in which the assumptions about universal features of human nature are minimized as much as possible, so that the particular circumstances in which people find themselves – the situation – carry a major explanatory role. The implication is that the study of moral phenomena in general has to take a cultural, often historical, approach. Thus armed, Smith rejects the moral philosophical tradition's attempts to reduce the moral life to clearly defined categories, especially rules, an endeavor that he saw epitomized in casuistry but which, he thought, had infected moral theory in general. At the same time, he was able to explain why one special part of morals *was* subject to strict rules, namely that part of justice which was concerned with the protection of subjective rights against injury. This was the modern discipline of 'natural jurisprudence', but since the injuries to which people may be subject are historically conditioned, the discipline was even more historical than 'natural'.

While Smith certainly had normative concerns in morals, politics, and law, they have to be understood as dependent upon his overall system. For in Smith's hands moral philosophy is first of all a grand anthropological theory within which language and literature, arts and sciences, politics and law, and, of course, economics are to be studied with the aim of establishing empirically – mainly historically – the balance between nature and culture. Through a unifying vision of the nature of interpersonal communication he helped diversify the study of humanity into several of the academic disciplines we take for granted today. It is only in relatively recent times, however, that this plurality of approaches has benefited the study of the man's own work. For most of the two and a half centuries since he started teaching and publishing our understanding of Smith has been severely hampered by narrow disciplinary boundaries. For the longest time, the subject was in the hands of economics as that discipline was shaped in the nineteenth and twentieth centuries; now normative moral philosophy as conceived by twentieth and twenty-first century readings of Kant and Mill is fast appropriating Smith in its search for historical respectability. Taken together, the essays in the present volume should help to further the diversification that is necessary when dealing with Adam Smith.

Acknowledgments

This volume is more the result of human action than human design. If the latter was simply our job, the former was much more fundamental. Knud Haakonssen, David Levy, Deirdre McCloskey and Sandra Peart are responsible for pushing this idea into action. Without their advice and encouragement this project would not have been possible. Another triggering human action for the development of this collection was a symposium generously organized by Liberty Fund. Some chapters of this collection were presented there, and we are very grateful to Samuel Fleischacker, James Otteson, James Buchanan, Ali Khan and Doug den Uyl for their helpful and illuminating comments at the conference, as well as their support throughout this project. In addition, Jerry Evensky, Clare Palmer, Vivienne Brown, Christopher Berry, Glenn Hueckel, Spencer Pack, Eugene Heath, Geoff Harcourt, Paul Russell, Jeremy Bendik-Keymer, Peter McNamara, and Ralph Lerner provided invaluable advice in helping us shape the volume. Moreover, we are grateful to acknowledge a Fondecyt grant from the Chilean government that allowed us some time together to plan and write our brief introduction. Also related to this activity in the very south of the world, Pelu's understanding and support were crucial for the development of this project.

We are also much indebted to three anonymous referees for their reports on our initial project; to our editor, Rob Langham, who was patient and supportive throughout this process; to institutions that offered employment and research support: Washington University in St Louis, Syracuse University, the University of Amsterdam, and Universidad Adolfo Ibáñez. Finally, we acknowledge the cooperation and enthusiasm of our contributors.

Abbreviations

We used the Liberty Classics editions (Liberty Fund) of Smith's works, which are exact, although less expensive, photographic reproductions of the editions published by Oxford University Press as the *Glasgow Edition of the Works and Correspondence of Adam Smith*, in the following manner:

Corr. *Correspondence of Adam Smith*, edited by E. C. Mossner and I. S. Ross, Oxford: Clarendon Press, 1977.

EPS *Essays on Philosophical Subjects*, edited by W. P. D. Wightman and J. C. Bryce, Oxford: Clarendon Press, 1980.

LJ *Lectures on Jurisprudence*, edited by R. L. Meek, D. D. Raphael, and P. G. Stein, Oxford: Clarendon Press, 1978.

LRBL *Lectures on Rhetoric and Belles Lettres*, edited by J. C. Bryce, Oxford: Clarendon Press, 1983.

TMS *The Theory of Moral Sentiments*, edited by D. D. Raphael and A. L. Macfie, Oxford: Clarendon Press, 1976.

WN *An Inquiry into the Nature and Causes of the Wealth of Nations*, edited by R. H. Campbell and A. S. Skinner, Oxford: Clarendon Press, 1976.

WN will be cited by book, chapter, section and paragraph, followed by page number (e.g. WN I.xi.e.8, 197) and TMS by part, section and paragraph, followed by page number (e.g. TMS V.2.6, 203). LRBL will be cited by lecture number, paragraph and page number (e.g. LRBL, lecture 6, I.62, 28). But when citing 'Considerations Concerning the First Formation of Languages' we will use only paragraph followed by page number (e.g. LRBL, Languages, 3, 205). The abbreviations we will use to refer to the essays in EPS are: Astronomy, Ancient Physics, Ancient Logics, External Senses, Imitative Arts (e.g. Astronomy, II.1, 37–8). *Correspondence* and *Lectures on Jurisprudence* will be cited by page number only (e.g. Corr. 145 or LJ 402).

David Hume will be cited in the Oxford edition: *A Treatise of Human Nature* by book, part, section and paragraph (e.g. Treatise 2.1.5.15); Hume's First Enquiry, *An Enquiry Concerning Human Understanding*, and his

Second Enquiry, *An Enquiry Concerning the Principles of Morals,* by section and paragraph (e.g. EHU 7.15 and EPM 2.23). Hume's *Essays* will be cited by page number to the Liberty Fund second edition of *Essays, Moral, Political, Literary* edited by Eugene Miller (e.g. *Essays,* 345).

1 Introduction

Leonidas Montes and Eric Schliesser

I

There is a general resurgence of interest in Adam Smith. Taking this phenomenon into consideration, we have put together a volume of original, commissioned, and refereed papers by scholars that defended doctoral theses on Adam Smith, or a closely related topic, between 2000 and 2004. By focusing on this recent and short period, an interesting selection of innovative and insightful new voices, representative of the intellectual fertility of this field, was gathered. Our search, by no means exhaustive, produced more candidates than we could include in this volume. While we aimed at publishing ten papers, after rejecting some good pieces, we ended up with fourteen contributions. Our selection criteria focused on quality, originality, and disciplinary as well as geographic diversity. Referees provided invaluable advice. Of course, the final decision was ours alone, and the usual caveats apply.

II

While the full story of the reception and study of Smith's works is not the purpose of this introduction, a brief, and no doubt very partial, reflection on the trajectory of the 'Smith industry' is not inappropriate. This will put the contributions collected in this volume in context. Of course, we leave out many works that are models of careful analysis.

Prior to 1976 the study of Smith was mostly the domain of historians of economic thought studying the classical period, and of Marxists searching for renowned predecessors to *Das Kapital*, especially to the labor theory of value and the four stages of development (e.g. Maurice Dobb, Ronald Meek). The focus was principally on the *Wealth of Nations*, which had received several commentaries and expositions throughout the first half of the nineteenth century, and continues today to be of interest to historians of economics (notably, Nathan Rosenberg, Mark Blaug, Samuel Hollander, Warren Samuels, David Levy, Jerry Evensky, Maurice Brown, Rory O'Donnell, Glenn Hueckel, and Walter Eltis). After the middle of the nineteenth century, study of Smith's economics and moral philosophy entered a period of relative neglect, except for the controversy known as *Das Adam Smith Problem.* German intellectuals were concerned with an apparent inconsistency between depictions of the nature of human beings in *An Inquiry Concerning the Wealth of Nations* (WN) and *The Theory of Moral Sentiments* (TMS). Smith's *Homo economicus* would rely upon self-interest, and his moral man, on benevolence. Skarżyński (1878) even suggested that, after his trip to the Continent, through his acquaintance with French *philosophes,* Smith had changed his mind. This produced an influential picture of Smith's intellectual development. However, Edwin Cannan's publication late in the nineteenth century of student lecture notes on Smith's treatment of jurisprudence and related topics offered conclusive evidence that this *Umschwungstheorie* was mistaken.

In the first half of the twentieth century, the noted economist Jacob Viner and the philosopher Glenn Morrow produced magnificent studies of Smith. Eckstein's introduction to the German edition of TMS (1926), and Scott's *Adam Smith as Student and Professor* (1937) are also noteworthy. During the 1950s, Joseph Cropsey offered a penetrating and provocative reading of Smith, but in his colossal overview of the history of economics, the famous economist Joseph Schumpeter dismissed Smith's originality and importance. Smith's status as a thinker reached its nadir, despite continuing studies (most notably Campbell 1971 and Lindgren 1973), until the events of 1976, marking 200 years after the publication of WN.

The launch of the *Glasgow Edition of the Works and Correspondence of Adam Smith,* published by Oxford University Press in six volumes between 1976 and 1983, a monumental achievement of the general editors A. S. Skinner, D. D. Raphael, and the volume editors A. L. Macfie, I. S. Ross, R. H. Campbell, W. P. D. Wightman, J. C. Bryce, P. G. Stein, E. C. Mossner, and T. Wilson, enabled future generations to have a comprehensive view of Smith's legacy. They established the canonical texts of Smith, including new scholarly editions of the found student lecture notes of Smith's treatment of Rhetoric and Belles Lettres (LRBL), and Jurisprudence (LJ). They also bring together Smith's miscellaneous and posthumous essays (EPS) and his correspondence. These volumes enabled a standardized notation for references to Smith. The authoritative introductions to each volume of the Glasgow Edition, together with a series of international conferences celebrating the bicentennial of the publication of WN in 1976, must be seen as a turning point in the scholarly study of Adam Smith. These conferences yielded several collections of papers. The editorial team of the Glasgow Edition has continued producing a number of influential scholarly monographs, including newly discovered texts. Some of these publications are formally associated with the Glasgow edition. Such activity triggered a renewed interest in the figure of Adam Smith in the last quarter of the twentieth century, as reflected in review essays by Recktenwald (1978), Brown (1997), and Tribe (1999).

Between 1981 and 1987, Liberty Fund released an inexpensive and high-quality edition of an exact photographic reproduction of the six original volumes of Smith's works of the Glasgow Edition. Recently, Liberty Fund included these, with searchable files, in *The Online Library of Liberty*. Together with the official *Index to The Works of Adam Smith* (edited by K. Haakonssen and A. S. Skinner), this made Smith's works easily available and thus encouraging research.

After the publication of the Glasgow Edition, Donald Winch's *Adam Smith's Politics* (1978), Knud Haakonssen's *The Science of a Legislator* (1981), the collection of papers edited by Istvan Hont and Michael Ignatieff, *Wealth and Virtue* (1985), and Richard Teichgraeber's *Free Trade and Moral Philosophy* (1986) initiated a second wave of scholarship. Although they presented different approaches, their influence continues to be felt through new studies of the context and reception of Smith's ideas. The latter received an unexpected boost of interest after the fall of the Berlin Wall in 1989. While the Smith's authority had been routinely appealed to by free-market thinkers associated with the political right, with the notable exception of Amartya Sen, and had even been the subject of serious studies by James Buchanan, Robert Coase, Friedrich von Hayek, Milton Friedman, Vernon Smith and George Stigler (see Glahe 1978 and Fry 1992), the decline of Marx's influence allowed a new look at Smith's legacy. Since then, several important books, most notably by Spencer Pack (1991), Samuel Fleischacker (1999, 2004), and Emma Rothschild (2001), reclaimed him for the political left. These works also call attention to the wide selection of classical (e.g. Aristotelian, Stoic, and Augustan) and literary sources Smith draws on.

In addition, Smith's intellectual and rhetorical resources were the focus of studies by Jerry Muller (1993), Stewart Justman (1993), Vivienne Brown (1994), Jeffrey Young (1997), and Gloria Vivenza (1984, translated in 2002). There are diverging positions on many important interpretive problems (cf. Salim Rashid, 1998), and the relevant intellectual contexts in understanding Smith, especially his relationship to Enlightenment thought. However, one important result of the internal development of this second wave is that it re-establishes TMS as a major work in the history of moral philosophy. Charles Griswold's *Adam Smith and the Virtues of Enlightenment* (1998) has been very influential in this respect. James Otteson (2002), by arguing that morality can be a basis for Smith's economics, is also a good example of this tendency. As evidence of the previous neglect of TMS, in the first three-quarters of the twentieth century there were only four republications of it, while there were over forty partial and complete reprints of WN in English alone. Moreover, today TMS influences the thought of well known contemporary moral philosophers such as Martha Nussbaum, Stephen Darwall, Ernst Tugendhat, and Charles Larmore, amongst others. An important trend in the second wave is that Smith's moral philosophy is increasingly being dissociated from the mainstream of utilitarianism. Another novel emerging consensus is that the rhetorical structure of Smith's texts is much more complex than previously imagined.

There is further evidence of the revival of interest in Smith. The International Adam Smith Society sponsors a regular newsletter. It informs members of recent dissertations, publications, and upcoming conferences. The society also promotes special sessions on Adam Smith, or works about him, at professional association meetings. As we write, the first issue of the *Adam Smith Review*, edited by Vivienne Brown, is in press. One exciting feature of this refereed new journal is that book reviews and book symposia allow an author's response, creating a lively atmosphere of discussion about Smith. Today it can be said that Smith studies, and the relevant contexts in which to analyze him, are flourishing. Moreover, at the time this introduction was written, Knud Haakonssen's long awaited *The Cambridge Companion to Adam Smith* was due to be released. This *Companion* gathers a distinguished group of established scholars writing about different aspects of Adam Smith.

Although it may seem from our account that Smith scholarship is largely confined to the English-speaking world, Japan, in particular, has a long-established and thriving community of scholars focused on Smith (see Mizuta, 2003) and the Scottish Enlightenment. We regret that we are unable to include a Japanese contribution in our collection. Nevertheless, this volume confirms that interest in Smith is a global and multi-disciplinary phenomenon. A large number of PhD dissertations on Adam Smith or a closely related topic have been written. These originate in many different academic disciplines (e.g. Economics, History, Philosophy, Women's and Gender Studies, Political Theory, Science Studies, Environmental Ethics, Sociology, and English Literature). The scholars whose work is represented in these pages had their dissertation research supervised by established academics in Germany, France, Spain, Great Britain, the United States, and the Netherlands. Moreover, the contributors are from the United States, Chile, Colombia, Scotland, the Netherlands, Germany, Spain, and Italy. There is no discernible ideological consensus among the selected papers. While firmly rooted in traditional disciplines, their research often takes on approaches from other areas of study. This is appropriate because Smith is an 'eclectic', in its original, Greek sense of 'choosing what's best', and he had a vast knowledge of what to choose!

It is noteworthy that about half the chapters included in this volume also draw on Smith's lesser-known essays on languages, the arts, the external senses, and the history of philosophy and science. These chapters continue to explore the details of Smith's arguments and their connection to an ever-expanding circle of subjects. This has stimulated a looking back at Smith's sources, reassessing influences on his work. Moreover, this debate is also fertile territory for making interesting connections between Smith and his contemporaries, and his relevance to later debates. The editors are especially pleased that this volume includes original research on all of Smith's writings. But important areas of study still await close scrutiny. For example, while Smith's relationship to the economic theories of the Physiocrats has been explored, his debt and contribution to the French Enlightenment, especially Montesquieu and Rousseau, still offers promising avenues of research. Smith's interest in botany and zoology is largely unexplored territory to scholars. So is his admiration of Swift. Even Smith's relationship to Plato or the ancient satirist Lucian, both of whom he praises, is, despite the attention given to other classical sources in his thought, still open to detailed study. Smith's known impact on Wollstonecraft, Paine, and Godwin awaits more enterprising scholarship.

III

We have grouped the chapters of this volume in four parts: 'Adam Smith, his sources and influence', 'Adam Smith and moral theory', 'Adam Smith and Economics' and 'Adam Smith and knowledge'. These labels are, of course, only rough guides to the reader because most of the papers we have selected do justice to more than one element in Smith's thought. For example, the first three chapters not only investigate Smith's response to his sources, but they also offer novel and more precise characterizations of Smith's moral and political commitments. So it is somewhat arbitrary that some of them did not end up in Part II, 'Adam Smith and moral theory'. Moreover, while the chapters were largely written independently from each other, often presupposing very different interpretive frameworks, with wildly differing theses, there are surprising areas of agreement among the contributors: four (Hanley, Flanders, Trincado, Frierson) undermine the utilitarian reading of Smith; two (Hanley, Brubaker) undercut the consensus on Smith's Stoicism; six (Mitchell, Montes, Trincado, Schliesser, Forman-Barzilai, Smith) reconsider claims about Smith's skepticism. The chapters by Kuiper and Hurtado-Prieto will force a reassessment of Smith's relationship to Mandeville. The following is a summary of our grouping of these chapters and an introduction to what they argue.

Part I, Adam Smith, his sources and influence

The first three chapters of this volume all deepen our understanding of Smith by calling attention to Smith's multi-layered response to various textual sources. While the authors of these three chapters offer different evaluations of Smith's thought, they all reveal that, befitting a professor of rhetoric and belles-lettres, Smith reflected critically on his very diverse (and immense) readings and that it is worth while to his readers to reflect critically on their own responses to his writings.

It is quite common to describe Smith as a utilitarian, while recently several commentators have explored proto-Kantian themes in Smith's moral philosophy. Against these two traditions comes Ryan Hanley's 'Adam Smith, Aristotle and virtue ethics' (Chapter 2). Hanley argues that in TMS Adam Smith describes an alternative approach to ethics, one which refocuses it on the education of character. In this respect, Smith deserves to be regarded as one of the eighteenth century founders of contemporary virtue ethics. Against the scholarly trend to read Smith as a latter-day Stoic, Hanley shows that Smith is quite indebted to Aristotle. Hanley's chapter forces one to rethink Smith's relationship to classical sources.

Edith Kuiper's 'Adam Smith and his feminist contemporaries' (Chapter 3) describes the feminist movement in eighteenth century Britain. She investigates the main topics discussed in the writings on gender equality and women's work by, for instance, Elizabeth Robinson Montagu, Priscilla Wakefield, Hannah More, and Mary Wollstonecraft. The chapter discusses two original texts in more detail: *The Woman's Labour* (1739), a poem by Mary Collier, and *Female Rights Vindicated. Or the Equality of the Sexes Morally and Physically proved* (1758) by an anonymous 'Lady'. Employing this wider discussion as her context, Kuiper explores critically Smith's positions on gender, work, and education. This chapter shows how basic concepts employed in political economy presuppose controversial assumptions about gender, labour, and education.

In Chapter 4, 'Beautiful and orderly systems: Adam Smith on the aesthetics of political improvement', Robert Mitchell engages recent scholarship of British Romanticism. This scholarship stresses the extent to which late eighteenth century British authors were obsessed with establishing the proper role of 'systems' in both political and literary thought and practice. Mitchell argues that Adam Smith's role in this discourse has generally been neglected. This chapter calls our attention to Smith's extensive comments on 'systems' that connect (in both the 1759 and 1790 editions of TMS) theorizing, aesthetic perception, and sacrifice. Mitchell claims that Smith's writings were formative for Romantic-era authors with political positions as diverse as those of Burke, Coleridge, and Godwin.

Part II, Adam Smith and moral theory

At first glance Smith's moral theory, rich in phenomenological detail and homely examples, often seems unpromising territory to professional philosophers looking for a highly theorized, systematic meta-ethics or ethical theory. Nevertheless, from very different angles, the first three chapters in Part III explore the resources within Smith's moral theory to handle issues of cultural relativity or moral pluralism. These chapters reveal that when pressed, Smith's writings contain complex and subtle reflections on fundamental and continuing problem in moral theory. This is also a major point of Flanders' interpretation of Smith's treatment of moral luck. Additionally, Brubaker's chapter suggests that Smith is methodologically self-aware about his rhetorical choices in presenting issues relevant to moral theory and political economy.

Fonna Forman-Barzilai's Chapter 5, 'Smith on "connexion", culture and judgment', addresses Smith's thoughts about affective and cultural impartiality. She argues, first, that while Smith's description of moral judgment generates an affective sort of coolness that succeeds in moderating our selfishness, it does not explain how we might become critical of our cultural experiences and biases. Forman-Barzilai then explores how Smith might have responded to the cultural relativity that emerges from his description of moral judgment. Smith could offer his theory of negative justice as a candidate for universal normativity; our negative affective reaction to pain and cruelty might have had the positive effect of opening a critical space for reflection about ourselves and others.

Carola von Villiez's Chapter 6, 'Double standard – naturally! Smith and Rawls: a comparison of methods', interprets three concepts developed by Smith in TMS – his idea of sympathy as a principle in human nature, his idea of a communal moral standard of propriety and his thought-model of the impartial spectator – as implying three dimensions of moral judgment. She argues that with this, Smith can be said to mediate between the factual moral convictions of moral communities and the demands of a procedural morality of impartiality. So from a methodological perspective, TMS could be a forerunner of the method of reflective equilibrium developed by John Rawls in his influential *A Theory of Justice*. This analogy of methods makes TMS an important resource for a contemporary contextual theory of morality designed for handling a characteristic of modern societies: moral pluralism.

Patrick Frierson's 'Applying Adam Smith: a step towards Smithian environmental virtue ethics' (Chapter 7) argues that Smith's moral theory can be seen as an undervalued resource in contemporary environmental ethics. Frierson shows that Smith provides a rich and insightful virtue ethics that can specifically support environmental virtues. He addresses the challenge that a virtue ethics cannot convince the 'anti-environmentalist' of the value of environmental virtues. According to Frierson, Adam Smith can give a non-anthropocentric defense of these virtues. Smith's specific suggestions for dealing with challenges to his virtue ethics are particularly well suited for responding to the kinds of problems that arise in contemporary environmental debates. Frierson illustrates this by using Smith's treatment of the role of custom in perverting moral sentiments. Smith's sensitivity to details, his awareness of problems that generate ethical disagreement, and his hopeful accounts of the laws of human psychology that make agreements possible, all could provide a basis for a realistic but optimistic environmental philosophy.

In both his moral and economic theories Smith frequently praises the wisdom of nature while contrasting it with the folly of man. This has led many scholars to see in his works a reliance on a Stoic picture of the providential harmony of nature leading to human happiness and perfection, a harmony disrupted by human frailty or corruption. Yet Smith is often critical of Stoicism, calls his own system of natural liberty 'utopian', and outlines great and universal causes of moral corruption that can be traced to the same moral sentiments that in other circumstances he relies on to generate virtue. Chapter 8, Lauren Brubaker's 'Does the 'wisdom of nature' need help?, argues that Smith rejects both Stoic resignation and utopian hubris. Brubaker analyzes Smith's claim that there is a conflict within nature between her own laws and the laws she prompts human nature to follow. Brubaker's chapter explains that Smith's complex understanding of nature's wisdom and human nature's efforts to help nature entail a limited, cautious and often indirect, but nevertheless essential, program of philosophical and political statesmanship. According to Brubaker this is why Smith reserves his highest praise for the superior prudence of philosophers and legislators.

In Chapter 9, ' "This irregularity of sentiment": Adam Smith on moral luck', Chad Flanders offers a sympathetic reading of Adam Smith on moral luck. In TMS, Smith observes that our sentiments are 'irregular' because we praise and blame people based on the consequences of their actions, which are never completely in their control. Our sentiments then seem to imply that our worthiness for praise or blame can be affected by luck. Critics have read Smith as giving a 'utilitarian' justification for our irregular sentiments. In his chapter, Flanders does not so much dispute this reading as show that it is incomplete. Smith explains how our 'irregular' sentiments might be appropriate as well as useful.

Part III, Adam Smith and economics

The part of this volume on Adam Smith's economics is among the shortest. It would be misleading to conclude, however, that historians of economics have turned away from the study of Adam Smith. In fact, five of the fourteen contributors to this volume are trained economists. Even so, it is clear that this volume reflects, in part, a broadening of the study of Smith rather than the wholesale revision of previous scholarship focused on reconstructing his views in economics. Nevertheless, the suspicion that the paucity of present contributions on economic issues suggests a lack of sustained engagement with the core of Smith's economics is not borne out by the three chapters in Part III. All three contributors emphasize that it is rewarding to read Smith as a systematic thinker in political economy. When we do so, Smith is revealed as less familiar and more profound than we have come to expect.

Chapter 10, Jimena Hurtado-Prieto's 'The mercantilist foundations of "Dr Mandeville's licentious system": Adam Smith on Bernard Mandeville', reinvestigates the relation between Smith and Mandeville. Whereas Smith's criticism of Mandeville's moral system has been widely noted – if only because it is clear that Smith does not want to be associated with Mandeville's 'scandalous' system – less attention has been given to Smith's criticism of the economic foundations of Mandeville's views. Hurtado-Prieto uses the student notes to Smith's *Lectures on Jurisprudence* to show that Smith's criticism of Mandeville's system is based not only on moral, but also on economic arguments. One original feature of Hurtado-Prieto's chapter is that it implies that Mandeville is, according to Smith, much closer to mercantilism than he is to Smith's own economic analysis. If Hurtado-Prieto is correct, this implies that Smith's criticism of mercantilism in WN may also be an extension of his moral views.

In Chapter 11, 'On Adam Smith's Newtonianism and general economic equilibrium theory', Leonidas Montes argues that Smith in general, and his invisible hand in particular, have been too readily associated with general economic equilibrium theory. Montes challenges this view by arguing that the emphasis in scholarly literature on Newton's influence on Smith is correct, but its nature misunderstood. He shows that Smith is a sophisticated reader of Newton, but that Newton's methodology does not necessarily lead to a notion of equilibrium as in modern general economic equilibrium theory. Smith's reading of Newton is interpreted as a consequence of a particular and distinctively Scottish reception of Newton. The members of the Scottish Enlightenment did not attribute to Newton an axiomatic-deductive methodology. Rather, it is suggested that the French tradition, which interpreted Newton in context of a Cartesian emphasis on deduction, adopted and adapted a particular Newtonianism fostering a methodology similar to that of Walras, the forerunner of general economic equilibrium theory.

In Chapter 12, 'Vanity and the Daedalian wings of paper money in Adam Smith', Maria Pia Paganelli argues that even such a highly technical issue as Smith's understanding of paper money is closely connected to his broader views on political economy. Paganelli addresses what appears to be a very strange omission in WN: even though Smith presents a careful analysis of paper money, he does not seem to recognize the full potential of public credit as a policy instrument. This is surprising because many of Smith's contemporaries, including his close friend David Hume, explore this theme. Paganelli argues that the reason for this omission may be traced to Smith's views on moral psychology and its connection to his political economy. This chapter shows that Smith's argument on paper money may be justified if we understand him as exploring commercial society, where vanity is the predominant motivational force behind human conduct.

Part IV, Adam Smith and knowledge

The three chapters in this part represent the continuing recovery of Smith's interest in traditional philosophic issues of metaphysics and epistemology. All three chapters draw to different degrees on Smith's posthumous publications to offer not only new interpretations of familiar elements of Smith's corpus but also a more rounded picture of Smith's philosophic self-understanding. While these chapters arrive at Smith from very different intellectual and interpretative traditions, they all paint a surprisingly 'au courant' picture of Smith: Smith's epistemology and metaphysics illuminates and are illuminated by issues in moral and political philosophy.

The role and growth of knowledge is a crucial point in Adam Smith's analysis of the development of commercial society. Craig Smith's 'Adam Smith on progress and knowledge' (Chapter 13) examines this issue. It argues that two of Smith's most noted theoretical arguments, the 'four stages' of subsistence theory of social change and the analysis of the progressive force of the division of labor, can be put into clearer relief. Craig Smith considers them in the light of arguments about the spontaneous generation of social order and the growth of human knowledge. By looking anew at many passages familiar in the scholarly literature, the chapter advances the view that Smith's theory of social change and progress is best understood as a process of the development and efficient utilization of human skills and knowledge.

In Chapter 14, 'Adam Smith's criticism of the doctrine of utility: a theory of the creative present', Estrella Trincado offers the original thesis that the Smithian concept of time can be seen as a core element of Smith's 'system'. She investigates the role of time in Smith's metaphysics and ethics, offering insights into the Smithian theory of law or political economy. Trincado argues that, unlike theories based on utility, Smith's system can be labelled a *creative present theory*. In Trincado's view Smith presents a phenomenologically rich account of depth perception which is based on active principles – such as gratitude, joy, curiosity, game playing and creation – that are lived in the present.

In Chapter 15, 'Adam Smith's benevolent and self-interested conception of philosophy', Eric Schliesser argues that Adam Smith's conception of philosophy is best understood in light of his engagement with Rousseau's rhetorical challenge to the worth of commercial society. Schliesser claims that Smith offers an endorsement of commercial life as a means to philosophy. Smith's task is complicated because he needs to navigate the relationship between philosophy and common life (as manifested by politics, religion, public opinion, etc.), on the one hand, and the new emerging relationship between natural science and philosophy, on the other hand. Schliesser argues that Smith adopts a theoretical viewpoint in which the results of Newtonian science are critically examined and potentially endorsed with the often tacit norms available within science. This chapter draws on Smith's moral psychology to reconstruct Smith's position. Then, it explains the dual political role of philosophy for Smith: as an adviser to statesmen, philosophy helps design an equitable, institutional framework; within the polity, philosophy is needed to vaccinate the citizens against the dangers of religion and factionalism.

Finally, if this volume inspires our peers and future research, and, as Smith would write to his publisher, 'sells well' (Corr. 229), we shall have succeeded in our task.

Selected references

Blaug, M. (1997) *Economic Theory in Retrospect*, fifth edition, Cambridge: Cambridge University Press.

Brown, M. (1988) *Adam Smith's Economics: His Place in the Development of Economic Thought*, London: Croom Helm.

Brown, V. (1994) *Adam Smith's Discourse: Canonicity, Commerce, and Conscience*, London: Routledge.

—— (1997) 'Mere Inventions of the Imagination', *Economics and Philosophy* 13: 281–312.

Buchanan, J. M. (1976) 'The Justice of Natural Liberty', *Journal of Legal Studies* 5: 1–16.

—— (1992) 'The Supply of Labour and the Extent of the Market', in Fry.

Campbell, R. H. and Skinner, A. S. (eds) (1982) *The Origins and Nature of the Scottish Enlightenment*, Edinburgh: Donald.

—— (1982) *Adam Smith*, New York: St Martin's Press.

Campbell, T. D. (1971) *Adam Smith's Science of Morals*, London: Allen and Unwin.

Cannan, E. (1896) *Lectures on Justice, Police, Revenue and Arms, delivered in the University of Glasgow by Adam Smith*, Oxford: Clarendon Press.

Clark, J. M. *et al.* (1928) *Adam Smith, 1776–1926: Lectures to Commemorate the Sesquicentennial of the Publication of The Wealth of Nations*, Chicago: University of Chicago Press.

Coase, R. H. (1976) 'Adam Smith's View of Man', *Journal of Law and Economics* 19: 529–46.

Cropsey, J. (1957) *Polity and Economy: an Interpretation of the Principles of Adam Smith*, The Hague: Nijhoff.

Darwall, S. (1998) 'Empathy, Sympathy, and Care', *Philosophical Studies* 89: 261–82.

—— (1999) 'Sympathetic Liberalism: Recent Work on Adam Smith', *Philosophy and Public Affairs* 28: 139–64.

Den Uyl, D. J. and Griswold, Charles L. Jr (1996) 'Adam Smith on Friendship and Love', *Review of Metaphysics* 49: 609–37.

Dickey, L. (1986) 'Historicizing the "Adam Smith Problem": Conceptual, Historiographical, and Textual Issues', *Journal of Modern History* 58: 579–609.

Dobb, M. (1973) *Theories of Value and Distribution since Adam Smith*, Cambridge: Cambridge University Press.

Eckstein, W. (1926) *Einleitung*, in Adam Smith, *Theorie der etischen Gefühle*, Leipzig: Meiner.

Eltis, W. (1984) *The Classical Theory of Economic Growth*, Basingstoke: Palgrave.

Evensky, J. (2001) 'Adam Smith's Lost Legacy', *Southern Economic Journal*, 67: 497–517.

—— (2005) *Adam Smith's Moral Philosophy: A Historical and Contemporary Perspective on Markets, Law, Ethics, and Culture*, Cambridge: Cambridge University Press.

Fleischacker, S. (1999) *A Third Concept of Liberty: Judgment and Freedom in Kant and Adam Smith*, Princeton, NJ: Princeton University Press.

—— (2004) *Adam Smith's Wealth of Nations: A Philosophical Companion*, Princeton, NJ: Princeton University Press.

Friedman, M. (1978) 'Adam Smith's Relevance for 1976', in Glahe.

Fry, M. (ed.) (1992) *Adam Smith's Legacy: His Place in the Development of Modern Economics*, London: Routledge.

Glahe, F. R. (ed.) (1978) *Adam Smith and the Wealth of Nations*, Boulder, CO: Colorado Associated University Press.

Griswold, C. L. (1998) *Adam Smith and the Virtues of Enlightenment*, Cambridge: Cambridge University Press.

Haakonssen, K. (1981) *The Science of the Legislator: the Natural Jurisprudence of David Hume and Adam Smith*, Cambridge: Cambridge University Press.

Harman, G. (1986) *Moral Agent and Impartial Spectator*, the 1986 Lindley Lecture, published by the Philosophy Department, Lawrence, KS: University of Kansas.

Hayek, F. A. (1978) 'Adam Smith's Message in Today's Language', in *New Studies in Philosophy, Politics, Economics, and the History of Ideas*, Chicago: University of Chicago Press.

Hollander, S. L. (1973) *The Economics of Adam Smith*. Toronto: University of Toronto Press.

Hont, I. and Ignatieff, M. (eds) (1985) *Wealth and Virtue: The Shaping of Political Economy in the Scottish Enlightenment*, Cambridge: Cambridge University Press.

Hueckel, G. R. (2000) 'On the "Insurmountable Difficulties, Obscurity, and Embarrassment" of Smith's Fifth Chapter', *History of Political Economy* 32: 317–45.

Justman, S. (1993) *The Autonomous Male of Adam Smith*, Norman, OK: University of Oklahoma Press.

Larmore, C. (1987) *Patterns of Moral Complexity*, Cambridge: Cambridge University Press.

Levy, D. M. (1995) 'The Partial Spectator in the Wealth of Nations: A Robust Utilitarianism', *European Journal of the History of Economic Thought* 2: 299–326.

—— (1997) 'Adam Smith's Rational Choice Linguistics', *Economic Inquiry* 35: 672–8.

—— (1999) 'Adam Smith's Katallactic Model of Gambling: Approbation from the Spectator', *Journal of the History of Economic Thought* 21: 81–92.

—— and Peart, S. J. (2004) 'Sympathy and Approbation in Hume and Smith: A Solution to the Other Rational Species Problem', *Economics and Philosophy* 20: 331–49.

Lindgren, J. R. (1973) *The Social Philosophy of Adam Smith*, The Hague: Nijhoff.

Macfie, A. L. (1959) 'Adam Smith's Moral Sentiments as Foundation for his *Wealth of Nations*', *Oxford Economic Papers* 2: 209–28.

—— (1967) *The Individual in Society: Papers on Adam Smith*, London: Allen and Unwin.

—— (1971) 'The Invisible Hand of Jupiter', *Journal of the History of Ideas* 32: 595–9.

Meek, R. L. (1977) *Smith, Marx and After: Ten Essays in the Development of Economic Thought*, London: Chapman and Hall.

Mizuta, H. (2003) 'Adam Smith in Japan', in *The Rise of Political Economy in the Scottish Enlightenment*, ed. Tatsuya Sakamoto and Hideo Tanaka, London: Routledge.

Morrow, G. R. (1923) 'The Significance of the Doctrine of Sympathy in Hume and Adam Smith', *Philosophical Review* 32: 60–78.

—— (1923) *Ethical and Economic Theories of Adam Smith*, repr. New York: Kelly, 1969.

Muller, J. Z. (1993) *Adam Smith in His Time and Ours: Designing the Decent Society*, New York: Free Press.

Nussbaum, M. C. (2003) *Upheavals of Thought: The Intelligence of Emotions*, Cambridge: Cambridge University Press.

—— (2004) *Hiding from Humanity: Disgust, Shame, and the Law*, Princeton, NJ: Princeton University Press.

O'Donnell, R. (1990) *Adam Smith's Theory of Value and Distribution: A Reappraisal*, New York: St Martin's Press.

O'Driscoll, G. P. Jr (ed.) (1979) *Adam Smith and Modern Political Economy: Bicentennial Essays on The Wealth of Nations*, Ames, IA: Iowa State University Press.

Otteson, J. (2002) *Adam Smith's Marketplace of Life*, Cambridge: Cambridge University Press.

Pack, S. J. (1991) *Capitalism as a Moral System: Adam Smith's Critique of the Free Market Economy*, Cheltenham: Elgar.

Raphael, D. D. (1973) 'Hume and Smith on Justice and Utility', *Proceedings of the Aristotelian Society* 73: 87–103.

—— (1985) *Adam Smith*, Oxford: Oxford University Press.

Rashid, S. (1998) *The Myth of Adam Smith*, Cheltenham: Elgar.

Raynor, D. (1984) 'Hume's Abstract of Adam Smith's *Theory of Moral Sentiments*', *Journal of the History of Philosophy* 22: 51–79.

Recktenwald, H. C. (1978) 'An Adam Smith Renaissance Anno 1976? The Bicentenary Output: A Reappraisal of his Scholarship', *Journal of Economic Literature* 16: 56–83.

Redman, D. A. (1997) *The Rise of Political Economy as a Science: Methodology and the Classical Economists*, Cambridge, MA: MIT Press.

Rosenberg, Nathan (1960) 'Some Institutional Aspects of the *Wealth of Nations*', *Journal of Political Economy* 68: 557–70.

—— (1965) 'Adam Smith on the Division of Labour: Two Views or One?', *Economica* 32: 127–39.

—— (1968) 'Adam Smith, Consumer Tastes, and Economic Growth', *Journal of Political Economy* 76: 361–74.

—— (1975) 'Adam Smith on Profits – Paradox Lost and Regained', in Skinner and Wilson.

Ross, I. S. (1995) *The Life of Adam Smith*, Oxford: Clarendon Press.

Rothschild, E. (2001) *Economic Sentiments: Adam Smith, Condorcet, and the Enlightenment*, Cambridge, MA: Harvard University Press.

Samuels, W. J. (1973) 'Adam Smith and the Economy as a System of Power', *Review of Social Economy* 31: 123–37.

—— (1977) 'The Political Economy of Adam Smith', *Ethics* 87: 189–207.

Schumpeter, J. A. (1954) *History of Economic Anylysis*, ed. Elizabeth Boody Schumpeter, New York: Oxford University Press.

Scott, W. R. (1937) *Adam Smith as Student and Professor*, Glasgow: Jackson.

Sen, A. K. (1986) 'Adam Smith's Prudence', in *Theory and Reality in Development: Essays in Honour of Paul Streeten*, ed. S. Lall *et al.*, New York: St Martin's Press.

—— (1987) *On Ethics and Economics*, Oxford: Blackwell.

Skarżyński, W. von (1878) *Adam Smith als Moralphilosoph und Schöpfer der Nationalökonomie. Ein Beitrag zur Geschichte der Nationalökonomie*, Berlin: Theobald Grieben.

Skinner, A. S. (1974) *Adam Smith and the Role of the State*, Glasgow: University of Glasgow Press.

—— (1996) *A System of Social Science: Papers relating to Adam Smith*, 2nd edn, Oxford: Clarendon Press.

—— and Wilson, T. (eds) (1975) *Essays on Adam Smith*, Oxford: Clarendon Press.

—— (1976) *The Market and the State: Essays in Honour of Adam Smith*, Oxford: Clarendon Press.

Smith, V. (1998) 'The Two Faces of Adam Smith', *Southern Journal of Economics* 65: 2–20.

Stigler, G. J. (1965) *Essays in the History of Economics*, Chicago: University of Chicago Press.

—— (1975) 'Smith's Travels on the Ship of State', in Skinner and Wilson.

Teichgraeber, R. F. III (1986) *Free Trade and Moral Philosophy: Rethinking the Sources of Adam Smith's Wealth of Nations*, Durham, NC: Duke University Press.

Tribe, K. (1999) 'Adam Smith: Critical Theorist?', *Journal of Economic Literature* 37: 609–32.

Tugendhat, E. (1997) *Vorlesung über Ethik*. Frankfurt am Main: Suhrkamp.

—— (forthcoming) 'Universally Approved Intersubjective Attitudes: Adam Smith' (trans. Bernard Schriebl), *Adam Smith Review*, 1.

Viner, J. (1927) 'Adam Smith and *laissez-faire*', *Journal of Political Economy* 35: 198–232.

—— (1972) *The Role of Providence in the Social Order*, Philadelphia: American Philosophical Society.

—— (1991) *Essays on the Intellectual History of Economics*, ed. Douglas Irwin, Princeton, NJ: Princeton University Press.

Vivenza, G. (2002) *Adam Smith and the Classics: The Classical Heritage in Adam Smith's Thought*, Oxford: Oxford University Press.

Winch, D. (1978) *Adam Smith's Politics: An Essay in Historiographic Revision*, Cambridge: Cambridge University Press.

—— (1995) 'Scottish Moral Philosopher as Political Economist', *Historical Journal* 35: 91–113.

—— (1996) *Riches and Poverty: An Intellectual History of Political Economy in Britain, 1750–1834*, Cambridge: Cambridge University Press.

Wood, J. C. (ed.) (1983–84) *Adam Smith: Critical Assessments*, 4 vols, London: Routledge.

—— (ed.) (1994) *Adam Smith: Critical Assessments*, V–VII, London: Routledge.

Young, J. T. (1997) *Economics as a Moral Science: The Political Economy of Adam Smith*, Cheltenham: Elgar.

Part I

Adam Smith, his sources and influence

2 Adam Smith, Aristotle and virtue ethics

Ryan Patrick Hanley

Among the most important developments in contemporary moral philosophy has been the emergence of virtue ethics as a viable alternative to utilitarian and consequentialist approaches to ethics on the one hand and deontological or Kantian approaches on the other. In contrast to these systems, which evaluate actions on the grounds of their capacity to maximize good effects (as do consequentialists) or their willed adherence to universally valid moral rules (as do Kantians), virtue ethicists have focused on describing the virtues and vices that determine good and bad characters. In shifting attention from actions to characters, virtue ethicists are often said to replace the question of 'what should I do?' with the question of 'what should I be?'[1]

The inspiration for this turn is often credited to the resurgence of neo-Aristotelianism.[2] To a lesser extent, and more recently, the antecedents of contemporary virtue ethics have been traced to eighteenth century British moral philosophy, and particularly to the systems of Hutcheson and Hume.[3] But to these names that of Adam Smith deserves to be added, for among the intentions of *The Theory of Moral Sentiments* is to describe an alternative approach to ethics, one which directs attention away from moral rules and refocuses it on the education of character. Further, like contemporary virtue ethicists, Smith too is indebted to Aristotle.[4] By setting their systems next to each other here I hope to call attention to certain of these debts and thereby explore Smith's investigation of the question of 'wherein does virtue consist?' – or, as he glosses it, 'what is the tone of temper, and tenour of conduct, which constitutes the excellent and praise-worthy character, the character which is the natural object of esteem, honour, and approbation?' (TMS VII.i.2, 265).[5] Smith's Aristotelian answer to this fundamental question of virtue ethics will, I hope, be of interest to both Smith specialists and contemporary moral philosophers.[6]

The forms of ethics and the place of rhetoric

In the final Section of the final Part of TMS Smith sets forth his understanding of the role of ethics in the education of character. He does this in the course of an investigation of the methods appropriate to 'the science which is properly called Ethics' (TMS VII.iv.6, 329). The passage itself further develops a distinction that Smith has already drawn between 'two different manners' of treating ethical rules (TMS VII.iv.2, 327). The first he associates with those philosophers who focus on justice and aim to articulate rules for just action which are 'accurate in the highest degree, and admit of no exceptions or modifications'. Smith agrees that such rigor is wholly appropriate to the rules of justice; he too thinks it necessary for the stability of society that such rules be held by all in 'the most sacred regard' (TMS III.6.10, 175). But he also insists that such rigor cannot be expected of the rules that govern all other virtues. Justice, he notes, 'is the only virtue with regard to which such exact rules can properly be given' (TMS VII.iv.7, 329). Its rules 'are the only rules of morality which are precise and accurate', whereas 'those of all the other virtues are loose, vague, and indeterminate' (TMS VII.iv.1, 327). To expect the same rigorous adherence to the rules for other virtues as we do for the rules of justice 'would evidently be the most absurd and ridiculous pedantry' (TMS III.6.9, 174).[7]

On these grounds Smith suggests that ethicists who would treat virtues apart from justice require a method different from those who focus solely on justice. Now, in some sense the entire goal of this final Section of the final Part of TMS is to distinguish the different methods proper to ethics and natural jurisprudence. But Smith also means to show that the conflation of these two different methods by ethicists has led to unnecessary confusion within moral philosophy as a whole. Thus he distinguishes two methods in ethics: that of 'critics' who applied to the whole of the virtues 'that loose method to which they were naturally directed by the consideration of one species of virtues', and that of 'grammarians' who in treating the virtues have 'universally endeavoured to introduce into their precepts that sort of accuracy of which only some of them are susceptible' (TMS VII.iv.2, 327). Both species of ethics are in some measure in the wrong in so far as each applies to the whole of virtue methods appropriate only to a part of it. Yet Smith prefers the method of the critics on the grounds that it is better suited to the virtues that are the proper subjects of ethics, whereas that of the grammarians is only suited to justice, the proper subject of natural jurisprudence.[8] Smith develops this point in his critique of the casuists. Both 'the casuists of the middle and latter ages of the christian church' and 'all those who in this and in the preceding century have treated of what is called natural jurisprudence', he explains, draw on the approach of the grammarians (TMS VII.iv.7, 329).[9] Yet the natural lawyers used this method to establish rules of justice more successfully than did those casuists who sought 'to prescribe rules for the conduct of a good man' (TMS VII.iv.8, 330).[10] Smith cannot condone such methods for such ends; hence his critique of casuists for attempting 'to no purpose, to direct by precise rules what it belongs to feeling and sentiment only to judge of'. As contributions to ethics their works are worthless: 'dry and disagreeable' and full of the 'frivolous accuracy' they sought to impose on 'subjects which do not admit of it'. Smith's critique of casuistry ends with his insistence that their works abound 'in abstruse and metaphysical distinctions', but are 'incapable of exciting in the heart any of those emotions which it is the principal use of books of morality to excite'. In so doing they fail to 'animate us to what is generous and noble' or 'soften us to what is gentle and humane' (TMS VII.iv.33, 339–40). Yet where the moral grammarians fail the moral critics succeed; they 'present us rather with a general idea of the perfection we ought to aim at, than afford us any certain and infallible directions for acquiring it' (TMS VII.iv.1, 327; III.6.11, 175–6).[11] They 'present us with agreeable and lively pictures of manners' in an effort to 'inflame our natural love of virtue, and increase our abhorrence of vice'. When dressed with 'the embellishments of eloquence', Smith insists, their moral portraits are 'capable of producing upon the flexibility of youth, the noblest and most lasting impressions', which in time confirm in them the noblest and most useful habits (TMS VII.iv.6, 329).[12]

Smith generally identifies the critical method in ethics with the works of the 'ancient moralists' who reject the 'nice exactness' characteristic of casuistry and instead seek to describe the excellent character (TMS VII.iv.34, 340; VII.iv.3, 328). Smith even has some favorite examples in mind, naming 'Cicero, in the first book of his Offices' and 'Aristotle in the practical parts of his Ethics' as particularly excellent (TMS VII.iv.5, 329). Now the debts of the Scottish Enlightenment in general and Adam Smith in particular to Cicero have been extensively examined.[13] Yet Smith's endorsement of Aristotle might give readers reason to pause. On its face, a significant divide seems to separate Smith from Aristotle. We need only remind ourselves here of several crucial differences already noted, including Smith's seeming silence on teleology,[14] his seeming silence on the intellectual virtues,[15] his seeming advocacy of the commercial life that Aristotle dismisses as hedonistic,[16] his seeming egalitarianism,[17] and his seeming redefinition of the flourishing life as one of social cooperation rather than individual self-perfection.[18] These differences may well be insurmountable, and it may well be the case that Smith's project and Aristotle's project simply cannot cohere. Yet at the same time, to attempt to 'rescue' Smith from such challenges may be misguided; in any case, it is not what shall be attempted here. What is of more interest to me is to attempt to reconstruct the grounds of Smith's admiration of that 'philosopher who certainly knew the world' (TMS VI.iii.44, 258).[19] Given the profound divide that seems to separate Aristotle's world from Smith's – a gap of which Smith himself could not possibly have failed to have been aware – precisely what elements of Aristotle's ethics did Smith admire and seek to recover?

Smith himself points to certain substantive elements, as evident in his observation that Aristotle's account of virtue corresponds 'pretty exactly' with what he himself has said in TMS about propriety and impropriety (TMS VII.ii.1.12, 270–1). But more suggestive than this similarity in their substantive accounts are several similarities in their conceptions of the methods and ends of ethics itself. Smith, we have seen, insists that ethics should animate its students to what is noble, and in so doing he closely follows Aristotle's repeated insistence that the principal goal of ethical inquiry is our improvement in fact (*Nicomachean Ethics* [NE] 1103b26–31; 1179a33–1179b4). Smith's own interest in the practical result of ethical inquiry is no less pronounced; hence his lament that the genius of his age has inclined towards 'abstract and Speculative reasonings which perhaps tend very little to the bettering of our practise', and particularly in the 'the Practicall Sciences of Politicks and Morality or Ethicks' (LRBL lecture 8, i.101–2, 41). Now, Smith's conscious distinction of the abstract and speculative sciences from the practical sciences of politics and ethics invites further examination of his conception of the differing methods of inquiry appropriate to each type of science. Smith's claim that the science of ethics 'does not admit of the most accurate precision' recalls Aristotle's characteristic insistence that the level of precision which can be expected in more rigorous sorts of inquiry can hardly be expected in theories of ethics, owing to the nature of their subject matter (TMS VII.iv.6, 329; VII.iv.33, 339–40; cf. NE 1094b11–14; 1098a26–9; 1103b34–1104a11). Like Smith, Aristotle too claims that the aim of ethics is less to establish general rules for action than to cultivate the judgment or practical wisdom necessary for right action in particular situations (NE 1104a5; 1109b18–23; 1126a31–1126b4). (This claim is helpfully developed in Sherman 1989: 13ff.) Both thinkers thus conclude that precision is not a proper goal for ethicists; indeed Smith's distinction of grammarians from critics is anticipated in Aristotle's distinction of the rough-and-ready science of carpenters from the more precise science of geometricians (NE 1098a29–32), and in his claim that the same degree of exactness ought not be expected from orators as from mathematicians (NE 1094b25–7).

Smith's and Aristotle's shared conception of the imprecise nature of the science of ethics leads them to a certain understanding of how ethical premises should be presented by authors to their audiences. The subject matter of ethics being what it is, Aristotle teaches that authors will do better to present broad outlines of the truth rather than exacting definitions, especially at the outset (NE 1094a24–6; 1094b19–23; 1098a20–6). His *Ethics* of course does just this. Starting with the given ('the that'), his inquiry begins with a 'rough sketch' drawn from what is already familiar to his audience, and fills this in over time as he moves gradually from common opinion towards truth (cf. 1145b2–7). Such an approach, while necessary because of the nature of the subject matter of ethics, is also necessary because of the nature of the audience to which books on ethics are commonly directed. None but the best-disposed students can be led to virtue through theoretical accounts alone, Aristotle knows; most men are driven by a love of gain and a love of pleasure rather than a love of what is noble (NE 1179b4–16). Consequently, if one hopes to steer an audience composed of lovers of pleasure or lovers of honor to the love of nobility, it is necessary to appeal, at least at the outset, to their instinctive inclinations and opinions.[20] Thus he concludes that the form of rhetoric appropriate for treatises on ethics differs from that of treatises on metaphysics. Most men, unable 'to reason from distant starting points' or see many things at once, are moved only by more immediate appeals (*Rhetoric* [R] 1357a1). Long, intricate arguments built on universals will always have much less sway with them than arguments grounded in particulars already familiar from experience (R 1395b25–1396a1).

Aristotle's understanding of the centrality of rhetoric to ethics is mirrored by Smith. In particular Smith embraces Aristotle's distinction between those approaches that lead up to first principles and those which take first principles as a departure point (NE 1095a30–b4). Aristotle's claim here is that ethical and political inquiries should take for their departure point that which is already familiar to their audience rather than begin with first principles. It is a conviction shared by Smith. At the conclusion of his twenty-fourth rhetoric lecture Smith explains that the method of writing and inquiry that is 'undoubtedly the best in all matters of Science' is inappropriate to 'rhetorical discourses', owing to their differing audiences. Like Aristotle, he insists that the people to which these latter are commonly directed 'have no pleasure in these abstruse deductions; their interest, and the practicability and the honourableness of the thing recommended is what alone will sway with them and is seldom to be shewn in a long deduction of arguments' (LRBL lecture 24, ii.135, 146).

Smith's ethics is as much shaped by this insight as Aristotle's. Virtue's beauty, he says, is 'chiefly perceived by men of reflection and speculation, and is by no means the quality which first recommends such actions to the natural sentiments of the bulk of mankind' (TMS IV.2.11, 192). Aware of this, in making his first recommendations of virtue, he emphasizes its utility rather than its beauty, or even the beauty of its utility. Smith of course hardly denies virtue's abstract beauty; he simply thinks that it is better introduced over time than at the start. The training of that 'natural eye of the mind' is a long, hard process (TMS III.iii.2, 135; cf. NE 1104a11–14). To raise us to that point where we, like Aristotle's *phronimos*, might 'know the original when we meet with it' will take time and practice, and thus cannot be approached head-on (TMS VII.iv.4, 328; cf. V.i.8, 198–9). Like Aristotle, Smith thus begins with an appeal to that which is commonly praised, only coming to the praiseworthy or noble in time.

The dialectic of self-love and benevolence

In developing its moral education of character *The Theory of Moral Sentiments* employs the ascending dialectic described in the *Lectures on Rhetoric.*

The movement of Smith's work is from that which is commonly honored and praised to that which is genuinely honorable and praiseworthy. As a moral educator, Smith's task is to elevate the self-love that prompts our concern with the goods of self-interest and show how self-love, when ennobled, might lead to the love of nobility which distinguishes men of wisdom and virtue. Our task then is to sketch this dialectical movement of TMS and to demonstrate its relationship to the dialectic of the *Ethics*.[21]

Provisionally we might first note that both books begin their arguments for ethical virtue by insisting on its utility in assisting in the attainment of commonly valued external goods. TMS begins with an appeal to precisely that concern with honor and interest that the *Lectures on Rhetoric* insists drives most men. In so doing, Smith acts on the principle underlying his explicit response to Epicurus: when men by their acts 'manifestly show that the natural beauty of virtue is not like to have much effect upon them, how is it possible to move them but by representing the folly of their conduct, and how much they themselves are in the end likely to suffer by it?' (TMS VII.ii.2.13, 298–9) In accord with such advice, Smith begins TMS with a discussion of propriety and the virtues related to the promotion of interest. Now, even in noting this, we must remember that Smith hardly defends naked self-interest; a once fashionable portrait of his work notwithstanding, Smith in fact took great pains to dissociate his moral system from the 'licentious systems' of La Rochefoucauld and Mandeville and other proponents of psychological egoism who reduced all virtue to interest (see especially TMS VII.ii.4, 308ff.). As the first sentence of the work indicates, Part I does not argue for the supremacy of either the other-directed or the selfish passions, but rather aims to explain how they work together. In treating this question, Part I lays the foundation of Smith's answer to the second of the two questions described at VII.i.2, namely the question of the sources of moral judgment. But in so far as Part I also treats the first question described at VII.i.2 – the 'wherein does virtue consist' question – it also presents propriety and the virtues of self-regard as preparative for a full appreciation of genuine virtue.

Part I indeed seems to focus on the role of self-regard in both individual and social life. It is here that Smith tells us that vanity and ambition, the source of our desire to become the object of the attention and approbation of others, govern our most characteristic activities: our attempts to better our condition through the pursuit of wealth and to better our position through the pursuit of political power and social rank (TMS I.iii.2.1, 50–1). The rich and great, we are further reminded, are always more widely admired than the wise and virtuous; more men esteem that life 'gaudy and glittering in its colouring' which forces itself 'upon the notice of every wandering eye' than the life 'more exquisitely beautiful in its outline' which attracts the attention 'of scarce any body but the most studious and careful observer' (TMS I.iii.3.2, 62; cf. WN V.i.b.5, 711). Aristotle too knows of course that honor and wealth command more admirers than do virtue and wisdom; the popular conception of happiness is founded on attaining the visible goods of pleasure, wealth or honor (NE 1095a17–28; cf. TMS VI.ii.1.20, 225–6). Further, Aristotle too notes that at its root the use of wealth is intimately tied to love of esteem and admiration (NE 1123a18–27; TMS I.iii.2.1, 50–1; VI.i.3, 212–13). Yet, rather than lament this common disposition, both thinkers put it to work at the outset, as each knows that the most effective way of leading popular audiences to virtue is to appeal to its utility in helping such audiences attain the objects of their native desires. Thus to those who hope to better their condition Smith recommends probity and prudence, industry, independence of spirit, and fortitude in suffering and distress (TMS I.iii.2.5, 54–6). To those who find themselves successful, he counsels prudence and discretion so as not to court the envy of others (TMS I.ii.5.1, 40–1; R 1387a15). Emphasizing the utility of the virtues in helping claim and maintain rewards, Smith speaks to his audience in a language to which they seem predisposed. By so doing he reveals his commitment to the belief that success in the pursuit of wealth and external honors is 'the reward most proper for encouraging industry, prudence, and circumspection' (TMS III.5.8, 166–7).[22]

Yet if Part I shows its readers a better way of acquiring external goods, Part II marks the beginning of an ascent. In shifting the focus of the inquiry from propriety to merit, Part II turns from claiming goods to deserving them. Here Smith moves beyond what is commonly honored to examine those activities for which men deserve to be honored. By the end of Part II, no doubt remains as to what these activities are. 'Actions of a beneficent tendency, which proceed from proper motives, seem alone to require reward' (TMS II.ii.1.1, 78). As we now learn, the virtuous self-advancement with which Smith's work began is only the first leg of a much longer journey; these activities in fact run a distant second in naturalness and nobility to those activities which promote the well-being of others. This he makes clear in his scathing critique of pity. For all his fame as an exponent of sympathy, Smith hardly considers all forms of sympathy valuable. Hence his critique of that 'illusive sympathy' which leads us to shed 'sympathetic tears' – such tears, he insists, are 'but a small part of the duty' that we owe to the afflicted. Better than 'the indolent and passive fellow-feeling' of this sympathy is thus the 'more vigorous and active sentiment' that leads us to approve of positive exertions (TMS II.i.2.5, 70–1). Hence his critique of 'mere good inclinations and kind wishes':

> Man was made for action, and to promote by the exertion of his faculties such changes in the external circumstances both of himself and others, as may seem most favourable to the happiness of all. He must not be satisfied with indolent benevolence, nor fancy himself the friend of mankind, because in his heart he wishes well to the prosperity of the world. That he may call forth the whole vigour of his soul,

> and strain every nerve, in order to produce those ends which it is the purpose of his being to advance, Nature has taught him, that neither himself nor mankind can be fully satisfied with his conduct, nor bestow upon it the full measure of applause, unless he has actually produced them.
>
> (TMS II.iii.3.3, 106)

Mere 'indolent benevolence' never measures up to positive beneficence; good dispositions run distant second to good actions which realize results. Hence Smith's critique of the affected or 'extreme sympathy' with those whose conditions we cannot remedy; such a disposition he calls 'perfectly useless' (TMS III.3.9, 140). So too he insists that, while amiable, the pity that fails to prompt positive actions capable of benefiting others is of limited value (TMS I.ii.4.3, 40; VI.iii.15, 243). In sharp contrast, by 'being productive of the greatest good', active exertions of beneficence 'deserve the highest reward' – far greater than the deserts of the man of pity or even the just man who 'does no real positive good' by simply sitting still and harming none (TMS II.ii.1.9, 81–2; cf. NE 1155a22–8).[23] Thus if indeed man is made for action and beneficent activity in particular, to promote the well-being of others is to discover the very ends of our nature. The implication of the quote above seems to be that only in beneficent activity do we find our fullest flourishing as a unified being, purposefully at work in promoting the ends for which we have been made.

In recommending beneficent activity as the proper end of man's nature, Smith seems far from Aristotle. As everyone knows, according to Aristotle the best life for a man is discovered not in the life of ethical virtue – much less the life dedicated to the specific virtue of beneficence – but in the life of contemplation, the active exercise of the soul's rational principle (NE 1098a7–18; 1178a6–8).[24] Yet, this famous conclusion notwithstanding, Aristotle also offers an account of beneficent activity quite similar to Smith's. In his discussion of friendship he explains that beneficent activity offers individuals an opportunity to flourish. Hence, he explains, benefactors love the recipients of their gifts more than the recipients love their benefactors (NE 1168a3–9). But Smith's distinction between indolent benevolence and active beneficence particularly finds its parallel in Aristotle's distinction between good-willing (*eunoia*) and good-doing (*euergeia*). Like Smith, Aristotle believes that we are fashioned by nature in such a manner as to sympathize with others prior to reflection; *eunoia*, he notes, may spring up suddenly, as for 'competitors in a contest; the spectators conceive goodwill and sympathy for them, though they would not actively assist them'. Also like Smith, Aristotle too recognizes that such goodwill 'is a sudden growth, and the kindly feeling is only superficial' (NE 1166b34–1167a3). Left unto its own devices, the spectator's goodwill is feeble; in the absence of affection, *eunoia* never develops into that deeper and more substantial concern which might lead one to act. Hence spectators conceive goodwill for those they see, but never 'actively assist them' or allow themselves to 'be put to any trouble on their behalf' (NE 1167a10). Thus *eunoia* is only friendship's starting point, the first glimmer of a truly useful disposition (NE 1167a3).[25]

Thus, like Smith, Aristotle emphasizes the superiority of actual good deeds to the mere potentiality for good deeds that goodwill represents. But with this Aristotle faces a problem. If *eunoia* is only a beginning, what leads us to *euergeia*? By what means is the potential of the virtuous disposition to be made actual? Smith too must confront the same problem: if merit consists in performing good deeds but benevolence is too feeble to effect them, to what more forcible mechanism might we appeal to move us to our proper ends? Smith and Aristotle seem to offer the same answer: to be beneficent in practice, it is not to benevolence that we must appeal, but to its inverse: namely, self-love. Of course the self-love which Smith and Aristotle have in mind is hardly the self-love of vanity. This self-love takes its highest pleasure in the consciousness of deserved self-approbation rather than the actual approbation of others. Aristotle explicitly distinguishes these two forms of self-love in IX.viii, explaining that self-love can be taken in more than one sense. Its most common usage is as a term of reproach for those who 'assign to themselves the larger share of money, honors, or bodily pleasures' – 'the things which most men desire and set their hearts on as being the greatest goods, and which accordingly they compete with each other to obtain'. This 'ordinary kind' of self-love exhibited by 'most men' he dismisses as mere selfishness, insisting that those who take more than their share of external goods are 'rightly censured' (NE 1168b15–23). But beyond this ordinary self-love lies another, namely that of the 'lover of self in an exceptional degree', who 'takes for himself the things that are noblest and most truly good'. Just as 'living by principle differs from living by passion, and aiming at what is noble from aiming at what seems expedient', so does this noble self-love differ from self-love of the ordinary sort (NE 1168b28–1169a6). It is precisely this distinction that Smith himself recovers in Part III of TMS. Where the familiar sort of self-love examined in Part I trains its eye on claiming wealth and power so that their possessor might better enjoy the attention and approbation of his peers, the higher self-lover is concerned to deserve what is genuinely noble and honorable.[26] One driven by this sort of self-love takes his highest pleasure not in the opinions of others, but in his 'pleasing consciousness of deserved reward' for having performed the most praiseworthy actions, which are 'acts of beneficence' (TMS II.ii.3.4, 86).

Magnanimity

With this distinction in place we might restate the organization of Smith's education of moral character. It begins with a study of praise-claiming (Part I), and proceeds to examine the actions that deserve praise (Part II).

In Part III these two discussions are brought together; here Smith encourages his reader to obtain honor by performing actions deserving of honor. Here we learn that we seek 'not only to be loved, but to be lovely; or to be that thing which is the natural and proper object of love', and we desire 'not only praise, but praiseworthiness; or to be that thing which, though it should be praised by nobody, is, however, the natural and proper object of praise' (TMS III.2.1, 113–14). The inquiry that focused on the claiming of honor thus here gives way to an inquiry into moral nobility. Thus in what follows, Smith's focus is on the noble man's hopes 'not merely of obtaining, but of deserving the approbation and applause of his brethren' (TMS III.2.26, 126–7; cf. III.1.7, 113).

The key move of Smith's shift from claiming praise to praiseworthiness is his recovery of the noble self-love described by Aristotle. In his well known account of the earthquake in China Smith offers his fullest account of the nobler self-love that corrects vulgar self-love and alone can move its possessor to act. Thus the central question of his examination here: 'When our passive feelings are almost always so sordid and so selfish, how comes it that our active principles should often be so generous and so noble?' Aware that we are 'always so much more deeply affected by whatever concerns ourselves, than by whatever concerns other men', Smith wants to know what 'prompts the generous, upon all occasions, and the mean upon many, to sacrifice their own interests to the greater interests of others'. Like Aristotle, he again rejects the idea that friendly feeling alone might be sufficient: 'It is not the soft power of humanity, it is not that feeble spark of benevolence which Nature has lighted up in the human heart' that enables us to resist natural selfishness. To correct this we require 'a stronger power, a more forcible motive':

> It is not the love of our neighbour, it is not the love of mankind, which upon many occasions prompts us to the practice of those divine virtues. It is a stronger love, a more powerful affection, which generally takes place upon such occasions; the love of what is honourable and noble, of the grandeur, and dignity, and superiority of our own characters.

Vulgar selfishness thus can be remedied and our true ends can be realized only by an appeal to a higher self-love. By attending to what is truly worthy in us, we allow ourselves to be guided by 'a voice capable of astonishing the most presumptuous of our passions' – a voice that, seemingly paradoxically, teaches the lesson that 'we are but one of the multitude, in no respect better than any other in it'. Having learned this lesson, our propensity to 'prefer ourselves so shamefully and so blindly to others' is no longer countenanced. With 'the real littleness of ourselves, and of whatever relates to ourselves' implanted in our minds, we turn our backs on narrow selfishness, and 'the natural misrepresentations of self-love can be corrected' (TMS III.3.4, 136–7).

Smith's description of this phenomenon might return us to Aristotle's account of how the 'feelings of regard which we entertain for ourselves' in time give rise to friendship (NE 1166a5). Having shown the vulgarity of that self-love which aims at external goods, Aristotle now reveals the benefits of the sort of self-love which drives the man 'who loves and indulges the dominant part of himself' and can rightly be called the 'lover of self in the fullest degree (NE 1168b33–4)'. Aristotle leaves no doubt as to the highest part of our being; throughout this book it is repeatedly insisted that it is 'the intellectual part' which 'appears to be a man's real self' (NE 1166a17).[27] On this point he might depart from Smith, yet the consequences Aristotle traces to this higher love of self are the same traced by Smith. So far from leading the greatest self-lover to prefer himself to others, the truest self-love instead promotes our concern for others. Thus Aristotle insists that the good man should be the greatest lover of himself not only because by so doing he lives in accord with what is highest in himself, but because by so doing he is led to act in a certain way toward others; only by being a lover of self in this highest sense can he 'both benefit himself by acting nobly and aid his fellows' (NE 1169a6–15).[28]

Elsewhere in his text Aristotle personifies this man. His portrait of the great-souled man offers a glimpse of how the noble self-lover is disposed towards honor and how he acts towards others. On the surface, the great-souled man seems to be principally concerned with honor; that is to say, he seems to be driven principally by the selfish love of external goods, the sort likely to claim much and deserve much (NE 1123b1–4). But Aristotle's study of greatness of soul, like the whole of which it is a part, operates dialectically.[29] In time we learn that the great-souled man is in truth the sort of man 'to whom even honor is a small thing' (NE 1124a17–20), and that it is not truly honor, but perfect moral nobility, *kalokagathia*, that is the object of his desires. Thus as the chapter develops we learn that the magnanimous man's greatness consists not in claiming honor – to which he is, by the end of the chapter, indifferent – but in deserving it on account of the way in which he is disposed towards others. Thus at the end of NE IV.iii Aristotle gives evidence for the *Rhetoric*'s provocative (though largely overlooked) definition of magnanimity as a virtue that produces great benefits (*euergetēmatōn*) (R 1366b17). Such benefactions are not performed in a spirit of compassion or pity, but rather from a desire to claim superiority in nobility through exceptional actions (NE 1124b9–18).

Magnanimity is of course an important concept for Adam Smith as well (TMS VII.ii.1.7, 268; VII.ii.1.12, 271; VI.iii.44, 258). (Cf. Cropsey 1957: 26, 56–61; see also Den Uyl and Griswold 1996: 625 n. 46.) At several points he calls attention to the beauty of magnanimous self-command and the fortitude that enables its possessor to steel himself against fortune's assaults and prevents him from depressing his companions through sympathetic commiseration with his misfortunes; indeed, in so far as Smith's admiration of self-command is tied to his admiration of magnanimity, it may have an Aristotelian as well as a Stoic provenance (TMS I.i.5.8, 25–6; I.iii.1.13–14, 47–9; NE 1100b30–3). But his magnanimous man particularly resembles Aristotle's in so far as he is more concerned to deserve than to claim; like Aristotle's, in the midst of the most profound suffering such a man consoles himself by reflecting on 'the applause and admiration which he is about to deserve by the heroic magnanimity of his behaviour' (TMS I.iii.1.14, 49). Further, he too appears to be genuinely indifferent to the opinions of others; he takes 'some reference to the sentiments of others' only in so far as he cares for what they ought to think rather than what they actually do think:

> The man of the greatest magnanimity, who desires virtue for its own sake, and is most indifferent about what actually are the opinions of mankind with regard to him, is still, however, delighted with the thoughts of what they should be, with the consciousness that though he may neither be honoured nor applauded, he is still the proper object of honour and applause, and that if mankind were cool and candid and consistent with themselves, and properly informed of the motives and circumstances of his conduct, they would not fail to honour and applaud him.

Thus while the man 'who while he desires to merit approbation is at the same time anxious to obtain it' may be 'laudable in the main', Smith insists that his motives have 'a greater mixture of human infirmity' than those of the one who acts only out of a desire to deserve and not obtain. Only the man of real magnanimity acts for the sake of the noble as opposed to acting for the sake of the opinions of others – 'the most sublime and godlike motive which human nature is even capable of conceiving' (TMS VII.ii.4.10, 310–11). Such faith in self is necessary for such a man, Smith insists. Even the greatest acts of beneficence are rarely celebrated with the level of esteem they deserve; with Aristotle he agrees that benefactors seem to love the recipients of their benefactions more than such recipients love them in return (NE 1167b17–28). Knowing this, Smith counsels that those who magnanimously serve others will do well to take their pleasure within, 'secure that, however misunderstood or misrepresented', they are yet 'the natural and proper objects of approbation' – a faith in self that leads us to become 'indifferent about the applause, and, in some measure, despise the censure of the world' (TMS III.1.5, 112). The more confident we are in our judgments of our merit, the more indifferent we will become about their praise, having less need for them to confirm our formerly tottering judgments of ourselves (TMS III.2.16, 122; NE 1095b26–30). In this respect such a man resembles Aristotle's ideal friend who labors without asking for reward; 'when he wishes a person's good', he 'wishes it for that person's own sake, even though nobody will ever know of it' (NE 1168b1–3). Confident in his self-worth, such a man is indifferent to both the malice and the praise of others.

But where are such men to be found? Politics would seem an unlikely arena for his genius; on the whole, Smith is more prone to find in political men 'excessive self-admiration' than genuine indifference to the praises or censure of others (TMS VI.iii.27, 249; cf. VI.ii.2.18, 234). But at his best, the exemplary political man – 'the reformer and legislator of a great state' who shows himself able to 'secure the internal tranquillity and happiness of his fellow-citizens for many succeeding generations' – seems to reach this peak of magnanimity. His efforts on behalf of peace and stability, Smith suggests, constitute the most extensive beneficence realizable in politics and render him worthy of the high regard in which he holds himself (TMS VI.ii.2.14, 232). In such a man perhaps we catch a glimpse of that exemplary human being who is able to combine the amiable and the awful virtues (TMS I.i.5.5, 25; III.3.35, 152). He is perhaps the most visible example of Smith's hope that the peak ancient virtue of magnanimity might be joined to the representative modern virtue of benevolence.

The character of virtue and the wise and virtuous man

Smith's virtue ethics receives its most sustained exposition in Part VI of TMS, 'Of the Character of Virtue', newly added to the sixth (1790) edition. Here Smith offers his most direct treatment of those ethical virtues which are least amenable to the rule-bound treatment, namely 'prudence' and 'just magnanimity' and 'proper beneficence' (TMS III.6.11, 176). Smith's methods here will be of particular interest to virtue ethicists; here we see his skill at moral portrait painting at its best, and particularly in his portraits of the prudent man, the magnanimous statesman, and the wise and virtuous man (cf. NE 1095b14–19). But this section is also of particular interest for a second reason. The dialectical movement that we have traced in TMS as a whole is repeated in Part VI in microcosm, as Part VI itself ascends from an examination of the role of virtue in the pursuit of external goods to an examination of the sort of virtue necessary for moral nobility via a systematic consideration of the virtues of prudence, magnanimity and proper beneficence.

The moral education offered in both TMS as a whole and especially in Part VI seems to be governed by its author's fidelity to what he calls 'the great secret of education', namely 'to direct vanity to proper objects' (TMS VI.iii.46, 259). In both Part VI and the book as a whole Smith regards self-love as in fact educable and capable of being directed to more noble objects.[30] Thus Part VI too begins with the common perspective of the pursuit of external goods. Smith's examination of 'inferior prudence' there represents not only his study of the virtue most closely associated with the commercial world of WN, but also the virtue most closely associated with the discussion of propriety and instrumentality in TMS I. Now, interestingly Aristotle too notes that prudence sometimes takes the form of a capacity to deliberate about what is immediately advantageous to one's self (NE 1140a24–31). This recognition leads him to pass quickly to more elevated virtues (NE 1141a20–2). In particular it leads him immediately to distinguish between the prudence that limits itself to guiding the acquisition of individuals to a more elevated prudence dedicated to political ruling (NE 1141b29–1142a11). Smith's distinction of inferior from superior prudence is of course made on precisely these same grounds. For all his respectability, the man of inferior prudence, deaf to 'the real and solid glory of performing the greatest and most magnanimous actions', can neither elicit nor deserve our highest approbation (TMS VI.i.13, 216). His circumspection is amiable, but never can we regard it as one 'of the most endearing, or of the most ennobling of the virtues'; such a man can elicit only our 'cold esteem' and 'seems not entitled to any very ardent love or admiration' (TMS VI.i.14, 216).[31] What once seemed admirable is thus little more than 'vulgar prudence' in contrast to the 'superior prudence' which encompasses not only propriety but also valor, justice, self-command and benevolence (TMS VI.conc.5, 263; VI.i.15, 216). Such a distinction of inferior from superior prudence reveals Smith's recognition that virtue can take more and less noble forms, and perhaps might itself be regarded as a development of his claim that in fact 'there is no virtue' in the common degree of moral or practical qualities, since 'virtue is excellence, something uncommonly great and beautiful, which rises far above what is vulgar and ordinary' (TMS I.i.5.6, 25).

Thus just as Aristotle's magnanimous man represents a peak of excellence in the ethical virtues, so too does Smith's man of superior prudence represent a political excellence superior to the individualistic excellence represented by inferior prudence. But even in praising this fellow, Smith clearly sees his faults. The self-love of inferior prudence is useful but narrow in its horizons; the magnanimous man's self-love, though more elevated than the self-love of inferior prudence, is also potentially far more destructive. For all his well intended preference of the praiseworthy to praise, the aspirant to magnanimity is occasionally prone to lose sight of the former in his love of the latter. Both Aristotle and Smith are profoundly aware of the dangers to which such excessive self-admiration can lead; the image of the tyrannical conqueror whose lust for honor leads him to do battle with both men and gods is never far from either of their minds (TMS VI.iii.28, 250–2). Indeed, this excessive self-admiration that 'dazzles the multitude' and elicits their 'foolish admiration' would be amusing were it not so dangerous. The best sort of men, Smith would have you know, 'secretly smile' at such men and their 'extravagant and groundless pretensions' (TMS VI.iii.27, 249–50).

But who are these best men? Having illustrated the dangers of magnanimity, Smith turns to an explication of his understanding of ethical self-perfection. His presentation of the wise and virtuous man is thus in some sense analogous to Aristotle's presentation of the superiority of the life of contemplation; both conceptions of self-perfection are indeed presented by their authors as attempts to transcend the problems which emerge from the unrestrained competition for nobility by men of ethical virtue (NE 1169a6–15). Smith particularly insists that wise and virtuous men take their pleasures elsewhere than in the restless pursuit of either honor or nobility. Popular glory he never courts, for 'to a real wise man the judicious and well-weighed approbation of a single wise man, gives more heartfelt satisfaction than all the noisy applauses of ten thousand ignorant though enthusiastic admirers' (TMS VI.iii.31, 253). Such a distinction between the merited praises of knowing judges and the 'foolish' praises of the 'common people' or the 'mob of mankind' is in fact a near-constant throughout Smith's work (TMS I.iii.3.8, 64–6; VI.iii.27, 249–50; VI.iii.30, 253). While not always so explicitly contemptuous of popular praise, it is evident that Smith thinks soliciting such praises is beneath the dignity of the wise and virtuous man.

But the wise and virtuous man is not only distinguished by his disposition towards honor. In a way he resembles the magnanimous man; like him, the wise and virtuous man enjoys a pleasant consciousness of having performed beneficent actions. He too acts from his love of nobility and reverence for the superiority of his own character. But here the wise and virtuous man parts company with the magnanimous man. Earlier Smith suggested that greatness consists not simply in the love of nobility and what is highest within us, but also in the realization that it produces: that even the best man is 'but one of the multitude, in no respect better than any other in it' (TMS III.3.4, 137; II.ii.2.1, 82–3; VI.ii.2.2, 227–8). But it is precisely this that the magnanimous men cannot expect. Even if they despise honor, their pursuit of nobility is yet plagued by their desire for superiority, and this love of superiority forbids them full acceptance of their 'real littleness' (TMS III.3.4, 137). Wise and virtuous men, however, carry with them always an awareness of precisely that which Alexander, Caesar and Socrates forgot. Unlike magnanimous men constantly comparing themselves with others, the wise and virtuous man keeps before him a higher standard of absolute perfection. Never forgetting that higher standards than those of others exist, he is always 'much more humbled by the one comparison, than he ever can be elevated by the other'. Remembering with 'concern and humiliation' how far short he falls of the image of absolute perfection which he carries with him always, he alone never forgets his real littleness. Yet the wise and virtuous man's understanding of the limits of human perfectibility does not lead him simply to reject self-perfection and embrace humility. Instead, this understanding forms the foundation of a modern understanding of self-perfection. His resulting combination of profound pride and profound humility colors not only his conception of himself, but also his relations with others:

> He is never so elated as to look down with insolence even upon those who are really below him. He feels so well his own imperfection, he knows so well the difficulty with which he attained his own distant approximation to rectitude, that he cannot regard with contempt the still greater imperfection of other people. Far from insulting over their inferiority, he views it with the most indulgent commiseration, and, by his advice as well as example, is at all times willing to promote their further advancement.
>
> (TMS VI.iii.25, 247–8)

Even in the consciousness of his genuine superiority, he has no interest in lording his superiority over his inferiors; his is, on the contrary, of a decidedly more humane disposition.[32]

But how does the wise and virtuous man promote the well-being of others by advice and example? Elsewhere Smith offers a clue. 'Political disquisitions', he explains, 'if just, and reasonable, and practicable, are of all the works of speculation the most useful' (TMS IV.1.11, 187). If true, works of political speculation might restore to theory the possibility of its providing the very benefits neglected by those speculators who neglect their active duties (TMS VI.ii.3.6, 237). Of course Aristotle likewise agrees that in so far as the end of politics is to make others better, inquiry into the nature of politics may be a quite useful sort of inquiry (NE 1099b29–32; 1102a7–13). In light of this similarity, it is important to note that both Smith's and Aristotle's ethics end on a remarkably similar note which nods in this direction: namely a promise of another, explicitly political project that will build on the moral project (TMS VII.iv.37, 341–2; cf. NE 1181b12–15). Thus in his final chapter Aristotle reminds us that 'in the practical sciences the end is not to attain a theoretic knowledge of the various subjects, but rather to carry out our theories in action' (NE 1179a35–1179b2; cf. TMS VII.ii.1.14, 272). Yet if one hopes 'to assist his own children and friends to attain virtue', he insists, one must first know something of 'the science of legislation' (NE 1180a29–34). Furthermore, in so far as the science that aims at promoting the happiness of men aims at what is best in specific instances, it may be that knowledge of general rules will not be enough (NE 1180b7–16; cf. TMS VII.iv.35ff., 340–2). Thus it is incumbent on us to examine specific constitutions and positive legal systems so that we may better know 'what is the best constitution absolutely, and what are the best regulations, laws, and customs for any given form of constitution' (NE 1181b20–2). This seems to be Smith's method as well. He too thinks that other thinkers have only evaluated the available regimes, and have failed to give an account of the best regime. This is hardly useless information, he agrees, but it is on the basis of these studies that he seeks to march forward and, like Aristotle, inquire into 'the natural rules of justice independent of all positive institution', leading to 'a theory of the general principles which ought to run through and be the foundation of the laws of all nations' (TMS VII.iv.37, 341–2). If *The Theory of Moral Sentiments* is in some sense meant to be his modern *Ethics*, the political disquisition to which Smith nods at the end of his ethics may well be his *Politics.*[33]

Smith of course never completed this political disquisition, but he at least got far enough to give us some sense of where he was headed. In what we have of it we find the wise and virtuous man at work. *The Wealth of Nations* opens with a caution to philosophers; whatever solace they might find in their superiority, Smith reminds them that by nature they are in fact no better than porters (WN I.ii.4, 28–9). But Smith not only reminds the philosopher that the porter is his equal; he also will remind him that he may yet owe the porter something more than the smallest active duty. 'The most dissimilar geniuses are of use to one another' (WN I.ii.5, 30). How porters might serve philosophers is easily enough imagined, but how might the philosopher serve the porter?

The *Lectures on Jurisprudence* offer a suggestion. There we learn that 'even wisdom and virtue in all its branches derive their lustre and beauty with regard to utility merely from their tendency to provide for the security of mankind' in necessities and conveniences. Wisdom and virtue is thus discovered not in honor or nobility, but in fulfilling ends that have commonly been regarded as 'the objects of the labour of the vulgar alone'. Such an approach seems meant as a reproach to those who consider such banality beneath them. Perhaps it is to these that Smith means to direct his observation that:

> in a certain view of things all the arts, the sciences, law and government, wisdom, and even virtue itself tend all to this one thing, the providing meat, drink, rayment, and lodging for men, which are commonly reckoned the meanest of employments and fit for the pursuit of none but the lowest and meanest of the people.
>
> (LJ 338)[34]

But this is of course the project of the *Wealth of Nations*, which aims to effect the practical betterment of the conditions of the poor through the achievement of 'that universal opulence which extends itself to the lowest ranks of the people' (WN I.i.10, 22). Through the authorship of the *Wealth of Nations* Smith himself therefore may be said to offer his own self as an illustration of the character of wisdom and virtue. In particular, Smith's authorship is meant to show how the ethical virtues of the wise and virtuous man might be harmonized with the intellectual virtues of the political speculator. And in so far as this character also represents an attempt to recover an understanding of self-perfection deeply informed by Aristotle, it may also point to another mechanism for the 'preservation of desirable aspects of ancient thought' within modernity (Griswold 1999: 7).

Notes

Earlier versions of this chapter were presented at the 2001 annual meeting of the Eighteenth Century Scottish Studies Society in Arlington, VA, and the 2001 annual meeting of the American Political Science Association in San Francisco. I am grateful to both audiences – and especially to Lauren Brubaker, Doug Den Uyl, Sam Fleischacker, Leon Montes, Jim Otteson and Eric Schliesser – for their many helpful suggestions.

1 The growing literature on virtue ethics is usefully surveyed and its central claims presented in Trianosky (1990), Stohr and Wellman (2002) and Copp and Sobel (2004). For important challenges to virtue ethics as a coherent third alternative to utilitarianism and Kantianism, see especially Nussbaum (1999) and Singleton (2002).
2 The recovery of Aristotle's approach to ethics is the departure point for several of the seminal statements of virtue ethics; see for instance Anscombe (1958). Aristotle's place as the originator of the virtue ethics tradition is underlined by Alasdair MacIntyre in several of his writings and perhaps most clearly in MacIntyre (2001). For critiques of the misappropriation of Aristotle by modern virtue ethicists on the grounds that their theories overemphasize Aristotle's egoism and neglect his understanding of the place of politics in human flourishing, see Simpson (1992) and Buckle (2002).
3 Darwall (2003) includes readings from three philosophers prior to the twentieth century: Aristotle, Hutcheson and Hume; cf. MacIntyre (2001: 1760). On Hume's virtue ethics, see Homiak (2000a, b). For a critical evaluation, see Hursthouse (1999a: 80–1). Douglas Den Uyl also makes a strong case for Shaftesbury as a 'classical virtue ethicist' in Den Uyl (1998: 276ff.).
4 Other commentators have nicely developed Smith's debts to Aristotle on other points. On justice, see Berns (1994); on friendship, see Den Uyl and Griswold (1996: esp. 616, 634); on the commercial virtues, see Calkins and Werhane (1998); on practical wisdom, see Fleischacker (1999) and Carrasco (2004); on self-command and the mean, see Vivenza (2001: 46ff.) and Montes (2004: 81–6). The present study seeks to complement these by pointing to yet another point of agreement on the grounds of their shared understanding of character and the role of ethics in its education.
5 References to Aristotle's works are as follows: NE *Nicomachean Ethics;* P *Politics;* R *Rhetoric.* In quoting the *Ethics* and the *Rhetoric* I have generally followed, respectively, Rackham's (Loeb) and Kennedy's (Oxford) translations.
6 In setting Smith and Aristotle in conversation my intention is not to make a historical case for the former's direct appropriation of the latter. This ground, in any case, has been well covered in Vivenza's admirable *Smith and the Classics.* I have also benefited from the same author's warning not to search for a 'particular interpretive key . . . grounded on a classical philosophy reworked by modern minds' (Vivenza 2004: 117). I am grateful to Professor Vivenza for allowing me to read her manuscript in advance of its publication.
7 Compare Smith's critique to the critiques of contemporary moral philosophy set forth in Baier (1985) and Hursthouse (1999b); cf. Stohr and Wellman (2002: 55).
8 Smith's recognition that the nature of justice requires that it be treated in a manner different from the other ethical virtues anticipates and thereby avoids one of the most common objections to contemporary virtue ethics, namely that it fails to provide a sufficient defense for justice itself; see, for example, Stohr and Wellman (2002: 68).
9 In WN Smith uses the example of casuistry to illustrate the fundamental dif-

ference between 'the ancient moral philosophy' and 'the modern philosophy', namely that where in the former 'the duties of human life were treated of as subservient to the happiness and perfection of human life', modernity has replaced the aspiration to 'the perfection of virtue' and 'the happiness and perfection of a man' with an ascetic morality focused on the afterlife (WN V.i.f.30, 771).

10 For an excellent discussion of the origins and operation of these general moral rules with respect to justice, see Fleischacker (1999: 41–55).

11 Smith's formulation recalls Hume's own distinction between 'two different manners' of moral philosophy in the first section of EHU 1.1–2, and especially his distinction between the artist and anatomist at EHU 1.8.

12 Of course Smith's qualifications need to be remembered throughout. Such systems, he here insists, achieve all that 'precept and exhortation can do to animate us to the practice of virtue' (TMS VII.iv.6, 329), yet the limits of such systems have already been clearly noted (TMS VII.ii.4.5, 307).

13 Smith's specific debts to Cicero are noted especially in Waszek (1984); cf. Vivenza (2001: 3–4, 42, 66, 191–4); and the response offered in Montes (2004: 124–8).

14 See especially Griswold (1999: 4–5, 315–16, 332–3). See also Werhane (1991: 49); cf. Fleischacker (1999: 147–51).

15 See especially Cropsey (1957: esp. 49–50).

16 See especially Calkins and Werhane (1998: 43ff.).

17 See especially Fleischacker (1999: 161); cf. Waszek (1984: 591ff.).

18 See especially Den Uyl (1998: 316): 'For Smith, then, the problem of virtue in modern times is solved by rejecting the classical elitism that defines virtue in terms of the perfection of one's soul and focusing instead on sentiments conducive to social cooperation'; cf. Den Uyl and Griswold (1996: 617); Den Uyl (1991: 137); Cropsey (1957: 38); cf. Fleischacker (1999: 140–4).

19 Fleischacker notes that 'Aristotle is the only moral philosopher coming in for no criticism' in the whole of TMS; see Fleischacker (1999: 122).

20 See especially NE 1098b9–12. My understanding of Aristotle's dialectic and his appeal to *endoxa* is particularly indebted to Tessitore (1996) and Jaffa (1952). Griswold also identifies Smith's methods as 'broadly Aristotelian' in this fashion; see Griswold (1999: 58).

21 On Smith's 'dialectic', see also Den Uyl and Griswold (1996: 611); Lerner (1999: 65); Skinner (1979: 45). See also Griswold's account of TMS as a 'story that unfolds in steps' (Griswold 1999: 61, 331); and Macfie's claim that TMS sets forth a 'theory of graduated individual values' and a 'psychological account of the progress from vanity to magnanimity' (Macfie 1967: 54, 72) – an understanding quite close to the notion of the dialectic of self-love that I mean to set forth here.

22 Thus while Aristotle and Smith clearly address different audiences, both seek to elevate well disposed elements in their respective audiences to a life better than the characteristic life of their fellows. Smith perhaps faces the greater challenge in so far as his audience begins from the lower point of pleasure in external goods that Aristotle dismisses as beneath his inquiry. The fact that Smith is compelled to begin from this lower point may explain if not excuse his failure to ascend to a full defense of the intellectual virtues. In any case, Smith seems to wish to transcend what MacIntyre regards as the irreconcilable divide that separates the classical or Aristotelian world of gentlemen from the modern 'Franklinian' world of commerce; see MacIntyre (1984: 181–203).

23 Montes provides an excellent summary of the distinction between benevolence and beneficence in Smith's (and in Hutcheson's and Bentham's) thought in Montes (2004: 106 n. 14). The same distinction is also central to contemporary moral philosophy. Thus William Frankena explains that '[b]enevolence is a

matter of intention, not of outcome; beneficence is one of outcome, not intention, though it may be intentional'. Frankena does, however, qualify this claim in a way that would have been unfamiliar to Smith, insisting that benevolence should be distinguished 'from mere well-*wishing* or *meaning*-well', as benevolence 'means *willing*, and genuinely *trying* to do or bring about good and not evil' (Frankena 1987: 2); the point is further developed in Livnat (2004: 309–10).

24 Of course this understanding has itself been the subject of a great debate; for its most recent instantiation, see the response of Lear (2004) to Kraut (1989).

25 Contemporary virtue ethicists have been troubled by Aristotle's seeming lack of commitment to humanitarianism; see for instance Slote (2000: esp. 335, 344). But Aristotle's conscious distinction between *eunoia* and *euergeia* and Smith's elaboration of this in TMS perhaps provide adequate resources for a substantial and robust form of active beneficence within virtue ethics, if not for the cosmopolitan compassion and caring that Slote means to defend. On this idea see also Berns's study of the relationship of Smith's sympathy to Aristotelian *philanthropia* (Berns 1994: 72–4).

26 Some commentators have distinguished self-love from vulgar selfishness on the grounds that the latter directly harms others whereas the former gives rise to the virtues of enlightened and prudential self-interest. See, for example, the editors' introduction to TMS, 22; and Samuel Hollander's claim that for Smith the 'motive of "self-love" is synonymous with that of "prudence"' (Hollander 1977: 138). But Smith yet seems to realize a higher self-love beyond mere enlightened self-interest, one similar to the Aristotelian self-love, which, so far from reaffirming the pursuit of external goods, transcends it.

27 Smith does claim that 'reason, principle, conscience' is the seat of what is noble within us, though his emphasis on reason is hardly so pronounced as Aristotle's; cf. Berns (1994: 87–9). But how sharp a divide should we draw? Aristotle of course argues for the supremacy of intellect, whereas for Smith the origin of morality lies in sentiment and not reason; the very notion of a 'moral sentiment' seems foreign to Aristotle, who explicitly claims that emotions, in so far as they are irrational, cannot be ethical (NE 1105b28–1106a2). Yet at the same time Aristotle is also aware of the need to discover a mechanism whereby the irrational might be made to participate with the rational (NE 1102b13–28; cf. Sherman 1989: 2, 162–4), just as Smith seems to suggest that the impartial spectator should serve to bring reason to bear on sentiment through judgment.

28 On the relationship of self-love to other-directed activity in Aristotle, see especially Kraut (1989: chapter 2).

29 The ideas introduced here – and particularly the relationship between beneficent actions and the love of superiority – are treated at greater length in Hanley (2002).

30 See also Hursthouse: 'our passions, which we are born with an inescapable and unchangeable tendency to feel, are themselves malleable: We can be trained, and can then go on to train ourselves further, through reflection, to feel our passions in certain ways and not others' (Hursthouse 1999a: 81); cf., in a different context, Cropsey: 'Moral philosophy is still to work upon men to seek good and avoid evil, but their passionate self-regard will be employed as the means' (Cropsey 1957: 29).

31 Smith's distinction between the men of inferior and superior prudence might be compared to the difference between Aristotle's *phronimos* and *megalopsychos*. Others have also seen the influence of Aristotle's *phronimos* in Smith's work; see Vivenza (2001: 47–9, 83); Griswold (1999: 204–5); Fleischacker (1999: 120–39).

32 Similarly Aristotelian self-sufficiency requires not transcendence but right relations with friends, families and fellow citizens; see NE 1097b6–11. One must be

around others to be beneficent (NE 1155a5–11; 1171a21–7), and even contemplation benefits from friendship; cf. Vivenza (2001: 58).

33 Smith may not be alone in this respect; see John Danford's compelling argument for Hume's second *Enquiry* as an 'a *Nicomachean Ethics* for liberal commercial society, an ethics consistent with the political situation of modern man' (Danford 1990: 161).

34 Yet this formulation leads one to wonder whether Smith's account of wisdom and virtue falls victim to Aristotle's critique of unequal friendships. Aristotle's defense of contemplation is in part presented as an attempt to establish a genuinely equal friendship in contrast to the unequal friendships in which one reaps the merely useful and the other the noble (NE 1168a9–12). Yet at the same time, Smith's account of wisdom and virtue seeks to remedy a certain shortcoming in Aristotle's account that modern readers have been hesitant to accept. Aristotle draws a rigid line of demarcation between gentlemen and philosophers, but Smith's wise and virtuous man seems to aspire to a reconciliation of the ethical and the intellectual virtues; cf. Den Uyl and Griswold (1996: 634).

References

Anscombe, G. E. M. (1958) 'Modern Moral Philosophy', *Philosophy*, 33: 1–19; reprinted in *Ethics, Religion and Politics* (1981), Minneapolis, MN: University of Minnesota Press.

Aristotle (1932) *Politics*, trans. H. Rackham, Cambridge, MA: Harvard University Press.

—— (1934) *Nicomachean Ethics*, trans. H. Rackham, Cambridge, MA: Harvard University Press.

—— (1991) *Rhetoric*, trans. G. A. Kennedy. Oxford: Oxford University Press.

Baier, A. (1985) 'Doing Without Moral Theory', in *Postures of the Mind*, Minneapolis, MN: University of Minnesota Press.

Berns, L. (1994) 'Aristotle and Adam Smith on Justice: Cooperation between Ancients and Moderns?' *Review of Metaphysics* 48: 71–90.

Buckle, S. (2002) 'Aristotle's *Republic*: or Why Aristotle's Ethics is not Virtue Ethics', *Philosophy* 77: 565–95.

Calkins, M. J. and Werhane, P. H. (1998) 'Adam Smith, Aristotle, and the Virtues of Commerce', *Journal of Value Inquiry* 32: 43–60.

Carrasco, M. A. (2004) 'Adam Smith's Reconstruction of Practical Reason', *Review of Metaphysics* 58: 81–116.

Copp, D. and Sobel, D. (2004) 'Morality and Virtue: An Assessment of Some Recent Work in Virtue Ethics', *Ethics* 114: 514–54.

Cropsey, J. (1957 [2001]) *Polity and Economy*, South Bend, IN: St Augustine's Press.

Danford, J. (1990) *David Hume and the Problem of Reason*, New Haven, CT: Yale University Press.

Darwall, S. (ed.) (2003) *Virtue Ethics*, Oxford: Blackwell.

Den Uyl, D. (1991) *The Virtue of Prudence*, New York: Peter Lang.

—— (1998) 'Shaftesbury and the Modern Problem of Virtue', *Social Philosophy and Policy* 15: 275–316.

—— and Griswold, C. (1996) 'Adam Smith on Friendship and Love', *Review of Metaphysics* 49: 609–37.

Fleischacker, S. (1999) *A Third Concept of Liberty: Judgment and Freedom in Kant and Adam Smith*, Princeton, NJ: Princeton University Press.

Frankena, W. (1987) 'Beneficence/Benevolence', *Social Philosophy and Policy* 4: 1–20.

Griswold, C. (1999) *Adam Smith and the Virtues of Enlightenment*, Cambridge: Cambridge University Press.

Hanley, R. P. (2002) 'Aristotle on the Greatness of Greatness of Soul', *History of Political Thought* 23: 1–20.

Hollander, S. (1977) 'Adam Smith and the Self-interest Axiom', *Journal of Law and Economics* 20: 133–52.

Homiak, M. (2000a) 'Hume's Ethics: Ancient or Modern?' *Pacific Philosophical Quarterly* 81: 215–36.

—— (2000b) 'Does Hume Have an Ethics of Virtue? Some Observations on Character and Reasoning in Hume and Aristotle', in M. Gedney (ed.) *The Proceedings of the Twentieth World Congress of Philosophy*, VII, Bowling Green, OH: Bowling Green State University Press.

Hursthouse, R. (1999a) 'Virtue Ethics and Human Nature', *Hume Studies* 25: 67–82.

—— (1999b) *On Virtue Ethics*, Oxford: Oxford University Press.

Jaffa, H. V. (1952) *Thomism and Aristotelianism*, Chicago: University of Chicago Press.

Kraut, R. (1989) *Aristotle on the Human Good*, Princeton, NJ: Princeton University Press.

Lear, G. R. (2004) *Happy Lives and the Highest Good*, Princeton, NJ: Princeton University Press.

Lerner, R. (1999) 'Love of Fame and the Constitution of Liberty', in T. Angerer (ed.) *Geschichte und Recht*, Vienna: Böhlau Verlag.

Livnat, Y. (2004) 'On the Nature of Benevolence', *Journal of Social Philosophy* 35: 304–17.

Macfie, A. L. (1967) *The Individual in Society*, London: Methuen.

MacIntyre, A. (1984) *After Virtue*, South Bend, IN: Notre Dame University Press.

—— (2001) 'Virtue Ethics', in L. C. Becker and C. B. Becker (eds) *Encyclopedia of Ethics*, London: Routledge.

Montes, L. (2004) *Adam Smith in Context: A Critical Reassessment of Some Central Components of his Thought*, London: Palgrave Macmillan.

Nussbaum, M. (1999) 'Virtue Ethics: A Misleading Category?' *Journal of Ethics* 3: 163–201.

Sherman, N. (1989) *The Fabric of Character: Aristotle's Theory of Virtue*, Oxford: Oxford University Press.

Simpson, P. (1992) 'Contemporary Virtue Ethics and Aristotle', *Review of Metaphysics* 45: 503–24.

Singleton, J. (2002) 'Virtue Ethics, Kantian Ethics, and Consequentialism', *Journal of Philosophical Research* 27: 537–51.

Skinner, A. S. (1979) *A System of Social Science: Papers Relating to Adam Smith*, Oxford: Oxford University Press.

Slote, M. (2000) 'Virtue Ethics', in H. LaFollette (ed.) *The Blackwell Guide to Ethical Theory*, Oxford: Blackwell.

Stohr, K. and Wellman, C. (2002) 'Recent Work on Virtue Ethics', *American Philosophical Quarterly* 39: 49–72.

Tessitore, A. (1996) *Reading Aristotle's Ethics: Virtue, Rhetoric, Political Philosophy*, Albany, NY: State University of New York Press.

Trianosky, G. (1990) 'What is Virtue Ethics All About? Recent Work on the Virtues', *American Philosophical Quarterly* 27: 335–44.

Vivenza, G. (2001) *Adam Smith and the Classics: The Classical Heritage in Adam Smith's Thought*, Oxford: Oxford University Press.

—— (2004) 'Reading Adam Smith in Light of the Classics', *Adam Smith Review* 1: 107–24.

Waszek, N. (1984) 'Two Concepts of Morality: A Distinction of Adam Smith's Ethics and its Stoic Origin', *Journal of the History of Ideas* 45: 591–606.

Werhane, P. (1991) *Adam Smith and His Legacy for Modern Capitalism*, Oxford: Oxford University Press.

3 Adam Smith and his feminist contemporaries

Edith Kuiper

> The Novelty and Daringness of this Performance cannot avoid drawing upon me the Attention of the Female World and the Criticisms of the Male. To endeavour refuting an Opinion of so long standing as that of *the Superiority of the Men over the Women, with respect to Genius and Abilities* must appear to many a strange and impractible Attempt;...
>
> (A Lady, *Female Rights vindicated or the Equality of the Sexes, Morally and Physically proved*, 1758: preface)

Adam Smith scarcely mentions women and gender issues in his TMS and WN. Because his texts were generally read as value-neutral in relation to gender, historians of economics tended to conclude from this that there was no significant contemporary discussion of women's or gender issues. However, research into women's and gender history as well as into the history of political and social theory and philosophy shows that there was an emerging debate on issues of gender equality and women's subordinate position to men that started as individual expressions of discontent and grew into a broader movement by the end of the eighteenth century.

Smith did engage in discussions on gender equality, for example, in his teaching, the notes of which were published in LJ. However, the arguments on these topics remained distinct from his moral philosophy and political economy (see also Nyland 2003b on this point), and are barely mentioned in the books published during his lifetime – TMS (1759) and WN (1776). There is an emerging literature on Smith's views on women, pointing out his position concerning the social and economic position of women and his use of and approach to masculine and feminine virtues (Rendall 1987; Akkerman 1992; Folbre 1992; Pujol 1992; Justman 1993; Sutherland 1995; Kuiper 2001; Nyland 2003b; see also Brown 1997). This chapter investigates the feminist discourse on the differences and equality between the sexes in the eighteenth century, in France and England. It also explores the ways in which Adam Smith had been in contact with these views, and how they may have influenced his writings.

The next section discusses early feminisms especially in France and

England, focusing on British feminism in the second half of the eighteenth century. I discuss in the third section two texts which can be characterized as early feminist economic texts: the first is a poem by Mary Collier, *The Woman's Labour* (1739), and the second is *Female Rights vindicated; or the Equality of the Sexes Morally and Physically proved* (1758), which was authored by 'A Lady' (anonymous). In the fourth section, the ways Smith might have been in contact with these discourses are discussed, and the position he takes on feminist issues in LJ, TMS, and WN is explored. The fifth section contains the conclusion.

Early feminist waves

Generally speaking, we refer to the feminist waves of the 1960s and 1970s as the second feminist wave, and the suffragette movement in the 1890–1920 as the first. However, Karen Offen in her book on *European Feminisms, 1700–1950* indicates several more 'challenges to male hegemony' (Offen 2000: xi) throughout Western history.[1] Akkerman and Stuurman (1998) list the following common features of these feminist discourses: (1) criticism of misogyny and male supremacy; (2) the conviction that the condition of women is not an immutable fact of nature and can be changed for the better, and (3) a sense of group identity, the conscious will to speak 'on behalf of women', or 'to define the female sex', usually aiming to enlarge the sphere of action open to women (Akkerman and Stuurman 1998: 3–4).

In eighteenth-century France, women from the aristocracy organized cultivated conversation in their salons, to which women and men had equal access. Mme de Pompadour, mistress of Louis XV, and Mme de Staël were famous for their salons, to which they invited guests like Voltaire, Diderot, D'Alembert and Hume. Physiocrats like Turgot met in such salons with influential bankers and bureaucrats to discuss projects of all kinds (Ross 1995). At the same time, however, the newly founded scientific academies were closed to women scientists and scholars, some even until late into the twentieth century (Noble 1992: 231; see also Schiebinger 1989).

The salons played an important role in feminist discourse in France, England and the rest of Europe. The French Revolution brought radical social and political changes. Though the French Revolution has often been perceived as a masculine endeavor, the period of turbulence in the years around 1789–93 gave women the opportunity to state their views and claim new practices and options for women (Kelly 1984; Schröder 1989). Soon after that, the Napoleonic Code restored the principles of subordination and a domestic role for women, and set these rules for centuries to come (Pott-Buter 1993).

The position of women in Britain was subject to drastic changes over the eighteenth century, which were related to the fading influence of the Church and economic developments in which the extended family was increasingly replaced by the nuclear family and in which tasks previously done by women in the household and/or on the farm were increasingly taken over by workshops outside the house (see e.g. Wiesner 1993; Simonton 1998). Weaving and later also spinning shifted to the manufacturing workshops, where women and men initially worked together. Towards the end of the eighteenth century, however, with the rise of the bourgeois ideal of the non-working housewife, women were excluded from these workplaces (Wiesner 1993: 97–100). This period also saw considerable changes in marriage and property laws (Browne 1987; anonymous 1777). All these developments had a major impact on women's social and economic independence. In addition, traditional practices in education were being restructured. With the rise of public schools, girls' education was widely discussed. Although men as well as women had been advocating better education for women for some time (e.g. Defoe in *The Education of Women*, 1719), not many improvements had been made by the time Smith started his teaching.

From the mid-seventeenth century feminist poems, pamphlets and books were being written by women of good breeding and education such as Lady Chudleigh (1656–1710), and by lower-class women, like washerwoman Mary Collier (1689/90–after 1759). Moira Ferguson calls the period between the mid-1680s until about 1713 the first sizable wave of British secular feminism. Mary Astell, who wrote *A Serious Proposal to the Ladies* (1694) and *Some Reflections upon Marriage* (1700), is one of the best known authors of this period (Ferguson 1985: 15).

Around 1740 a new spur to feminist discussion developed in England. 'Sophia', an anonymous author, translated a work by Poulain de la Barre[2] and used large parts of his text in *Woman Not Inferior to Man: or, A short and modest Vindication of the natural Right of the Fair-Sex to a perfect Equality of Power, Dignity, and Esteem, with Men, by Sophia, A Person of Quality*. This publication was immediately followed by an anonymous reply from 'A Gentleman': *Man Superior to Woman; or, a Vindication of Man's Natural Right of Sovereign Authority over the Woman. Containing a plain Confutation of the Fallacious Arguments of Sophia, in her late Treatise intitled, Woman not inferior to Man. Interspersed with a Variety of Characters, of different Kinds of Women, drawn from Life. To which is prefix'd, a Dedication to the Ladies* (1740), which was later ascribed to Sophia as well. Later in 1740, Sophia responded with an answer with an even longer title: *Women's superior Excellence over Man; or, A Reply to the Author of a late Treatise, entitled Man Superior to Woman. In which, the excessive weakness of this Gentleman's Answer to Woman not inferior to Man is exposed; with a plain Demonstration of Woman's natural Right even to Superiority over Men in Head and Heart; proving their Minds so much more beautiful than the man's as their Bodies are, and that, had they the same Advantage of Education, they would excel them as much in Sense as they do in Virtue. The whole interspersed with a variety of mannish Characters, which some of the most noted Heroes of the present Age had the Goodness to sit for* (Brandon Schnorrenberg 2004: 2). These texts were collected and reprinted together in 1751. The text by 'A Gentleman' was in this volume explicitly attributed to Sophia. Feminist challenges to male hegemony began thus to bubble up through an increasing number of fissures, and according to Karen Offen, the debate on the woman question became a central feature of the Enlightenment exploration of human society (Offen 2000: 35).

Around the 1750s a group of women writers known as 'Bluestockings' held discussions and published pamphlets, plays, and poems.[3] They offered a new message to women, telling them 'to be assertive, take the lead, wait for no man, write, create, do not flinch from flouting custom' (Ferguson 1985: 21). The separation between the public and the private, which stated the public sphere to be the male realm and the private the female realm, thus limiting women's access to the public realm, was extensively discussed. Not all members of this group questioned these social boundaries set to women's conduct, though. In some cases, as for instance in the work of Hannah More (1745–1833) this had the paradoxical effect that while the author supported these boundaries in her words, by publishing her thoughts she transgressed them (Stott 2003). Hannah More was an important member of the Bluestocking group, as were Elisabeth Robinson Montagu (1720–1800) and Elisabeth Carter (1716–1806).

The Bluestockings regarded a better education for women as the main route to achieving their full potential. Many women felt they were bereft of power. Married higher-class women, for instance, were either confined to purely leisure activities, or faced deprivation and poverty if fate claimed their husbands, fathers or brothers, as they themselves were not equipped to act as their own providers. Sophia, Hannah More, and later Priscilla Wakefield (1751–1832) and Mary Wollstonecraft (1759–97) all made a strong case for women to become educated, for improvements to women's education, for men's jobs to be opened up to women and for measures to protect women's jobs from being taken over by men. All these proposals aimed to enable women to shake off their state of dependence on men.

It would probably be going too far to speak of a feminist movement in the second half of the eighteenth century, in the sense of a formal organization. There were, however, small groups and individuals who demonstrated a full-blown feminist consciousness and fuelled a debate that was taken up enthusiastically by leading and less enlightened critics (Offen 2000: 49).

Two feminist economic texts before *The Wealth of Nations*

To give an impression of the texts published in this period, I discuss two texts in more detail. Both texts show the changes going on in contemporary images of women. They are evidence of the shift away from the use of biblical images of Eve in defining the role of women that began in the seventeenth century, towards a representation of women's lives that was increasingly based on their own experiences. The first is a poem,

The Woman's Labour (1739), in which a lower-class woman mentioned earlier, Mary Collier, speaks up about the workload and tasks assigned to working women. In those days poetry was a fairly standard form for expressing views and taking part in social and political debate; this can also be seen in the poem by Bernard Mandeville (1670–1733) *Fable of the Bees* (1732). The second text I discuss, *Female Rights vindicated* (1758) by 'A Lady', is of a more political and philosophical character, and discusses women's economic dependence on men.

The Woman's Labour (*1739*)

The polemic poem by Mary Collier, *The Woman's Labour*, was written in response to Stephen Duck's tribute to male laborers: *The Thresher's Labour* (1736) (Ferguson 1985). Stephen Duck (1705–56) was a thresher who wrote poems at an early age, and who was 'discovered' after writing *The Thresher's Labour*, in which he describes the hardships endured by the common worker. In his poem Duck ignores the contribution made by women to the production process and, when he does mention women, it is in a misogynistic way. Queen Caroline brought him to court, where he held all kinds of small, mostly honorary jobs. He became a national literary celebrity (Ferguson 1985: 256).

Collier responds to Duck by pointing to the invisibility of women in his poem and criticizes his negative description of women and their work. In her poem she rails against women's double shift in labor, that assigns to women full tasks both in the field and in the household. Her poem is part of a tradition of lower-class poets in the second half of the eighteenth century in Britain (see e.g. Goodridge 2003). It is exceptional in the way it addresses working women's experiences, while most of the later feminist work is by upper-class and aristocratic women and concerns their experiences and problems.

An advertisement precedes the poem itself, in which Collier claims authorship of the poem. Being very modest about her authorship of this poem, she makes the point that if people in the same employment as her would do similar things, such as writing critical poems, 'the Peace in Families [would] be less disturbed' (Advertisement). She also mentions that she hopes for a 'small Sum of Money in her Pocket, as well as the Readers Entertainment' (Advertisement).

She begins the poem by addressing Stephen Duck, who is no longer poor, as he was taken up by the court. She urges him to listen to her.

> Immortal Bard! Thou Favorite of the Nine!
> Enrich'd by Peers, advance'd by Caroline!
> Deign to look down on One that's poor and low
> Remembering you yourself was lately so;
>
> (B)[4]

She continues the poem by explaining that she has no education and lives a life of slavery, and she stresses that in the past men held their women in high esteem, 'But now, alas!, that Golden Age is past' (7). In her view, people like Duck have no interest in or respect for women any more, but merely complain about their own workload, downgrading women's work while women work twice as hard as men. She describes a summer's day during hay gathering. After having done their normal share of work, women go home to take up their domestic duties: 'When ev'ning does approach, we homeward hie, And our domestic Toils Incessant ply' (9). In her description of women's work in the house, she describes how the husband comes home and sits down, while the wife makes dinner, cleans and mends clothes. During the night when he sleeps she gets up 'Because our froward Children cry and rave' (11). In the morning the children have to be fed and she has to work again in the field.

> What you would have of us we do not know:
> We oft' take up the Corn that you do mow;
> We cut the Peas, and always ready are
> In ev're Work to take our proper Share;
> And from the Time that Harvest doth begin,
> Until the Corn be cut and carry'd in,
> Our Toil and Labour's daily so extreme,
> That we have hardly ever *Time to dream.*
> (11; emphasis in original)

After the harvest, the winter comes, and Collier continues by describing her work at the Big House for her Mistress: she works in the Linen room with fine fabrics that need to be handled with care involving extremely long working days so she barely sees the sun once a day. Other work is also required: cleaning pots and pans, and sometimes fetching beer in the middle of the night: 'Alas! our Labours never know an End; On Brass and Iron we our Strength must Spend' (15). Talking about her changing shape and how she gets dirty all the time, she refers to Duck's remarks about peas, saying

> Colour'd with Dirt and Filth we now appear;
> Your threshing *sooty Peas* will not come near.
> All the Perfections Woman once could boast,
> Are quite obscur'd, and altogether lost.
> (16; emphasis in original)

Thus coming to the end of her poem:

> While you [Stephen Duck – E.K.] to *Sysiphus* yourselves compare,
> With *Danaus' Daughters* we may complain a Share;

For while *he* labours hard against the Hill,
Bottomless Tubs of Water *they* must fill.
(17; emphasis in original)

Again and again, Collier takes Duck's language and opposes it to the reality of working women's lives. In the end, with a Marxist twist *avant la lettre*, she blames not so much men but rather the 'sordid Owners' as the cause of the misery of the poor, since the wages they pay are too low.

So the industrious Bees do hourly strive
To bring their Loads of Honey to the Hive;
Their sordid Owners always reap the Gains,
And poorly recompense their Toil and Pains.
(17)

Although not explicitly, but still hard to overlook, the poem refers here to Mandeville's *Fable of the Bees*. This poem, in which he discusses society, using the metaphor of a beehive, was, by the time Collier wrote hers, widely known and discussed.[5] Since Collier claims that reading was an important part of her upbringing, and later in life remained a way of recreation (Collier 1762), Mandeville's poem apparently was part of this reading and provided inspiration.

The terms 'Toil and Trouble', or 'Toil and Pains' Collier uses here, which indicate the energies and effort put into the work done, also show up in Adam Smith's WN when he explains 'the real price of every thing' (WN I.v.2, 47). There Smith seems to align himself with Stephen Duck rather than with Mary Collier in the way he ascribes the results of labor to men without mentioning anywhere women's contribution to the process. I return to this point in the discussion on Smith's work later in this chapter.

Female Rights Vindicated (*1758*)

The text *Female Rights vindicated; or the Equality of the Sexes Morally and Physically proved* (1758) by 'A Lady', has been attributed to 'Sophia' as an edited version of *Woman not Inferior to Man* (Brandon Schnorrenberg 2004: 5) which goes back to Poulain de la Barre's *The Equality of the Sexes*, published in France in 1673. Poulain de la Barre's narrative is rewritten from a female perspective with the religious element removed, comments on the English situation inserted, and from a scientific analysis the texts are turned into a more political pamphlet.

Female Rights vindicated starts with 'A dedication to the Ladies' in which the author claims that this text should be seen as supporting women's interests. In the preface that follows, the pamphlet asserts that women have as much virtue, courage and chastity as men, in some cases even more. Many explicit examples are put forward, such as the Amazons, the biblical Judith, the prophetess Deborah, Jeanne d'Arc, and others, to underscore this point. Several biblical arguments for the inferiority of women to men are refuted, thus opening the way to the central discussion in the book of the issue of why and how women became perceived as inferior to men, and why this is unjustified.

The pamphlet makes the point that the sexes are equal; that the differences between them exist mainly in relation to the reproduction of the species and perhaps a difference in physical strength, which is in the author's view not of major importance (preface, 20). The rest, 'all the Difference in the Manners and Dispositions of the Men and Women, arises from no other Cause but the Difference in their Education' (96). A conjectural historical account is given, similar to those of Adam Smith and others (see Nyland 2003b), but with very different focus and content. This account tells about the way the exclusion of women from public professions came about, how male prejudice has been reproduced throughout history, from the ancient philosophers to today's ideas that women are inferior to men, and how women came to occupy a dependent position in relation to men. The issue of the dependence of women on men and their lack of access to education and to public professions is a central theme in this text (see e.g. 31). The idea that women and men are not equal, 'that [women's] intellectual Capacities are as different as their Bodies, and that there should be as much Distinction in the Function of their Lives, as in those of their Bodies', is perceived as 'founded, like most others, in Custom, nurtured by Appearances' (33).

In her arguments, this anonymous author claims access for women to public positions like those of lawyer, philosopher and surgeon, which was unheard of in those days. She emphasizes that although the idea of a woman lawyer 'making the full Argument before the Bar' (29) still may make people laugh, giving women full access to all professions is fully justified. It is the idea that women are inferior to men that is irrational, based solely on custom and interest, and will need to change (77).

There is an extended discussion on various sciences, the way these have influenced and contributed to maintaining the idea that women are inferior to men, and how use is being made of the authority scholars have over the minds of 'the Unlearned' to keep this idea intact. She points out that sciences such as astronomy, physics and medicine should be accessible to women. She claims that because women have similar talents for them as men – because their minds are the same as men's and because they carry out the tasks currently assigned to them very effectively – they have a rightful claim to access to experiments and the conduct of research on these topics just like men. Especially interesting is the way the author has a strong focus to bear on the role of the body in scientific research, claiming that training one's powers of observation is important here, and that women are equally as good observers as men. Taking up the Enlightenment discourse of natural rights and the power of rational reasoning, she challenges all academics, but philosophers especially, to make their case that women are inferior to men. She states that this case has never been fully made, and that philosophers, like other scientists (e.g. historians, orators and lawyers) have been building on prejudice, custom and interest, and are 'too busy in discovering new Worlds' (53) to discuss this important issue.

The text aims to convince its reader and make the point as clearly as possible, as it regularly repeats itself. The argument is, however, strongly made and surprising in the way it breaks away from essentialist reasoning, bringing in historical and institutional developments, the role of customs and interests, and of women themselves in the reproduction of gender and power differences: 'Women – they seem to look upon their Situation as natural, whether it be through a defect of properly reflecting upon what they are, or being born and educated in a State of Subjection, they consider the Evil as irremediable' (33). It takes the differences between the sexes as culture and context specific, analyzing the developments in English society that have led to the current situation of dependence for women.

Adam Smith and his feminist contemporaries

Research into women's writing in the British Enlightenment has mainly been conducted in the fields of women's and gender history and in English literature. Discussions of some of these early women's texts can be found in Robert Dimand's chapter on *Reflections on the present condition of the Female Sex* (1798) by Priscilla Wakefield, and in Evelyn Forget's 'Cultivating Sympathy: Sophie Condorcet's Letters on Sympathy', both published in Dimand and Nyland (2003).

There are more texts by women and/or feminist authors from this period that are relevant to the history of economics. Only a limited selection of these texts, however, have yet been reprinted and, when originally written in French or Dutch, translated into English. Women's writing in the eighteenth century can best be characterized as more or less feminist, instead of in dichotomous terms, as feminist or anti-feminist. Not all women writers in this period questioned the social boundaries set on women's activities and behavior, but most do so to a greater or lesser extent. Women's writing, especially the writing that takes the experience of women as its starting point, went against the silence on women's issues and experiences that marked the dominant discourse, which was defined by men (see e.g. Woolf 1929).

Even though the ongoing discussion on gender equality may have taken place largely outside the inner circle of early political economists, these men had to relate implicitly or explicitly to these discussions as they were writing about economic behavior and political institutions. The rest of this chapter addresses the ways in which Adam Smith has been in contact with people who were involved in this discourse, the extent to which he was familiar with the arguments and ideas, and how he positioned himself explicitly or implicitly in relation to them in his writings.

Adam Smith and the feminist discourse

In his personal life, Smith was, like each of his contemporaries, directly confronted with the economic position of women and their dependence on husbands, brothers and guardians. He will have noticed the difference of education of boys and girls; that boys were trained in Latin and Greek and went to schools, and that girls' education was at best fragmental and mostly directly related to the household tasks assigned to them; and that women did not have access to universities such as Oxford, where he went. And he may have realized that remaining unmarried, like he did, would for women have had severe consequences, as the professions open to them were limited to governess or housekeeper. An example of this was his cousin, Janet Douglas, who entered his household in 1754 after the death of her husband, and took care of his household until she died in 1788, two years before Smith's death (Ross 1995: 135).

Adam Smith was a member of various clubs, such as the Select Society in Edinburgh, the Literary Society of Glasgow, and he was one of the founders of the Edinburgh Poker Club in 1762 (Rae 1895: 134). We know that the Select Club for instance at one of its meetings discussed the position of women. Dugald Stewart reports on a meeting held December 1754 that was, by exception, preceded by David Hume, during which '[t]he Society entered upon the debate of the question appointed for this night, namely, – 'Whether [we] ought to prefer ancient or modern manners with regards to the condition and treatment of women?' (Stewart 1858: 204)

That Smith was indeed familiar with the changing position of women in early commercial society appears from his LJ, which reports on his teaching on this subject. In his stage theory, he indicates four stages in economic development: the age of the hunters, the age of pasture, the age of agriculture and the age of commerce. He argues that in the age of commerce, when defence activities became less important to daily life in society, women's social and economic position changed and improved. He discusses this change with particular reference to their property and inheritance rights (LJ 59–61, see also Nyland 2003b: 97–100).

When he went to France, women played an important role in introducing him to the French salons. Ross (1995) mentions Mme Necker, duchesse d'Enville, Mme Deflours, Mme de Boufflers, and others. In addition to his connection with David Hume, these women opened the door for Smith to the debates at the French court during the days of Louis XV's reign. Though not all these women were outspoken feminists, they wrote poems, plays and translated books; they published, acted and contributed to public life. Mme Necker, the mother of the Germaine de Staël – a famous publicist and feminist – propagated breast-feeding at a time that this was not at all widely accepted (Gutwirth 2004). Mme Riccoboni was an actress and published on various topics. In 1765 she published a novel, *l'Abeille*, in which she addressed the social injustice toward women (Schröder 1989, 101). Smith acknowledged Riccoboni's contributions on love and friendship (TMS III.3.14, 143; Ross 1995: 399). Smith's correspondence contains some letters to women in these circles: in 1765 Smith writes for instance to Marie Louis Denis, later the mistress of Voltaire (Corr. 109), and in 1772 he writes to Mme de Boufflers about a French translation of the TMS (Corr. 161). Smith's library contained two books by French women authors. One is by the Marquise de Lambert (*Oeuvres de Madame la marquise de Lambert*, Amsterdam, 1748) (Mituza 1967: 33), and the other is entitled *Lettres de Madame de Maintenon* (1756) (Mituza 1967: 37). Both these authors contributed substantially to the *querelles des femmes*, more in particular to the French discussion on girl's education.[6]

After Smith returned from France, he again took part in the political and literary clubs that were being founded all over Scotland and also attended friendly gatherings as for instance in London in 1775 at the house of Joshua Reynolds. Both Adam Smith's and Hannah More's biographers mention these meetings at the Reynoldses' without, however, mentioning direct meetings between Hannah More and Adam Smith (Rae 1895: 263; Stott 2003: 29). Ross assumes that Smith has attended the gatherings at Elizabeth Robinson Montagu's house in London. He mentions Montagu's visit to Scotland in 1766 and her as someone with whom Smith seemed to be on a good footing (Ross 1995: 228). He does not, however, offer an account of the content of their discussions. Mrs Montagu was acquainted with Burke, Johnson, Garrick and other persons with whom Smith was also in direct contact. In 1769 she published anonymously *An Essay on the Writings and genius of Shakespeare, Compared with the Greek and French Dramatic Poets. With Some Remarks upon the Misrepresentations of Mons. de Voltaire*, which was very well received. After the publication of the WN, Elizabeth Montagu commented positively on this book, stating, 'I heartily join in your wish, and would even convert it into a prayer, that the rulers of nations would listen to many of [Smith's] wise and salutary counsels' (Montagu, quoted in Ross 1995: 290).

Smith was sideways involved in a debate on the character and content of public education. In this debate Jean-Jacques Rousseau (1762), Fordyce (1765) and others claimed that girls requested a specialized education that would prepare them mainly for their role as mistress of the house and carer of her children. In her discussion on gender in eighteenth century English education, Michèle Cohen (2004) describes this debate on education in the eighteenth century as a highly gendered one. Public institutions for boys were over the years increasingly perceived as contributing to the methodological training of boys and as enhancing their virtues, while at the same time they were seen as threatening the virtue of girls (Cohen

2004: 589). As indicated earlier women such as Elizabeth Montagu, Catherine Macaulay in her *Letters on Education* (1790) and Mary Wollstonecraft in *Thoughts on the Education of Daughters* (1787) took different positions, stating that women's education was insufficient to prepare them for economic independence and a profession that would, if necessary, enable them to provide for themselves (Ferguson 1985: 25). These circles were not very extensive, and those active in literature, politics and cultural life met on various occasions. John Ross reports on a discussion between Adam Smith and Henry Mackenzie, in which they discuss the recent work of three feminist authors, Charlotte Smith (1749–1806), Ann Radcliffe (1746?–1810) and Hannah More, whose main work would be published in the years after Smith's death (Ross 1995: 399). All three of them were highly concerned about the access of women to decent occupations, without which women who depended on their own income might be pushed into prostitution (Ferguson 1985: 26). According to Ross, it was, however, mainly their work as novelists that was the topic of the conversation.

Adam Smith's texts on gender issues

Reviewing the discourse in British feminism in Smith's days, Alice Browne (1987) lists the three main points on the feminist agenda in this period: (1) a denial that men were superior to women and a call for women's equal access to education, (2) the legal and economic position, especially if they were married, and (3) the attack on the double standard in sexual morality that demanded chastity for women but not for men (Browne 1987: 1). I shall briefly discuss Adam Smith's position on these three points in reverse sequence, starting with his views on the double sexual standard.

In LJ Adam Smith addresses this point directly, and takes a sophisticated approach in this matter. He states it as a historical fact in his discussion of marriage laws and divorce that infidelity in the wife will make most people sympathize with the husband. This is because

> as in almost all contracts of marriage the husband has a considerable superiority to the wife, [therefore] the injury done to his honour and love will be more grievous, as all injuries done to a superior by an inferior are more sensibly felt than those which are done to an inferior by one whom they look upon as above them.
>
> (LJ 147)

In the TMS, on the other hand, he does not word it in this fashion. Perhaps due to the difference in the audience, he states in the TMS that chastity is particularly the wife's duty, and not so much the husband's (see also Folbre 1992), and that the reputation of the wife in the case of adultery is damaged beyond repair, which is different for men (TMS VII.iv.13, 332).[7]

In his LJ, Smith dwells for quite a while on the second point, the legal and economic position of women, especially married women. Throughout his lectures, man is the starting point of the analysis.

> The end of justice is to secure from injury. A man may be injured in several respects. 1st as a man; 2dly, as a member of a family; 3dly as a member of a state. As a man, he may be injured in his body, reputation, or estate. As a member of the family, he may be injured as a father, as a son, as a husband or wife, as a master or servant, as a guardian or pupil.
>
> (LJ, 399)

Women, married women especially, come in as a member of a family, under 2 and 3 concerning property and inheritance issues.

In the elaboration of these basic concepts, Smith refers to men – their professions, experiences, histories and concerns. In his stage theory, Smith discusses the rights of women and indicates that in the commercial stage women have more rights than during other stages, namely the right to inherit and to own property (LJ 66–7). The fact that Smith does not discuss here access to education, the (limited) rights of women to enter into contracts and earn a living, the sexual division of labor in the household, is partly due to the topic of jurisprudence itself, and the way he builds his framework starting from man as an individual and as the head of the family. The lack of attention for women's legal and natural rights was indicated and addressed in an anonymous publication of 1777, in which the well informed author provides the reader with an elaborate overview of women's legal position.[8]

Smith's TMS (1759) was initially written as an educational book for boys. That the TMS was a book on boys' or men's moral behavior, rather than that of girls or women's conduct, can also be read from the subtitle of the fourth edition: *An Essay towards an Analysis of the Principles by which Men naturally judge concerning the Conduct and Character, first of their Neighbours, and afterwards of themselves* (Raphael and MacFie 1984: 40). Women's moral behavior is only dealt with as a foil to the discussion of men's moral behavior. In the TMS they mainly figure in examples of vice[9] and weakness.[10] In opposition to Hume (Treatise, 2.2.11), the relation between the sexes is not discussed as a topic of moral behavior, but only in terms of women invoking men's passions 'that arise from the body and those that are derived from the imagination' (see TMS I.ii.1–2, 27–34).

In WN, we also see Smith's stages theory occur (WN V.1.a–c, 689–723) but the issue of women's changing social and economic position is neither discussed nor analyzed. Moreover, when we look at some central issues in WN, such as the division of labor and the definition of prices, we see that labor put into the production of goods by women is largely neglected, and in some instances denied or attributed to men. Kathryn Sutherland concludes on Smith's treatment of women that 'her labour is placed decisively outside the economic order' (Sutherland 1995: 99).

Pujol (1992), Rendall (1987), Sutherland (1995) and others have argued at great length that although Smith's analysis of the economy starts with the division of labor, which he perceives as the basic explanation for and engine of economic growth, the sexual division of labor in the family is hardly addressed. The sexual division of labor as a pre-condition for the division of labor between men is bypassed by Smith (Pujol 1992: 19).[11] He vaguely mentions the sexual division of labor in farming: 'The spinner is almost always a distinct person from the weaver; but the ploughman, the harrower, the sower of the seed, and the reaper of the corn, are often the same' (WN I.i.4, 16). The gendered character of this distinction, however, is not mentioned or discussed, nor is its change in character during the rise of early industrial society analyzed. Of the work done on the farm, around the house, the caring for children and the spinning, Smith mentions only spinning as work done by women.[12]

> [B]ut our spinners are poor people, women commonly, scattered about in all different parts of the country, without support or protection. ... It is not by the sale of their work, but *by that of the compleat work of the weavers*, that our great master manufacturers make their profits.
>
> (WN IV.viii.4, 644, emphasis added)

The productivity of women's work is here ascribed to that of the weavers (mostly men) who 'compleat their work'. This idea of women as incomplete men is an Aristotelian concept that comes up and informs Smith's reasoning without being further discussed or elaborated, here or elsewhere. It can be read as reflecting Smith's use of concepts of ancient Greek philosophers, here applied in a context where women's role extends that of wife and heiress; those he discussed in his LJ.

Smith defines 'the real price of every thing' in terms of men's work and the use of their bodies along similar lines to the poem by Stephen Duck we discussed earlier in this chapter. That women contributed to family income (and how this complicates the computations of labor value) is neither addressed nor acknowledged.

> The real price of every thing, what every thing really costs to the man who wants to acquire it, is the toil and trouble of acquiring it. ... What is bought with money or with goods is purchased by labour as much as what we acquire by the toil of *our own* body.
>
> (WN I.v.2, 47; emphasis added)

These observations by Smith stand in a long tradition of books on husbandry in which the relation between God, Man, and Nature is conceptualized, as Keith Tribe (1978) shows, as a relationship between 'Man and his Land'. These texts build on and at the same time reconceptualize this biblical image of Adam and the Earth. This, and the fact that the discourse on the role of Eve went along different lines, meant that the conceptualization of women's role on the farm lacked a basis, which will have contributed to the absence of women in theoretical statements such as these.

In addition, Smith's theorization of the real price of everything stresses the right to appropriate the results of toil and trouble taken, which was precisely that which was denied to married women at the time. *The Laws respecting Women* (1777) reports that

> [b]y marriage the very being or legal existence of a woman is suspended; or at least it is incorporated and consolidated into that of the husband; under whose wing, protection and *cover*, she performs everything; and she is therefore called in our law a *feme-covert, fœmina viro co-operta*; is said to be *covert-baron*, or under the protection or influence of her husband, her *baron*, or lord.
>
> (Anonymous 1777, 65)

Personal property and her income 'as such were the property of her husband, who could dispose of the money however he pleased' (Holcombe 1983: 31). Commercial society may have been more equal in respect to gender relations than other societies. Smith, however, was well aware that the marriage laws prevented most women from concluding contracts and from disposing of their own income.

Coming to the third and last point on the feminist agenda (the denial that men were superior to women and the call for equal access to education), we see that here Smith's position is clear and explicit. In the only reasonably extended paragraph in WN in which he pays explicit attention to women's social and economic position, he states that:

> [t]here are no publick institutions for the education of women, and there is accordingly nothing useless, absurd, or fantastical in the common course of their education. They are taught what their parents or guardians judge it necessary or useful for them to learn; and they are taught nothing else. Every part of their education tends evidently to some useful purpose; either to improve the natural attractions of their person, or to form their mind to reserve, to modesty, to chastity, and to oeconomy: to render them both likely to become the mistresses of a family, and to behave properly when they have become such.
>
> (WN V.i.47, 781)

Though Smith makes the case that education is the basis for the social differences between men (WN I.ii.4, 28–9), he refrains from making a similar claim about the differences between women and men. Opposing public education for women against the background of a debate going on about the aims and content of girls' education, and propagating private education exclusively directed to the performance of domestic tasks, was not exactly a feminist approach.

Adam Smith does not make the explicit argument that men are superior to women. His analysis, however, starts from men and their experiences, silencing women's concerns and contributions. For instance, in his conceptualization of exchange relations, self-interest and dependence in his famous quote on the baker, the butcher and the brewer (WN I.ii.2, 27), he claims that no one, 'not even a beggar', is fully dependent on other people (see also Kuiper 2002). When reading this in its historical gender context, we have to realize that married women were in fact fully dependent on their husbands, fathers and brothers. In a context in which dependence was widely discussed by men and women, Smith's focus on the market and market relations as a way to solve the problem of one's dependence on others is not gender-neutral. The dependence of married women on their husbands was an acknowledged social fact that Smith does not deal with, nor is the sex segregation of jobs, which goes against a further division of labor addressed. Smith is silent on these issues to a remarkable extent.

Conclusion

In the Enlightenment period in Britain, women's social and economic position was changing with the emergence of industrial society. In this chapter I outlined the feminist discourse and women's writing on gender inequality in eighteenth century France and England. To give an impression of the perspective and arguments put forward by those who were concerned about women's social and economic position in Adam Smith's day I discussed a poem by Mary Collier, *The Woman's Labour* (1739), and *Female Rights vindicated* (1758) by 'A Lady' in more detail. The first text speaks of women's double burden and the lack of recognition of women's work; the second deals with the subordination of women to men, their exclusion from scientific research and jobs and the dependence of women on men this results in. Although I did not find any direct evidence that Smith read either of these two texts, they were part of a discourse that Adam Smith encountered on a range of occasions: in persons and in groups that articulated and propagated them. He was in direct and indirect contact with several more and less outspoken feminists of his day in France, England and Scotland. His position on the main feminist issues of his day, however – on the denial that men were superior to women and women's access to education, the legal and economic position of married women, and the sexual double standard – is shown to be mostly adverse to these feminist claims. Although in his LJ he does not make explicit remarks concerning the inferiority of women and is rather sophisticated and aware of women's position, in TMS and WN Smith more directly adopts the *status quo* in these matters as the starting point of his analysis. Moreover, in some instances where attention for women would have been logical and even required he neglects or ignores women and their interests.

In Adam Smith's system of thought women, their contribution and their interests do not play an explicit role. In Mandeville's *Fable of the Bees*, on the other hand, the author discussed issues of luxury and lust – for instance the sexual double standard and prostitution – openly. This offended Smith, who talked about the importance of language and the way in which many aspects of reality and of behavior (luxury and lust in particular) should only be named by terms 'to mark rather the restraint and subjection which they are kept under, than the degree they are allowed to subsist in' (TMS VII.ii.4.11, 312). For Smith, Mandeville was too explicit in these matters, as will have been his feminist contemporaries, who tried to table issues Smith would rather not discuss.

Whatever Smith's intentions may have been in his conceptualization of women's work and his focus on that of men, the result was that he attributed most if not all the work done on the farm and in the family to men and thus lost sight of the division of labor in the family and the contribution of women's economic work more generally. I hope to have allowed the voices of some of the women writers contemporary with Smith to be heard once again regarding their concerns about women's experiences and their work, as relevant to understanding economic development.

Notes

1 Akkerman and Stuurman (1998) speak of six waves: the first being 'late medieval and Renaissance feminism' (1400–1600), the second 'rationalist feminism' (1600–1700), and the third 'enlightenment feminism' (1700–1800). They see 'Utopian feminism' (1820–50) as the fourth, 'liberal feminism' (1860–1920) as the fifth, and the last wave of 'contemporary feminism' since the 1960s as the sixth. Joan Kelly (1984) in her work on early feminisms placed Christine de Pisan (1363–1434) and *The Book of the City of Ladies* (1406) at the start of the discourse of the late medieval and Renaissance feminism.

2 Poulain de la Barre (1647–1723) lived and worked as a priest in France but left France after his conversion to Calvinism to live in Geneva. He referred in his arguments to natural-rights notions in *The Equality of the Sexes* (1673) and applied Descartes's method of deductive reasoning (Nyland 2003a: 21).

3 To explain the name 'Bluestocking', Anne Stott tells the story of the botanist Benjamin Stillingfleet who claimed as an excuse to decline an invitation to one of this group's meetings that he was not properly dressed. In response Elisabeth Vesey, at whose house the meeting was to take place, replied, 'Don't, mind dress! Come in your blue stockings!' Blue stockings were the informal stockings, where a more formal dress required silk stockings (Stott 2003: 51).

4 References are to pages. After the 'Advertisement' that is referred to as 'A',

and the first stanza of the poem numbered as 'B', the counting of the pages starts.

5 There have been quite a few editions and before the end of the century the book was translated into French and into German (Kaye 1924, xxxvi–xxxvii).

6 The book by De Lambert contains letters to her daughter, which are critical on girls' and women's education, and a feminist treatise on women's social position (*Sur les femmes*). *Lettres de Madame de Maintenon* (1756) was written by Francoise d'Aubigne (1635–1719), later Marquise de Maintenon, who was governess to Louis XIV's children and later married him. Besides her influence on Louis XIV, she was famous for her letters on girls' education and as the founder of a school for poor girls.

7 '[T]he violations of chastity in the fair sex, a virtue of which, for the like reasons, we are excessively jealous;... Breach of chastity dishonours irretrievably. No circumstances, no solicitation can excuse it; no sorrow, no repentance atone for it. We are so nice in this respect that even a rape dishonours, and the innocence of the mind cannot, in our imagination, wash out the pollution of the body' (TMS VII.iv.13, 332).

8 In his preface the author states that 'England has been stiled the Paradise of women; not can it be supposed that in a country where the natural rights of mankind are enjoyed in as full an extent as is consistent with the existence and well-being of a great and extensive empire, that the interests of the softer sex should be overlooked' (1777, Preface, iv).

9 As in: A woman who paints [to conceal her ugliness] could derive, one should imagine, but little vanity from the compliments that are paid to her complexion.... To be pleased with such groundless applause is a proof of the most superficial levity and weakness. It is what is properly called vanity, and is the foundation of the most ridiculous and contemptible vices, the vices of affectation and common lying; follies which, if experience did not teach us how common they are, one should imagine the least spark of common sense would save us from (TMS III.2.4, 115).

10 This comes to the fore for instance where Smith discusses '[t]ime, however, in a longer or shorter period, never fails to compose the weakest woman to the same degree of tranquility as the strongest man' (TMS III.3.32, 151).

11 Pujol states that Smith uses the sexual division of labor – the basis of the social division of labor – as evident and as 'natural', and together with his definition of productive labor excludes women's activities from the (later) consideration of economists (Pujol 1992: 22–3).

12 'The spinning of linen yarn is carried on in Scotland nearly in the same way as the knitting of stockings, by servants, who are chiefly hired for other purposes. They earn but a very scanty subsistence, who endeavour to get their whole livelihood by either of those trades. In most parts of Scotland she is a good spinner who can earn twenty-pence a week' (WN I.x.b.51, 134).

References

Anonymous (1777) *The Laws respecting Women, as they regard their Natural Rights or their Connections and Conduct, etc.*, London: J. Johnson.

Akkerman, Tjitske (1992) *Women's Vices, Public Benefits: Women and Commerce in the French Enlightenment*, Amsterdam: 't Spinhuis.

—— and Stuurman, Siep (eds) (1998) *Perspectives on Feminist Political Thought in European History: From the Middle Ages to the Present*, London and New York: Routledge.

A Lady (1758) *Female Rights Vindicated or The Equality of the Sexes, Morally and Physically Proved*, London: Burnet.

Brandon Schnorrenberg, Barbara (2004) 'Sophia: British Feminism in the Mid Eighteenth Century', paper presented at the 1980 meeting of the American Society for Eighteenth Century Studies, available online: http://www.pinn.net/~sunshine/biblio/sophia2.html (latest update 9 June 2004, accessed at 31 January 2005).

Brown, Vivienne (1997) '"Mere Inventions of the Imagination": A Survey of Recent Literature and Adam Smith', *Economics and Philosophy* 13: 281–312.

Browne, Alice (1987) *The Eighteenth Century Feminist Mind*, Brighton: Harvester Press.

Cohen, Michèle (2004) 'Gender and "Method" in Eighteenth-century English Education', *History of Education* 33 (5): 585–95.

Collier, Mary (1739) *The Woman's Labour*, Available online: http://duke.usask.ca/~vargo/barbauld/related_texts/collier.html (accessed 31 January 2005).

—— (1762) *Poems, on Several Occasions: Some remarks of the Author's Life Drawn by Herself*, Winchester. Reprinted in Moira Ferguson (ed.) *First Feminists. British women writers 1578–1799*, Bloomington, IN: Indiana University Press and Old Westbury, NY: Feminist Press (1985), 264–5.

Defoe, Daniel (1719) *On the Education of Women*, available online: Internet Modern History Sourcebook, http://www.fordham.edu/halsall/mod/1719defoe-women.html (last updated August 1998, accessed 31 January 2005).

Dimand, Robert (2003) 'An Eighteenth-Century English Feminist Response to Political Economy: Priscilla Wakefield's *Reflections* (1798)', in Robert Dimand and Chris Nyland (eds) *The Status of Women in Classical Economic Thought*, Aldershot: Elgar, 194–205.

—— and Nyland, Chris (eds) (2003) *The Status of Women in Classical Economic Thought*, Aldershot: Elgar.

Ferguson, Moira (ed.) (1985) *First Feminists: British Women Writers 1578–1799*, Bloomington, IN: Indiana University Press and Old Westbury, NY: Feminist Press.

Folbre, Nancy (1992) 'The Improper Arts': Sex in Classical Political Economy, *Population and Development Review* 18 (1 March): 105–21.

Fordyce, James (1765) *Sermons to Young Women*, London: Cadell.

Forget, Evelyn (2003) 'Cultivating Sympathy: Sophie Condorcet's Letters on Sympathy', in Robert Dimand and Chris Nyland (eds) *The Status of Women in Classical Economic Thought*, Aldershot: Elgar, 142–64.

Goodridge, John (ed.) (2003) *Eighteen-century English Labouring Class Poets*, London: Pickering and Chatto.

Gutwirth, Madelyn (2004) 'Suzanne Necker's Legacy: Breastfeeding as Metonym in Germaine de Staël's *Delphine*', *Eighteenth-Century Life* 28 (2): 17–40.

Holcombe, Lee (1983) *Wives & Property: Reform of the Married Women's Property Law in Nineteenth-Century England*, Toronto, Ont: University of Toronto Press.

Justman, Stewart (1993) *The Autonomous Male of Adam Smith*, Norman, OK and London: University of Oklahoma Press.

Kaye, F. B. (1924) 'Introduction: Life of Mandeville', in Bernard Mandeville, *The Fable of the Bees: or Private Vices, Publick Benefits*, Oxford: Clarendon Press.

Kelly, Joan (1984) *Women, History & Theory: The Essays of Joan Kelly*, Chicago and London: University of Chicago Press.

Kuiper, Edith (2001) *'The most valuable of all Capital': A Gender Reading of Economic Texts*, Amsterdam: Thela Thesis.

—— (2002) 'Dependency and Denial in Economic Texts', in C. Gerschlager and M. Mokre (eds) *Exchange and Deception: A Feminist Perspective*, Dordrecht: Kluwer, 75–90.

—— (2003) 'The Construction of Masculine Identity in Adam Smith's Theory of Moral Sentiments', in D. K. Barker and E. Kuiper (eds) *Towards a Feminist Philosophy of Economics*, London and New York: Routledge, 145–60.

Mandeville, Bernard (1732) *The Fable of the Bees, or Private Vices, Publick Benefits: With a Commentary Critical, Historical, and Explanatory* by F. B. Kaye, Oxford: Clarendon Press [1924].

Mizuta, Hiroshi (1967) *Adam Smith's Library: A Supplement to Bonar's Catalogue with a Checklist of the whole Library*, Cambridge: Cambridge University Press for the Royal Economic Society.

Noble, David F. (1992) *A World without Women: The Christian Clerical Culture of Western Science*, Oxford: Oxford University Press.

Nyland, Chris (2003a) 'Poulain de La Barre and the Rationalist Analysis of the Status of Women', in Robert Dimand and Chris Nyland (eds) *The Status of Women in Classical Economic Thought*, Cheltenham: Elgar, 21–39.

—— (2003b) 'Adam Smith, State Theory and the Status of Women', in R. Dimand and C. Nyland (eds) *The Status of Women in Classical Economic Thought*, Cheltenham: Elgar, 86–107.

Offen, Karen (2000) *European Feminisms, 1700–1950: A Political History*, Stanford, CA: Stanford University Press.

Pott-Buter, Hettie A. (1993) *Facts and Fairy Tales about Female Labor, Family and Fertility: A Seven-country Comparison, 1850–1990*, Amsterdam: Amsterdam University Press.

Poulain de la Barre, François (1673) *The Equality of the Sexes*, trans. Desmond M. Clarke, Manchester and New York: Manchester University Press (1990).

Pujol, Michèle (1992) *Feminism and Anti-feminism in Early Economic Thought*, Aldershot: Elgar.

Rae, John (1895) *Life of Adam Smith*, London: Macmillan, repr. New York: Augustus M. Kelley (1977).

Raphael, D. D. and MacFie, A. L. (1984) 'Introduction', in Adam Smith, *The Theory of Moral Sentiments*, Indianapolis, IN: Liberty Fund.

Rendall, Jane (1987) 'Virtue and Commerce: Women in the Making of Adam Smith's Political Economy', in Ellen Kennedy and Susan Mendus (eds) *Women in Western Political Philosophy: Kant to Nietzsche*, Brighton: Wheatsheaf, 44–77.

Ross, John (1995) *The Life of Adam Smith*, Oxford: Oxford University Press.

Rousseau, J. J. (1762) *Emile, of een Verhandeling over de opvoeding* (Emile, or A Treatise on Education), trans. into Dutch by Campen (1790–93).

Schiebinger, Londa (1989) *The Mind has No Sex? Women in the Origins of Modern Science*, London and Cambridge, MA: Harvard University Press.

Schröder, Hannelore (1989) 'Inleiding en commentaar' (Introduction and comments) in Olympes des Gouges, *Verklaring van de Rechten van de Vrouw en Burgeres* (1791), (Declaration of the Rights of Woman and Burgheress), Kampen: Kok Agora.

Simonton, Deborah (1998) *A History of European Women's Work, 1700 to the Present*, London and New York: Routledge.

Stewart, Dugald (1854–60) *The Collected Works of Dugald Stewart, Esq., FRSS*, ed. William Hamilton, Edinburgh: Constable. Reprinted by Thoemmes Press (1994).

Stott, Anne (2003) *Hannah More: The First Victorian*, Oxford: Oxford University Press.

Sutherland, Kathryn (1995) 'Adam Smith's master narrative: women and the *Wealth of Nations*' in Stephen Copley and Kathryn Sutherland (eds) *Adam Smith's Wealth of Nations: New Interdisciplinary Essays*, Manchester: Manchester University Press, 97–121.

Tribe, Keith (1978) *Land, Labour and Economic Discourse*, London: Routledge.

Wiesner, Merry E. (1993) *Women and Gender in Early Modern Europe*, Cambridge, MA: Harvard University Press.

Woolf, Virginia (1929) *A Room of One's Own*, London: Hogarth Press.

4 Beautiful and orderly systems

Adam Smith on the aesthetics of political improvement

Robert Mitchell

In recent years, scholars of British Romanticism have stressed the extent to which late eighteenth century British authors were obsessed with establishing the proper role of 'systems' in both political and literary thought and practice. Edmund Burke blamed the excesses of the French Revolution at least in part on 'the surfeit and indigestion of systems' (Burke 1869, vol. IV: 16); S. T. Coleridge warned the audience of his 'Moral and Political Lecture' (1795) not to confuse the destruction of 'pernicious systems' with the killing of their 'misguided adherents' (Coleridge 1971: 19); Thomas Paine argued that while '[w]e have heard the *rights of man* called a *levelling* system ... the only system to which the word *levelling* is truly applicable, is the hereditary monarchical system' (Paine 1942: 162); in William Blake's prophetic-epic poem *Jerusalem* (1804), Los exclaims that 'I must create a system or be enslav'd by another man's' (Blake 1988: 153); and William Godwin contended that governments tended to 'perpetually reduc[e] oppression into a system' (Godwin 1985: 92). In an attempt to unravel the complicated function (or functions) of 'system' in the political thought of the tumultuous 1790s, literary critics have sought to reconstruct the traditions to which this term belonged, as well as the discursive shifts that gave it new life in the 1790s. David Simpson, for example, has outlined a tradition of English antipathy toward philosophic 'systems' and 'theory' that extended back to the Civil War. Within this tradition, 'theory', 'method', and 'system' were associated with Puritan radicalism, political and social upheaval, and (by the mid eighteenth century), French philosophy and politics. Thus, when Burke labeled his opponents as 'systematizers' in the 1790s, he was able to draw on an implicit narrative that linked the stability of the nation with the triumph of common sense over the deceptive genre of system (Simpson 1993). Clifford Siskin, taking a slightly different tack, has noted that, *pace* what we might expect from Simpson's account, the 1790s 'was actually a watershed year for published systems in England', and he also urges us to attend to the ways in which systems became 'embedded in other genres', such as the lyric and novel (Siskin 1998: 10). These developments, he suggests, made it possible for people to begin blaming 'the System' as a 'primary modern means of totalizing and rationalizing our experience of the social' (9).[1]

Yet even as the contributions of Simpson, Siskin, and others have significantly expanded our understanding of the political valences of late eighteenth century discussions of systems, these accounts have generally neglected the role of Adam Smith in this discourse. Though Siskin describes Smith as 'the master systematizer of the Scottish Enlightenment', commentators have ignored Smith's explicit reflections on the psychological attractions, uses, and dangers of systems, which he first outlined in Section IV of the original 1759 edition of *The Theory of Moral Sentiments*, and to which he returned in Part VI of the 1790 edition. In both the original edition and his later revisions, Smith outlined an intriguing connection between aesthetics – or, more specifically, the love of beauty – and systems. He argued that the advance of civilization depends upon love of the *beauty* of systems, and he outlined two different ways in which systems encouraged the 'industry of mankind' (TMS IV.1.10, 183). In some cases, institutions were created because legislators fully perceived the beauty of a social system, such as a 'public police', and sought to instantiate this system in reality. In other cases, however, progress occurred because individuals mistook an element of a system for the system itself, and devoted enormous effort to acquiring these elements. People generally came to perceive their confusion of part for whole too late, yet while the 'sacrifice' of their energies was perhaps tragic from the perspective of the individual, it was efficacious for civilization as a whole. Smith seemed more comfortable with this latter mode of system-love than with the mode based on the conscious recognition of systems, for he warned – haltingly in 1759 and more stridently in 1790 – that the loveliness of explicitly perceived systems sometimes became so attractive that adherents ceased to attend to the actual social effects of emerging institutions, and this form of blindness was destructive of social stability.

It is unfortunate that Smith's reflections on systems and beauty have not caught the attention of Romantic literary critics, for in fact his analyses established the analytic framework for debates about the virtues of systems in the 1790s. Smith's distinction between two kinds of system-love – on the one hand, the love of the system *as* a whole, and on the other, a love based on the misrecognition of a part of the system for the whole – anticipated Burke's distinction between the good British system (which, Burke contended, was rarely explicitly recognized as a system) and the bad French 'philosophic system', which led to 'frauds, impostures, violences, rapines, burnings, murders, confiscations', and other evils. Smith's discussion of systems also established the framework within which an arguably more radical author such as Coleridge sought to theorize the nature of the system that true British patriots might follow. Drawing on Smith's suggestion that systems exacted sacrifices, Coleridge sought to explain the different modes of sacrifice by means of which good and bad systems could be distinguished. Even the much more radical political theorist William Godwin, who argued, *pace* Burke, that all governments and institutions are intrinsically oppressive, also sought (like Burke) to understand systems in terms of their beauty, and (like Coleridge) to distinguish good from bad systems through their relationship to sacrifice. This does not suggest that Godwin was 'really conservative' (or, conversely, that Burke was 'really radical'), but it does suggest that both of these terms should be understood in connection with an understanding of system first fully articulated in Smith's text on moral philosophy.[2]

My discussion here is divided into four parts. I begin by outlining four different senses of the word 'system' current in the eighteenth century, and I indicate several important modes of relationship between these different senses of the term. I then focus on the connections that Smith establishes between aesthetics and systems in the 1759 edition of *The Theory of Moral Sentiments* before turning, in the third section, to a discussion of his revisions in the 1790 edition. I conclude with a brief discussion of the ways in which Smith's paradigm helps us to understand the role of system in Edmund Burke's conservative political theory of the 1790s, as well as the more ambiguously conservative political philosophy articulated by Samuel Taylor Coleridge and William Godwin's decidedly radical anarchist political philosophy.

The four systems of the eighteenth century

'System' could mean a number of different things for eighteenth century authors. In the quote above from Burke, 'system' meant something like a deceptive theory about the proper structure of government, while Godwin and Paine, in the selections cited, employed the term to mean something more like the set of actually existing social institutions. It is thus useful to distinguish between four different eighteenth century senses of system: (1) system as *genre* (that is, a method of literary composition and an implied premise about how best to produce knowledge); (2) system as the *metaphysical structure of the universe*; (3) system as *a discrete set of institutions* designed to achieve a particular end, often with the support of the state (for example, the 'system of slavery'); (4) system as *the overarching set of social institutions* that collectively controlled all possibilities for individual action and dissent.[3] In what follows, I briefly outline each of these four meanings, illustrating each with examples drawn from early eighteenth century texts.

System as genre

Since at least the seventeenth century, 'system' referred to a genre of literary production. The guiding premise of the genre of system was that true knowledge was produced when one proceeded deductively from sound principles; in print form, this meant that an author should begin with an outline of principles and employ expository prose (Siskin 1998: 13–15). Hundreds, if not thousands, of works in this genre were produced in the late seventeenth and early eighteenth centuries, ranging from discussions of natural philosophy (e.g. Thomas Rutherford's *A System of Natural Philosophy*, 1748), to theology (e.g. Ralph Cudworth, *The True Intellectual System of the Universe*, 1678), to moral philosophy (e.g. Francis Hutcheson's *System of Moral Philosophy*, published posthumously in 1755), and oratory (e.g. John Stirling's *A System of Rhetoric*, 1733). Simpson has argued that system was often seen as a 'radical' genre in the seventeenth and eighteenth centuries, associated with Puritan radicalism, and by extension, political and social upheaval. Burke's late eighteenth century attack on systems, Simpson suggests, was part of a long tradition of attacks on the genre. In the seventeenth century, for example, Francis Bacon had criticized systems for their tendency to 'anticipat[e] nature' by restricting the possible field of investigation to phenomena consonant with the foundational principles of the system (rather than what might in fact be the case), and for later commentators, this epistemological shortcoming was aligned with the 'leveling' tendencies of extreme Protestant reform (Bacon 2000: 38; see Siskin 1998: 14–15). In place of the epistemologically problematic and politically dangerous genre of system, opponents proposed alternate genres. Bacon, for example, favored aphorisms as a literary mode more likely to capture the nature of things than the deductive premises of systems, while the 'miscellaneous style and diversified style' of Shaftesbury's *Characteristics of Men, Manners, Opinions, Times* (1711), was, according to Simpson, 'intended as a gesture of freedom against the constraints of form and system, tendencies [Shaftesbury] seems to have intuitively identified as the property of an emerging bourgeoisie' (Simpson 1993: 48).

System as order of the universe

Yet if conservative authors often attacked the genre of system, they no less frequently invoked the term in what we might call a 'morally prescriptive explanation' of the nature of reality: that is, as an explanation of the true nature of the world, that, once recognized by the reader, would morally improve him or her. Shaftesbury, for example, may have opted for an anti-systematic 'miscellaneous and diversified style' in the *Characteristics*, but he also contended in that text that the universe was best understood as a set of interlocking and co-dependent 'systems'.[4] He argued that apparently independent entities, such as individual animals, are more accurately perceived as parts of systemic wholes; thus, while 'every creature has a private good and interest of his own', each also 'points beyond itself' to other creatures (so, for example, 'if an animal has the proportions of a male, it shows he has a relationship to a female') (Cooper 1999: 167). Because each 'species of animals contribute to the existence or well-being of some other [species]', the 'whole species ... [is] a part only of some other system'. Shaftesbury claimed, for example, that

> to the existence of the spider that of the fly is absolutely necessary. The heedless flight, weak frame and tender body of this latter insect fits and determines him as much a prey as the rough make, watchfulness and cunning of the former fits him for rapine and the ensnaring part. The web and wing are suited for one another.
>
> (168)

Shaftesbury's use of metonymy – the web for the spider and the wing for the fly – simply emphasizes his point that every individual 'thing' should be perceived as a part of a whole. In turn, every living system – for example, the fly–spider system – can be understood as a part in the 'system of all animals', which itself is part of the 'systems of a globe or earth', and all of these are part of 'a system of all things and a universal nature' (169). In the section of *Characteristics* entitled *The Moralists, a Philosophical Rhapsody*, the character Theocles describes the same doctrine, and suggests that such a 'view' of harmony is registered aesthetically, as 'a plain internal sensation' of 'order and proportion' that also serves as the basis of the arts (273–4).

If, as Siskin and Simpson suggest, system as *genre* tended toward a progressive politics, a much more conservative politics was embedded in the sense of system as a description of the metaphysical structure of nature. Shaftesbury's examples suggest that the interests of any particular group, or 'part', could always be negated by appeals to the more expansive 'whole' within which these supposed conflicts are overcome. He suggested, in fact, that sacrifice was the necessary corollary to the love of nature's systems: in *The Moralists,* for example, 'Philocles' argues that 'in the several orders of terrestrial forms a resignation is required, a sacrifice and mutual yielding of natures one to another' (245), and this could be translated directly into political terms, for '[i]t happens with mankind that, while some are by necessity confined to labour, others are provided with abundance of all things by the pains and labour of inferiors' (214).[5] Yet Shaftesbury had argued in the first version of the *Inquiry* that these were only apparent sacrifices, 'for every particular in its System, to work *to the good of that System or Public,* and *to its own good,* is all one, and not to be divided' (cited in Klein 1994: 57–8). One part's apparent loss is recouped by the beauty of 'this wide system' of the universe (245). To love the beauty of these systems is to accept their fundamentally static nature, an aesthetic appreciation that is (thereby) also an instantiation of virtue.[6]

Shaftesbury's reflections on system as the structure of nature served as a starting point for a number of early eighteenth century texts. Francis Hutcheson, for example, contended that '[m]ankind are ... insensibly link'd together, and make one great *System*, by an invisible *Union*' (Hutcheson 1728: 178) and he argued that 'wherever we find a Determination among several rational Agents to mutual Love, let each Individual be look'd upon as a Part of a great Whole, or System, and concern himself in the publick Good of it' (Hutcheson 1729: 160). He also employed Shaftesbury's descriptions of factions as 'limited systems' to argue against those who would 'artfully raise and foment this Party Spirit; or cantonize them into several Sects for the Defence of very trifling Causes' (Hutcheson 1729: 209). In *An Essay on Man* (1733–34), Alexander Pope highlighted to an even greater extent than Shaftesbury the political implications of this understanding of system, noting in the first epistle of his poem that disturbances in one system have implications for all systems ('The least confusion but in one [system], not all/That system only, but the whole must fall' (Pope 1993: 279, lines 249–50)), and he reminded his readers in the fourth letter that, in the human system, harmony requires that 'Some are, and must be, greater than the rest' (300, line 50), for if 'fortune's gifts . . . each alike possessed,/And each were equal, must not all contest?' (300, lines 63–4).

System as a discrete set of institutions

In addition to denoting a genre committed to the production of knowledge, and a description of the part–whole division of nature, 'system' was also used to describe sets of institutions that were organized to achieve a particular result (often, though not always, with the help, or implicit support, of the state). Thomas Hobbes had provided the template for this understanding of system in *Leviathan* (1651), noting that '[b]y SYSTEMS, I understand any numbers of men joined in one interest, or one business' (Hobbes 1966, vol. III: 210). He provided a typology of different kinds of systems, distinguishing between regular and irregular; absolute and subject; political and private; and lawful and unlawful systems. During the course of the eighteenth century, 'system' was increasingly used to describe a number of 'interests' which coordinated the activities of large groups of people: for example, James Allan Park's *A System of the Law of Marine Insurances* (1787) or Bennett Cuthbertson's *System for the Compleat Interior Management and Oeconomy of a Battalion of Infantry* (1776). The term could also be used in a more negative sense, to describe a morally questionable set of institutions. An early example of such a use is William Wilkinson's *Systema Africanum, or, A treastise, discovering the intrigues and arbitrary preceedings of the Guiney Company* (1690), and by the late eighteenth century, commentators often sought to describe, and critique, the 'system of slavery' that tied together Britain, Africa, and the New World.[7]

System as social totality

By the early nineteenth century, 'system' had acquired an additional, and more sinister and totalizing, sense. As Kevin Gilmartin has documented, early nineteenth century radical authors frequently used the term to describe a corrupting and pervasive form of governmental and monied influence that had 'the strength of a giant' and the reach of the 'hundred hands of Briareus' (Wooler 1817: 97; cited in Gilmartin 1996: 16). System in this sense denoted a force of deception and influence that threatened to control all aspects of society, and Siskin suggests this totalizing understanding of the system provided the foundation of our contemporary notion of 'The System' as 'that which . . . works both too well – "You can't beat 'The System'" – and not well enough – it always seems to "break down"' (Siskin 2001: 202). Both Gilmartin and Siskin note that this understanding of 'the System' was plagued by a paradox: on the one hand, it was condemned as a 'corrupting' force that limited individual or collective choice; yet, on the other hand, it was described as *so* totalizing that it would seem to serve as the foundation of even those forms of subjectivity that purportedly resist it. Siskin suggests that we can observe this link between system and subjectivity in the example of the eponymous protagonist of William Godwin's *Caleb Williams*, who seeks to evade an apparently all-seeing British monitorial system, but at the same time 'comes to feel part of the very things that oppress him' (Siskin 2001: 211).

System in the first edition of *The Theory of Moral Sentiments*

These four different understandings of system were often used independently of one another. For example, an author might describe the universe as a series of systems without necessarily employing the genre of system, nor did the genre of system necessitate belief in nature as a hierarchy of systems. Institutions could be understood as systems without necessitating belief in either the system of the universe or 'the System' (in Siskin's sense of the totality of the social). At the same time, though, implicit links between these different kinds of systems were common: for example, many authors used the genre of system in order to describe the nature of existing (or proposed) practical or institutional systems, and descriptions of the universe as a series of systems often implied the legitimacy of existing social and political systems.

Adam Smith's *The Theory of Moral Sentiments* seems to have been the first text to provide something like a 'meta-theory' of the relationship between these different meanings of system. First published in 1759, this text is perhaps best known for Smith's contention that all moral sentiments and judgments are grounded in acts of sympathy through which we imaginatively 'enter into' the situation of another and 'become in some measure the same person with him' (TMS I.i.1.2, 7). However, Smith turned to a consideration of 'systems' in both Part IV ('Of the EFFECT of UTILITY upon the Sentiment of Approbation'), in which he examined the possible consequences of the love of systems, and Part VII ('Of Systems of Moral Philosophy'), in which he sought to subsume previous systems of moral philosophy into his own. In what follows, I shall focus on Smith's reflections in Part IV, for it was in this section that he developed at greatest length his understanding of the relationship between the different senses of 'system'.[8]

Smith does not explicitly define 'system' in Part IV of *The Theory of Moral Sentiments*, but it seems to denote any practical plan or institution that produces (or aims to produce) a certain end, often with the support of the state. Part IV is focused on the ways in which judgments about the beauty of objects and institutions are in fact really judgments about their usefulness, or utility – or, as Smith puts it, 'the fitness of an system or machine to produce the end for which it was intended, bestows a certain propriety and beauty upon the whole, and renders the very thought and contemplation of it agreeable' (TMS IV.1.1, 177). Smith contends that our perception of the beauty of a system or machine is a function of our perception of its ability to achieve the end for which it appears to us to be designed. So, for example, he contends that it is the 'beauty of order, or art and contrivance' that serves 'frequently to recommend those institutions which tend to promote the public welfare' (TMS IV.1.11, 185). Smith stresses that our love of the system is not a function of the benefits that a system actually delivers to us or to others, but rather its perceived capacity to achieve what it is designed to do. So, for example,

> When a patriot exerts himself for the improvement of any part of the public police, his conduct does not always arise from pure sympathy with the happiness of those who are to reap the benefit of it. It is not commonly from a fellow-feeling with carriers and waggoners that a public-spirited man encourages the mending of high roads. ... [rather] The perfection of police, the extension of trade and manufactures, are noble and magnificent objects. The contemplation of them pleases us, and we are interested in whatever can tend to advance them. They make part of the great system of government, and the wheels of the political machine seem to move with more harmony and ease by means of them. We take pleasure in beholding the perfection of so beautiful and grand a system...
>
> (TMS IV.1.11, 185)

It is the fitness of these institutions (public police; road mending; government) that is, in and of itself, attractive. Our perception of this beauty is, in one sense, disinterested, for it does not depend on any advantage that will accrue to us, either as individuals or as part of collectivity. However, this form of disinterest does not immobilize us; by contrast, it draws us forward, and 'interests' us in whatever can further these systems.

Smith acknowledges that the disinterested nature of system-love is not always clear to the individuals involved, and he notes that people often confuse *elements* of a system with the harmony and order that characterize the system as a whole. He suggests that people tend to view systems on the basis of a logic of unconscious synecdoche, taking a part for the whole, but then forgetting that they have done so. This confusion explains, for example, why some individuals become obsessed with obtaining what are, from an individual point of view, essentially useless objects, such as 'palaces', 'gardens', or 'the equipage, the retinue of the great'. Smith suggests that

> If we consider the real satisfaction which all these things are capable of affording, by itself and separated from the beauty of that arrangement which is fitted to promote it, it will always appear in the highest degree contemptible and trifling. But we rarely view it in this abstract and philosophical light. We naturally confound it in our imagination with the order, the regular and harmonious movement of the system, the machine or oeconomy by means of which it is produced.
>
> (TMS IV.1.9, 183)

The 'beauty' of these objects (palaces, gardens, etc.) is not simply admired, but encourages an individual to commit himself to forms of apparently irrational behavior, expending far more in effort than he could ever hope to receive in pleasure from the objects he pursues. Smith argues that disappointment inevitably results, for

> in the languor of disease and the weariness of old age, the pleasures of the vain and empty distinctions of greatness disappear. In his heart he curses ambition, and vainly regrets the ease and indolence of youth, pleasures which are fled forever, and which he has foolishly sacrificed for what, when he has got it, can afford him no real satisfaction.
>
> (TMS IV.I.8, 182)

This is a tragic narrative, for knowledge always arrives after action; we realize too late that we mistook the parts for the whole, and that our real love was for the harmony of the system that produced those parts, rather than the parts themselves.[9]

Yet Smith suggests that, however tragic this imaginary confusion of element for system is for the individual, it was precisely such a love of system that first enabled humans to liberate themselves from natural constraints, and which continues to make social progress possible. He argues that this misrecognition of part for whole 'rouses and keeps in continual motion the industry of mankind'. 'It is well that nature imposes upon us in this manner', Smith writes, for it is this

> which first prompted [humans] to cultivate the ground, to build houses, to found cities and commonwealths, and to invent and improve all the sciences and arts ... which have entirely changed the whole face of the globe, have turned rude forests into agreeable and fertile plains, and made the trackless and barren ocean a new fund of subsistence ... The earth by these labours of mankind has been obliged to redouble her natural fertility...
>
> (TMS IV.1.10, 183–4)

Where Bacon had criticized systems because they 'anticipated' nature, for Smith this is precisely their strength, for they transcend nature by going beyond what is given. Systems may be imaginary, corresponding to nothing in nature, but precisely because of this they allow humans to overcome what is 'given' by nature. Nor does such transcendence require that each individual consciously perceive the whole of this imaginary system, for the imaginary confusion of individual object for systemic harmony propels the advance of civilization, as individuals laboriously create ever more complex systems for obtaining objects. Thus, however 'foolish' these sacrifices to systems may appear from the perspective of the wise individual, they are nevertheless efficacious from the perspective of civilization itself. The tragedy of individual sacrifices benefits, and enables, the progress of civilization itself.

Smith's account thus outlines two different ways in which a spectator can perceive systems as beautiful. In some cases – for example, the public police – the system is consciously recognized as such, and in these cases the perception of beauty depends upon the extent to which the spectator can imagine all the parts of the system operating together. In these instances, no one *part* appears beautiful, but rather the reciprocal subordination of all the parts to one another creates the appearance of beauty. This is strikingly similar to Shaftesbury's claim that judgments of beauty result from the perception of nature as a set of systems. However, for Smith, such perceptions of system are tied to *changes* in social structure – for example, the transition from 'primitive' forms of social organization to the much more complex forms of life within 'cities and commonwealths' – while for Shaftesbury they were linked to a static social order. Yet in addition to this first mode of beauty, Smith also suggests that in some instances a system is only *implicitly* recognized, and in these cases an element of the system, for example, the palace, comes to take on the beauty of the whole. In these cases, the spectator finds him or herself bound to pursue the elements of the existing social system (though such pursuit may, over the long term, and unwittingly, cause changes in that system).

Even as he extolled the virtues of the love of system, Smith expressed some unease about the ways in which system-love could become an end in itself. He suggested that there was something almost inhuman about the love of systems such as public works, for proponents often seemed to pursue them whether or not they truly achieved the specified end. He suggested, for example, that

> [f]rom a certain spirit of system . . . from a certain love of art and contrivance, we sometimes seem to value the means more than the end, and be eager to promote the happiness of our fellow-creatures, rather from a view to perfect and improve a certain beautiful and orderly system, than from any immediate sense or feeling of what they either suffer or enjoy.
>
> (TMS IV.1.11, 185)

Even in these cases, aesthetics still assisted morality, for the love of the beauty of these systems generated social benefits. Yet it was clearly unsettling for Smith to recognize the ways in which the love of system could become fully self-referential, for it suggested a rather tenuous link between the good and the beautiful, at least in the context of our engagement with systems.

Smith concluded his reflections on system-love in this first edition of *The Theory of Moral Sentiments* with a reflection on the relationships between what I have outlined above as the first three senses of the term: that is, system as genre, as metaphysical structure of the universe, and as institution. Shaftesbury had argued that the love of the beauty of nature as an interlocking system of systems promoted morality, and while Smith's view is much more secular and far less extensive, he too argued that 'nature' employed the love of systems in a beneficial manner. By falling in love with systems (even if in the mode of mistaking a part for the whole), the 'industry of mankind' was roused in a beneficial way. However, he also connected this relatively 'unconscious' love of systems to both the genre of system, and institutional systems. He noted that discourse *on* institutional systems tended to produce converts to the systems described. He suggested, for example, that if one were to describe 'the great system of public police' *as* a system – that is, if one were to describe 'the connexions and dependencies of its several parts, their mutual subordination to one another, and their general subserviency to the happiness of the society' – then it was 'scarce possible that a man should listen to a discourse of this kind, and not feel himself animated to some degree of public spirit' (TMS IV.1.11, 186). In other words, institutional systems could be introduced and encouraged through the genre of system, which in turn promoted nature's goal of civilizing society. As a result, Smith suggested, 'political disquisitions', in which the 'several systems of civil government' were described, were 'of all works of speculation the most useful' (TMS IV.1.11, 187).

System in the 1790 edition of *The Theory of Moral Sentiments*

By 1790, however, Smith had come to reconsider some of his claims about the love of system. He left Part IV as it was, but expanded on the negative possibilities of the love of system in Part VI ('Of the CHARACTER of VIRTUE'), his major addition to the 1790 edition. In the second chapter of the second section of this part, entitled 'Of the order in which Societies are by nature recommended to our Beneficence', Smith sought to explain the principles that 'recommended' a society to an individual's beneficence. He argued that 'the state or sovereignty in which we have been born and educated' is, 'by nature, most strongly recommended to us' (TMS VI.ii.2.2, 227), primarily because it is the foundation for most of the other connections we have to other people (for example, 'our children, our parents, our relations, our friends, our benefactors') (TMS VI.ii.2.2, 227). Smith acknowledges that this beneficence entails a certain conservatism, for it encourages 'each particular order or society [i.e. limited part of society] to maintain its own powers, privileges, and immunities, against the encroachments of every other' (TMS VI.ii.2.9, 230–1). He does not rule out the possibility that our beneficence to the state may lead to the call for fundamental changes in its constitution, but he suggests that this 'spirit of innovation' ought to be accompanied by 'perhaps, the highest effort of political wisdom' (TMS VI.ii.2.12, 231–2).

Unfortunately, Smith argued, it was precisely such wisdom that seemed to be lacking in 'times of public discontent, faction, and disorder' (VI.ii.2.12, 231). He argued that '[a]midst the turbulence and disorder of faction', the love of beautiful systems – which under normal conditions, further civilized the world – could become separated from both morality and political stability. During these periods of instability

> a certain spirit of system is apt to mix itself with that public spirit which is founded upon the love of humanity, upon a real fellow-feeling with the inconveniences and distresses to which some of our fellow-citizens may be exposed. This spirit of system commonly takes the direction of that more gentle public spirit; always animates it, and often inflames it even to the madness of fanaticism.
>
> (VI.ii.2.15, 232)

This misappropriation of the reins of social change occurs, Smith argues, when the love of the beauty of systems becomes so fully self-referential as to become an end in itself. In these cases, '[t]he great body of the party are commonly intoxicated with the imaginary beauty of this ideal system, of which they have no experience, but which has been represented to them in all the most dazzling colours in which the eloquence of their leaders could paint it' (TMS VI.ii.2.15, 232).

While these reflections make clear that Smith was far more uneasy about the love of systems in 1790 than in 1759, the criteria by means of which he imagines his readers will be able to distinguish between good and bad – and real and ideal – systems, as well as real and 'imaginary beauty', is not so readily legible. He is clear that illusory systems are those which are grounded in an unrealistic combination of benevolence and belief in the possibility of perfection, for adherents of these systems imagine that they will 'not only remove the inconveniencies and relieve the distresses immediately complained of, but will prevent, in all time coming, any return of the like inconveniencies and distresses' (TMS VI.ii.2.15, 232). Such systems are unrealistic, Smith argues, because they combine a universal love of humanity with an absolute belief in perfection. He does not necessarily object to the humanitarian aspect of these would-be reformers, for he still condones that 'public spirit' that is 'founded upon the love of humanity, upon a real fellow-feeling'. However, he is clearly uncomfortable with the belief in perfection that motivates some reformers, arguing that while the perfection of a system may serve as a regulative ideal, it cannot be instantiated in reality.

In place of such visions of perfection, Smith outlines a practice for pursuing systems that was remarkably similar to the vision of conservatism being articulated at the same time by Edmund Burke. Smith argues that '[t]he man whose public spirit is prompted altogether by humanity and benevolence, will respect the established powers and privileges even of individuals, and still more those of the great orders and societies, into which the state is divided' (TMS VI.ii.2.16, 233). What Smith finds problematic is not change itself, nor even the love of system, for he acknowledges that '[s]ome general, and even systematical, idea of the perfection of policy and law, may no doubt be necessary for directing the views of the statesman' (TMS VI.ii.2.18, 234). He also acknowledges that even a *fanatical* love of system is occasionally necessary for social stability, as it enables socially beneficial forms of conscious self-sacrifice; the military, for example, creates conditions in which droves of '[g]ood soldiers' are able to 'cheerfully sacrifice their own little systems to the prosperity of a greater system' (TMS VI.ii.3.4, 236). What concerns Smith, however, is the *amount* and the *speed* of change. The problem with the 'man of system' is that he insists upon 'establishing all at once, and in spite of all opposition, every thing which that idea [of the system] may seem to require' (TMS VI.ii.2.18, 234). Smith suggests that systems must change slowly because they often have far-reaching and complex effects upon the multiple 'societies' of which every state is composed, but the relationship between the twin criteria of respect for the existing state and slow change is not always clear. So, for example, just a few years after Smith's death, Prime Minister Pitt encouraged the rapid development of a 'system of police' responsible for monitoring potentially treasonous activities of Britons: should the wisdom of such change be assessed in relationship to its capacity to support the existing state or the rapidity of its deployment? Smith suggests that in such cases, criteria of assessment may be lacking, and patriots will require 'the highest effort of political wisdom' to determine whether to support or oppose systemic change (TMS VI.ii.2.12, 231–2).

Commentators have suggested several different possible reasons for Smith's increased concern with system-love in the 1790 edition. In the introduction and notes to their edition of TMS, D. D. Raphael and A. P. Macfie suggest that the French Revolution served as the impetus for Smith's new reflections on system, and that his 'man of system' probably referred to Richard Price, whose 'The Love of our Country' had appeared the year before. (See TMS, pp. 18–19, 229 note 2, 231 note 6.) Within this interpretation, Smith's expanded comments on the perils of systems-love were an almost immediate response to events taking place just as he was finishing his revisions. Emma Rothschild proposes a slightly less immediate cause for Smith's revisions, suggesting that his reflections were aimed at 'the 'systematical' Prussian despotism of Frederick II', and she notes that Smith owned a copy of Frederick's memoirs, in which the king described the need for legislators to act 'from a determinate system of politics, war, finance, commerce, and laws' (Rothschild 2001: 55, 272 note 31). It is also possible that the increasing prominence of the anti-slavery cause, which became extremely visible and vocal in the period between 1787 and 1792, encouraged Smith to reconsider the speed with which systems should change. Anti-slavery advocates repeatedly railed against the 'system of slavery', which encouraged violence and immorality, and urged legislators to vote against this 'destructive system' (Nickolls 1788: Yearsley 1788; 26). Yet at the same time, even many anti-slavery advocates hesitated to endorse immediate emancipation for slaves, arguing that however evil the system of slavery might be, it must be dismantled slowly lest its destruction create more problems – and economic hardship – than its continued existence. As a number of critics have pointed out, Smith was himself critical of what he saw as the economic inefficiencies of the slave trade, but this same concern, emphasized in slave trade debates of the late 1780s, may have encouraged him to consider anew the speed with which systems ought to change.

Reassessing the politics of systems in the 1790s: Burke, Coleridge, Godwin

Since the 1980s, many literary critics of British Romanticism have sought to understand more fully the various explicit and implicit political positions adopted by authors such as William Blake, William Wordsworth, and Samuel Taylor Coleridge in both their prose and verse writings. Wordsworth and Coleridge have proven to be especially interesting cases, for both began the 1790s as strong supporters of the French Revolution, but within a decade and a half, each had adopted a much more conservative and pro-governmental political position. In seeking to understand the causes and vectors of Wordsworth's and Coleridge's changing political allegiances, literary critics have often positioned Edmund Burke as a fixed point of arch-conservatism, and judged these literary authors' politics by their convergence or divergence from elements of Burke's political philosophy. Simpson, for example, argues that Coleridge's reflections on system and method in both his writings from the 1790s as well as subsequent texts such as *The Friend* (1808, 1818) was simply Burkeanism in a more philosophical style (Simpson 1993: 59). In the case of Wordsworth, James Chandler argues that between 1793 and 1798 the poet moved away from an early commitment to the genre of system to the opposite position, a 'profound reversal' that was a result of his adoption of Burkean political principles (Chandler 1984: 81).

While this contextualization of Coleridge's and Wordsworth's reflections on systems against the figure of Burke is by no means unwarranted, Smith's reflections on system in both 1759 and 1790 should be part of this discussion, for his discussion established the framework within which both 'conservative' and 'radical' political positions could be mapped out. In order to make this case, I first outline the way in which Burke's conservative political philosophy can be seen as adoption of Smith's understanding of unconscious system-love. I then consider two Romantic authors: the radical political theorist and novelist William Godwin and the poet and philosopher S. T. Coleridge. All three authors, I suggest, follow Smith's lead in attempting to distinguish between good and bad forms of system-love, and do so by employing variants of Smith's reflections on the relationship of both sacrifice and beauty to systems.

In recent literary criticism on system, Burke has generally figured as an author vigilantly opposed to both the genre of 'system' as well as any attempt to found political practices on systems. Simpson, for example, notes that '[t]hroughout the 1790s Burke kept up and indeed stepped up his campaign against "the surfeit and indigestion of systems"' (Simpson 1993: 59), and he suggests that in Burke's most unsystematic text, the *Reflections on the Revolution in France*, he successfully depicted more radical authors, such as Price and Paine, as 'systematizers' (59). Burke outlined a horrifying vision of the social consequences of placing trust in systems, for he argued in his *Reflections* that the Revolutionary 'philosophic system' had engendered 'frauds, impostures, violences, rapines, burnings, murders, confiscations', and in the first of his *Letters on a Regicide Peace*, he argued that '[w]e are at war with a system' (Burke 1869, vol. III: 395; Burke 1869, vol. V: 250). The result, Simpson suggests, was the consolidation of a 'conservative' distrust of the genre of system that persists even into the present.

Yet Simpson also acknowledges (though does not fully address) that even as Burke criticized the *genre* of system, his philosophy of conservatism was grounded on an explicit appeal to the 'lovely' British system which (Burke claimed) mediated between culture and nature. In the *Reflections*,

Burke extolled the British 'political system' as one that was 'placed in a just correspondence and symmetry with the order of the world', with the result that 'the parts of the system do not clash', and '[o]ne advantage is as little as possible sacrificed to another' (Burke 1869, vol. III: 275, 457). Like Shaftesbury, Burke sought to contain the dangers of philosophical systems by appealing to a political system that 'harmonizes' with the natural order.[10] However, where Shaftesbury's meta-system was fundamentally static, Burke followed Smith's lead in imagining a meta-system that changed over time, and which was capable of a 'well-sustained progress' (457). For Burke, cultural systems can speak to themselves, gradually altering their principles and elements. However, Burke, again like Smith, sought to limit the speed with which this social feedback would occur, arguing that change must happen so slowly that 'its operation is ... in some cases almost imperceptible' (456). The systems of nature and culture must appear to blend ('the Mind must conspire with time'), for only by this means will one promote a harmonious social order within which 'the parts of the system do not clash'.[11] Burke, in other words, did not object to systems, per se, but rather to systems that promoted rapid change.

Like Smith, Burke positioned beauty as the index of this harmony between nature and the British system. Burke argued that the perceived continuity between the past and the present 'carries an imposing and majestic aspect' (276) and created a series of 'pleasing illusions which [make] power gentle and obedience liberal' (332). Burke contended that the 'love of country' demands that the 'country ought to be lovely', and he tied this to a 'system of manners' that spreads a pleasing patina on the British system, and thereby prevents it from collapsing (334). For Burke, as for Smith, progress does not depend solely on rational decisions, but it also depends even more fundamentally upon aesthetic judgments concerning the beauty of systems.[12] However, Burke valorized the second of Smith's two modes of beauty (the beauty that results when the whole is misrecognized in a part), describing the beauty of royalty as one of 'pleasing illusions which made power gentle and obedience liberal' (332).

Yet Burke, like Smith, also found himself struggling with the question of distinction: *how* fast is too fast? By means of what criterion can one determine whether a system is encouraging 'slow' or 'fast' progress? And are all beautiful systems good? In the *Reflections*, Burke provided an answer to this question by drawing on the metaphor of 'sacrifice' that Smith had emphasized in his 1759 comments on system. Burke and Smith agreed that the 'evolution' of social systems was not always a painless process, but where Smith had focused on the tragic consequences for the individual (who often discovered too late that he or she had mistaken an element for system, and thereby sacrificed his energy and youth), Burke suggested that legislators could catch sight of, and compare, possible sacrifices to the system before they happened. The legislator will seek to avoid sacrifice as much as possible; the 'parts of the system do not clash', Burke explained, when '[o]ne advantage is as little as possible sacrificed to another'.[13] Burke does not seem to believe that sacrifice can be avoided entirely, for he contends in the third of his *Letters on a Regicide Peace* that the British upper classes are those who are characterized by a 'fortitude' that,

> undisturbed by false humanity, can calmly assume that most awful moral responsibility of deciding when victory may be too dearly purchased by the loss of a single life, and when the safety and glory of their country may demand the certain sacrifice of thousands.
>
> (Burke 1869, vol. V: 469)

However, while beautiful systems may sometimes require sacrifices, they do not – *pace* Smith's claims – demand them on a regular basis. The system of the National Assembly, by contrast, encouraged precisely the sort of 'shouting of multitudes' that Burke had associated with the sublime in his much earlier *A Philosophical Enquiry into the Origin of our Ideas of the Sublime and Beautiful* (Burke 1869, vol. I: 159). Burke also aligned the National Assembly with sublimity by arguing that the new French government, considered simply as a system, and without comparing that ideal with its realization, painted for the imagination an 'awful image' which casts such a 'light' so as to 'subdue' all inquirers. The consequence of such aesthetic intimidation is a system that demands ever more sacrifices (for example, 'everything human and divine [is] sacrificed to the idol of public credit') (Burke 1869, vol. III: 282). As Tom Furniss notes, Burke's *Reflections* silently inverts the aesthetic theory he had outlined in *A Philosophical Enquiry into the Origin of our Ideas of the Sublime and Beautiful* (1756, 1759). Where in that earlier text Burke had seemed to valorize the sublime over the beautiful (Ferguson 1992; Furniss 1993), in his political prose of the 1790s, he sought to represent the revolution 'as an example of the way the sublime in its highest degree can run out of control' (Furniss 1993: 119), and his recommendation in the *Reflections* that 'the powerful submit to the lovely . . . reverses what the early aesthetics presents as both crucial and inevitable power relations' (176). Yet, Burke suggests, even these 'sacrifices' can hardly be called by that name, for in the case of the French systematizers,

> [n]ot one drop of *their* blood have they shed in the cause of the country they have ruined. They have made no sacrifices to their projects of greater consequence than their shoebuckles, whilst they were imprisoning their king, murdering their fellow citizens, and bathing in tears and plunging in poverty and distress thousands of worthy men and worthy families.
>
> (Burke 1869, vol. III: 283)

Burke criticizes the architects of the French Revolution, in other words, not because of their commitment to system, per se, but rather on account of their unwillingness to make sacrifices to their systems.

While Burke explicitly argues that sacrifices to systems ought to be avoided as much as possible, his critique of French systematizers implied that *self*-sacrifice could serve as an acceptable criterion for more moderately paced progress, and this suggestion was amplified in Samuel Taylor Coleridge's more radical political prose of the mid 1790s. While Coleridge occasionally attacked what he viewed as 'pernicious systems', he was no enemy of system, *per se*, for he and fellow poet Robert Southey were attempting to develop their own 'System' of Pantisocracy, a quasi-communistic society to be established on the banks of the Susquehanna river in Pennsylvania. Moreover, in his published prose, Coleridge attempted to theorize the different forms of sacrifice that systems demanded, and to provide a criterion by means of which British patriots could commit themselves to true systems.

Coleridge's efforts to distinguish between good and bad systems was most clearly articulated in 'A Moral and Political Lecture' and the nearly identical text *Conciones ad Populum*. In this lecture and text, Coleridge uses 'sacrifice' as a means of distinguishing between four classes of 'professed Friends of Liberty'. Members of the first class of the friends of liberty sincerely desire reform, but their efforts are inefficacious because they offer 'no sacrifices to the divinity of active Virtue' (Coleridge 1971: 8). The second class, by contrast, is made up of those who are all too willing to offer human sacrifices to Freedom, for they desire to make the 'Altar of Freedom stream with blood' (9). This second class is also characterized by confused aesthetic judgments: they mistake revenge for sacrifice, and as a result '[t]he Groans of the Oppressors make fearful yet pleasant music' to this second class of friends (10).[14] The third class of professed friends, like the first, are unwilling to sacrifice anything at all, but in this case this refusal is based on self-interest, as they simply want to topple those above them in order to occupy the highest slot in the social hierarchy. The fourth and final class of the friends of liberty – and the only class of which Coleridge approves – practice the only proper form of sacrifice. This group is composed of 'thinking . . . Patriots' and they have 'cultivat[ed]' their 'moral taste' to such an extent that they are willing to 'sacrifice all energies of heart and head' (12, 15).

Coleridge also links the sacrifices of the fourth class of patriots to a form of aesthetic judgment. Citing a passage from Mark Akenside's *The Pleasures of the Imagination*, Coleridge argues that this fourth class are those who are able to 'appea[l] to Nature, to the winds/And rolling waves, the suns unwearied course,/The elements and the seasons' and read in these natural events the message 'be great like [God]/Beneficent and active' (41). This fourth class of friends of liberty are like religious mediators, who are both able to hear the 'Strange Rumblings and confused Noises' that are part of the quasi-natural processes of political change, but are also able control these processes by practicing proper forms of sacrifice (the sacrifice of the energies of heart and head). Coleridge positions himself as a devotee of this mode of sacrifice in the final lines of his poem 'Reflections on having Left a Place of Retirement' (1796), contending that rather than imitating those who 'sigh for Wretchedness, yet shun the Wretched', he will 'go, and join head, heart, and hand,/Active and firm, to fight the bloodless fight/Of Science, Freedom, and the Truth in Christ' (Coleridge 1966: 107–8; lines 57, 60–2).

In *Conciones ad Populum*, Coleridge further explained that the four classes' different modes of sacrifice are a function of their differing relationships to systems. The first three classes of professed Friends, that is, the 'majority of Democrats', confuse systems with their parts, for they 'attribute to the system which they reject, all the evils existing under it' (Coleridge 1971: 37). This confusion is motivated by a tendency toward abstraction (citing Burke, Coleridge suggests that they 'contemplat[e] truth and justice "in the nakedness of abstraction"'). Yet the fourth class of patriots is *not* made up of those who eschew systems entirely, but rather of people who accept what Coleridge in his 1795 *Lectures on Revealed Religion* called Jesus's 'system of morality' and God's 'perfect system of morality' (160, 161). Coleridge's fourth class of patriots thus mixes elements from Smith's two categories of system-love: rather than describing self-sacrifice as characteristic of the unconscious love of system, as Smith had suggested, Coleridge instead connects it with the conscious recognition of system.

While Coleridge was arguably at least quasi-'Burkean' in his political sentiments, William Godwin certainly was not. *An Enquiry Concerning Political Justice* (1793, 1796, 1798) outlined an essentially anarchist position, for Godwin argued that any system of government – or, more generally, *any* institution – served to obstruct the progress of reason and social relations. 'By its very nature,' Godwin wrote, 'political institution has a tendency to suspend the elasticity, and put an end to the advancement of mind,' and he bemoaned the fact that '[h]undreds of victims are annually sacrificed at the shrine of positive law and political institution' (Godwin 1992: 185, 9).[15] Moreover, of the three authors I consider in this section, Godwin was the most committed to the genre of system; as Siskin notes, Godwin's *Enquiry* took the 'standard form of written system: a list of "principles" followed by expository prose' (Siskin 1998: 14–15). At points, the author of the *Enquiry* even seemed to fit Burke's image of the heartless man of system, for Godwin argued (especially in the first edition of the *Enquiry*) against feeling as a ground for decisions, and instead in favor of calm reason, which could steel itself to the need for sacrifice. Through the application of reason, an individual could determine his or her absolute value with respect to others and, if necessary, 'perceive either that my prosperity or existence must be sacrificed to those of twenty men as good as myself, or theirs to mine' (Godwin 1992: 346).[16]

Yet even as Godwin extolled the virtues of system, reason, and sacrifice, he retained the focus on aesthetic perception that characterized Smith's paradigmatic descriptions of system-love. Godwin argued that '[n]o man can love virtue sufficiently, who has not an acute and lively perception of its beauty', and he also contended that when the beauty of virtue was perceived, the irresistible force it exerted upon the perceiver was a function of its aesthetic quality: '[i]t is impossible not to see the beauty of equality, and to be charmed with the benefits it appears to promise' (Godwin 1992: 233, 830). Moreover, he claimed that such aesthetic perceptions of truth demanded to be instantiated in social forms, as these perceptions spread from an enlightened elite to the more general population:

> As soon as any important truth has become established to a sufficient extent in the mind of the enterprising and the wise, it may tranquilly and with ease be rendered part of the general system; since the uninstructed and the poor are never the strenuous supporters of those complicated systems by which oppression is maintained.
>
> (Godwin 1992: 188)[17]

Where Burke had connected beauty to illusion, Godwin argued that beauty was a guide to truth, though this complicated the relationship between system and temporality in Godwin's text. Burke had argued that commitment to fully recognized systems accelerated change beyond control, and he argued that beauty moderated progress by dressing up the British system in 'pleasing illusions'. Godwin did not dispute Burke's claim that social change must proceed slowly – he agreed that '[g]radual improvement is the most conspicuous law of [human] nature' – but Godwin implied that perception of the beauty of truth contained its own principle of moderation (Godwin 1992: 221). In the first edition of *Enquiry*, he suggested that 'systematizers' could play an important role in such moderate change, noting that while the progressive effects initiated by Helvetius's writings were not apparent to that French author, nevertheless, 'the work of renovation was in continual progress' between the publication of his texts and the start of the French Revolution (224). However, in subsequent editions, Godwin found himself agreeing with Burke that fidelity to systems could lead to uncontrolled changes. In the 1796 edition of *Political Justice*, he imagined a radical opponent of the *Enquiry* complaining that

> It is easy for a reasoner to sit down in his closet, and amuse himself with the beauty of this conception [of the progress of society]; but in the meantime mankind are suffering, [and] injustice is hourly perpetrated...
>
> (Godwin 1796: 224)

While this imaginary critic urged the adoption of a system and 'method' which would speed up reform, Godwin tried to convince his readers that perceptions of the beauty of social change in fact encouraged relatively patient and slow-moving change. Moreover, in a discussion of 'good and evil', he argued that the nature of this distinction had been obscured by those who made virtue unattainable, as well as by 'those who, spurring the narrow limits of science and human understanding, have turned system-builders, and fabricated a universe after their own peculiar fancy' (Godwin 1985: 390).

Conclusion: Smith, system, and Romanticism

My point in drawing attention to these similarities between the political theories of Burke, Coleridge, and Godwin is not to suggest that their political positions were identical. Instead, I am stressing the extent to which all three sought to understand, and control, the mechanism of social progress by making recourse to the framework of systems first articulated in Smith's original 1759 edition of *Theory of Moral Sentiments* and again stressed in the 1790 edition. Smith's text made it possible for these authors to think (or more likely, impossible not to think) of social change and progress as a function of the sacrifices entailed by the conscious and unconscious recognition of the beauty of systems. Where Smith had argued for the utility of both modes (though he was clearly more uneasy about conscious system-love), Burke's conservative political philosophy sought to valorize only the unconscious mode of system-love. Godwin, by contrast, distrusted anything but Smith's conscious mode of system-love, while the early Coleridge developed an interesting hybrid of modes, favoring conscious system-love, but linking it to the mode of self-sacrifice that Smith had attributed to unconscious system-love.

Recognizing Smith's role in this discourse has significant implications for our understanding of the politics of Romantic figures. My analysis highlights the fact that both conservatives and radicals found themselves drawn to systems, and both groups also sought to assess these in aesthetic terms (beauty). Thus, rather than using commitment to system as the litmus test to distinguish between conservative and radical authors (or conservative and radical moments in an author's work), we need to consider more carefully the multiple ways in which systems and beauty could be linked by Romantic-era authors. In addition, while Burke has functioned as the reference point for assessing the politics of Romantic authors, my analysis suggests that Smith should factor into this discussion as well. This is not to suggest that Smith was a Romantic author, but acknowledging his role in the context of debates about systems in the 1790s helps us to understand the 'Romantic turn' to models of organicism first articulated by Burke. While Smith's reflections on systems do not easily fall into either the conservative or radical label, they arguably establish the possibility of such labels in the first place.

Notes

1 For other discussions of systems in the Romantic era, see Rothstein (1975: 1–21, 208–242); Rajan (1981, 1992, 1996); Chandler (1984: 32–5, 73, 231, 238); Gilmartin (1996: 51–2, 158–94); Kaufmann (1995); Burgess (2000: 10–16).
2 My use of the term 'conservative' draws on the accounts of Quinton (1978) and O'Gorman (1986), who argue that conservatism is founded on the beliefs that: (a) humans are inherently imperfect, but (b) the dangers of this failing are limited by the 'organic' nature of society, which in turn mandates that (c) polities rely on tradition, rather than political innovation. Quinton and O'Gorman date the origins of conservatism differently, but both position Burke as its first major proponent. My thanks to Katey Kuhns Castellano for her work and help on this point. 'Radical' is a far more contested term, but I follow Jacob (1981) and Gilmartin (1996) in using it to refer to a commitment to instantiate republican forms of government which would overcome the Whig/Tory division, a political goal that was often underwritten by pantheistic and/or materialist natural philosophies. Useful discussions of this term include McCalman (1988); Morton and Smith (2002: 1–26); Andrews (2003). Thanks to Tim Fulford and Stuart Andrews for helpful discussions on this topic.
3 Siskin (1998) implies a threefold typology that corresponds roughly to my first, third and fourth meanings above. Unfortunately, he does not mention the second element of my typology, which – as my analysis below will suggest – is particularly important for understanding Smith's discussion of systems.
4 Shaftesbury introduced the term 'system' in his *Inquiry Concerning Virtue and Merit*, which is unarguably the most generically systematic section of the *Characteristics*. The *Inquiry* had been published independently in 1699, probably without Shaftesbury's permission, and thus its inclusion in the more stylistically diverse *Characteristics* was perhaps an attempt to undercut the genre of system which the *Inquiry*, as an independent publication, had seemed to privilege. For a discussion of the relationship between the 1699 *Inquiry* and *Characteristics*, see Klein (1994).
5 I expand on the relationship between sacrifice and systems in Mitchell (2005 and forthcoming).
6 This notion of system was related, but not identical, to the notion of the 'great chain of Being', the history of which Arthur O. Lovejoy has described. As Lovejoy notes, a central premise of eighteenth century discussions of the great chain of Being was that 'the true *raison d'être* of one species was never to be sought in its utility to any other', which was precisely the opposite of Shaftesbury's claims about systems (Lovejoy 1960: 186).
7 For examples of the slave trade described as a 'system', see p. 74 below.
8 My discussion of the role of system in Smith's thought has been greatly facilitated by Knud Haakonssen's distinction between 'contextual knowledge' and 'system knowledge' in Smith; see Haakonssen (1981: 79–82, 89–93); see also Schliesser (2005).
9 According to Rosen, Smith did not believe that such unhappy conclusions would vex many people, since they occur only in 'time of sickness or low spirits' (Rosen 2000: 90). However, Smith also mentions old age as an initiating cause of such reflections, which makes it much more likely that they will come to disturb most people.
10 Simpson points out that Burke's opponents detected 'method' and 'system' in

the *Reflections*, despite Burke's apparent opposition to that genre. Thomas Cooper, for example, argued that in fact Burke was the 'systematic opponent of every Species of Reform', and despite his supposed distrust of systems, he had in fact developed a systematic 'THEORY of *privileged orders*' (Cooper 1792: 66, 82; cited in Simpson 1993: 54).

11 Burke's objection to philosophic systems, as Simpson notes, is precisely that they are supposed to be 'ready and easy way[s] that spee[d] up mental and social processes and economiz[e] on human energy' (Simpson 1993: 58).

12 For a useful discussion of the role of concepts of beauty in Burke's political prose of the 1790s, see Furniss (1993: 113–265).

13 Burke reiterated this claim in the second of his *Letters on the Regicide Peace*, contending there that '[t]he British State is, without question, that which pursues the greatest variety of ends, and is the least disposed to sacrifice any of them to another, or to the whole' (Burke 1869, vol. V: 374).

14 In *Conciones ad Populum* Coleridge implies that this second mode of sacrifice is inefficacious: 'A system of fundamental Reform will scarcely be effected by massacres mechanized into Revolution' (Coleridge 1971: 48).

15 Godwin published three editions of the *Enquiry*, in 1793, 1796, and 1798. The latter two editions differ in some significant ways from the first, but unless otherwise indicated, all citations are drawn from the first edition.

16 In the 1798 edition Godwin adopted a more Smithian position, arguing that '[w]e are able in imagination to go out of ourselves, and become impartial spectators of the system of which we are a part', and as a result of such a disinterested view, 'it is possible for a man to sacrifice his own existence to that of twenty others' (Godwin 1985: 381).

17 In a footnote to *Edmund Burke's Aesthetic Ideology*, Furniss contends, though without explanation, that Godwin's 'system may be said to advocate a politics of radical beauty rather than that of the radical sublime' (Furniss 1993: 289 n. 35). I agree entirely with Furniss's suggestion, but as my analysis suggests, this point alone does not necessarily distinguish his project from more conservative systems such as that of Burke.

References

Andrews, Stuart (2003) *Unitarian Radicalism: Political Rhetoric, 1770–1814*, New York: Palgrave Macmillan.

Bacon, Francis (2000) *The New Organon*, ed. Lisa Jardine and Michael Silverthorne, Cambridge: Cambridge University Press.

Blake, William (1988) *The Complete Poetry and Prose of William Blake, Newly Revised Edition*, ed. David Erdman, New York: Doubleday.

Burgess, Miranda J. (2000) *British Fiction and the Production of Social Order, 1740–1830*, Cambridge: Cambridge University Press.

Burke, Edmund (1869) *The Works of the Right Honorable Edmund Burke*, 3rd edn, 12 vols, Boston, MA: Little Brown.

Chandler, James (1984) *Wordsworth's Second Nature: A Study of the Poetry and Politics*, Chicago: University of Chicago Press.

Coleridge, Samuel Taylor (1966) *The Complete Poetical Works of Samuel Taylor Coleridge: Including Poems and Versions of Poems Now Published for the First Time*, ed. Ernest Hartley Coleridge, Oxford: Clarendon Press.

—— (1971) *The Collected Works of Samuel Taylor Coleridge*: I, *Lectures on Politics and Religion*, ed. Lewis Patton and Peter Mann, Princeton, NJ: Princeton University Press.

Cooper, Anthony Ashley, Third Earl of Shaftesbury (1999) *Characteristics of Men, Manners, Opinions, Times*, ed. Lawrence E. Klein, Cambridge: Cambridge University Press.

Cooper, Thomas (1792) *A Reply to Mr Burke's Invective against Mr Cooper and Mr Watt, in the House of Commons, on the 30th of April, 1792*, 2nd edn, London: J. Johnson.

Cudworth, Ralph (1678) *The True Intellectual System of the Universe; wherein all the Reason and Philosophy of Atheism is Confuted and its Impossibility Demonstrated*, London: Richard Royston.

Cuthbertson, Bennett (1776) *System for the Compleat Interior Management and Oeconomy of a Battalion of Infantry*, Bristol: A. Gray.

Ferguson, Frances (1992) *Solitude and the Sublime: Romanticism and the Aesthetics of Individuation*, New York: Routledge.

Furniss, Tom (1993) *Edmund Burke's Aesthetic Ideology: Language, Gender, and Political Economy in Revolution*, Cambridge: Cambridge University Press.

Gilmartin, Kevin (1996) *Print Politics: The Press and Radical Opposition in Early Nineteenth-Century England*, Cambridge: Cambridge University Press.

Godwin, William (1796) *An Enquiry Concerning Political Justice, and its Influence on Morals and Happiness*, Philadelphia: Bioren and Madan.

—— (1985) *An Enquiry Concerning Political Justice, and its Influence on Modern Morals and Happiness*, New York: Penguin Books.

—— (1992) *An Enquiry Concerning Political Justice, and its Influence on General Virtue and Happiness*, 2 vols, London: G. G. J. and J. Robinson, 1793; reprint edn, ed. Jonathan Wordsworth, New York: Woodstock Books.

Haakonssen, Knud (1981) *The Science of a Legislator: The Natural Jurisprudence of David Hume and Adam Smith*, Cambridge: Cambridge University Press.

Hobbes, Thomas (1966) *The English Works of Thomas Hobbes of Malmesbury*, 11 vols, ed. Sir William Molesworth, London: John Bohn, 1839–45; 2nd reprint edn, Darmstadt: Scienta Verlag Aalen.

Hutcheson, Francis (1728) *An Essay on the Nature and Conduct of the Passions and Affections; with Illustrations on the Moral Sense*, London: Printed by J. Darby and T. Browne for J. Smith and W. Bruce.

—— (1729) *An Inquiry into the Original of Our Ideas of Beauty and Virtue: In Two Treatises*, 3rd edn, London: J. and J. Knapton.

—— (1755) *A System of Moral Philosophy: in three books, written by the late Francis Hutcheson; published from the original manuscript, by his son Francis Hutcheson; to which is prefixed some account of the life, writings, and character of the author, by William Leechman, D.D.*, London: A. Millar and T. Longman.

Jacob, Margaret C. (1981) *The Radical Enlightenment: Pantheists, Freemasons and Republicans*, London: Allen & Unwin.

Kaufmann, David (1995) *The Business of Common Life: Novels and Classical Economics between Revolution and Reform*, Baltimore, MD: Johns Hopkins University Press.

Klein, Lawrence E. (1994) *Shaftesbury and the Culture of Politeness: Moral Discourse and Cultural Politics in Early Eighteenth-Century England*, Cambridge: Cambridge University Press.

Kramnick, Isaac (1990) *Republicanism and Bourgeois Radicalism: Political Ideology in Late Eighteenth Century England and America*, Ithaca, NY: Cornell University Press.

Lovejoy, Arthur O. (1960) *The Great Chain of Being: A Study of the History of an Idea*, New York: Harper Torchbooks.

Makdisi, Saree (2003) *William Blake and the Impossible History of the 1790s*, Chicago: University of Chicago Press.

McCalman, Ian (1988) *Radical Underworld: Prophets, Revolutionaries and Pornographers in London, 1795–1840*, Cambridge: Cambridge University Press.

Mitchell, Robert (2005) 'Adam Smith and Coleridge on the Love of Systems' *Coleridge Bulletin* 25 (summer): 54–60.

—— (forthcoming) 'The Fane of Tescalipoca: S. T. Coleridge on the Sacrificial Economies of Systems in the 1790s', *Studies in Romanticism*.

Morton, Timothy and Nigel Smith (2002) *Radicalism in British Literary Culture, 1650–1830: From Revolution to Revolution*, Cambridge: Cambridge University Press.

Nickolls, Rev. Robert Boucher (1788) *Letter to the Treasurer of the Society Instituted for the Purpose of Effecting the Abolition of the Slave Trade*, London: James Phillips.

O'Gorman, Frank (1986) *British Conservatism: Conservative Thought from Burke to Thatcher*, London: Longman.

Paine, Thomas (1942) *The Rights of Man*, New York: Wiley.

Park, James Allan (1787) *A System of the Law of Marine Insurances, with three chapters on bottomry; on insurances on lives; and on insurances against fire*, London: Printed by His Majesty's law printers for T. Whieldon.

Pope, Alexander (1993) *Alexander Pope: A Critical Edition of the Major Works*, ed. Pat Rogers, Oxford: Oxford University Press.

Quinton, Anthony (1978). *The Politics of Imperfection: The Religious and Secular Traditions of Conservative Thought from Hooker to Oakeshott*, London: Faber.

Rajan, Tilottoma (1981) 'In Search of System', *University of Toronto Quarterly* 51 (1): 93–102.

—— (1992) 'En-Gendering the System: The Book of Thel and Visions of the Daughters of Albion', in J. Douglas Kneale (ed.), *The Mind in Creation: Essays on English Romantic Literature in Honour of Ross G. Woodman*, Montreal: McGill Queen's University Press, 74–90.

—— (1996) 'Dis(Figuring) the System: Vision, History, and Trauma in Blake's Lambeth Books', *Huntington Library Quarterly* 58 (3–4). 383–411.

Rosen, F. (2000) 'The Idea of Utility in Adam Smith's *The Theory of Moral Sentiments*', *History of European Ideas* 26: 79–103.

Rothschild, Emma (2001) *Adam Smith, Condorcet, and the Enlightenment*, Cambridge, MA: Harvard University Press.

Rothstein, Eric (1975) *Systems of Order and Inquiry in Later Eighteenth-Century Fiction*, Berkeley, CA: University of California Press.

Rutherford, Thomas (1748) *A System of Natural Philosophy, being a course of lectures in mechanics, optics, hydrostatics, and astronomy*, London, n.p.

Schliesser, Eric (2005). 'Some Principles of Adam Smith's Newtonian Methods in *The Wealth of Nations*', *History of Economic Thought and Methodology* 23A: 35–77.

Simpson, David (1993) *Romanticism, Nationalism, and the Revolt against Theory*, Chicago: University of Chicago Press.

Siskin, Clifford (1998) '1798: The Year of the System', in *1798: The Year of the Lyrical Ballads*, ed. Richard Cronin, New York: St Martin's Press, 9–31.

—— (2001) 'Novels and Systems', *Novel: A Forum on Fiction* 34 (2): 202–15.

Stirling, John (1733) *A System of Rhetoric, in a method entirely new: containing all the tropes and figures*, London: Thomas Astley.

Wilkinson, William (1690) *Systema Africanum, or, A treastise, discovering the intrigues and arbitrary preceedings of the Guiney Company and also how prejudicial they are to the*

American planters, the woollen, and other English manufactures, to the visible decay of trade, and consequently greatly impairing the royal revenue, which would be infinitely encreased, provided merchants and mariners were encouraged, who can discover several places not yet known, or traded accound of their fortifications, humbly submitted to Their Majesties, and to the consideration of both houses of Parliament, London, n.p.

Winch, Donald (1985) 'The Burke–Smith Problem and Late Eighteenth-Century Political and Economic Thought', *Historical Journal* 28 (1): 231–47.

Wooler, T. J. (1817) *The Black Dwarf*, London: T. J. Wooler.

Yearsley, Ann (1788) *A Poem on the Inhumanity of the Slave-trade*, London: G. G. J. and J. Robinson.

Part II

Adam Smith and moral theory

5 Smith on 'connexion', culture and judgment

Fonna Forman-Barzilai

Adam Smith was especially sensitive to the ways that our affective 'connexions' to particular people and groups tend to color our sentiments and undermine the objectivity and impartiality of our moral judgments. He granted that it is natural and good for us to care more for ourselves and our beloved – indeed, that through a sort of divine œconomy humanity thrives as each takes care of his own. But he was concerned that these passive affections sometimes inspire judgments and actions that neglect or actively violate the well-being of those 'not particularly connected' to us. It was therefore one of Smith's central objectives in the *Theory of Moral Sentiments* to *enlarge* the perspective of ordinary spectators whose judgments were easily led astray and often blinded by affective entanglements.

On balance, I think Smith's descriptions of sympathy and the impartial spectator are together a plausible account of how people learn to surmount affective bias. We might say that Smith succeeds in his project of affective enlargement. But surely there are other sorts of bias than affective bias that a successful moral theory must address. I am thinking specifically of *cultural* bias, a subject of considerable importance in the twenty-first century. In this chapter, I argue that Smith's accounts of sympathy and the impartial spectator, on their own, do not explain sufficiently how people might surmount cultural bias. My argument rests on an assertion, which I shall explore here at length, that Smith's account of the moral life should be read as a highly original anthropology of culture formation – thicker, more textured and complex than perhaps any other in the eighteenth century.[1] In the TMS Smith described in rich detail how moral culture is shaped, sustained and perpetuated by its own participants, without a value-giver, without traditional forms of authority. Smith's description of the moral life, understood anthropologically, confirms that the standards people use when they judge themselves and others derive from their own social experiences and are thus particular to those experiences. I am not arguing here that moral cultures cannot overlap and coincide with one another and therefore become in varying degrees intelligible to one another on Smith's model, but there is nothing in his anthropology to suggest that they must or will. Coincidence is left to chance. For this reason I argue that while Smith's theory does generate a transitory, affective sort of coolness, moderating our selfishness and enlarging us by reminding us that 'we are but one of the multitude, in no respect better than any other in it' (TMS III.3.4, 137), it is ultimately incapable of generating the sort of impartiality necessary for calling our own cultural experiences into question, a critical space in which we might come to know ourselves better and to evaluate those who are culturally remote without assimilating them to ourselves. In other words, different sorts of judgment require different sorts of impartiality. I argue here that Smith's theory succeeds in demonstrating affective impartiality but not cultural impartiality.

The 'point of propriety' that Smith so often spoke of, which served to orient and constrain sentiment and action, is not a universally normative measure that can be grafted on to any moral context. What is proper in one moral culture might be rude and insensitive in another. You belch at my table and I am put off; I wear shoes at yours and you are. Smith's anthropology reveals that the *content* of propriety – that which designates a given sentiment or action as 'praise-worthy' and 'proper' – is particular to those who articulate it, part of a moral culture and as such deeply consensual. We might say that the formal category of propriety is universal for Smith (all moral cultures have some understanding of it), but that the content is necessarily plural. It must not be confused with what some might wish to characterize as universally normative or transcultural. In due course we will encounter thinkers who have attempted to draw cosmopolitan and universalist conclusions from Smith's account of the moral life – but we will discover, with Knud Haakonssen (2003: xi), that Smith 'does not have access to a universal morality nor is an underlying logos any part of his system'.

Of course, Smith might not have been troubled by late modern questions driven by concerns about universal normativity and cross-cultural intelligibility – especially if he was concerned chiefly with social coordination, as I shall argue he was. But anyone interested in Smith's salience in an age of global interconnectedness must wonder whether his anthropological account of the moral life exposes him to charges of moral insularity and relativity. In the second part of this chapter, I will speculate how Smith might have responded to the specter of moral relativity. I suspect that he might have pointed us to another dimension of his thought, an alternative resource for cross-cultural understanding and judgment which he himself had described as 'universal' and independent of positive institution. I am referring to Smith's theory of justice, notably his assertion that justice is a 'negative virtue' grounded not in sympathetic concord which was inherently unstable and its product subject to great cultural variation, but in what he described as a *human aversion to cruelty*, which struck him as universal among people.

This chapter proceeds in two parts. In the first part, I explore Smith's concerns about affective bias and the process by which he believed we are capable of enlarging our moral judgments. I argue, however, that the activity of enlarging our judgments in the case of *cultural* bias is a very different matter, and that Smith's description of sympathetic exchange fails to provide the resources necessary for doing so. Nevertheless, in the second part, I demonstrate that Smith might have responded to the relativity that emerges from his anthropological description of moral judgment by offering his theory of negative justice as a candidate for universal normativity – that our negative affective reaction to pain and cruelty has the positive effect of opening a critical space for reflection about ourselves and others. Surely, one must pass Smith's universal gesture through a critical sift, but we must first establish evidence that such a gesture lies awaiting critique in the pages of Smith's TMS. This is not an obvious thing. My goal in the second half of the chapter is to establish that Smith's theory of justice is situated within the larger context of his concerns about impartial judgment, to merge Smith's negative justice with his preoccupation with bias and stabilizing the standards by which we judge. Once this connection is established – whether or not we ultimately agree that negative justice does the universalizing work that Smith apparently believed it can – we shall see that Smith becomes relevant to twenty-first century moral and political theory in very new ways.

Affective concentricity and moral judgment

We begin by exploring Smith's thoughts on the effects of affective 'connexion' on moral judgment, and his description of how we learn to surmount bias and enlarge our judgments through the mechanisms of sympathy and the impartial spectator. What exactly was affection for Smith, and why was it morally problematic? He argued that affection was the emotional product of 'association' and 'connexion' among people who share physical space over time.[2] This orientation to human affection reflects Smith's deep appreciation of Stoic moral psychology. Adam Smith's interest in the Stoics is generally well acknowledged, thanks to substantial contributions in recent years (see notably TMS Editors' Introduction, 5–10; Waszek 1984; Brown 1994; Griswold 1999; Vivenza, 2002: ch. 2; 191–212; Montes 2004). Here I am most interested in Smith's appropriation of the Stoic idea of *oikeoisis*, initiated by Hierocles and developed by Cicero.[3] The word *oikeoisis* derives from the Greek root *oikos*, which referred in ancient democratic life to the private realm of the household as opposed to the public realm of the *polis*. *Oikeoisis* was a Stoic extrapolation from the familiarity one develops over time with those who inhabit the *oikos*, with those who share one's physical space. When offered as a more general account of the nature of human affection, *oikeoisis* described a phenomenon of fading or weakening sentiment that corresponds to an increase in physical distance and a corresponding lack of familiarity. Thus, the Stoics mapped our affections concentrically, claiming that the circles of affection weaken as the object radiates further from the self.

Smith embraced Stoic *oikeoisis* as an empirical fact about human 'affection'. He agreed that we tend to feel affection for those with whom we share physical space and are most familiar, and likewise, as Jacob Viner (1972: 80–1) put it, that 'spatial distance operates to intensify psychological distance'. This Stoic way of understanding human connectedness is captured in Smith's observation that 'affection, is in reality nothing but habitual sympathy':

> Our concern in the happiness or misery of those who are the objects of what we call our affections; our desire to promote the one, and to prevent the other; are either the actual feeling of that habitual sympathy, or the necessary consequences of that feeling. Relations being usually placed in situations which naturally create this habitual sympathy, it is expected that a suitable degree of affection should take place among them. We generally find that it actually does take place; we therefore naturally expect that it should. . . .
>
> (TMS I.ii.1.7, 220)[4]

For Smith, affection evolves through our experiences living in close proximity with others over time. It does not originate in blood, a fallacy which holds force for him 'no-where but in tragedies and romances' (TMS VI.ii.1.11, 222). Nor is it an abstract entity like benevolence or compassion, which moralists traditionally attempted to teach and to shift about from object to object. For Smith, the Stoic circles were firmly grounded in human experience and were therefore resistant to philosophical or religious manipulation. As such, while he was greatly impressed with and indebted to Stoic moral psychology, Smith rejected the Stoic's 'absurd and unreasonable' cosmopolitan assertion that we should aspire to collapse the concentric, affective structure of human relationships through the proper use of reason (TMS III.3.9, 140). He simply could not accept that our highest human aspiration is to nourish apathy toward the near and to become 'citizens of the world' (TMS III.3.11,140).[5]

The concentric structure of familiarity and affection therefore explains why we tend to sympathize more vibrantly with some people than others – why, as Viner described it:

> the sentiments weaken progressively as one moves from one's immediate family to one's intimate friends, to one's neighbors in a small community, to fellow-citizens in a great city, to members in general of one's own country, to foreigners, to mankind taken in the large, to the inhabitants, if any, of distant planets.
>
> (Viner 1972: 80–1)

Of course, Smith believed that affective concentricity was natural and good – indeed, that 'the great society of mankind would be best promoted by directing the principal attention of each individual to that particular portion of it, which was most within the sphere both of his abilities and of his understanding' (TMS VI.ii.2.4, 229). But he also recognized that this natural structure threatened to bias the sympathy process, to distort our perceptions and judgments, ultimately to divide and factionalize humankind. As Smith put it, 'feeling too strongly' tends to delude us into fantastic over-evaluations of ourselves and our loved ones, of our own pains and joys, the importance of our place in the world relative to others (TMS III.3.38, 153–4). In a well known passage, he speculated that most of us would be considerably more distressed by the loss of our pinky finger than by the sudden death of millions of distant strangers swallowed up in a massive earthquake (TMS III.3.4, 136–7).

In the next breath, however, Smith introduced his reader to the 'impartial spectator', a conscience-like faculty inside each of us that ensures that our passive sentiments will not give way to radically partial judgments and actions. (The best account of reflective judgment in Smith is Fleischacker 1999.) This 'inhabitant of the breast, the man within, the great judge and arbiter of our conduct' succeeds in cooling us off, 'astonishing the most presumptuous of our passions' (TMS III.3.4, 137), protecting the weak and innocent, Smith maintained, because it forces us to imagine how we would appear to a 'third person who has no particular connexion' with us – an impartial person – if we were to lose control and surrender to our passive sentiments (TMS III.3.3, 135). We might say that the impartial spectator imposes a sort of affective distance on us and prompts us to reflect, to be less partial, more objective, judges:

> Should those passions be, what they are very apt to be, too vehement, Nature has provided a proper remedy and correction. The real or even the imaginary presence of the impartial spectator, the authority of the man within the breast, is always at hand to overawe them into the proper tone and temper of moderation.
>
> (TMS VII.ii.1.44, 292)

Since Smith employed his spectator model to bridge the distance between spectators and those they would potentially harm through their self-preference, some interpreters have claimed that his theory has cosmopolitan significance – that it can help spectators transcend cultural bias and understand and generate fellow feeling for those who are physically, affectively and *culturally* remote. In what follows I argue that this kind of appropriation forces an alien agenda on Smith – and more important, that it neglects one of his most original insights: that sympathy is a social practice oriented around criteria that vary from one forum of ordinary experience to another. I am referring to the constructed, historical nature of the criteria spectators deploy when they judge – or, to use Smith's language, the 'standards and measures' against which they discern 'propriety' in other people (TMS I.i.3, 16–19). We saw above that Smith's spectator was able, with varying degrees of success, to transcend affective bias and to enlarge her moral judgments. I argue next that because Smith's theory of moral sentiment was ultimately a description of how moral culture develops and sustains itself, and not a theory of how we become conscious about that process or how we might transcend it when necessary, this enlargement is substantially more complex and difficult to realize in the case of cultural bias.

Cultural plurality and moral judgment

On Smith's account, our moral criteria are disciplined over time through our experiences participating in sympathetic exchange, primarily with those around us. He described our moral criteria in the following way:

> I judge of your sight by my sight, of your ear by my ear, of your reason by my reason, of your resentment by my resentment, of your love by my love. I neither have, *nor can have*, any other way of judging about them.
>
> (TMS I.i.3.10, 19, emphasis mine)

And again:

> when we judge . . . of any affection . . . it is scarce possible that we should make use of any other rule or cannon but the correspondent affection in ourselves.
>
> (TMS I.i.3.9, 18)

On Smith's description, spectators do not judge others with an abstract criterion, a 'view from nowhere' (Nagel 1986). Spectators employ what we might call a *self-referential* standpoint, which means that we judge the actions and opinions of others 'as right, as accurate, as agreeable to truth and reality . . . *for no other reason* but because we find that it agrees with our own' (TMS I.i.4.4, 20, emphasis mine). But, where does *our own* perspective come from? How do we know what we know? For Smith, a spectator comes to know who she is, what she believes, and the standards by which she will judge others, through a lifetime of gazing into the 'mirror of society', of participating in sympathetic exchange with those around her. In a well known passage Smith speculated that a person who grew up in solitude 'could no more think of his own character, of the propriety or demerit of his own sentiments and conduct, of the beauty or deformity of his own mind than of the beauty or deformity of his own face' (TMS III.1.3, 110). Society provides the mirror of self-knowledge, and engenders

– indeed, disciplines – the criteria by which the self will come to mirror and judge others.

A central theme in this chapter is that Smith's account of the origins of our moral criteria culminates in a culturally insular portrait of the moral life.[6] Our desire for love and approval motivates us to accommodate ourselves to what we believe spectators can indulge, to what Smith called a 'point of propriety'. We come to know what this point is, what our world generally approves and disapproves of, through our experiences moving through it. Compounded over time, these experiences progressively constrain my understanding of myself and others, and serve to condition the moral criteria ('my ear', 'my reason', 'my resentment', and so on) that I will deploy when I inevitably find myself in the position of spectator. This is what I mean when I say that Smith provided a rich account of culture formation. He described how what 'we' know is engendered and transmitted through the process of sympathetic exchange: I absorb moral culture as I gaze into the mirror of society, draw judgment upon myself, and adjust to what my society expects of me as a member of it; in turn, I generate culture as I become a mirror for others who gaze at me and are judged and disciplined by me. What emerges is a moral culture that is particular to those of us who participate in it. We share a language, shared understandings and expectations. And because this process is a universal one for Smith, a description of how all moral cultures unfold, we are left with a picture of deep moral diversity – moral cultures particular to their participants, overlapping and communicable in some ways *perhaps*, but profoundly and deeply pluralistic.[7]

The consequence of cultural plurality for moral judgment, of course, is that the criteria we deploy will be more appropriate when we judge those who share our cultural experiences, and less appropriate with those who don't – indeed, that we may be woefully imprecise when judging a person just before our eyes, or on our television screens, clearly as our eyes may receive the 'facts'.[8] In the case of affective bias, we recall, Smith had invoked the impartial spectator to help enlarge our perspective and refine our judgments; but I will argue here that the transitory sort of enlargement that Smith achieved with his spectator model is not the sort of enlargement that is required to facilitate cross-cultural intelligibility and judgment.

Smith seems to have acknowledged this when he observed that a spectator will always sympathize more 'precisely' with members of his family than with his neighbors, and with his neighbors than with his fellow citizens:

> He is more *habituated* to sympathize with them. He *knows better how everything is likely to affect them*, and his sympathy with them is more *precise and determinate*, than it can be with the greater part of other people. It approaches nearer, in short, to what he feels for himself.
>
> (TMS VI.ii.1.2, 219, emphasis mine)

Because we share a history I am likelier than a stranger is to make 'precise and determinate' judgments about my family, friends, co-workers and fellow citizens (in this concentric order). I already understand their worlds of meaning and 'how everything is likely to affect' them. This would seem to entail that when the moral imagination is thrust beyond the sphere of the spectator's experience and understanding, it can misfire and yield judgments that are at best '*im*precise' and '*in*determinate' and at worst based on narrow criteria foisted on to a reified other.

Still, some have suggested that Smith's spectator model enables impartial judgment of others culturally recognizable or not. Martha Nussbaum (1995: 134 n. 23) for instance drew parallels between Smith's spectator model and John Rawls's device of the original position.[9] Charles Griswold (1999: 92, 96–9) argued that Smith's theory gets us beyond the trap of cultural perspectivism because sympathy is 'spectator-centered' rather than 'agent-centered' and because this 'asymmetrical relation of actor and spectator becomes lexical insofar as judgments of value and truth are concerned'. Luc Boltanski (1993) agrees when he claims that Smith's spectator model can sustain a 'politics of pity' with regard to distant suffering. (For further discussion, see my review of Griswold 1999 in Forman-Barzilai 2000.) But we need to ask Smith and those persuaded of the transcultural significance of his theory: how do spectators overcome cultural bias, detach themselves from their own experiences as agents disciplined in a world of values? How does sympathy avoid speculation and assumption, avoid becoming an arrogant, smothering intrusion? How, within the terms of Smith's thick description of the disciplinary process through which spectators come to be proper members and gatekeepers of social morality, do they now become critical of and transcend these experiences when they imaginatively enter into the conditions of others with potentially very different histories?

This brings us again to Smith's idea of the 'impartial spectator', a conscience-like faculty he invoked at various points throughout the TMS to overcome the nearsightedness of our passive sentiments. Most claims about Smith's transcultural significance hang on the impartial spectator, for obvious reasons. Smith maintained that this ideal 'third person' (whom he sometimes called 'reason', 'principle', 'conscience', 'the man within') helps us to become impartial judges, to rise above the natural consequences of having private interests, of living in families and communities and thus feeling affection and concern for some people more than others. As such, the impartial spectator would seem to be the perfect cosmopolitan device for getting us beyond ourselves.

But I argue that different sorts of impartiality are required for different sorts of judgment, and that the sort of impartiality achieved by Smith's impartial spectator might be effective for adjusting affective shortsightedness, but is *not* the sort required to render unbiased cross-cultural judgments. On its own terms, Smith's spectator model succeeds in producing a transitory sort of coolness, mediating our self-regarding and other-regarding tendencies, disciplining propriety, and ensuring relatively stable and sociable communities. But rendering cross-cultural judgments that don't simply reduce the other to oneself requires something much different: that a spectator be able to transcend not merely his *affective* 'connexions' to self and specific others, but more fundamentally, to question and sometimes to subvert the *very measure* by which he has become accustomed to judging himself and the world. In other words, while Smith is primarily concerned with social coordination, the problem of historical consciousness and critique is an epistemic one and in many respects beyond the scope of his theory.[10]

Therefore, to say that sympathetic judgment is 'an ongoing process of adjustment, a continual search for equilibrium', as Griswold (1999: 102), Haakonssen (1981: 58–9), and Hope (1989: 87) have, does not get us closer to an explanation of how Smithian spectators might transcend cultural bias. On Smith's account it seems that making better judgments involves becoming better and better interpreters of our own cultural signals, becoming more disciplined, in 'command' of ourselves, proper, sociable, polite – whatever these things might mean in our particular social world. Haakonssen (1981: 58) is helpful when he observed that the 'process' of refining our judgments 'is a continual weeding out of behaviour which is incompatible with social life'. Again, the emphasis here is on social coordination. But how does this process of becoming a more mature, proper and congenial member of my society better help me understand someone who has learned (through the same process as I have, for sympathy is a universal process) what it means *in her world* to be 'in command' of herself, proper, sociable, polite, etc.? In fact, it seems that as my capacity for sympathetic judgment 'progresses' and 'matures' in Smith's theory, I become more deeply entrenched culturally, more tractable and docile, less critical, less inclined to understand myself and others. Smith's theory of moral maturity seems to deny the reflective space that is necessary for critical self-awareness and cross-cultural judgment.

At various points, no doubt, Smith argued that a mature spectator will have learned to distinguish what is inherently praiseworthy from that which is conventional, merely praised, and therefore less worthy (TMS III.2.7, 117; 2.32, 130–1). This would seem to provide the spectator with some measure of critical distance from her own history, and a capacity for cultivating a more impartial, less insular view of the world. Indeed, Smith believed he was advancing on Humean conventionalism when he proposed his idea of the impartial spectator. It will be useful at this point to pause and consider relevant differences between Hume and Smith. In his general concerns about affective bias, Smith agreed with Hume in the *Enquiry Concerning the Principle of Morals* that 'sympathy . . . is much fainter than our concern for ourselves, and sympathy with persons remote from us, much fainter than that with persons near and contiguous' (EPM

5.2.42). Hume observed that this sentimental bias, while natural and appropriate, often wreaks havoc on our morals, leading us to exaggerate the importance of that which affects us and to underestimate that which does not. Accordingly, he argued that moral judgment demands a firmer, more impartial foundation than our sentiments can provide. Hume believed this foundation could be derived from the 'general unalterable' standards that emerge through social intercourse:

> it is necessary for us, in our calm judgments and discourse concerning the characters of men, to neglect all these differences, and render our sentiments more public and social. . . . The intercourse of sentiments, therefore, in society and conversation, makes us form some general unalterable standard, by which we may approve or disapprove of characters and manners.
>
> (EPM, 5.2.42)

Although Smith drew substantially upon the Stoic concept of *oikeoisis* to establish the relation between affection and sympathy, as we saw, he aligned with Hume's basic insight that our sympathy tends to fade as the object becomes further removed affectively. And, like Hume, Smith sought to divert us from ourselves and our beloved by *enlarging* the natural bias of our passive feelings. But one of the most interesting differences between them, I believe, is that Smith was less confident than Hume that common sense was the surest way of accomplishing this. In fact, we can say that convention troubled Smith. (I discuss this at greater length in Forman-Barzilai 2002.) He agreed with Hume that convention was often efficient in diverting us from ourselves and enlarging the natural bias of our passive feelings. Indeed, his own account of sympathetic exchange greatly resembled Hume's 'intercourse of sentiments'. But for Smith efficiency was not reason enough to surrender our moral judgments to convention, to what is merely praised. What if convention happened to be corrupt, profane, bellicose – or, we might say, racist, sexist, homophobic? Corrupt societies might be successful in socializing selfish souls, but they would nevertheless, inevitably, breed deeply disturbing judgments – for example, when a slaveholder feels affirmed by the values of his slaveholding society, or when a Hitler youth is exalted as a brave young patriot. As Smith described the problem in his underappreciated discussion of 'custom', people 'brought up amidst violence, licentiousness, falsehood, and injustice ... have been familiarized with it from their infancy, custom has rendered it habitual to them, and they are very apt to regard it as, what is called, the way of the world. . . .' (TMS V.2, 201). In this sense, convention tends to deny us a critical space for analyzing deeply held beliefs and the practices they sustain – particularly when convention is sanctioned and fortified by power.

Concerns about moral relativity have a distinctly contemporary ring to them. I am perfectly aware that my reading of Smith is driven by my twenty-first century discomfort with culturally sanctioned violations of human liberty and dignity – and that, to the extent that Smith was troubled by moral relativity, he was motivated less by humanitarian or cosmopolitan concerns and more by the corruption of European social morals. Corrupt people (Smith singled out profligates and politicians) too often paraded themselves as 'virtuous' in eighteenth century European life, and succeeded in deluding a pliable and envious public into honoring and emulating them (TMS I.iii.2–3, 50–66). The corrupt few, in other words, tended to set the standards of taste and value for the many. This is one way that common sense – 'the way of the world' – was very easily perverted. Now, understanding *when* common sense is perverted – understanding the difference between what is praiseworthy and what is merely praised – requires a critical distance that convention, by its very nature, fails to supply. That Smith was troubled by the relativity of Hume's commonsense approach to coordinating our sentiments seems to be one key reason he attempted to locate a more stable foundation for moral judgment in the 'impartial spectator'.

The problem is that Smith's foray into 'is' and 'ought', his distinction between that which is praiseworthy and that which is conventionally praised, never explains *how* spectators come to know the difference, *where* this new knowledge about the world comes from. How does a spectator carve out a space for critical reflection in Smith's description of moral life? How does the impartial spectator inside of me know more than the less mature me that is attuned to the clamor of the world? Has Smith really progressed on Hume here? His opacity has led some observers to conclude that the impartial spectator is just another a cultural artifact, subject to the ebb and flow of human experience, ultimately little more than the voice of conventional morality speaking though us. While Smith wanted his impartial spectator to enlarge us, to attune our judgments to something stable and universal, he simultaneously gave us good reason to believe that it is little more than an internalization of social norms, what Sam Fleischacker (forthcoming: 8) has called a 'an idealized version of our friends and neighbors … built *out* of actual spectators', or what Sheldon Wolin (1960: 343–51) might have called a 'socialized conscience', a social censor constructed in the mind over time that has strong affinities with the Freudian super-ego. (See Campbell 1971: 149, 165; Raphael 1975: 97–8, 1985: 41–4; Fleischacker 1991: 259.) An agent internalizes her experiences with actual spectators, so that at a certain point of moral maturity she can avert her eyes from the world and turn instead to the representative of society within her.

Given the likely complicity of Smith's impartial spectator in reinforcing 'the way of the world', how do we 'enter into' contexts and worlds of meaning that are unfamiliar to us without speculating about the other, and forcing their practices into our own frames of reference, demanding that they conform to 'my sight', 'my ear', 'my reason', and so on?[11] I submit that Smith's sympathy model fails to enlarge the perspective of spectators entangled within cultural space. Rather, it thickly describes how deeply entrenched our perspectives really are, how difficult it is to cultivate a critical distance from ourselves. It is for this reason, I submit, and not for his alleged cosmopolitanism, that Smith speaks most insightfully to moral and political theory today.

Animating critique: Smith's negative justice

How might Smith have responded to the charge that his impartial spectator was merely a psychic internalization of common sense? How might he have sought to generate universality without abstracting morals from their empirical roots?

In what follows I shall pursue Smith's idea of 'justice', what he sometimes referred to, following Hugo Grotius, as 'natural jurisprudence'. Overall, Smith had relatively little to say about justice in the TMS, and what he did say was sporadic and unsystematic. (For discussion see Fleischacker 2004: 146–73.) He made frequent references to the 'plainest and most obvious rules of justice', to the 'most sacred laws of justice', to 'what justice demands', to the attempt of 'all well-governed states' to prescribe positive laws that 'coincide with those of natural justice', to 'the natural rules of justice independent of all positive institution', to 'the general principles which ought to run through and be the foundation of the laws of all nations ... without regard to the particular institutions of any one nation', and so on (for example, TMS VI.ii.intro.2, 218; II.ii.2.2, 84; III.3.41, 155; VII.iv.7–114, 329–33; VII.iv.37, 341–2). In other words, he often gestured toward the universality of justice – but about content he said very little. He acknowledged that 'natural jurisprudence' is 'of all the sciences by far the most important, but hitherto, perhaps the least cultivated', but that 'it belongs not to our present subject to enter into any detail' (TMS VI.ii.intro.2, 218). In the closing paragraph of the TMS he promised his readers a more 'complete' account in 'another treatise' (TMS VII.iv.37, 341–2),[12] but his promise stood unfulfilled for thirty years and his notes on the subject were consigned to the flames upon his death. Fortunately Smith's ethics students at the University of Glasgow heard his lectures on jurisprudence, and their notes are now available to us in *Lectures on Jurisprudence.*[13]

In an early unpublished manuscript written before the TMS appeared in 1759, Smith claimed that 'natural jurisprudence, or the Theory of the general principles of Law ... *make a very important part of the Theory of moral Sentiments*' (TMS, Appx. II, 389, emphasis mine).[14] Although he never pursued the linkages between jurisprudence and moral sentiment in future work, offering surprisingly few words on the subject in the TMS itself, he did declare there quite explicitly that 'no social intercourse can take place among men who do not generally abstain from injuring one another' (TMS II.ii.3.6, 87). And even more boldly:

> Justice ... is the main pillar that upholds the whole edifice. If it is removed, the great, immense fabric of human society ... must in a moment crumble into atoms.
>
> (TMS II.ii.3.4, 86)

Let's unpack what Smith did say about justice in the TMS (drawing occasionally on the *Wealth of Nations* and *Lectures on Jurisprudence*) with an eye to understanding (1) why justice was 'a very important part of the Theory of moral Sentiments'; (2) why he believed that the demands of justice transcended variations of culture and nation, practice and institution; and (3) why therefore we might accurately characterize Smith's theory of justice as a response to the relativity of moral standards that emerges from his description of the moral life in Parts I–III of the TMS.

Nowhere do we learn more about Smith's idea of justice than in a modest section of the TMS which he devoted to a distinction between 'justice' and 'beneficence' (TMS II.ii, 78–91). In the course of his comparative account, we learn several important things about justice: that it is what Smith calls the 'foundation' of social life and is therefore unique among the virtues; that nature has assured its observance by planting in human nature an instinctive and immediate 'appetite' for it and for the means necessary to obtain it; that justice is a 'negative virtue', which means that it consists in refraining from doing things that are unjust, rather than in doing 'good' things; that it is therefore precise and easily codified, what we might call today 'minimal' but also absolutely imperative; and that it doesn't merit praise yet can be extorted legitimately by force.

How do all of these characteristics hang together for Smith? To begin, he maintained that 'society flourishes and is happy' when people are 'bound together by the agreeable bands of love and affection, and are, as it were, drawn to one common centre of mutual good offices' (TMS II.ii.3.1, 85). He observed that beneficent action always pleases the spectator and merits praise and gratitude; and inversely, that callous disregard to the needs of others – 'a want of beneficence' – always jars the spectator and merits condemnation.[15] Yet we may never legitimately 'extort' kindness from a 'brute' or 'punish' someone who has committed no willful, affirmative act of harm, or 'injustice' (TMS II.ii.1.3–10, 78–82).[16] Beneficence is 'free' and a 'matter of choice'. But because it merits approbation and gratitude when offered and social condemnation when withheld (TMS II.ii.1–5, 78–80), Smith believed, beneficence is sufficiently regulated by the sympathy process and needs no additional support. Moreover, beneficence can be effectively *substituted* by considerations of utility:

> But though the necessary assistance should not be afforded from such generous and disinterested motives, though among the different members of the society there should be no mutual love and affection, the society, though less happy and agreeable, will not necessarily be dissolved. Society may subsist among different men, as among different merchants, *from a sense of its utility*, without any mutual love or affection; and though no man in it should owe any obligation, or be bound in gratitude to any other, it may still be upheld by a mercenary exchange of good offices according to an agreed valuation.
>
> (TMS II.ii.3.2, 85–6, emphasis mine)

When pressed on the lack of good will among men, Smith frequently turned to the invisible hand of utilitarian rationality. But we mustn't inflate the utilitarian dimension of Smith's thought beyond proper bounds. In the TMS utility seems to be little more than a supplement to moral sentiment when self-love spoke too loudly, an insurance policy implanted in the world by Nature through what Smith often referred to as her benevolent 'œconomy'.

But he was less cavalier with justice. Society may 'subsist, though not in the most comfortable state' without 'beneficence', Smith speculated, but 'the prevalence of injustice must utterly destroy it' (TMS II.ii.3.3, 86). While beneficence is an 'ornament which embellishes' social life, making it lovelier and easier to bear, justice is the 'main pillar that upholds the whole edifice'. Like the 'foundation of a building', if justice is 'removed', the 'immense fabric of human society must in a moment crumble into atoms'. This is why Smith maintained that injustice is punishable, but a want of beneficence is not (TMS II.ii.1.2–8, 79–81). The 'observance' of justice may be 'extorted by force', and its 'violation . . . exposed to punishment' (TMS II.ii.1.5, 79). And yet justice merits 'very little gratitude' (TMS II.ii.1.9, 81–2). I feel no gratitude to someone who allows me to pass on the street unharmed or who refrains from taking my child's lunch money. 'The man who barely abstains from violating either the person, or the estate, or the reputation of his neighbours, has surely very little positive merit' (TMS II.ii.1.9, 81–2). Indeed, justice most often requires very little of us. In a passage that has become red meat for libertarians, Smith asserted that 'we may often fulfil all the rules of justice by sitting still and doing nothing':

> Mere justice is, upon most occasions, but a *negative virtue*, and only hinders us from hurting our neighbour.
>
> (TMS II.ii.1.9, 82, emphasis mine)

And again:

> A sacred and religious regard *not to hurt or disturb* in any respect the happiness of our neighbour, even in those cases where no law can

> properly protect him, constitutes the character of the perfectly innocent and just man.
>
> (TMS VI.ii.intro.2, 218, emphasis mine)

In his description of justice as a 'negative virtue', Smith was resuscitating an ancient legal distinction between what Aristotle called 'commutative justice' and 'distributive justice' and what Hugo Grotius later called 'the *justicia expletrix*' and 'the *justicia attributrix*'. Smith described these two senses of law both in his *Lectures on Jurisprudence* and in Section VII of the TMS, distinguishing 'perfect' from 'imperfect rights', aligning the former with commutative justice, and the latter with distributive justice. He claimed that he would confine his reflections to the elaboration of perfect rights, since 'the latter do not belong properly to jurisprudence, but rather to a system of moralls as they do not fall under the jurisdiction of the laws' (LJ(A) i.14–15, 9). In a theory of distributive justice or 'the *justicia attributrix*':

> we are said not to do justice to our neighbour unless we conceive for him all that love, respect, and esteem, which his character, his situation, and his connexion with ourselves, render suitable and proper for us to feel, and unless we act accordingly. . . . [it] consists in proper beneficence, in the becoming use of what is our own, and in the applying it to those purposes either of charity or generosity, to which it is most suitable, in our situation, that it should be applied. In this sense justice comprehends all the social virtues.
>
> (TMS VII.ii.1.10, 269–70)

This active and affirmative orientation to justice is espoused today by those who would argue that sitting idle in the midst of suffering when one has resources and capacity to intervene can be as hurtful, *as unjust*, as a willful, affirmative act of harm. One thinks of the myriad arguments for social welfare, for Good Samaritan laws, for humanitarian intervention, the Kitty Genovese case, German citizens who rescued Jews during the Holocaust, and so on. But because Smith believed that withholding benevolence does 'no positive hurt' (TMS II.ii.1.3, 79), that the 'social fabric' could 'subsist' without such assistance, he left the imperative of 'charity and generosity' to the ordinary governance of moral approbation and utilitarian substitution (TMS II.ii.3.4, 86). Smith regularly condemned ancient and modern 'casuists' (among whom he included Cicero, Augustine, Pufendorf, Barbeyrac and Hutcheson) for attempting to 'lay down exact and precise rules for the direction of every circumstance of our behaviour' – for attempting to '*prescribe* rules for the conduct of a good man' (TMS VI.iv.7–8, 329–30, emphasis mine). Smith's orientation to justice as commutative was inspired by a belief that human ends are plural and contentious. A modern polity that permitted individuals to pursue their own ends, and tolerated the result, was prohibited from codifying the 'exact and precise' demands of justice. Law must be minimal, consensual, codifying only what we can know for sure. And for Smith, the only thing we can know for sure is that 'injury' is bad – that 'it does real and positive hurt' (TMS II.ii.1.5, 79) – and that we must therefore 'abstain from doing [our neighbor] any positive harm, and do not directly hurt him either in his person, or in his estate, or in his reputation' (TMS VI.ii.1.10, 269). Minimal though it was, however, commutative justice was not 'free' or a matter of 'choice'. It was perfect, strict, an imperative in the Kantian sense: we are 'tied, bound, and obliged' to it (TMS II.ii.1.5, 80).

But, how did Smith believe justice recommends itself to us? How do we agree to its terms? How does it 'tie, bound and oblige' us? For one thing, Smith took issue with Hume's well known claim in the *Enquiry* that 'public utility is the *sole origin* of justice' (EPM 3.1.1; emphasis added) – that 'this virtue derives its existence entirely from its necessary *use* to the intercourse and social state of mankind' (EPM 3.1.7). Smith insisted that justice was *not simply* a function of its utility, and that in saying it was, Hume had mistaken an efficient for a final cause.[17] Smith agreed that justice was useful for the maintenance of society; but efficiency alone did not explain *why* we are drawn to justice and away from injustice:

> As society cannot subsist unless the laws of justice are tolerably observed, as no social intercourse can take place among men who do not generally abstain from injuring one another; the consideration of this necessity, it has been thought, was the ground upon which we approved of them and enforcement of the laws of justice by the punishment of those who violated them.... But though it commonly requires no great discernment to see the destructive tendency of all licentious practices to the welfare of society, it is seldom this consideration which first *animates* us against them. *All men, even the most stupid and unthinking, abhor fraud, perfidy, and injustice, and delight to see them punished. But few men have reflected upon the necessity of justice to the existence of society, how obvious soever that necessity may appear to be.*
> (TMS II.ii.3.6, 87; II.3.9, 89, emphasis mine)

And yet, if not through a Humean sense of utility, or a Hutchesonian benevolence, or Lockean reason, or Rousseau's general will, or raw coercion, how did Smith believe justice recommended itself to us? In his own words, how did it 'animate' itself to us?

Smith believed that justice was unique among 'all the other social virtues' in the following way:

> we *feel ourselves* to be under a stricter obligation to act according to justice, than agreeably to friendship, charity, or generosity; that the practice of these last mentioned virtues seems to be left in some

> measure to our own choice, but that, *somehow or other*, we *feel ourselves* to be in a peculiar manner tied, bound, and obliged to the observation of justice.
>
> (TMS II.ii.1.5, 80, emphasis mine)

In this very important passage, Smith claimed that 'somehow or other' we '*feel* ourselves to be' under such an obligation, which makes the feeling seem somewhat mystical. But Smith the sober empiricist did not go in for such things. He established very clearly in the surrounding pages *just how* we come to *feel* this way. Since justice was essential to the 'fabric of human society' and since maintaining social order was the 'peculiar and darling care of Nature', nature had ways of assuring our feeling (TMS II.ii.3.4, 86). This, Smith argued, was the 'remarkable distinction between justice and all the other social virtues' (TMS II.ii.1.5, 80). The 'Author of Nature' did not 'entrust' justice to 'sympathy' nor to 'the slow and uncertain determinations' of man's 'reason' (as she had with benevolence) but instead had 'endowed' man with an 'appetite' – 'an *immediate and instinctive* approbation' of 'justice' and of everything that is 'most proper to attain it' (TMS II.i.5.10, 77; II.ii.3.4, 86, emphasis mine). And as further guarantee, as an extra 'precaution', nature gave us an instinctive sense that force is appropriate to constrain its observation (TMS II.ii.1.5, 80; II.ii.3.4, 86). In 'well-governed states', Smith observed, this charge is handed over to 'the public magistrate' who is 'under a necessity of employing the power of the commonwealth to enforce the practice of this virtue' (TMS VII.iv.36, 340; see also WN V.i.b, 708–23). No 'end' in the book *but justice* was endowed with these two unique qualities: first, of being untutored and 'immediate' – a 'natural sense', an 'appetite', an 'end' that nature has 'implanted in the human breast', 'stamped upon the human heart in the strongest and most indelible characters' – and second, that it was enforceable by the 'power of the commonwealth'. Indeed, as 'nature's favourite end', justice was unique among the virtues.

In his distinction between justice and beneficence, Smith acknowledged the work of 'an author of very great and original genius', referring possibly to David Hume, possibly to Henry Home who, in his *Essays on the Principles of Morality and Natural Religion*, noted that justice is 'less free' than generosity.[18] I have no quarrel with either hypothesis, but I submit that Smith's claim that *justice was unique among the virtues* may well have been influenced by Bishop Joseph Butler who, in his *Dissertation upon the Nature of Virtue* in 1726, argued in striking parallel that *injustice was unique among the vices.* Although Smith ranked virtues and Butler vices, the criteria they used to *order* their rankings were identical. Observe:

> nature has not given us so sensible a disapprobation of imprudence and folly, either in ourselves or others, as of falsehood, injustice and cruelty; I suppose, because that constant habitual sense of private

> interest and good, which we always carry about with us, renders such sensible disapprobation less necessary, less wanting, to keep us from imprudently neglecting our own happiness ... and also because imprudence and folly appearing to bring its own punishment more immediately and constantly than injurious behaviour, it needs less the additional punishment which would be inflicted upon it by others had they the same sensible indignation against it as injustice and fraud and cruelty. . . .
>
> (Butler 1900: 72)

Smith must have been attracted to the reasons behind Butler's distinction here between the vice cluster falsehood–injustice–cruelty and the other less destructive vices, such as imprudence and folly. Like Butler, who claimed that most vices were matters of 'private interest' and therefore subjected the violator to their 'own punishment', their own immediate negative consequences – as, say, foolishly wasting one's money makes one poor – Smith claimed that the virtue of beneficence was sufficiently governed by sympathy and that if need be, it could be effectively supplemented by utilitarian calculation. Because they were self-policing, neither Butler's ordinary vices nor Smith's ordinary virtues required additional assurances. But the similarities went deeper. Like Butler, who argued that nature had assured against the vices of injustice, falsehood and cruelty by giving to mankind a 'sensible disapprobation' and 'indignation' against them, Smith concurred that justice was unique among the virtues because of our natural and instinctive 'appetite' for it. Neither Smith nor Butler was willing to entrust 'nature's favorite end' to the misfirings of utilitarian calculation, as Hume had. For both of them, *appetite, not utility, was the final cause of justice.* Smith argued:

> With regard to ... the *favourite ends of nature,* she has constantly in this manner not only endowed mankind with an appetite for the end which she proposes, but likewise with an appetite for the means by which alone this end can be brought about...
>
> (TMS II.i.5.10, 77, emphasis mine; see also TMS II.ii.3.4–5, 86–7; VII.iii.1.2, 316)

And, in a stunning passage with Hobbesian intonations, Smith more urgently noted how essential the 'sense' of merited punishment becomes when human temptation is unconstrained by our 'particular connexion' with others:

> In order to enforce the observation of justice ... *Nature has implanted in the human breast* that consciousness of ill-desert, those terrors of merited punishment which attend upon its violation, as the great safeguards of the association of mankind, to protect the weak, to curb the

> violent, and to chastise the guilty. Men, though naturally sympathetic, feel so little for another, with whom they have no particular connexion, in comparison with what they feel for themselves; the misery of one, who is merely their fellow-creature, is of so little importance to them in comparison even of a small conveniency of their own; they have it so much in their power to hurt him, and may have so many temptations to do so, that *if this principle did not stand up within them* in his defence, and overawe them into a respect for his innocence, they would, like wild beasts, be at all times ready to fly upon him; and a man would enter an assembly of men as he enters a den of lions.
>
> (TMS II.ii.3.4, 86, emphasis mine)

In this passage, Smith described an 'appetite' for justice and those things necessary to attain it – an appetite that compensates for our lack of 'feeling' for those who are 'not particularly connected' with us (TMS II.1.5.10, 77). In other words, without this 'appetite' sympathy is incapable of *restraining* our self-love when we are faced with 'inconveniency' and 'temptation'. When inconvenienced or tempted, we tend to refrain from harming *only* those affectively related to us in our innermost circles of sympathy. Our appetite for justice is thus intended to protect everyone else – those innocent and endangered mere 'fellow-creatures' with whom we have no 'particular connexion'.[19]

Now, it makes sense to speak of an appetite for something that satisfies a physical urge. Smith himself referred to 'hunger, thirst, the passion which unites the two sexes, the love of pleasure, the dread of pain', and so forth (TMS I.ii.1 9, 27–31). But how did he go on to include justice among these goods? What does it mean to have an 'appetite' for an abstract thing like justice? What does an appetite for justice consist in? Smith believed that this question could be addressed only in the *negative.* Surely he characterized justice as 'nature's favourite end', but nature did not fasten justice to a *summum bonum,* a positive conception of the good which was subject to radical contestation. Striking a chord with pluralists today, Smith believed that positive goods make for necessarily precarious foundations.[20] And yet, eager to prevail over relativity, he claimed that all people seem to agree that unjust acts do 'real and positive hurt' to individuals and to society (TMS II.ii.1.5, 79). Smith insisted that nature had safeguarded her 'favourite end' by anchoring it on something that transcends contention, an experience he described as a shared human aversion to *cruelty,* much like Judith Shklar (1998) did 200 years later with her *summum malum* of cruelty.[21] Like Smith, Shklar did not want to rest liberal 'ends' on a '*summum bonum* toward which all political agents should strive' (since this is fundamentally incompatible with an individual's liberty to chose her own ends) but rather on a '*summum malum,* which all of us know and would avoid if only we could' (Shklar 1998: 10–11).

Shklar (1998: 11) sought to develop a liberalism whose primary objective was to prohibit 'cruelty', defined as the 'deliberate infliction of physical, and secondarily emotional, pain upon a weaker person or group by stronger ones in order to achieve some end, tangible or not, of the latter'. She acknowledged that in modern life 'sources of oppression are indeed numerous', but she was urgently focused on 'agents of the modern state' who have 'unique resources of physical might and persuasion at their disposal' (Shklar 1998: 3). Although Smith didn't stress particular agents of cruelty in his account, he would likely have sympathized with Shklar's preoccupation with the perils of unrestrained governmental power. But I believe the affinity between Smith and Shklar is interesting for two less obvious reasons: first, although their language differed (Shklar 'intuition', Smith 'appetite'), both described a non- or pre-rational aversion to cruelty that derives from negative human experience; and second, both asserted that our aversion to cruelty produces knowledge that cruelty is 'an absolute evil' (Shklar 1998: 5), and ultimately engenders a minimalist political morality that is intelligible across contexts, independent of positive institution.

Smith, like Shklar (1984), often discussed 'ordinary vices' such as greed, envy, mean-spiritedness, misanthropy, vengeance, resentment, and so on; but evidence for the uniqueness of cruelty abounds in the TMS. Smith often referred to our aversion to cruelty as a 'horror', a 'repugnance', a 'hatred', an 'abhorrence', an 'indignation', a reaction that is 'immediate and instinctive' (see for example TMS II.i.3.1, 71; II.i.5.6, 76; II.ii.3.9, 89; VII.iii.3.9, 323; VII.iii.3.14, 325). Cruelty speaks to us in a different language and inspires a different sort of discord than ordinary vices do:

> Our *horror* for cruelty has no sort of resemblance to our contempt for mean-spiritedness. . . . It is quite a *different species of discord* we feel at the view of those two different vices.
>
> (TMS VII.iii.3.14, 325, emphasis mine)

Note how our discord with cruelty differs: when we imaginatively 'enter into' lesser vices to determine whether or not they are 'proper', Smith said that we generally seek to understand the circumstances that motivate an agent to engage in the given behavior. Knowledge of the agent's circumstances helps me better understand why is she being so greedy, so obstinate, so puerile – helps me understand the 'whole case . . . with all its minutest incidents' as Smith put it (TMS I.i.4.6, 21). Propriety is always a contextual matter. But our engagement is very different in the case of cruelty. Coming upon it, we instantly become consequentialists according to Smith; our attention is drawn away from the circumstances and motivations of the person who committed the cruel act, and immediately toward the *consequences* of his action: the bloody victim, the torn flesh. Smith observed that we feel the most visceral, 'most lively sympathy' with 'cutting or tearing of the flesh' (TMS III.3.15, 143–4). No doubt, this affinity with the sufferer relates to our own experiences regarding suffering, and our own 'dread of death', which, according to Smith, is 'the great restraint upon the injustice of mankind which, while it affects and mortifies the individual, guards and protects the society' (TMS I.i.1.13, 13). Our horror of cruelty, thus, rests not on our sympathetic 'abhorrence' and 'disapprobation' of the person who committed the cruel act, but on a 'more sensible' and visceral sympathy with the sufferer which 'naturally boils up in the breast' (TMS II.i.5.6, 76). Only through our sympathy with the sufferer's 'unavoidable distress' and his 'anguish' do we arrive eventually at a 'fellow-feeling' with his 'just and natural resentment' toward the person who caused him harm.

> When we bring home to ourselves the situation of the persons whom those scourges of mankind insulted, murdered or betrayed, what indignation do we not feel against such insolent and inhuman oppressors of the earth.
>
> (TMS II.i.5.6, 76)

But we must press those who insist on the universal and transcultural significance of cruelty: can it stand up against contextual variation? Does it give moral and political theory a way to condemn certain cultural practices? Shklar of course insisted on the universal and cosmopolitan significance of her 'liberalism of fear', since she believed that the intuition upon which it rests is itself universal:

> Because the fear of systematic cruelty is so universal, moral claims based on its prohibition have an immediate appeal and can gain recognition without much argument ... If the prohibition of cruelty can be universalized and recognized as a necessary condition of the dignity of persons, then it can become a principle of political morality.
>
> (Shklar 1998: 11)

Knud Haakonssen (1981: 148) suggested that Smith would have agreed here – that 'some situations involving injury are so basic to human life that the spectator's verdicts will always be recognizably similar'.[22] And yet, in a seriously understudied chapter in the TMS devoted to the subject of 'Custom' (TMS V, 194–211), Smith observed that 'custom' sometimes sanctions practices – 'particular usages', 'actions' – that strike modern readers as cruel and 'warpt'. His example was Greek infanticide. Smith characterized the exposure of infants as a 'dreadful violation of humanity' – 'can there be greater barbarity ... than to hurt an infant?' – but at the same time seemed oddly indulgent toward Plato and Aristotle, who were 'led away by the established custom' and 'instead of censuring, supported the horrible abuse' (TMS V.2.1, 209–10). In Chapter V, Smith's reflections on culture foreshadow assumptions that are axiomatic for anthropologists today – the deep diversity and frequent incommensurability of cultural practices, the extent to which culture conditions cruelty and often accommodates practices perceived by outsiders as cruel.[23] Think of the great variety of cultural phenomena in which a supposed human aversion to cruelty seems to be sidelined, bypassed, overcome: for example, the normalization of and desensitization to cruelty experienced by children overexposed to violence; the tendency of some cultures to rank the values of beauty, profit, piety, safety, or nation above cruelty; the modern sterilization of violence in Foucault's history of punishment; the inversion of morals captured chillingly in Himmler's claim that the SS 'stayed decent'; Arendt's banality of evil; Milgram's surrender to authority, and so on. In a relativist key, Smith conceded that 'we may well imagine that there is scarce any particular practice so gross which [custom] cannot authorise' (TMS V.2.15, 210).[24]

And yet in other places Smith was perfectly and unapologetically contemptuous of practices that violated humanity – for example, African slavery, in which 'Fortune never exerted more *cruelly* her empire over mankind' (TMS V.2.9, 206, emphasis mine) and the 'savage injustice' committed by Europeans against aboriginals in 'America' (WN IV.i.32, 448; IV.vii.c.80, 626). I believe we are left with a clear idea of what cruelty is for Smith himself, but with a hazy sense of whether he believed it signifies something stable across contexts, or whether, like propriety, cruelty is an artifact of cultural experience, necessarily particular to the person/group who experiences it, and ultimately compatible with 'particular usages'.

Conclusion

Whether we ultimately believe that cruelty is intelligible across contexts and that our aversion to it sustains a cosmopolitan morality – indeed, whether we conclude that Smith's turn from sympathy to justice in this essay adequately confronts cultural bias – for generating and reflecting on such questions, Smith is remarkably relevant to current thinking about moral and political judgment in a pluralist world. We might say in fashionable parlance that Smith was attempting to weave a course between the inherent *relativity* of common sense and the contentious *certitude* of various positive conceptions of the good, when he attempted through his account of negative justice to articulate a *universal* perspective for moral judgment. And we might say, further, that his attempt to ground this universal perspective in a *summum malum* derived from a shared human aversion he believed to be confirmed though experience, rather than an abstract *summum bonum* which is always partial and contentious, resonates today with those who are interested in developing a minimal, or thin, conception of moral goods. There is no space in a short essay to analyze Smith's brand of minimalism. But if I have demonstrated his relevance by situating his thoughts about affective 'connexion' (part one) and culture (part two) in a larger problematic of moral judgment, I believe I have accomplished much.

Notes

I would like to thank Sam Fleischacker, Lloyd Rudolph, Stephen White, fellow new voices Eric Schliesser and Leon Montes, an incisive anonymous referee, and especially David Forman-Barzilai for their insightful comments. Sincere thanks as well to David Levy and Sandra Peart for inviting me to present some of these ideas at their 2004 Liberty Fund symposium 'New Voices Explore Adam Smith'. A special note of gratitude, long overdue, to Larry Dickey for his encouragement over so many years.

1 That Smith can be read as perhaps 'the most anthropologically sensitive' of seventeenth and eighteenth century moral philosophers see Fleischacker (forthcoming: 5).
2 Although Smith acknowledged that we can feel affection, regardless of such connection, for a person who has demonstrated exceptional 'personal qualities', for someone exceptionally needy, or for someone from whom we have experienced 'past services' (TMS VI.ii.1.15–20, 223–6).
3 See Hierocles' fragment on concentric circles in Long and Sedley (1987: I, 349–50; II, 347–8). For Cicero's formulation, see Griffin and Atkins (Cicero 1991: I.46–59, 20–5). The following treatment of Stoic *oikeoisis* draws substantially upon my discussion in Forman-Barzilai (2005). For further discussion of Smith's appropriation of the Stoic circles, see Forman-Barzilai (2002: 393–401); and Montes (2004: 241, n. 41). Montes challenges Vivenza (2002: 204–5), who doubts the Stoic origin of Smith's thinking about degrees of fellowship. On Stoicism in modern thought generally see the essays in Blom and Winkel (2004).
4 For discussion of the 'familiarity principle' in Smith (in both WN and TMS), see Otteson (2002: 183–9). An interesting discussion of Smith's 'spheres of intimacy' and the way it helps resolve the 'Adam Smith Problem' can be found in Nieli (1986).
5 Elsewhere Smith concluded: '[B]y the perfect apathy which [the 'stoical philosophy'] prescribes to us, by endeavoring, not merely to moderate, but to eradicate all our private, partial, and selfish affections, by suffering us to feel for whatever can befall ourselves, our friends, our country ... [it] endeavors to render us altogether indifferent and unconcerned in the success or miscarriage of every thing which Nature has prescribed to us as the proper business and occupation of our lives' (TMS VII.ii.1.46, 292–3). That Smith conceived of a commercial substitute for cosmopolitan feeling, see Forman-Barzilai (2002), and for a similar formulation (Nieli 1986). That Smith, in this sense, was participating in an eighteenth century discourse in which free trade was linked conceptually to the cultivation of humanitarian values, see Dickey (2004).
6 In the argument that follows, I concur with Fleischacker's claim that Smith's 'procedure of moral judgment' makes 'the standards of one's society largely determinative of one's moral judgment' (Fleischacker, forthcoming: 4). See also Fleischacker (2004: 80–2).
7 The possibility of overlap renders Smith a pluralist to my mind, rather than a relativist.

8 The discussion that follows will draw heavily from, but build upon, relevant portions of Forman-Barzilai (2005).
9 But surely there is a crucial difference. Impartial judgment for Smith did not entail a 'standing back', a 'veiling' of self, but the imaginative insertion of a fully developed self into the circumstances of another. Rawls himself noted the crucial 'contrast': for Smith, he wrote, spectators 'possess all the requisite information' and 'relevant knowledge' of their 'natural assets or social situation', while in the original position, parties are 'subject to a veil of ignorance' (Rawls 1971: 183–7). See also Campbell (1971: 127–41), Raphael (1975: 96–7), and Haakonssen (1996: 151–2).
10 That Smith was concerned more with moral action than with moral epistemology see Fleischacker (1991: 255–6).
11 A reference again to Smith's description of the 'measure' spectators use when they determine the propriety of others (at TMS I.i.3.10, 19).
12 Also see Smith's discussion of the natural jurisprudence of Grotius, Hobbes and Pufendorf in LJ (B) 1–3, 397–8.
13 On balance, however, Smith's *Lectures* were devoted primarily to a dry, academic enumeration of public, domestic and private laws. LJ (A) i.1–iii.147, 5–199; LJ (B) 1–201, 397–485). But he did offer one revealing lecture entitled 'Of the Laws of Nations' (LJ (B) 341–58, 545–54) in which we get some elaboration on what he referred to in the TMS as 'the general principles which ought to run through and be the foundation of the laws of all nations . . . without regard to the particular institutions of any one nation' (TMS VII.iv.37, 341–2).
14 Glasgow University Library, MS. Gen 1035/227. These were most likely lecture notes for his ethics course in the University of Glasgow.
15 'Those whose hearts never open should, we think, be shut out in the same manner, from the affections of all their fellow creatures' (TMS II.ii.1.10, 81).
16 'When a father fails in the ordinary degree of affection towards a son; when a son seems to want that filial reverence which might be expected to his father; when brothers are without the usual degree of brotherly affection; when a man shuts his breast against compassion, and refuses to relieve the misery of his fellow creatures, when he can with the greatest ease; in all these cases, though everybody blames the conduct, nobody imagines that those who might have reason, perhaps, to expect more kindness, have any right to extort it by force' (TMS II.ii.1.7, 81).
17 On differences between Hume and Smith on justice and utility, see Haakonssen (1981: 87–9) and Raphael (1972/73: 94–5).
18 See the editors' note at TMS II.ii.1.5, 80 n. 1; cf. Haakonssen 1981: 203 n. 20.
19 Robert C. Solomon (1995: 206) noted perceptively that for Smith 'a sense of justice is needed to supplement sympathy, which by itself is not nearly powerful enough to counter the inevitable self-serving motives of most people'.
20 Fleischacker (1999: 144–9) observed that Smith also resisted making positive assertions about human 'happiness', preferring instead to stress 'failings that take away from happiness'. Haakonssen (1981: 83–4) attributed this to the greater 'pungency' and 'universal' identifiability of pain over joy, and linked this prioritization to Smith's negative justice.
21 Shklar noted in passing her affinity with Smith on this point in Shklar (1990: 117–18).
22 Yet Haakonssen (2003: ix) later noted that 'what *counts* as injury is not a universal matter', that it 'varies dramatically from one type of society to another'. Fleischacker strenuously takes issue with Smith's assumptions about injury. Because 'harm is an essentially *social* good', he believes that Smith's theory of justice emphatically fails as a response to cultural bias (Fleischacker, 2004: 145–73, at 156).

23 Although I would argue that Smith's recourse to 'human nature' in TMS V ultimately makes him a pluralist and not a relativist. He noted that customs vary and that some become 'warpt' – but since the 'sentiments of moral approbation and disapprobation are founded on the strongest and most vigorous passions of human nature' these customs 'cannot be entirely perverted' (TMS V.2.1, 200) This suggests that Smith believed that human nature embeds all cultural variations. Cultural survival, he believes, is the proof. Indeed, 'no society could subsist a moment in which the usual strain of men's conduct and behavior was of a piece with the horrible practice [infanticide] I have just now mentioned' (TMS V.2.16, 211).

24 Of course Shklar (1998: 15–16) flatly condemned 'relativists' (Michael Walzer was a favorite) who 'argue that the liberalism of fear would not be welcomed by most of those who live under traditional customs, even if these are as cruel and oppressive as the Indian caste system'. She insisted that we will never know whether people 'really enjoy their chains' until 'we can offer the injured and insulted victims of most of the world's traditional as well as revolutionary governments a genuine and practicable alternative to their present condition' (Shklar 1998: 16).

References

Blom, H. W. and Winkel, L. C. (eds) (2004) *Grotius and the Stoa*, Assen: Van Gorcum.

Boltanski, L. (1993) *La Souffrance à distance*, trans. Graham Burchell (1999) *Distant Suffering: Morality, Media and Politics*, Cambridge: Cambridge University Press.

Brown, V. (1994) *Adam Smith's Discourse: canonicity, commerce and conscience*, London: Routledge.

Butler, Joseph (1900) *Fifteen Sermons Preached at the Rolls Chapel*, in J. H. Bernard (ed.) *The Works of Bishop Butler* I, London: Macmillan.

Campbell, T. D. (1971) *Adam Smith's Science of Morals*, London: Allen & Unwin.

Cicero (1991) *Of Duties*, ed. M. T. Griffin and E. M. Atkins, Cambridge: Cambridge University Press.

Dickey, L. (2004) '*Doux-commerce* and humanitarian values: free trade, sociability and universal benevolence in eighteenth-century thinking', in H. W. Blom and L. C. Winkel (eds) *Grotius and the Stoa*, Assen: Van Gorcum.

Fleischacker, S. (1991) 'Philosophy in Moral Practice: Kant and Adam Smith', *Kant-Studien* 82: 249–69.

—— (1999) *A Third Concept of Liberty: Judgment and Freedom in Kant and Adam Smith*, Princeton, NJ: Princeton University Press.

—— (2004) *On Adam Smith's* Wealth of Nations, Princeton, NJ: Princeton University Press.

—— (forthcoming) 'Smith and Cultural Relativism' to appear as 'Smith und der Kulturrelativismus', in C. Fricke (ed.) *Adam Smith als Moralphilosoph*, Berlin: De Gruyter.

Forman-Barzilai, F. (2000) 'Review Essay, Griswold, *Adam Smith and the Virtues of Enlightenment*', *Political Theory* 28 (1): 122–30.

—— (2002) 'Adam Smith as Globalization Theorist' *Critical Review* 14 (4): 391–419.

—— (2004) 'And thus spoke the spectator: Adam Smith for humanitarians', *Adam Smith Review* I: 167–74.

—— (2005) 'Sympathy in Space(s): Adam Smith on Proximity', *Political Theory* 33 (2): 189–217.

Griswold, Jr, C. L. (1999) *Adam Smith and the Virtues of Enlightenment*, Cambridge: Cambridge University Press.

Haakonssen, K. (1981) *The Science of a Legislator: The Natural Jurisprudence of David Hume and Adam Smith*, Cambridge: Cambridge University Press.

—— (1996) *Natural Law and Moral Philosophy: From Grotius to the Scottish Enlightenment*, Cambridge: Cambridge University Press.

—— (2003) 'Introduction' to K. Haakonssen (ed.) *Theory of Moral Sentiments*, Cambridge: Cambridge University Press.

Hope, V. (1984) 'Smith's Demigod', in V. Hope (ed.) *Philosophers of the Scottish Enlightenment*, Edinburgh: Edinburgh University Press.

—— (1989) *Virtue by Consensus: The Moral Philosophy of Hutcheson, Hume and Adam Smith*, Oxford: Clarendon Press.

Long, A. A. and Sedley, D. N. (1987) *The Hellenistic Philosophers*, 2 vols, Cambridge: Cambridge University Press.

Montes, L. (2004) *Adam Smith in Context: A Critical Reassessment of some Central Components of his Thought*, London: Palgrave Macmillan.

Nagel, T. (1986) *The View from Nowhere*, Oxford: Oxford University Press.

Nieli, R. (1986) 'Spheres of Intimacy and the Adam Smith Problem', *Journal of the History of Ideas* 47 (4): 611–24.

Nussbaum, M. C. (1995) *Poetic Justice: The Literary Imagination and Public Life*, Boston, MA: Beacon.

Otteson, J. R. (2002) *Adam Smith's Marketplace of Life*, Cambridge: Cambridge University Press.

Raphael, D. D. (1972/73), 'Hume and Adam Smith on Justice and Utility', *Proceedings of the Aristotelian Society* 73: 87–103.

—— (1975) 'The Impartial Spectator', in A. S. Skinner and T. Wilson (eds) *Essays on Adam Smith*, Oxford: Clarendon Press.

—— (1985) *Adam Smith*, Oxford: Oxford University Press.

Rawls, J. (1971) *Theory of Justice*, Cambridge, MA: Belknap Press.

Shklar, J. N. (1984) *Ordinary Vices*, Cambridge, MA: Belknap Press.

—— (1990) *Faces of Injustice*, New Haven, CT: Yale University Press.

—— (1998) 'Liberalism of Fear' in S. Hoffman (ed.) *Political Thought and Political Thinkers*, Chicago: University of Chicago Press.

Solomon, R. C. (1995) *A Passion for Justice: Emotions and the Origins of the Social Contract*, Lanham, MD: Rowman & Littlefield.

Van Holthoon, F. L. (1993) 'Adam Smith and David Hume: with Sympathy', *Utilitas* 5 (1): 36–48.

Viner, J. (1972) *The Role of Providence in the Social Order: An Essay in Intellectual History*, Princeton, NJ: Princeton University Press.

Vivenza, G. (2002) *Adam Smith and the Classics: The Classical Heritage in Adam Smith's Thought*, Oxford: Oxford University Press.

Waszek, N. (1984) 'Two Concepts of Morality: A Distinction of Adam Smith's Ethics and its Stoic Origin', *Journal of the History of Ideas* 45: 591–604.

Wolin, S. (1960) *Politics and Vision: Continuity and Innovation in Western Political Thought*, Boston, MA: Little Brown.

6 Double standard – naturally!

Smith and Rawls: a comparison of methods

Carola von Villiez

Introduction

Adam Smith's *Theory of Moral Sentiments*, while marking an important station on the way to the ethics of Immanuel Kant, is surpassed by the latter – such is the conception prevalent within the German-speaking world. Yet to conceive of Smith merely as some kind of 'Kant Junior' is to misjudge the relevance of his theory.[1] Smith proceduralizes the notion of the moral standpoint as one of detached impartiality in order to apply it to the concrete moral convictions of factual communities. And, although he does not himself reflect on this, by doing so he takes a middle way between universalism and particularism in the sense of a contextualist approach to morality. This explains the current relevance of his theory. For such a contextual approach is indispensable not only for a theory of justice, which is to handle pluralism, as John Rawls has convincingly argued (Rawls 1971, 1993, 1999). It can be considered of equal importance for a *theory of morals* faced with the task of accommodating that moral pluralism characteristic of modern societies.[2] This chapter attempts to clarify some of the concepts of TMS that seem to be especially significant in this regard: Smith's idea of *sympathy* as a principle in human nature, his idea of a *communal moral standard* of propriety and his thought experiment of the *impartial spectator*. Smith's remarks on these can be interpreted as pointing to a distinction between *three dimensions of moral judgment*. So that, from a methodological perspective, TMS displays equivalents to the method of reflective equilibrium developed by Rawls in *A Theory of Justice*.[3] It is exactly this analogy of methods that designates TMS to be an important resource for a contemporary contextual theory of morality designed for handling moral pluralism.

Adam Smith: sympathy as a principle in human nature

Adam Smith stands in the tradition of British theorists who ascribe to sentiments a significant function in moral judgments.[4] The sentiment relevant for moral judgments in Smith is *sympathy*. (For a detailed examination of Smith's concept of sympathy see especially Andree 2003 and Montes 2004, esp. 2: 45–55.) Sympathy, for Smith, represents a general *affective receptivity* toward other humans, a faculty that Ernst Tugendhat in his *Vorlesungen über Ethik* has aptly called a capacity of 'affective tuning in' or 'mutual vibrating' (cf. Tugendhat 1997: 15. Lecture, esp. 286ff.). Yet 'sympathy' in Smith also stands for concrete *sympathetic sentiments.* As the following passage shows, he does not confine these to feelings of compassion or pity:

> Pity and compassion are words appropriated to signify our fellow-feeling with the sorrow of others. Sympathy, though its meaning was, perhaps, originally the same may now, however, without much impropriety, be made use of to denote our fellow-feeling with *any passion* whatever.
>
> (TMS I.i.1.5, 10; my emphasis)

Smith's use of the term in the sense of a *faculty* cannot be substantiated with only one pointed quote. It can, however, be reconstructed from the context of passages like the following, in which Smith presents the mutual wish for sympathy as a nature-given force:

> Nature, when she formed man for society, endowed him with an original desire to please, and an original aversion to offend his brethren. She taught him to feel pleasure in their favourable, and pain in their unfavourable regard.... But ... nothing pleases us more than to observe in other men a fellow-feeling with all the emotions of our own breast; nor are we ever so much shocked as by the appearance of the contrary.
>
> (TMS III.2.6, 116 and I.i.2.1, 13)

The motivation for developing and applying this faculty flows from the general *sociability* of human beings. It is this natural sociability which occasions a desire for interacting with others not only on an intellectual but also an affective level – one might even say a desire for 'affective communication' (Tugendhat 1997: 295). For this reason, Smith considers altruism (a principal willingness to consider the interests of others along with one's own interests) to play a substantial role in human motivation. (For a similar definition of altruism, see Nagel 1970.) The fundamental relevance of this assumption for his moral theory is evident from the very first words of TMS on:

> However selfish man may be supposed, there are evidently some principles in his nature, which interest him in the fortune of others, and render their happiness necessary to him, though he derives nothing from it except the pleasure of seeing it.
>
> (TMS I.i.1.1, 9)

Smith assumes the *capacity* for sympathy to be a principle in human nature. Moreover, as a human disposition it is universal in reach. Smith speaks of *universal benevolence* induced by sympathy in this context. For instance: 'Though our effectual good offices can very seldom be extended to any wider society than that of our own country; our good-will is circumscribed by no such boundary, but may embrace the immensity of the universe' (TMS VI.ii.3.1, 235). This already indicates that the immediate perception of affect-manifestations need not be the only trigger for sympathetic feelings. And indeed, knowledge of the relevant features of situations also suffices for this purpose. As will be explained in the following section, comprehensive knowledge of the relevant features of situations is in fact a *precondition* of *proper moral judgment*. Aided by the power of imagination, it allows sympathetic participation in the fate even of distant people or historical personalities who have been subjected to injustice.[5]

The concept of sympathy is the backbone of Smith's theory.[6] It figures in his analysis of the processes commonly at work in reaching everyday moral judgments and it also provides the reason for individuals to defer to a procedure, which pays equal account to self-interest and the interests of others in moral judgments (or in examining personal motives). As will be demonstrated in the following section, Smith uses the notion of sympathy not only with view to a mere description of everyday moral practices, but also for designing a normative procedure that satisfies rational criteria of judgment – comprehensive knowledge of relevant facts and adequate consideration of the interests of all those concerned – and can serve as a testing device for everyday moral judgments. Sympathy, that is, plays a decisive role in the *formation* and *justification* of moral judgments. Yet sympathetic feelings induced by the mere perception of affections, i.e. *first-degree* sympathetic feelings, do *not* suffice for purposes of justification. They specify a first dimension of what might be called *natural moral judgments*. These natural moral judgments are subject to review against the background of a comprehensive knowledge of the situation's relevant features as well as – at the very least – of the particular moral context from which the affections are to be judged. As shall be explained below, Smith's demand for reciprocal role reversal indicates the overriding significance of comprehensive information for proper moral judgment in TMS.

The review of our natural moral judgments opens up a second dimension of what might be called *social moral judgments*, which refers to *second-degree* feelings of sympathetic approbation. Although these social moral judgments can be ascribed a justificatory status superior to that of natural moral judgments, they are yet subject to further review. Thus, the examination of social moral judgments from a perspective of *well informed impartiality* occasions *third-degree* sympathetic feelings, characteristic for judgments, which – on account of their genetic connection with the first two dimensions of moral judgment – are impartial and yet contextual.

In the following, I will try to demonstrate how these three dimensions of moral judgments can be reconstructed from Smith's own remarks.

Adam Smith: a reconstruction of three dimensions of moral judgment

The *first dimension* of moral judgment is characterized by a form of immediate sympathetic communication. It refers to the interaction between manifestations of affects – like grief and joy – or rather their perception, and *emotive reactions* thereby immediately induced in the observer. The following passage brings this to the point:

> Upon some occasions sympathy may seem to arise merely from the *view* of a certain emotion in another person. The passions, upon some occasions may seem to be *transfused* from one man to another, *instantaneously* and antecedent to any knowledge of what excited them in the person principally concerned.
>
> (TMS I.i.1.6, 11; my emphasis)

These emotive reactions already contain an implicit judgment on the situation observed. Yet, judgments owed to this form of immediate sympathetic communication are *not* grounded in a *comprehensive knowledge* of the factual situation, but solely in an observation of affects. One might say, they contain an *advance* on *benevolent affections* (like compassion), which, however, may prove unjustified at close sight. This is why, although 'the very appearances of grief and joy inspire us with some degree of the like emotions [. . ., e]ven our sympathy with the grief or joy of another, before we are informed of the cause of either, is always extremely imperfect' (TMS I.1.1.8–9, 11). The case is clearer still with displays of anger and resentment. As Smith remarks, we readily sympathize with persons who are subjected to the anger of another, 'and are immediately disposed to take part against the man from whom they appear to be in so much danger' (TMS I.1.1.7, 11). So that the 'furious behaviour of an angry man is more likely to exasperate us against himself than against his enemies' (TMS I.1.1.7, 11). The explanation he gives for this is that the unsocial passions – like anger and hatred – 'are by nature the objects of our aversion', because they 'drive men from another' (TMS I.2.3.5, 37).

Yet, expressions of anger and resentment are sometimes justified. So that, although the unsocial passions 'are the only passions of which the expressions . . . do not dispose and prepare us to sympathize with them, before we are informed of the cause which excites them', when we learn that they were in fact *justly* incited, it seems like we must revise – if not even *revoke* – our initial sympathetic feelings for the alleged sufferers in order to be able to adequately share the resentment of the person *factually* wronged (TMS I.ii.3.5, 36). For, since with regard to the unsocial passions 'our sympathy is *divided* between the person who feels them, and the person who is the object of them', one should think that an increase in our sympathetic indignation surely goes along with a decrease in sympathetic compassion (TMS I.2.1, 34; my emphasis). This appears to be even more so, since resentment 'is the safeguard of justice and the security of the innocent' (TMS II.ii.1.4, 79).[7]

Proper moral judgment requires us to assess a (display of) passion in relation to its *cause* (cf. TMS I.3.6, 18). This is why sympathy actually 'does not arise so much from the view of the passion, as from that of the situation which excites it' (TMS I.1.1.12, see also TMS I.1.4.6, 21). Assessing passions in relation to their causes requires more than observation: it requires reflection on the *relevant features* of a situation. Yet, even though first-degree sympathetic feelings from mere observation are no basis for proper moral judgments, they nevertheless provide the very motivational impetus for us to engage in a process of moral communication. This leads to a second dimension of moral judgments.

While the first dimension of moral judgment is marked by our primary desire for affection, the *second dimension* is marked by a desire for *approbation*. For human beings, Smith argues, feel pleasure in the *approval* of their fellow humans, while their disapprobation is 'most mortifying and most offensive' to them (TMS III.2.6, 116). Second-degree sympathetic feelings are, accordingly, to be understood as feelings of approbation. As for judgments of approbation, individuals initially only have their *own* respective standard at their disposal: 'Every faculty in one man is the measure by which he judges of the like faculty in another' (TMS I.i.3.10, 19). Smith dedicates a complete paragraph, entitled 'Of the manner in which we judge of the propriety or impropriety of the affections of other men, by their concord or dissonance with our own', to this assertion (TMS I.i.3, 16ff.).

Judgments made solely with view to one's own subjective standard, however, have little chance at *intersubjective authority*, for Smith does not assign any context-independent, substantial criterion for the correctness of moral judgments, which would be intuitively accessible to individuals. He does indeed demand to assess sentiments with a view to their *cause*. Yet, since he also believes individuals' judgment competence to vary (cf. TMS VI.iii.23–5, 247), one should expect their conclusions to differ even on one and the same situation. His remarks regarding proper degrees of different sentiments (cf. TMS I.ii) appear to add little in this respect. The lack of a *context-independent*, substantial criterion for the propriety of kind and intensity of sentiments in relation to their cause suggests that, in Smith, *second-order* moral judgments require *social communication* along with comprehensive knowledge of relevant situational features. This interpretation is supported by the *reciprocal role reversal* he presupposes (cf. TMS I.4.6, 21 and TMS I.1.4.8, 22). By means of this role reversal, moral actors try to gain as much information as possible on the (rational and emotive) interests of all those affected by an action, for the purpose of judgment. On the basis of this information, the propriety of the action in question is initially judged from the perspective of a communal spectator.

Thus, Smith's numerous remarks regarding the relevance of mutual moral commenting clearly indicate propriety to be a function of social interaction (similar to Haakonssen 1981: 54). For example:

> Were it possible, that a human creature could grow up to manhood in some solitary place, without any communication with his own species, he could no more think of his own character, of the propriety or demerit of his own sentiments and conduct,... than of the beauty or deformity of his own face.
>
> (TMS III.1.3, 110)

Not only does our very moral development depend on the *looking-glass* function of society (cf. esp. TMS III.1.3–5, 110–12). It is also in the course of moral interaction, i.e. observing others' reactions to our own behavior and *vice versa*, that general rules of behavior are formed (cf. TMS III.4.7–8). So that *factual spectators* mutually judging and commenting on each other's behavior can be taken to play a decisive role in moral judgment. Second-dimension morality, for Smith, is a function of the mutual adjustment of sentiments and judgments within a particular moral community. Since, moreover, he considers moral communication to be a precondition for harmonious social relations (cf. TMS I.i.4.7, 22), one can assume the judgments of factual spectators to more or less reflect the norms and intuitions of their moral community, so that second-order judgments might be understood as moral judgments justified *from within the context of a factual moral community*. (See also Fleischacker 1999, esp. ch. 3.3.) This second dimension of moral judgments, then, would rest not so much on people perceiving each other as sentient beings, but *acknowledging* each other as *moral actors* belonging to a *common moral community* and acting according to what Smith comprises under the *standard of approximation* (cf. TMS I.i.5.8–10, 26 and VI.iii.23, 247).

Although, as remains to be demonstrated, social moral judgments are an integral component of reflective equilibrium, they cannot be considered ultimately justified merely because they represent the convictions prevalent in a moral community, for the latter may very well reflect mere prejudice or rest on factual mistakes. Accordingly, Smith distinguishes between *judgments of approximation* well founded from within the context of a moral community and *judgments of exact propriety and perfection*. (The relation between the two is addressed below.) So the dimension of *social moral judgments*, resulting from an interest in mutual moral commenting, does not represent the final instance of justification for Smith. For the *third dimension* of moral judgments thus opening up, it is no longer the 'moral applause of society' – its approbation or disapprobation – that is decisive, but rather the *praiseworthiness* of actions. Smith makes this distinction with the following words: 'Praise and blame express what actually are; praise-worthiness and blame-worthiness, what naturally ought to be the sentiments of other people with regard to our character and conduct' (TMS III.2.25, 126).[8] As the following quote illustrates, this superior human desire for praise*worthiness* locates proper moral judgment *beyond* the horizon of *popular opinion*:

> But this desire of the approbation, and this aversion to the disapprobation of his brethren, would not alone have rendered him fit for that society for which he was made. Nature, accordingly, has endowed him not only with a desire of being approved of, but with a desire of being *what ought to be approved of*: or of being *what he himself approves of in other men.*
>
> (TMS III.2.7, 117; my emphasis)

At this stage, moral judgment is (to some extent!) removed from the reach of external moral sanctions and, to speak in Kantian terms, transferred to the internal sphere of autonomous judgment. Therefore, as far as the critical questioning of judgments well founded from within the context of a moral community is concerned, it is no longer the opinions of factual spectators that are decisive. Their place is rather taken by an *idealized spectator*: the 'impartial spectator'. This idea is most impressively established in the following passage:

> But though man has, in this manner, been rendered the immediate judge of mankind, he has been rendered so only in the first instance; and an appeal lies from his sentence to a much higher tribunal, to the tribunal of their own consciences, to that of the supposed impartial and well-informed spectator, to that of the man within the breast, the great judge and arbiter of their conduct.
>
> (TMS III.2.32, 130–1)

For moral judgments of this dimension, third-degree sympathetic sentiments are relevant, the sentiments of a *well informed and impartial spectator*. Only actions and dispositions this imagined person within can (emotively and rationally) go along with can be considered completely justified. At this point, Smith obviously is no longer concerned with the mere description of moral practice within an existing moral community. Rather, with the impartial spectator he ultimately introduces a *procedural standard* that this practice must measure up to.

Adam Smith: the impartial spectator

The figure of the impartial spectator can be understood as a heuristic aid for assessing the propriety of others' judgments regarding our own conduct as well as determining the moral quality of actions we are about to perform. Thus, we do not only 'examine our own conduct, and endeavour to view it in the light in which the impartial spectator would view it . . . after we have acted', but 'when we are about to act' as well (TMS III.4.2, 157). It serves as a thought experiment to define the praiseworthiness of actions or dispositions and (in its simplest constellation) works according to the following pattern: I perform an action *A*. My performance of this action (or the disposition it manifests) is the cause for approbation or disapprobation in a person *P* whose rational or emotive interests are affected by it. Rather than simply adopting her judgment of approbation or disapprobation regarding my action, I examine its praiseworthiness. In a first step, I enter the situation of person *P* to this avail. The underlying intention in this is not a merely intellectual definition of her rational interests, but moreover the ascertainment of the sentiments – the *emotive interests* – connected with her situation. That is, I assume *P*'s position not only mentally, but also emotively. Not only do I think myself into *P*, I *feel* myself into *P*, in order to let the intellectual and affective information thus gained enter into my judgment.

In order to be able to counterbalance our *natural affective partiality* (that 'natural inequality of our sentiments'; TMS III.3.3, 136), we must undertake the reciprocal role reversal sketched above to begin with. In this first-order role reversal, we completely enter into the situation of the other person and ascertain her initial conditions including her self-affections. So the state of comprehensive informedness thereby aimed at seems to equally presuppose two efforts. First, an intellectual apprehension of the interests of persons affected (by an action or disposition) by means of a *rational operation*. Reason does indeed play an important role in moral judgments for Smith. For, 'when we come to particular cases, the actual consequences which happen to proceed from any action, have a very great effect upon our sentiments concerning its merit or demerit, and almost always either enhance or diminish our sense of both'; and, for anticipating the actual consequences of an action, one of the 'qualities most useful to ourselves' is 'superior reason and understanding, by which we are capable of discerning the remote consequences of all our actions, and of foreseeing the advantage and detriment which is likely to result from them' (TMS II.iii.intro.5, 93 and IV.2.6, 189). The second effort involved in the first-order role reversal consists in the sensory apprehension of the affective interests of persons affected by means of an *emotive operation*. This way, the reciprocal role reversal provides us with a richer notion of what is at stake for the parties involved, as would be the case if the interests imputed to others were supported only by our own situational and personal features or rational choices.[9] On this basis, we are then able to make second-dimension moral judgments, i.e. moral judgments which are grounded in a comprehensive knowledge of all the interests involved and which – on account of their correspondence with the existing moral intuitions – may be considered well founded from within the context of a particular moral community.

Yet, for the reasons named above, such judgments must be considered provisional for so long as they have not been validated from the third-person perspective of an (in the above sense) well informed and *impartial* spectator. This requires a *second-order role reversal*, which 'habit and experience have taught us to do' (TMS III.3.3, 135), and which Smith describes as follows:

> Before we can make any proper comparison of those opposite interests, we must change our position. We must view them, neither from our own place nor yet from his, neither with our own eyes nor yet with his, but from the place and with the eyes of a *third person*, who has no particular connection with either, and who judges with *impartiality* between us.
>
> (TMS III.3.3, 135: my emphasis)

According to Smith, this *well informed impartiality* is the precondition for moral judgments that may be considered justified in a superior sense than that of mere agreement with the prevailing convictions. A judgment is then really justified only when it can be presented as result of the execution of an impartiality procedure. (I will explain the operationalization of this procedure further below.)

In the previous remarks, a decisive difference between Smith's theory of moral sentiments and other moral conceptions, taking the moral standpoint to be embodied in a concept of impartiality (exemplary Barry 1989, 1995; Habermas 1994; Nagel 1970; Rawls 1971, 1993), has suggested itself. Other authors try to generate impartiality by means of a complete abstraction from the concrete person and situation of moral actors and, most of all, from their sentiments. One could call this a 'thin' notion of impartiality. Rawls, for instance, takes account of this with his concept of a 'thick veil of ignorance', which initially excludes all information from the judgment situation in order to allow just the information considered absolutely necessary for a decision.[10] In contrast to this, Smith proposes a *thick* notion of impartiality that does not even exclude the natural partiality of individuals toward their own person from the judgment situation. Rather, the latter is entered into the impartiality procedure to balance the scales: if you cannot expect an individual to ignore her natural partiality toward herself, you must also account for the partiality of the Other toward himself. With this assumption, Smith seems to stand in direct opposition to Kantian models of impartiality and especially to that proposed by Rawls.[11] However, on the basis of a comparison of methods, affinities between both conceptions can be made apparent that make the seemingly incommensurable impartiality procedures of both authors compatible with each other. And it is just this similarity in methods which moves Smith along with Rawls in the proximity of a contextualist conception of morality.

Adam Smith as a proponent of a contextualist approach to ethics

There are two features which characterize a contextualist conception of morality: it puts moral judgments into the care of procedural operations, by means of which the quality of actions can be determined, and it ties back the results of these operations to the moral intuitions of individuals in social contexts of action. By uniting these two features on the methodical level, such a conception acknowledges morality to be a historically and culturally grown phenomenon, yet doesn't uncritically accept the moral moods of a moral community. It lays claim to a culture- and time-transcending justification of moral judgments and norms, which is yet not owed to an ahistorical or acultural perspective. On this account, it can be considered to take an intermediary position between a universalist and a particularistic stance on morality. I will demonstrate the legitimacy of ascribing to Smith such a contextualist conception of morality on the basis of his remarks about the two standards of moral judgment, for which the judgments of factual spectators and the judgment of the impartial spectator are representative respectively.

Although Smith does not make this explicit, there is reason to assume that the standard defining the judgments of factual moral spectators is developed in the course of their continually squaring their moral sentiments amongst one another, constantly holding up a mirror to one another (cf. TMS III.i.3–5, 110ff.). For the development and application of their moral standards, human beings are thrown back on to one another (cf. TMS III.i.3, 110), so that the development of morality in Smith represents a social process, a form of 'moral circuit', in which the moral convictions of individual and society mutually require and further each other. His numerous references to the necessity of a mutual adjustment of the sentiments of actors and spectators (e.g. TMS I.i.4.6–10, 21ff.) point in this direction. At this point he refers to *factual* spectators mutually evaluating and commenting on each other's moral conduct within the confines of a moral community. In this context, Smith speaks of an imperfect formulation of the ideal of impartiality, a standard of approximation, exhibited in the moral conduct of the majority of society (cf. TMS I.i.5.8–10, 26 and VI.iii.23, 247).

Smith contrasts this standard of approximation with a notion of perfect impartiality, an 'archetype of perfection' (cf. TMS I.i.5.8–10, 26 and VI.iii.23–5, 247). By characterizing the latter as the *ideal* standard, Smith expresses his conviction that, although the perfect judgment of a well informed impartial spectator might well be unattainable for human beings, it must nevertheless always be *striven for* by means of the second change of positions.[12] Our moral judgments thus always move in between these two standards:

> In estimating our own merit, in judging of our own character and conduct, there are two different standards to which we naturally compare them. The one is the idea of exact propriety and perfection, so far as we are each capable of comprehending that idea. The other is that degree of approximation to this idea which is commonly attained in the world, and which the greater part of our friends and companions, of our rivals and competitors, may have actually arrived at. We very seldom (I am disposed to think, we never) attempt to judge of ourselves without giving more or less attention to both these different standards. But the attention of different men, and even of the same man at different times, is often very unequally divided between them; and is sometimes principally directed towards the one, and sometimes towards the other.
>
> (TMS VI.iii.23, 247)

The following passage, in which Smith describes the *generation* of the ideal standard, suggests that the perfect judgment of the impartial spectator might be understood as the ideal outcome of an analysis both of our own character and conduct and that of others and the constant application of the impartiality procedure to these observations in the sense of a process of *social-contextual reconstruction.*

> There exists in the mind of every man, an idea of this kind [exact propriety and perfection], gradually formed from his observations upon the character and conduct both of himself and of other people. It is the slow, gradual, and progressive work of the great demigod within the breast [the impartial spectator], the great judge and arbiter of conduct. This idea is in every man more or less accurately drawn, its colouring is more or less just, its outlines are more or less exactly designed, according to the delicacy and acuteness of that sensibility, with which those observations were made, and according to the care and attention employed in making them. . . . Every day some feature is improved; every day some blemish is corrected.
>
> (TMS VI.iii.25, 247)

It is instructive to note in this context how, between editions, Smith modified the passage concerning the relation between the tribunal of the man without and that of the man within. Apparently, the first edition must have suggested conscience to be a mere *reflection* of social attitudes, prompting questions as to its supposed distinctness from and superiority to popular opinion (cf. Raphael and MacFie 1982: 16). In the second edition, Smith still considered the jurisdiction of conscience to be 'in a great measure derived from the authority of that very tribunal, whose decisions it so often and so justly reverses' (TMS ed. note, p. 129 (2nd edn III.1.8 and draft of 1759)). In edition 6, he then finally replaced the foregoing as follows:

> The jurisdictions of those two tribunals are founded upon principles which, though in some respects resembling and akin, are, however, in reality different and distinct. The jurisdiction of the man without, is founded altogether in the desire of actual praise, and in the aversion to actual blame. The jurisdiction of the man within, is founded altogether in the desire of praise-worthiness, and in the aversion to blame-worthiness.
>
> (TMS III.2.32, 130–1)

It should be safe to assume that the common standard of approximation is specified by the judgments of the man without, i.e. man as the 'immediate judge of mankind' (TMS III.2.32, 130). The standard of exact propriety, in contrast, is a result of the workings of the man within, that impartial spectator (a.k.a. *conscience*) assessing the second-dimension judgments of common morality. So that, although '[a]ccording to Smith, conscience is a product of social relationship', it should not be taken to simply *reflect* 'the feelings of real external spectators' (Raphael and MacFie 1982: 15). Yet, the 'man within the breast, the abstract and ideal spectator of our sentiments and conduct, requires often to be awakened and put in mind of his duty, by the presence of the real spectator' (TMS 3.38, 153).[13] Exact moral judgment, in Smith, is the result of an *interaction* between conscience and common moral judgment.

Principles play an important role in this process.[14] They are developed in the course of the observation of our social moral practice: 'Our continual observations upon the conduct of others, insensibly lead us to form to ourselves general rules concerning what is fit and proper either to be done or to be avoided' (TMS III.4.7, 159). On account of our natural desire for affection and approbation, the appraisals of persons from within our moral surroundings are highly significant in this context. Following the foregoing quote, Smith speaks about how certain actions shock or satisfy our 'natural sense of merit and propriety' (TMS III.4.8, 159). If these sentiments are reinforced by others, our own affective needs are satisfied. And it is just this observation – that certain actions 'excite all those sentiments, for which we have by nature the strongest desire; the love, the gratitude, the admiration, of mankind' – which 'naturally' motivates us to 'lay down to ourselves a rule of another kind. That every opportunity of acting in this manner is carefully to be sought after' (TMS III.4.7, 159). This, according to Smith, is the origin of principles:

> It is thus that the general rules of morality are formed. They are ultimately founded upon experience of what, in particular instances, our moral faculties, our natural sense of merit and propriety, approve or disapprove of.
>
> (TMS III.4.8, 159)

At first we judge the propriety of actions on the basis of the moral convictions of our surroundings. Significant for our intuitions and rules and the judgments built thereon, then, are first- and second-degree sympathetic feelings and not the sentiments of the impartial spectator, which are owed only to a *reflection* upon these first- and second-degree feelings and judgments. According to this interpretation, the talk of a 'natural sense of merit and propriety' refers to the basic sympathetic disposition of human beings living in social contexts. Then Smith's assumption, that moral judgments do not *originally* refer to general principles, becomes intelligible:

> We do not originally approve or condemn particular actions; because, upon examination, they appear to be agreeable or inconsistent with a certain general rule. The general rule, on the contrary, is formed by finding from experience, that all actions of a certain kind, or circumstanced in a certain manner, are approved or disapproved of.
>
> (TMS III.4.8, 159)

Yet, if these general principles are owed to the activities of our natural moral faculty in the last instance, and if the latter is controlled by our natural desire for sympathetic affection and approbation, they cannot hold for the final justification of moral judgments. For in Smith, the praise*worthiness* of actions or dispositions is decisive for this purpose. And the latter is not defined by whether or not actions are the cause for first- or second-degree sympathetic feelings. The praiseworthiness of an action or disposition rather results from its being apt to excite the sympathetic sentiments of the well informed impartial spectator. In criticism of other theories of propriety Smith remarks:

> None of those systems either give, or even pretend to give, any precise or distinct measure by which this fitness or propriety of affection can be ascertained or judged of. That precise and distinct measure can be found nowhere but in the sympathetic feelings of the impartial and well-informed spectator.
>
> (TMS VII.ii.1.49)

Nevertheless, general principles have a corrective function with regard to our moral sentiments:

> Those general rules of conduct, when they have been fixed in our mind by habitual reflection, are of great use in correcting the misrepresentations of self-love concerning what is fit and proper to be done in our particular situation.
>
> (TMS III.4.12, 160)

That means: general principles are owed to sympathetic feelings, yet at the same time serve as a corrective for the latter in concrete situations. One could speak of an interaction between *principles* and *moral intuitions*, in which neither one can lay claim to ultimate authority. The latter is reserved for the impartial spectator affirming the results of their interaction. It is in this sense that the procedure developed by Smith can be conceived of as a process of social-contextual reconstruction which aims at bringing into accord our moral intuitions and principles under conditions of impartiality. An approximation to the perfect judgment of the impartial spectator requires us to go back and forth between intuitions and principles under conditions of impartiality. Yet, despite our efforts, we never quite reach perfect judgment, so that even our thus reflected judgments always remain open to revision on the basis of further evidence or refinement of sensibilities. Against this background, Smith's remark that our moral judgments always contain a hidden reference to the *factual* judgments of others or those judgments that we *believe to be able to expect* of them, or those judgments that *could be expected under certain conditions* (cf. TMS III.1.2, 110) becomes intelligible: the factual judgments of others are immediate expressions of their moral intuitions, the judgments we believe to be able to expect are those we expect taking into consideration the principles underlying our moral practice, and the last are the perfect judgments we approximate by bringing the impartiality procedure to bear on them.

Thus, in Smith, justified moral judgments are those that are in accord with the critical self-understanding of a moral community. The latter follows from an execution of the procedure described above, in which the impartiality ideal of a procedural conception of morality is related to the practice of a moral community on the methodical level. In this sense, one can ascribe to him a contextualist view of morality. Obviously, Smith develops a theory of *individual ethics* and not one of justice. Yet, from a *methodological perspective*, his approach can be shown to display a principal closeness to a concept of *reflective equilibrium* which Rawls posits as the methodical framework of his conception of justice as fairness.

John Rawls: the idea of reflective equilibrium

John Rawls is known for his reformulation of social contract theory. The significant element of his theory in this respect is his so-called *original position* – an imaginary state, to be entered for the purpose of evaluating the justice quality of society's basic structure – which is to be understood as a thought experiment. By means of this original position, Rawls simulates a situation of rational decision under conditions of uncertainty, in which parties are to reach a binding agreement on principles of justice for their society. Certain conditions of reason (which are not up for choice) are to set the frame for an impartial decision. The condition relevant for the present context is the so-called *veil of ignorance*. In contrast to Smith, Rawls holds that judgments of impartiality can be reached only under *exclusion* of concrete information. For this reason, his metaphorical veil of ignorance hides such information as may provide the actors (in the imaginary agreement situation of the original position) with clues for a judgment on their own behalf, that is, primarily information regarding their individual social standing and chances in life.

By excluding this information, Rawls seeks to define his original position – in explicit contrast to the model of an impartial sympathetic spectator – as a decision situation under uncertainty (cf. Rawls 1999: 161ff.). This fact raises expectations of grave differences between Rawls and Smith. To begin with, however, one must note that Rawls misinterprets Smith as an early utilitarian, so that his anti-utilitarian arguments in *A Theory of Justice* would apply with full force.[15] Besides, his rejection of the impartial spectator rests on a misunderstanding regarding the notion of sympathy underlying Smith's theory of moral sentiments and its function within the same. Thus, he seems to share the popular view that Smith takes moral action to depend on *philanthropic inclinations*.[16] Yet, as explained above, Smith explicitly distinguishes between the notion of sympathy and that of pity or benevolence. And although he presupposes a principal human sociability, he considers moral action decidedly *not* to be owed to simple feelings of benevolence but to moral sentiments. Moral sentiments, however, do not require complete altruism, but only a general willingness to engage in the complex role reversal described above.

In addition, it is significant for the present context that the original position represents only one part of Rawls's justification programme. Besides his reference to contract theory, he recurs to coherence theory as a strategy for norm justification with his concept of reflective equilibrium.[17] His conjunction of these two justificatory strategies rests on the conviction that a theory of justice cannot be fully justified from the rationalistic presumptions of normative construction alone (cf. Rawls 1999: 19). It must, moreover, be apt for being brought into agreement with the basic moral intuitions of the society it is designed for. And thus, the idea of reflective equilibrium denotes a process of mutual adjustment of original position premises, justice principles derived therefrom and moral intuitions.

> By going back and forth, sometimes altering the conditions of the contractual circumstances, at others withdrawing our judgments and conforming them to principle, I assume that eventually we shall find a description of the initial situation that both expresses reasonable conditions and yields principles which match our considered judgments duly pruned and adjusted. This state of affairs I refer to as reflective equilibrium. It is an equilibrium because at last our principles and judgments coincide; and it is reflective since we know to what principles our judgments conform and the premises of their derivation.
>
> (Rawls 1999: 18)[18]

In contrast to the initial decision on justice principles in the original position, this process does not take place behind the veil of ignorance, but in full knowledge of the previously excluded information. So, with his idea of reflective equilibrium, Rawls ties together two views of morality that are usually thought of as either–or choices: that of the moral point of view as one of detached impartiality and that of morality as a historically and culturally grown phenomenon with social norms having to be understood as resulting from the thick morality of particular moral communities. It is this mediating approach which reveals him as a proponent of a contextualist notion of ethics.

Smith and Rawls: a comparison of methods

Smith's method in TMS has been interpreted as one of reflective equilibrium. The notions of moral sentiments and a dual role reversal in the light of two standards of judgment were taken to be the relevant elements of his theory in this regard. They can also be found in Rawls in a similar form. Interestingly, Rawls does not consider himself an exclusive advocate of a rationalistic ethical tradition, but explicitly puts his conception of justice as fairness into the tradition of moral sentiments theory: 'Justice as fairness is a theory of our moral sentiments as manifested by our considered judgments in reflective equilibrium' (Rawls 1999: 104). With the talk of moral sentiments fit for reflective equilibrium, Rawls does not refer to unreflected out-of-the-stomach judgments, but to *well considered* moral judgments, i.e. judgments which have been cleared from obvious epistemic distortions and sufficiently generalized (cf. Rawls 1999: I.9).[19]

Similarly, in Smith morally relevant sentiments do not enter the judgment process in their crude form of unreflected, first-degree sympathetic feelings. Rather, they must be toned up or down first (cf. TMS I.i.3.4, 18 and I.i.4.7–10, 22ff.). Apart from *sympathy*, the basic capacity for affective interest in the fate of others, this requires *self-command*. (For discussions of self-command in Smith, see Montes 2004: 3.5.1 and Griswold 1999.) Our capacity for sympathy enables us to confront the rational and affective interests of others with the care we owe our fellow human beings and, that way, to balance emotive deficits owed to our own natural partiality. By means of self-command, in contrast, we tone down excessive feelings toward our own person (or that of others). So that sympathy and self-command are, so as to speak, two sides of the same coin:

> Our sensibility to the feelings of others, so far from being inconsistent with the manhood of self-command, is the very principle upon which that manhood is founded. The very same principle or instinct which, in the misfortune of our neighbour, prompts us to compassionate his sorrow; in our own misfortune, prompts us to restrain the abject and miserable lamentations of our own sorrow. . . . The man of the most

> perfect virtue, the man whom we naturally love and revere the most, is he who joins, to the most perfect command of his own original and selfish feelings, the most exquisite sensibility both to the original and sympathetic feelings of others.
>
> (TMS III.3.34–5)

Smith considers self-command to be a virtue which must be *cultivated.* While a 'very young child has no self-command' yet, as it grows older, it 'enters into the great school of self-command' learning to moderate all its passions 'to the degree which its play-fellows and companions are likely to be pleased with' in order to 'gain their favour, and avoid their hatred or contempt' (TMS III.3.22, 145). By subjecting our feelings to such fine-tuning, we create the basis for harmonious relations on an interpersonal and societal level. Accordingly, the motivation for the mutual adjustment of sentiments is to be sought in the human desire for affection and approbation. We transpose our emotions to a 'pitch' that factual spectators from within our moral community can go along with, because the kind and intensity of our emotions then correspond to their own emotions (cf. TMS I.i.4.7–10, 22). And, although Smith does not make this explicit, one might say that with this mutual tuning into each other we bring our emotions to a level required for judgments to be socially acceptable. We turn them into emotions, which – from the internal viewpoint of our own moral community – are appropriate to their cause.

Yet in Smith, moral judgments cannot be considered fully justified merely because of their social acceptability, but only if they can moreover be presented as results of a *dual* role reversal. Whereas the first, reciprocal role reversal creates the preconditions for well informed moral judgments according to the shared convictions of a moral community, the second-order role reversal constitutes the critical questioning of these very judgments from a perspective of detached impartiality. Rawls also works with such a dual change of perspective. In order to reach an instrumental decision, the imaginary participants to the original position must enter the situation of different groups of persons and ask themselves how the various justice principles at their choice would impact their lives.[20] Because they do in fact belong to one of these groups (even though they do not know which one), one could say that the uncertainty of the original position motivates a reciprocal role reversal. The second-order role reversal is warranted by the informational politics of the original position. The restrictions on information externally imposed on its participants by the veil of ignorance (together with the stipulation of mutual disinterestedness) are to lead to a decision on the basis of appropriate reasons. So, by and large, reasons considered *appropriate* in this context can well be equated with what in Smith proves to be appropriate from the perspective of an *impartial spectator*, for they result from Rawls's own impartiality device (see Rawls 1999: 118–23 and 232f.).

The observation that Rawls, in contrast to Smith, starts with a 'thin' notion of impartiality *prima facie* seems to mark a decisive difference between both theories. Yet this apparent difference is cancelled by the fact that both authors tie their impartiality procedure into an idea of reflective equilibrium, which refers to comprehensive information about the moral sentiments and social circumstances of factual moral communities. Even though one might object that in Rawls, other than in Smith, such comprehensive information is only provided *after* (in form of justice principles) a substantial decision on the criteria of appropriate action has been reached. However, this objection misses the very *pointe* of Rawls's idea of reflective equilibrium. For reflective equilibrium does not mean linear adjustment from 'thin impartiality' toward 'everyday moral life', but goes both ways. It denotes a dynamic equilibrium, a state of *mutual* adjustment. Thus, 'this equilibrium is not necessary stable. It is liable to be upset by further examination of the conditions which should be imposed on the contractual situation and by particular cases which may lead us to revise our judgments' (Rawls 1999: 18). That is, the principles agreed upon under lack of information are not accorded an ultimate corrective claim with regard to moral judgments formed under conditions of full information. Rather, these well informed judgments *themselves* are anew to interact with the principles agreed upon in the original position (as well as with the impartiality conditions externally imposed upon the same). (See also Daniels 1979, 1980.)

In Smith, the ideal of perfection does not appear to interact in the same way with our well informed judgments at first sight. However, one must once again consider his remarks regarding the *generation* of the ideal. It is formed by continuous observation of our own conduct and that of others and application of the impartiality procedure to these observations. It is, thus, not static, but rather subject to continuous improvement. Moreover, Smith's remarks regarding the social process of moral development (e.g. TMS III.i.3–5, 110ff.) suggest a constant interaction between individual and collective morality. The ideal, that is, does not remain within, but is always thrown back into the social realm to interact with the communal standard. In this manner, the ideal of perfection interacts with our well informed judgments. The fact that the relation between factual and ideal norm is thus not linear in Smith, but goes both ways, explains how moral progress is possible. And, thus, the difference between the two conceptions actually isn't quite as grave as Rawls himself holds.

Although Rawls's rejection of the notion of an impartial, sympathetic spectator – so far as aimed at Smith – is owed to an incorrect reception of the latter's concept of sympathy and relation to utilitarianism, the following difference between their impartiality models is to be noted in this context. Rawls and Smith provide different explanations for the *motivation* of actors to engage in a complex role reversal in social contexts of moral decision. In Smith, the first- and second-order role reversal is motivated by the sympathetic disposition, the *fundamental sociability*, of human beings, whereas in Rawls the *rational self-interest* of actors in situations of decision under uncertainty stands in the foreground. Accordingly, he models the original position by postulating *mutual disinterestedness*, thus seeking to exclude positive interest (benevolent altruism) in the fate of others as well as negative interest (envious egoism) as motivational basis. So that instead of 'mutual disinterestedness' one might alternatively speak of *socially compatible self-interest*. The latter, however, is at no rate precluded by Smith's notion of a fundamental sympathetic disposition of human beings either, because, according to his view, social affections and selfish affections (as well as unsocial affections) are equally part of human constitution. Rawls tries to avoid such anthropological premises altogether, and as a merely heuristic aid for defining criteria for the justice quality of societal basic structures, the original position can very well do without them.[21]

In an effort to preclude personal contingencies from influencing the initial choice of justice principles, Rawls models the participants in the original position as free and equal (*Kantian*) moral subjects, rather than as actual people with personal features. Communitarian thinkers, especially Sandel and Taylor, have contested this liberal notion of 'atomistic individuals' without social contexts. Neither moral development nor individuation itself, they insist, is possible without a social context, so that moral motivation as well as moral beliefs can be understood only against the background of the traditions of moral communities (cf. Sandel 1982; Taylor 1985, 1988). On this account, so the communitarian line of thought, Kantian concepts of free and equal moral subjects as well as abstract universalism in general must be rejected as defining features of moral theories. Yet, whereas arguments against strong forms of abstract universalism that negate the relevance of culture for morality are justified, arguments against a wholesale rejection of abstraction and universalization in moral justification are equally so. For moral theories that reject abstraction and universalization as methodical instruments are incapable of supplying a *critical standard of judgment*, i.e. one that does not simply amount to the existing *mores*. Smith, in contrast, provides just such a critical standard with the impartial spectator. He is fully aware of the fact that a principal capability and willingness to 'divide myself, as it were, into two persons', so 'that I, the examiner and judge, represent a different character from that other I, the person whose conduct is examined into and judged of', are indispensable for purposes of moral justification (TMS III.1.6, 113).

In Rawls, the original position provides for that impartial perspective. However, in discussing the relevance of anthropological presuppositions for his theory, one must bear in mind that the original position is part of his justificatory programme of reflective equilibrium. And the latter requires us to assess the justice quality of basic structures by *mediating* between the perspective of the idealized participants to the original position and our standpoint as factual members of existing societies. At this point, he is inevitably thrown back to the question of what should motivate people to examine their moral intuitions and social moral practices in the first place and, further, what should motivate them to engage in the proposed impartiality operation to this avail, if not a fundamental interest in the fate of others, as assumed by Smith. It is here that the communitarian critique of Rawls's owing a convincing explanation for the motivational effectiveness of his conception cannot quite be dismissed (e.g. MacIntyre 1993: 99–100). For, while Smith produces a compelling explanation for our motivation to engage in a process of mutual justification by complex role reversal – namely our basic sympathetic disposition – Rawls refers only to a vague 'sense of justice'. And it is not clear from his remarks that this sense of justice is anything more than a very abstract idea of mutuality – which again raises questions about the motivation to accept mutuality as a guiding principle of conduct. In this respect, Rawls's conception might well profit from a Smithian concept of sympathy.[22]

A contextualist approach to ethics: double standard – naturally!

At first sight, Smith seems to waver hopelessly between normative construction and moral-sociological description in TMS. Yet his approach gains quite a bit of intelligibility when examined from a meta-theoretical perspective. From this viewpoint he aims neither at the construction of a purely formalistic moral conception nor at a mere description of a society's moral practices, but rather at a mediation of both. Such mediation characterizes a contextualist approach to ethics, which critically-normatively refers to the fundamental convictions of a moral community by means of a reconstructive interpretation of moral culture. This requires assuming an external standpoint, which must yet not be a culture-external standpoint in the strict sense, for it needs to be developed from within the very confines of the moral context, for whose assessment it is to serve. The conviction that Smith implicitly aims at such a construction of the critical moral standard from within is supported by his remarks regarding the ideal standard, which must be understood as the perfect judgment of an impartial spectator. This perfect judgment is the ideal result of a procedural operation, in which the moral sentiments of individuals or collective moral intuitions and the principles underlying the same are brought into interaction with each other under conditions of impartiality with the goal of reaching reflective equilibrium.

This procedure is operationalized by means of the dual role reversal rendered possible and motivated by the fundamental sympathetic constitution of human beings. With his model of a sympathy-induced dual role reversal, Smith provides directives for reaching context-sensitive judgments which are yet impartial in a superior sense. He demonstrates that the notion of the moral point of view as one of detached impartiality does not require a complete abstraction from the judgment contexts of moral communities and that feelings may be accorded a constitutive role in processes of moral justification, without thereby rejecting rational justification.

Notes

This chapter is a revised and extended translation of 'Sympathische Unparteilichkeit. Adam Smith's moralischer Kontextualismus' in Ch. Fricke and H.-P. Schütt (eds) *Adam Smith als Moralphilosoph*, Berlin and New York: De Gruyter (2005). Many thanks go to Eric Schliesser and Leonidas Montes for critical comments.

1 Accordingly, this view is currently being revised in German literature on Adam Smith. A good example for this is the essay 'Unparteilichkeit in der Moral', in which Georg Lohmann 'wants to suggest differentiations in our views of moral judgment'. In this, moral sentiments and impartiality play an important part (cf. Lohmann 2001). For a comparison of judgment and freedom in Kant and Smith see Fleischacker (1999). For a complementary reading of Smith as a proto-Kantian see Montes (2004).

2 Another important resource for the designing of a contextualist theory of morals can be found in neo-Kantian culture theory. For a constructive (re-) formulation of a concept of legal cultures cf. exemplary Mohr (1997, 1998, 2001), Mohr and von Villiez (2002) and von Villiez (2004).

3 The following refers exclusively to *A Theory of Justice*. The modification and supplementation of Rawls's conception of justice as fairness undertaken especially in *Political Liberalism*, although of major relevance for his theory as such, do not add anything for the present subject. For a comparison of Smith and Rawls with regard to Smith's 'system of natural liberty', see Buchanan (1976).

4 Particularly Shaftesbury, Francis Hutcheson and David Hume are to be named in this context. For a detailed examination of the development of moral-sense theory from Shaftesbury to Hume see Schrader (1984). In Darwall (1995), Stephen Darwall examines the views of several important authors of the British Enlightenment on the nature of obligation in moral judgments. He distinguishes advocates of an empirical naturalist tradition, like Hume, from those who like Shaftesbury might be understood as predecessors of a notion of moral autonomy, which comes to full development in Kant's practical philosophy. There are good reasons for considering Smith, whom Darwall does not examine in this work, as a connecting link between these latter and Kant.

5 The account of the role of rhetoric, examples and narrative in TMS provided in Griswold (1999, esp. ch. 1) is very interesting in this context.

6 In this sense also Tugendhat (1997: 284; my translation): the 'core of Smith's ethics . . . wholly refers to a universally imperative reference of the own affectivity on to that of others, to an affective openness to others and i.e. to their affections resp. affect capability'.

7 Admittedly, Smith's notion of resentment as well as the interaction between resentment and sympathetic compassion is rather complex. These complexities need not be pursued any further for the present purpose.

8 Smith doesn't clearly separate his remarks regarding the assessment of self-conduct from those regarding the assessment of others. Because he assumes the same mechanism for both cases (similarly TMS Editors' Introduction, 17), a differentiation does not seem compelling for the present purpose. See TMS

III.1.1, 109: 'The principle by which we naturally either approve or disapprove of our own conduct, seems to be altogether the same with that by which we exercise the like judgments concerning the conduct of other people.'

9 In this context, Tugendhat points to a difference between Smith's concept of affective communication and Kantian concepts of consideration like, for instance, Habermas's concept of communicative action. While the latter refers to mutual communication *about* the *interests* of those affected, Smith aims at communication *with* the *affects* of others, aiming not at a balance of interests but rather at harmony of affects (cf. Tugendhat 1997: 295f.). Yet, it seems like the pre-assessment of consequences, which Smith demands, can be read (or at least easily adapted) to cover a concept of (communicative) consideration of interests as well. It is this very inclusiveness which makes Smith such an interesting source for developing a contextual moral theory.

10 Rawls considers his theoretical framework capable of covering a normative theory of individual action in addition to a theory of institutional justice. Thus, '[t]he principles that hold for individuals, just as the principles for institutions, are those that would be acknowledged in the original position' (Rawls 1999: 99). It is unclear whether Smith would, in turn, apply his impartial spectator procedure to institutional justice theory. Yet, as this chapter merely aims at a general comparison of methods for the sake of establishing that TMS can ultimately serve as a resource for a contemporary contextual theory of *morality*, the question does not seem to be of central importance at this point.

11 For a discussion of the impartiality models of Smith, Rawls and Barry with a view to a defense of impartiality as a basic principle of justice theory see Mohr (2003).

12 Smith notes that judgments of *exact propriety* are ultimately accessible only to a divine being. Nevertheless, the 'wise and virtuous man' will always try to approximate the ideal standard (TMS VI.iii.25, 247f.). Interesting in this context: Schliesser on Smith's description of Hume's ability to live up to the divine standard of judgment (Schliesser 2003).

13 As Fleischacker has put it: 'On Smith's general view of moral development, we are awakened to reflecting on our own conduct only by the approval and criticism of others ... We then internalize these external responses' (Fleischacker 1999: 50–1). Yet, this must not be understood as a linear relation, but rather as a constant interaction between the internal and the external, which explains the mutual development of individual and social morality.

14 Smith deals with principles in a chapter on the origin and purpose of general rules. For critical thoughts on the status of principles in TMS see Griswold (1999, esp. ch. 2) and Fleischacker (1999, esp. ch. 3).

15 Rawls' comments on Smith's concept of the impartial spectator in the course of his critique of Hume's judicious spectator. To him, the model of a 'sympathetic spectator' ultimately flows into a utilitarian cost–advantage calculation and is, thus, beset with the same difficulties as utilitarianism (cf. Rawls 1999: ch. 3.30). According to Rawls, the judgment of the impartial spectator will equal the principle of utility. Yet this principle resp. the model of an impartial spectator, so Rawls is only generally acceptable under conditions of a complete *altruism* of human beings (cf. Rawls 1999: 165). Rawls shares the common misconception of Smith's notion of sympathy. For, although in one place he correctly speaks of a 'capacity for sympathetic identification' (Rawls 1999: 163), for the most part he uses the term 'sympathy' in the sense of 'altruism', 'benevolence' or 'love of mankind'. Smith's notion of sympathy, however, cannot without further ado be equated with that of Hume (see also Tugendhat 1997: 285).

16 The alleged *Adam-Smith-Problem* is also owed to this misconception of the notion of sympathy. It essentially rests on the mistaken opinion that Smith

bases his moral philosophy in TMS on a concept of benevolence, and his economic theory, in contrast, on a concept of egoism. The actual terminological content and status of 'sympathy' in Smith's conception has, however, been explained above, and the 'egoism' allegedly carrying his economic theory is better entitled 'rational self-interest' (cf. esp. WN I.ii.2, 26–7). Smith (similar to Shaftesbury) presumes human beings to be characterized by a basic sympathetic disposition as well as a natural striving for self-preservation. See also Raphael and Macfie (1982, I.2.b) and Montes (2003).

17 For a discussion of coherence theory in Rawls cf. Daniels (1979, 1980), Hoerster (1977), Lyons (1975), and Raz (1982, 1992).

18 It is important to note that reflective equilibrium, according to Rawls, is always provisional and subject to further improvement and approximation to the ideal against the background of new evidence. In Smith, just the same, we never quite live up to the ideal standard (cf. TMS VI.iii.23–5, 247–8).

19 Yet in Rawls, moral sentiments do not only play a part in the shape of well-considered judgments. Conceptually basic is also his notion of a *sense of justice*, which he postulates as one of two moral capacities of human beings (cf. Rawls 1999: ch. 8).

20 In this context, Rawls introduces a concept of 'representative persons', which, together with his assumption of a 'chain connection' between their different positions, is to have the effect of making a detailed assessment of positions superfluous when one considers the position of the least advantaged representative person (Rawls 1999: 69–72). This assumption has, however, been widely contested, for it rests on unproven empirical premises. Should the assumption of chain connection prove wrong, a comprehensive role-reversal becomes inevitable. For problems related to Rawls's assumption of chain connection see Koller (1998: 60–1), Barber (1975), Rae (1975), and Sen (1970: 138). Interesting in this context: Barry suggests transfer of the function of chain connection to a principle of solidarity (Barry 1973).

21 Because he aims at a theory of justice, Rawls refers to *principles of justice* as manifest in a society's accepted conceptions. Whereas the impartiality conditions in the original position model the decision on justice principles defining the conduct of institutions – and thus only indirectly the conduct of individuals within these institutions – in Smith, the impartiality procedure immediately yields directives for individual conduct.

22 Also a reformulation of Rawls's 'sense of justice' with view to Smith's notion of resentment might be interesting in this context. For the relation between resentment and justice in Smith cf. Schliesser and Pack (2006).

References

Andree, G. J. (2003) *Sympathie und Unparteilichkeit. Adam Smiths System der natürlichen Moralität*, Paderborn: Mentis.

Barber, B. R. (1975) 'Justifying Justice: Problems of Psychology, Politics and Measurement in Rawls', in N. Daniels (ed.) *Reading Rawls: Critical Studies on Rawls'* A Theory of Justice, Oxford: Blackwell, 292–318.

Barry, B. (1973) *The Liberal Theory of Justice: A Critical Examination of the Principal Doctrines in* A Theory of Justice *by John Rawls*, Oxford: Clarendon Press.

—— (1989) *Theories of Justice*, Berkeley, CA: University of California Press.

—— (1995) *Justice as Impartiality*, Oxford: Clarendon Press.

Buchanan, J. (1976) 'The justice of natural liberty', *Journal of Legal Studies* 76, 5 (1): 1–16.

Daniels, N. (1979) 'Wide Reflective Equilibrium and Theory Acceptance in Ethics', *Journal of Philosophy* 76: 256–82.

—— (1980) 'Reflective Equilibrium and Archimedean Points', *Canadian Journal of Philosophy* 10 (1): 83–103.

Darwall, S. (1995) *The British Moralists and the Internal Ought, 1640–1740*, Cambridge: Cambridge University Press.

Fleischacker, S. (1999) *A Third Concept of Liberty: Judgment and Freedom in Kant and Adam Smith*, Princeton, NJ: Princeton University Press.

Griswold, Ch. (1999) *Adam Smith and the Virtues of the Enlightenment*, Cambridge: Cambridge University Press.

Haakonssen, K. (1981) *The Science of a Legislator: The Natural Jurisprudence of David Hume and Adam Smith*, Cambridge: Cambridge University Press.

Habermas, J. (1994) *Faktizität und Geltung. Beiträge zur Diskurstheorie des Rechts und des demokratischen Rechtsstaats* (4th edn 1998), Frankfurt am Main.: Suhrkamp.

Hoerster, N. (1977) 'John Rawls' Kohärenztheorie der Normenbegründung', in O. Höffe (ed.) *Über John Rawls' Theorie der Gerechtigkeit*, Frankfurt am Main: Suhrkamp.

Koller, Peter (1998) 'Die Grundsätze der Gerechtigkeit', in O. Höffe (ed.) *John Rawls. Eine Theorie der Gerechtigkeit*, Berlin: Akademie Verlag.

Lohmann, G. (2001) 'Unparteilichkeit in der Moral', in L. Wingert and K. Günther (eds) *Die Öffentlichkeit der Vernunft und die Vernunft der Öffentlichkeit. Festschrift für Jürgen Habermas*, Frankfurt am Main: Suhrkamp.

Lyons, D. (1975) 'Nature and Soundness of the Contract and Coherence Arguments', in N. Daniels (ed.) *Reading Rawls: Critical Studies on Rawls*' A Theory of Justice, Oxford: Blackwell.

MacIntyre, A. (1993) 'Ist Patriotismus eine Tugend?' in A. Honneth (ed.) *Kommunitarismus. Eine Debatte über die moralischen Grundlagen moderner Gesellschaften*, Frankfurt am Main: Campus.

Mohr, G. (1997) 'Der Begriff der Rechtskultur als Grundbegriff einer pluralistischen Rechtsphilosophie', in B. Falkenburg and S. Hauser (eds) *Modelldenken in den Wissenschaften*, Hamburg: Meiner (=Dialektik 1997/1).

—— (1998) 'Zum Begriff der Rechtskultur', in W. Goldschmidt (ed.) *Kulturen des Rechts*, Hamburg: Meiner (=Dialektik 1998/3).

—— (2001) 'Rechtskultur', *Information Philosophie* 3 (August): 40–4.

—— (2003) 'Das Prinzip der Unparteilichkeit. Drei Modelle: Moralisch, gesellschaftlich, global', in H. J. Sandkühler and F. Triki (eds) *Der Fremde und die Gerechtigkeit. L'étranger et la justice*, Frankfurt am Main: Peter Lang.

—— and von Villiez, C. (2002) 'Europa zwischen nationaler und globaler Rechtskultur', in R. Elm (ed.) *Europäische Identität. Paradigmen und Methodenfragen, Zentrum für Europäische Integrationsforschung*, Baden-Baden: Nomos.

Montes, L. (2003) '*Das Adam Smith Problem:* Its Origins, the Stages of the Current Debate, and one Implication for our Understanding of Sympathy', *Journal of the History of Economic Thought* 25 (1): 63–90.

—— (2004) *Adam Smith in Context: A Critical Reassessment of some Central Components of his Thought*, Basingstoke: Palgrave Macmillan.

Nagel, Th. (1970) *The Possibility of Altruism*, Princeton, NJ: Princeton University Press.

Rae, D. W. (1975) 'Maximin Justice and an Alternative Principle of General Advantage', *American Political Science Review* 69: 630–47.

Raphael, D. D. and Macfie, A. L. (1982) 'Introduction', in *Adam Smith: The Theory of Moral Sentiments*, Indianapolis, IN: Liberty Fund.

Rawls, J. (1971) *A Theory of Justice*, Cambridge, MA: Harvard University Press, 1999.

—— (1993) *Political Liberalism* (2nd edn 1996), New York: Columbia University Press.

—— (1999) *The Law of Peoples*, Cambridge, MA: Harvard University Press.

Raz, J. (1982) 'The Claims of Reflective Equilibrium', *Inquiry* 25: 307–30.

—— (1992) 'The Relevance of Coherence', *Boston University Law Review* 72: 273–321.

Sandel, M. (1982) *Liberalism and the Limits of Justice*, Cambridge: Cambridge University Press.

Schliesser, E. (2003) 'The Obituary of a Vain Philosopher: Adam Smith's Reflections on Hume's Life', *Hume Studies* 29 (2): 327–62.

—— and Pack, Sp. (2006) 'Adam Smith's "Humean"' Criticism of Hume's Account of Origin of Justice', *Journal for the History of Philosophy* 44 (1): 47–63.

Schrader, W. (1984) *Ethik und Anthropologie in der Englischen Aufklärung. Der Wandel der Moral-sense-theorie von Shaftesbury bis Hume*, Hamburg: Meiner.

Sen, A. (1970) *Collective Choice and Social Welfare*, San Francisco: Holden Day.

Taylor, Ch. (1985) 'Atomism', in *Philosophy and the Human Sciences Philosophical Papers 2*, Cambridge: Cambridge University Press, 187–210.

—— (1988) *Negative Freiheit? Zur Kritik des neuzeitlichen Individualismus*, Frankfurt am Main: Suhrkamp.

Tugendhat, E. (1997) *Vorlesungen über Ethik*, Frankfurt am Main: Suhrkamp.

Von Villiez, C. (2004) 'Cultural Integrity and Human Rights: A Four-level Model of Legal Culture', in H. J. Sandkühler and H. B. Lim (eds) *Transculturality: Epistemology, Ethics, and Politics*, Hamburg: Peter Lang.

7 Applying Adam Smith

A step towards Smithian environmental virtue ethics

Patrick Frierson

> A wealthy eccentric bought a house in a neighborhood I know. The house was surrounded by a beautiful display of grass, plants, and flowers, and it was shaded by a huge old avocado tree. But the grass required cutting, the flowers needed tending, and the man wanted more sun. So he cut the whole lot down and covered the yard with asphalt. After all, it was his property and he was not fond of plants.
>
> (Hill 1983: 98)

I

Largely through the work of J. Baird Callicott, David Hume and Adam Smith are familiar to those seeking to provide a philosophical framework for environmental ethics.[1] In his *In Defense of the Land Ethic*, Callicott traces the philosophical pedigree of the land ethic from Hume and Smith through Darwin to Aldo Leopold. He sees the key philosophical move made by both Hume and Smith as an extension of intrinsic value from narrower to wider circles, so that Hume, for example, 'insisted that things other than oneself (or one's own experiences) may be valued for their own sakes' (Callicott 1989: 85). Leopold and Callicott then extend this trajectory further to include the welfare of nature, or the 'land' (Leopold 1949; Callicott 1989, 1999, 2001). Unfortunately, Callicott's inclusion of Smith in his lineage of the land ethic is misleading because Smith's most fruitful contributions to environmental ethics come not from using his theory to extend 'intrinsic value' to nature, but from an appropriation of Smith to show how an environmental ethic can be philosophically rigorous *without* needing to invoke notions of intrinsic value.[2] This can be done by drawing from Smith's rich and insightful virtue ethic to support specifically environmental virtues.

This chapter began with a story from Thomas Hill's article, 'Ideals of Human Excellence and Preserving the Natural Environment' (Hill 1983), an article which first drew widespread attention to a virtue ethical approach to environmental ethics. Hill remarks that the story, in which a man destroys a garden because he is annoyed at taking care of it and wants more sun,[3] leaves 'even apolitical observers with some degree of moral discomfort' (Hill 1983: 98). Hill asks how to account for this discomfort and rejects approaches that depend on the 'untenable' claim that 'plants have rights or morally relevant interests' (Hill 1983: 100). Instead, he suggests virtue ethics as a better approach to environmental problems. Even if Hill overstates the case against rooting environmental ethics in the intrinsic value of nature,[4] an environmental ethic that defends environmental virtues without entering the murky waters of intrinsic value is valuable, given the unsettled nature of the present debates about what entities have intrinsic value.[5]

Like Hill, Adam Smith can explain what is wrong with environmental degradation without first needing to solve contentious issues about intrinsic value. But Smith goes further than Hill in laying out a philosophical account of the nature of moral evaluation, so Smith avoids some key ambiguities in Hill's account.[6] Like Hill (and any other virtue ethic), a Smithian defense of environmental virtue will depend on psychological claims about which there may be disagreement.[7] Smith provides sufficient detail about the nature of moral evaluation that although Smith himself did not focus on applying his theory to environmental ethics, one can use Smith's account of moral sentiments to defend environmental virtues.

I show how Smith's moral theory can improve on Hill when it is used to defend environmental virtues. In focusing on 'virtues' and in calling Smith's ethic a 'virtue ethic', I am not concerned primarily with specific virtues that Smith discusses, nor even with his account of 'virtue' *per se*.[8] Rather, in discussing Smith's 'virtue ethics', I have in mind Smith's concern with what Hill identifies as a new approach in environmental ethics, a focus on 'what kind of person' one should be (Hill 1983: 101) and what sorts of attitudes towards nature one should have.[9] Adam Smith, like Hill, focuses on the kinds of attitudes that it is proper for human beings to have, and in that sense a Smithian environmental ethic will be a virtue ethic that does not depend upon any particular outcome of discussions about intrinsic value. In part II of this chapter, I lay out the overall contours of that ethic.

After offering a general account of how a Smithian approach to attitudes towards the environment would look, I take up the question of whether a Smithian environmental ethic is fundamentally question-begging. In responding to this challenge, I point out (in section III) the role of 'laws of sympathy' in Smith's account. These regularities of sentiment ensure relative uniformity of ethical evaluation and decision, at least among impartial spectators.

My discussion of these regularities of sentiment in section III might seem to conflict with a true virtue ethic, within which 'we may be able to formulate rules ... but no set of rules will exactly ... anticipate every decision in a new situation' (Schneewind 1990: 43). Thus in section IV, I highlight how Smith's ethics, like many contemporary virtue ethical approaches, encourages sensitivity to particulars of human psychology and ethical situations in a way that differs from many deontological and consequentialist approaches in ethics. Although Smith discusses both general rules and regularities of sentiment, the general rules are ultimately secondary to the considered responses of an impartial spectator to the nuances of moral situations,[10] and the regularities of sentiment are always responsive to particular details. In that sense, Smith's ethics includes a sensitivity to particulars that characterizes a virtue ethic.

Finally, because Smith's ethics depends on the capacity to evaluate and even deliberate as an impartial spectator, one might question whether it is ever possible to be free from sources of partiality. In section V, I take up one example of a particularly pernicious form of partiality – custom – and I show how Smith addresses the 'warping' influence of custom. This provides an opportunity to highlight the distinctive way in which Smith envisions moral progress, and it shows one example of the ethical fruit of Smith's attention to possible problems with his theory. Overall, this chapter provides a taste of the richness of Smith's theory and a beginning to the process of applying that theory to environmental ethics.

II

Smith was a contemporary and friend of David Hume, and Smith's own ethical theory extends some of the insights of Hume's theory. But whereas Smith and Hume are often seen as having nearly identical moral theories, in part because both develop sentimentalist accounts based on sympathy, Smith takes Hume's insights in a very new direction. Thus although sympathy lies at the foundation of Smith's moral theory, it functions in moral evaluation quite differently for Smith than for Hume. For Hume, one sympathizes with the pleasures and pains of others. When a character trait causes pleasure, one feels a sympathetic pleasure and approves of that trait. Thus for Hume, the scope of moral considerability is the scope of sympathy. That is, because one evaluates character traits based on their tendencies to promote pleasure or pain to the person with the trait or to others affected by it,[11] only those with whom one can sympathize are morally considered in deciding the virtue or vice of a character trait. To avoid anthropocentricism, a Humean environmental ethic must show that one can extend sympathy beyond human beings, that one can 'feel the pain' of nature.[12]

Within Smith's moral theory, sympathy functions differently, and this allows Smith to provide an environmental virtue ethic that does *not* depend on the extension of sympathy beyond human beings (cf. Darwall 1998; Otteson 2002; Levy and Peart 2004 For Smith, when we feel sympathy for another 'we place ourselves in his situation . . . and become in some measure the same person with him' (TMS I.i.1.2, 9). By imagining oneself in the place of another, one 'feel[s] something which, though weaker in degree, is not altogether unlike' the feelings of the 'person principally concerned' (TMS I.i.1.2, 9).[14] But for Smith, unlike for Hume, moral evaluation is not a matter of simply approving of pleasant feelings and disapproving of unpleasant ones. Instead, it comes from a distinctive pleasure associated with successfully sympathizing with another fully.[15]

To understand the importance of this distinctive pleasure, it is important to realize that for Smith, the sympathetic union between the spectator's feelings and those of the person principally concerned is seldom complete. There is often a gap between the idea one forms of the sentiments of another and the feelings one acquires sympathetically. Our *idea* of what another feels is usually based on *effects* of the other's feelings, which we know by observing what the other says and does. Smith explains, 'It is, indeed, scarce possible to describe ... internal sentiment or emotion' in any way other than 'by describing the effects which they produce without, the alterations which they occasion in the countenance, in the air and external behavior, the resolutions they suggest, the actions they prompt to' (VII.iv.5, 328–9).[16] In contrast to the *idea* that one forms of the feelings of another, sympathetic feeling is a genuine *feeling*. This feeling is not acquired, as it is for Hume, simply from the idea that one has of the feelings of another.[17] A spectator can know that another is sad without the spectator herself feeling sad. Nor is the feeling acquired by considering what one would feel in the place of another. This consideration can give a conditional judgment about one's feelings, but it does not provide an actual feeling. In the case of bodily passions, for example, one can know that one would feel hungry if one were actually in the situation of another – such hunger might be, as Smith says, 'natural' and 'unavoidable' – but one will still not feel sympathetic hunger because one does not feel that hunger when one *imagines* being the other. One comes to feel something sympathetically by vividly imagining oneself in the place of the other and then *actually responding* to that imagined situation. Normally this response will be a feeling, and this feeling is typically similar to that felt by the object of one's sympathy, but it need not be identical. Usually, in fact, the expressed emotion of the object of sympathy is stronger than what the sympathetic spectator feels. Although it can cause some sympathetic feeling, imagining oneself in the place of another generally does not have the same emotional effect as actually being in that place.

Smith argues, however, that when the gap of sentiment is overcome, when people share the same feelings, there is a distinctive pleasure: 'Nothing pleases us more than to observe in other men a fellow feeling with all the emotions of our own breast' (TMS I.i.2.1, 13). The pleasure of mutual sympathy is, moreover, a mutual pleasure, sought after by both the person principally concerned – the agent or sufferer – and the spectator who sympathizes. Thus both the agent and the spectator seek to modify their own passions to fit those of the other:

> The spectator must . . . endeavour, as much as he can, to put himself in the situation of the other, and to bring home to himself every little circumstance of distress which can possible occur in the sufferer. He must adopt the whole case of his companion with all its minutest incidents; and strive to render as perfect as possible, that imaginary change of situation upon which his sympathy is founded. After all this, however, the emotions of the spectator will still be very apt to fall short of the violence of what is felt by the sufferer. . . . The person principally concerned is sensible of this, and at the same time passionately desires a more complete sympathy. . . . In order to produce this concord, as nature teaches the spectators to assume the circumstances of the person principally concerned, so she teaches this last in some measure to assume those of the spectators.
>
> (TMS I.i.4.6–7, 21–2)

Because complete sympathy brings pleasure, both spectator and person principally concerned seek to bring their sentiments in line with those of the other. The spectator imaginatively enters as fully as possible into the situation of the agent in order to feel the agent's passions more intensely, and the agent moderates her passions to the level with which they can be sympathized.

Smith's moral theory arises out of this process, such that the right or 'proper' pitch of any passion is defined by the mutual compromise between person principally concerned and spectator. In so far as the spectator enters into one's passions, she approves of those passions.

> When the original passions of the person principally concerned are in perfect concord with the sympathetic emotions of the spectator, they necessarily appear to this last just and proper, and suitable to their objects. . . . To approve of the passions of another, therefore, as suitable to their objects, is the same thing as to observe that we entirely sympathize with them.
>
> (TMS I.i.3.1, 16)

On this account of sympathy (unlike Hume's), one can morally approve of passions that are unpleasant, because the basis for moral approval is not the pleasure of the feelings with which one sympathizes but the pleasure of sympathy itself. This also implies, again contrary to Hume, that one can morally approve or disapprove of character traits as 'unsuitable to their objects' independent of any benefit or harm to those objects. A 'proper' sentiment is simply one that can be sympathized with.

For environmental ethics, this account of sympathy implies that a Smithian will not primarily focus on extending sympathy beyond human beings.[18] The extension of sympathy to non-human entities would be important if the only entities that count morally are those with which one can sympathize. But while this is arguably true in the case of Hume, it is not true for Smith. For Smith, the scope of sympathy tracks moral *accountability*, not moral *considerability*. That is, one can hold an entity morally accountable only if one is capable of sympathizing with it, because the way in which one holds others accountable depends upon the degree of concord between their sentiments and one's own sympathetic emotions. Still, one can hold entities such as people morally accountable for actions, even if one cannot sympathize with the entities affected *by* those actions. Thus a Smithian virtue ethic need not engage in the task of showing that nature or non-sentient beings have 'interests' or other attitudes with which an observer would be able to sympathize. Smith can discuss proper attitudes towards nature *directly*, since any attitude towards nature is proper if one can sympathize with it (or improper if one cannot). In this sense, Smith gives a basis for making claims about the virtue or vice of certain attitudes, a basis lacking in Hill's virtue ethical approach.

Thus Smith can address the case of the wealthy eccentric, for example, by showing why the attitudes of that eccentric are improper. The problem with this eccentric is that we cannot sympathize with him. Based on his actions, we conclude that he has little or no affection for his garden. And when we imagine ourselves in his situation, looking out over his garden, we simply cannot enter into this indifference. With great imaginative effort we can sympathize to some degree with his annoyance at needing to take care of the plants in his garden and his desire to have more sun. But we cannot sympathize with these sentiments to the degree that would justify destroying the garden. Thus we rightly deem the eccentric's attitudes to nature to be morally wrong.

With respect to more complex cases, the evaluation is more complex, but its overall structure is the same. One can sympathize with the feelings of loggers seeking to preserve their way of life, and with strip miners seeking to make efficient use of natural resources. In some cases, one may be able to sympathize with these loggers and miners to a degree that will justify actions such as logging and mining, but one will never be able to sympathize with a total disregard for nature. Ultimately, for Smith, moral evaluation is based on the particular details of each situation, and so Smith's theory, as a virtue ethic, gives no fixed rule for settling every case. But his account of the nature of moral evaluation shows that the details that will matter morally are those that influence one's emotional response to imagining oneself in the situations of eccentrics, loggers, and miners. And this provides a non-arbitrary way to engage in ethical reflection.[19]

III

The appeal to sympathy provides Smith with a basis for environmental virtues that need not appeal, as Hill's does, to the role of those virtues in furthering anthropocentric virtues, and that does not directly depend on any appeal to intrinsic values in nature. But one might worry that this appeal to sympathy only works when the sympathizer already shares a concern for the natural world. Although Smith provides an account for how one makes moral judgments, one might think that this amounts to little more than a rigorous intuitionism, and thus that it suffers from the same problems as intuitionism when facing moral disagreement. Thomas Hill's criticism of intuitionism seems to apply to Smith as well. Hill argues, 'those prone to destroy natural environments will doubtless give one answer, and nature lovers will likely give another' (Hill 1983: 101).[20] As applied to Smith, one might argue that there are variations in sentiments that undermine any Smithian defense of environmental virtues. Appeals to sympathy seem particularly problematic precisely 'when an issue is as controversial as the one at hand' (Hill 1983: 101). One might think that anti-environmentalists *will* sympathize with the wealthy eccentric, and thus that Smithian ethics will have little to add, unless it can somehow ground environmental virtues on shared sympathetic reactions about anthropocentric virtues. And in that case, Smith would be little better than Hill.

Smith's responses to the objection that sympathies vary elucidate the insightfulness of his overall approach to ethics. The first response, on which I focus in the rest of this section, is that ethical judgments *will* be more or less uniform, despite various differences between individuals, because of basic laws that govern sympathy. Human nature is simply not as variable as the criticism suggests. People are not generally 'prone to destroy natural environments' for no reason. And even those who destroy natural environments in a particular context – say, loggers who cut old-growth forests – will generally be unsympathetic to the destruction of a garden by our wealthy eccentric. For Smith, 'if everyone were an impartial, knowledgeable, and attentive spectator, then each person would react with the same passion to the same situation' (Heath 1995: 452).

Smith does not simply make this general point, however. He lays out several natural 'laws of sympathy' (Campell 1971: 98), *universal* tendencies that affect the degree of sympathy with various emotions. These are not laws in the strict sense – Smith never uses the term 'law' to describe them – but they do reflect *relatively* consistent generalities of human sympathy. In that sense, Smith's ethic reflects the attentiveness to particularity that should characterize a virtue ethic, but he still recognizes the importance of general, though not exceptionless, laws. To show how these work in a concrete case, I discuss three that are relevant to the way in which people are likely to respond to the wealthy eccentric (for more on laws of sympathy, cf. Campbell 1971; Griswold 1999). The way that these laws apply to the wealthy eccentric is based on the particular details of that case, and one will need to give different arguments for other cases. Many of these will draw on other laws of sympathy than those discussed here. The discussion of this case is given as a sample of the kind of ethical argument that

Smith can make, an example that justifies further study of Smith's laws of sympathy and further application of these to environmental virtues.

The first law that is relevant to the case of the eccentric is that 'our propensity to sympathize with joy is much stronger than our propensity to sympathize with sorrow' (TMS I.iii.1.5, 45, cf. VI.iii.15, 242–3). Moreover, 'we are generally most disposed to sympathize with small joys and great sorrows'; thus small pains are harder to enter into than small pleasures (TMS I.ii.5.1, 40). The pains involved in taking care of a garden are so small that one can hardly enter into them, and the pleasures associated with spending time in a garden are, even if small, particularly easy to enter into. In the WN, in fact, Smith emphasizes the pleasures of 'cultivating the ground', arguing that this activity has 'charms that more or less attract every body' (WN III.i.3, 378).[21] Thus people will find it difficult to sympathize with the wealthy eccentric, and they will therefore deem his attitudes and behavior towards his garden morally improper.

The impropriety of the wealthy eccentric's behavior will be highlighted by a second law of sympathy, that spectators can more easily enter into 'passions which take their origin in the imagination' than those 'which take their origin from the body' (TMS II.ii.1.6, 29; II.ii.1.3, 27). The small joys associated with spending time in the garden are not specifically bodily. One does not sympathize with the physical pleasure of sitting under the avocado tree as much as with the imaginative or aesthetic pleasure of spending time in the garden. And sympathy with the imaginative pleasures of the garden will generally be greater than sympathy with the bodily pains of taking care of it.

A third relevant law of sympathy is that 'passions ... which take their origin from a particular turn or habit ... are ... but little sympathized with' (TMS I.ii.2.1, 31). The wealthy eccentric is eccentric, and passions that are rooted in eccentricity are harder to sympathize with because the spectator cannot easily enter into them. Eccentricity can sometimes be entered into, when it is rooted in aspects of one's upbringing or situation with which a spectator can sympathize. When Aldo Leopold describes how he 'love[s] all trees, but [is] in love with pines' (Leopold 1949: 74), he gives a sufficiently vivid description of the circumstances of this love to induce the reader, at least when reading his book, to sympathize with him. (To feel this, of course, I refer the reader to Leopold's essay 'Ax in Hand' (Leopold 1949: 72–7). I would need to quote most of that essay to generate the proper sympathy with Leopold.) But the wealthy eccentric seems incapable of any equivalent account of his eccentricity, incapable, that is, of describing his situation such that a spectator can sympathetically share his eccentricity.

Of course, there may be factors that would make it easier to sympathize with the wealthy eccentric. He may lack the resources to care for his garden properly (and thus not really be wealthy), or he may have other responsibilities that preclude such care, or it may be particularly painful for him to care for it. All of these factors will affect our sympathy with the eccentric (who may even cease to be eccentric), and thus our moral evaluation. But in all of these cases, our capacity to sympathize will be governed by the laws governing sympathy in general. Thus if the eccentric paves his garden because he lacks the resources to care for it properly and still provide for himself and his children (not the case of our 'wealthy' eccentric), then one will easily enter into the pains of seeing one's children suffer, both because these pains are intense (and hence easier to enter into by the first law above) and because they are largely imaginative rather than bodily (and hence easier to enter into by the second law). This will help one to sympathize with his desire to destroy the garden, and thus make it more morally appropriate. One of the strengths of Smith's theory is that it provides a framework for thinking about how various factors will affect our sympathies, one that requires attending to all the details that can affect one's sympathies without getting so lost in these details that one cannot make any moral assessments at all.

It is important to note here that Smith's criterion for moral evaluation is the sympathy of *spectators*, not the feelings of actors involved in the situation, and for moral judgments that are stable and reliable, these spectators must be 'impartial'.[22] Often moral disagreements arise when those who stand to benefit in various ways are the main interlocutors about the propriety of various policies. Smith is acutely aware of the fact that human interests differ, and that these different interests lead to different attitudes towards situations. Hunters, loggers, biologists, hikers, and environmentalists may have different views about who should get access to a particular natural environment, but these are differences between sentiments of 'persons principally concerned', not differences between *moral* evaluations of *spectators*. And Smith insists that moral judgment strictly speaking involves judging from the standpoint of a true – and hence impartial – *spectator*. From this standpoint psychological laws governing sympathy will override one's contingent interests, and moral judgments will be more or less uniform.

Smith defends his turn to the impartial spectator on two grounds. First, the quest for complete concord between one's own sentiments – as a person principally concerned – and the sentiments of partial spectators will be constantly frustrated. Smith explains this process in detail:

> When we first come into the world, from the natural desire to please, we accustom ourselves to every person we converse with ... and for some time fondly pursue the impossible and absurd project of gaining the good-will and approbation of every body. We are soon taught by experience, that this universal approbation is altogether unattainable.... The fairest and most equitable conduct must frequently obstruct the interests or thwart the inclinations of particular persons, who will seldom have candor enough to ... see that this conduct ... is

> perfectly suitable to our situation. In order to defend ourselves from such partial judgments, we . . . conceive ourselves as acting in the presence of . . . an impartial spectator who considers our conduct with the same indifference with which we regard that of other people.
>
> (III.2.36, 129)[23]

The effort to secure actual praise meets with frustration when actions and attitudes fail to receive the praise that one knows they are due. Thus one learns to discount the judgments of those who decide on purely partial grounds and to evaluate one's own attitudes, and eventually those of others as well, on the basis of the judgments of an impartial – and hence more 'candid and equitable' – spectator. The tendency to turn to an impartial spectator is heightened, for Smith, by humans' natural tendency to seek not only praise – actual concord of sentiments – but praise*worthiness*: 'Nature . . . has endowed [people] not only with a desire of being approved of, but with a desire of being what ought to be approved of, or of being what he himself approves of in other men' (III.2.7; for a discussion of these arguments in the context of Hobbes and Mandeville, cf. Muller 1993: 105ff.)

This shift from mere spectators who give praise to *impartial* spectators who affirm praise*worthiness* has implications for moral evaluation of others as well. For Smith, truly ethical reflection involves a double movement of the imagination. One first seeks to put oneself imaginatively in the place of an impartial spectator, to look at the person principally concerned from a disinterested standpoint. Then, from the perspective of the impartial spectator, one imaginatively enters the position of the person principally concerned. Once this double act of imagination is complete, one responds naturally to the situation in which one imaginatively finds oneself. One judges sentiments to be proper if one feels those sentiments when imagining oneself in the place of an impartial spectator imagining herself in the place of the person principally concerned.

It is important to note here that 'impartial' does not mean purely rational or distant from the concrete particulars of life.[24] In this sense, Smith's impartial spectator is quite different from an 'ideal observer' who is 'dispassionate', even 'in the sense that he is incapable of experiencing emotions of the kind – such emotions as jealousy, self-love, . . . and others which are directed towards particular individuals as such' (Firth 1952: 55). The impartial spectator must be a *sympathetic* spectator, one who enters into the particulars of the situation and responds emotionally to them. As Martha Nussbaum explains, the perspective of impartial spectator

> is a viewpoint rich in feeling. Not only compassion and sympathy, but also fear, grief, anger, hope, and certain types of love are felt by this spectator, as a result of his active, concrete imagining of the circumstances and aims and feelings of others.
>
> (Nussbaum 1990: 338)

Rather than a lack of emotion, the impartiality of the spectator reflects the fact that one's emotional response must be entirely sympathetic, rather than tainted by various particular and purely personal interests. Such impartiality is necessary in order to achieve the 'concord' of sentiments with others that human beings naturally seek.

In addition to being impartial, spectators who hope to make good ethical judgments must be 'well-informed' (III.2.32, 130). Spectators must know all the information that is relevant to properly evaluating the passions of the person principally concerned. This will include detailed particular knowledge about the situation causing those passions, as well as information about the effects of expressing those passions. It will also include knowledge of what the person principally concerned knows. Thus a well informed spectator evaluating the eccentric will need to know that the eccentric's disregard for his garden is likely to disturb the nesting patterns of the birds that live in the garden's trees, but the spectator will also need to know that the eccentric does not realize this.[25] With respect to the capacity to sympathize with the eccentric when imagining oneself in his position, knowledge of the eccentric's state of mind will moderate, though not completely eliminate, the effects of the spectator's knowledge of the effects of the eccentric's attitudes.

Finally, Smithian spectators must be 'attentive' (TMS I.i.1.4, 10). Attentiveness refers to the degree to which the spectator makes use of her knowledge of the situation, the extent to which she actually uses her imagination to enter into the situation of the person principally concerned. Thus it is distinct from being well informed. The clearest case of being well informed but not attentive comes in Smith's discussion of what happens when 'a stranger passes by us in the street with all the marks of the deepest affliction; and we are immediately told that he has just received the news of the death of his father' (I.i.3.4, 17). In this case, Smith suggests, 'it may often happen ... that, so far from entering the violence of his sorrow, we should scarce conceive the first movements of concern upon his account' (I.i.3.4, 17). One might think that the discord of sentiment would be a kind of disapproval, but Smith points out that it need not be. Instead, we can explain the failure to sympathize in terms of a lack of attentiveness. As Smith says, 'we [may] happen to be employed about other things, and do not take time to picture out in our imagination the different circumstances of distress which must occur to him' (I.i.3.4, 18). The problem here is not that we are too partial, nor that we do not *know* the relevant circumstances of distress, but simply that we do not imaginatively attend to those circumstances. We are imaginatively inattentive.[26] But we can still correct our moral judgments, and even our actions, based on what we know we would feel if we were more attentive.

Ethical evaluation, then, comes when an impartial, well informed, and attentive spectator imagines herself in the place of another. When imagining herself in that situation, the spectator will feel various sentiments and begin to adopt certain attitudes. These sentiments and attitudes define what is morally right or 'proper', and in so far as they correspond to those of the person with whom she sympathizes, that person is virtuous.[27] *Environmental* virtues, then, will be those attitudes towards nature with which impartial and attentive spectators can fully sympathize. And while these attitudes will depend largely on the particulars of each situation, they are likely to include such virtues as humility, respect, cherishing, gratitude (or something like it) and aesthetic appreciation (cf. Hill 1983, Cafaro 2001, and Frasz 1993). Environmental vices will be any attitudes towards nature with which a spectator cannot sympathize, and are likely to include indifference, abusive exploitation, domineering attitudes, violence, and ingratitude. Smith provides a framework that offers hope that people with widely different interests can, when they assume the position of impartial spectators, come to agreement about the nature of environmental virtues and vices.

IV

Unfortunately, however, impartiality may be difficult to discern, and people often have hidden interests that affect their sympathies. Moreover, even those who are impartial may be ignorant of information that is relevant to assessing the propriety or justice of various attitudes towards nature. And these people may not only be uninformed but may not even realize that they are uninformed. Finally, even those who ingenuously seek to be impartial may not be sufficiently attentive, or not attentive to the most important details of situations. Thus differences will persist, even among those who ingenuously seek moral agreement.[28] It is hard to imagine approving of the wealthy eccentric, but it is easy to imagine ingenuous anti-environmentalists defending even more drastic forms of environmental degradation, such as clear-cutting old-growth redwoods or allowing greenhouse gases to get out of control. What resources does Smith have for discussions between environmentalists and ingenuous anti-environmentalists?

Unlike deontological and consequentialist approaches to ethical problems, virtue ethicists such as Smith do not provide litmus tests for determining which party to a disagreement should be declared victor. Smith cannot simply call both sides to tally overall pleasure and pain, nor will he be able to show rational inconsistency in those who are ethically wrong. With Hume, Smith would agree that ''tis not contrary to reason to prefer the destruction of the whole world to the scratching of my finger' (*Treatise* 2.3.3.7).[29] Charles Griswold points out that because of his absence of exceptionless rational principles of morality, 'Smith always resists easy descriptions of what [moral improvement] might entail' (Griswold 1999: 214).[30] But the absence of overriding principles for settling disputes does not mean that Smith has nothing to say to those engaged in ethical debates. For one thing, Smith does outline various *virtues* – prudence, generosity, self-command, and justice (TMS VI) – that are relevant to these debates.[31] For another, Smith's resistance to quick solutions to complex disputes comes from his appreciation of the fact that what makes for a successful ethical conversation depends not only on universal facts about human nature – the so-called 'laws of sympathy' – but also on details of the situation being discussed and the histories of the interlocutors. For the case of the wealthy eccentric, relevant details of the situation discussed might include the background and other obligations of the eccentric himself, specifics about the history and health of the plants and animals in the garden, attitudes of neighbors towards the garden, and relevant ecological impacts that the destruction of the garden will have. Relevant details of the interlocutors might include a variety of hidden sources of partiality or blindness, their past experiences with gardens and trees, their scientific backgrounds, and any connections with the eccentric himself.

Despite the limitations imposed by its sensitivity to particulars, Smith's account of moral judgment helps show the kinds of moral conversations that will be required. Part of the discussion between proponents and opponents of environmental virtues would involve helping one's interlocutor be more well informed about and attentive to relevant features of the situation. An environmentalist may need to bring the anti-environmentalist – physically or through words and pictures – to an old-growth forest and a recent clear-cut. The anti-environmentalist may introduce the environmentalist to the loggers whose livelihood depends on logging and show towns decimated by restrictions on logging. Part of the point here is to teach one's interlocutor new facts, to help her be more 'well informed'. But even if one already knows all the relevant facts, new experiences may be needed to give the capacity to enter more attentively *in imagination* into the full context of assessing the proper attitude towards the forest.[32] This attentiveness depends on being able to see nature from a variety of different perspectives and to be aware of features that are ethically relevant but that one might too quickly pass over as one seeks to quantify the value of nature.

The important role of imagination and attentiveness in Smith's ethical theory helps explain the importance of environmental literature and poetry as essential components of a philosophically rigorous environmental ethic (cf. Griswold 1999: 59, 214–15). As philosophers become more attuned to the importance of the emotions and of sensitivity to particulars in ethical life, they emphasize the role of literature. Martha Nussbaum, for example, points out,

> There may be some views of the world and how one should live in it – views, especially, that emphasize the world's surprising variety, its complexity and mysteriousness, its flawed and imperfect beauty – that cannot be fully and adequately stated in the language of conventional

> philosophical prose . . . but only in language and in forms themselves more complex, more allusive, more attentive to particulars.
>
> (Nussbaum 1990: 3)

Although Nussbaum primarily has in mind in this passage the variety, mystery, and beauty of the human social world, her description perfectly fits the nature writing of such authors as Thoreau, Muir, Leopold, Gilbert White, Rachel Carson, Loren Eiseley, Mary Hunter Austin, Annie Dillard, and Wendell Berry. Environmental ethics that focuses on philosophical theorizing about intrinsic value or various 'rights' risks failing to see the important role that environmental literature can play in explaining humans' responsibility to nature. A Smithian environmental virtue ethic, by contrast, will depend on sensitively written literature to explain and expand its claims about the nature of environmental virtues.

Smith is widely recognized as an important precursor to contemporary interest in the intersection between philosophy and literature. Nussbaum herself takes Smith as an example of one who 'attaches considerable importance to literature' (Nussbaum 1990: 339).[33] Charles Griswold has gone further, pointing out that 'plays, novels, and poems, but particularly tragedies . . . completely overshadow [Smith's] relatively rare references to properly philosophical texts' (Griswold 1999: 59). Perhaps more importantly, 'so permeated with examples, stories, literary references and allusions, and images is the *Theory of Moral Sentiments* that at times it presents the character of a novel; narrative and analysis are interwoven throughout' (Griswold 59–60). Even if Griswold may overstate his case here,[34] it is clear that Smith not only recognizes the value of literature as a resource for moral philosophy, but also incorporates literary elements into his own philosophical analysis.

Literature, examples, and stories play three important roles in Smith's ethic, three roles that are particularly well served by environmental literature. First, as Nussbaum frequently emphasizes, literature is uniquely well suited to capture the particulars of situations in a way that addresses one's emotions. Philosophical analysis tends to be abstract, but Smith's ethics depends on attentiveness to particular details. In environmental writing in particular, literature is needed to communicate the intricate beauty of nature, its complexity and mystery. Second, literature is needed to learn to imagine oneself in the place of another. For Smith, ethics is fundamentally an effort of imagination, a response to fully seeing oneself in the place of another. And literature places one in a position to sympathize with characters in that literature. When one feels grief at the end of a tragedy or gets excited at the prospects for a character in a novel, one is more easily able to feel the grief or hopefulness of others in one's life. In this respect, non-fiction environmental literature is particularly powerful, because one learns to sympathize with the real-life authors of such literature, entering into their love of nature in a way that carries directly into one's own life. Finally, reading literature teaches one to assume the stance of spectator in a way that is emotionally engaged but still 'impartial' in Smith's sense. This makes it easier to assume this 'impartial' stance when evaluating one's actions and attitudes.

However, even as literature, conversation, and new experiences make one more attentive to relevant features of a situation, hidden partiality may continue to cloud one's judgment. The logger may feel or at least claim to feel some sympathy with the wealthy eccentric's antipathy to the plants in his garden. This might arise from a vague sense that caring too much about the eccentric's garden could force her to care more about the forests she logs every day. Or it may even come from a defense mechanism needed for her daily life; she needs to disregard the welfare of plants and trees in order to live with herself, and she takes that disregard into her attempt to sympathize with the eccentric. In either case, she evaluates the eccentric from a standpoint that is closer to that of a person principally concerned than that of an impartial spectator. Impartiality can have profound indirect effects. Those engaged in environmentally destructive activities, even if only implicitly, will be less likely to be moved by environmental literature and will thus remain ill informed about and inattentive to ethically important features of nature.

Thus an important part of ethical conversation will involve drawing the attention of one's interlocutor to her partiality, so that she can begin to work through it. In some cases, becoming more aware of partiality will help people actually overcome that partiality and assume a more truly impartial, and thus more properly ethical, perspective. But Smith also emphasizes the importance of being aware of partiality even if one cannot actually change the way one feels, because one can at least change one's moral *judgments* (see TMS I.i.3.3–4, 17). One will not always have the time or ability to reform one's sentiments themselves, and some forms of partiality may simply be impossible to overcome. But one can change one's judgments and even modify the expression of one's sentiments to correspond to what one knows one *would* feel were one truly impartial. And whether they lead to changes in sentiments or simply in moral judgments, conversations that draw attention to hidden sources of partiality can bring about greater agreement about environmental virtues.

In this context, one of the greatest strengths of Smith's moral theory is his sensitivity to the sources of hidden partiality, such as self-deception, vanity, and custom. In the rest of this chapter, I focus on one particularly pernicious source of partiality: custom.[35] Smith's response to the problem of custom helps address concerns about relativism in Smith and will provide the opportunity to show how Smith's account of moral progress differs from at least some other approaches (especially those of Callicott and Leopold) in contemporary environmental ethics.

V

Smith claims that the way people are raised, the company one keeps, and the overall attitudes of one's culture all have effects on one's moral sentiments. Smith describes 'custom' as a 'principle ... which ha[s] a considerable influence upon the moral sentiments of mankind, and [is] the chief cause ... of the many irregular and discordant opinions which prevail in different ages and nations concerning what is blamable or praise-worthy' (TMS V.1.1, 194; cf. V.2.2, 200–1). Within societies, custom can have dramatic effects on one's attitudes towards virtue and vice. And across different societies, 'the different situations of different ages and countries are apt ... to give different characters to the generality of those who live in them, and their sentiments concerning the particular degree of each quality ... vary according to that degree which is usual in their country' (V.2.7, 204). All of these influences of custom reflect a potentially hidden partiality that should be uncovered and overcome.[36]

Fortunately, the effects of custom are limited: 'the sentiments of moral approbation and disapprobation are founded on the strongest and most vigorous passions of human nature; and though they may be somewhat warpt, cannot be entirely perverted' (TMS V.2.1, 200). In particular, the differences introduced by custom affect *degrees* of approval more than which traits will be approved (V.2.13, 209). In the context of environmental ethics, this diagnosis seems particularly apt. There are few whose moral sentiments are so perverted that they do not recognize *something* wrong with a wealthy eccentric who paves his garden. But those accustomed to environmental destruction may prefer the virtues of frugality and industry in the eccentric efficiently saving the time and resources of maintaining a garden. The case of the wealthy eccentric is extreme, of course, in part because it can seem like a stretch to say that the 'duties' of frugality and industry here really encroach on the important virtues of cherishing natural beauty. But the conflicts between virtues can play particularly large roles in precisely the debates that most occupy environmentalists, debates where what is at stake are trade-offs of goods or even trade-offs of relevant virtues – compassion towards human beings and respect for nature, for example.

Moreover, Smith suggests that when it comes to particular kinds of *action*, custom can have a more profound influence on moral evaluation than it can in the case of moral evaluation of character traits (V.2.14, 209). Smith's main example of such 'wide departure' from good morals is infanticide, approved of by 'almost all the states of Greece, even among the polite and civilized Athenians' (V.2.15, 210),[37] and several aspects of Smith's discussion of infanticide are instructive for environmental ethics.

First, the *scope* of example is extreme. Smith's comments about the limited capacity of custom to 'warp' moral sentiments imply only that 'custom should never pervert our sentiments with regard to *the general* style and character of conduct' (V.2.16, 211). In particular cases, custom can *dramatically* warp moral sentiments. In the environmental arena, this suggests that it will be helpful to discuss environmental virtues, on which there will be more agreement, before getting to specific practices. Difficult conversations about practices will be more fruitful when preceded by easier discussions about virtues.

Second, the *proximate cause* of this perversion of moral sentiment is important for identifying such perversions in one's own moral evaluations. As Smith explains, 'the uniform continuance of the custom had hindered [people] from perceiving [infanticide's] enormity' (V.2.15, 210). When people engage in a practice for a long time, they are more likely to be morally blinded. Importantly, the barbarity of the practice is one that societies themselves could and should have censured, *if* they had adopted a truly impartial standpoint. Smith emphasizes that the 'helplessness' and natural 'amiableness' of infants '*call forth* the compassion, even of an enemy', and the efforts of philosophers to defend infanticide forced them into increasingly 'far-fetched considerations' (V.2.15, 210, emphasis added). An environmentally relevant example of such a custom may be 'familiarity' with eating animals (cf. Singer 1990). Our culture packages those animals – both literally in supermarkets and linguistically as 'beef' rather than 'cow' – to distract imaginative and emotive attention from uncomfortable facts about what one is doing. Such a long-standing custom of eating other animals is likely to make us approve of the practice even when it is a 'barbarous prerogative' (V.2.15, 210). Of course, the fact that eating meat is an established custom does not settle the debate about whether eating meat is naturally barbarous or not. It may be that humans have a custom of eating meat precisely *because* there is nothing morally repulsive about that practice. In fact, Smith insists that custom can 'never pervert our sentiments with regard to the general style and character of conduct' because 'no society could subsist' in which this were the case (V.2.16, 211). But this does not take away from the fact that custom *can* conceal the injustice of virtually any single practice (V.2.15, 210). The fact that one is part of a culture with a long history of meat eating suggests a source of partiality to which we should be particularly attentive, though it does not in itself decide regarding the propriety of the practice.

Third, the *initial cause* of the ancients' approval of infanticide can be explained naturally. Smith explains that 'the extreme indigence of a savage is often such that he . . . dies of pure want, and it is frequently impossible for him to support both himself and his child' (V.2.15, 210). This explanation is important for showing that the custom of infanticide is a cause of its moral approval, not vice versa. There are many practices that are customary, such as parents caring for their children or victims seeking some sort of retaliation for harm done to them. These practices are customary in part *because* they are proper, so custom alone cannot constitute a reason (not even a *prima facie* reason) to reject a practice. But by explaining the origin of infanticide, Smith shows how a practice that may initially have been engaged in with ambivalence – because necessary but repugnant – could eventually pervert one's moral sense.[38] Without such an explanation, there would be no way to make sense of the ancients' *initial* approval of infanticide other than to say that they have a fundamentally different moral sense. Similarly in the case of eating meat, a plausible story about why people would initially have eaten meat despite the repugnance of killing animals – say, because there were no vegetarian ways to get sufficient calories and nutrition – can help one defend the claim that a natural condemnation of meat eating is obscured by custom. And Smith even suggests that there is a natural basis for not wanting to kill animals, claiming that 'Nature has ... implanted in man' a 'fellow-feeling' and even 'some degree of respect' for 'all ... animals' ('Of the External Senses', ¶7).[39]

The previous points all suggest that when confronting someone – including oneself – whose sentiments are perverted by custom, one should point out proximate causes of such perversion as a way of highlighting the possible influence of custom, as well as the initial cause, to show that the original basis of the custom no longer applies and should no longer affect our judgments. But all of these attentions to the perverting influence of custom are merely means of promoting a more impartial stance. The final judgment must be based on a person's natural sympathies, 'what *naturally* ought to be the sentiments of' an impartial spectator (II.2.25, emphasis added). These natural sentiments are not, of course, the raw and partial sentiments of a person principally concerned, but the reflective and educated sentiments of an impartial spectator. But even impartial spectators imagine themselves in the place of another and respond naturally, though not partially, to being in that position.[40] This suggests that the way in which moral progress will take place will not be through an evolution of moral sentiments in the traditional sense. For Smith, the problem raised by custom is that moral sentiments are perverted or impeded from functioning as they naturally would. Thus the primary task for those seeking to cultivate environmental virtues is not to generate *new* moral sentiments but to clear away the corrupting influences of custom to reveal natural moral sentiments that have been impeded.[41]

VI

Indifference towards environmental problems is among the most important ethical crises facing the world today. Ecologists, nature writers, and environmentalists have all made valuable contributions to reflecting on the proper relationship between human beings and the nature on which we depend. Philosophers have also played an important role, especially in explaining and defending core claims and concepts underlying better attitudes towards nature. But environmental ethics has remained too narrowly focused, and the resources of the history of ethics have not been sufficiently brought to bear on reflections about nature. Meanwhile, studies in ethics and the history of ethics have generally ignored ethical issues related to the environment in particular. Early modern ethics in particular has often suffered from its association with metaphysical views about the differences between humans and nature and from the fact that early modern moral philosophers themselves generally did not apply ethics to environmental issues. But the history of ethics in general, and Adam Smith in particular, can help open new approaches within environmental ethics. Although many of these thinkers did not focus on human relationships with nature, their careful ethical reflection can be fruitfully extend to deal with the greatest ethical issues – including environmental issues – faced today.

Specifically, Adam Smith develops an ethic that can helpfully be applied to discussing environmental virtues. Like Thomas Hill's environmental virtue ethics, Smith does not depend on controversial notions such as intrinsic value or the interests of nature. But unlike Hill, Smith is able to explain the propriety and moral importance of specifically environmental attitudes, without appealing to the role that these attitudes play in cultivating other more human-centered virtues. He can do this by showing how sympathy provides a rigorous but flexible standard for determining the moral appropriateness of an attitude.

The full strength of a Smithian approach to environmental ethics, however, comes in the details. Like other virtue-based ethical theories, Smith's ethics is sensitive to details in a way that precludes sweeping claims about environmental problems, but his specific suggestions for dealing with challenges that his virtue ethics faces are particularly well suited for responding to the kinds of problems that arise in contemporary environmental debates. Conversations about the proper attitudes towards nature can benefit from Smith's attention to the role of literature, the danger of custom, and the importance of rules grounded in particular cases.

There is, of course, considerably more to be done to develop a full Smithian environmental ethic. The account offered here is at best incomplete. I have left numerous details to be filled in, and several contentious issues unresolved. Moreover, Smithian ethics depends essentially on conversations in which partiality is uncovered and remediated and in which details play a large role. There is a certain amount of risk to doing environmental ethics from a Smithian perspective; it may turn out that love of nature will be difficult to sympathize with and wanton destruction of it may turn out to be proper in the end. Or it may turn out that Smith is wrong about his optimistic hope that human beings are capable of reaching unity of sympathy when we strip away partiality. Both of these cases seem to me unlikely, but they are potential dangers of a Smithian approach.

This chapter offered an initial taste of how the overall framework of Smith's moral theory can be applied to environmental ethics. With its sensitivity to details, its awareness of problems that generate ethical disagreement, and its hopeful accounts of the laws of human psychology that make agreement possible, Smith's theory is one that is particularly well suited to the complex environmental problems we face today. My treatment of his theory here points the way to areas for further research and provides a basis for hope that a fuller exploration of Smith's philosophy in the light of recent environmental ethics will provide a richer understanding of both Smith's ethics and the environmental problems to which it is applied.

Notes

1 Callicott's use of Hume has not been uncontested. For some critiques of Callicott's use of Hume, see Lo (2001a and b) and Varner (1998). For other attempts to use Hume to develop an environmental ethic, see Carter (2000) and Boomer (2004).

2 The reason for this is not, as Callicott has suggested (Callicott 1999: 209), because Smith is a poorer resource for environmental philosophy than Hume and Darwin; he is a better one.

3 Here, I take Hill's brief account of this case at face value. Given the arguments presented in this chapter, of course, this brief account is not wholly sufficient for moral evaluation. Smith's arguments depend on details of the case, and Hill's unsympathetic approach to the eccentric is probably unfair in various respects. Still, for the purposes of this chapter, his account will serve as a useful, even if overly simple, example.

4 The debate between defenders and opponents of extending rights to ecological wholes is among the most developed in contemporary environmental ethics literature. For some examples of defenders, see Leopold (1949), Stone (1974), Goodpaster (1979), Callicott (1989, 1999), and Naess (1973). For some opponents, see Singer (1975), Taylor (1989), and Varner (1998).

5 Katie McShane has put the advantage of this approach well: 'The environmental ethics literature is filled with attempts to run all of these lines of [metaethical] argument. But ... [a] book [that] has nothing at all to say about [such] conflicts ... surely ... is an asset. The debates about biocentrism and ecocentrism are well-worn at this point' (McShane 2003b). I do think that Smith's approach offers a way to think about intrinsic value that will move that discussion forward in productive ways (see my 'Adam Smith and Intrinsic Value', unpublished manuscript), and discussions of intrinsic value in nature have yielded philosophical and practical fruit in environmental ethics. The approach outlined here, however, is an alternative to those discussions.

6 Hill provides no overarching theory of virtue. Rather than working from a clear account of what makes something a virtue and showing that certain attitudes towards nature are virtues on that account, Hill defends the importance of various environmental attitudes on the basis of their connection with virtues that an 'anti-environmentalist' – Hill's term – will endorse. As Hill explains, 'though indifference to nature does not *necessarily* reflect the absence of virtues, it often signals the absence of certain traits which we want to encourage because they are, in most cases, a natural basis for the development of certain virtues' (Hill 1983: 102). For example, 'it may be that, given the sort of beings we are, we would never learn humility before persons without developing the general capacity to cherish ... many things [including nature] for their own

sakes'(Hill 1983: 105–6). Unfortunately, this argument ties the value of environmental virtues to their contingent connection with specifically human-centered character traits. Hill does not sufficiently defend the value of environmental virtues in their own right.

7 Elizabeth Anscombe, whose 'Modern Moral Philosophy' is often regarded as the origin of contemporary interest in virtue ethics, famously insisted that 'it is not profitable . . . to do moral philosophy . . . until we have an adequate . . . psychology' (Anscombe 1956: 26). Although Anscombe and Smith would disagree about the precise psychology that underlies good moral philosophy, Smith's ethics reflects his deep appreciation of the need to get one's psychology right before doing moral philosophy. In that sense, Smith shares with virtue ethics a concern with psychology as an important component of moral philosophy. And of course, that leaves Smith open to criticism on psychological grounds (see e.g. Darwall 1998), and these psychological issues may turn out to be just as much of a morass as the meta-ethical issues related to intrinsic value.

8 Thus there is considerably more work to be done to fully lay out a Smithian virtue ethic and apply that ethic to environmental issues. Smith develops a detailed account of specific human virtues, focusing his account on prudence, benevolence, self-command, and justice. Moreover, Smith carefully distinguishes between virtue in the strict sense and what he calls 'propriety', the moral category that will be the primary focus of this chapter (I.i.5.7, 25). (Briefly, the distinction is that propriety is conformity of one's attitudes to what they should be, whereas virtue includes a consideration of how far from the norm one's actions or attitudes are. Smith points out, for example, that 'to eat when we are hungry is certainly, upon ordinary occasions, perfectly right and proper, . . . [but] nothing can be more absurd that to say it was virtuous', whereas by contrast 'there may frequently be . . . virtue in . . . actions which fall short of the most perfect propriety because they may still approach nearer to perfection than could well be expected' (I.i.5–6, 25).) Both of these specifically virtue-oriented aspects of Smith's theory are relevant to environmental ethics, and both are important for Smith's overall theory. For the purposes of this chapter, however, I have chosen to focus on two other distinctive features of Smith's account – his emphasis on evaluating *attitudes* rather than deciding on intrinsic value or looking at actions or states of affairs, and the focus on rich description and concrete particulars that goes with his account of moral life.

9 For Hill, the relevant contrast here is between environmental virtue ethics and environmental ethics that depends on claims about intrinsic value. A similar point can be made about the contrast between virtue ethics and deontological and consequentialist approaches to ethics more generally. Unlike those approaches, virtue ethics focuses on issues of character, attitudes, and emotions rather than the rightness or wrongness of actions (deontology) or the goodness of states of affairs (consequentialism). Cf. Darwall (2003: 3), Crisp and Slote (1997), Slote (1992), and Hursthouse (1999).

10 Although I have a detailed discussion of 'laws of sympathy' in Smith in section III, I have cut my discussion of Smith's account of general rules for the sake of length. Smith introduces general rules as a way of dealing with the problem of self-deception. Although these rules play an important part in his ethics and reflect a quasi-deontological stance in ethics, they are ultimately derivative of particular responses to particular situations (cf. III.iv.8–10, 159–60).

11 Hume says to be 'useful or agreeable to the person himself or to others' (*Treatise* IX.i.1). Hume's account is a bit more complicated in the *Treatise*, primarily because of his emphasis there on artificial virtues, which do not fit this account of sympathy as neatly. For more, see Boomer.

12 Hume does extend sympathy beyond human beings, claiming that we 'observe

the force of sympathy thro' the whole animal creation and the easy communication of sentiments from one thinking being [which in the context clearly includes animals] to another' (*Treatise*, II.ii.5.15) and that 'sympathy ... takes place among animals no less than among men' (II.ii.12.6). Hume does not go beyond sentient beings, however. (For a discussion of whether Hume's account of patriotism commits him to concern for wholes, see Callicott 1989: 75–100 and Varner 1998: 12–16.)

13 Thus Callicott is wrong to claim that because 'the sentiment of sympathy [is] so central to it' Smith cannot provide for 'ethical holism' (Callicott 1999: 209). The argument against holism in Smith might work given the role of sympathy in *Hume's* theory, but the role of sympathy in Smith's account does not preclude ethical holism, as the rest of this section will show.

14 TMS I.i.1.2, 9. 'Person principally concerned' is Smith's term for the person with whom one sympathizes (see e.g. I.i.3.1, 13). This way of describing the object of sympathy is neutral between agents and those who passively respond to situations. For Smith, both action-guiding passions and mere responses to situations are susceptible to moral evaluation. This has important implications for environmental ethics in that the scope of environmental virtues will extend beyond those that guide actions. Feeling the right way about nature is a virtue, even if such feelings are volitionally inert.

15 Smith and Hume are explicit about this difference between their accounts. (See TMS I.iii.1.9, footnote, and related notes in the Glasgow/Liberty Fund Edition, 46.) Cf. too Raynor (1984) for an examination of this difference. Raynor sees Hume's criticisms of Smith as having more merit than I do, but a full discussion of the differences between Smith and Hume on this point is beyond the scope of this chapter.

16 Cf. too II.i.5.11, 78; I.i.3.1, 16–17; III.1.3, 110; Heath (1995: 452–3), and Campbell (1971: 97). The fact that one gets an idea of what another feels largely from the expression of that feeling is important for Smith's overall moral theory, and it helps explain why Smith's discussion of moderating one's passions often focuses on the *expressions* of those passions. However, this fact can be obscured by the way that Smith introduces his discussion of sympathy, where Smith claims that 'as we have no immediate experience of what other men feel, we can form no idea of the manner in which they are affected, but by conceiving what we ourselves should feel in the like situation' (TMS I.i.1.2, 9). As a means of introducing sympathy, this approach is quite effective, but it proves confusing when Smith discusses the comparison of one's sympathetic feeling with the actual feelings of another. Fortunately, in the passages referenced above, Smith clears up the confusion by admitting that the expression of emotion provides some basis for inferring the actual feelings of another.

17 Admittedly, this account of Hume is somewhat simplified for the purposes of comparison with Smith. Although this account fits some of Hume's descriptions of sympathy in the *Treatise* well (see e.g. 2.i.9, 318–20), there are other passages in the *Treatise* (e.g. 3.3.1, 576) that seem to allow for different mechanisms of sympathy, and the EPM account can be read as quite different from the one I have presented here.

18 In 'Adam Smith and the Possibility of Sympathy with Nature' (forthcoming in *Pacific Philosophical Quarterly*), I show that Smith *can* extend sympathy beyond human (and even sentient) beings, but my focus here is on the contribution that Smith can make to environmental ethics even *without* this extension.

19 Incidentally, this also provides a helpful way to think about Sylvan's 'last man' argument (see Routley 1973 and Routley and Routley 1980). In that argument, Richard Routley (now Sylvan) imagines the case of the last human being alive, whose last act is to destroy a forest. The thought experiment is generally used

to show that without some account of the non-instrumental value of the forest we cannot explain what is wrong with this action. On a Smithian account, however, we would explain the wrongness of this action by our inability to sympathize with such a last man. Of course, this depends on giving a richer account of the circumstances of that last man than Routley offers. If his desire to destroy the forest was due to the fact that the forest had (somehow) been responsible for destroying the human race, then it would be easier to sympathize with his resentment, though it is arguable whether this would justify destroying the forest. But a random and callous act of destruction would be difficult if not impossible for an impartial spectator to sympathize with, given the nature of human sympathy. And thus, for Smith, the last man's destruction of the forest would be morally improper. (I thank an anonymous commentator for recommending that I include some discussion of this case in this chapter. I regret that space prevents me from offering a fuller Smithian account of various 'last man' scenarios.)

20 This objection is similar to a more general objection to Smith's moral theory, that it depends on importing into the sympathetic spectator the very moral norms that Smith seeks to get out of him. See Campbell (1971: 119ff.) for a detailed explanation of and response to this more general problem in Smith.

21 I thank Eric Schliesser for drawing my attention to this important passage.

22 There are degrees of impartiality here, and similar degrees of stability and reliability. Judgments based on custom can be *relatively* impartial in that they depend upon communal rather than purely individual forms of partiality, and they can thus be *relatively* stable. The case of infanticide discussed later is a clear example of just how stable these ultimately partial moral judgments can be.

23 This passage is not in the first or last editions of TMS. For details about its inclusion, see the footnote in TMS, 128–9.

24 Impartiality may be the most widely discussed issue in Smith's ethics, so the relevant secondary literature is vast. For two insightful accounts, see Griswold (1999) and Campbell (1971). My contrast of Smith's impartial spectator with Firth's 'ideal observer' largely follows Griswold's account, though I take Smith's impartial spectator to be closer to the ideal observer than Griswold does. In particular, on my reading the impartial spectator is primarily an imaginative construct, though many actual spectators will respond impartially.

25 Some might think that for Smith one would need to know about a situation only what the person principally concerned knows. After all, if one is trying to imagine oneself in that person's situation, any knowledge beyond knowledge that is known by the person principally concerned might be thought to interfere with one's sympathetic imagination. In a sense, this is correct. Knowing details that the person principally concerned does not know *is* likely to inhibit one's sympathy with that person, since the spectator cannot fully ignore what she knows, even if she knows that the agent does not know it. But Smith thinks that this limitation on sympathy is appropriate. Smith's clearest admission that the spectator takes into account information of which the agent is unaware or to which the agent is inattentive comes in his discussion of unsocial passions, where the welfare of others affected by the agent affect the spectator's judgment. In his account of the influence of fortune (II.iii), it is clear that this effect on the spectator applies even when the agent is unaware of or not focused on the effects of his actions on others.

26 Incidentally, Smith points out in this context that this inattentiveness can be present 'without any defect of humanity on our part' (TMS I.i.3.4, 17). This suggests that one need not always assume the role of an attentive (or for that matter of an impartial and well informed) spectator. Such careful sympathetic

imagining takes effort and often will simply not be worth the time. Part of living a virtuous life is knowing which issues call for detailed moral consideration and which can simply be passed by in the business of life. And that will apply to environmental cases as well. One need not always carefully think through every attitude towards nature. It is enough to reflect periodically on one's relationship with nature and to think particularly carefully about attitudes that are particularly significant. Given the current environmental crises that the world faces, however, attitudes towards nature demand more attention than people often give them.

27 This account is simplified in that it ignores the distinction between virtue and propriety.

28 Here it is important that Smith is not trying to come up with an ethical theory that can coerce the most resistant opponent to change her mind. Often environmental philosophers assume that those who disagree are stubbornly fixed to speciesist positions that environmental philosophy must somehow break through. Hill's description of the 'anti-environmentalist' (Hill 1983: 103) is typical in this respect. Smith has very little to say, however, to a truly stubborn antagonist. (He might adopt Hume's strategy from the introduction to the *Enquiry*: 'The only way ... of converting an antagonist of this kind, is to leave him to himself. For, finding that nobody keeps up the controversy with him, it is probable he will, at last, of himself, from mere weariness, come over to the side of common sense and reason.') For Smith 'nothing pleases us more than to observe in other men a fellow-feeling with all the emotions of our own breast' (TMS I.i.2.1, 13). Thus there is a natural impulse to seek congruence of sentiment with others, and when this impulse is overcome, there is no reason to believe that ethical arguments of any kind will have any effect. (Simon Blackburn has pointed out in his development of a Humean–Smithian ethic, the futility of these kinds of attempts to 'prove to the annoying character that he is thinking contrary to reason', Blackburn 1998: 215. See his discussion for more on the dangers of making such attempts.)

29 Smith would agree with this, of course, only if he were to use the term 'reason' in Hume's sense. In fact, Smith sometimes conflates the term 'reason' with 'principle, conscience, the inhabitant of the breast' (III.3.4, 137). In *this* sense of reason, neither Hume nor Smith would take preferring the destruction of the world to be 'reasonable'. I thank Eric Schliesser for encouraging me to be clearer about this point. For a much more detailed examination of Smith as developing an account of practical 'reason', see Carrasco (2004). I disagree with Carrasco's emphasis on reason in that essay, but even in her discussion she admits that in the 'account of practical reason which I [Carrasco] am taking as a reference, perception is constitutive of practical reason and it may occur via emotions' (Carrasco 2004: 88). In so far as Carrasco is admitting the possibility of a practical 'reason' that is just a refined and impartial kind of sentiment, she and I agree.

30 Griswold includes detailed descriptions of the kinds of ethical conversation that Smith will encourage and specific illustrations of these, such as Smith's account of slavery.

31 As noted earlier in note 8, the present chapter does not focus on these virtues, though they are an important element of Smith's overall theory, and one with implications for environmental ethics (I discuss the virtues of benevolence and justice in relation to the environment in 'Adam Smith and the Possibility of Sympathy with Nature', forthcoming in *Pacific Philosophical Quarterly*).

32 It is worth pointing out here that, like Hill, Smith does not limit his focus to the morality of *actions* specifically. Smith's focus is on the *attitudes* that it is proper to take towards nature, and actions become relevant as expressions of these attitudes.

33 She ultimately takes issue with a particular claim of his – that we do not sympathize with romantic love – on the basis of her reading of *David Copperfield*. I refer the reader to Nussbaum (1990) as an example of how philosophically rigorous debate can be furthered by reference to literature, and to chapter 14 in particular as a use of such debate to challenge Smith in several important respects.

34 Smith does, after all, devote a whole section of the TMS to discussing the relationship between his views and those of his *philosophical* predecessors (TMS VII), and the TMS includes more implicit allusions to philosophical texts than Smith's explicit references might suggest.

35 Smith's treatments of self-deception and vanity also have implications for environmental ethics, but I have cut discussions of those for the sake of brevity.

36 Some have argued that the role of custom in ethical evaluation is a fact of ethical life, one that Smith was willing to accept. Alan Gibbard, for example, claims that 'If Smith's ... story supports his detached observer theory, it supports the theory in a relativized form. The proper feelings for a person, Smith must say, are those of a detached observer who belongs to that person's own culture. The feelings people have, after all, depend greatly on their acculturation' (Gibbard 1990: 280). There seems to be some merit to this claim. If the impartial spectator is developed in response to the failure to elicit praise from the partial spectators one faces in daily life (as explained in section III, above), it might seem reasonable to think that the impartial spectator will share the general cultural traits of those whose praise one initially sought. And as a psychological fact, this is no doubt true, at least to a point. Custom will influence the moral judgments that people make, even when those people *think* that they are assuming the role of impartial spectators. As Charles Griswold points out, 'for most people, most of the time, the conception of the virtues and their relative is shaped by convention (V.2.7)' (Griswold 1999: 351). But Smith does not claim that this psychological fact about moral evaluators applies to the impartial spectator itself. Griswold rightly insists, '[Smith] never suggests that we are so fully governed by convention or history that we cannot accurately or impartially understand [or evaluate] ... temporally distant philosophies. ... The possibility of critical moral reflection is reiterated even in the section of the *Theory of Moral Sentiments* on custom (V.2.5); the reactions of the impartial spectator continue to serve as the standard (cf. V.2.13)' (Griswold 1999: 350–1). Smith's treatment of both other cultures and his own shows Smith's willingness to apply moral categories to criticize opinions that are accepted on the basis of cultural norms. And Smith explains how custom can be 'destructive of good morals' (V.2.14, 209), which makes sense only if the standard for good morals is not itself based on custom. Moreover, Smith's twofold argument for the impartial spectator – based on the innate desire for praise*worthiness* and on the contingency of praise from partial spectators – provides good reasons to move beyond merely culture-bound moral norms towards an inter-culturally impartial spectator. Once one seeks praise not from actual peers in one's society but from a spectator who captures 'what *naturally* ought to be the sentiments of other people with regard to our character and behaviour' (III.2.25), there is no reason to limit this imaginative construction by one's own culture. Thus Maria Carrasco has rightly emphasized that 'the impartial spectator ... might err ... when the standard he internalized, though approved by most of the people in that society, is actually mistaken' (Carrasco 2004: 106). While I disagree with Carrasco about the process of correcting these mistakes, she is certainly correct that internalizing customary norms of one's society is a form of partiality from which the impartial spectator must free herself.

37 TMS V.2.15, 210. Importantly, Smith adds that it was approved even by 'the

doctrine of [ancient] philosophers, which ought to have been more just and accurate'. Smith was acutely aware of the fact that philosophers are often behind the times when it comes to moral progress.

38 Smith's language in describing the case suggests that the parent has ambivalence here. He describes that case in which 'it is frequently impossible for him to support both himself and his child' and he asks movingly, 'what then should we imagine must be the heart of a parent who could injure that weakness which even a furious enemy is afraid to violate?' (V.2.15, 210). But Smith does not explicitly say that there is any ambivalence here, and in the case of eating meat, the evidence for ambivalence is even weaker. Still, it is reasonable that, in at least some cases, people engage in activities with ambivalence, and become so accustomed to the activity that the ambivalence gradually fades. Reading Smith's account of infanticide in this light is particularly plausible and helps one see the way in which Smith attributes the earliest cases of infanticide not to a morally depraved 'savage barbarity' but to an 'excusable' necessity (V.2.15, 210).

39 I thank Eric Schliesser for drawing this passage to my attention. It is important to note in this context that neither Smith nor this reconstruction of Smith depends on claiming that there was a point in the past at which human beings were vegetarians. In his lectures on Jurisprudence, Smith outlines 'four distinct states which man passes through', of which the first is 'the Age of Hunters' (LJ (A) i.27, 14, cf. too WN V.i, 689–90). Because the hunting and killing of animals is the primary 'means of sustenance' (LJ i.27, 14) for human beings at this (and the next) stage of human history, the respect for animals that is implanted in humans by 'Nature' (External Senses, ¶7, 136) is overridden by necessity. It is only late in human development that our respect for animals could lead human beings to refrain from killing them, but by those late stages the custom of eating meat has the potential to counteract this natural respect.

40 My account here differs in language, though only partially in principle, from that of Carrasco (2004). Carrasco claims that 'it is clear that Smith does not believe that our notions of moral good and evil arise from our brute or natural sentiments' (Carrasco 2004: 87). But, as the context of this quotation makes clear, what Carrasco means by natural sentiments are sentiments that are not 'informed by the impartial spectator' (Carrasco 2004: 87). In that sense, I agree. Moral sentiments are not the partial sentiments that we might be said to have 'naturally' in response to a situation in which we are a person principally concerned. But 'natural sentiments', as I use the term, are natural in the sense that they are not shaped by custom or even education, except in so far as the latter makes one impartial. Smith may use the term 'natural sentiments' occasionally to refer to sentiments that are unsuitable for moral evaluation (see II.ii.3.10, 90), although this case is debatable. But Smith's predominant use of the term is to refer to natural *but impartial* sentiments (for a few examples, see II.ii.3.13, 91 (ed. 1–5); II.iii.2.8–9, 103; III.2.9, 119; III.4.7, 159; III.5.9–10, 167–8; III.6.12, 176). Even in these cases, however, Carrasco is correct to distinguish these impartial natural sentiments from those sentiments that proceed from our partiality – which is 'natural' in a different sense – or from custom.

41 This account of the progress of morals is notably different from those of Leopold, Callicott, and their philosophical predecessors Darwin and Hume. For Darwin, human moral sentiments literally evolve to become more holistic because this is evolutionarily advantageous. For Hume, Leopold, and Callicott, the sentiments evolve as well, though these thinkers more clearly explain that the evolution is social and cultural rather than biological (cf. Callicott 2001: 211). But for Smith, moral sentiments do not need to evolve to meet changing situations, and it is unlikely that they even *could* evolve in this way. What is required is that as situations change one *removes* cultural *impediments* to one's

natural sentiments. This attitude towards progress suggests a humility towards nature lacking in Hume, Leopold, and Callicott, all three of whom seek to use human reason and culture to *improve on* the sentiments that are natural to us. Smith, by emphasizing that our natural sentiments are good but corrupted, favors a return to community with nature.

References

Anscombe, Elizabeth (1956) 'Modern Moral Philosophy', *Philosophy*, 33, reprinted in Roger Crisp and Michael Slote (eds) *Virtue Ethics*, Oxford: Clarendon Press (1997).

Blackburn, Simon (1998) *Ruling Passions: A Theory of Practical Reasoning*, New York: Oxford University Press.

Boomer, Allison (2004) 'Can We Ethically Care for Non-human Life? A Humean Approach to Environmental Ethics' (unpublished manuscript).

Cafaro, Phillip (2001) 'Thoreau, Leopold, and Carson: Toward an Environmental Virtue Ethics', *Environmental Ethics* 23: 3–17.

Callicott, J. Baird (1989) *In Defense of the Land Ethic*, Albany, NY: State University of New York Press.

—— (1999) Beyond the Land Ethic, Albany, NY: State University of New York Press.

—— (2001) 'The Land Ethic', in *A Companion to Environmental Philosophy*, ed. Dale Jamieson, Oxford: Blackwell.

Campbell, T. D. (1971) *Adam Smith's Science of Morals*, Totowa, NJ: Rowman & Littlefield.

Carrasco, M. A. (2004) 'Adam Smith's Reconstruction of Practical Reason', *Review of Metaphysics* 58: 81–116.

Carter, Alan (2000) 'Humean Nature', *Environmental Values* 9: 3–37.

Crisp, Roger and Slote, Michael (eds) (1997) *Virtue Ethics*, Oxford: Clarendon Press.

Darwall, S. (1998) 'Empathy, Sympathy, Care', *Philosophical Analysis* 89: 261–82.

—— (2003) *Virtue Ethics*, Oxford: Blackwell.

Darwin, Charles (1871) *The Descent of Man*. Reprinted 1981 with introduction by John Tyler Bonner and Robert M. May, Princeton, NJ: Princeton University Press.

Figueroa, Robert and Claudia Mills (2001) 'Environmental Justice', in *A Companion to Environmental Philosophy*. ed. Dale Jamieson, Oxford: Blackwell.

Firth, Roderick (1952) 'Ethical Absolutism and the Ideal Observer', *Philosophy and Phenomenological Research* 12: 317–45.

Frasz, Geoffrey (1993) 'Environmental Virtue Ethics: A New Direction for Environmental Ethics', *Environmental Ethics* 15: 259–74.

Gibbard, Alan (1990) *Wise Choices, Apt Feelings*, Cambridge, MA: Harvard University Press.

Goodpaster, K. E. (1979) 'On Being Morally Considerable', *Journal of Philosophy* 75: 308–25.

Griswold, Charles R., Jr. (1999) *Adam Smith and the Virtues of Enlightenment*, New York: Cambridge University Press.

Heath, Eugene (1995) 'The Commerce of Sympathy: Adam Smith on the Emergence of Morals', *Journal of the History of Philosophy* 33: 447–66.

Hill, Thomas E., Jr. (1983) 'Ideals of Human Excellence and Preserving the Natural Environment', *Environmental Ethics* 5: 211–24. Reprinted in Lori Gruen and Dale Jamieson (eds) *Reflecting on Nature*. New York: Oxford University Press (1994), 98–110. (Page numbers refer to the anthologized version.)

Hursthouse, Rosalind (1999) *On Virtue Ethics*, Oxford: Oxford University Press.

Leopold, Aldo (1949) *A Sand County Almanac*, New York: Oxford University Press.

Levy, David M. and Peart, Sandra J. (2004) 'Sympathy and Approbation in Hume and Smith: A Solution to the Other Rational Species Problem', *Economics and Philosophy* 20: 331–49.

Lo, Yeuk-Sze (2001a) 'Non-Humean Holism, Un-Humean Holism', *Environmental Values* 10: 113–23.

—— (2001b) 'A Humean Argument for the Land Ethic?', *Environmental Values* 10: 523–39.

McShane, Katie (2003a) 'What environmentalists should mean by "intrinsic value"'. (Unpublished manuscript, presented at Colby College, March 2003.)

—— (2003b) Review of *Environmental Justice: Creating Equality, Reclaiming Democracy* by Kristin Shrader-Frechette. *Notre Dame Philosophical Reviews*, http://ndpr.icaap.org/content/archives/2003/9/McShane_Shrader-Frechette.html.

Muller, J. Z. (1993) *Adam Smith in his Time and Ours*, Princeton, NJ: Princeton University Press.

Naess, Arne (1973) 'The shallow and the deep, long-range ecology movement', *Inquiry* 16: 95–100. Reprinted in Alan Drengson and Yuichi Inoue (eds) *The Deep Ecology Movement*, Berkeley, CA: North Atlantic Books (1995).

Norton, Bryan (1988) 'The Constancy of Leopold's Land Ethic', *Conservation Biology* 2: 93–102.

—— (1991) *Toward Unity Among Environmentalists*, Oxford: Oxford University Press.

Nussbaum, Martha (1990). *Love's Knowledge: Essays on Philosophy and Literature*. Oxford: Oxford University Press.

O'Neill, John (1993) *Ecology, Policy, and Politics*, New York: Routledge.

Otteson, James (2002) *Adam Smith's Marketplace of Life*, Cambridge: Cambridge University Press.

Raynor, D. (1984) 'Hume's Abstract of Adam's Smith's *Theory of Moral Sentiments*', *Journal of the History of Philosophy* 22: 51–79.

Routley, Richard (1973) 'Is There a Need for a New, an Environmental Ethic?' in *Proceedings of the Fifteenth World Congress of Philosophy*. Sophia, Bulgaria: Sophia Press.

Routley, Richard and Routley, Val (1980) 'Human Chauvinism and Environmental Ethics' in Don Mannison, Michael McRobbie, and Richard Routley (eds) *Environmental Philosophy*, Canberra: Australian National University.

Schneewind, J. B. (1990) 'The Misfortunes of Virtue', *Ethics* 101: 42–63.

Shrader-Frechette, Kristin (2002) *Environmental Justice: Creating Equality, Reclaiming Democracy*. Oxford: Oxford University Press.

Singer, Peter (1975/1990) *Animal Liberation: A New Ethics for our Treatment of Animals*. New York: Avon Books.

Slote, Michael (1992) *From Morality to Virtue*, Oxford: Oxford University Press.

Stone, C. D. (1972) 'Should Trees Have Standing? Towards Legal Rights for Natural Objects', *Southern California Law Review* 45: 450–501.

—— (1974) *Should Trees Have Standing? Towards Legal Rights for Natural Objects*, Los Altos, CA: William Kaufman.

Taylor, Paul (1989) *Respect For Nature*, 2nd edn, Princeton, NJ: Princeton University Press.

Varner, Gary E. (1998) *In Nature's Interests?*, New York: Oxford University Press.

8 Does the 'wisdom of nature' need help?

Lauren Brubaker

Shortly after the publication in 1759 of the first edition of TMS, Adam Smith's close friend David Hume writes to him from London to thank him for some presentation copies of the book. Hume reports that he gave them away to those he 'thought good Judges, and proper to spread the reputation of the Book'. If you entertain any suspicions that the two descriptions might not exactly or regularly coincide, you would find your skepticism amply supported by the rest of the letter. Twice Hume starts to give Smith a report on the reception of TMS in London, only to break off in mid-sentence due to some 'foolish impertinent' interruption, which he then proceeds to describes at length. After the second of these, he admonishes Smith: 'have Patience: Compose yourself to Tranquillity: Show yourself a Philosopher in Practice as well as Profession: Think on the Emptiness, and Rashness, and Futility of the common Judgements of Men: How little they are regulated by Reason in any Subject, much more in philosophical subjects.' As if this was not sufficiently insufferable, after a few more comments he adds this further instruction:

> A wise man's Kingdom is his own Breast: or if he ever looks farther, it will only be to the Judgement of a select few, who are free from Prejudices, and capable of examining his Work. Nothing indeed can be a stronger Presumption of Falsehood than the Approbation of the Multitude.

At last relenting, he gets to the point: 'I proceed to tell you the melancholy news, that your Book has been very unfortunate: for the Public seem disposed to applaud it extremely.'[1]

This would not have nearly the humor or the bite if we, along with Hume, weren't convinced that Smith was surely very concerned with the success of his book, however much he also agreed with Hume's admonitions. In this entertaining yet telling exchange among friends we see raised questions of serious import for both philosophers: the ambition for reputation based on the praise of the multitude versus the approbation of one's 'own breast' or of a 'select few', the prejudiced nature of most, perhaps all, actual judges of virtue and merit, the problematic relation between philosophy and public opinion, the futility of popular enlightenment, and even the nature of philosophy or philosophic tranquillity itself. The seemingly personal questions concerning the success and reputation of one's book suggest the larger questions of the possible influence of philosophy on public opinion or politics and the possibility of public enlightenment.[2] Is Smith as skeptical as Hume seems here about the possibility of philosophy enlightening society and opinion?[3] The common understanding of such well known Smithian doctrines as his reliance on the 'invisible hand', his praise of Stoic tranquillity, and his invocation of providential harmony would suggest that he has little need or concern for popular enlightenment. The wisdom of nature is sufficient. Human efforts are likely either impotent or pernicious. But if resignation to the will of nature or providence is Smith's true position, why did he write books that are, to put it mildly, hardly a defense of the way things have always been? How does he understand the wisdom of nature and what is his stance toward human efforts to help?

Smith's systems: public enlightenment?

In many ways Smith's writings exemplify and promote Enlightenment ideals. It is not without reason that he is considered among the founders of modern liberalism. He advocates individual liberty, equal justice for all, progress in commerce, science and the arts, and the disestablishment of religion and its relegation to the private sphere. He is hardly a slave to tradition, describing his political economy as the 'very violent attack I had made upon the whole commercial system of Great Britain' (Letter 208 to Andreas Holt, 26 October 1780, Corr. 249–53). It would be fair to say that his attack on the reigning orthodoxies is not limited to economics, but extends as well to philosophy, religion and politics. In place of the prejudices and self-interested corruption that seemed to prevail everywhere, he proposes a series of natural systems that he argues will result in the opulence of nations and the 'perfection and happiness of human nature' (TMS III.5.8, 166). These are not the ideas or activities of one preaching resignation to the wisdom of nature.

And yet, his systems all seem to rely on that wisdom. First, his theory about our moral sentiments explains how pursuing our natural sentiments in the transactions of everyday life leads us, through sympathy and the desire of the approval of others, to recognize and follow common moral standards. This happy result is obtained through the operation of natural passions common to all of us. It may thus be thought to preclude the necessity of strenuous intervention by political and especially religious authorities on behalf of public morality.[4] Second, his system of natural jurisprudence, also relying on natural sentiments, elevates justice as the primary political virtue and seems to provide a natural standard against which all positive law can be judged.[5] Finally and most famously, he outlines an 'obvious and simple system of natural liberty' regarding political economy which he claims 'establishes itself of its own accord' (WN IV.ix.51, 687). This combination of natural systems in morals, politics, and economics appears to offer the path to 'the order of the world, and the perfection and happiness of human nature' (TMS III.5.9, 168). Such a strong reliance on the wisdom of nature has led some to characterize Smith as an anti-enlightenment traditionalist or Burkean conservative (Otteson 2002: 322).

There is just one troublesome question. If such perfection is so natural, the result of natural processes representing the benevolent wisdom of nature, why isn't it visible almost everywhere? The perfection of human nature and the system of natural liberty could hardly be seen in Smith's time. Dare we claim they are widespread today? One obvious answer to this inconvenient fact would attribute the failure of these natural systems to human folly. Due to the prevalence of corruption, prejudice, or superstition we fail to realize the benefits of this natural harmony. Distortions of the natural moral equilibrium and of the natural progress of opulence would then plausibly be remedied by the removal of economic, religious and political prejudices, by popular enlightenment. To accomplish this, a more enlightened understanding is needed by philosophers, legislators, and moral authorities – whoever shapes public opinion. Smith's books then would provide just such an enlightened remedy through his description of the systems of natural morals and natural liberty. Most scholars of Smith hold some such account of Smith's systems and intention, whether like Hayek they approve of him as offering a laudable defense of liberty and freedom, condemn him for contributing to the modern moral degeneration (Minowitz 1993; Manent 1998) or join with Marx to fault him for a hopelessly misguided optimism, one perhaps even obscuring an underlying class or cultural partiality.[6]

There is much in Smith to justify such views. Why else would he publish such sustained attacks on the regnant orthodoxies? Doesn't he intend to expose them as prejudice and false philosophy in order to replace them with the truth based on nature? Yet our earlier glance at Hume's letter should alert us to the possibility that Smith may have shared Hume's reservations about the possibility of popular enlightenment and political reformation that would undermine such sanguine optimism. In what follows I explore the complexities of Smith's discussion of the wisdom of nature. At times he encourages an interpretation of his natural systems as the wisdom of nature, seemingly deprecating any need for human help. Yet he also is aware of and makes use of the imaginative appeal of the beauty of simple and elegant systems to motivate public-spirited statesmen to attempt public enlightenment and aid nature in realizing natural liberty. At other times, however, he bemoans the dangers of faction and fanaticism that result when men of system become enamored of beautiful systems. Finally, he provides ample if sometimes muted arguments that despite his seeming praise of nature, the wisdom of nature (and thus Smith's own natural systems) neither guarantees its results nor is unambiguously beneficent. Specifically I investigate Smith's claim that there is a conflict within nature between nature's own laws and the laws nature prompts human nature to attempt to enforce, a conflict that makes problematic any simple invocation of nature in understanding his views. I conclude that Smith rejects both Stoic resignation and utopian hubris. He is neither a naïve optimist nor a resigned determinist. His complex understanding of nature's wisdom and human nature's efforts to help nature results in a limited, cautious and often indirect, but nevertheless essential, program of philosophical and political statesmanship.

Smith's systems reconsidered

Smith's systems appear 'simple and obvious'. Close examination reveals that they are complex and nuanced. The wisdom of nature and providential harmony are frequently ambiguous and qualified. In TMS, despite the frequent invocation of natural harmony, he recognizes problems that are both sufficiently serious and systemic to justify a characterization of them as Adam Smith's problem.[7] In brief, our natural desire for the approval of actual spectators, while a major inducement to conventional morality, is often in conflict with the love of virtue for its own sake (TMS III.ii.6, 116). Further, this desire for sympathy can, depending on whose sympathy we seek, lead either to conformity with social norms and thus social harmony or to the aggravation of political faction and the encouragement of enthusiasm or superstition (III.3.12–3, 154). The opinion of the impartial spectator, Smith's standard for moral judgments, is often opposed and even overwhelmed by the prejudiced opinions of actual spectators (III.2.31–3, 128). Even the love of virtue and the love of wisdom, when embodied in false religious or philosophical doctrines, are not immune to fanaticism (Brubaker, 2002). Thus his theory of our moral sentiments, while it liberates individual sociability and morality from the need for strenuous intervention by moral authorities of whatever sort, ultimately offers no guarantee of decent social morals or a moderate or humane politics. Our natural sociability, while a more accurate understanding of human nature than the 'selfish system of morals' of Hobbes, Locke, and Mandeville, turns out to be a mixed blessing.[8] Nature or natural morality needs help.

We turn next to his political economy. The famous invisible hand that guarantees socially favorable outcomes from the unfettered pursuit of individual self-interest, while an important advance in understanding certain social and particularly economic processes, is admitted by Smith to apply only in limited situations. His single use of the phrase in WN makes no claim to universality: 'he is in this, as in many other cases, led by an invisible hand...' (IV.ii.19, 456). Even in those cases the successful operation of the invisible hand requires several prerequisites, most importantly personal liberty and the administration of impartial justice by very human hands. In many other areas the natural progress of opulence has severe negative consequences with the result that, as Smith dryly remarks concerning the deleterious effects of the expansion of the division of labor, 'some attention of government is necessary in order to prevent the almost entire corruption and degeneracy of the great body of the people' (WN V.i.f.49, 781). Further, the 'obvious and simple system of natural liberty' requires that trade and the movement of labor and capital be freed from all restrictions. Smith dismisses such an expectation. It is 'as absurd . . . to expect that an Oceana or Utopia should ever be established' as to expect such complete freedom (WN IV.ii.43, 471, IV.ix.51, 687). Here again nature or the natural progress of opulence is a mixed blessing, and the invisible hand and the system of natural liberty need human help in a way similar to the natural system of morals.

Contrary to the usual view of Smith, I think that the pervasive problems with the wisdom of nature suggested by these systemic obstacles to natural harmony in morals, politics and economics are not merely the result of corruption or prejudice, real as those problems are. For Smith they are endemic in human nature and the human situation, fully as natural as the benefits. If this is so, he would be wildly optimistic to conclude that they are easily ameliorated by more enlightened opinions provided by a philosophic advisor to legislators. Making matters more complex, Smith sees an additional problem. If nature needs help, she at the same time resists human efforts to improve or mitigate her irregularities. Further, Smith insists that the help offered by various reformers and moralists is more often harmful than helpful. Sometimes what religion or philosophy considers the folly of man is in fact the wisdom of nature, and our efforts to intervene are either impotent or pernicious. In other cases when intervention is needed, false religion and philosophy or false political economy mistake the problem and make matters worse. An investigation of Smith's references to system and philosophy show that he is frequently and persistently a critic of men of system as dangerous, and of philosophy and reason as, in his words: slow, uncertain, abstract, refined, abstruse, quibbling and whining (TMS VI.ii.2.15–18, II.i.5.10, III.3.7–9, 21, III.5.4).

When philosophy and system are not impotent against the natural current, they are usually harmful. There is a systematic reason for this as well. In order to motivate partisans and bring about change, political/economic or philosophical/religious systems necessarily present the complexity of the human problem in a simplified and thus partial and distorted way (WN Introduction, 7–8, 11 and Book IV; TMS III.3.43, 155, III.6.12, 176, VI.ii.2.15, 232, VII.i.1, 265). The true philosophic stance – skeptical moderation and humility – is not a battle cry that can rally public opinion and drive reform or revolution. Only dogmatic and thus partial or false systems can serve this purpose. Smith the philosopher understands and describes the appeal of the beauty of elegant systems as well as their limitations (TMS IV.i.11, 185 and VI.ii.15–18, 232). He himself proposes a set of elegant natural systems designed to appeal to the imagination of legislators, but we have seen that he also indicates, sometimes bluntly and sometimes quietly, that the apparent natural harmony they claim is systematically flawed. It can be said in his defense that if his systems too become 'simple and obvious' dogma, he has reason to think that opinions or prejudices based on his systems are more beneficial, or less harmful, than the opinions they replace.[9]

These observations suggest that despite his solid credentials as a reformer, Smith is keenly aware of the limits of enlightenment and of the dangers of systematic philosophy, not excluding his own systems of moral sentiments and natural liberty. How then are we to understand these seemingly irreconcilable sides of Adam Smith and his systems? A closer look at what Smith means by nature in such phrases as natural liberty, natural harmony, and the wisdom of nature will shed further light on this question.

Natural harmony?

Many readers of Smith take his references to 'God', the 'Deity', the 'all-wise Author of Nature', the 'invisible hand', and 'Providence' to refer to an eternal benevolence and wisdom that Smith found necessary to invoke in order to guarantee harmony and happiness here below. Most recent scholars, on the other hand, have almost universally concluded that Smith's theories can do very well without such final causes (Waterman 2002 and Kleer 1995 are notable exceptions). Jacob Viner in a famous formulation found such a belief essential to TMS, but absent in WN. He concluded that the books were incompatible and WN was superior on just these grounds (Viner 1927). Peter Minowitz more recently spent a good portion of his book deconstructing such religious or providential talk in TMS in order to prove Smith's consistency, a consistency based on the conclusion that Smith in both books is really a skeptic and atheist like Hume (Minowitz 1993). Both Macfie and Haakonssen agree that nothing important rides on the theological talk, and that Smith provides a careful explanation of immediate or efficient causes to explain everything for which the all-wise author of nature is invoked as the final cause (Macfie 1967: 12; Haakonssen 1981: 77).[10] If one accepts, as I do, this claim that Smith generally works from the bottom up, we are still left with the question: why does Smith use the language of providential natural harmony so frequently and prominently? At issue is the status of Smith's defense of natural liberty and natural moral sentiments. Some account of why or how nature guarantees the 'perfection and happiness of human nature' would seem necessary for Smith to sustain this defense. While we have argued that his account of nature is more complex and ambiguous than usually recognized, we also contend that he remains committed to a substantial and meaningful role for natural morals and natural liberty, and that much of his liberal political and economic project depends on his ability to make such arguments. What does he mean by natural harmony?

The Smith-as-Stoic argument

Macfie, among others, accounts for what he calls Smith's 'optimistic Theism' by reference to 'the attitude of his period' and more specifically to the influence of the 'ancient stoics' on both Smith and Francis Hutcheson, Smith's teacher at Glasgow (1967: 110, 112, 116). To substantiate this claim, he quotes as proof (and repeats the quote in the editors' Introduction to TMS) Smith's apparently favorable description of the idea of a general order in the universe (1967: 116; TMS *8*).

> The ancient stoics were of the opinion, that as the world was governed by the all-ruling providence of a wise, powerful, and good God, every single event ought to be regarded, as making a necessary part of the plan of the universe, and as tending to promote the general order and happiness of the whole: that the vices and follies of mankind, therefore, made as necessary part of this plan as their wisdom or their virtue; and by that eternal art which educes good from ill, were made to tend equally to the prosperity and perfection of the great system of nature.
>
> (I.ii.3.4, 36)

Macfie is correct that many of these Stoic themes are present in Smith: that self-regarding motives on the part of individuals (vice) can have unintended beneficial consequences, that these lead to the prosperity of all under certain conditions (the invisible hand argument), that the folly of man is often turned by the wisdom of nature to a useful purpose, and that nature is a 'great system' that seems to promote the order, happiness and perfection of the whole. It is thus understandable that he and many others have seen strong evidence of Stoicism in Smith.[11] Our problem is to understand just what Smith means by these claims, to figure out the importance and role of 'optimistic Theism' in his system. The attribution of this to Stoicism, disregarding the condescending reference to the attitude of the times, does not shed much light on this question except by way of contrast. For Smith is, both in this context and in general, explicit about his distance from the Stoic understanding of providential natural harmony.

After the seemingly sympathetic presentation of the Stoic view just noted, Smith continues: 'No speculation of this kind, however, how deeply soever it might be rooted in the mind, could diminish our natural abhorrence for vice, whose immediate effects are so destructive, and whose remote ones are too distant to be traced by the imagination.' Smith is arguing, in a chapter on the unsocial passions of hatred and resentment, that while there is certainly some utility in these passions when considered in a broad or speculative view, their immediate effects are often disagreeable and pernicious. The impartial spectator is thus always cautious in approving unsocial passions, and usually does so only in a much qualified form. Smith is making a comparison to the case of vice. While it may in the Stoic view be a contribution to some ultimate universal good, it is properly the object of our 'natural abhorrence'. As for the unsocial passions, Smith continues: 'It was, it seems, the intention of Nature, that those rougher and more unamiable emotions, which drive men from one another, should be less easily and more rarely communicated' (I.ii.3.5, 37). As he often does, Smith is here *contrasting* the intentions of nature, which are found in our natural sentiments, with the abstract or philosophic view.[12] In this case our natural negative reaction to anger or hatred on the one hand, and to vice on the other, is contrasted with the Stoic version of optimistic Theism that sees in them an ultimate beneficial harmony. Thus the key 'Stoic' passage relied on by Macfie is introduced by Smith to provide the basis for his critique of the Stoic version of natural harmony.

Smith's final discussion of Stoicism, extensively revised in the last edition, confirms and even sharpens this contrast between the wisdom of nature and Stoic philosophy.[13] After an extensive and sympathetic discussion of the Stoic system and the 'stoical wise man', he draws this conclusion:

> The plan and system which Nature has sketched out for our conduct seems to be altogether different from that of the Stoical philosophy ... the perfect apathy which it prescribes to us ... endeavours to render us altogether indifferent and unconcerned in the success or miscarriage of every thing which Nature has prescribed to us as the proper business and occupation of our lives.
>
> (VII.ii.1.43–6, 292)

Smith could hardly be more explicit in his rejection of Stoic natural harmony. It is nature and not philosophy that provides guidance in our ordinary and common activities of life. Smith does allow a place for 'sublime contemplation' of the benevolent wisdom that directs the great machine of the universe, but it is a limited place. If, after all our 'most faithful exertions', we find that we are faced with unpleasant or unfavorable results, we can then turn to reliance on and submission to that 'divine Being'. Nature points out such contemplation as the proper 'consolation of our misfortunes', but it should neither be our main occupation nor prevent us from performing even the 'smallest active duty' (VII.ii.1.43–6, 292–3; VI.ii.3.5–6, 236–7). We will return to the exceptional case, or what we may call the consolation issue, in our conclusion.

Immediately, however, Smith is primarily concerned with the promptings of nature (and thus, indirectly, of the Author of nature) as most important in the everyday or normal situation. These promptings are understood by all in common life, without benefit of philosophy. As regards the 'proper occupation and business of our lives' Stoic philosophic tranquillity is detrimental and misleading; it is contrary to nature. But if Stoic philosophy or the Stoic understanding of nature provides little help in understanding Smith's view, how ought we to understand his idea of natural harmony?

The ambiguous nature of Nature

Smith has much to say about nature, natural sentiments, natural liberty and even the wisdom of nature. Charles Griswold in his analysis lists no fewer than seven different uses of the concept of nature in Smith's writings (1999, 311–17). The present discussion is not meant to be exhaustive, but will concentrate on the aspect that is relevant to our topic: Smith's understanding of how it is that nature 'teaches' us, the nature referred to in such phrases as 'nature's intention' or what 'nature has prescribed'. It is nature as the efficient cause of those factors that leads to 'perfection and happiness'. If we want to understand what Smith means by the wisdom of nature, we must decipher his meaning here.

Let us begin with the obvious or traditional understanding of the 'Author of nature'. As far as I can determine, Smith is consistent in holding that whatever is useful and enduring about religion is 'first impressed by nature, and afterwards confirmed by reasoning and philosophy' (TMS III.5.3–5, 163). While he is carefully respectful of many religious teachings, he neither invokes revelation nor depends on its support for any important conclusion (Waterman 2002: Part IV). It is human reasoning, not nature, which he often calls into question: the 'slowness and uncertainty of philosophical researches'. Nature or natural principles prompt or lead us to certain religious conclusions, including belief in a benevolent deity. But the causal relation never runs the other way: religion and the deity are not used to account for or explain nature. Rather, religion itself is in danger when it strays from its 'natural principles' under the influence of 'factious and party zeal'. Such 'false notions of religion' are 'almost the only causes which can occasion any very gross perversion of our natural sentiments' (III.5.13, 170; III.6.12, 176). Whatever Smith is going to teach about the Author of nature he intends us to learn from observing nature herself.

R. H. Coase argues that Smith's frequent use of such circumlocutions as Author of Nature indicates his reluctance to make a definitive statement about the ultimate cause of the harmonies he observed. He suggests that the missing link in the causal chain, about which Smith had an intimation, but only an intimation, and thus suspended judgment, is what is now known as evolution or 'natural selection' (Coase 1976: 539; see also

Campbell 1971: 75). Smith was ahead of his time in understanding this, and thus can do very well without God or teleology. But we must ask: does nature intend self and species preservation, or does it intend some nobler end such as human happiness or perfection?

Throughout much of TMS the teaching of nature seems indeed to be 'Darwinian'. 'Thus self-preservation, and the propagation of the species, are the great ends which Nature seems to have proposed in the formation of all animals.' These are the 'favourite ends of nature' and the 'beneficent ends' intended by the 'great Director of nature' (II.i.5.10, 77–8). Throughout nature we see and admire 'how every thing is contrived for advancing the two great purposes of nature, the support of the individual, and the propagation of the species' (II.ii.3.5, 87).[14] Such talk is now familiar enough and would seem to coincide with the Smith you think you know: the advocate of free and competitive markets where only the fittest prosper. Might we call this the libertarian Smith? Yet Smith also insists that nature has grander aims. At one point he analyzes the persistent human tendency to take into account the consequences or lack thereof of actions, which is to say fortune, when deciding on punishment. From the point of view of reason or philosophy, we should consider only intention. Fortune is beyond anyone's control. Yet he argues 'Nature, however, when she implanted the seed of this irregularity in the human breast, seems, as upon all other occasions, to have intended the happiness and perfection of the species' (II.iii.3.2, 105). Elsewhere he notes that

> [t]he happiness of mankind, as well as of all other rational creatures, seems to have been the original purpose intended by the Author of nature, when he brought them into existence ... this opinion ... is still more confirmed by the examination of the works of nature, which seem all intended to promote happiness, and guard against misery.
> (III.5.7, 166)

Self-preservation is one thing. It is something that even we, in the post-Darwin age, can plausibly attribute to nature. Happiness and perfection are more exalted, and more problematic, claims. They are not something that can be easily reconciled with Darwinian nature, especially by a philosopher intent on keeping his analysis grounded in nature and common life, free from philosophical abstractions. Such a claim would seem to strain the now generally accepted view of a thoroughly modern Smith for whom nothing important depends on teleology or theology. Smith's account of nature, just as his account of his natural systems, seems ambiguous or conflicted. I do not claim to have discovered yet another Adam Smith Problem. Smith himself makes this conflict explicit in TMS, and to that we now turn.

In the context of his discussion of whether general moral rules are 'justly regarded as the Laws of the Deity' Smith makes an extraordinary, even implausible, observation, at least for one defending the harmony of nature. The rules that nature follows, rules that promote self-preservation, often shock and offend the 'natural sentiments' of man. Nature opposes nature, or nature simply and human nature are at odds.

> Thus man is by Nature directed to correct, in some measure, that distribution of things which she herself would otherwise have made. The rules which for this purpose she prompts him to follow, are different from those which she herself observes . . . The rules which she follows are fit for her, those which he follows for him: but both are calculated to promote the same great end, the order of the world, and the perfection and happiness of human nature.
>
> (III.5.9, 168)

If we are going to make sense of Smith's idea of the wisdom of nature, and thus of natural morals and natural liberty, we will have to come to terms with this amazing claim of a *conflict within nature*, a claim generally downplayed or neglected by those who either defend or deny his reliance on a providential *harmony* in nature.

Let us look first at nature's laws. Smith claims that 'notwithstanding the disorder in which all things appear to be in this world, yet even here every virtue meets with its proper reward'. Since this is not intuitively obvious, we must ask: what does he mean by 'its proper reward'? His answer: the one which will most effectively promote that particular virtue. Thus prudence and industry are rewarded with success and with wealth, the ends which they seek. But what about wisdom, truth, justice, humanity? They clearly don't guarantee wealth and greatness. Philosophers since Thales have been asked some variant of 'If you're so smart, why aren't you rich?' Smith argues that these virtues should not result in vulgar success. They guarantee instead the esteem of those we live with. Wisdom and virtue desire to be seen as praiseworthy, not to achieve worldly greatness. 'It is not in being rich that truth and justice would rejoice, but in being trusted and believed.' These rewards, Smith adds, these virtues 'almost always acquire'. In fact, once we develop a reputation for virtue, or the opposite, there is a halo effect. A good man will receive the benefit of the doubt even when he strays, a knave will be assumed to act basely even when he acts from the best of motives. Vice and virtue thus receive 'more than exact and impartial justice' at the hand of nature (III.5.8, 166).

But perhaps you are thinking this is all well and good, but what about the numerous cases where injustice triumphs and virtue is trampled? Smith acknowledges the problem. His description up to now, he admits, is based on examining nature's laws in a 'cool and philosophical light'. He has adopted something like the position of Stoic philosophy. But that is not the perspective of common life. Our natural sentiments recoil when we see 'violence and artifice prevail over sincerity and justice'. Smith's description of the conflict is memorable:

> Magnanimity, generosity, and justice, command so high a degree of admiration, that we desire to see them crowned with wealth, and power, and honours of every kind, the natural consequences of prudence, industry, and application; qualities with which those virtues are not inseparably connected. Fraud, falsehood, brutality, and violence, on the other hand, excite in every human breast such scorn and abhorrence, that our indignation rouses to see them possess those advantages which they may in some sense be said to have merited, by the diligence and industry with which they are sometimes attended. The industrious knave cultivates the soil; the indolent good man leaves it uncultivated. Who ought to reap the harvest? who starve, and who live in plenty? The natural course of things decides in favour of the knave; the natural sentiments of mankind in favour of the man of virtue.
>
> (III.5.9, 167–8)

Our natural sentiments balk at the harshness of what I will call nature simply, nature red in tooth and claw, where those who are industrious succeed through just or unjust means. Thus the natural sentiments of mankind lead to the creation of human laws. These are an effort to mitigate the distribution of rewards that nature simply, nature as the survival of the fittest, would make on her own. (If we are not naturally social democrats, we are at least compassionate conservatives.) Human laws, and human moral teachings more generally, attempt to provide fairness, justice, and equality of opportunity, to remove the advantage that natural strength or cunning provides.[15] As Smith makes clear in another context, justice is the one virtue necessary to society. It is 'the main pillar that upholds the whole edifice' (II.ii.3.4, 86). But human justice is clearly different from nature's justice.[16]

As we have seen, Smith finds the Stoic view of natural harmony faulty because it is unnatural: it sought to transform or transcend human nature and our natural moral sentiments in order to bring them into agreement with a postulated harsh but ultimately beneficent natural order of the universe. Would Stoicism be necessary or appealing if we commonly felt that the world was benign and just? If successful, such Stoic resignation, attained through strenuous effort, would lead to an unnatural passivity regarding human things, to a suppression of those impulses of human nature such as indignation at vice and injustice that strive to mitigate the harshness of nature simply. While Smith makes this critique most bluntly in the case of Stoicism, one must keep in mind the close similarities of this Stoic apathy with some versions of Christian otherworldliness: the devaluation of success or failure in this world and a recognition that what appears to us as evil is part of God's mysterious plan. On the other hand nature simply, or the nature of harsh survival, if the only aspect of nature, would reduce human nature to the laws of animal nature, to a mere struggle for survival. Smith insists on the importance of both aspects of nature: nature simply and the tendency of human nature to intervene through law and morality.

Why are both required for the order of the world and man's perfection and happiness? The harshness of nature simply guarantees our constant striving to survive and even better our condition. While utopian reformers of various stripes have persisted in trying to banish this aspect of nature, Smith will have none of it. If we could really transcend or ignore nature simply, we would be divine and no longer human. We would have neither a need to strive nor a need to moderate our striving through law and morality. Such visionaries represent the flip side of Christian or Stoic resignation to the harshness and vice that pervade this world. Smithian humans are neither utopian nor tranquil. They are led by nature to improve on nature through society, but they can't transcend or ignore nature simply.

The argument that both nature's rules and human rules are necessary to the 'great end, the order of the world and the perfection and happiness of human nature' is consistent with other aspects of Smith's system. Nature's rules, harsh though they may be, are not only 'necessary and unavoidable', but 'useful and proper for rousing the industry and attention of mankind' (III.5.10, 168). Earlier in TMS he makes a similar point about pain. In retaining our self-command under physical distress, we are rewarded by the knowledge that we are upholding our own dignity and honor. But by nature's 'unalterable law' we still suffer. And it is 'fit' that we should. Otherwise, Smith observes: a man 'could, from self-interest, have no motive for avoiding an accident which must necessarily diminish his utility both to himself and to society' (III.3.28, 148).[17] In matters of self and species preservation, nature does not act through the 'slow and uncertain determinations of our reason', but through 'original and immediate instincts', through 'hunger, thirst, the passion which unites the two sexes, the love of pleasure, and the dread of pain' (II.i.5.10, 77). These laws of natural necessity are common to man and animals.

But nature has also 'directed' human nature to justice and benevolence, to the love of virtue and the love of beauty. Most of TMS and WN are descriptions, not of nature simply, or of animal instinct and appetite, but of social nature, of human nature. Smith is concerned with 'the immense great fabric of human society, that fabric which to raise and support seems in this world, if I may say so, to have been the peculiar and darling care of Nature' (II.ii.3.4, 86). He is concerned to show, in explicit contrast to Mandeville and Rousseau (EPS *Letter:* 250), that man is naturally social and that there is a natural basis in sentiment and the conditions of ordinary social life for morality and law. Nature, not just human convention, is concerned to promote 'the order of the world, and the perfection and happiness of human nature' through morality, law, and society. These are the laws suitable for man, prompted by nature but different from her own laws of self-preservation, of survival of the strongest and most cunning. Human preservation depends on immediate appetite and instinct. These are the necessary but not sufficient conditions for happiness and perfection. Human perfection and happiness require those additional aspects of human nature and sentiment that are developed in human society. Nature simply needs the help of human efforts to correct nature and human nature. Natural harmony, at least in the sense of human happiness and perfection, depends crucially on this help, on this conflict within nature. Yet Smith claims only that such help is 'prompted' by nature through our human nature. Its success is not guaranteed by nature and depends on the wisdom of human efforts.[18]

So what?

Does this duality of nature help us understand the complexities or ambiguities of Smith's natural systems? Let's look first at his moral system. Smith has a nuanced understanding of the perfection of human nature. This is clear from his accounts of the gradual development of the idea of an impartial spectator from our experience of the original actual spectators of our actions, and of the development of the love of virtue as the basis of morality rather than merely the love of praise, to name only two of the most crucial discussions. While these start in our immediate natural sentiments, their maturation requires judgment and reflection. Through such 'slow, gradual and progressive work' we all develop to some extent an 'idea of exact propriety and perfection' (TMS VI.iii.25, 247). As a result our evolving understandings of the impartial spectator's viewpoint and of the love of virtue for itself come to restrain some of our other natural sentiments. These developed or perfected sentiments can even come into conflict with the natural sentiments from which they first arose. The impartial spectator can render a judgment contrary to the judgment of actual spectators, the original or natural tribunal. The love of virtue or the desire to be praiseworthy can sustain us even under conditions in which we lose the praise of actual spectators, our original or natural desire.[19] Nature sets us on the course to 'happiness and perfection' through human society, but that achievement requires that we develop standards of judgment and motivations for virtue at odds with what first appeared to be the natural standard. Nature is here at odds with herself. Under the right circumstances, our natural sociability prompts us toward the perfection of human nature. Those who achieve a measure of success in this effort gain some ability to transcend their original and powerful natural desire for the praise of actual spectators. Smith's natural system of morals rests on this higher understanding of natural 'harmony' born of the conflict within in nature and the efforts of human nature and society to ensure happiness and perfection. So far so good. If this natural perfection were guaranteed, a kind of natural harmony on a higher level would be maintained and Smith's systems, more complex than usually understood, would nevertheless constitute his natural account of human perfection and happiness. Such might be a sophisticated libertarian reading of Smith. But of course Smith never claims that such natural perfection is inevitable.

A similar understanding of nature can be seen in Book IV of WN, in Smith's discussion of the 'obvious and simple system of natural liberty' that 'establishes itself of its own accord' (IV.ix.51, 687). This is the classic statement of natural harmony in the realm of economics, as bold and comprehensive as any alleged in TMS in the realm of human sociability in general. But what exactly is Smith saying here? The quoted phrases are part of a conditional sentence. The beginning reads: 'All systems either of preference or restraint, therefore, being thus completely taken away...' Only if this condition is met will the natural harmony of the system of natural liberty come into being. But this is precisely the problem. What would be required to meet this condition of 'completely' removing all systems of 'preference or restraint' in order to reach what Smith properly thinks would constitute a great advance for mankind? Earlier in this same Book IV, Smith offers his analysis of the political problems involved: 'To expect, indeed, that the freedom of trade should ever be entirely restored in Great Britain, is as absurd as to expect that an Oceana or Utopia should ever be established in it.' The obstacles, stated over-simply, are the prejudices of the public and the private interests of various individuals and groups (IV.ii.43, 471). Thus natural liberty is an admirable goal and one to which we are prompted by many natural sentiments. But like the perfection and happiness of human nature just discussed, it appears to be a goal or possibility suggested but certainly not guaranteed by nature in either of her two aspects.

Furthermore, Smith is consistent, here and elsewhere, in prescribing several other preconditions for the functioning of natural liberty. Foremost among these are justice and personal security. Only when these are guaranteed are individuals free to make decisions on the economic criteria that allow natural liberty to function efficiently (Werhane 1991). As in the case of natural morality, Smith suggests that there are obstacles based not just in nature simply, but even in our human nature, that make the attainment of impartial justice difficult. This is particularly a problem for commercial society, owing to the divergent interests of the different orders of society, a problem that only becomes more complex and intense with the increasing division of labor.[20] Lest one think that the achievement of these preconditions are themselves simple, obvious or natural, it should be remembered that Smith spends much of Book III and part of Book V of WN describing the convoluted history of the development, and more often the lack of development, of these very factors. His friend and mentor David Hume filled six volumes of his *History of England* with a much longer and more detailed account of the difficulties that had to be surmounted to achieve the modicum of impartial justice and personal security that Britain had then attained.[21] 'Natural liberty' in economics thus resembles nature's direction of the 'happiness and perfection' of man in society. Nature, not to mention the benevolent Author of nature, is going to need considerable human help to overcome the obstacles that unalloyed nature has erected. Nature, of course, helps herself to some extent, through the 'natural' moral sentiments she has implanted in human nature. But nature also needs perhaps more than Hume's small amount of 'wisdom and foresight' provided by statesmen and philosophers. Of course, such intervention may not merely be lacking, even when the present is frequently more harmful than helpful.

This understanding of what Smith means by natural harmony, the wisdom of nature, and natural liberty is a significant departure from the standard understanding. A comparison with a recent sophisticated account is perhaps useful to highlight these differences and clarify what is at stake. Many commentators recognize that natural liberty requires the appropriate institutions, and that one of Smith's main aims was to specify those institutions (see especially Rosenberg 1960). But despite this, they generally attribute to Smith belief in a benevolent nature in the sense of nature simply. The corruption of this natural harmony is then attributed to human frailty. Thus natural liberty would be the normal state, but for instances of human corruption, corruption that could be prevented or eliminated by the proper institutions. As Jerry Evensky puts it: 'Human reason gives us the ability to impose the distortions of our frailty into the course of human events ... and thereby to perturb the regularity and distort that natural harmony that we would enjoy in the human condition if there were no vice' (2001, 502).[22] He goes on to describe the 'ideal harmonious liberal society' as a 'limit that can be approached but never reached' (504). This conclusion – that for Smith 'natural liberty' is an ideal or limit – is similar to our argument. The disagreement concerns the understanding of nature in this 'natural harmony'. Smith's description of the complex interaction of nature simply and the human institutions to which nature directs human nature comports well with the idea of perfection and happiness as a limit that is approached. It is my contention, however, that 'vice' or the drive to self-preservation and to better our condition, the success of the strongest (which Smith, in discussing nature's own laws, called the natural and proper reward of industry and prudence), and the corruption of our moral sentiments by the natural desire to admire the rich and great and to seek the approval of actual spectators, are all emphatically a part of nature and human nature. Smith denies that such natural impediments can ever be completely overcome. They are evils for which 'the nature of human affairs can scarce admit of a remedy'

(WN IV.iii.c.9, 493).[23] Smith's nature does not contain Rousseau's noble savage, unaffected by vice or vanity. Thus it is hard to imagine how this ideal natural harmony or natural liberty can be understood as the normal or natural condition subject to distortion or perturbation by human frailty. The normal condition is the conflict or tension between harsh nature, including natural human appetites and desires, and the equally natural human desire for justice, benevolence, and sociability more generally. The problem is not simply to remove the corruption introduced by humans into some natural or pre-human condition. Human happiness and perfection, to the limited extent that they exist, are ongoing human achievements prompted by human nature under the partly hostile and partly beneficial conditions created by nature simply. 'Natural liberty' and natural morals are the victory of human institutions and laws over nature simply and even human nature in its merely self-preserving form.

Smith's picture is further complicated by the fact that this constant effort of humans to mitigate nature simply is both a blessing and a curse. We are at least as likely to oppress and injure one another in the pursuit of religious or political improvement or perfection as we are to perfect impartial justice. Frequently, this harm is a result of underestimating the power of what Smith calls nature simply, believing that these aspects of human nature are not natural, but accidental and therefore remediable aspects of the human situation. By describing traits as 'human frailty' Evensky may contribute to such a misunderstanding. Smith insists that *both* nature simply (emphatically including human selfishness, ambition and the like) *and* the natural human striving to mitigate nature are necessary to the 'happiness and perfection of human nature' (III.5.9, 167). Furthermore, even the aspects of human nature which prompt us to mitigate nature simply have contradictory tendencies. For example, the desire for the approval of others, to which Smith traces much of our sociability and much of our motivation to be moral, can also be the basis of faction and fanaticism (TMS III.3.42–3, 154; Brubaker 2004). Any account of natural liberty or natural harmony that doesn't take both aspects of nature into account, that assumes either that nature on her own is harmonious or that human intervention is either sufficient or consistently beneficial, misrepresents the complexity of Smith's understanding.[24]

The system of natural liberty in economics is a limiting case, and can be approached only through a sustained, although qualified, intervention of statesmen and their philosophic advisors. Nature's intention to promote the happiness and perfection of man is also a limiting case or ideal, and similarly depends on qualified and limited human intervention through law and morality. Qualified and limited, and emphatically anti-utopian, because in each case nature has her own laws which cannot be ignored without paying a price. Limited also because, as we have seen, Smith is keenly aware that many efforts at human intervention are counterproductive. Smith understands natural harmony and natural liberty to rely on limited but essential and fallible human help. My analysis coheres with Smith's occasional and occasionally vehement praise for statesmen and philosophers and with his stinging denunciation of the otherworldliness of Stoicism and some versions of Christianity (TMS VI.i.15, 216; VI.ii.2.14, 232). Such praise and condemnation are both evident in his critique of the 'eloquent and philosophical Massillon'. Smith finds it 'contrary to all the principles by which nature has taught us' that Massillon would extol the 'futile mortifications of a monastery' as superior to 'the ennobling hazards and hardships of war', or would raise the contemplative life of monks and friars above

> all the heroes, all the statesmen and lawgivers, all the poets and philosophers of former ages: all those who have invented, improved, or excelled in the arts which contribute to the subsistence, to the conveniency, or to the ornament of human life; all the great protectors, instructors, and benefactors of mankind; all those to whom our natural sense of praise-worthiness forces us to ascribe the highest merit and most exalted virtue.
>
> (TMS III.2.34–5, 133–4; see also WN V.I.f.30, 771)

We are reminded of his criticism of the philosophy of the Stoics as contrary to nature.

Conclusion

Smith's human nature is designed for action, not for resignation to or contemplation of benevolent natural harmony. Humans are compelled by the very principles that nature has implanted in them to strive to 'better their condition' individually and to create society, political institutions, law, and morality (TMS VI.ii.3.6, 237). Smith continues his discussion of the two different kinds of 'natural' laws with this description of mankind:

> Like the gods of the poets, he is perpetually interposing, by extraordinary means, in favour of virtue, and in opposition to vice, and, like them, endeavours to turn away the arrow that is aimed at the head of the righteous, but to accelerate the sword of destruction that is lifted up against the wicked.
>
> (III.5.10, 168)

Prompted by nature, man intervenes to correct the outcomes that nature alone would produce, 'the distribution of things that natural events would make, if left to themselves'. To do that, man – like the gods of old – has to use 'extraordinary means', means natural to man but in tension with nature simply. There is no natural harmony in human things that exists without the conscious and conscientious intervention of wise humans.

There is no such thing as nature left to herself. The 'simple and obvious system of natural liberty' is, perhaps, conceptually simple, but it is certainly not politically simple. The perfection of man is a goal to which human nature is 'directed' by nature, a goal that human nature is 'calculated to promote' (III.5.9, 168). Such language suggests a tendency or a proclivity, not a certainty. Such ends are far from natural in the sense of ordinary or average. They cannot be understood as natural in the modern scientific sense of nature as what is universal and predictable. Like the viewpoint of the impartial spectator, or the standpoint of 'exact propriety and perfection', our best efforts can only approach these ends (VI.iii.23–5, 247). For Smith, true Enlightenment or true philosophy means recognizing, against the Stoics, that nature needs human help. It also means recognizing, against utopian Enlighteners, that nature resists and limits that help and that the human tendency to intervene on behalf of perfection and happiness is fraught with danger.

But what has happened to Providence, to natural harmony? If man is like the gods, what place is left for God or the gods? Why all the talk of religion, the Author of nature, of God? Smith continues: 'The natural course of things cannot be entirely controlled by the impotent endeavours of man: the current is too rapid and too strong for him to stop it.' When 'violence and artifice prevail over sincerity and justice' and when virtue suffers under the 'success of the oppressor', our natural sentiments are shocked. 'We are equally grieved and enraged at the wrong that is done, but often find it altogether out of our power to redress it.' Then we

> naturally appeal to heaven, and hope that the great Author of our nature will himself execute hereafter, what all the principles which he has given us for the direction of our conduct, prompt us to attempt even here ... and thus we are led to the belief of a future state, not only by the weaknesses, by the hopes and fears of human nature, but by the noblest and best principles which belong to it, by the love of virtue and the abhorrence of vice and injustice.
>
> (III.5.10, 169; see also III.2.11–12, 119–21 E6; II.ii.3.12, 91)

To bring home this point, Smith turns again to Massillon, Bishop of Clermont: 'Does it suit the greatness of God, to leave the world which he has created in so universal a disorder? To see the wicked prevail almost always over the just....' (III.5.11, 169). Human nature is led not only to the 'general rules' of morality, but also to a belief in an 'All powerful Being, who watches over our conduct, and who, in a life to come, will reward the observance, and punish the breach' of those rules (III.5.12, 170; see also III.2.33, 131).[25] Nature teaches us this also, as a consolation in our misfortune. But if this teaching is so natural and universal, doesn't it suggest that Smith's beneficent natural harmony must be of a peculiar sort? The natural course of events, even with the human help prompted by nature, so frequently fails to produce the desired happiness and perfection that '[i]n every religion ... that the world has ever beheld' there has been some version of reward and punishment in a future life (TMS, II.ii.3.12, 91).

Smith's account of the harmony of nature and of Nature's teaching is complex. We are directed, by nature and by Smith, to strive for order and perfection. But we are also taught that our power against the natural current is very limited. We strive for justice upon earth, but recognize that it is often unattainable, and that our efforts often go astray. Some of us try to understand these ambiguities of nature from a 'cool and philosophical view'. The danger is that if philosophy fails to remain tied to natural sentiments and common life it risks producing 'men of system' and promoting 'civil and ecclesiastical' 'faction and fanaticism' (TMS III.3.43, 155; see also WN V.i.g.7–9, 791). Nature needs our help to achieve her ends of the 'order of the world' and human 'happiness and perfection', but our abilities and wisdom are often not up to the task. Nature 'directs' and 'prompts' human nature towards justice and virtue, but she herself rewards the 'industrious knave'. Both aspects of nature are 'calculated to promote' those great ends. There is no money-back guarantee. It is a lesson both of hope and of moderation, of striving and of humility.

Smith might best be thought of as a proponent of a limited and cautious enlightenment. He sees clearly both the limits of enlightenment as well as the need for philosophy and statesmanship. Finally, if neither our natural sentiments nor our unaided reason can know for certain all the intentions of the Author of nature, or the assurance of a life to come, neither do they know for certain that we are abandoned in this world. We can recognize the natural impulses that lead to the 'sublime contemplation' of the harmony of the universe and the importance of such contemplation as a consolation in our misfortunes. Smith's attitude towards natural harmony and the human situation is neither Stoic resignation nor utopian hubris. It is neither the cynical resignation of Mandeville nor the romantic activism of Rousseau. He thus displays a combination of superior prudence and skeptical humility. One may ask whether he does not also display more benevolence than the aggressive enlighteners, with their utopian imprudence and dogmatic skepticism. We need only recall that benevolence and self-command also rank among the Smithian virtues.

Notes

1 Letter 31 from David Hume, 12 April 1759 (Corr. 33–6). Hume continues by reporting: 'Three Bishops called yesterday at Millar's Shop in order to buy Copies ... You may conclude what Opinion true Philosophers will entertain of it, when these Retainers to Superstition praise it so highly.'

2 Ryan Hanley explores Hume's substantial ambitions for literary fame and its relation to philosophy, with reference also to Smith and Benjamin Franklin (2002). Eric Schliesser critiques Hanley's argument and extends it to Smith

(2003). Ralph Lerner offers a concise, detailed, and nuanced discussion of Smith's ambiguous views of ambition (1999).

3 Smith reports a conversation he had with Hume on his deathbed in which Hume imagines excuses he might make to Charon for not getting in his boat (Letter 178 to William Strahan, 9 November 1776, Corr. 219). The last was: 'Have a little patience, good Charon. I have been endeavouring to open the eyes of the Public. If I live a few years longer, I may have the satisfaction of seeing the downfall of some of the prevailing systems of superstition.' But Charon would then lose all temper and decency. 'You loitering rogue, that will not happen these many years . . . Get into the boat this instant.'

4 '*The Theory of Moral Sentiments* is a book that seeks to show that the "sentiments" (also termed "passions" or "emotions") can suffice for morality, virtue, liberty, and in general for a harmonious social order' (Griswold 1999: 13). Griswold makes this picture somewhat more complex as his book proceeds.

5 Smith never published this part of his system. It is available to us only as two sets of student notes published as *Lectures on Jurisprudence* (LJ).

6 James Alvey (2003) offers an exhaustive examination of the question of Smith's optimism or pessimism, concluding that he provides ample grounds for opposing interpretations.

7 This play on the phrase 'the Adam Smith Problem' is intended to distinguish my treatment from that now generally discredited one. The two interpretations see the specific issues involved very differently. More important, unlike the claim in the earlier version of the problem that Smith failed to see or resolve the tension between TMS and WN, I argue that Smith is quite conscious of serious tensions, and that they occur within his moral theory and economics as a whole and not between his two books. For an account of the original Adam Smith Problem, see Teichgraeber (1981, 1986: 133–9 and n. 33) and more recently Montes (2004: Chapter 2). For a more detailed discussion of the tensions within his moral theory, see Brubaker (2003).

8 See TMS III.ii.27, 127 and VII.ii.4.7, 308 for Smith's critique of Mandeville and VII.iii.1, 315 for his discussion of Hobbes. The phrase is Hume's (EPM App. 2.2).

9 See the provocative characterization by McNamara: Smith's 'is a system that avoids the dangers of system' (1998: 32ff.).

10 Eric Schliesser points out to me that some arguments for God are inductive arguments based on design. It is certainly possible to argue in this manner, and Smith could be considered as offering a version of such an argument. The important issue for this chapter (and the point at which the argument ceases to be inductive) is whether the conclusion, a benevolent God, is then used to explain or account for anything that cannot be or is not accounted for otherwise.

11 '[A] Stoic idea of nature and the natural forms a major part of the philosophical foundations of TMS and WN alike.' 'Despite these criticisms, it is not too much to say that Adam Smith's ethics and natural theology are predominately Stoic' (Macfie, Intro. to TMS, 7, 10).

12 Vivienne Brown finds Smith's rejection of Stoicism to be based on 'a denial of the coincidence of reason and nature' (1994: 73–4). Vivenza (2002) offers a detailed examination of the possible Stoic influences on Smith. Montes discusses numerous reservations about Vivenza's analysis and sees much less Stoic influence (2004).

13 Samuel Fleischacker is one of the few to recognize this critique of Stoicism in Smith: 'the long chapter in which Smith officially seems to be declaring his sympathies for Stoicism turns out rather to urge an Aristotelian moderation, in relation to one's passions, over Stoic attempts to eliminate or ignore them'

(1999: 122). Fleischacker also correctly rejects the consensus view and argues that Smith becomes less Stoic later in his life (2004).

14 Joseph Cropsey provides a detailed and thorough analysis of this aspect of Smith's understanding of nature (1957: viii and chapter 1). Much of Smith's account of the differences between savage and civilized morals and of the wide agreement on 'the general style and character of conduct' turns on adaptation to circumstances and the fact that 'no society could subsist a moment' (it would destroy itself) if certain basic principles of conduct were not widely followed (TMS V.2). See also his comparison of human and animal population growth as determined by the 'means of their subsistence' (WN I.viii.39, 97; see also I.viii.26–7, 90). I take all these to show Smith's awareness that nature herself sets harsh and unforgiving limits on human alternatives, limits enforced through death and the collapse of societies: those societies and individuals that choose wisely survive, those that don't meet the challenge die.

15 Is this not precisely the aspect of modern society that provoked F. Nietzsche's polemic in the *Genealogy of Morals* that 'slave morality' elevates the weak?

16 Cropsey is one of the few to draw attention to the peculiarity of this passage from III.5: 'Smith's solution implies the simultaneous naturalness and arbitrariness of the normative ranking of the virtues: man is naturally disposed to reverse the natural. Then human nature is in some sense *sui generis*, not wholly an aspect of nature but partly a denial or negation of it. This is the dubious position Smith occupies in order to maintain the distinction between the noble and the ignoble while at the same time conceding the indifference of nature to nobility' (1957: 40).

17 Cropsey, consistent with his emphasis on Smithian nature as self-preservation, interprets this passage as follows: 'In other words, the self-love which is the desire for self-preservation was meant by nature to prevail over the self-love which is self-respect and which corresponds to the requirements of dignity' (1957: 53). I find Smith to argue for a balance of the two, a view supported by Smith's emphasis that humans sometimes choose injury and death despite the natural drive to self-preservation (TMS III.3.5, 138, IV.2.10, 191).

18 Haakonssen argues that 'with one bold move he set aside the ancient divide over the issue of nature versus artifice in morality. This is perhaps his most original contribution to moral philosophy. Smith suggested that artifice is natural to humankind.' He does not, however, discuss the III.5 passage or recognize any tension or problem that this conflict between nature and human nature might pose for Smith's claim of natural harmony and perfection. He dismisses any such claims in Smith: 'he does not have access to a universal morality, nor is an underlying *logos* any part of his concern' (2002: xii).

19 In his revisions for the second and sixth editions of TMS Smith wrestled with this question. His final version leaves his position ambiguous. He postulates two separate 'natural' desires, one for the approval of actual spectators and one for being actually praiseworthy (III.2.6–7 and editors' note, 116. See also III.2.31–2 and note r, 128). For a detailed discussion of Smith's revisions and how they make his natural system of morals more complex, see Brubaker (2003).

20 See his blunt analysis that it is in the interest of merchants and manufacturers to 'deceive and even to oppress the publick' (WN I.xi.p.10, 267) as well as his running critique of the political machinations of merchants and manufacturers throughout Book IV.

21 Volume II of the *History*, the last written by Hume, concludes with his justification for the work: the study of history is important because it instructs even the English, 'who have happily established the most perfect and most accurate system of liberty that was ever found compatible with government', concerning

'the great mixture of accident, which commonly concurs with a small ingredient of wisdom and foresight, in erecting the complicated fabric of the most perfect government' (1983: II, 525).

22 Evensky's Smith displays considerable providential optimism. 'Smith established a few basic principles with respect to human nature, societal constructs, and societal change. Then, with these principles in mind, he sifted through his historical/anthropological sources trying to identify those connecting principles that would, if unimpaired by human frailty, guide the course of humankind's evolution toward the constructive outcome that he took on faith as the human prospect' (2001: 503). Compare Cropsey: 'This social form [commercial society] is highest (not in the sense of "noblest") precisely because it best suits the end of nature, namely the preservation of man's existence. Yet there is nothing in the nature of things which will or might "inevitably" lead to the coming into being of the natural or most expedient social arrangement' (1957: 63).

23 Waterman quotes this passage as part of his claim that Smith's theology can be understood to follow the Augustinian or Pauline 'doctrine of Original Sin'. He wants to 'construe the text [WN] as containing, and possibly even as shaped by, a quasi-Augustinian account of the way in which God responds to human sin by using the consequences of sin both as a punishment and as a [partial] remedy' (2002, Part 4). While he thus agrees that Smith is anti-utopian, as 'legal and moral reform can never be sufficient', he echoes the Stoics, claiming that nature always acts 'wisely and well, so as to make creative use of human folly and wickedness in ways that bring good out of evil'.

24 While agreeing in great measure with his description of Smith's project, I differ with Cropsey in seeing Smith as retaining a sense of natural perfection, if not returning to a full sense of natural teleology. Cropsey insists that Smith's version of nature is entirely modern and mechanistic: 'Articulating man entirely within nature, yet declining to see a question of man's freedom *vis-à-vis* nature, Smith has adopted an ancient simplicity: man's integration in the order of nature is beneficial rather than threatening to humanity, and is concordant with man's sociality and his virtue. Smith's project for liberal commercial society is part of his wider project for accommodating man's sociality and morality to the environment of mechanistic nature, although the traditional setting for that conception of man in nature is the older and teleological vision of nature' (1977: 88). If Cropsey is right that Smith thinks mechanistic nature produces consistently beneficial results (and Cropsey elsewhere seems to question this (1957: ch. 3)), why isn't liberty and justice for all the default condition of mankind? The libertarian account of Smith faces the same problem: how to account for the nearly universal absence of natural liberty (Otteson 2002: 287, 297). See Brubaker (2005), where I argue against Otteson that the political efforts necessary to achieve even modest libertarian liberty contradict any 'Burkean conservatism'. My Smith is less sanguine about the beneficence of nature and places more emphasis on the human effort needed to even approach perfection and happiness.

25 Griswold discusses Smith's key assertion about the two aspects of nature and his claim that both are proper and necessary for the perfection of human nature. He concludes that this claim is 'not credible' and that Smith's invocation of Massillon is proof: 'Smith neither prepares us for this outburst, nor has a word to say in response to it' (1999: 326).

References

Alvey, J. (2003) *Adam Smith: optimist or pessimist?* Aldershot: Ashgate.

Brown, V. (1994) *Adam Smith's Discourse: canonicity, commerce and conscience*, London: Routledge.

Brubaker, L. (2002) 'A Particular Turn or Habit of the Imagination: Adam Smith on love, friendship and philosophy' in E. A. Velásquez (ed.) *Love and Friendship: rethinking politics and affection in modern times*, Lanham, MD: Lexington Books.

—— (2003) 'Smith's Moderate Response to Rousseau's Critique of Modern Commercial Society', annual meeting of the American Political Science Association, Philadelphia, August.

—— (2004) 'Adam Smith's Enduring Relevance: Review of *On Adam Smith* by Jack Weinstein, *Adam Smith Review* 1: 188–93.

—— (2005) 'Why Adam Smith is neither a Conservative nor a Libertarian', round table on *Adam Smith and the Marketplace of Life* by James Otteson, *Adam Smith Review*, 2.

Campbell, T. D. (1971) *Adam Smith's Science of Morals*, London: Allen & Unwin.

Coase, R. H. (1976) 'Adam Smith's View of Man' *Journal of Law & Economics* 19: 529–46.

Cropsey, J. (1957) *Polity and Economy: an interpretation of the principles of Adam Smith*, The Hague: Nijhoff.

—— (1977) 'The Invisible Hand: Moral and Political Considerations', in J. Cropsey *Political Philosophy and the Issues of Politics*, Chicago: University of Chicago Press.

Evensky, J. (2001) 'Adam Smith's Lost Legacy', *Southern Economic Journal* 67 (3): 497–517.

Fleischacker, S. (1999) *A Third Concept of Liberty: judgment and freedom in Kant and Smith*, Princeton, NJ: Princeton University Press.

—— (2004) *On Adam Smith's* Wealth of Nations*: a philosophical companion*, Princeton, NJ: Princeton University Press.

Griswold, C. L. Jr (1999) *Adam Smith and the Virtues of Enlightenment*, Cambridge: Cambridge University Press.

Haakonssen, K. (2002) 'Introduction', in K. Ameriks and D. M. Clarke (eds) *Adam Smith: The Theory of Moral Sentiments*, Cambridge Texts in the History of Philosophy, Cambridge: Cambridge University Press

—— (1981) *The Science of the Legislator: the natural jurisprudence of David Hume and Adam Smith*, Cambridge: Cambridge University Press.

Hanley, R. (2002) 'Hume's Last Lessons', *Review of Politics* 64 (4): 659–85.

Hume, David (1983) *The History of England from the Invasion of Julius Caesar to the Revolution in 1688*. Based on the 1778 edn, 6 vols, Indianapolis: Liberty Classics.

Kleer, R. (1995) 'Final causes in Adam Smith's *Theory of Moral Sentiments*', *Journal of the History of Philosophy* 33: 275–300.

Lerner, R. (1999) 'Love of Fame and the Constitution of Liberty', in T. Angerer, B. Bader-Zarr and M. Grandner (eds) *Geschichte und Recht. Festschrift für Gerald Stourzh zum 70. Geburtstag*, Vienna: Bohlau.

Macfie, A. L. (1967) *The Individual in Society: papers on Adam Smith*, London: Allen & Unwin.

Manent, P. (1998) *The City of Man*, trans. M. A. LePain, Princeton, NJ: Princeton University Press.

McNamara, P. (1998) *Political Economy and Statesmanship*, DeKalb, IL: Northern Illinois University Press.

Minowitz, P. (1993) *Profits, Priests, and Princes*, Stanford, CA: Stanford University Press.

Montes, Leonidas (2004) *Adam Smith in Context: a critical reassessment of some central components of his thought*. New York: Palgrave Macmillan.

Otteson, J. (2002) *Adam Smith's Marketplace of Life*, Cambridge: Cambridge University Press.

Rosenberg, N. (1960) 'Some Institutional Aspects of the *Wealth of Nations*', *Journal of Political Economy* 68: 557–70.

Schliesser, E. (2003) '"The Obituary of a Vain Philosopher": Adam Smith's reflections on Hume's life', *Hume Studies* 29 (2): 327–62.

Teichgraeber, R. F. III (1981) 'Rethinking *Das Adam Smith Problem*', *Journal of British Studies* 20 (2): 106–23.

—— (1986) *'Free Trade' and Moral Philosophy: rethinking the sources of Adam Smith's Wealth of Nations*, Durham, NC: Duke University Press.

Viner, J. (1927) 'Adam Smith and *Laissez faire*', *Journal of Political Economy* 35: 198–232.

Vivenza, G. (2002) *Adam Smith and the Classics: the classical heritage in Adam Smith's thought*, Oxford: Oxford University Press.

Waterman, A. M. C. (2002) 'Economics as Theology: Adam Smith's *Wealth of Nations*', *Southern Economic Journal* 68: 907–21.

Werhane, P. (1991) *Adam Smith and his Legacy for Modern Capitalism*. Oxford: Oxford University Press.

9 'This irregularity of sentiment'

Adam Smith on moral luck

Chad Flanders

Smith's writings on moral luck, mostly found in a short section in his *Theory of Moral Sentiments* entitled 'On The Influence of Fortune upon the Sentiments of Mankind, with regard to the Merit or Demerit of Actions', have been almost totally neglected in the contemporary literature on the subject. Perhaps this is unsurprising. After all, it is only recently that philosophers have begun to take Smith seriously as a moral philosopher. Moreover, debates on moral luck are for the most part conducted ahistorically, dating themselves only as far back as Bernard Williams's and Thomas Nagel's influential essays on the subject (Williams 1981; Nagel 1979).[1] But the most significant reason for the neglect of Smith in debates on moral luck may be that his arguments attempting to justify our 'irregular' sentiments regarding moral praise and blame appear on a first reading as almost unaccountably weak. While Smith acknowledges it may be unjust that we praise or blame people according to the good or bad consequences of their actions rather than what they have intended, he also seems to suggest that this injustice should be tolerated for the overall beneficial consequences it produces. In other words, on a first reading, Smith gives what appears to be a baldly utilitarian justification in defense of our irregular sentiments. In the only article-length treatment of Smith on moral luck, Paul Russell charitably suggests that even Smith knew his utilitarian arguments weren't very good: '[i]n the final analysis, it seems fair to conclude that Smith is never entirely convinced by his own effort to rationalize the irregularities in moral sentiment in the way that he describes' (Russell 1999: 46).

In this chapter, I endeavor to show that Smith had many insightful things to say about consequential moral luck[2] – some in spite of himself – especially when we consider Smith's stance towards moral luck not merely in the one section of TMS mentioned above, but in light of TMS as a whole. My chapter divides into three parts. In the first part, I outline Smith's understanding of our irregular sentiments regarding praise and blame, and why they present for him such a puzzle. In the second and the third parts, I proceed dialectically. That is, I begin by presenting Smith's arguments in the putatively utilitarian light in which they sometimes ask to be read. I then go on to show that Smith, on a closer reading and one which takes into account the arguments of TMS as a whole, actually holds a much more nuanced and plausible position on how our irregular sentiments might be justified – one which defies easy categorization into 'utilitarian' or 'deontological'.

I

In his introduction to the section on the 'influence of Fortune upon the Sentiments of Mankind, with regard to the Merit or Demerit of Actions', Smith seems to be setting himself up for an answer to the problem of moral luck which, it turns out, he never gives. He begins by saying, rather strongly, that if we divide an action into (1) the intention, (2) the external movement of the body, and (3) the good or bad consequences it produces, then it is 'abundantly evident' that praise or blame cannot be based on (2) or (3), that is, one's external movements, or the consequences of one's action (TMS II.iii.intro.I, 92). In the case of external movement, Smith writes, innocent and blamable actions can both have the same form, but it cannot be true that they deserve the same blame or praise. A person who shoots a bird, Smith writes, 'perform[s] the same external movement' as a person who shoots a man (TMS II.ii.intro.2, 93). So we have to look back to the intention behind the external movement, to affix praise or blame rightly: was he trying to shoot a man, or just a bird? Still less is it proper to judge a person based on the accidental or unforeseen consequences of his action because, Smith says, these don't depend upon the agent 'but upon fortune' (TMS II.ii.intro.2, 93). The only consequences for which we can be judged are those that we intended, or at least those which 'show some agreeable or disagreeable quality in the intention of the heart' from which we acted, for example, if someone didn't intend to cause somebody harm, but was being reckless, or negligent, and because of this ended up causing harm (TMS II.ii.intro.3, 93). These consequences matter because they are consequences that are ultimately traceable to a person's 'design' in acting. And so all praise or blame, Smith says, must ultimately belong to a person's design, 'the intention or affection of his heart' (TMS II.ii.intro.3, 93).

Thomas Nagel, in his seminal essay on 'Moral Luck', reads these opening passages and attributes the following position to Smith: in order to assess an action, we should 'pare down each act to its morally essential core, an inner act of pure will assessed by motive and intention' (Nagel 1979: 31). If the intention of two acts is the same, then no matter, Smith says, 'how different soever the accidental, the unintended and unforeseen consequences' of the different actions, the two acts have the same merit because in deciding merit, only the intention should come into play (TMS II.iii.intro.4, 93). This idea gets put more formally in terms of Smith's 'equitable maxim', which is that 'to the intention or affection of the heart

... all approbation or disapprobation, of any kind, which can justly be bestowed upon any action, must ultimately belong' (TMS II.iii.intro.3, 93). Nagel is not wrong in attributing this idea to Smith. Moreover, Smith asserts that the 'self-evident justice' of the equitable maxim is 'acknowledged by all the world, and there is not a dissenting voice among all mankind' (TMS II.iii.intro.4, 93).

The problem, however, is that we honor the equitable maxim more in the breach than in the observance. Even though we can all agree in the abstract that unintended and unforeseen consequences should not be the basis of any judgment of moral worth, and that external movements are unreliable as objects of praise and blame because the same movements can represent different actions, we do not act like we believe in the 'equitable maxim'. In particular cases, we let the unintended and unforeseen consequences of people's actions make a difference in how we assess them. This is a species of something that is referred to as 'hindsight bias': we feel we have a better sense of what the person has intended based on the consequences (or the lack of consequences) his action has (see Royzman and Kumar 2004). What is wrong with this is that it sometimes distorts our understanding of the person's intention. The person who fails to bring about some consequence, even if this is the result of an accident, is thought to have not really intended that consequence at all. The person who accidentally harms somebody is thought to have had that harm in his plans all along. So on the one hand, we agree that only a person's intention should matter in how we judge him. On the other hand, we also let consequences affect how we judge a person: they distort our picture of that person's intention, making us think it is better or worse than it really is. 'Scarce, in any one instance, perhaps', Smith writes, 'will our sentiments be found, after examination, to be entirely regulated by this rule [the equitable maxim] which we acknowledge ought entirely to regulate them' (TMS II.iii.intro.5, 93).

In the first paragraph of this part, I said that Smith seems to set himself up for an answer which he in the end fails to give, and now we can see the outlines of that answer: man should revise his judgments so that they are in line with the equitable maxim! (This seems to be the position that Nagel ascribes to Smith.) Fortune simply should not be allowed to have some influence 'where we should be least willing to allow her any' (TMS II.iii.3.1, 104). If we are judging people for things that they did not intend and were out of their control, we ought to stop doing so, because this is unfair. At best, we are being ungrateful, for not acknowledging the person who meant to do us well but who, wholly because of an accident, wasn't able to carry out his design. At worst, we are plainly being unjust, by blaming someone for a harm he didn't intend, or blaming him out of proportion to the harm he did intend but which resulted in more harm than he could have foreseen. In sum, we should 'pare down each act to its morally essential core' (its intention or design), and then judge according only to that and not by anything else. To be sure, in so far as our habits of blaming and praising according to the 'event and not the design', as Smith puts it, are ingrained in our customs, habits, and laws, we should be careful in making any radical change: this may do more harm than good, as Sanford Kadish (citing Smith) cautions (Kadish 1994: 699). But to accommodate our irregular sentiments would be a second best, a falling short of the ideal.[3]

So we might expect Smith, in this section, to perhaps give some examples of our irregular sentiments (which he does) and explain how we are led to blame and praise in this manner (which he also does), but then to say that we are, in fact, quite irrational in doing this. Smith often makes claims to this effect, e.g. that we often resent a harm done to us entirely out of proportion to the actual harm and so we should revise our judgments (TMS II.ii.2.1, 82–3). Indeed, this seems the whole point of the 'impartial spectator', that we are sometimes too rash in our judgments, and so we need to step back from them, and see them in a different light. When we are in the grip of our various passions, Smith says, paraphrasing Malebranche, they seem to justify themselves, 'and seem reasonable and proportional to their objects, as long as we continue to feel them' (TMS III.4.3, 157). However, when we look more coolly at our conduct we can see that, perhaps, the passion was unjustified after all – that the anger or resentment we felt was too much, given how slight the injury was, and how short-lived the pain. And we can see Smith proposing something similar with regard to our irregular sentiments. In the heat of the moment, we may judge on consequences, but when we reflect, we see that we should stick to the 'rule' that only somebody's intentions matter in judging him, because he couldn't have controlled the accidental and unforeseen consequences of his act. Therefore it shouldn't be lost on us that Smith calls the equitable maxim a 'rule' which ought 'entirely to regulate our conduct', because rules are precisely those things that are 'fixed in our mind by habitual reflection' (TMS III.4.12, 160) as opposed to the judgments made on the spot, in particular cases (for more on Smith on rules, see Fleischacker 1990: 143–9).

What is interesting is that Smith does not give the answer we might expect, namely, that we should revise our judgments to be more in line with the equitable maxim. Smith says, instead, that he is going to consider the 'end' to which our irregular sentiments answer, or 'the purpose which the Author of nature seems to have intended' by them (TMS II.iii.intro.6, 93). Clearly, Smith means by this that the Author of nature brings good out of what seems to be irregular: the Author of nature by his 'eternal art' educes good from ill (TMS I.ii.e.4, 36). The 'great disorder' in our sentiments, Smith says elsewhere, is 'not without its utility' (TMS VI.iii.31, 253).[4] The question is whether Smith sees our irregular sentiments *only* as (possibly unjust) means to a good end, or whether he sees them as sometimes proper and as making ethical sense in their own right.

I suggest, in the next two parts of this chapter, that Smith may also be offering a type of argument for keeping our irregular sentiments as they are which we might put under the category of 'reconciliation'. That is, our irregular sentiments might not be things we need to be resigned to, or brute forces of unreason that we are giving in to – perhaps for the overall utility they provide – but parts of our social world that we can accept and even affirm (cf. Rawls 1996: 171). This is another, non-utilitarian, way we might understand Smith's more general belief that 'every part of nature, when attentively surveyed, equally demonstrates the providential care of its Author' (TMS ii.III.3.2, 105).

II

Smith puts up some roadblocks in the way of this 'non-utilitarian' interpretation, though. In his chapter on the 'final cause of this irregularity of sentiments' Smith writes that Nature 'when she implanted the seeds of this irregularity in the human breast, seems, as upon all other occasions to have intended the happiness and perfection of the species' (TMS II.iii.3.1, 105). This quotation by itself is perhaps not all that worrisome. What is more worrisome is the gloss Smith later puts on the first quote, which is that 'every part of nature, when attentively surveyed, equally demonstrates the providential care of its Authors, and we may admire the wisdom and goodness of God even in the weakness and folly of man' (TMS ii.III.3.2, 106). The word that is particularly worrisome here is 'folly' which suggests that our sentiments are at best quite off the mark, and at worst, vicious. Smith seems to make the latter association when he writes earlier in TMS of 'the vices and follies of mankind' as an equally necessary part of God's plan as man's virtue, because both tend to the 'prosperity and perfection of the great system of nature' (TMS i.II.3.4, 36). The phrasing of the chapter on the final ends of our irregular sentiments, then, strongly implies that Smith is giving a flatly 'utilitarian' justification of our irregular sentiments, where our mistaken sentiments get vindicated in spite of their impropriety and because of their utility.

The problem with this interpretation of Smith, however, is that Smith's arguments for the utility of our sentiments are pretty weak, and in places even go against what Smith affirms elsewhere in TMS. And if Smith's arguments are truly of this utilitarian type, and they do not succeed, then what we are left with is not merely the irregularity of our sentiments but their irrationality: they neither are in line with the equitable maxim, nor do they serve to bring about some greater good. We would have no reason, then, not to try to change our irregular sentiments, or if we could not change them, at least to regret them.

In this part and the next, I try to read Smith's arguments along a different line, one less utilitarian and more of the kind the impartial spectator could endorse, that is, a kind of explanation which shows the sentiments might be proper whatever utility they might also have. This is not to say that the utilitarian arguments Smith does give are hopelessly wrong and to be completely rejected, only that they do not have to bear all the weight. Smith makes two utilitarian-sounding arguments for the 'final cause' of our irregular sentiments; the first argument will take up the rest of this part, and I will consider the second argument in part III.

Smith's first argument

The first argument Smith gives deals mainly with one kind of case, namely, those cases where we punish or resent unequally because of the different consequences of similar actions. Some people intend to do something bad, go through all the right motions to accomplish that bad thing, but nonetheless, because of luck, never are able to actually do the bad thing. These people, who end up only attempting to do bad, are punished less harshly than those who actually succeed in doing bad – even though what separates the two classes of people is nothing relevant to blame, because what separates them is their good or bad fortune. Now, Smith wants to convince us that it is a good thing that this asymmetry exists. He says that if it did not and we punished people based on the malevolent designs, 'every court of judicature would become a real inquisition. There would be no safety for the most innocent and circumspect conduct' (TMS II.iii.3.2, 105). There would not be any 'safety' because even a person who behaved innocently enough might still be suspected of harboring 'bad wishes, bad views, and bad designs', though none of these designs had yet 'broke[n] out into any action' (TMS II.iii.3.2, 105). Smith actually has a pretty good point here, but what he does with it (as I go on to explain) may not be the best way of expressing it. There is a trade-off between freedom and action and nipping potentially bad conduct in the bud. We value the fact that actions which do not cause harm presumptively deserve protection. Of course, sometimes we pay for this, when we could have stopped a bad action before it caused the harm, but there is undoubtedly a trade-off on the other side, too. There are costs involved with having a 'very accurate police' (TMS II.iii.2.8, 102) which punish any person 'in whose breast we suspect or believe such [hurtful] designs or affections were harboured' (TMS II.iii.3.2, 105). The trade-off is not merely that sometimes the police would punish someone who didn't deserve it, but that in general, we would feel less free because 'even the most innocent and circumspect conduct ... might still be suspected' (TMS II.iii.3.2, 105). We are better off, we think, if punishment is limited to those cases of 'actual evil, or [the] attempt to produce it' (TMS II.iii.3.2, 105) and doesn't also include punishing 'the affections of the heart only, where no crime has been committed' (TMS II.ii.3.3, 106).

So Smith has a valid point, albeit a pretty modest one, of a roughly rule-utilitarian variety. We value freedom of action, and believe innocent conduct (as Smith defines it) deserves at least presumptive protection, so we make it a rule not to punish merely bad thoughts or malevolent affections. Yet Smith says things in the course of making this modest point which I do not think we should follow him on, and which indeed go against things Smith elsewhere has endorsed. He ends up making his case in rather bold strokes and heated rhetoric, and in the process fails to make some fundamental distinctions. Let me lay out two of these distinctions in the abstract before I go on to show how Smith, in addition to the modest rule-utilitarian point he makes, gives us a real insight into our nature as agents, and how we come to know the intentions of others and even our own intention.

First, Smith seems to group our 'sentiments, thoughts, [and] intentions' as if they were all of one kind. Smith makes no distinction between what may be a mere passing fancy or a whim, considered for a moment and then disposed of, and a more sincere disposition, on which we have reflected for some period of time and which we now endorse (Russell 1999: 44). All of these are put together by Smith, because all of them exist in us prior to the moment of action. But I take it that we do distinguish between the passing thoughts and the more considered judgments of others, and this is shown in how we variously react to them. On the one hand, we rarely resent the mere passing fancies or idle thoughts of others, partly because we are rarely in a position to know them, and partly because we don't view them as actually endorsed by the agent. These do not register as appropriate objects of our resentment, and rightly so: we do not know if these are really part of the agent that he would affirm, rather than reject, were he to consider them. Still less are these thoughts the objects of punishment. On the other hand, we do resent the more fully formed intentions and designs of agents, and sometimes even view these as appropriate objects of punishment. Indeed, to use an example Smith invokes elsewhere in the section on our irregularity of sentiments, 'a treasonable consort, though nothing has been done, or even attempted in consequence of it, nay, a treasonable conversation, is in many countries punished in the same manner as the actual commission of treason' (TMS II.iii.2.4, 100). Already, when we recognize that all thoughts are not alike, and that some will be resented either because of the evident resolution with which they are held or because of the sensitivity of their content, we begin to blur the line between what is merely a hurtful design or malevolent affection, and what is an evil act that merits resentment and punishment. When Smith indiscriminately groups all thoughts as alike, he ignores that there are some sentiments which we do resent even though they never 'break out into any action'. In fact, he ignores distinctions that he clearly makes elsewhere in TMS.

Second, Smith fails to note that not all hurtful actions are of a piece and that we make important distinctions between them. Surely an action which causes harm accidentally is treated very differently than a harm deliberately caused. Therefore, we should be skeptical of Smith when he says that the 'great judge of hearts' has placed the 'sentiments, designs, [and] affections' of people 'beyond the limits of every human jurisdiction' and has reserved judgment of these 'for the cognizance of his own unerring tribunal' (TMS II.iii.3.2, 105). This is a somewhat striking claim for Smith, someone who throughout TMS has emphasized our ability to imagine ourselves in the place of others; does this not imply, also, that we can enter into their sentiments, designs and affections? Moreover, it is not only clear that we do judge evils and attempted evils based on the designs behind them, but that it is proper that we should do so, as Smith clearly recognizes elsewhere. (We need only recall the example Smith gives of the person who shoots a bird and the person who shoots a man: 'both of them', he says, 'perform the same external movement: each of them draws the trigger of a gun'; TMS II.iii.intro.2, 93.) We feel that the person who has accidentally brought about an evil is very different than someone who has premeditated that evil; the former seems an inappropriate object of resentment, where the latter is a fit object both of resentment and punishment. What Smith in some of his more strident rhetoric seems to be advocating, as Paul Russell points out, is akin to a regime of strict liability, where we would base punishment on actual harm caused by an action without looking at the intent behind the harmful action (Russell 1999: 43). But this ignores how we do make distinctions between harmful acts, and at the same time ironically overlooks the significant disutility we would incur if we did punish all harm-causing actions the same way, without regard to intention. To use Smith's term, 'innocent conduct' would likewise be at risk in a regime of strict liability, because one who was as 'circumspect' as we could reasonably expect could still be held strictly liable for those harms he inadvertently caused. This, too, would mean potentially sharp reductions in freedom of action, because we could never be sure if and when he might be held responsible for a harm we had caused purely by accident. As Russell comments, 'in these circumstances every person must be afraid and anxious that, through no fault of her own, she might become the object of resentment and retribution' (Russell 1999: 43).

Smith's first argument: another interpretation

So we need to be careful when reading Smith's first argument along utilitarian lines. He undoubtedly has a point, but our practice of blaming is much more nuanced than the blunt construal he gives of it in his brief chapter on the 'final cause' of our irregularity of sentiment. For we do base blame on intentions, both in the sense that sometimes 'mere' thoughts, designs, and affections can be the appropriate object of resentment, and in the sense that an appraisal of another's intention is a nearly indispensable part of deciding whether he ought to be punished for his bad action. Yet I want to step away from the question of the usefulness, strictly speaking, of our tendency to punish and resent based on consequences. I want to look at our dependence on consequences not in terms of their utility, but in terms of their epistemic value. For the fact is that although we can know a person's intentions, we cannot know them infallibly, and for this reason we may sometimes realize what a person has intended only when his intentions 'break out into action' and produce either a good or bad consequence. This allows us to give a different spin on Smith's first argument, by not reading it as an argument about how our irregularity of blame leads to our 'happiness and perfection'. What I will suggest is that we read it, instead, as showing us a truth about our nature as finite and imperfect agents: we cannot read one another's minds, and many times we do not even fully know the content of our own minds.

The relevant example here is the one Smith gives of a man who rides a horse but who loses control of the horse after it takes fright, and ends up injuring his neighbor's slave. Smith writes about that case:

> [When] an accident of this kind happens, we are apt to think that he ought not have rode such a horse, and to regard his attempting it as an unpardonable levity; though without this accident we should not only have made no such reflection, but should have regarded his refusing it as the effect of timid weakness.
>
> (TMS II.iii.2.9, 104)

That is, the only way we can find out that the person should not have been riding the horse in the first place is when that person gets into an accident. If his ride was accident-free, we would not have learned about his lack of skill in riding a horse, a lack of skill that made it dangerous for him to be on the horse. Now, Smith's point in that example was really that the person did take care in riding the horse, and that we (unfairly) consider him to be reckless in riding the horse when he was not. But we can certainly apply his point to those cases where a person is reckless or negligent but we do not know this until something bad happens. To take a more contemporary example, we sometimes become aware that a person has been driving too fast or not paying enough attention to the road only after he gets into an accident.

Of course, we do not always wait to discover someone's intention or design until after something bad has happened. Sometimes we know enough beforehand to set guidelines about what is and what is not an acceptable degree of care. We know that having a certain amount of alcohol in your blood is highly likely to make you an unsafe driver, so we do not wait for an accident to happen in order to make an arrest (or to take away the car keys from a friend who's been drinking too much). This is why we also aren't shy in punishing criminal acts that are 'carried to the length of the last attempt' (TMS II.iii.2.4, 100): we feel that in those cases we have all the evidence we could ask for. Yet there will always be a considerable degree of doubt in many cases. Where an intention is never fully manifested in an actual harm caused, there still remains room to question whether the person really intended to do harm. As Smith rightly notes, 'we are capable, it may be said, of resolving, and even of taking measures to execute, many things which, when it comes to the point, we feel ourselves altogether incapable of executing' (TMS II.iii.2.4, 100). That is, if our intentions 'give birth to no action', we are left to wonder if they really were our intentions at all, if we truly meant to cause the harm in the first place. Perhaps our heart was never entirely in it, and that is why our effort failed. It is, then, not only the minds of others that are not transparent to us; even in our own case we may not be sure of our intention until we see its effects in the world. We may know our minds better, less because of some privileged access we have to them, than because we have been around ourselves more, and have seen more of the consequences of our actions, and through them know what we are truly capable of (TMS III.2.15, 122).[5]

In the examples of the negligent horse rider and the person who got into a car accident, we imagined that the negligence (or the recklessness) was there all along, prior to the bad consequences. But there are other cases where the intention is coincident with the action itself. This need not be only cases where we decide, on a whim, to do something. It can also involve cases where we are torn between two courses of action, and then finally decide on one and do it. In these cases the moment of action and the moment where our intention gets formed will be one and the same. Smith gives the example of a person who is deliberating whether to commit a crime, and who goes back and forth between his intention to do it and his intention not to do it.

> He changes his purpose every moment [Smith writes]; sometimes he resolves to adhere to his principle, and not indulge a passion which may corrupt the remaining part of his life with the horrors of shame and repentance; and a momentary calm takes possession of his breast, from the prospect of that security and tranquillity which he will enjoy when he thus determines not to expose himself to the hazard of a contrary conduct.
>
> (TMS III.4.12, 161)

Until he has taken the 'last fatal and irrecoverable step', Smith says, we will not be able to ascribe an intention to him, not because we can never know that intention, but because the intention does not exist. The ambiguity of the intention is there until the moment of choice, which Smith expresses vividly by the metaphor of the man throwing himself off a precipice. The man seems to fall into the decision, rather than simply at some discrete moment resolve to do it and then at some later time carry it out.

So far, we have considered two types of examples, each of which, I think, shows something different about why we need to rely on consequences in figuring out someone's intention. In the case of the rider on the horse who runs somebody over, we need consequences as evidence that there was a bad (negligent) will there, even though without any bad consequences we would have never suspected it. With the most recent example, of the man whose intention is not really fixed until it 'breaks out into action', we come nearer to relying on consequences because it is the appropriate thing to do. It would be wrong to resent the person for thinking about a bad action that it is not even clear he fully means to do. In the next moment, he might change his mind, and decide to straighten up and fly right. At least in some cases, our irregular sentiments are regular, because it is only when the pain and pleasure are caused that we have a definite intention come into view.

All of this is not to say that the rule-utilitarian argument Smith gives for our irrational sentiments isn't a good one. It is just that it has some flaws, especially in the form Smith sometimes presents it, and that anyway it isn't the whole story: there is another way of describing our sentiments and why we find it necessary to rely on consequences. We certainly do save ourselves a lot of trouble and protect our freedom of action by not punishing thoughts. But this is not because we do not (or cannot) know the thoughts, designs, plans and intentions of others, because sometimes we do. Rather, it is that we cannot know these things infallibly, which is why it is 'proper' given our nature to rely on consequences to make inferences about people's intentions.

But our irregular sentiments might not just be proper given our nature, as a way of correcting for our flaws, but proper full stop. Intentions are not always fully formed prior to the moment of action, and it is only by waiting to see what happens that we can know whether a person deserves to be resented or not. In respecting this last point, we of course might go too far, and imagine someone might still change his mind even though his intention seems pretty fully formed. Here our sentiments risk turning irregular again, but we can still see the ethical sense in them. We seem ready to pay the cost of allowing some possibly preventable harm in order to be fair to others, and not restrict anyone's action unless we are reasonably confident it will 'break out' into a harmful action. This may sometimes result in our unhappiness, but I think we can still find some value in it, even if it is only the value of wishing that people were better than they usually are (Schmidtz 2002: 783–4). Perhaps it was something like this thought that led Smith to say, in comparison to benevolent affections, our malevolent affections towards another 'can scarce be too tardy, too slow, or deliberate' (TMS II.iii.3.3, 106).

III

Smith's second argument

I now turn to Smith's second argument for the 'utility' of our irregular sentiments, which builds on two types of cases: first, those cases where we have tried with good intent to perform a beneficial or important action, but due to unlucky circumstances this leads to nothing, and second, the cases where, though our intentions are entirely innocent, we end up causing harm anyway. What unites these two cases for Smith is that they show how our irregular sentiments provide us with incentives for certain types of good behavior. The fact that we are not praised (or praised only faintly) for having good intentions, but given the 'loudest acclamations' (TMS II.iii.3.3, 106) only for actions that are effective and prove concretely beneficial, moves us to try harder to make actual our designs for the happiness of others. 'Man', Smith declares, 'was made for action, and to promote by the exertion of his faculties such changes in the external circumstances both of himself and others, as may seem most favourable to the happiness of all' (TMS II.iii.3.3, 106). Man is not to be satisfied (and we cannot let him be satisfied) merely with trying hard and not succeeding, or with wishing the good of others but doing nothing about it, as if it were true that 'it's the thought that counts'.[6] Smith also thinks that being resented by others just for accidentally causing harm leads us to be more careful. It's important that the harm we unintentionally cause others is regarded as our 'misfortune', Smith says, because man is

> thereby taught to reverence the happiness of his brethren, to tremble lest he should, even unknowingly, do any thing that can hurt them, and to dread that animal resentment which, he feels, is ready to burst out against him, if he should, without design, be the unhappy instrument of their calamity.
>
> (TMS II.iii.3.4, 106)

So Smith sees a kind of economy of rewards and punishments being fortuitously set up by our irregular sentiments: we praise only those intentions that are successful, even thought it may be a matter of chance that a good intention does succeed, and this leads people to try harder, to 'strain every nerve' (TMS II.iii.3.3, 106); plus we resent even those harms that are accidentally caused, and this leads people to be extra cautious.

So here we have two ways in which what looks, from one angle, as an irregularity, a mistake, actually leads to the happiness of mankind. The sentiments have a utility, just like our chasing after trinkets and baubles has its utility (TMS IV.1.6, 180). And surely we would not be wrong to concede that Smith has a point here. We will feel that our action is not fully complete when it does not have the effects we intend it to have, even when our failure is due to bad luck rather than lack of effort. If our purposes aren't realized in the world, we are not 'fully satisfied with [our] conduct', as Smith says. It is also true that part of why we work hard is for the sake of praise, although being over-anxious about praise even for praiseworthy actions is a sign of weakness (TMS III.2.29, 127–8). It is better to be satisfied that we have tried our best, or done the right thing, even if no one notices. Finally, we simply do care whether we have harmed or helped others, contributed to the 'happiness of [our] brethren' not merely because we want praise or fear blame for what we have done, but because that happiness matters in itself, is worth something in its own right.

Still, as I even began suggesting in the last paragraph, there is something wrong with the utilitarian way Smith puts his argument. Sometimes the reason we do not want to hurt someone accidentally is because we are afraid other people might resent us for it. But mostly we do not want to hurt someone accidentally, because if we do we will have *hurt somebody*, and this is a bad thing in its own right. In an interesting and subtle shift from the first five editions of TMS to the sixth, Smith seems aware of this point. In the first five editions, he wrote that it was of 'considerable use' that we regard the evil we do to another as our misfortune. But in the sixth edition, he says it is of 'considerable importance' (TMS II.iii.3.4, 106) that we regard those evils as our misfortunes. This is slight evidence, to be sure, but it does seem to show that Smith realized that casting his arguments for our irregular sentiments in terms of their usefulness might not be the best way of putting them. In any case, let me make two general points about the utilitarian way in which Smith sometimes presents his second argument, before I go on to suggest an alternative reading of it.

First, I wonder if Smith is in fact playing fair with the examples he gives, because it looks like he may be grouping together two sorts of cases that should be kept distinct. One kind of case involves someone who has, as Smith says, only an 'indolent benevolence' and 'fanc[ies] himself the friend of mankind because in his heart he wishes well to the prosperity of the world' (TMS II.iii.3.3, 106). Another kind of case involves a person who truly 'strain[s] every nerve' in order to advance the prosperity of mankind, but through unfortunate circumstances never really succeeds in his efforts. In the former type of case, we might well suspect that the person is not really sincere in his sentiments, and so we rightly withhold our praise from him: he is not, in fact, doing all he can to bring about the 'prosperity of the world'. E. M. Forster criticizes such a character in his novel *Where Angels Fear to Tread*: 'You told me once that we shall be judged by our intentions, not by our accomplishments. I thought it a grand remark. But we must intend to accomplish – not sit intending on a chair' (quoted in Fleischacker 1990: 293 n. 36). In the second sort of case, it seems clear that the person is sincere in his wishes for the happiness of mankind given how hard he works (he is obviously 'intending to accomplish'). But if Smith wants his point to have force, the examples he gives need to be on a level – he needs to be comparing two people who are working equally hard, but who succeed or fail based just on luck. By taking two cases where the intentions are in fact different, Smith fails to capture the point he wishes to make, which is that it is only because actual results are praised that man is moved to work hard to produce the actual happiness of mankind. If it is truly *only* luck that separates the second case from success, where the person exerts himself mightily, then there should be nothing wrong with praising him, because no perverse incentive will result. For if we praise those cases like him, we are praising those people who will be most likely, luck willing, to actually benefit mankind.

Second, if we imagine the cases rightly, it may be that the incentives our irregular sentiments provide may be the exact opposite of what Smith supposes they provide. In the real world, success does not always track real effort, and so to praise simply those actions which happen to benefit mankind may not be to praise the type of action which will, over the long run and for the most part, benefit mankind. That is, praising consequences rather than effort may create perverse incentives by encouraging the wrong sorts of behavior. Smith actually makes something like this point later on in TMS when he considers the 'real merit' of 'spirited, magnanimous, and high-minded persons'. 'Success', Smith says, 'covers from his eyes, not only the great imprudence, but frequently the great injustice of their enterprises; and, far from blaming this defective part of their character he often views it with the most enthusiastic admiration' (TMS VI.iii.30, 252). In other words, success can make foolish and unwise (even vicious) actions appear as actually good, winning our praise, and making it seem as if those actions should be emulated. In fact, it has only been the luck of the magnanimous person that has made his actions appear in a flattering light. 'Fortune has in this', Smith continues, 'great influence over the moral sentiments of mankind, and according as she is either favourable or adverse, can render the same character the object, either of general love and admiration, or of universal hatred and contempt' (TMS VI iii.30, 252–3). The fact that fortune colors the way we perceive actions can lead to perverse incentives for behavior in two ways. One way, as I have already mentioned, is that it can make actions which will usually be unjust or harmful appear good and beneficial. People may be led to see those actions as the type which they should perform, rather than those virtuous actions which will, in most cases, actually increase the happiness of mankind. Another way is by leading some to conclude that no matter what they do, how hard they work, the real basis of others' esteem for them will be on the basis of consequences which, we know, depend on luck – so what's the use of really trying? It is perhaps for reasons like these that Smith remarks that to judge 'by the event, and not by the design, has been in all ages the complaint, and is the great discouragement of virtue' (TMS II.iii.3.1, 104–5). When we shift our praise from those people who actually sincerely try to do good and who by no fault of their own may fail, to those who simply succeed, whatever their underlying motivation or virtue, we risk creating incentives for behavior that have no real relation to the happiness of mankind, except the contingent one that in *this* case *this* behavior has turned out to be successful.[7]

Smith's second argument: another interpretation

Even after we point all this out, what Smith says still has some merit, and not just in a utilitarian way (i.e. we should withhold praise until good consequences occur to provide an incentive for people to work hard, and we should blame even when the harm is accidental, in order to get people to be more careful, and even to refrain from engaging in some activities altogether). There is still something to the idea that if a virtue never becomes actual, we may legitimately wonder whether the agent really possesses that virtue, or only wishes that he possessed it. We cannot know with any certainty all the 'latent virtues' (TMS II.iii.3.3, 106) a person has, and when a latent virtue breaks out into a good action, we may have better grounds for believing that there was a virtuous character trait there from the beginning. We may not even know that we ourselves possess a virtue until we have realized it in action. As Charles Griswold asks, 'if you have no chance to display these virtues in action, can you, or spectators, be certain that you possess them?' (Griswold 1999: 241). In sum, just as we might not know a harmful intention until bad consequences happen, so too we may not know a real virtue until it produces good consequences. In both cases consequences can help us support our inferences about the character of an agent's intentions. Of course, the point by now has to be hedged about with qualifications, especially given what Smith himself says about how luck and not actual virtue can be what is primarily responsible for the beneficial consequences, and that this can distort how we perceive the merit of somebody's actions. Consequences can serve as evidence for someone's intention, but not indefeasible evidence.

And we should emphasize a point made in passing above, which is that it matters to us in itself whether we end up helping someone or harming them. Here we might make a distinction made by Michael Zimmerman in his discussion of moral luck (Zimmerman, 2002). Two people with similar intentions may cause very different results, and this merely because of fortune rather than anything in what they intended. What we should say about these cases, Zimmerman writes, is that neither party is *more responsible* than the other, even though one person may *be responsible for more.* Neither one, that is, is more deserving of our praise or blame than the other, in terms of intentions or designs. Yet we might nonetheless honor more the one who has by his good fortune ended up helping us, simply because he has caused us a benefit, whereas the other has not. The point of the honor, however, is not best interpreted as providing an incentive for others to work harder, as Smith in his utilitarian mode sometimes appears to hold. The point of the honor is simply that it is good to be the bringer of benefits, as opposed to somebody who only attempts to be one. This is why, Smith correctly points out, we may 'esteem' and 'love' the person with good intentions, but the person who has actually helped us is the one to whom praise and reward are owed, for she has produced an 'actual service' for us (TMS II.iii.3.3, 106).

The idea of praising someone for a consequence he has produced with the help of fortune is plausible when his intention and effort were geared towards that result. It is less plausible when it was only his intention and was not accompanied by sincere effort. It is still less so when there is only the good wish, an 'indolent benevolence'. But Smith will say that even in this latter case, a 'shadow of merit' falls over the person. We tend to feel grateful to the person who has provided us with a benefit even when this was mostly a matter of luck. Our joy in the good result spreads to the agent connected with it and besides, with praise, we need only the slightest of reasons to justify our gratitude (TMS II.iii.2.6, 102).

More disturbingly, perhaps, Smith wants to insist that some resentment is justified for harms we only accidentally cause, and that we are not wrong in feeling somewhat guilty for causing them. His most developed example is the person who has run down someone with his horse, which I mentioned above in discussing Smith's first argument. Smith said that the rider will 'have some sense of his own ill desert' with regard to the person he has injured (TMS II.ii.2.10, 106). If the rider doesn't apologize, or atone for what he did, Smith says, it would be regarded as 'the highest brutality' (TMS II.ii.2.10, 106) by others. So we have it from Smith that in cases where even when we are not strictly speaking liable (Smith says that the rider has taken the utmost degree of care), we feel guilty when we have hurt somebody, and other people expect us to act as if we were really at fault, at pains of engaging in 'the highest brutality' and pretending that we are innocent. But wasn't the rider really innocent? Why is the rider not entitled to consider the accident as part of nature, and not of his design? After all, that comes closer to being the correct explanation, certainly closer than that the rider set out to deliberately hurt the neighbor's slave. Smith (anticipating these worries) asks why should the rider, 'since he was equally innocent with any other bystander, be thus singled out from among all mankind, to make up for the bad fortune of another' (TMS II.ii.2.10, 106)? And Smith replies that our sympathies are at least in part with the injured person, who feels, Smith revealingly writes, a 'resentment' that 'may be regarded as unjust' (TMS II.ii.2.10, 106).

However, Smith also says that the 'man of humanity' who has accidentally caused another person injury, 'without the smallest degree of blamable negligence', will feel a sense of guilt, even though he is not really guilty (TMS II.iii.3.4, 106). By invoking the 'man of humanity' Smith seems to be saying that the 'fallacious' sense of guilt is appropriate, even mandatory, when we have unintentionally hurt someone.[8] But it seems wrong to see this guilt as simply useful: as if the importance of avoiding accidental harm is to avoid fallacious guilt, rather than simply to avoid harming somebody. This fallacious guilt demands being analyzed in its own right, to see whether we can make any sense of it.

On 'fallacious' guilt

There are two things that it seems plain this guilt is not. First, the guilt is 'fallacious' because Smith, by hypothesis, is ruling out that there was any actual wrong involved. In discussing the main characters in several tragedies, Smith writes that all of them feel guilty even though 'not one of them is in the smallest degree guilty' (TMS II.iii.3.5, 107). So we should dismiss the explanation that would say this fallacious guilt is due to our uncertainty about whether we really did everything to avoid the accident. (Were we paying enough attention to the road?) At least, these are not the type of cases in which Smith is interested. Second, this fallacious guilt is not, or not only, a form of sympathy with the person we have injured accidentally. Sympathy is something that the innocent bystander might feel. But I take it that what we are looking for is the special connection we might feel with the person we have harmed, by virtue of the fact that we have caused him harm. Since sympathy can be felt by those who are not at all causally related to the injured party, it's not what we're looking for.[9]

We should also note something else, which is related to 'fallacious guilt' not being simply a form of sympathy. We could imagine an innocent bystander being obliged to help the injured person, but we could not imagine him being obliged to make an apology or that his help might be a form of atonement or expiation. What is interesting about the guilt Smith talks about is that it looks like guilt for something we are morally responsible for, and bears the marks of it, but in fact we are not really morally responsible for the wrong. (Nor, by hypothesis, were we negligent or reckless in causing the accident.) At the same time, neither our guilt or apologies nor our efforts to make expiation are simply acts of beneficence. Smith is famous for drawing a contrast between justice and beneficence, yet here we have a phenomenon which resists analysis entirely in terms of either concept. A person who failed to make an apology or feel guilt over an accidental harm would not be unjust, for this is reserved for deliberate wrongs: Smith writes that a person violates a duty of justice who does 'real and positive hurt to some particular persons, from motives which are naturally disapproved of' (TMS II.ii.1.4, 79). In the cases we are discussing the motives are pure, by hypothesis. But neither would the person who has accidentally injured another be beneficent in offering his assistance, for we feel in some way that this is what he owes to the injured party; he is 'tied, bound, and obliged' to him, although not by force (TMS II.ii.1.6, 79).

With these distinctions in mind, we should turn more explicitly to what Smith says. In explaining why we feel the fallacious guilt, Smith supplies us with an elaborate metaphor. He compares our accidentally injuring another with treading on the holy ground 'which has been consecrated to some god' (TMS II.iii.3.4, 107). He says in these cases, the person who has even 'ignorantly' violated the precinct of the god would incur 'the vengeance of that powerful and invisible being to whom it had been set apart' (TMS II.iii.3.4, 107). In a similar vein, Smith says, the wisdom of nature has made 'the happiness of every innocent man' a sacred place, so that even accidental violations of an innocent person's happiness require 'some atonement' (TMS II.iii.3.4, 107). The provenance of the comparison should make us, I think, a little wary. The cost of violating the holy ground of the god is to risk the god's vengeance. However, might we not say that the god in this instance is being unnecessarily cruel? Perhaps we cannot change what the god will do, but we can change how we feel about others who have involuntarily harmed another person. Do we have to mimic the cruelty of the god?

However, Smith does offer something in the way of a justification. He says that it is a good thing that we regard even being the 'unhappy instrument of another's harm, as something that we should feel guilty about, and that others might resent us for. Smith explains that this teaches us to 'reverence the happiness' of our brethren, and 'to tremble lest' we should 'even unknowingly, do any thing that can hurt them' (TMS II.iii.3.4, 106). I have discussed this type of utilitarian argument above, but mostly in the context of praise for consequences, not blame for them. The argument Smith offers here unmistakably has the same form – that of a utilitarian justification for feeling guilty about hurting another person unintentionally and having others resent us. But like many good, utilitarian arguments, it can seem, on closer examination, to involve some injustice.

The idea behind Smith's argument can be cashed out in terms of justification for some strict liability statutes. We have strict liability for selling adulterated milk, for instance. This is to deter some people from getting into the business of selling milk in the first place; they will 'tremble' lest they sell adulterated milk, and their solution will be to not sell it at all. For those who do sell milk, the point of the statute is to get them to be overly careful, absurdly careful, about how they package and prepare milk. But note that in a particular instance where adulterated milk is found, and the company is punished, it will be hard to avoid the thought that it involves some injustice. All things considered, it is a good thing we have the statute, because it deters some from producing milk in the first place, and it will make the company that is punished by the statute even more careful in preparing milk in the future. However, by hypothesis, the company that gets punished for violating the statute could have been as careful as you wish, and still they are guilty.

Now translate into the case of a person who accidentally or unknowingly causes a person harm. By hypothesis, we can say that he has done everything he could reasonably have been expected to do, in order to avoid hurting the other person. He of course could have stayed home and done nothing, but surely (and Smith would agree) this is too much to ask. What Smith seems to be saying is that it is a good thing that our 'animal resentment' might burst out against a person who unintentionally causes harm, because it will teach others, and him, to be more careful in the future. However, it strikes me that even though there might be good utilitarian reasons for resenting him, this resentment is more than a little unjust: after all, he has done nothing wrong! Perhaps this is why strict liability is mostly confined to regulatory infractions, and does not show up in the criminal law too often. Strict liability is more about regulating an industry than about punishing individuals for their wrongdoing, more about fines than about jail terms (see Schulhofer and Kadish, 2001: 255).

We ought to concede what Smith has right: when we harm someone unintentionally we do feel a kind of guilt, and the injured party does feel a kind of resentment. But, Smith adds, we should not confuse these cousins to guilt and resentment with the real things. The guilt for some harm we have caused by accident is 'fallacious' guilt and the resentment the injured party feels is an 'animal resentment'. Smith also talks in terms of a 'shadow' of demerit falling over the person who has caused the harm (TMS I.iii.1.7, 107). The shadow imagery does some real work here, on several levels. First, and most obviously, a shadow lacks substance – this shows that the 'demerit' Smith refers to exists at one remove from real guilt, although it is not completely unrelated to that guilt. Fallacious guilt is to real guilt as a person's body is to his shadow. Second, our shadow is of our likeness, and not of the likeness of anybody else. Only we can cast our own shadow, so our shadow bears our mark and is connected to us (and just to us). Finally, we do not intend to cast our shadow; when the sun is out, our shadow appears. So our shadow is not something we go about causing intentionally, it is something that happens to us, in the same way that the harm we cause accidentally is less something we do and more like something that happens to us. Smith seems to be asking us: how much of our lives is constituted by the shadows we cast over things, as opposed to those things we have deliberately caused?

It is a fact that irrational guilt and irrational resentment are still feelings, sometimes powerful ones; they are psychological facts we have to deal with. With this in mind, we might construct ways of rationalizing the need for the person who has caused harm to have to make an apology, offer atonement, etc. He needs to do these things to 'appease that animal resentment' (TMS II.iii.2.10, 104) of the injured party (and those close to him); he may also need to do these things to rid himself of his own irrational guilt feelings. Doing these things may make him feel better. After all, the fallacious guilt he feels is nonetheless something which he feels, and something he would like to get rid of; the emotional pain others feel is still there, even if it is 'animal'. So we can understand why the fallaciously guilty party might be moved to propitiate the unjust resentment of others by his actions and also, at the same time, lessen his own irrational guilt at the harm he has caused.

Such a justification of our acts of atonement and our apologies, however, is bound not to satisfy. It leaves the feelings themselves unjustified. Would it not be better if no one felt the mistaken feelings in the first place? It may be that we end up doing all sorts of slightly irrational things in order to deal with the compulsive emotions we feel, but surely this is a second-best solution. It would be better not to have the compulsive feelings at all, rather than to have to go to absurd lengths to get rid of them. And if others feel an irrational resentment against us for the harm we have done, and that resentment is unjustified, surely this is more their problem than ours.

But I think Smith is right about more than just the psychology. I believe he is right that if a person didn't feel the 'fallacious guilt' or that a 'shadow of demerit' had fallen over him, we would suspect that something was missing that ought to be there. There is a character who appears in Bernard Williams' famous essay 'Moral Luck' (Williams 1981). The person has accidentally hit a child with his car, but he fails to show remorse. Why should he, since it was an accident? He considers his obligations fulfilled when his insurance pays the family of the child, and he otherwise shrugs the accident off and goes about his business as usual. Something, clearly, is missing in this person's response: he is falling below the line not merely of expected conduct, but of morally acceptable conduct.

We should be careful in stating what is missing here. It is not the fact that the person has not gone to jail, or admitted his guilt. That would be to say that what we demanded was strict liability for the harm caused. I do not think we want to say that. Smith is right to say that what is missing here is not an expression of guilt, but an expression of guilt's shadow. The person in Williams' essay should not feel that he has hit the child on purpose, but he should feel terrible about it – he should feel almost tainted by it. He is in a special relationship with the harm caused, even though his responsibility, as per the equitable maxim, is no greater than a bystander to the event. Somehow, the fact of brute causation gains a moral salience, and we want the driver to recognize that salience.

I mentioned Bernard Williams a few paragraphs ago. Williams has also written on the moral significance of the things that we cause, though not intending to. He writes, in a representative passage from *Shame and Necessity*, that regret for the unintended consequences of our actions

> is not just regret about what happened, such as a spectator might have. It is an agent's regret, and it is in the nature of action that such regrets cannot be eliminated, that one's life could not be partitioned into some things that one does intentionally and other things that merely happen to one.
>
> (Williams 1993: 70)

Williams helpfully sets out a category that is different from the things one did intentionally, and the things that happen to us. He calls this category of actions the 'things that one did'. These things, the things one did, are more intimately mingled with one's sense of self; these are the 'shadows' of merit or demerit that Smith talks about.

Williams writes that the things one did can change people 'radically', and change them 'because they did that thing, not just because of what happened to them' (Williams 1993: 74). Smith also writes in this vein. He gives the example of a man who, 'without the smallest degree of blamable negligence', has caused the death of another man. 'During his whole life', Smith comments, 'he considers this accident as one of the greatest misfortunes that could have befallen him' (TMS II.iii.3.4, 107). What Williams and Smith both say about this type of case seems to me very acute. Our association with the things we unintentionally cause can indeed radically change our life. But without saying anything more, this remains on the level of a psychological point. We are not interested, or not only interested, in how our connection with the harm we unintentionally cause makes us feel and how it might change our lives, but with the question: should it make us feel this way?

In response to this question, Williams answers that '[t]hose who have been hurt need a response; simply what has happened to them may give them a right to seek it, and where can they look more appropriately than to you, the cause?' (Williams 1993: 70). But answering in this way just begs the question, because it assumes that causing a harm has a moral weight in itself without explaining how it gets that weight. Perhaps, although those hurt need a response, there is (like the case of a typhoon wiping out a village) no one that they can appropriately turn to, except maybe God. Or perhaps they should seek out a wealthy benefactor, who has the funds to compensate them for their hurt. We need a reason why causation assumes such importance here, why the person who has caused the harm is the one they might 'appropriately' turn to, and Williams doesn't give us one. In any event, Williams seems more concerned with the tragic fact that harming someone, even accidentally, can decisively shape one's life for the worse.[10] He seems less concerned about the relationship it might create with the person we have harmed.

Among contemporary philosophers, Susan Wolf seems to me to come closest to capturing what is at stake here. She calls what goes missing in the case of the man who shrugs off the accident a 'nameless virtue', but likens it to a kind of generosity (Wolf 2000–01: 14; see also Walker 1991).This goes some of the way, I think, towards articulating the nature of the man's mistake. It is hard to articulate, because the person is not strictly speaking responsible so there is nothing really wrong with him not acting as if he were strictly speaking responsible. So it is generous of him if he does atone for what he has done, to apologize, and to make amends, as if he were a guilty party. This makes it sound supererogatory, however, although it does not really seem that way. It is something we might reasonably expect of the person who has accidentally injured us, not something he is going above and beyond the call of duty in doing.

So this 'nameless virtue' seems hard to fit into any neat category. It is not like the paying off of a debt, nor is it like the giving of a gift. It is somewhere in between. Wolf, I think, helps us to see that the nameless virtue that gets exercised when we feel terrible, apologize, etc., for harming someone intentionally is part of a much larger class of virtues. We could define ourselves as pure wills, and not take responsibility for anything that we accidentally or unintentionally caused. However, if we did this, Wolf writes, if we 'define ourselves in ways that aim to minimize the significance of contingency and luck, we do so at the cost of living less fully in the world, or at least at the cost of engaging less fully with the others who share that world' (Wolf 2000–01: 15). What is Wolf getting at when she says this?

Some of our relationships are based simply on a contract: we agree to perform some service in exchange for some good. The relationship may not last beyond the fulfillment of the contract. But many, indeed, most of our relationships are not like this. They are not tit for tat. Smith writes of the 'trifling circumstance' of living in the same neighborhood as someone else. From a certain point of view, the property of 'being a neighbor' to someone is an accident, not having any moral importance in itself. Why should I favor someone who just happens to live in a close geographical relationship to me? There are many other people I could help, and who are perhaps even more deserving of my help. My neighbor may never have benefited me in any concrete, tangible way. I may not even especially like her. Nonetheless, Smith writes, that 'there are certain small good offices, accordingly, which are universally allowed to be due to a neighbour in preference to any other person who has no such connection' (TMS VI.ii.1.16, 224).

Consider family relationships also. We may believe that we owe a debt to our family members for the service they have provided in the past, and so our present kindnesses towards them are a way of repaying that debt. We could think this, but it would be a remarkably shallow way of regarding our relationship to our family members: we owe debts to them, not merely through some cold accounting of past services rendered, but because they're family. At the same time, if we ignore the services our family has provided for us, what are we left with, when talking about the importance of family? It was just an accident of birth that we are members of a particular family, and why should an accident create relations of such moral importance? Still, the accident that this person is my brother rather than that person, may give me reason to favor him. Smith says that it would be 'the highest impropriety, and sometimes even a sort of impiety', if we felt otherwise towards those related to us (TMS VI.ii.1.5, 220).

What Smith is getting at is that sometimes mere 'accidents' can create moral relationships with other people. At the very least, they can be the basis for such relationships. It is perhaps not that our causal relationship with the person we have injured has a moral importance in itself, but that we can confer an importance on it, just as we can confer an importance on the relationship with the person who is our neighbor and who gains our favor simply because we see his face every day. The failure of the person who feels no 'fallacious guilt' at the harm he has accidentally caused is not (or not necessarily) that he misses how the harm he has caused will psychologically affect him, and will radically change his life. His failure is that by denying that a moral relationship can be based on little more than an accident he is being churlish, because many, if not most, of our moral relationships are based on accident – including ones that have benefited him.

Smith describes a kind of bargaining that goes on between the person who has caused the harm, and the person who has been injured. If the person hurt is poor, and the person who has caused the harm is in 'tolerable circumstances', he will offer financial compensation and take the injured person 'under his protection' (TMS II.iii.3.4, 107). If the situation is the other way around, the person who has done the harm will express his sorrow, and try to render them 'every good office which he can devise' (TMS II.iii.3.4, 107). What is interesting in this passage is that the important thing is not the compensation for the wrong, which is why it would be inappropriate for the injured family to look to a wealthy benefactor. What is more important is that a kind of recognition has occurred, that the two people share a relationship with one another, even though that relationship, at bottom, was an accident.

In an arresting phrase, John Rawls writes that 'in justice and fairness, men agree to share one another's fate' (Rawls 1971: 102). Rawls is of course talking about institutional arrangements, and in particular the so-called difference principle, where the talents of some will not be allowed to benefit them without at the same time helping the least well-off. What the case of making amends for the harms we accidentally cause shows is that there are many non-institutional ways in which we can show that we share one another's fate. And in these cases, we share our fate not as citizens, participating in a 'cooperative venture for mutual advantage', but as human beings, meeting accidentally. It is in a sense arbitrary that we should be lumped together in these ways, by something so seemingly morally arbitrary as brute causation: a car hitting a child. But if I am right, many of our relationships are like this, founded on accidents, and by recognizing that we in some cases may suffer in ways we strictly speaking do not deserve may heighten our recognition that perhaps in many more cases we are treated much better than we deserve.[11]

Conclusion

I have written in defense of Smith on the incipient rationality of our moral sentiments. It is arguable, however, whether I have written anything on the problem of moral luck *per se.* That is, my interpretation of Smith's arguments has not touched on whether luck really might make a difference to our moral worth, our moral credit or demerit. It has touched only on whether good or bad consequences might perform an epistemic function in determining the true moral worth of others (they can) or whether our fallacious guilt in causing bad things to happen to other people might show us something deep about our relationships to one another (it does). Does this mean that Smith as I have interpreted him has nothing to contribute to contemporary debates on moral luck? By way of conclusion, let me briefly address this important question.[12]

So, first: did Adam Smith really believe in moral luck? Or did he rather deny it? In the closing paragraph of his discussion of our irregular sentiments, Smith explicitly states that should we be unjustly praised or blamed by others, we have this consolation, namely, that we can regard our action as if it *had* gone off without the interference of luck, and to imagine how people would have reacted to the action. The 'more candid and humane part of mankind', Smith says, will wholly go along with this effort (TMS II.ii.3.6, 108). This shows, I believe, that the true standard of moral worth for Smith is ultimately what he calls the 'equitable maxim', which is that we should not be judged based on 'those events that did not depend upon our conduct' (TMS II.iii.3.6, 108).[13] In this way, Smith seems simply to deny the problem of moral luck, if by this we mean that our moral worth can be contingent on the things we cause but do not intend to cause. Smith seems simply to deny that moral worth can be contingent in this way; in fact, I think he does deny it. To put the point in religious terms (terms which I believe would be acceptable to Smith), there is such a thing as our moral credit and demerit in the eyes of God, and this worth cannot be affected by fortune but only by what we intend to do (cf. Schneewind 1998: 388–93, especially 391–2).

But to regard the problem of moral luck as raising a problem only if luck affects our moral credit and demerit *directly* seems to take an unhelpfully narrow view of what that problem can involve. For even if our moral worth is not contingent in the way in which Smith denies that it is, there still may be a problem about the fact that we often cannot tell another person's true intentions (and therefore what he truly deserves) and a problem about how to deal with the harms which we have accidentally caused. We may be unlucky or lucky in what people find out about our moral worth, and we may be unlucky or lucky in what things we cause without meaning to. Both of these things will affect how our lives will go, and even how our lives will go morally speaking. The most significant and enduring reason to study Smith on our irregularity of sentiments may not be that Smith provides a solution to the contemporary problem of moral luck (although he has certainly has worthwhile things to say about it), but that he directs our attention to the true scope of the problem.

Notes

I am grateful to Eric Schliesser for inspiring this chapter and for his encouragement and criticism, to Charles Larmore, Leonidas Montes and Jennifer Rubenstein for their written comments, and to Dan Brudney for conversations which greatly improved the structure and argument of the chapter, especially section III. Although I depart from its overall assessment of Smith and moral luck, Russell (1999) has importantly structured my thinking on the topic.

1 See e.g. Thomson (1989: 213 n. 7), who cites Bernard Williams as 'the first philosopher to have noticed and taken seriously the fact' of agent regret. For a rare acknowledgment (but only that) of Smith's role in the formulation of the problem of moral luck, see Domsky (2004: 445 n. 1). Nussbaum (1986) is the great exception to the claim that work on moral luck has been conducted ahistorically.

2 'Consequential moral luck' is luck in how our actions turn out, and is the kind of luck with which Smith is most concerned. For discussion, see Nagel (1979), which distinguishes consequential moral luck from other kinds of moral luck.

3 Smith suggests this type of defense in his other use of the term 'irregularity' (TMS III.3.12, 141).

4 Fleischacker writes that Smith 'notes approvingly, in [*Wealth of Nations*], that certain types of actions contribute to the public good without their agents ever intending them' but 'we must be careful not to confuse this endorsement with *moral* approval' (Fleischacker 2004: 47; his emphasis). It strikes me that Fleischacker is here imputing to Smith a moral/ethical distinction that Smith doesn't have, and that Smith would have no trouble seeing the utility which results from our irregular sentiments as *morally* good.

5 As Fleischacker notes in comparing Smith to Kant, we are also prone to self-deception in interpreting our own motives (Fleischacker 1991). Eric Schliesser writes that 'Smith's philosophy departs from the confidence of the Cartesian ego' (Schliesser 2006: 334). How dire must our epistemic straits be if we are even strangers to ourselves!

6 Isn't this phrase usually uttered with less than complete sincerity? That is, doesn't it become clear when someone says of an unwanted gift that 'it's the thought that counts' he is at the same time expressing some disappointment?

7 Eric Schliesser (personal communication) argues that we might read Smith's aim in *Wealth of Nations* as promoting institutions that make success less a matter of (some forms of) luck and more a matter of real effort.

8 Smith draws a contrast between humanity and generosity (TMS IV.2.10, 190–1), but the 'humanity' discussed in the text seems to combine qualities of both humanity and generosity as they are later defined: it involves both fellow feeling and sacrifice.

9 Also, the causer of harm has a certain *proximity* to the harm he has caused. He is the first person on the scene of the accident, as it were. But this proximity might also be shared by an innocent bystander.

10 See Bittner (1992) for an incisive criticism of Williams on this score.

11 In a longer version of this chapter (Flanders 2004) I connect the point made in this section with what I call Smith's 'anti-Stoicism'.

12 I address this question in more detail in the 'Introduction' and 'Epilogue' to Flanders 2004.

13 A fuller defense of this claim would require a further investigation of what Smith means by 'consolation' (see, for instance, its use in TMS VII.ii.1.45, 292).

References

Bittner, Rüdiger (1992) 'Is it Reasonable to Regret the Things One Did?' *Journal of Philosophy* 89 (5): 262–73.

Domsky, Darren (2004) 'There is no Door: Finally Solving the Problem of Moral Luck', *Journal of Philosophy* 101 (9): 445–64.

Flanders, Chad (2004) 'Responsibility and Objectivity', Ph.D. dissertation, University of Chicago.

Fleischacker, Samuel (1990) *A Third Concept of Liberty*, Princeton, NJ: Princeton University Press.

—— (1991) 'Philosophy and Moral Practice: Kant and Adam Smith', *Kant Studien* 82: 249–69.

—— (2004) *On Adam Smith's Wealth of Nations*, Princeton, NJ: Princeton University Press.

Griswold, Charles (1999) *Adam Smith and the Virtues of Enlightenment*, Cambridge: Cambridge University Press.

Kadish, Sanford (1994) 'The Criminal Law and the Luck of the Draw', *Journal of Criminal Law and Criminology* 84: 679–702.

Nagel, Thomas (1979) *Mortal Questions*, Cambridge: Cambridge University Press.

Nussbaum, Martha (1986) *The Fragility of Goodness*, Cambridge: Cambridge University Press.

Rawls, John (1971) *A Theory of Justice*, Cambridge, MA: Harvard University Press.

—— (1996) *Political Liberalism*, New York: Columbia University Press.

Rothstein, Paul (1987) 'Causation in Torts, Crimes, and Moral Philosophy: A Reply to Professor Thomson', *Georgetown Law Journal* 76: 151–66.

Royzman, Edward and Kumar, Rahul (2004) 'Is Consequential Luck Morally Inconsequential? Empirical Psychology and the Reassessment of Moral Luck', *Ratio* 17 (3): 329–44.

Russell, Paul (1999) 'Smith on Moral Sentiment and Moral Luck', *History of Philosophy Quarterly* 16 (3): 37–58.

Schliesser, Eric (2006) 'Adam Smith's benevolent and self-interested conception of philosophy', this volume: 328–57.

Schmidtz, David (2002) 'How to Deserve', *Political Theory* 30 (6): 774–99.

Schneewind, J. B. (1998) *The Invention of Autonomy*, Cambridge: Cambridge University Press.

Schulhofer, Stephen, and Kadish, Sanford (2001) *Criminal Law and its Processes*, New York: Aspen Law and Business.

Thomson, Judith Jarvis (1989) 'Morality and Bad Luck', *Metaphilosophy* 20 (3–4): 203–21.

Walker, Margaret Urban (1991) 'The Virtues of Impure Agency', *Metaphilosophy* 22 (1–2): 15–27.

Williams, Bernard (1981) 'Moral Luck', in *Moral Luck*, Cambridge: Cambridge University Press.

—— (1993) *Shame and Necessity*, Berkeley, CA: University of California Press.

Wolf, Susan (2000–01) 'The Moral of Moral Luck', *Philosophic Exchange* 31: 5–19.

Zimmerman, Michael (2002) 'Taking Luck Seriously', *Journal of Philosophy* 99 (11): 553–76.

Part III

Adam Smith and economics

10 The mercantilist foundations of 'Dr Mandeville's licentious system'

Adam Smith on Bernard Mandeville

Jimena Hurtado-Prieto

The relationship between Bernard Mandeville and Adam Smith has been widely acknowledged in the history of economic thought. In spite of their clear divergence on moral grounds most scholars consider that Mandeville and Smith did not differ considerably on economic matters.[1] However, morals and economics were two sides of the same explanation through which moral philosophers began to describe commercial society during the seventeenth and eighteenth centuries.

This chapter focuses on how Smith perceives Mandeville and the way in which he tries to mark his differences with the latter's shocking and paradoxical result: private vices are necessary for national prosperity. As Schumpeter remarks, Smith is well aware of the apparent close connection between his own theory and Mandeville's,

> Smith cannot have failed to perceive Mandeville's argument was an argument for Smith's own pure Natural Liberty couched in a particular form. The reader will have no difficulty in realizing how this fact must have shocked the respectable professor – particularly if it should be the case that he learned something from the offending pamphlet.
>
> (Schumpeter 1954: 184)

Bernard Mandeville's *Fable of the Bees or Private Vices, Publick Benefits* was a *succès de scandale* when it appeared in 1714[2] and was the object of continuous debate during most of the eighteenth century.[3] In 1756 Smith sent a letter to the *Edinburgh Review* presenting Mandeville as the source of inspiration for Jean-Jacques Rousseau's *Discourse on the Origin of Inequality*.[4] Smith considers the *Discourse* as a progress on Mandeville's principles, where Rousseau has 'softened, improved and embellished, and stript of all that tendency to corruption and licentiousness which has disgraced them in their original author' (EPS 250).

In TMS Smith comments on 'Dr Mandeville's licentious system'. One of the reasons Smith gives for rejecting Mandeville's system of moral philosophy is its dangerous effects on the understanding of social *mores*, 'There is, however, another system which seems to take away altogether the distinction between vice and virtue, and of which the tendency is, upon that account, wholly pernicious, I mean the system of Dr Mandeville' (TMS VII.ii.4.6, 308).

The Letter to the *Edinburgh Review* and the section on Mandeville in TMS have also led people to explore the connection between both authors from their opposition on moral matters (cf. Werhane 1991). Smith refutes Mandeville's theory of a selfish human nature. However, it has been recognized that their relationship is more complex than this (Winch 1992). Less attention has been given to the relation between the economic and moral aspects of their connection (Colletti 1972; Hurtado-Prieto 2004). By analyzing both aspects simultaneously, it can be shown that Smith does not criticize Mandeville's paradoxical result only on moral grounds. Smith has economic arguments to show that what he considered to be Mandeville's erroneous views are based on the latter's misunderstanding of economic concepts and mechanisms.

The aim of this chapter is to understand the connection between the moral and the economic criticism Smith addresses to Mandeville. We believe Smith himself gives us the clue to this dual relationship in LJ. There we find that Mandeville's 'licentious system' comes from a common confusion between wealth and money. This confusion prevails in what Smith calls the commercial or mercantile system, which he strongly criticizes in WN. Mandeville's paradoxical result would be an example of the mistaken 'notions with regard to foreign commerce and home expence' derived from the mercantile system.

The chapter is divided into three sections. The first section deals with Smith's rebuke of the commercial system and with the points Mandeville shares with it. Smith takes up each point and shows why he believes the commercial system and thereby Mandeville's theory rest upon shaky foundations.

The second section deals with the moral implications of the mercantile system present in Mandeville's thought. The first implication has to do with luxury, its moral status and its social function. Mandeville believes luxury is a private vice of capital importance for the wealth and power of a nation. This explains the subtitle of his *Fable* 'private vices, publick benefits'. Smith interprets this subtitle as, 'private vices *are* public benefits' and aims at showing that, contrary to Mandeville's assertion, virtue and wealth are compatible.

The third section shows the different views these authors have concerning commercial society. This society is no doubt inequitable, but this does not mean, according to Smith, that the poor are condemned to a life of misery (cf. Hont and Ignatieff 1983). On the contrary, they are entitled to decent living conditions, which include enjoying not only the *necessaries* but also the *conveniencies* of life (cf. Pack 1991, Rothschild 2001).

Mandeville and the commercial system

Political economy, according to Smith, is 'a branch of the science of a statesman or legislator' that 'proposes to enrich both the people and the sovereign' (WN IV.intro.1, 428). In Book IV of WN Smith analyzes the two systems of political economy that have existed, the system of commerce and the system of agriculture. Eight of the nine chapters in this book deal with the former, 'the modern system ... best understood in our country and in our times' (WN IV.intro.2, 428).

Smith also analyzes this system in LJ when he explains Police or the 'regulation of government in general' (LJ 331). Police comprises 'the attention paid by the public to the cleanliness of the roads, streets, etc.; 2d, security; and thirdly, cheapness or plenty' (LJ 331; 486). Smith passes rapidly over the first two and focuses on the third point. He concentrates on opulence 'or what are those things which ought to abound in a nation' (LJ 333; c.f. LJ 487). Opulence, according to Smith, corresponds to the easiness to provide necessaries and conveniencies through labor. In treating of opulence, Smith divides his topic into five items: the rule of exchange or what regulates prices; money as a measure of value and instrument of commerce; the cause of the slow progress of opulence; taxes or public revenue; and the effects of commerce (LJ 353, 494).

In the lectures on money Smith analyzes the commercial system.[5] Here we find that several writers had hinted at this system 'but Mr Mun was the first who formed it into a regular system' (LJ 381). According to LJ, Mun attacks paper money because it banishes gold and silver from the country, producing its ruin (LJ 506). The central argument is that 'Money never decays, a stock of it will last for ever, and by keeping up great quantities of it in the country we shall insure our riches as long as the world stands' (ibid.). Since then, many authors have adopted this system, including Locke (LJ 381, 508): 'Gold and silver, therefore, are according to him, the most solid and substantial part of the moveable wealth of a nation, and to multiply those metals ought, he thinks, upon that account, to be the great object of political œconomy' (WN IV.i.3, 430).

According to Smith, the mercantile system is built upon the popular confusion that money is wealth. Hence, the main concern of economic policy should be the balance of trade in order to guarantee that exports will always be greater than imports, avoiding outflows of money. Likewise, the tenants of this view believe that no luxury or extravagance in national goods can be hurtful to the nation's wealth because all money remains within the country:

> There is still another bad effect proceeding from that absurd notion that national opulence consists in money. It is commonly imagined

> that whatever people spend in their own country cannot diminish public opulence, if you take care of exports and imports. This is the foundation of Dr Mandeville's system that private vices are public benefits. What is spent at home is all spent among ourselves, none goes out of the country.
>
> (LJ 513; cf. LJ 576)[6]

Mandeville then would have constructed his theory upon the arguments of the commercial system. Smith believes it is important to show why these arguments are false because they have had 'bad effects . . . both in speculation and practice' (LJ, 576). In speculation Smith refers to the systems of Mun and Gee and 'of Mandeville who built upon them' (ibid.). In practice this system leads to partial economic policies that promote the manufacturers' interests, 'contrary to that justice and equality of treatment which the sovereign owes to all the different orders of his subjects' (WN IV.viii.30, 654). Because the main architects of the system are, according to Smith, the merchants and the manufacturers, it takes into account only their interests, sacrificing the rest. These policies also infringe 'the boasted liberty of the subject, of which we affect to be so very jealous; but which, in this case, is so plainly sacrificed to the futile interests of our merchants and manufacturers' (WN IV.viii.47, 660). In brief, such policies give prevalence to the interests of the producers because 'in the mercantile system, the interest of the consumer is almost constantly sacrificed to that of the producer; and it seems to consider production, and not consumption, as the ultimate end and object of all industry and commerce' (WN IV.viii.49, 660).

In the rest of this section we will analyze the three points Smith identifies with the commercial system, the confusion between money and wealth, the importance of the balance of trade and the effect of luxury spending within the country. In each case we will show not only Smith's view but also Mandeville's position in order to determine the latter's proximity with the commercial system.

Money and wealth

The foundation of the commercial system is what Smith considers to be the confusion between wealth and money. Smith believes it is important 'to examine at full length this popular notion' because of the negative effects we have just mentioned in speculation and practice.[7]

> Money in common language, as I have already observed, frequently signifies wealth; and this ambiguity of expression has rendered this popular notion so familiar to us, that even they, who are convinced of its absurdity, are very apt to forget their own principles, in the course of their reasonings to take it for granted as a certain and undeniable

> truth. Some of the best English writers upon commerce set out with observing, that the wealth of a country consists, not in its gold and silver only, but in its lands, houses, and consumable goods of all different kinds. In the course of their reasonings, however, the lands, houses, and consumable goods, seem to slip out of their memory, and the strain of their argument frequently supposes that wealth consists in gold and silver, and that to multiply those metals is the great object of national industry and commerce.
>
> (WN IV.i.34, 450)

In fact, money, says Smith, is the measure of value and the instrument of commerce (LJ 367–9; 499–500). It is certainly important because on the one hand it gives 'a plain, clear and ready measure of value' (LJ 374) and on the other, as a medium of exchange it upholds transactions of commodities and this 'promotes the industry of the people and facilitates and encourages the division of labour' (LJ 374). There is then a link between money and wealth, but this does not mean they are the same thing. 'The great wheel of circulation is altogether different from the goods which are circulated by means of it. The revenue of the society consists altogether in those goods, and not in the wheel which circulates them' (WN II.ii.14, 289).

Smith believes there is a distinction between the means of circulation and opulence because 'the greater part of the foods, cloaths, etc. that is laid out to procure this circulation the less of food, cloaths, and lodging is there in the country' and, therefore, the greater the poverty 'for it is not this money which makes the opulence of a nation, but the plenty of food, cloaths, and lodging which is circulated' (LJ 378, 503, 576). Money then only helps to increase opulence as a means of circulation, but opulence itself 'consists in the abundance of necessarys and conveniencies of life and the industry of the people' (LJ 378, 504; WN intro.1–2, 10; I.v.1,3, 47–8; I.xi.e,33, 207–8). Hence, wealth neither consists in nor depends upon the quantity of money in the country (LJ 576; WN IV.1.15, 437).

The functions of money as a measure of value and an instrument of commerce lead to the confusion between wealth and money (WN IV.i.1, 429) evidenced in the 'ambiguity of expression' mentioned before. But just looking at individuals' everyday behavior it is obvious that '[i]t is not for its own sake that men desire money, but for the sake of what they can purchase with it' (WN IV.i.18, 439). Individuals keep money because it procures the means to obtain all the necessaries and conveniencies they might wish for (LJ 384, 509). Money is not wealth because it is not consumable, it cannot be used 'for any of the purposes of life' (LJ 508). An individual's revenue does not really consist in money 'but in the power of purchasing, in the goods which can successively be bought with [it] as [it] circulates from hand to hand' (WN II.ii.22, 291). Money is part of the circulating capital of the country and allows the distribution of wealth among individuals but makes no part of their revenue (WN II.ii.23, 291).

What is Mandeville's position regarding this 'confusion'? It is important to establish what Mandeville actually believes because, according to Smith, this is the cornerstone of the commercial system. The question then is to know if, at least on this account, Mandeville is a true representative of the mercantile system.

Mandeville believes 'it is impossible to name another [thing], that is so absolutely necessary to the Order, Œconomy, and the very Existence of the Civil Society' (Fable ii.349) and asserts 'there is no living without Money' (Fable i.100). In this society, Mandeville says, due to the variety of wants all individuals stand constantly in need of others' services. The only way to obtain them is bartering, that is exchanging one thing for another and this is possible thanks to money.

> Therefore the Invention of Money seems to me to be a thing more skilfully adapted to the whole Bent of our Nature, than any other of human Contrivance. There is no greater remedy against Sloth or Stubbornness; and with Astonishment I have beheld the Readiness and Alacrity with which it often makes the proudest Men pay Homage to their Inferiors, It purchases all Services and cancels all Debts.
>
> (Fable ii.353–4)

However, this does not mean Mandeville assimilates money and wealth. Actually, he believes 'too much Money can undo a Nation' as the case of Spain proves (Fable i.194). Mandeville states that 'the surest Wealth consists in a Multitude of laborious Poor; for besides that they are the never-failing Nursery of Fleets and Armies, without them there could be no Enjoyment, and no Product of any Country could be valuable' (Fable i.287). Wealth then, according to Mandeville, is the labor of the poor 'and not the high or low value that is set on Gold or Silver' because it is this labor that produces 'all the Comforts of Life' (Fable i.302; cf. Fable i.197–8). Therefore, in order to increase wealth it is necessary to keep a portion of the population poor so they are forced to work to guarantee their subsistence.[8] These poor people will certainly work for money, because they need it to get the food, clothes and lodging necessary for their survival. Thus, the main use of money is paying the labor of the poor (Fable i.193–4).

Certainly, Mandeville does not go as far as Smith when the latter establishes a clear-cut distinction between money and real wealth. Smith refers to Hobbes when he asserts that wealth is power (WN I.v.3, 48): 'The power a commodity gives to its owner, who has no intention of consuming it, is the power to command others' labor.' Thus, wealth corresponds to the power of commanding labor. As owners of commodities, individuals meet at the market to make use of this power over each other. This is why the real price of any commodity is labor (WN I.v.1–2, 47). Therefore, exchanging goods corresponds to exchanging labor itself. 'What is bought with money or with goods is purchased by labour as much as what we acquire by the toil and trouble of our own body' (WN I.v.2, 47).

This means there is no difference between barter and monetary exchange: money only makes exchange easier, but the real price of a commodity is always labor, hence exchanging directly the products of labor or indirect exchange using money amounts to the same operation. Money is only a veil that must be removed in order to see the true essence of economic relationships. Such a view allows Smith to leave money aside in his investigation of the nature and causes of the wealth of nations. Mandeville, like mercantilists, believes wealth has to be socially recognized by means of a social institution such as money (Diatkine 1989: 10). This implies he cannot leave money aside in his analysis of commercial society. In contrast to Smith's position, Mandeville seems to believe the invention of money precedes exchange rather than exchange leading to the invention of money. In other words, Mandeville's view presents money as a condition for exchange, an institutional arrangement necessary for the existence of the market, whereas Smith's position regards money as an outcome of exchange.

The balance of trade

Smith believes the identification between wealth and money leads to the special concern that authors of the commercial system place on the balance of trade. The balance of trade is the only way for a country with no mines to accumulate gold and silver and therefore 'it necessarily became the great object of political œconomy to diminish as much as possible the importation of foreign goods for home-consumption, and to increase as much as possible the exportation of the produce of domestick industry' (WN IV.i.35, 450; IV.viii.1, 642).

Smith considers there is nothing 'more absurd' than this doctrine as the foundation of all the regulations of commerce (WN IV.iii.c.2, 488). Economic policy, according to Smith, passes from one useless concern, the ban of metal exports, to another even more useless and more complex, the regulation of imports and exports (WN IV.i.10, 434). This means abandoning internal trade, the 'trade in which equal capital affords the greatest revenue, and creates the greatest employment' (WN IV.i.10, 435). The doctrine of the balance of trade leads to a misallocation of resources.

This particular concern for foreign trade reveals the partial character of these policies because those who promoted them 'did not really know how foreign trade enriched the country', they only knew it enriched themselves (WN IV.i.10, 434). The tenants of this view do not realize, according to Smith, that free trade is always advantageous (LJ 390, 511; WN IV.iii.c.2, 488–9). The benefit of commerce, says Smith, is not bringing money into the country but promoting industry, manufactures and opulence (LJ 367, 499).

In fact, these policies are, in Smith's view, incapable of accomplishing the goal they set themselves. Smith believes controlling the balance of trade cannot regulate the flow of precious metals. Furthermore, the depreciation of the exchange rate does not increase the commercial deficit:

> They [the arguments of the commercial system] were sophistical too, perhaps, in asserting that the high price of exchange necessarily increased, what they called, the unfavourable balance of trade, or occasioned the exportation of a higher quantity of gold and silver. That high price indeed was extremely disadvantageous to the merchants who had any money to pay in foreign countries.... The high price of exchange too would naturally dispose the merchants to endeavour to make their exports nearly balance their imports, in order that they might have this high exchange to pay upon as small a sum as possible. The high price of exchange, besides, must necessarily have operated as a tax, in raising the price of foreign goods, and thereby diminishing their consumption. It would tend therefore, not to increase, but to diminish, what they called the unfavourable balance of trade, and consequently the exportation of gold and silver.
>
> (WN IV.i.9, 433–4)

Smith's argument can be interpreted as a comparison between the price effect and the volume effect of a depreciation of the exchange rate. If the price elasticity of the supply of exports and of the demand for imports of the country are high the volume effect compensates for the price effect and the commercial deficit decreases. If this is not the case the mercantilists have a point. The correct understanding of an economic mechanism determines if a policy is advantageous or adverse for national wealth. Smith concludes then that

> [n]o nation can be ruined by the ballance of trade being against them ... and not withstanding of this [an unfavorable balance of trade] the nation has continually improved in riches, in strength, in opulence; and money when wanted is raised in greater abundance and with greater facility now than ever.
>
> (LJ 393; cf. 512–13)

Mandeville insists on the 'great Regard that is to be had to the Balance of Trade' (Fable i.248–9) making sure imports should never be greater than exports (Fable i.115–16, 304). This policy ensures that foreign luxury will never be hurtful:

> If what I urg'd last be but diligently look'd after, and the Imports are never allow'd to be superior to the Exports, no Nation can ever be

> impoverish'd by Foreign Luxury; and they may improve it as much as they please if they can but in proportion raise the Fund of their own that is to purchase it.
>
> (Fable i.116)

Regulating the balance of trade implies that the policy makers know and pursue the interest of the country (Fable i.115), which is to ensure national prosperity. This primary objective is what Mandeville calls 'the great Art' of making 'a Nation happy and what we call flourishing'; this art consists in offering all those who need it an opportunity to be employed; keeping the poor at work through subsistence wages; promoting fishery and agriculture in order to keep labor cheap; protecting property and administering justice impartially (ibid.; cf. Fable i.197). These policies guarantee that luxury will never hurt the country, precisely the point Smith attacked.

Luxury spending

Smith does not claim that Mandeville confuses money and wealth. Nevertheless, he asserts, as mentioned above, that Mandeville builds his theory upon one of the consequences of this confusion. This theory, according to Smith, posits that it does not matter what people spend their money on as long as they spend it at home. This spending includes luxury and one of Mandeville's main conclusions is that luxury is necessary for the wealth of a nation.

Mandeville knows that luxury is perceived as contrary to the wealth of a nation as it is to that of an individual but he refuses to follow the idea of presenting frugality as the source of wealth (Fable i.108–9). He uses the following example to explain his position. If Britain were to diminish its imports from Turkey by half, the excess of commodities resulting in Turkey would bring their price down and the Dutch and the French would profit, buying more Turkish commodities and increasing their exports to this market, leaving Britain without the Turkish trade; or, if half of the goods imported from Turkey were to be re-exported, Britain would also lose this trade because it would not be profitable to British merchants, for, on the one hand, they would be supplying already supplied markets – as the other European countries already trade with Turkey – and, on the other, the cost of opportunity of re-exporting the commodities would be too high (Fable i.111–12). So the interest of foreign trade is not money flows but commodity flows: 'Buying is Bartering, and no Nation can buy Goods of others that has none of her own to purchase with them' (Fable i.111).[9]

This example leads Mandeville to assert that all the negative effects normally imputed upon luxury are actually the results of bad public administration: 'Good Politicians by Dextrous Management' are capable of regulating foreign exchange in the best interest of the nation, that is, ensuring there will not be a commercial deficit (Fable i.115–16). Therefore, bounties and taxes should be used to control which nations are the best trade partners and which commodities are brought into the country.

This 'Dextrous Management' also implies influencing people's desires, making some commodities more worthy of admiration than others. Hence, using people's desire to be admired and their tendency to seek this admiration through their material possessions, the government can guarantee economic growth. Mandeville is straightforward: people want goods, luxuries if possible, not only to satisfy their material needs but also to satisfy their desire for others' approval. Besides, luxury increases consumption, thereby stimulating industry and increasing employment. A nation to be rich must allow its inhabitants to indulge their passions (Fable i.84):

> I am reconciled likewise with the Luxury of the Voluptuous, ... because now I am convinced that the Money of most rich Men is laid out with the social Design of promoting Arts and Sciences, and that in the most expensive Undertakings their principal Aim is the Employment of the Poor.
>
> (Fable ii.43)

Smith argues that prodigality reduces the national stock. In order to understand this argument one must have in mind Smith's distinction between productive and unproductive labor (WN II.iii.1, 330). The first one refers to labor that increases the value of the object to which it is applied and the second to labor that leaves nothing in terms of value after it is bestowed. An individual can grow richer if she invests in productive labor and poorer if she invests in unproductive labor (ibid.). The distinction between both types of labor is also important to understand the wealth of a nation. The reproduction of the national stock depends upon the proportion between productive and unproductive labor employed with it (WN II.iii.3, 332). Most of what is invested in productive labor is reinvested as capital, which keeps the industry going (WN II.iii.4, 332). Capital is then the central element for the reproduction and increase of the national stock. As 'Capitals are increased by parsimony and diminished by prodigality and misconduct' (WN II.iii.14, 337) Smith considers that a major source of wealth is saving, the consequence of frugality (WN II.iii.13–16, 337). Prodigality, on the contrary, means spending on unproductive labor and on entertaining an entourage, leaving nothing after the expenditure is over.

Though the expense of the prodigal should be altogether in homemade, and no part of it in foreign, commodities, its effect upon the productive funds of society would still be the same. Every year there would still be a certain quantity of food and clothing which ought to have maintained productive, employed in maintaining unproductive hands. Every year, therefore, there would still be a diminution in what would otherwise have been the value of the annual produce of the land and labor of the country. (WN II.iii.21, 339).

Prodigality reduces the annual value of the country's production (WN II.iii.26, 340), '[E]very prodigal appears to be a publick enemy, and every frugal man a publick benefactor' (WN II.iii.26, 340). However,

> It can seldom happen, indeed, that the circumstances of a great nation can be much affected either by the prodigality or misconduct of individuals; the profusion or imprudence of some always being more than compensated by the frugality and good conduct of others.
> (WN II.iii.27, 341)

This, according to Smith, happens because profusion comes from the desire of 'present enjoyment' which is but a momentary impulse (WN II.iii.28, 341). Most individuals know the way to better their condition is through saving, which makes prodigals relatively few (WN II.iii.28, 341–2).

In short, if we are to follow Smith, Mandeville's attack on frugality and his defense of luxury[10] must be softened. Frugality leads to the increase in the capital stock of the nation, thus to accumulation. The more capital in a country the more industrious it will be (WN II.iii.12, 335–6) and hence the greater its annual produce. Mandeville does not consider accumulation as a source of growth. He believes prosperity has to do with circulation and therefore perceives frugality only as the characteristic of indolent people, incapable of undertaking any industrious activity, and who do not contribute to national wealth (Fable i.05). Mandeville seems to make no difference between saving and hoarding wealth, which means he considers that frugality keeps money from circulating and thus slows down economic activity (Fable i.183, 223, 251, 355). The contrary of frugality, prodigality is therefore beneficial because, according to Mandeville, it makes money circulate, encouraging industry and commerce. And as prodigals tend to spend their money on luxury goods, this means luxury is beneficial for economic growth (Fable i.23).

Smith's analysis uses elements of Mandeville's argument but in a subtler fashion. First, frugality leads to savings that are not dormant capitals. Second, luxury spending can be beneficial if and only if it employs productive labor. Smith's claim in the LJ amounts to showing there is an economic mistake behind Mandeville's paradoxical moral philosophy and continues showing Mandeville also relies on an erroneous view of human nature.

The moral implications of mercantilism

We have established that Mandeville does not believe wealth consists in money. Nevertheless, he gives an important place to its circulation.

Furthermore, he believes keeping a commercial surplus is important and asserts that spending in general and luxury spending in particular are beneficial. Though there are differences in relation to Smith's characterization of the commercial system, Mandeville posits issues in common with it, especially regarding the last point. It is precisely this point which Smith underlines when relating Mandeville and the mercantile system: people can spend as much as they like on any kind of goods or services; this will never diminish the nation's wealth. This, says Smith, is the basis for Mandeville's 'private vices, public benefits'.

This means, on the one hand, that Mandeville presents luxury as a vice and on the other that this vice contributes to the public interest. These are the two points we analyze in this section. First, we look at Mandeville's defense of luxury even if it is a vice, and Smith's reformulation of this notion, removing the vicious connotation. Second, Mandeville never said, as Smith asserts, that private vices *are* public benefits, he said they should be handled in order to become beneficial, that is, individuals following their passions under certain rules, determined by legislators, promote public interest. Mandeville did not believe human virtue within commercial society was very likely and therefore virtue could not be the foundation of society.

Luxury

Mandeville says regarding luxury,

> Whatever has contributed since to make life more comfortable, as it must have been the Result of Thought, Experience and some Labour, so it more or less deserves the Name of Luxury, the more or less trouble it required, and deviated from the primitive Simplicity.
>
> (Fable i.69)

Smith finds this definition is too broad:

> Every thing according to him [Mandeville] is luxury which exceeds what is absolutely necessary for the support of human nature, so that there is vice even in the use of a clean shirt, or of a convenient habitation.
>
> (TMS VII.ii.4.11, 312)

Mandeville himself considers this critique (Fable i.248, 330) because he knows that presenting all that is not immediately necessary for human subsistence as a luxury might seem exaggerated (Fable i.107). However, he believes that softening his definition and making it depend upon circumstance and habit leads to erasing all limits between luxury and other goods. Taking his position to the extreme, this implies that either everything is luxury or nothing is, '[i]f every thing is to be Luxury (as in strictness it ought) that is not immediately necessary to make Man subsist as he is a living Creature, there is nothing else to be found in the World' (ibid.).

After considering all the problems this definition implies, Mandeville concludes that 'in one Sense every Thing may be call'd so [luxury], and in another there is no such Thing' (Fable i.123). Mandeville affirms that if we are to have an objective definition of luxury we cannot introduce considerations of time and place (Fable i.169). This would lead to a purely subjective definition of luxury, where each individual would decide what is necessary for her own subsistence (Fable i.107–8, 248, 330).

Mandeville, according to Smith, forgets something in his account of human nature that prevents him from changing his definition of luxury. Human beings have an aesthetic need: 'Such is the delicacey of man alone, that no object is produced to his liking' (LJ 206, 487). Nature has endowed human beings with reason, ingenuity, art and the capacity to improve the things that surround them (LJ 333–6, 487), to compensate for human frailty and weakness compared with other animals. Human beings, besides satisfying their basic needs, have a natural tendency to make things agreeable. This is the case with food, clothes and lodging. Smith asserts savages prove humans can eat raw food 'but this does not seem to be the way most agreable or beneficial to him' (LJ 334); the same happens with clothes and lodging through which the human being 'forms to himself around his body a sort of a new atmosphere, more soft, warm, and comfortable than that of the common circumambient air' (LJ 334). In fact, most of human needs could be supplied by the labor of a single individual (LJ 487) but:

> This way of life appears rude and slovenly and can no longer suffice him; he seeks after more elegant niceties and refinement. Man alone of all animalls on this globe is the only one who regards the differences of things which no way affect their real substance or give them no superior advantage in supplying the wants of nature.
>
> (LJ 335)

Humans are the only animals that take pleasure in diversity and refinement and it is this pleasure that explains the creation of arts and sciences (LJ 336–7, 488), 'the causes which prompt man to industry and are peculiar to him of all animalls, the natural feebleness of his frame and his desires for elegance and refinement' (LJ 337).

This taste for beauty and refinement explains the existence of conveniences that go beyond the simple satisfaction of physiological needs. This aesthetic need leads to reconsidering the distinction between necessaries and luxuries. Smith states that all consumable goods can be classified as one or the other (WN V.ii.k.2, 869). He defines necessaries as 'not only the commodities which are indispensably necessary for the support of life, but whatever the custom of the country renders it indecent for creditable people, even of the lowest order, to be without' (WN V.ii.k.3, 869–70).

Among human basic needs there is a need for beauty and refinement that makes appearing in public without shame as important as providing for food and clothes. This notion of appearing in public without shame changes with time and place (WN V.ii.k.3, 870). Thus, luxury corresponds to the objects that 'Nature does not render ... necessary for the support of life; and custom no where renders it indecent to live without them' (ibid. 870–1). Smith then reformulates the definition of luxury, taking into account elements Mandeville seems to have left aside. Thus the diversity of commodities proper to commercial society is no longer the result of a human vice but of a natural inclination which implies no moral corruption.

Private vices, public benefits

Mandeville writes most of the *Fable of the Bees* as an explanation of the original fifteen-page-long poem and the subtitle, *Private vices, publick benefits*, he gives his book. The most common interpretation of this phrase is that a society of selfish individuals only concerned with the satisfaction of their desires and the indulgence of their passions would achieve general material well-being. Even if Mandeville believes that it is impossible to enjoy 'all the most elegant Comforts of Life that are to be met with in an industrious, wealthy and powerful Nation, and at the same time be bless'd with all the Virtue and Innocence that can be wish'd for in a Golden Age' (Fable i.6–7), this does not mean he opposes any type of morality, as the common interpretation might lead to believe. Mandeville considers the current definition of virtue makes it a practical impossibility, so social order cannot rely on it.

The definitions of virtue and vice are contrary to human nature, which Mandeville considers to be passionate:

> every thing, which, without Regard to Publick, Man should commit to gratify any of his Appetites, [is] VICE; if in that Action there cou'd be observed the least prospect, that it might either be injurious to any of Society, or ever render himself less serviceable to others, And to give the Name of VIRTUE to every Performance, by which Man, contrary to the impulse of Nature, should endeavour the Benefit of others, or the Conquest of his own Passions out of a Rational Ambition of being good.
>
> (Fable i.48–9; cf. ii.109)

This definition contains clear traces of Jansenism and therefore can be classified as a rigorist one (Kaye 1924: lxxxi–lxxxiii, ciii; Maxwell 1951: 249; Horne 1978: 22–3; Viner 1991: 180; Force 2003). This definition implies morality is dependent on reason, which, in the context of this same definition, is contrary to passions. Therefore, that which is contrary to reason is vicious because it implies indulging passions. Virtuous behavior implies that all actions must proceed from a 'rational ambition of being good' (Fable i.260) and this ambition is associated with absolute control of passions or even self-denial (Fable i.156). Mandeville believes this definition is unrealistic and cannot direct human action within commercial society.

Mandeville addresses the issue of the survival of a society composed of selfish individuals concerned only with their own interest. He presents the causes and the consequences of a behavior that cannot be considered as virtuous but that corresponds to the one followed by honest folks. The aim of human life is not virtue but happiness and, according to Mandeville, they do not necessarily coincide. A virtuous character implies peace of mind, wisdom, temperance and humility but happiness is made up of pleasures that are always earthly and sensory (Fable i.151, 166; ii.108).

Mandeville believes individuals always act according to their self-love, which means that pleasure accounts for all their actions (Fable i.348–9; cf. Hundert 1994). As he defines virtue as self-denial, Mandeville cannot accept that virtue and pleasure are compatible. An individual who acts virtuously goes against her own nature; she will have fewer desires and supplying her needs will be easier than in the case of someone who follows her self-love (Fable i.355). But, according to Mandeville's view on luxury spending, she does not contribute to the wealth of the nation. Hence, virtue means acting contrary to human nature and does not promote industry.

However, making public benefits follow from private vices is not automatic, as Smith seems to believe when he says Mandeville's theory resumes to private vices *are* public benefits. Nowhere in Mandeville's work is this phrase to be found.[11] Considering the whole sentence is enlightening. 'Private Vices by the dextrous Management of a skilful Politican may be turned into Publick Benefits' (Fable i.369). This is what Mandeville tries to explain in his *Fable* to a specific public, modern deists and the *Beau Monde*.

> It is those he wants to come at. To the first he sets forth the Origin and Insufficiency of Virtue, and their own Insincerity in the Practice of it, to the rest he shews the Folly of Vice and Pleasure, the Vanity of Worldly Greatness, and the Hypocrisy of all those Divines who pretending to preach the Gospel, give and take Allowances that are inconsistent with, and quite contrary to the Precepts of it.
>
> (Fable ii.102)

But Mandeville's intention can be thought to be more far-reaching. According to him, 'things are only Good and Evil in reference to something else, and according to the Light and Position they are placed in'

(Fable i.367). Regarding moral judgments this means two criteria may be put forward, one that evaluates individual virtue and the other public benefits. Mandeville states that, on the one hand, trying to make human nature agree with virtue is hypocrisy (Fable i.331; ii.109). So, even if the pursuit of self-love produces public benefits the actor should not be considered virtuous. Individuals should be judged only according to the motivation of their action in order to determine if they are virtuous or not. 'But Men are not to be judg'd by the Consequences that may succeed their Actions, but the Facts themselves, the Motives which it shall appear they acted from' (Fable i.87).

On the other, 'it is manifest, that when we pronounce Actions good or evil, we only regard the Hurt or Benefit the Society receives from them, and not the Person who commit them' (Fable i.248), that is, there is a social criterion that allows judging individual actions separately from the actor. That is why

> The short-sighted Vulgar in the Chain of Causes seldom can see further than one link; but those who can enlarge their View, and will give themselves the leisure of gazing on the Prospect of concatenated Events, may, in a hundred Places, see Good spring up and pullulate from Evil, as naturely as Chickens do from Eggs.
>
> (Fable i.91)

Smith strives at surmounting the incompatibility between virtue and passionate human nature. Kaye (1924: cxxviii–cxxx) and Hirschman (1997 [1977]: 19) note that Smith, following David Hume,[12] overcomes Mandeville's apparent contradiction because in his definition of virtue passions are not excluded and even if virtue implies control of passions and self-command it does not necessarily imply self-denial. Virtue, according to Smith, joins self-control and fellow feeling, it means command of passions but not their denial. Hence, virtue does not imply going against the natural impulses of human beings as Mandeville said. On the contrary, Smith explains why virtue is desirable based not on reason but on feeling:

> Pleasure and pain are the great objects of desire and aversion, but these are distinguished not by reason, but by immediate sense and feeling. If virtue, therefore, be desirable by its own sake, and if vice be, in the same manner, the object of aversion, it cannot be reason which originally distinguishes those different qualities, but immediate sense and feeling.
>
> (TMS VII.iii.2.8, 320)

This is opposite to Mandeville's presentation of the current definition of virtuous behavior as deriving from a 'rational ambition of being good'. Pleasure and pain determine the desirability of virtue and the aversion against vice, thus virtuous or vicious actions respond to sensitive motivations. Reason, known to be the slave of passions, does not play a significant role in determining the moral character of human behavior.

Changing the definition of virtue allows Smith to consider that passions are not necessarily disruptive of social order.[13] One of these passions is the desire to better one's condition and it is central to our analysis due to its role in the accumulation of wealth. Both authors consider this desire as a characteristic of human nature. Mandeville believes it is particular to individuals within society and explains the development of techniques and industry (Fable ii.128, 181). Individuals not only want to enjoy a growing number of commodities to render their life more comfortable, they also want others to admire them because of their belongings.

Smith presents this desire as the principle behind the tendency to save:

> But the principle which prompts us to save, is the desire of bettering our condition, a desire which, though generally calm and dispassionate, comes with us from the womb, and never leaves us till we go into the grave.
>
> (WN II.iii.28, 341)

As individuals always look for admiration (TMS I.iii.2.1, 50) they strive to increase their fortune because this seems to be the promptest way to achieve their goal (WN II.iii.28, 341). This explains accumulation and thereby the increase in national stock (cf. Diatkine 1991: 35–6; Winch 1996: 89). Individuals looking for others' sympathy display their riches and hide their poverty because it is easier to sympathize with joy than with grief (TMS I.iii.2.1, 50). It is through their social relations that human beings discover the way to satisfy their desire to better their condition and enjoy the sympathy of their fellows through the accumulation of wealth. Individuals will be successful if they are capable of being prudent, that is, of exercising their self-control. Human beings learn to postpone their consumption in order to achieve a better situation. This means, individuals, following their natural desire of bettering their condition learn to control their immediate desires. Smith thus shows how the motive for the endless search for wealth also acts as a regulator of endless desires and passions. The desire to better one's condition is not harmful, and it teaches individuals the importance of frugality and self-control.

Two elements are central in this argument: Smith changes Mandeville's definition of virtue so as to include passions and he shows virtue and wealth are not opposed due to the action of the desire of bettering one's condition on human behavior. This desire is then related to the desire of enjoying the pleasure of mutual sympathy. Their compound action explains why individuals acquire luxurious objects. Contrary to Mandeville, Smith shows the attraction human beings feel for luxuries does not imply vice or corruption.

Commercial society

Having shown what Smith considers as the erroneous foundations of Mandeville's system, he is then able to show a brighter picture of commercial society: a society where every member can profit from necessaries and conveniences or in other words from opulence. Smith begins with Mandeville's description of commercial society and gives a brighter view of the negative characteristics the latter presents. Commercial society is undoubtedly a society characterized by social inequalities where a majority work so that a minority might enjoy a life of comfort and ease. But the important point is that in this kind of society a worker or a peasant is better off than in any other social organization (LJ 563; WN I.i.11, 24; cf. Pack 1991, Rothschild 2001, amongst many others). Smith's starting point is that, in spite of crying inequalities, the material conditions of those who work in commercial society are better than those of the richest members of any other social organization (LJ, 399, 489, 562; WN I.i.11, 22).

In the terms of Hont and Ignatieff (1983: 1–6), thanks to the division of labor, inequality within commercial society assures satisfying the needs of the poorest better than equality in misery within primitive societies. Smith, following Mandeville (Fable i.366), argues that the division of labor increases labor productivity and thus individuals have a larger variety of goods at their disposal (WN I.i.10, 22). Furthermore, they both consider division of labor a condition for the pacific enlargement of commercial society. As individuals specialize they implicitly accept their place in the social division of labor and therefore their mutual dependence, for the satisfaction of their needs is peaceful. Mandeville believes the division of labor leads to the peaceful enlargement of society because each individual is occupied in her own specialized productive activity (Fable i.367). Passions keep each individual focused on her own work and make them accept their position within social hierarchy (Fable i.366). According to Smith, the division of labor and the expansion of the market, consequences of the disposition to truck, barter and exchange, allow individuals to profit from others' talents because the different products are 'brought, as it were, into a common stock, where every man may purchase whatever part of the produce of other men's talents he has occasion for' (WN I.ii.5, 30). This is how commercial society is established, a society where individuals supply the greater part of their wants through exchange (WN I.iv.1, 37).

However, Smith, contrary to Mandeville, does not consider that the fate of the workers in commercial society is limited to the satisfaction of their basic needs. Smith does not share Mandeville's defense of the doctrine of the utility of poverty.[14] Mandeville justifies the extreme inequalities of commercial society and of maintaining the workers in a situation of relative poverty because he believes

> It is impossible that a Society can long subsist, and suffer many of its Members to live in Idleness, and enjoy all the Ease and Pleasure they can invent, without having at the same time great Multitudes of People that to make good this Defect will condescend to be quite the reverse, and by use and patience inure their Bodies to work for others and themselves besides.
>
> (Fable i.286)

According to Mandeville, those who accept this task must be willing to accept the harshest material conditions and the only way is that they should see this kind of life as the only way to avoid starvation,

> No Man would be poor and fatigue himself for a Livelihood if he could help it, The absolute necessity all stand in for Victuals and Drinks, and in cold Climates for Clothes and Lodgings, make them submit to any thing that can be bore with. If no body did Want no body would work; but the greatest Hardships are look'd upon as solid Pleasures, when they keep a man from starving.
>
> (Fable i.287)

Experience shows individuals will work only in order to guarantee their subsistence (Fable i.192). The reason is, according to Mandeville, human beings have a natural tendency to pleasure and laziness (Fable i.239). Work is perceived as a pain and, Mandeville believes, the only motivation for an individual to work is to avoid greater pain. This means that only their needs push the poor to work (Fable i.194) and therefore they will work only if they really need to (Fable i.92–3, 287, 302). Letting the poor save by paying them high salaries has a direct and negative consequence on the supply of labor and produces a slowdown of economic activity (Fable i.193).

Smith argues that high wages are not only an indicator of the state of society but also an incentive for workers (LJ 567; WN I.viii.44, 99). The demand for labor, according to Smith, is directly affected by the increase in income and the national stock, which means that the demand for labor depends upon the progress of the wealth of the nation (WN I.viii.21, 86–7). The high price of labor must then be seen as a sign of economic growth and therefore the improvement in the material conditions of the working poor is beneficial for society as a whole (WN I.viii.36, 96). High wages are the cause of an increasing population, which is an essential element of prosperity (WN I.viii.42, 99).

Smith has thus transformed Mandeville's description: social inequalities are undeniable but they do not mean the poor are condemned to a life of misery. Within commercial society human beings work knowing that the wage they receive assures them decent living conditions. Subsistence wages in Smith's theory become wages that allow workers to buy the goods considered as necessary to keep a decent standard of living given the society they live in.

Conclusion

Smith's appraisal of Mandeville's 'licentious system' goes beyond moral arguments. Even if Smith's system of sympathy can be seen as a response to what Hume called the selfish hypothesis present in Hobbes's and Mandeville's work, Smith uses economic arguments to dismantle Mandeville's paradox. Smith understands Mandeville's conclusion as stating that private vices *are* public benefits and indicates this result is built upon the commercial system. In particular, Smith believes this result comes from the idea that no spending – luxury spending – within the country can hurt its wealth and this claim stems from the confusion between wealth and money.

We have shown that even if Mandeville clearly distinguishes wealth and money and identifies wealth with the labor of the poor; he shares the mercantilists' concern for the balance of trade and for the need to regulate commerce. He also gives a central role to money in economic activity, far more important than the one Smith gives it as the instrument of commerce and the measure of value. Therefore, even if Mandeville does not completely fit in Smith's view of the mercantile system, some of the arguments the latter uses against it can be applied to Mandeville. This is especially the case regarding luxury. Mandeville considers almost all commodities in commercial society to be luxury and he believes the multiplication of goods is due to the indulgence of human passions. This indulgence, according to Mandeville, is contrary to virtue but promotes national wealth. Smith, by changing the notion of virtue and giving a positive connotation to the desire of bettering our condition, avoids Mandeville's contradiction between human nature and virtue and thereby between virtue and wealth.

Exploring the connection between both authors from Smith's point of view reveals aspects that have been overlooked in recent literature, in particular, the significant connection between morals and economics. Smith presents a unique and systematic critique of Mandeville that reveals new ways of understanding the mechanisms underlying social order. This is certainly just a first step in revising the connection between both authors.[15] There are undoubtedly elements Smith takes from Mandeville, but in fact, they are not only found in Mandeville. The important link between them is that Smith takes Mandeville's description of commercial society, he begins his analysis with the same question on commercial society's ability to provide for all its members in spite of social inequalities and he radically transforms it. An extension of this text would lead to exploring the authors' view on social coordination and thereby on the role of government. Is the natural harmonization of interests possible? Do the functions of the 'skilful politician' include guaranteeing social coordination? These questions have already been raised in the literature but we believe the contrast between the authors shown in this text could be another step to reconsider them.

Notes

This chapter builds on some of the arguments developed in my PhD dissertation where I explore the place Jean-Jacques Rousseau, Adam Smith and Jeremy Bentham give to economics within their social and political philosophies as a response to a challenge Mandeville launches concerning the explanation of society beginning from a particular anthropological conception. The chapter corresponds to a much revised version of a text presented at the Séminaire XVIIIème Siècle organized by PHARE, the research center where I wrote my dissertation. I thank Daniel Diatkine, Gilles Dostaler, Jérôme de Boyer des Roches and Gilbert Faccarello as well as other participants for their questions and comments. Special thanks to Raphaël Dépinoy for his insightful suggestions. A second draft was presented at the eighth annual conference of the European Society for the History of Economic Thought where I benefited from comments from Annie L. Cot, Sergio Cremaschi and Anthony Brewer. I also wish to thank Andrés Alvarez and Arnaud Berthoud for their attentive reading. I am indebted to Leonidas Montes and Eric Schliesser, who through their detailed remarks allowed me to revise and considerably improve those early drafts. Finally, I thank an anonymous referee for observations which led to a reformulation of the text. All remaining errors and omissions are my responsibility.

1 E. Halévy (1991 [1901]: 114) states the continuity between Mandeville and Smith, arguing that Smith's economic theory is Mandeville's doctrine under a rational and scientific form. Smith would follow Mandeville in his theory of the unintended effects of individual actions or in his explanation of the division of labor as the source of the wealth of nations. Hayek (1978 [1966]), for instance, is an example of the first view, Smith continues Mandeville's tradition by presenting social order as the unintended consequence of individual actions. For an insightful and contradictory analysis see E. Le Jalle (2003). Because our aim is to analyze Smith's appraisal of Mandeville's system and not to establish a comparison between both authors we will not deal with these points in this chapter. The generalized view of a continuous line between both authors can also be found in Wilson (1967), West (1976) and Dumont (1985, even if he recognizes Mandeville's ambiguity), among others.

2 Mandeville first published the poem *The Grumbling Hive or Knaves turn'd Honest* which constitutes the first part of the *Fable* anonymously in 1705. The *Fable* went through at least thirteen successive editions between 1714 and 1806 in England (Kaye 1924: xxxiii–xxxviii; Primer 1975: xvii, x–xi; Carrive 1983: 65–118). The two volumes of the *Fable* include the essays *An Enquiry into the Origin of Moral Virtues, An Essay on Charity, and Charity-schools, A Search into the Nature of Society*, Mandeville's index, *A Vindication of the Book* and six dialogues. Quotations in the text will follow the standard usage citing the volume in roman numbers followed by the page in arabic numbers.

3 After the scandal produced by the *Fable*, Mandeville was condemned to oblivion until the twentieth century when he has been described as a forerunner of economic liberalism (Halévy 1991 [1901]), of utilitarianism (Kaye 1924, who also considers Mandeville is a continuator of the Augustinian tradition), as a mercantilist (Heckscher 1955; Keynes 1969 [1936]; Viner 1991), as an

evolutionist (Rosenberg 1994 [1963]), as a transition author between mercantilism and liberalism (Chalk 1991 [1966]), as a predecessor of the theory of emerging effects (Hayek 1978 [1966]), as a moral relativist (Scott-Taggart 1991 [1966]), as a libertine (Rashid 1985), or as a representative of Epicureanism (Hundert 1994). For a summary of existing interpretations of Mandeville's work see M. Perlman (1996: 105–14) and S. Rashid (1985: 313–17). In this chapter we will focus only on the way he was perceived by Adam Smith.

4 For a detailed analysis of the letter, its implications in relation to Mandeville, Rousseau and Smith, and the literature on this connection see Hurtado-Prieto (2004).

5 The lecture notes do not use the phrase 'system of commerce'. In fact, in the notes there is no specific name to allude to this system. The editors of the LJ note that seven pages are missing in the 1762–63 report where probably it is made clear that the system referred to corresponds to 'the theory or hypothesis that opulence consists in or can be measured by [the nation's] stock of gold and silver' (LJ n. 55, 381). The link between this theory and the system of commerce analyzed in the WN is also confirmed by the authors Smith mentions as representatives of the system in LJ and in WN, Mun and Locke.

6 'From hence {Sir John Mandeville, author of the *Fable of the Bees*} formed his theory that private vices were publick benefits. It was thought that no luxury or folly whatever, not the greatest extravagance imaginable, if laid out on commodities of home production could in the least be prejudiciall, many were even beneficiall; that if we kept out all other goods, let one spend as much as he pleased, the nation was as rich as before; the money is not sent abroad to France or Holland but is still at home' (LJ 169, 393). Smith obviously makes a mistake on Mandeville's name, as the editors of the LJ remark.

7 According to Smith, Hume also wrote showing the absurdity of this idea; however, 'he seems . . . to have gone a little into the notion that public opulence consists in money' (LJ 252–3, 507–8).

8 In the last section we will come back to the doctrine of the utility of poverty.

9 This also indicates that the idea of regulating the balance of trade in order to accumulate metals is not so important to Mandeville because, as his example suggests, reducing imports from Turkey with exports remaining constant would mean that the balance was paid in money, but this would not compensate for the final loss of the Turkish market.

10 National wealth, according to Mandeville, comes from commerce (Fable i.116) and commerce greatly depends upon luxury (Fable i.124): 'Great Wealth and Foreign Treasure will ever scorn to come among Men, unless you'll admit their indispensable Companions, Avarice and Luxury' (Fable i.185).

11 The subtitle of the *Fable* is 'private vices, publick benefits' and Mandeville constantly repeats in this work as in other texts he never meant to say private vices were public benefits or private vices were naturally transformed into public benefits. Not taking seriously this claim leads to considering his arguments as contradictory (Hume 'Of Refinement in the Arts') or hollow (Hutcheson 1750) or as favoring a libertine position (Rashid 1985; Viner 1991:182). Presenting an explanation of human behavior as completely dependent upon egoistic motivations (Hundert 1994: 17) and confronting this explanation with a rigorist definition of virtue leads to a *reductio ad absurdum*, as remarked by Kaye (1924), not to a rejection of all morality. Let us quote just some examples. 'When I assert, that Vices are inseparable from great and potent Societies, and that it is impossible their Wealth and Grandeur should subsist without, I do not say that the particular Members of them who are guilty of any should not be continually reprov'd, or not be punish'd for them when they grow into Crimes' (Fable i.10); 'Now I cannot see what Immorality there is in shewing Man the

Origin and Power of those Passions, which so often, even unknowingly to himself, hurry him away from his Reason; or that there is any Impiety in putting him upon his Guard against himself, and the secret Stratagems of Self-love, and teaching him the difference between such Actions as proceed from a Victory over the Passions, and those that are only the result of a Conquest which one Passion obtains over another; that is, between Real, and Counterfeited Virtue ... What hurt do I do to Man if I make him more known to himself than he was before?' (Fable i.230); according to Mandeville his book is 'a Book of severe and exalted Morality, that contains a strict Test of Virtue, an infallible Touchstone to distinguish the real from the counterfeited, and shews many Actions to be faulty that are palmed upon the World for good ones, It describes the Nature and Symptoms of human Passions, detects their Force and Disguises; and traces Self-love in its darkest Recesses' (Fable i.404–5).

12 In his essay *Of the Refinement in the Arts* Hume tries to correct what he considers as extreme views on luxury which present vicious luxury as beneficial for society and innocent luxury as threatening to social order. Hume strives at showing luxury contributes to social happiness and virtue and when it becomes vicious it ceases to be beneficial. Hume concludes his essay declaring in reference to Mandeville, 'Let us, therefore, rest contented with asserting, that two opposite vices in a state may be more advantageous than either of them alone; but let us never pronounce vice in itself advantageous. Is it not very inconsistent for an author to assert in one page, that moral distinctions are inventions of politicians for public interest; and in the next page maintain, that vice is advantageous to the public? And indeed it seems upon any system of morality, little less than a contradiction in terms, to talk of a vice, which is in general beneficial to society' (Hume, *Essays*, 280). On Hume's appraisal of Mandeville's position see, for example, Goldsmith (1988: 601–3).

13 This is an important point because it shows that whereas Smith believed in natural sociability Mandeville did not. In the letter to the *Edinburgh Review* Smith explains that Mandeville and Rousseau share two principles on which they build their systems: sociability is not inherent to human nature and law is an instrument of oppression (EPS, 250–1).

14 The defense of subsistence wages was common at the time and Heckscher (1955: ii.164) considers it to be another proof of Mandeville's mercantilism. However, as Heckscher (1955: ii.169–71) himself shows, other mercantilist authors defended the opposite view and believed high wages would increase purchasing power and therefore sales or they would act as an incentive to work or be a symbol of national prosperity (cf. Steiner 1992: 130). This shows the difficulty in finding a unique voice within mercantilism.

15 This revision can be seen in the larger context of the debate between mercantilism and liberalism as Berthoud (1989: 72–3) presents it: 'Mercantilism represents at the same time a model and a failure for economic liberalism. The model of a doctrine that for the first time is built upon a conception of an individual free from all ends that are not his own and for whom wealth ceases to be a good and becomes power, as such, independent from place and from its particular use. The failure of a unitary theory, because it shamelessly assumes the immorality of an unfair exchange and of accumulation not unqualified by false appearance.... In other words, is it possible to keep mercantilist freedom without the suspicion of injustice and the illusion attached to economicism and monetary measure. If these questions are relevant, it can be understood in what sense the theories of economic liberalism regarding the market and accumulation can be seen as answers mobilized by a moral problem' (our translation).

References

Berry, Ch. (1994) 'The Eighteenth Century Debate', in C. Berry, *The Ideas of Luxury: A Conceptual and Historical Investigation*, Cambridge: Cambridge University Press, 126–76.

Berthoud, A. (1989) 'Liberté et libéralisme économique chez Walras, Hayek et Keynes', in A. Berthoud and R. Frydman (eds) Le libéralisme économique, interprétations et analyses, *Cahiers d'économie politique* 16–17: 43–73.

Campbell, T. D. (1971) *Adam Smith's Science of Morals*, London: Allen & Unwin.

Carrive, Paulette (1983) *La Philosophie des passions chez Bernard Mandeville*, Lille: Atelief national de reproduction des thèses, Université Lille III, Paris: Didier.

Chalk, A. F. (1991) [1966] 'Mandeville's Fable of the Bees, A Reappraisal', *Southern Economic Journal* 33 (1): 1–16. Repr. in M. Blaug (ed.) *Pre-classical Economists* III, *John Law (1671–1729) and Bernard Mandeville (1670–1733)*, Pioneers in Economics Series 8, Aldershot: Elgar, 149–64.

Coleman, D. C. (ed.) (1969) *Revisions in Mercantilism*, London: Methuen.

Colletti, L. (1972) 'Mandeville, Rousseau et Smith', in L. Colletti, *De Rousseau à Lénine*, trans. Alexandre Bilous, Paris, London and New York: Publications Gramma, Gordon and Breach, 208–92.

Diatkine, D. (1989) 'Hume et le libéralisme économique', in A. Berthoud and R. Frydman (eds) Le libéralisme économique, interprétations et analyses, *Cahiers d'économie politique* 16–17: 3–19.

—— (1991) Introduction', in A. Smith, *Recherche sur la nature et les causes des richesses des nations*, trans. Germain Garnier, rev. Adolphe Blanqui, 2 vols, Paris: Flammarion.

Dumont, L. (1985) *Homo Aequalis* I, *Genèse et épanouissement de l'idéologie économique.* Paris: NRF, Gallimard.

Fitzgibbons, A. (1995) *Adam Smith's System of Liberty, Wealth and Value: The Moral and Political Foundations of the Wealth of Nations*, Oxford: Clarendon Press.

Force, P. (2003) *Self-interest before Adam Smith*, Cambridge: Cambridge University Press.

Goldsmith, M. M. (1985) *Private Vices, Public Benefits: Bernard Mandeville's Social and Political Thought.* Cambridge: Cambridge University Press.

—— (1988) 'Regulating Anew the Moral and Political Sentiments of Mankind: Bernard Mandeville and the Scottish Enlightenment', *Journal of the History of Ideas* 49 (4): 587–606.

Halévy, E. (1991) [1901] *La Formation du radicalisme philosophique*, 3 vols, Paris: Presses Universitaires de France.

Hayek, F. A. (1978) [1966] 'Dr Bernard Mandeville', in F. A. Hayek, *New Studies in Philosophy, Politics, Economics and the History of Ideas*, London: Routledge, 249–66.

Hecksher, E. F. (1955) *Mercantilism* II, 2nd edn, rev. Heckscher, ed. E. F. Soderlund, trans. Mendel Shapiro. London: Allen and Unwin.

Hirschman, A. (1997) [1977] *The Passions and the Interests: Political Arguments for Capitalism before its Triumph*, twentieth anniversary edn, Princeton, NJ: Princeton University Press.

Hont, I. and Ignatieff, M. (eds) (1983) *Wealth and Virtue: The Shaping of Political Economy in the Scottish Enlightenment*, Cambridge: Cambridge University Press.

Horne, Th. A. (1978) *The Social Thought of Bernard Mandeville: Virtue and Commerce in Early Eighteenth Century England*, New York: Columbia University Press.

Hundert, E. J. (1994) *The Enlightenment's Fable: Bernard Mandeville and the Discovery of Society*, Cambridge: Cambridge University Press.

Hurtado-Prieto, J. (2003) 'The Risks of an Economic Agent: A Rousseauian Reading of Adam Smith', *Colombian Economic Journal* 1 (1): 193–220. Online: http://fce.unal.edu.co/cej/number1/7-J-Hurtado.pdf (accessed 10 December 2004).

—— (2004) 'Bernard Mandeville's Heir: Adam Smith or Jean-Jacques Rousseau on the way to Economic Analysis', *European Journal of the History of Economic Thought* 11 (1): 1–31.

Hutcheson, F. (1750) 'Publishing on the Internet', *Remarks upon the Fable of the Bees*. Online: http://socserv.socsci.mcmaster.ca/~econ/ugcm/3113/hutcheson/remarks.htm (accessed 15 November 2004).

Kaye, F. B. (1924) 'Commentary Critical, Historical and Explanatory', in B. Mandeville, *The Fable of the Bees or Private Vices, Publick Benefits*, Oxford: Oxford University Press. Repr. Indianapolis, IN: Liberty Fund (1988).

Kerkhof, B. (1995) 'A Fatal Attraction? Smith's "Theory of Moral Sentiments" and Mandeville's "Fable"', *History of Political Thought* 16 (2): 219–33.

Keynes, J. M. (1969) [1936] 'Notes sur le mercantilisme, les lois contre l'usure, la monnaie estampillée et les théories de la sous-consommation', in J. M. Keynes, *Théorie générale de l'impôt, l'intérêt et la monnaie*, trans. Jean de Largentage, Paris: Payot, 333–65.

Landreth, H. (1975) 'The Economic Thought of Bernard Mandeville', *History of Political Economy* 7 b(2): 193–208.

Le Jalle, E. (2003) 'Hayek, lecteur des philosophes de l'ordre spontané: Mandeville, Hume, Ferguson, *Astérion*, 1: 88–111. Online: http://asterion.revues.org/document17.html#_nref_22 (accessed 20 November 2004).

Magnusson, L. (ed.) (1995) *Mercantilism*, London: Routledge.

Mandeville, B. (1924) *The Fable of the Bees or Private Vices, Publick Benefits*, With a Commentary Critical, Historical, and Explanatory by F. B. Kaye, 2 vols, Oxford: Oxford University Press. Repr. Indianapolis, IN: Liberty Fund (1988).

de Marchi, N. (2001) 'Exposure to Strangers and Superfluities: Mandeville's Regime for Great Wealth and Foreign Treasure', in P. Groenewegen (ed.) *Physicians and Political Economy: Six Studies of the Work of Doctor Economists*, London: Routledge, 67–92.

Maxwell, J. C. (1951) 'Ethics and Politics in Mandeville', *Philosophy* 26 (98): 242–52.

Moss, L. S. (1987) 'The Subjectivist Mercantilism of Bernard Mandeville', *International Journal of Social Economics* 14 (6): 167–84.

Otteson, J. R. (2000) 'Adam Smith on the Emergence of Morals: A Reply to Eugene Heath', *British Journal for the History of Philosophy* 8 (3): 545–51.

Pack, S. (1991) *Capitalism as a Moral System: Adam Smith's Critique of the Free Market Economy*, Cheltenham: Elgar.

Perlman, M. (1996) 'The Fable of the Bees, Considered Anew', in Marc Perlman, *The Character of Economics, Economic Characters, and Economic Institutions*, Ann Arbor, MI: University of Michigan Press, 87–120.

Primer, I. (ed.) (1975) *Mandeville Studies: New Explorations in the Art and Thought of Dr Bernard Mandeville (1670–1733)*, The Hague: Nijhoff.

Rashid, S. (1985) 'Mandeville's Fable: Laissez-faire or Libertinism?' *Eighteenth Century Studies* 18 (3): 313–30.

Rosenberg, N. (1994) [1963] 'Mandeville and *laissez-faire*', *Journal of the History of Ideas*, April. Repr. in N. Rosenberg, *The Emergence of Economic Ideas: Essays in the History of Economics*. Economists of the Twentieth Century, Cheltenham: Elgar, 1–14.

Rothschild, E. (2001) *Economic Sentiments: Adam Smith, Condorcet, and the Enlightenment*, Cambridge: Cambridge University Press.

Schumpeter, J. A. (1954) *History of Economic Analysis*. London: Allen & Unwin.

Scott-Taggart, M. J. (1991 [1966]) 'Mandeville: Cynic or Fool?' *Philosophical Quarterly* 16 (6): 221–32. Repr. in M. Blaug (ed.) *Pre-classical Economists: John Law (1671–1729) and Bernard Mandeville (1660–1733)* III, Cheltenham: Elgar.

Steiner, Ph. (1992) 'Marchands et princes. Les auteurs dits "mercantilistes"', in A. Béraud and G. Faccarello (eds) *Nouvelle histoire de la pensée économique. Des scolastiques aux classiques* I, Paris: La Découverte, 95–140.

Viner, J. (1948) 'Power versus Plenty as Objectives of Foreign Policy in the Seventeenth and Eighteenth Centuries', *World Politics* 1 (1): 1–29.

—— (1991) Introduction to Bernard Mandeville, A Letter to Dion (1723) in D. A. Irwin (ed.) *Jacob Viner: Essays on the Intellectual History of Economics*, Princeton, NJ: Princeton University Press, 176–88.

Werhane, P. H. (1991) *Adam Smith and his Legacy for Modern Capitalism*, New York: Oxford University Press.

West, E. G. (1976) *Adam Smith*, Indianapolis, IN: Liberty Classics.

Wilson, Charles (1967) 'Trade, Society and the State', in E. E. Rich and C. H. Wilson (eds) *The Cambridge Economic History of Europe, IV*, Cambridge: Cambridge University Press.

Winch, D. (1992) 'Adam Smith: Scottish Moral Philosopher as Political Economist', *Historical Journal* 35 (1): 91–113.

—— (1996) *Riches and Poverty: An Intellectual History of Political Economy in Britain, 1750–1834*, Cambridge: Cambridge University Press.

11 On Adam Smith's Newtonianism and general economic equilibrium theory

Leonidas Montes

In her classic and influential *Man and Society: The Scottish Inquiry of the Eighteenth Century* (1945), Gladys Bryson called our attention to the evident importance of Newton for the Scottish Enlightenment, linking this influence to a tradition initiated by Francis Bacon. According to her, Adam Smith, 'eager to bring some order into the chaotic field of social phenomena' (1968 [1945]: 20), would think of his own contribution to 'social sciences' as following Newton's successful model. Certainly Smith was another inheritor of an intellectual tradition that, except for a few notable exceptions, venerated Newton and his legacy. Newton's discoveries were the paradigmatic result for subsequent scientific progress, but the nature of Newtonianism within the Scottish Enlightenment is still a matter of debate.

An intellectual appreciation of the eighteenth century context, which was thoroughly pervaded by Newton's enormous influence, has led important scholars to assess Newton's influence on Adam Smith. Mark Blaug, an authority on the history of economic thought, argued that the pivotal role of sympathy in TMS, and that of self-interest in the WN, 'must be regarded as deliberate attempts by Smith to apply this Newtonian method first to ethics and then to economics' (1992 [1980]: 52). Andrew Skinner, an authority on Adam Smith, also believes that Smith's economics 'was originally conceived in the image of Newtonian physics' (1979: 110). Indeed, Adam Smith was very much influenced by Newton. Therefore, the story goes according to some modern economists, he applied Newton's method to political economy, leading to general economic equilibrium theory. The language of 'gravitation' and 'center of repose' in chapter 7 of the first book of WN would be a simple proof for this reading. Smith's admiration for Newton, in addition to Newton's atomistic/mechanistic description of the celestial order, would constitute evidence that Smith initiated the tradition of general economic equilibrium theory relying upon the same ontological preconceptions. In this chapter I challenge this view by arguing that emphasizing Newton's influence on Smith is right, but for different reasons. Smith was a real Newtonian, but his methodology does not necessarily lead to a notion of general economic equilibrium theory. Neither does it fully rest upon an axiomatic-deductive methodology. This has been generally attributed to Newton, but Newtonianism was not conceived in that way by the Scottish Enlightenment. It was the French who adopted and adapted an axiomatic-deductive Newtonianism, fostering a methodology similar to that of Walras.

In the next section I will prove that Newton's methodology is much more complex and subtle than commonly thought. I describe Newton's method of analysis (method of resolution) and synthesis (method of composition) as well as his conception of a potentially open-ended process of successive approximation. The third section will broadly discuss Smith's approach to Newton, with special emphasis on chapter 7 of WN. In the last section special emphasis will be given to the context of the Scottish Enlightenment. I argue that Smith's intentions in his *History of Astronomy* are a consequence of a particular and distinctly Scottish reading of Newton. I show not only that Adam Smith was a careful interpreter of Newton, but also that he mastered Newton's methodology in a very sophisticated manner. This research concludes with a brief reflection on the methodological approach followed in this chapter, and its import for our understanding of Smith's Newtonianism.

Newton's methodology

After reading some of Newton's manuscripts, John Maynard Keynes was perhaps the first to uncover the other face of the father of modern science. In 1936 an auction at Sotheby's sold rather cheaply 329 lots of Newton's manuscripts, nearly 3 million words. Keynes managed to buy, and gradually reassemble, more than one-third of the collection (Spargo 1992). After assessing this first-hand evidence, in his posthumous 'Newton, the Man',[1] Keynes wrote: 'Newton was not the first of the age of reason. He was the last of the magicians, the last of the Babylonians and Sumerians' (Keynes 1972: 364). While Newton's reputation was built upon his scientific discoveries in mechanics, cosmology, optics and mathematics, the fact that he had spent much energies dealing with alchemy, theology, prophesies and ancient wisdom had been simply ignored. After Keynes's path-breaking essay, different biographies have offered a more detached and objective account of the real Newton,[2] leading to renewed interest in Newton's 'private science'.

Newton was not only exceptionally well read in alchemical literature, but also an eminent practitioner. He was also a voracious reader of the scriptures and theological treatises. Convinced that ancient sages knew the law of universal gravity, he spent much of his energies studying the prophecies in the Book of Daniel and the Book of Revelation. Nowadays scholars would agree that Newton's speculations about the nature of matter might have been influenced by his alchemical, theological and his ancient wisdom knowledge. As Patricia Fara nicely put it: 'for him gravity, alchemy, and God were intimately linked . . . Newton's alchemical pursuits were not ancillary to his natural philosophy but rather formed an essential part of his religious endeavour to study God's activities from as many aspects as possible' (2003: 501). But what is the real nature of Newtonianism? Before answering this question, we must first investigate what Newton said about his methodology.

Principia and *Opticks* are the most important public sources for understanding Newton's method. *Principia*'s complete title *Philosophiae Naturalis Principia Mathematica* resembles, and explicitly pretends to supplant, Descartes's *Principia Philosophiae* (1644).[3] Newton's *magnum opus* was purposely written in 'the mathematical way', expressly to avoid 'being baited by Smatterers in Mathematicks' (quoted in Westfall 1980: 459). It is undeniable that mathematics plays a crucial role in developing Newton's methodology, but one of the greatest achievements of Newton's 'experimental philosophy' resides in his method of resolution (analysis) and composition (synthesis). In his famous *General Scholium*, appended to the end of *Principia*'s second edition, Newton refers to the nature of his 'experimental philosophy' in which 'propositions are deduced from the phenomena and are made general by induction' (Newton 1999 [1687]: 943). In the last query 31 of his *Opticks*[4] he declares that 'analysis consists in making Experiments and Observations, and in drawing general Conclusions from them by Induction . . . Synthesis consists in assuming the Causes discover'd, and establish'd as Principles, and by them explaining the Phaenomena proceeding from them' (Newton 1979 [1704]: 404–5). In sum, the method of resolution allows us to infer causes from phenomena, and the method of composition a (or some) principle(s) from which we can explain other phenomena (on this issue and its relation to Smith see different views in Hetherington 1983 and Montes 2003).

At the end of the first paragraph of *Principia*'s preface, concerned and aware of the unknown nature of the force of gravity, Newton speculates that

> many things lead me to have a suspicion that all phenomena may depend on certain forces by which the particles of bodies, by causes not yet known, either are impelled toward one another and cohere in regular figures, or are repelled from one another and recede. Since these forces are unknown, philosophers have hitherto made trial of nature in vain.
>
> (Newton 1999 [1687]: 382–3)

concluding that: 'But I hope that the principles set down here will shed some light on either this mode of philosophizing *or some truer one*' (*ibid.*, emphasis added). This is the whole issue regarding gravity force. Newton was attacked for appealing to occult qualities, as he would be following the discredited Aristotelian-scholastic tradition. His efforts to rebut this accusation, or to explain his system, uncover another very interesting facet of Newton's methodology: a desire to uncover the real nature of things that, and this is crucial, even allows the existence of another possibility (recall *or some truer one*).

Elsewhere, the father of the universal law of gravitation, talking about attraction in the last query of his *Opticks*, was also open to the possibility 'that there may be more attractive Powers' (Newton 1979 [1704]: 376). Moreover, the four 'rules for the study of natural philosophy' have become emblematic to understanding Newton's 'experimental philosophy'. In particular, the controversial rule 4, which was added for the *Principia*'s third edition, states:

> In experimental philosophy, propositions gathered from phenomena by induction should be considered either exactly or very nearly true notwithstanding any contrary hypothesis, until yet other phenomena make such propositions either more exact or liable to exceptions.
>
> (Newton 1999 [1687]: 796)

This statement is very different from the commonly received view of Newton's legacy. Instead of an emphasis on the apodictic character of a theory, or a concern on its permanent explanatory powers, Newton simply leaves theories as open-ended. This is important evidence corroborating that an axiomatic-deductive model of science is neither Newton's, nor Smith's inheritance, as will be shown in the next section. Schliesser (2005a) has given additional and substantial evidence for interpreting Smith's Newtonian theory of science as a research tool for a potentially open-ended process of successive approximation.[5] Newton accepts that the progress of natural philosophy is open-ended, arguing for provisional truth until proven otherwise. Moreover, he does not consider mathematical event regularities as the hallmark of scientific progress. Laws, for Newton, including the law of gravity, can be open to refinement as part of this successive approximation process. Adam Smith, as will be shown soon, understood this very well.[6]

As it was first published in English, Newton's *Opticks* was more popular, and certainly more accessible to the general public.[7] In addition, he finishes his work 'proposing only some queries, in order to allow a farther search to be made by others' (Newton 1979 [1704]: 339). This successive thirty-one queries give the chance to read Newton's speculations and research proposals about many difficult things. The corpuscular theory of light entailed difficult questions, especially about the inner nature of matter. In particular there is another important suggestion about Newton's actual methodology at the end of query 28:

> And though every true Step made in this Philosophy brings us not immediately to the Knowledge of the first Cause, yet it brings us nearer to it, and on that account is to be highly valued.
>
> (*Ibid.*: 370)

In the last query 31, Newton follows explaining this argument:

> And if no Exception occur from Phenomena, the Conclusion may be pronounced generally. But if at any time afterwards any Exception shall occur from Experiments, it may then begin to be pronounced with such Exceptions as occur. By this way of Analysis we may proceed ... in general, from Effects to their Causes, and from particular Causes to more general ones, till the Argument end in the most general. This is the Method of Analysis: And the Synthesis consists in assuming the Causes discover'd and establish'd as Principles, and by them explaining the Phenomena proceeding from them, and proving the Explanations.
>
> (*Ibid.*: 404–5)

These passages are a clear reflection of Newton's method of approximation to reality.[8] Not denying truth, he is confident that deviations from actual phenomena actually bolster the advancement of scientific knowledge. If there are no deviations, our conclusions will stand, but if disruptions from phenomena do appear, we should simply enhance the pursuit of scientific truth through reiterative analysis that will successively lead to a new synthesis. However, this kind of dialectical methodology acknowledges not only a process of successive approximation to reality, but also a prioritization of the method of resolution (or analysis). Indeed: 'in Natural Philosophy, the Investigation of difficult Things by the Method of Analysis, ought ever precede the Method of Composition' (*ibid.*: 404). This is a crucial point that has been relatively ignored: analysis precedes, and moreover, has pre-eminence over synthesis.[9]

Cautious as he is about truth, Newton never denies its existence. In fact, Newton's account of scientific progress suggests his realism. In his *General Scholium*, he refers to God and gravity. Probably with the famous blind mathematician, Nicholas Saunderson (1682–1739) in mind, Newton makes a analogy of God with colors. 'As a blind man has no idea of colors' (Newton 1999 [1687]: 942), the same happens with God. Reality is not necessarily actualized. Then, searching for the cause of gravity, Newton argues that what really matters is that gravity 'exists' (*ibid.*: 943). This is not only the best example to understand what Eric Schliesser has termed as Newton's 'modest realism', but also it is most likely the source of Newton's late concern with methodology.[10] Newton had the answer for how the world worked, but he didn't know why it worked that way. In other words, he could describe gravity as a cause but he could not explain its causal powers.

I have only concentrated on *Principia* and *Opticks*, but it must be mentioned that Newton's unpublished papers do present further evidence for the interpretation I have been trying to develop.[11] Just to give one example, in a fragment that was probably intended for the *Opticks*, Newton refers to the method of resolution and composition, adding that 'he that expects success must resolve before he compounds. For the explication of Phaenomena are Problems much harder than those in Mathematicks' (McGuire 1970: 185). Scientific progress is not only a matter of simply achieving mathematical regularity, nor is the latter a precondition of Newton's method. If his discoveries created a mathematical system of nature, this does not necessarily imply that Newton's natural philosophy encouraged a particular mathematical-positivistic interpretation of his method.[12]

Smith on Newton

Leaving aside EPS for the moment, with its many references to Newton mainly in his *History of Astronomy*, there are scant direct references to Newton in Smith's works (none in WN, some in LRBL, one in his LJ, and one in TMS). But the only reference to Newton in TMS, in Chapter 2, Part III, is within an interesting passage added to the sixth edition. After noting the sensibility of poets and men of letters towards public opinion, Smith goes on to declare that 'Mathematicians, on the contrary . . . are frequently very indifferent about the reception which they may meet with from the public' (TMS III.3.20, 124). He mentions Robert Simson and Matthew Stewart as his first-hand examples. Then he writes:

> The great work of Sir Isaac Newton, his *Mathematical Principles of Natural Philosophy*, I have been told, was for several years neglected by the public. The tranquillity of that great man, it is probable, never suffered, upon that account, the interruption of a single quarter of an hour. Natural philosophers, in their independency upon the public opinion, approach nearly to mathematicians, and, in their judgements concerning the merit of their own discoveries and observations, enjoy some degree of the same security and tranquillity.
>
> (*Ibid.*)

Smith continues, adding that:

> Mathematicians and natural philosophers, from their independency upon public opinion, have little temptation to form themselves into factions and cabals, either for the support of their own reputation, or for the depression of that of their rivals. They are almost always men of the most amiable simplicity of manners, who live in good harmony with one another, and the friends of one another's reputation, enter

into no intrigue in order to secure the public applause, but are pleased when their works are approved of, without being either much vexed or very angry when they are neglected.

(TMS III.2.22, 125)

This is one of the few occasions when he directly refers to Newton, and it is worth examining its content. When Smith refers to having heard that Newton's *Principia* had been neglected by the public, probably his source is Robert Simson, his mathematics teacher at Glasgow. But after his account of Newton and natural philosophers, Smith was not only another inheritor of Newton's highly idealized image, but also idealistic about mathematicians in general. He ignores the Newton–Leibniz debate over the invention of calculus, and he naively contemplates mathematicians regardless of the intrigues and factions that we know about now. I presume that the former might reflect the general view about Newton as the British intellectual hero who had the keys of nature,[13] and the latter is probably influenced by his personal acquaintance with some Scottish mathematicians, mainly perhaps Simson.[14]

Smith's account of Newton's methodology is in his essay *History of Astronomy* (EPS, 31–105), 'the pearl of the collection', according to Schumpeter (1994 [1954]: 182). While Smith was ill in 1773, he sent a letter to Hume, declaring:

> As I have left care of all my literary papers to you, I must tell you that except those which I carry along with me there are none worth the publishing, but a fragment of a great work which contains a history of the Astronomical Systems that were successively in fashion down to the time of Des Cartes. Whether that might not be published as a fragment of an intended juvenile work, I leave entirely to your judgement; tho I begin to suspect myself that there is more refinement than solidity in some parts of it.
>
> (Corr. 168)

This shows that though Smith was committed to rescue *History of Astronomy* (hereafter Astronomy) from burning, he was not fully convinced about its quality. However, as Smith's modesty is evident throughout his correspondence, it might simply be a rhetorical and polite sentence to his friend Hume. There is some debate regarding the quality of Astronomy. Some scholars simply consider it a 'juvenile' work,[15] which could have been written while he studied in Oxford. Nevertheless, the editors of the Glasgow Edition believe that Astronomy 'is one of the best examples of theoretical history' (EPS, *2*), concluding that 'Smith's view of science appears more perceptive today than it will have done in the eighteenth century' (*ibid.*, p. 21). But soon after Wightman, editor of EPS, considers that '[t]o none of them [Smith's main essays] would a modern scholar turn for enlightenment on the history of the sciences' (EPS, 5). Specifically, Astronomy, '[t]hough acceptable to a modern historian in its main lines, it contains so many errors of detail and not a few serious omissions as to be no longer more than a museum specimen of its kind' (EPS, 11).[16] The actual nature of Newton's methodology suggested in Astronomy has been relatively neglected in comparison with the comments and research on the triad 'surprise, wonder and admiration', and it can be argued that it has even been underestimated. For example, Longuet-Higgins concludes that 'Smith's approach to the history of astronomy was that of a psychologist rather than a philosopher of science' (1992: 91).[17]

Smith reflected the British reaction towards mechanical philosophy. He refers to Descartes as 'that ingenious and fanciful philosopher' (Astronomy, IV.61, 92). In his Astronomy he clearly understood how Newton's system had surpassed the Cartesian theory of vortices. The full title of this essay reads 'The Principles Which Lead and Direct Philosophical Enquiries; Illustrated by the History of Astronomy', immediately calling our attention to its methodological import. Although it begins with a psychological account of scientific progress, from the history itself some conclusion can be drawn. Surprise, wonder and admiration are successive steps towards scientific progress. The psychological stages from 'what is unexpected', through 'what is new and singular', finishing up in 'what is great and beautiful', respectively, form the ground to understanding the nature of scientific progress as an abstract mental process. Although this underlying abstraction is already present in the classics, it is noteworthy how Smith situates his history within this psychological process. The latter, as an abstraction, underpins and precedes Astronomy,[18] but his history has a peculiar nature.

Smith defines the role of the philosopher as the study 'of the connecting principles of nature' (Astronomy, II.12, 45), a definition that carries forward throughout this essay. Indeed, this idea of 'connecting together' demands something to be connected, implying that such connections exist. Moreover, before proceeding to develop his Astronomy, Smith states:

> Let us endeavour to trace it, from its first origin, up to that summit of perfection to which it is at present supposed to have arrived, and to which, indeed, it has equally been supposed to have arrived in almost all former times ... Let us examine, therefore, all the different systems of nature ... [that] have successively been adopted by the learned and ingenious.
>
> (Astronomy, II.12, 46)

The conditional nature of scientific progress implicit in this passage, in an epoch that deemed Newton's discoveries as the scientific climax per se, is an aspect of Smith's understanding of Newton that has been neglected.

For Smith science is an open-ended process of successive approximations which resembles Newton's real methodological legacy. Newton discovered that

> he could join together the movements of the Planets by so familiar a principle of connection, which completely removed all the difficulties the imagination had hitherto felt in attending them ... Having thus shown, that *gravity might be the connecting principle* which joined together the movements of the Planets, he endeavoured next to prove that it really was so.
>
> (Astronomy, IV.67, 98, emphasis added)

Smith's use of *might* is not casual; it only reinforces my argument.

Smith finishes his account of Newton's discoveries with the following sentence: 'Such is the system of Sir Isaac Newton, *a system whose parts are all more strictly connected together*, than those of any other philosophical hypothesis' (Astronomy, IV.76, 104, emphasis added). Neither is casual here Smith's use of *more*. The recurrent idea of connections in nature that exist is skeptically subject to approximation in Smith's account of Newton. The idea that 'gravity might be the connecting principle', or the characterization of Newton's system as 'a system whose parts are all more strictly connected together', simply reflect that Newton's system is the most precise humankind has reached, but not the final truth. Newton's scientific success with his connecting principles prompts Smith to assert that we should take his principles '*as if* they were the real chains which Nature makes use of to bind together her several operations' (Astronomy, IV. 76, 105, emphasis added). Note again the 'as if'. Indeed, these examples show that Smith fully understood the open-ended nature of scientific inquiry. This is distinctively Newtonian, as we have shown in the preceding section of this chapter. Smith was aware that we could approximate successively to reality, and this is also quite Newtonian.

Now let's turn to Smith and general economic equilibrium theory. Joseph Schumpeter, not a fan of Adam Smith, in his monumental *History of Economic Analysis*, praises 'the rudimentary equilibrium theory of Chapter 7, by far the best piece of economic theory turned out by A. Smith' (1994 [1954]: 189), simply because it would be a theoretical predecessor pointing towards Walras. Referring to the prices and quantities that constitute 'the economic "system"', if Isnard, Smith, Say and Ricardo 'struggled or rather fumbled for it', for Schumpeter it was Walras who made the 'discovery' of economic equilibrium, 'the Magna Carta of economic theory' (*ibid.*: 242). Since then, it has been generally accepted that Smith would be a forerunner, if not the founder, of general economic equilibrium theory.[19] Some modern economists, considering Walrasian general economic equilibrium as 'the peak of neoclassical economics' (Samuelson 1952: 61), conclude that Adam Smith, 'father of our science', could have better reasons to claim his title. Moreover, the most famous (and most elusive) metaphor in the history of economic thought, the invisible hand, has been interpreted as 'a poetic expression' that confirms Smith as 'a creator of general equilibrium theory' (Arrow and Hahn 1971: 2). One way or another, microeconomics textbooks too readily link Smith's invisible hand to some sort of equilibrium.[20]

Smith's general attempt to uncover the nature of political economy, and in particular to illuminate the 'the particular accidents ... natural causes, and ... particular regulations of police' (WN I.vii.20, 77) of the market mechanism, is Newtonian in terms of its methodology and realism. He did not foresee a theoretical model of the market mechanism from which a conjunction of events can be deduced, as Schumpeter might have wished. His broad project of a social science including ethics, jurisprudence and political economy was to find out the real structures underlying social phenomena. His intellectual pursuit relates to the 'nature and the causes' (recall the full title of WN) of social phenomena. Both Newton and Smith react against reducing phenomena to mechanical causes, sharing a common philosophical project. Therefore it is no coincidence that Smith's words in his Astronomy reflect a realism that is much embedded of Newton's influence. The purpose of our inquiries is to 'lay open the concealed connections that unite the various appearances of nature' (Astronomy, II.3, 51). This is further evidence, *pace* Blaug, who claims that Smith 'had a naïve view of what constituted Newton's method' (1992 [1980]: 53), that Smith understood Newton better than has been generally granted.

The source of the debate on Smith and general economic equilibrium theory is principally, but not exclusively, concentrated on Chapter 7, 'Of the natural and market Price of Commodities', in the first book of WN. This would be the supposed foundation of general equilibrium theory, or the germ of this theory. According to Smith the natural price differs from the market (or actual) price that is determined by effective demand. He defines this process as:

> The natural price, therefore, is, as it were, the central price, to which the prices of *all* commodities are continually *gravitating*. Different accidents may sometimes keep them suspended a good deal above it, and sometimes force them down even somewhat below. But whatever may be the obstacles which hinder them from settling in this *centre of repose and continuance*, they are constantly tending towards it.
>
> (WN I.vii.15, 75, emphasis added)

The idea of *all* prices, the use of the word *gravitating* and the idea of a *center of repose* appear as additional evidence of Newton's influence, but one has also to remember that '[i]n Smith's day invoking Newton's name and borrowing his terminology was a commonly used rhetorical device'

(Redman 1993: 225). After a couple of pages discussing some facts about how price fluctuations affect rent, wages and profits, Smith continues:

> But although the market price of every particular commodity is in this manner continually *gravitating*, if one may say so, towards the natural price, yet sometimes particular accidents, sometimes natural causes, and sometimes particular regulations of police, may, in many commodities, keep up the market price, for a long time together, a good deal above natural price.
>
> (WN I.vii.20, 77, emphasis added)

Note that Smith carefully adds 'if one may say so' after *gravitating*, perhaps underlining its metaphorical character, or maybe aware that gravitation actually implied a different phenomenon. Indeed, Smith's use of gravitation in terms of prices emulates Newton's third law of action and reaction: 'to every action there is always an opposite and equal reaction', but it differs in a very important way. For Newton action and reaction are always equal, and bodies are gravitating not only towards some central body, but they are *all* also mutually gravitating toward one another. In other words, if Smith's depiction of the price mechanism were actually Newtonian, all prices should gravitate towards one another, implying that the natural price should also gravitate to the 'prices of all commodities'. This would be much rather like a kind of dis-equilibrium. The late Bernard Cohen argued that because of this difference, Smith's application of Newtonianism to the price mechanism 'was perfectly correct *up to a point*; it was merely incomplete' (Cohen 1994: 65, emphasis in the original). This is a serious argument against any interpretation of Smith as a forerunner of general equilibrium relying on Newton.

Another point of divergence is that general equilibrium theory, since Walras's early contributions, has become increasingly mathematical, basically emulating the results of what Cohen (1980) terms the *Principia*'s 'Newtonian style'. But it must be remembered that Smith is very cautious, and rather skeptical about the use of mathematics in moral philosophy (which, of course, included political economy). In a letter regarding Webster's compilation of Scottish population figures for a pension scheme, Smith declares: 'You know that I have little faith in Political Arithmetic and this story does not contribute to mend my opinion of it' (Corr. 288). Then, in WN, Smith states: 'I have no great faith in political arithmetic' (WN IV.v.b.30, 534). Although within this tradition initiated by William Petty there was a lot of guesswork in applying political arithmetic during the eighteenth century, at least it can be granted that Smith's method in economics (and *a fortiori* in ethics), with the exception of some simple arithmetical operations such as averages, is not mathematical.

Moreover, regarding Smith's teleological view of the market, he is considering a process, not a final state. Mark Blaug has expressed this view bluntly:

> The effort in modern textbooks to enlist Adam Smith in support of what is now known as the 'fundamental theorems of welfare economics' is a historical travesty of major proportions. For one thing, Smith's conception of competition was . . . a process conception, not an end-state conception.
>
> (Blaug 1997 [1962]: 60)[21]

Smith did not share a mechanical reductionism that, applied to economics, would demand the use of sophisticated mathematics to explain the harmony of market forces within an idealized general equilibrium model. This reductionism presupposes a closed system, an assumption that is at the core of neoclassical economics, especially in relation to general equilibrium theory. Smith's political economy is that of an open system.

The conviction that social phenomena can be treated mechanically, and individuals atomistically, has been wrongly ascribed to something that might be called 'Smithian Newtonianism'. The latter is a doubly spurious interpretation of Newton and Smith that has pervaded neoclassical economics and underlies the development of modern economic general equilibrium theories. If economists have simply relegated Newtonianism to forces in equilibrium, neglecting Newton's actual meaning of his laws and his complex methodology, this mechanical order does not necessarily follow from Smith's conception of the market mechanism. Smith's realistic account of economic phenomena did not pave the way for the ontologically atomistic-mechanistic pre-assumption of neoclassical economics that has been epitomized by general economic equilibrium.

Finally, unconditional faith in a rational order, characterized by harmony, stability, balance or equilibrium, was a particularly French phenomenon, pervasive in Lavoisier, Laplace, Condillac, Lagrange and Condorcet. This tradition led to Walras. However, the thinkers of the Scottish Enlightenment, and Smith in particular, did not consider that social phenomena could be reduced simply to a kind of mechanical equilibrium. Indeed, Smith used the word 'equilibrium' only once in the WN, when he criticizes the doctrine of the balance of trade (WN IV.iii.c.2, 489). In this context, how Smith understood Newton is directly related to how the Scots assimilated Newtonianism, as I argue in the next section. The role that the Scottish Enlightenment played in the dissemination of Newton's ideas is an important feature that illuminates further the context of Smith's approach towards Newton's methodology.

Newton and the Scottish Enlightenment

Just in the last paragraph of *Opticks*'s, in query 31, Newton declared '[a]nd if natural Philosophy and all its Parts, by pursuing this Method, shall at length be perfected, the Bounds of Moral Philosophy will also be enlarged' (Newton 1979 [1704]: 405). This sentence was taken seriously by the eighteenth century savants. George Turnbull fully reproduced this quotation on the title page of the first edition of *The Principles of Moral Philosophy* (1740). Francis Hutcheson, founding father of the Scottish Enlightenment, attempted a mathematical morals, probably inspired by Newton. David Hume wished to build his 'science of man' explicitly emulating Newton's experimental method. Smith was no exception in this setting; therefore, as already mentioned, it is not surprising that he refers to '[t]he great work of Sir Isaac Newton' (TMS III.2.20, 124). Thomas Reid was another inheritor of this Newtonian tradition, as his explicit references to Newton's 'four rules for the study of natural philosophy' evince. Newton's influence on moral philosophy, mathematics, political economy, physiology, and medicine, among other disciplines, is tremendous and very complex. But one of the more puzzling questions is how these intellectuals understood Newton's method.

Therefore, it would be no surprise that Smith might have also echoed Newton's desire at the end of his *Opticks* in his LRBL:

> in the manner of Sir Isaac Newton we may lay down certain principles known or proved in the beginning, from whence we count for the severall Phenomena, connecting all together by the same Chain. – This latter which we may call *the Newtonian method is undoubtedly the most Philosophical, and in every science whether of Moralls or Natural Philosophy* etc., is vastly more ingenious and for that reason more engaging than the other [Aristotle's].
>
> (LRBL, lecture 24, ii.133, 145–6, emphasis added)[22]

It is very difficult and highly nuanced to define what Newtonianism is all about, but the Scottish Enlightenment played a crucial role in spreading Newtonianism.[23] Indeed, Paul Wood has recently argued that 'his writings [Newton's] were read in such radically different ways that it is difficult to identify a unified Newtonian tradition in the moral sciences' (Wood 2003: 802). Eighteenth century *philosophes* carefully adopted Newton's successful discoveries as a paradigm, but many of them uncarefully adapted his methodology. I argue that in France there was a tendency to interpret Newton within a context in which its scientific institutions were still backing the Cartesian legacy. The Scottish were not only determined in disseminating Newton's legacy, but also had a different understanding of what Newtonianism was. The latter shaped the British reception of Newton. In my view this context might explain why Smith understood Newton so well.

There is evidence that Scottish universities were not only prominently Newtonian, but also determinant to establish Newtonianism in Britain. From the 1690s onwards, they 'led the way in the institutionalization of the Newtonian system' (Wood 2003: 810). Christine Shepherd (1982) has done archival research on Newton's rapid acceptance at the Scottish universities from the 1660s up to the early eighteenth century, concluding that Scotland witnessed 'a considerable degree of progress in natural philosophy at the end of the seventeenth century and during the early years of the eighteenth' (*ibid.*: 83).[24] This phenomenon was no doubt due to the enormous influence of the Gregories at St Andrews and Edinburgh,[25] but was by no means exclusive to them. For example, John Keill (1671–1721), a Scotsman, began lecturing on Newton's natural philosophy in Oxford perhaps as early as 1699, becoming Savilian professor there in 1712, initiating an experimental course in Newtonian physics.[26]

In Britain perhaps the most influential and popular accounts of Newton's new system during the first half of the eighteenth century were Henry Pemberton's (1694–1771) *A View of Sir Isaac Newton's Philosophy*, published in 1728, a year after Newton's death, and Voltaire's (1694–1778) *The Elements of Sir Isaac Newton's Philosophy* (1738). But Colin Maclaurin's (1698–1746) notable *An Account of Sir Isaac Newton's Philosophical Discoveries*, which was published in 1748, is perhaps the best account written in the first half of the eighteenth century.[27]

Colin Maclaurin was an exceptionally gifted Scottish mathematician who early in his life, when he was only fifteen, submitted a sophisticated thesis in which he expounded Newton's law of gravity. He rapidly assimilated Newton's calculus, and 'was arguably the most capable and energetic exponent of Newtonianism working in Scotland, if not in Britain, during the first half of the eighteenth century. He helped not only to consolidate the Newtonian hold on Scottish academe, but also to create public science in the Scottish Enlightenment' (Wood 2003: 102). Maclaurin grasped the importance and the essence of Newton's legacy, and his influence through his *An Account of Sir Isaac Newton's Philosophical Discoveries* was considerable in Scotland and in England. Adam Smith was just another savant who benefited from Maclaurin's sophisticated interpretation of Newton; although this book apparently was not in his library, there are good reasons to believe that he read it.[28]

The French reception of Newton, and its context, were completely different from what happened in Britain. Initially it was through Newton's optical work and his reflecting telescope that he first became famous in French scientific circles. Newton's *Principia* was not ignored in France, simply rebutted within a Cartesian framework. Additionally Huygens and Leibniz were competent critics of Newton's law of gravity, and as inheritors of mechanical philosophy they did their best to explain matter and its interaction as a cause for attraction. If in France it was difficult to accept the notion of a void, the idea of bodies attracting one another without any material cause was generally deemed as preposterous. Indeed, the most entrenched notion in France was the insistence on mechanisms and contact between bodies. The latter clashed with Newton's existence of universal gravitation as a force operating universally and independently of any direct mechanical contact. Descartes had defined matter as an infinitely extended plenum, but Newton formulated his concept of universal gravitation operating in bodies *in vacuo*.

Voltaire's celebrated *Letters Concerning the English Nation* (1733)[29] not only popularized Newton, but also evince the context of a great divide between French Cartesianism and Britain's Newtonianism. The new system of natural philosophy had to break through the well established Cartesian regime that was deeply institutionalized in the French scientific community.[30] Just to give one example, if in Scotland Glasgow University took longer to initially accept Newtonianism, as early as 1711 it became part of the Newtonian network with the election of Robert Simson (1687–1768) to a Chair in mathematics (Wood 2003: 100). In the University of Paris the first Newtonian lectures were in the 1740s, as it had remained under the reign of Cartesianism (see Jacob 1988: 201). In fact, '[g]iven the tenacity with which members of the French *Académie des Sciences* in the first three decades of the eighteenth century attempted to find a mathematical defense of Cartesian vortex . . . it is unsurprising that Newton's phenomenological physics was slow to take root in the Continent's colleges and universities' (Brockliss 2003: 61, see also 85). Britain, relying on a tradition initiated by Francis Bacon, gave more emphasis to Newton's 'experimental philosophy'. This created two rival traditions of physics: 'one mathematical and one experimental, which have affected the two countries approaches to natural science ever since' (*ibid.*: 86). It was only at the end of the eighteenth century that Laplace, who dubbed himself 'the French Newton', could finally impose his own 'Newtonian agenda on the French scientific community' (Brockliss 2003: 85).

But the development of both traditions was firmly linked to the history of mathematics. Although Guicciardini (1989) offers a more nuanced account, Florian Cajori, in his influential *A History of Mathematics* (1901), declared:

> Mathematical studies among the English and German people had sunk to the lowest ebb [1730–1820]. Among them the direction of original research was ill-chosen. The former adhered with excessive partiality to ancient geometrical methods, the latter produced the combinatorial school, which brought forth nothing of value. The labours of Euler, Lagrange, and Laplace lay in higher analysis, and this they developed to a wonderful degree.
>
> (*Ibid.*, 246)

This categorical judgment remains a cause of debate, and many contributions have proved it to be exaggerated. But, to put it simply, there was a difference. If in Britain the geometrical approach to mathematics, initiated by Newton, was followed, the French took another road. This analytical approach, although more successful, is quite different from what the Scottish understood by science. It was theoretical, not always practical; it was elegant, not always real. On the role of mathematics, the Scottish tradition interpreted Newton's underlying idea that mathematics is an instrument to describe nature, not a model of reality.[31] Additionally, they generally conceived mathematics, and especially differential calculus, in the geometrical tradition unintentionally initiated by Newton. The superiority of analytical mathematics and abstract thinking was more pervasive and generally accepted by the French Enlightenment. The Scottish mathematical mind was deeply influenced by Colin Maclaurin and Robert Simson's geometrical approach (see Olson 1971).

The idea of a struggle between Cartesian mechanism and Newtonianism is not original,[32] neither can it be defended as a general phenomenon. But in my personal view there are grounds to assume that Britain and France stood by the side of their intellectual heroes. In addition, not only was Scotland an early advocate of Newtonianism, but, more important, the Scottish Enlightenment provided a unique setting for rapidly assimilating and applying original approaches to Newton's ideas. Natural philosophy induced a debate about metaphysics in general (see Stein 2002), theology, and moral philosophy. Disagreement over the nature of gravity and the nature of matter entailed different metaphysical and theological aspects. This discussion was especially fruitful in Scotland, and it was through the Scots that Britain rapidly became Newtonian.

The methodological differences between the French and British traditions of thought are a consequence of Newton's legacy, but by no means part of his legacy. Patriotism, personal rivalries, different scientific agendas, and political and cultural idiosyncrasies, among others, contributed to this divide. If France generally promoted an axiomatic-deductive method, and Britain an inductive methodology based on experiment and observation, Newton defended a process of continuous approximation to reality framed by an analytic-synthetic method. The latter confirms the thesis that Adam Smith was a sophisticated interpreter of Newton's methodology, but the Scottish context might have been more than a simple indirect influence on Smith.

Conclusion

In this chapter I have attempted to uncover what Newtonianism was all about, showing that Smith was a sophisticated interpreter of Newton's actual methodology. By questioning the generally accepted view that Smith, relying on Newton's pervasive influence, would be the father of general economic equilibrium theory, I argued that Adam Smith, for some important methodological reasons, cannot be considered as a forerunner of this theory, neither can Newton. If general economic equilibrium theory relies on an axiomatic-deductive methodology, and if its evolution has been closely attached to a mathematical development,[33] Newton's methodology was more nuanced.

In my opinion, careful reading of the legacy of an author should emphasize not only *what* the author said, but *why* and *how* he said it, i.e. text, context and language play a significant and interdependent role. The real meaning of ideas requires more than simple textual analysis. I believe the success of intellectual history lies in the often elusive combination of each of these three components. Emphasizing only the text would run the risk of reading an author as though the text were written by a contemporary (a common practice in reading Adam Smith as a modern economist). Focusing exclusively on the context might mean missing the real essence of what the text says and what the author's intentions were in using particular words. It is a stubborn truth that words, apparently simple, but at the same time deeply complex, do matter. However, overemphasis only on hermeneutic approaches would risk a process in which the author, and his or her context, might simply disappear.

In economics we have generally taken for granted a kind of equilibrium in Smith, a germ that developed in a well known direction. Standard references to the invisible hand reflect this widespread popular account. However, Newton's equilibrium applied to economics would rather become a kind of disequilibrium. Moreover, at the level of the history of ideas, I argued that there was a scientific and historical shift. If the Scottish Enlightenment had a 'geometrical' way to understand reality, very much influenced by Newton, it was a transition on the Continent, especially in France, that paved the way towards general economic equilibrium theory. The former account has realist overtones that contrast with an emphasis on abstraction. Many rational reconstructions and speculations can derive from this intuition, but one unintended consequence of this investigation is that Adam Smith, as a member of the Scottish Enlightenment, understood Newtonianism much better than has generally been granted.

Notes

An earlier and shorter version of this chapter will be published in *History of Scottish Political Economy* (forthcoming), edited by Sheila and Alisdair Dow. I am much indebted to Eric Schliesser for his helpful comments.

1 As far as I know this essay was read posthumously by Sir Geoffrey Keynes (John Maynard Keynes's brother) in July 1946, as part of Newton's tercentenary celebrations at Trinity College. Gleick (2003: 188) seems to believe that John Maynard Keynes had read this essay.

2 The classic accounts of Newton's life are by Bernard le Bovier de Fontenelle, who published in 1728 *The Elogium of Sir Isaac Newton*; William Stukeley, Newton's friend and follower, who wrote in 1752 *Memoirs of Sir Isaac Newton's Life*, and Sir David Brewster's one-volume *The Life of Sir Isaac Newton* (1831) and

then his two volumes *Memoirs of the Life, Writings, and Discoveries of Sir Isaac Newton* (1855). The latter remained the classic biography of Newton as the father of the 'Age of Reason'. Although many biographies of Newton have been written since Keynes's essay, in my view Richard Samuel Westfall's *Never at Rest: A Biography of Isaac Newton* (1980), remains the best account of Newton's life and his intellectual context (a condensed version entitled *The Life of Isaac Newton* was published in 1993). Manuel's *Portrait of Isaac Newton* (1968) gives a provocative and rather Freudian reading of Newton, Hall's *Isaac Newton: Adventurer in Thought* (1992) is also an excellent biography, and White (*Isaac Newton: The Last Sorcerer*, 1998) and Gleick (*Isaac Newton*, 2003) have published good accounts of Newton's life.

3 The first edition was published in 1687, thanks to Edmond Halley, by the Royal Society; the second, edited by Roger Cotes, in 1713, and the third, edited by Henry Pemberton, was published in 1726. The first English translation of Newton's *Principia* was by Andrew Motte and published posthumously in 1729. A revised version by Florian Cajori was published in 1934, and in 1999 Bernard Cohen and Anne Whitman published the new and long-awaited complete translation of *Principia*, preceded by Cohen's excellent *A Guide to Newton's Principia.*

4 After Newton was appointed President of the Royal Society in 1703, he followed John Wallis's advice to publish his work on Optics. The first edition of Newton's *Opticks* was finally published in 1704, thirty years after it had been written, and only a year after the death of his lifelong rival Hooke (he had promised not to publish it while he was alive). In *The Advertisement* to the first edition, Newton explained that he had suppressed this work from publication since 1675 in order to 'avoid being engaged in Disputes'. The last query, numbered 31, was added for its first Latin edition, *Optice*, published in 1706. The latter was translated and prefaced by Newton's friend and staunch advocate, Samuel Clarke. The Latin edition added seven new queries (numbered 25–31), and the second English edition, published in 1717, added eight more queries (numbered 17–24).

5 In fact, Bernard Cohen, George Smith, and Howard Stein are the leading Newtonian scholars that have investigated Newton's commitment to an open-ended process of successive approximation. For example, Smith (2002: 159) refers to rule 4 arguing that '*quam proxime* amounts to an evidential strategy for purposes of ongoing research', and then brilliantly underlines that 'the process of successive approximations issuing from Newton's *Principia* in these fields has yielded evidence of a quality beyond anything his predecessors ever dreamed of' (*ibid.:* 162).

6 Andrew Skinner (1979, 2001) already had underlined connections between Smith, Kuhn and Shackle in terms of his philosophy of science, but Schliesser is more precise in his treatment of 'Smith as a realist about Newton's theory' (Schliesser, 2005b). For excellent analysis of this and other issues see also Smith (2002) and Stein (2002).

7 This simple difference between both *oeuvres* also entails two 'rather different traditions of doing science' (see Cohen and Smith 2002: 31). However, I should add that methodologically, as it will be implicitly suggested here, more than differences between late life and early editions of Newton's works, there is methodological evolution.

8 In Montes (2003: 741–3), I pointed out some similarities between Newton's actual method and the approach known in economics as 'critical realism'. A year after that piece was submitted *The Cambridge Companion to Newton* was published. In it the editor, George E. Smith, in his essay 'The Methodology of the Principia', analyzes Newton's four rules and refers to his second rule, writing that '*same effect, same cause* – authorizes inferences that Charles Saunders Peirce

would have labeled abductive in contrast to inductive' (Smith 2002: 160–1, emphasis in the original). Considering that critical realism has defended a retroductive model of inference that very much resembles Peirce's abductive inference (see Lawson 1997: 294, n. 14), it is encouraging to read an eminent scholar like George E. Smith making the same link.

9 The editors of the Glasgow Edition rightly point out in their introduction to EPS that 'Smith's methodology would seem to conform to the requirements of the Newtonian method properly so called in that he used the techniques of analysis and synthesis in the appropriate order' (EPS, 12).

10 In a very suggestive essay, Strong (1952) argued for a sort of 'Newton Problem' (*à la* Smith), as his *Principia* and *Opticks* were originally delivered without reference to God. (The *General Scholium* was added twenty-six years after the first edition of *Principia* in 1687, and the queries mentioning God first appeared in the Latin edition *Optice* in 1706 and especially for the second English edition of 1718.) Certainly Newton's need to somehow explain the cause of gravity, the main attack from the Cartesians, might have influenced his reliance on a theological argument. But in my view Strong's argument can be extended towards Newton's concern with his methodology as an open-ended process of successive approximation. It is undeniable that Newton was self-aware about his experimental philosophy, but his works acquired significant methodological nuances as he grew older.

11 For example Kuhn underlines that although Newton 'has seemed to support the further assertion that scientific research can and should be confined to the experimental pursuit of mathematical regularity ... [c]areful examination of Newton's less systematic published writings provides no evidence that Newton imposed upon himself so drastic a restriction upon scientific imagination' (1958: 45).

12 Expanding on this view, see Montes (2003: 725–32). Strong (1951) investigates Newton's 'mathematical way', noting not only that his Method of Fluxions is first and foremost geometric, but also arguing for a 'mathematical experimentalism in which measurements and rules of measure prepare the mechanical principles' (*ibid.*: 107). Mathematics, for Newton, 'is a tool devised to assist in the solution of physical problems' (*ibid.*). Elsewhere he defends the thesis of a Newtonian 'mathematical conceptualism' followed by Maclaurin, Pemberton and 'sGravesande, which contrasts with Keill's 'mathematical realism' (Strong 1957). Moreover, Newton's views on mathematics give pre-eminence to geometry. The way he developed his 'calculus of fluxions' (differential calculus) and his 'method of flowing quantities, or fluents' (integral calculus) reflects the importance he gave to classical geometry before pure mathematics (see especially Guicciardini 1989, 1999, 2002).

13 Simply remember Alexander Pope's intended epitaph for Newton: 'Nature and nature's laws lay hid in night:/God said, Let Newton be! And all was light (1730). Voltaire and Fontenelle might have inspired Smith on this account, as they refer to Newton's tranquillity of mind. In fact, soon after the last quoted passage from TMS, Smith refers to Fontenelle, who, writing about mathematicians and natural philosophers, 'has frequent opportunities of celebrating the amiable simplicity of their manners' (TSM III.2.23, 125).

14 According to Alexander Carlyle, Robert Simson was 'of a Mild Temper and of Engaging Demeanour, and was Master of all Knowledge ... which he Deliver'd in an Easy Colloquial Style, with the Simplicity of a Child, and without the Least Sympton of Self-sufficiency or Arrogance' (quoted in Ross 1995: 46).

15 It was definitely written before 1758 (cf. Astronomy, IV.75, 103).

16 Also Cleaver (1989), by contrasting theoretical and scientific discourse, resorts to Astronomy, identifying three principles on the basic pre-assumption that

there is a sort of equilibrium or uniformity that prompts Smith into an epistemology that lacks an environmental/cultural setting. I disagree with this preassumption.

17 Contrary to the common view, Bernard Cohen suggested that 'Smith was well educated in Newtonian science' (1994: 66). Schliesser (2005a and 2005b) and Montes (2003) have attempted a revival of the methodological import of Smith's Astronomy, especially in some of its Newtonian aspects.

18 However, it must be warned that at the end of his essay on astronomy Smith has recourse to his initial intention: 'while we have been endeavouring to represent all philosophical systems as mere inventions of the imagination, to connect together the otherwise disjointed and discordant phaenomena of nature' (Astronomy, IV.76, 105).

19 For example, Lionel Robbins praises the achievement of the WN, which is 'in harmony with the most refined apparatus of the modern School of Lausanne' (1962 [1932]: 69). Samuel Hollander, applying our modern knowledge of general equilibrium to an understanding of Smith's price mechanism, refers to 'the remarkable chapter' (1973: 117). Later he argues that 'still a price-theoretic orientation to the *Wealth of Nations*' has not been contradicted (Hollander 1987: 61), concluding that Chapter 7 'contains an embryonic account of general equilibrium theory' (*ibid.*: 65). Buchanan and Yoon (2000) argue that Smith's increasing returns are compatible with competitive equilibrium. This would imply Smith as a forerunner of competitive equilibrium as an end-state. For different views, see Chandra (2004) and Negishi (2004).

20 Mas-Collel *et al.*'s popular *Microeconomic Theory* reads: 'The first fundamental theorem of welfare economies states conditions under which any price equilibrium with transfers, and in particular any Walrasian equilibrium, is a Pareto optimum. For competitive market economics, it provides a formal and very general confirmation of Adam Smith's asserted 'invisible hand' property of the market' (Mas-Colell *et al.* 1995: 549; see also 327 and 524).

21 Winch also convincingly argues against those who still want to view Smith as a precursor of general equilibrium theory, but he too readily suggests that '[w]hat Smith praised as "Newtonian method" fits his own work as well as that of general equilibrium theorists' (1997: 399).

22 As caveat, this passage appeared while Smith was lecturing on methods of presentation. There is another incidental reference to Newton in (LRBL, Languages, 1, 204) and (LJ 399), also a reference in a footnote to Isaac Newton's *Representation to the Lords of the Treasury* (WN I.xi.h, 229). Very important is the reference to Newtonian philosophy in Smith's letter to the authors of the *Edinburgh Review* (EPS, 244).

23 Shepherd (1982) and Wood (2003) have notably shown how Scottish intellectuals contributed to the spread of Newtonianism in Britain.

24 Brockliss (2003) states that '[b]y the 1690s his [Newton's] theory of universal gravitation, as well as his work on light and color, was being discussed by professors of philosophy in the Scottish universities' (*ibid.*: 47).

25 James Gregory (1638–75) invented the reflecting telescope, was a Fellow of the Royal Society, corresponded with Newton, became professor of mathematics in St Andrews in 1668, and then professor in the new mathematics chair at the University of Edinburgh in 1674. David Gregory (1659–1708) succeeded his uncle James Gregory as professor of mathematics at the University of Edinburgh in 1683. In 1692 he was admitted to Balliol College, Oxford, and then, supported by Newton, David Gregory was appointed to the Savilian chair of astronomy at Oxford. He was an important disciple of Newton and a member of his intimate circle.

26 John Keill, according to his successor, Desaguliers, was the first one to teach

Newtonian physics 'by experiments in a mathematical manner' (quoted in Guerlac 1981: 118)

27 Initially Maclaurin's contribution was conceived as a companion to a biography of Newton projected by John Conduitt, who was married to Newton's niece, Catherine Burton. Once Conduitt died (1737), Colin Maclaurin continued to work on his project, which was finally published two years after his death (see Strong, 1957: 54). Other popular and influential works were Francesco Algarotti's (1712–64) *Sir Isaac Newton's Philosophy Explain'd for the Use of the Ladies* (1737), and Bernard de Fontenelle's (1657–1757) popular *The Elogium of Sir Isaac Newton* (1728). Notable is *The Newtonian System of Philosophy, adapted to the Capacities of Young Gentlemen and Ladies* (1761) which contain the famous teachings of Tom Telescope (see Secord 1985).

28 His library contains only Maclaurin's *A Treatise of Fluxions* (see Bonar 1966: 107). But when Smith talks about Cassini's observations he mentions Maclaurin, 'who was more capable of judging' (Astronomy, IV.58, 90). This is a good reason to believe that Smith was familiar with Maclaurin's popular and famous *An Account of Sir Isaac Newton's Discoveries.*

29 Especially Letter XIV '*On* Des Cartes *and Sir* Isaac Newton', and to a lesser extent Letter XV '*On Attraction*' and Letter XVI '*On Sir* Issac Newton's *Opticks*'. I am indebted to Eric Schliesser for pointing out that Voltaire also published a separate treatment in 1738 as a (rather long) book, *Elémens de la Philosophie de Neuton.*

30 As Guerlac (1981) has argued, it was Malebranche and his followers, especially Maupertius and Clairaut, who disseminated Newton's legacy in France, though it has also been argued that they basically attempted to reconcile Newton with Descartes (see Gascoigne 2003: 299). On Malebranche and his followers' great influence on Newton's acceptance in France see Hankins (1967).

31 Guicciardini (1989) presents an analysis of British mathematics during the eighteenth century.

32 On Newton's reception in France, Pierre Brunet's *L'Introduction des théories de Newton en France au XIII siècle I, Avant 1738* (second volume never appeared) states that Cartesians opposed Newtonianism in France, but Guerlac (1981) argues that there was no such academic division. See also Hall (1975). Certainly Newton's *Opticks* was more popular especially through Malebranche and his followers, and Fontenelle's popular *Eloge*, first read to the Royal Academy of Sciences in Paris in 1727. A curious but representative feature of the British–French divide is that Leibniz's notation for calculus was adopted in France (and the Continent), while in Britain, Newton's notation prevailed during the eighteenth century. This is the famous ' the dot against d's'.

33 Within this framework Roy Weintraub's suggestive contribution *How Economics Became a Mathematical Science*, together with the other side of the coin currently developed by Judith Klein on *How Mathematics Became Economics*, basically reflect this idea. At a general level Philip Mirowski's contributions are also inspiring in this respect. My modest contribution is just a footnote to their research.

References

Arrow, K. J. and Hahn, F. (1971) *General Competitive Analysis*, San Francisco: Holden Day.

Blaug, M. (1992) [1980] *The Methodology of Economics or How Economists Explain*, Cambridge: Cambridge University Press.

—— (1997) [1962] *Economic Theory in Retrospect*, Cambridge: Cambridge University Press.

Bonar, J. (1966) *A Catalogue of the Library of Adam Smith*, New York: Kelley.

Brewster, D. (1831) *The Life of Sir Isaac Newton*, London: John Murray.

—— (1855) *Memoirs of the Life, Writings, and Discoveries of Sir Isaac Newton*, Edinburgh: Constable.

Brockliss, L. (2003) 'Science, the Universities, and Other Public Spaces: Teaching Science in Europe and the Americas', in *The Cambridge History of Science, Eighteenth Century Science*, IV, ed. R. Porter, Cambridge: Cambridge University Press, 44–86.

Brunet, P. (1931) *L'Introduction des théories de Newton en France au XIII siècle* I, *Avant 1738*, Paris: Libraire Scientifique Albert Blanchard.

Bryson, G. (1968) [1945] *Man and Society: The Scottish Inquiry of the Eighteenth Century*, New York: Kelley.

Buchanan, J. M. and Yoon, J. Y. (2000) 'A Smithian Perspective on Increasing Returns', *Journal of the History of Economic Thought* 22 (1): 43–8.

Cajori, Florian (1901) *A History of Mathematics*, New York: Macmillan.

Chandra, R. (2004) 'Adam Smith and Competitive Equilibrium', *Evolutionary and Institutional Economics Review* 1 (1): 57–83.

Cleaver, K. C. (1989) 'Adam Smith on Astronomy', *History of Science* 27 (76): 211–18.

Cohen, I. B. (1980) *The Newtonian Revolution: With Illustrations of the Transformation of Scientific Ideas*, Cambridge: Cambridge University Press.

—— (1994) 'Newton and the Social Sciences, with Special Reference to Economics, or, The case of the Missing Paradigm', in *Natural Images in Economic Thought: 'Markets Red in Tooth and Claw'*, ed. P. Mirowski, Cambridge: Cambridge University Press, 55–90.

—— and Smith, G. E. (2002) *The Cambridge Companion to Newton*, Cambridge: Cambridge University Press.

Dow, S. C. (1987) 'The Scottish Political Economy Tradition', *Scottish Journal of Political Economy* 34 (4): 335–48.

Fara, P. (2003) 'Marginalized Practices', in *The Cambridge History of Science* IV, *Eighteenth Century Science*, ed. R. Porter, 485–507, Cambridge: Cambridge University Press.

Gascoigne, J. (2003) 'Ideas of Nature: Natural Philosophy', in Roy Porter (ed.) *The Cambridge History of Science* IV, *Eighteenth Century Science*, Cambridge: Cambridge University Press, 285–304.

Gleick, J. (2003) *Isaac Newton*, New York: Pantheon Books.

Guerlac, H. (1981) *Newton on the Continent*, Ithaca, NY: Cornell University Press.

Guicciardini, N. (1989) *The Development of Newtonian Calculus in Britain, 1700–1800*, Cambridge: Cambridge University Press.

—— (1999) *Reading the Principia: The Debate on Newton's Mathematical Methods for Natural Philosophy from 1687 to 1736*, Cambridge: Cambridge University Press.

—— (2002) 'Analysis and synthesis in Newton's mathematical work', in *The Cambridge Companion to Newton*, ed. I. B. Cohen and G. E. Smith, Cambridge: Cambridge University Press.

Hall, A. R. (1975) 'Newton in France: A New View', *History of Science* 13: 233–56.

—— (1992) *Isaac Newton: Adventurer in Thought*, Cambridge: Cambridge University Press.

Hankins, T. L. (1967) 'The Influence of Malebranche on the Science of Mechanics during the Eighteenth Century', *Journal of the History of Ideas* 28: 193–210.

Hetherington, N. S. (1983) 'Isaac Newton's Influence on Adam Smith's Natural Laws in Economics', *Journal of the History of Ideas*, 44 (3): 497–505.

Hollander, S. (1973) *The Economics of Adam Smith*, London: Heinemann.

—— (1987) *Classical Economics*, Oxford: Blackwell.

Jacob, M. C. (1988) *The Cultural Meaning of the Scientific Revolution*, New York: Knopf.

Keynes, J. M. (1972) 'Newton, The Man', in *Essays in Biography*, vol. X in *The Collected Writings of John Maynard Keynes*, ed. D. Moggridge, London: Macmillan for the Royal Economic Society, 363–81.

Kuhn, T. S. (1958) 'Newton's Optical Papers', in *Isaac Newton's Papers & Letters on Natural Philosophy*, ed. I. B. Cohen, Cambridge: Cambridge University Press.

Lawson, T. (1997) *Economics & Reality*, London: Routledge.

Longuet-Higgins, H. C. (1992) '"The History of Astronomy": a twentieth-century view', in *Adam Smith Reviewed*, ed. P. Jones and A. Skinner, Edinburgh: Edinburgh University Press.

Maclaurin, C. (1750) [1748] *An Account of Sir Isaac Newton's Philosophical Discoveries*, London: Printed for A. Millar.

Manuel, F. E. (1968) *Portrait of Isaac Newton*, Cambridge, MA: Belknap Press of Harvard University Press.

Mas-Colell, A., Whinston, M. D. and Green, J. R. (1995) *Microeconomic Theory*, Oxford: Oxford University Press.

McGuire, J. E. (1970) 'Newton's *Principles of Philosophy*: An Intended Preface for the 1704 *Opticks* and a Related Draft Fragment', *British Journal for the History of Science* 5: 178–86.

Montes, L. (2003) 'Smith and Newton: some Methodological Issues concerning General Economic Equilibrium Theory', *Cambridge Journal of Economics* 27 (5): 723–47.

—— (forthcoming) 'Adam Smith: Real Newtonian', in *History of Scottish Political Economy*, ed. Sheila and Alisdair Dow, London: Routledge.

Negishi, T. (2004) 'Adam Smith and Disequilibrium Economic Theory', *Adam Smith Review* 1: 30–9.

Newton, I. (1979) [1704] *Opticks. or, a Treatise of the Reflections, Refractions, Inflections and Colours of Light*, London: William Innys.

—— (1999) [1687] *Mathematical Principles of Natural Philosophy*, ed. I. B. Cohen and A. Whitman, Berkeley, CA: University of California Press.

Newton-Smith, W. H. (1990) 'Realism', in *Companion to the History of Modern Science*, ed. R. C. Olby, G. N. Cantor, J. R. R. Christie and M. J. S. Hodge, London: Routledge, 181–95.

Olson, R. (1971) 'Scottish Philosophy and Mathematics, 1750–1830', *Journal of the History of Ideas* 32 (1): 29–44.

Redman, D. A. (1993) 'Adam Smith and Isaac Newton', *Scottish Journal of Political Economy* 40 (2): 210–30.

Robbins, L. (1962) [1932] *An Essay on the Nature and Significance of Economic Science*, New York: Macmillan

Ross, I. S. (1995) *The Life of Adam Smith*, Oxford: Clarendon Press.

Samuelson, P. (1952) 'Economic Theory and Mathematics. An Appraisal', *American Economic Review* 33 (2): 56–66.

Schliesser, E. (2005a) 'Some Principles of Adam Smith's 'Newtonian' Methods in the *Wealth of Nations*', *Research in History of Economic Thought and Methodology* 23A: 35–77.

—— (2005b) 'Realism in the Face of Scientific Revolutions: Adam Smith on Newton's "Proof" of Copernicanism', *British Journal for the History of Philosophy* 13 (4): 697–732.

Schumpeter, J. A. (1994) [1954] *History of Economic Analysis*, London: Routledge.

Secord, J. A. (1985) 'Newton in the Nursery: Tom Telescope and the Philosophy of Tops and Balls, 1761–1838', *History of Science* 23 (60): 127–51.

Shepherd, C. M. (1982) 'Newtonianism in Scottish Universities in the Seventeenth Century', in *The Origins & Nature of the Scottish Enlightenment*, ed. R. H. Campbell and A. S. Skinner, Edinburgh: John Donald.

Skinner, A. S. (1979) 'Adam Smith: An Aspect of Modern Economics?' *Scottish Journal of Political Economy* 26 (2): 109–25.

—— (2001) 'Adam Smith, the Philosopher and the Porter', in *Knowledge, Social Institutions and the Division of Labour*, ed. P. L. Porta, R. Scazzierir and A. Skinner, Cheltenham: Elgar.

Smith, G. E. (2002) 'The Methodology of the *Principia*', in *The Cambridge Companion to Newton*, ed. I. B. Cohen and G. E. Smith, Cambridge: Cambridge University Press.

Spargo, P. E. (1992) 'Sotheby's, Keynes, and Yahuda: The 1936 Sale of Newton's Manuscripts', in P. M. Harman and A. E. Shapiro (eds) *Investigations of Difficult Things: Essays on Newton and the History of the Exact Sciences in Honour of D. T. Whiteside*, Cambridge: Cambridge University Press.

Stein, H. (2002) 'Newton's metaphysics', in *The Cambridge Companion to Newton*, ed. I. B. Cohen and G. E. Smith, Cambridge: Cambridge University Press.

Strong, E. W. (1951) 'Newton's "Mathematical Way"', *Journal of the History of Ideas* 12 (1) 90–110.

—— (1952) 'Newton and God', *Journal of the History of Ideas* 13 (2): 147–67.

—— (1957) 'Newtonian Explanations of Natural Philosophy', *Journal of the History of Ideas* 18 (1): 49–83.

Stukeley, W. (1936) [1752] *Memoirs of Sir Isaac Newton's Life*, London: Taylor and Francis.

Voltaire (1994) [1733] *Letters Concerning the English Nation*, Oxford: Oxford University Press.

Weintraub, E. R. (2002) *How Economics Became a Mathematical Science*, Durham, NC: Duke University Press.

Westfall, R. S. (1980) *Never at Rest: A Biography of Isaac Newton*, Cambridge: Cambridge University Press.

—— (1993) *The Life of Isaac Newton*, Cambridge: Cambridge University Press.

White, M. (1998) *Isaac Newton: The Last Sorcerer*, London: Fourth Estate.

Winch, D. (1997) 'Adam Smith's Problems and Ours', *Scottish Journal of Political Economy* 44 (4): 384–402.

Wood, P. (2003) 'Science, Philosophy, and the Mind', in *The Cambridge History of Science, Eighteenth Century Science*, IV, ed. R. Porter, Cambridge: Cambridge University Press, 800–24.

12 Vanity and the Daedalian wings of paper money in Adam Smith

Maria Pia Paganelli

George Stigler (1971) claimed that: 'it is uncomfortable to explain Smith's failure by the failure of everyone else, for he is a better man than everyone else' (214). Diverging from Stigler, the problem presented in this chapter is: how can we explain Smith's failure when others did not fail, for Smith is a better man than everyone else?

The failure by Smith diagnosed in this chapter is his lack of vision for the potential uses and/or misuses as policy instruments of paper money in general and of public credit in particular – vision that Smith's contemporaries did not lack. Paper money could be used not only as a cheaper substitute for metallic money, as Smith well realized, but also as a relatively cheaper policy tool to create more money and try to gain control over the economy. Public credit could be used not only to finance wars, as Smith observed, but also to try to fix and stimulate the economy, as some contemporaries known to him as well as many future economists would claim (see among others Viner 1930, Monroe 1966, Friedman 1969, Pribram 1983, Pocock 1985, Albertone 1992, Humphrey 1993, 2004, Keynes [1936] 1997, Smithin 2003.) And that paper money may cause hyperinflation, not just more or less beneficial inflation, is recognized among many others by Smith's friend, David Hume, but not by Smith. Why then does not Smith recognize the potential, either positive or negative, of using paper money as a policy instrument to gain control over the economy rather than just as a monetary instrument?

This chapter proposes a *possible* justification for Smith's silence, within the limitations generally associated with all explanations of silences. Smith's contemporaries (and successors) tend to use either benevolence or love of power to justify the positive or negative effects of using paper money as a policy instrument. Smith, on the other hand, considers neither love of power nor benevolence as fundamental motivational forces in human conduct in a commercial society. The downplaying of benevolence as a major motivational force suggests downplaying the possible use of paper money to stimulate the economy; and the downplaying of the love of power suggests downplaying the possible misuse of paper money that causes hyperinflation. A *commercial society* like the one Smith describes is based on forces such as self-centered vanity instead. And vanity, mediated through commerce and market forces, strips paper money of its negative as well as positive potential as a policy instrument: the analysis of paper money as a policy instrument becomes superfluous because money has no motivational basis to become a policy instrument. Money remains simply a unit of account, a means of exchange, and a credit instrument.

The chapter develops as follows. The first section presents a general overview of the eighteenth century debate on money, in which Smith does not participate. The second section presents Smith's analysis of the different forms of paper money. A brief account of his analysis of the benefits and the costs associated with paper money follows. The subsequent sections show how vanity, rather than love of power or benevolence, seems to motivate Smithian human beings, and how, in a commercial society based on self-interested vanity, public credit is neither a threat nor a blessing, as some of Smith's contemporaries thought.

Policy instrument: a new function of money

Before proceeding a clarification is due. While it is true that paper money, paper credit, and public credit are not necessarily equivalent, it is also true that in the eighteenth century these distinctions were not necessarily as well defined as they are today. They were often treated as synonymous.[1] In this chapter there is no attempt to modernize or correct the eighteenth century understanding of money, but simply to report it.

In the eighteenth century the State begins to have the achievement of public happiness as one of its objectives. The State now has the opportunity to be active in the betterment of society and of the economy.[2] The explicit claim of direct control over society, in one form or another, is accompanied by the search for appropriate tools. Money begins to show its potential for being one of these tools.

Money has two traditional functions: unit of account and medium of exchange. In the eighteenth century money debates, a third function is added: money can be a policy instrument to progress toward public happiness. Money could now become a policy instrument to promote economic growth and public happiness, and to pay for it. Paper money, especially when irredeemable, makes money a more malleable and controllable policy instrument than any commodity money. Paper money is generated by both private credit as well as public credit. Control over the economy is achieved by controlling either or, better, both.

Many eighteenth century authors begin their treatises on money declaring that the purpose of their work is to contribute to the achievement of public happiness. Something like this is typical: 'I have the Interest and Advancement of Trade (on which the Welfare and Happiness of Mankind so much depends) really at Heart' (Vanderlint [1734] 1970, dedication). The State is justified to expand its activities to include not only warfare but also welfare[3]: 'what I understand by political oeconomy ... the object of the art ... is, to provide food, other necessaries, and employment to every one of the society.... To provide a proper employment for all the members of a society is the same as to model and conduct every branch of their concerns' (Steuart [1767] 1966, 28).

Focusing on how to achieve public happiness helps in the analysis of different conceptions of the role of inflation. Traditionally inflation, via debasement, is generated simply to finance an increase in military expenditures. Indeed:

> I am very glad to pursue this matter somewhat further, so that an example will not be made of something that is not one. In the First Punic War the as, which was supposed to be of twelve ounces of copper, weighed only two, and in the Second Punic War, it weighed only one. This retrenching corresponds to what we today call expansion of the currency.... The [Roman] republic [inflated because it] was not in a position to pay its debt.
>
> (Montesquieu [1748] 1989, 413)

Debasement, or inflation, is in fact traditionally thought of only as a 'dirty trick' to get rid of debts that were too big to be paid otherwise. No intention to control, regulate, stabilize, fine-tune, or improve the economy is present: only paying off a very large debt. Indeed, calls for inflation are justified either as a backward-looking 'patch'[4] or as the result of vicious behaviors.[5] In Montesquieu's words: '*bad faith or need* makes them withdraw part of the metal from each piece of money, leaving it with the same name' (Montesquieu [1748] 1989, 400, emphasis added).

But in the eighteenth century, starting with John Law, among others, we see calls for inflation based on the idea that increasing the quantity of money would increase wealth and therefore the happiness of the people. Money becomes an important ally of the new order. Money, being required to pay for the re-creation or the improvement of the new social order, and, if controllable and active on the economy, becomes an important policy instrument to be used to construct progress and achieve happiness in a country. But if money has to be a fine-tuning instrument, using metals is not easy. The technology of debasing becomes too complicated and expensive, as shown in the debate on recoinage of the seventeenth century.[6] Paper, issued both through private credit channels and through public credit, is an easier and cheaper technology to produce a more malleable and controllable form of money that better fits its new role of promoter of new advantages, independently of the needs of financing wars.

This eighteenth century debate opens the door to the conception, development, and eventual acceptance of present-day fiat money. But, while most of Smith's contemporaries take part in this debate in one way or the other, Smith's voice is absent. Adam Smith has a meticulous account of money, but only in its traditional functions. Money for Smith is only a unit of account and a means of exchange, and public credit is only a form of paper money, useful to pay for expensive wars. Furthermore, not only is money not a policy instrument to Smith, but he does not even seem to consider it as a conceivable option for others, as he quickly dismisses those who think otherwise. Smith looks at the same phenomena as his contemporaries but sees different things.

What is paper money?

Smith describes the use of different kinds of money in detailed fashion. He has a meticulous account of paper money, which mirrors his contemporaries'. Smith's unique signature is present in his description of the origins of paper money and in his policy prescriptions. But let us start with a brief explanation of the different forms of paper money that Smith observes.

Smith claims that money is an instrument that facilitates trade, decreasing the transaction costs involved in barter (WN I.iv.2, 37–8). Money may take different forms in different times and places (WN I.iv.3–5, 38–9). Precious metals, such as gold and silver, are commonly used as money in the Western world, both within each country and among different countries. But the eighteenth century sees the increasing use of another kind of money: paper. Paper money takes various forms, two of the major forms being receipts and credit. Paper money could be issued, at different times, both privately, by individuals and banks, and by the government.

Paper money in the form of receipts takes place when receipts for bank deposits circulate as money (bank money), while the precious metals are safely kept in a bank. The circulating receipts are the claims on deposits. Banks issuing these papers, in theory, could either be banks with 100 percent reserves or with just fractional reserves. Banks with fractional reserves are banks that accept deposits, giving a paper claim on it to the depositor, and offer loans and lines of credit, lending out a part of the deposits received and therefore keeping only a fraction of their reserves. Borrowers pay interest on the loan, generating revenue for the bank. When the bank issues loans or credit, they could be in metal or in paper notes. Some notes go back to bankers for payment, while others keep circulating. According to Smith, bankers need only about 20 percent of gold as reserve for immediate demands, the economy running on a fifth of the gold and silver otherwise required (WN II.ii.29, 292–3). In practice, all the banks are fractional reserve banks, even if some, like the Bank of Amsterdam, claim otherwise. Smith describes the practical difficulties of sustaining a 100 percent reserve: how could the Bank of Amsterdam operate with no revenue? His conclusion is that what the bank claims in words is not present in the facts (WN II.ii.104, 328). On the other hand, other thinkers, such as David Hume, propose an alternative view. Hume, who thinks 100 percent reserve banks are the only acceptable banks, also understands the operational problem of banks with no revenue. But he suggests the introduction of government subsidies to maintain the operations of the banks as a possible way to keep the banks in business (Hume, *Essays*, 285).

Credit takes different forms. It could be backed with collateral (cash accounts) – 'melting' non-liquid assets – or it could be backed not by tangible goods but by the creditworthiness granted to men 'of credit'. The guarantee might come from the creditor's good reputation or from other people's good words vouching for his good reputation. Credit could be granted to individuals or companies, as well as to the government. Public credit is indeed the credit granted to the government, which could also be either backed or unbacked. Backed public credit usually consists of mortgaging future tax revenue. Unbacked credit could be granted on the basis of trust in the current government. The duration of the debt might vary. It might be short-term – with a fund that would allow paying back the interest and the principal – or 'for perpetuity' – with a fund large enough to pay only the interest (WN V.iii.12, 912).

Finally, notes may be traded at a discount if their real value is less than their nominal value, usually due to a decrease in trust in the issuer or due to over-issuing. They could be traded with *agio*, that is, notes may be traded at more than their nominal value because of the extra security offered by a well respected bank (WN II.ii.104, 328).

Benefits of paper money

But why are England, and Europe in general, developing these different forms of money? Are not gold and silver good enough monies?

Smith claims that, with the development of commerce, paper money develops as a cheaper form of money. (For an account of Smith's theory of banking see Gherity 1994.) He describes the benefits of private paper credit in a commercial society in Book II, and the benefits of public paper credit in a commercial society in Book V.

In a commercial society, using gold and silver as domestic currency has a high opportunity cost. Gold and silver in their monetary forms can be used either domestically as currency or can be sent abroad to buy cheaper consumption or investment goods. Given the opportunity to use precious metals, it is natural to observe the emergence of substitutes like paper to be used as domestic currency while the precious metals are sent abroad (WN II.ii.26, 292). Smith indeed explains that money is not part of the revenue of a country, but, due to its function as means of exchange, it is the 'great wheel' on which revenue and goods circulate in society (WN II.ii.14, 289, and WN II.ii.23, 291).

Echoing Hume, Smith considers demand for money constant, given a certain level of economic activity: if money supply is increased via paper, 'whatever is poured into it beyond this sum cannot run in it [in the economy], but must overflow ... it will, therefore, be sent abroad, in order to seek that profitable employment which it cannot find at home. But the paper cannot go abroad; because at a distance from the banks which issue it, and from the country in which payment of it can be exacted by law, it will not be received in common payments. Gold and silver, therefore ... will be sent abroad' (WN II.ii.30, 293) to buy goods and bring home profits (WN II.ii.31–2, 294). When paper substitutes for gold, gold increases funds for maintenance of industry, the quantity of that industry, and the annual product of land and labor. Therefore, wherever cash accounts are used 'every merchant can, without imprudence, carry on a greater trade than he otherwise could' (WN II.ii.46, 299–300).

Smith explains further that using paper rather than gold frees gold from unproductive uses by the following suggestive image of paper money as an aerial highway that frees fertile ground for more productive uses:

> It is not by augmenting the capital of the country, but by rendering a greater part of that capital active and productive than would otherwise be so, that the most judicious operations of banking can increase the industry of the country ... The part of his capital which a dealer is obliged to keep by him unemployed, and in ready money for answering occasional demands, is so much dead stock, which ... produces nothing either to him or his country. The judicious operations of banking enable him to convert this dead stock into active and productive stock ... The judicious operations of banking, by substituting paper in the room of a great part of this gold and silver, enables the country to convert a great part of this dead stock into active and productive stock ... The gold and silver money which circulated in any country may very properly be compared to a highway, which, while it circulates and carries to market all the grass and corn of the country, produces itself not a single pile of either. The judicious operations of banking, by proving, if I may be allowed so violent a metaphor, a sort of wagon-way through the air; enable the country to convert, as it were, a great part of its highways into good pastures and corn fields, and thereby to increase very considerably the annual produce of its land and labour.
>
> (WN, II.ii.86, 320–1)

When the increase in commerce renders metals expensive as domestic currency, metals will leave an opening for paper, seeking cheaper (more productive) employments. With some caveats to be presented later in this work, paper money is therefore a beneficial consequence of the increased commerce in a commercial society.

In the form of public credit, paper money allows smoothing revenue collection over time, which is useful especially in the case of wars:

> By means of borrowing they are enabled, with a very moderate increase of taxes, to raise, from year to year, money sufficient for carrying on the war, and by the practice of perpetual funding they are enabled, with the smallest possible increase of taxes, to raise annually the largest possible sum of money.
>
> (WN V.iii.37, 919–20)

For the purposes of this chapter, the most interesting part of Smith's account of the benefits of paper money is what Smith does *not* mention. The eighteenth century experiences the first calls to try to manipulate the money supply to stimulate the economy, mostly through easing or tightening private and public credit. Some of these calls were less sophisticated than others. But Smith does not seem to pay much attention either to this potential or to those who claim its relevance.

In the eighteenth century a (not very sophisticated) way to justify money creation is the attempt to fight poverty. Poverty is associated with the lack of money. A way to claim to be fighting poverty is to generate money, something more easily done with paper[7] than with precious metals. (See, for example, Vanderlint [1734] 1970.) Another way to justify money creation is to claim that

> public incumbrances are advantageous, independent of the necessity of contracting them; that any state, even though it were not pressed by a foreign enemy, could not possibly have embraced a wiser expedient for promoting commerce and riches, than to create funds, and debts, and taxes, without limitation.
>
> (Hume, *Essays*, 352; critical of this view)

Money and riches tend to go hand in hand just like lack of money and poverty tend to be observed at the same time. The traditional understanding, to which Smith subscribes, sees wealth generating money, and poverty lack of money. The competing view that makes its way through the eighteenth century reverses the direction of causation, or, according to Hume, it 'mistake[s], as is too usual, a collateral effect for a cause' (Hume, *Essays*, 290). The mechanisms through which an increase in money supply 'quickens' industry are not always clear. Sometimes they are recognized as mysterious, as for example by Isaac de Pinto ([1774] 1969) who claims that 'Circulation and credit are two springs, the play of which is not thoroughly understood' (115). Sometimes they simply sound alchemistic, such as Berkeley's query No. '233. Whether the credit of the public funds be not a mine of gold to England; and whether any step that should lessen this credit, ought not to be dreaded?' (Berkeley [1735] 1979), or de Pinto's explicit reference to magic: 'This mass of wealth has been successively produced with the same specie, by the magic of credit and circulation' (de Pinto [1774] 1969, 20).[8] Nevertheless, many think,

'The more notes the Banks can circulate ... the more will industry and trade be promoted. Nor can there be any limit' (Wallace [1734] 1969, 19). Smith remains silent instead. His only words[9] are his comments (or lack thereof) on John Law's 'visionary project', which is dismissed simply as 'the most *extravagant* project both of banking and stock-jobbing that, perhaps, the world ever saw' (WN II.ii.78, 317, emphasis added).

Costs of paper money

Just as Smith deals with some of the common benefits (real or perceived) of paper money, but not all of them, so he deals with some of the common costs (real or perceived) of paper money, but not all of them. Smith tells us that the costs of paper money in a commercial society are associated with the tendency of over-issuing paper money. He does not tell us that using paper money to stimulate the economy can cause hyperinflation. For Smith, creditors tend to like promissory notes more than loans in precious metals because they free idle capital, and because they could pay back a little at a time. The interest on the notes is revenue to the bank. The more notes issued, the more interest collected, the more revenue generated, and most likely, the higher the profits for the bank. And, if banks discount bills of exchange with promissory notes, they could make more profit than with gold (WN II.ii.43, 298–9). Creditors, therefore, are tempted to ask for over-issuing of credit, and banks are tempted to over-issue credit.

In addition, 'over-trading of some bold projectors ... was the original cause of this excessive circulation of paper money' (WN II.ii.57, 304). Because of their high profits, certain commercial activities attract merchants' attention. Merchants ask for money to participate in these profitable trades. But as more and more merchants enter these markets, profits are eaten away (over-trading) and with them the resources to pay the banks back (over-issuing).

Furthermore, banks should lend 'that part of it [capital] only, which he would otherwise be obliged to keep by him unemployed, and in ready money for answering occasional demands' (WN II.ii.58, 304). 'Fixed capital' pays back only after many years: too much time for a bank. The capital that could be repaid only after years should therefore not be borrowed through banks, but through mortgages and/or bonds from private people (WN II.ii.64, 307). But, when wise banks reject a credit extension, traders use 'shift of drawing and redrawing' to raise the money used to over-trade (WN II.ii.65, 308).

And because, according to Smith, paper and metallic money are substitutes in the domestic market, over-issuing paper generates an oversupply of money. But paper and metals are not substitutes in international markets, as paper cannot be sent abroad. The domestic quantity of money would return to its natural level by reconverting paper into gold and silver, and sending the precious metals abroad. Banks, therefore, have to be ready to convert paper into gold and silver at all times. If they over-issue, they might not be as ready. And if they signal hesitation or difficulties, they might generate bank runs (WN II.ii.48, 300–1).

This intrinsic instability and potential for runs caused Smith to say:

> The commerce and industry of the country, however, it must be acknowledged, though they may be somewhat augmented, cannot be altogether so secure, when they are thus as it were, suspended upon the Daedalian wings of paper money, as when they travel about upon the solid ground of gold and silver.
>
> (WN II.ii.86, 320–1)

As far as costs associated with public credit, Smith seems to believe that public debt may be abundantly issued because paper credit 'is always an obvious and easy expedient for getting out of the present difficulty' (WN V.iii.40, 920–1), the present difficulty being the cost of wars. For Smith, the danger of using public credit is therefore not over-issuing, but the decrease in the cost of wars, which may increase their length (WN V.iii.50, 926).

Smith's apparent lack of concern about the possible over-issuing of public credit 'independent[ly] of the necessity of contracting [it] . . . even though [a state] were not pressed by a foreign enemy', as Hume said, is puzzling, especially in light of the famous attacks his friend Hume makes against public credit ('[E]ither the nation must destroy public credit, or public credit will destroy the nation' (Hume, *Essays*, 360–1)). Hume claims that an economic collapse is near as money manipulations are raising prices. Smith simply and quickly dismisses the higher prices to which Hume refers as due 'probably, to the badness of the seasons' (WN II.2.96, 324).

So, why does Smith seem to close his eyes to what others considered positive as well as negative potentials of paper money?

Blinding vanity

A possible explanation for why Smith seems to stop short in his analysis of paper money may be that his project is to analyze the potential of *commercial* society. As shown below, most of the reflections of Smith's contemporaries base the potential of paper money either on the assumption of benevolence or on the assumption of desire for power. On the other hand, for Smith, in a *commercial* society the most relevant force in its different expressions is a self-interested vanity, not benevolence and not power. Smith may be able to dismiss some theoretical and/or practical effects of paper money as not relevant for an apparatus built on vanity and commerce such as his.

Those who advocate the benefits of increasing money supply (by increasing money to stimulate the economy) generally justify their claims as motivated by what today we call the 'benevolent dictator' assumption:[10] the sovereign wants to act upon the economy because he is moved by benevolence, by genuine care for the well-being of society. So, for example, Bishop Berkeley ([1735] 1979) claims not only that the State should encourage the industry of its members (query 3) but also asks in query No.:

> 346. Whether, therefore, a legislator should be content with a vulgar share of knowledge? Whether he should not be a person of reflexion and thought, who hath made his study to understand the true nature and interest of mankind, how to guide men's humours and passions, how to incite their active powers, how to make their several talents co-operate to the mutual benefit of each other, and the general good of the whole?

The idea of the 'benevolent dictator' is restated, among others, by Sir James Steuart when he combines the interests of individuals and the interest of the public in the interest of the sovereign and says: 'Virtue and justice, when applied to government, mean no more than a tender affection for the whole society, and an exact and impartial regard for the interest of every class' (Book 1, 20).

On the other hand, those who emphasize the perniciousness of paper money, and of its increases, tend to see knavery and desire for power as the motivation for action of the sovereign (for example, Hume, *Essays*). (For an account of knavery in Hume see Farrant and Paganelli 2006.)

Benevolence and love of power may not necessarily be considered as major forces driving human conduct. If they are not, the theories based on them may be quickly dismissed as 'extravagances' or, at worst, short-term problems. And this seems to be what Smith does. To understand this claim, let us walk though Smith's system.

Let us take as a starting point the view that TMS and WN are to be read together and are not in contradiction with each other. One of the most convincing accounts of this view comes from James Otteson (2002). Otteson describes the moral system of TMS as similar to the market system of WN. This communality is based on the fact that the Smithian man is a man hard-wired to desire the attention and approbation of others. The same self-interest (or desire for approbation) that drives every man to better his material conditions drives every man to better his moral conditions.

> From whence, then, arises that emulation which runs through all the different ranks of men, and what are the advantages which we propose by that great purpose of human life which we call *bettering our*

> *condition?* To be observed, to be attended to, to be taken notice of with sympathy, complacency, and approbation, are all the advantages which we can propose to derive from it. It is the *vanity*, not the ease, or the pleasure, which interests us. But *vanity* is always founded upon the belief of our being the object of attention and approbation.
>
> (TMS I.iii.2.1, 50, emphasis added)

Similarly, man's moral development depends on the presence of the impartial spectator, whose approbation human vanity wants:

> We endeavour to examine our own conduct as we imagine any other fair and impartial spectator would examine it. If upon placing ourselves in his situation, we thoroughly enter into all the passions and motives which influence it, we approve of it, by sympathy with the approbation of this supposed equitable judge.
>
> (TMS III.i.2, 110)[11]

The entire Smithian apparatus seems therefore to revolve (or collapse?) around the innate human vain desire to attract the attention of other people.[12] The desire of power boils down to vanity, and public benevolence boils down to vanity as well. The desire to pursue 'power and preheminence ... [is motivated by the same human desire] to be observed, to be attended to, to be taken notice of with sympathy, complacency, and approbation ... It is the vanity ... which interest us' (TMS I.iii.2.1, 50). The alleged 'public benevolence' of the sovereign boils down to 'his own interest, his own vanity, the interest and vanity of many of his friends and companions' (TMS VI.ii.2.6, 230; cf. TMS VI.ii.2.16, 233). In the Smithian system, we are left with only vanity. (On the importance of vanity in Smith, see also Lerner 1999 and Schliesser 2003.)

The analysis of the origins of both private and public paper credit confirms that vanity is the force at its base. In fact, the development of private paper money is linked to human vanity because paper money is an instrument that facilitates commerce. As we just saw, commerce is the instrument through which a man fulfills his hard-wired desire to 'better his condition', which in its turn, Smith claims, is a function of the hard-wired human vanity which is at the very base of all human actions. Furthermore, even the development of public credit is linked to vanity, as dealt with in Book V of the WN.

Smith's most interesting, albeit less explored, characterization of the origins of paper money comes from Book V, where he deals with public credit. There, Smith presents the common explanation that public credit is a product of war financing: 'The want of parsimony in time of peace, imposes the necessity of contracting debt in time of war. When war comes, there is no money in the treasury but what is necessary for carrying on the ordinary expence of the peace establishment' (WN V.iii.4, 909).

What is interesting for our purposes is the reason for 'the want of parsimony in time of peace'. The 'want of parsimony' is, for Smith, caused by the presence of commerce. In non-commercial societies, tastes are unrefined, and luxuries and useless trinkets basically unknown. The natural and unavoidable human vanity and the human desire for ostentation are therefore much constrained:

> The same disposition to save and to hoard prevailed in the sovereign, as well as in the subjects. Among the nations to whom commerce and manufactures are little known, the sovereign, it has already been observed in the fourth book, is in a situation which naturally disposes him to the parsimony requisite for accumulation. In that situation the expence even of a sovereign cannot be directed by that vanity which delights in the gaudy finery of a court. The ignorance of the times affords but few of the trinkets in which that finery consists.
>
> (WN V.iii.2, 908)

The wealth that accompanies commerce allows vanity to bring extravagances so that

> In a commercial country abounding with every sort of expensive luxury, the sovereign, in the same manner as almost all the great proprietors in his dominions, naturally spends a great part of his revenue in purchasing those luxuries. His own and the neighbouring countries supply him abundantly with all the costly trinkets which compose the splendid, but insignificant pageantry of a court.
>
> (WN V.iii.3, 909)

If Smith's account of the origins of paper money could be given in a nutshell, with all the limitations of such brevity, it would go more or less as follows: vanity generates paper money thanks to the development of commerce. The more *commercial* a society is, the more vanity is freed from constraints, the more money is spent on unproductive trinkets, the less cash is left, the more credit and paper is needed. Smith is indeed exploring the potential of (building?) a tight commercial society. To Smith benevolence and love of power are not commercial motivations, but vanity is. Benevolence and love of power do not enter in Smith's commercial picture and as a consequence neither do the sub-systems built on them. On the other hand, for Smith vanity is a driving force of commerce and the sub-systems that he describes are based on it.

Cost–benefit analysis

A commercial society may be a feasible society for Smith, as it possesses not only the seeds for development and prosperity (vanity), but also the mechanisms to persist (mostly[13] free markets). A commercial society generates wealth, in part, through the natural introduction of credit. But, as we saw, paper money may threaten a commercial society because of its intrinsic instability associated with over-issuing. But this instability may not be irremovable, as its cause may eventually be removed. And the processes through which instabilities are removed seem to be built into paper money itself.

Smith implies that neither merchants nor banks should over-issue as it may bring all into bankruptcy. But Smith's recriminations do not prevent banks from over-issuing (WN II.ii.41–87, 297–320). The reason for over-issuing is, for Smith, ignorance – banks do not always understand what is best for them (WN II.ii.53, 302). Indeed, he reiterates more than once, 'every particular banking company has not always understood or attended to its own particular interest, and the circulation has frequently been over-stocked with paper-money' (WN II.2.56, 303).

The ignorance of banks shows in different ways. First, banks fail to understand that paper should be issued only to replace idle reserve money, not to fund entire projects (WN II.ii.71, 311). Projectors fool banks when traders draw and redraw upon one another. If they do it from the same bank, the bank will realize what is going on. But traders use different banks, and may add more projectors in the circle. Distinguishing between a real bill of exchange and a fraudulent one becomes more difficult. And when a banker realizes he is discounting fake bills, it is too late (WN II.ii.72, 311–12). Finally, banks also tend to overestimate the inflow of money and underestimate their outflow (WN II.ii.76, 315–16).

Fortunately, 'nature' takes care of it, as competitive markets are generally good schools.[14] If a bank that had over-issued tried to fulfill its promises to convert paper into metal upon demand, it would face an outflow of precious metal larger than its inflow. The acquisition of precious metals to fulfill its demand might quickly become very expensive. It is therefore in the bank's interest not to over-issue, because what it would gain, if not more, it would have to spend to keep its coffers ready. And the bank, losing profits, would decrease the amount of issuing (WN II.ii.49–51, 301–2).

Moreover, competition among banks brings an additional check on issuing too much paper. And if something goes wrong, the damage is more limited. (For a general account of decentralized systems in Smith, see Paganelli 2005.)

> The late multiplication of banking companies in both parts of the United Kingdom, an event by which many people have been much alarmed, instead of diminishing, increases the security of the publick. It obliges all of them to be more circumspect in their conduct, and, by not extending their currency beyond its due proportion to their cash, to guard themselves against those malicious runs, which the rivalship

> of so many competitors is always ready to bring upon them. It restrains the circulation of each particular company within a narrower circle, and reduces their circulating notes to a smaller number. By dividing the whole circulation into a greater number of parts, the failure of any one company, an accident which, in the course of things, must sometimes happen, becomes of less consequence to the publick.
>
> (WN II.ii.106, 329)

Ignorance is therefore a curable disease for Smith. Once banks understand what they have 'not always understood' banks will not over-issue. And because every man is driven by his desire to better his condition, there is no reason to believe that banks will forever 'not attend to [their] own particular interest'. To a potential destructive force there is therefore a market antidote. The instability seen in the past does not have to persist in the future.[15]

Similarly, the problems associated with public credit are not really problems. First, longer wars due to their decreased immediate cost may not always be a cost to all, as some people may enjoy the longer length (WN V.iii.37, 919). To Smith the real problem seems to be over-expenditure by the government, rather than the credit issued to pay for it. The problem seems to be war,[16] not paper money. WN concludes by recommending to Great Britain a 'diminution of her expenditure ... [as] it is surely time that Great Britain should free herself from the expence of defending those provinces in times of war, and of supporting any part of their civil or military establishments in time of peace' (WN V.iii.92, 946).

The fact that public credit is not a problem for Smith is confirmed by the explicit reference that in a commercial society debts are usually mitigated by the prosperity commerce generates. So Smith reassures:

> The same commercial state of society which, by the operation of moral causes, brings government in this manner into the necessity of borrowing, produces in the subjects both an ability and an inclination to lend. If it commonly brings along the necessity of borrowing, it likewise brings along with it the facility of doing so.
>
> (WN V.iii.5, 910)[17]

An additional constraint on possible abuses of paper money, which is actually an additional benefit of the introduction of paper money, is the development of an ethical system and of a system of justice, or at least of a system that uses credit as a signal of virtue. Smith echoes Wallace, among others, when he realized that 'None will give credit but to men of integrity, prudence, and activity, or to men of substance. Here then are natural checks and limits, beyond which credit will not be extended' (Wallace [1734] 1969, 28). Chiara Baroni (2002) superbly presents how

Smith sees credit as an instrument to develop a 'man of credit', a virtuous man to whom it is worth lending. And, similarly, at the government level, as Wallace claims, 'WHEN a free government is able to contract great debts by borrowing from its subjects, this is a certain sign, that it has gained the confidence of the people' (Wallace [1734] 1969, 53), so Smith states that a government that is able to have credit is a just government – a government that is trusted with the use of private property:

> Commerce and manufactures, in short, can seldom flourish in any state in which there is not a certain degree of confidence in the justice of government. The same confidence which disposes great merchants and manufactures, upon ordinary occasions, to trust their property to the protection of a particular government; disposes them, upon extraordinary occasions, to trust that government with the use of their property ... The security which it grants to the original creditor, is made transferable to any other creditor, and, from the universal confidence in the justice of the state, generally sells in the market for more than was originally paid for it.
>
> (WN V.iii.7, 910; see also Rosenberg 1990)

The commercial society that Smith analyzes (or proposes?) is therefore a sound society. It requires vanity to generate it and markets to sustain it. Paper money is an example of one of the sub-systems that contribute to its subsistence and development (cf. Skaggs 1999). Vanity is at the base of a commercial society that generates, among other things, paper money. The limitations that paper money generate may be corrected by commerce itself. Not much more is needed.

Conclusion

During the eighteenth century the introduction of paper money in the form of paper credit begins to flourish. Its functioning is described by many, including Smith. Its potential as a policy instrument is a topic of debate for many, but not for Smith.

The expansionary monetary policies associated with the positive effects of paper money are usually rooted in benevolent motivations. The fears of monetary expansion associated with paper money are usually rooted in the fear of the love of power. Smith is aware of the claims that paper money may be the instrument that solves a country's economic problems, as benevolent leaders will use it wisely. Indeed, he is aware of the attempts to use paper money to solve a country's problems such as the scheme developed by John Law. He is also aware of the claims that paper money may be the instrument of a country's destruction, as knavish leaders will use it to increase their power. Indeed, he is aware that the then high prices may be the first symptom of the pending destruction, as argued by

David Hume. But Smith simply and quickly dismisses Law's scheme as 'extravagant' and Hume's high prices as due to 'bad weather' rather than a sign of the pending catastrophe caused by paper money. Using money as a policy instrument does not seem to be part of Smith's view of the world.

This chapter claims that what looks like Smith's lack of vision for using paper money as a policy instrument to stimulate the economy is due to his focus on understanding a purely commercial society. In a commercial society like the one Smith describes, not only is there little need for government, but there is also little need for love of power and for benevolence. Smith seems to imply that a world in which power is the predominant motivation of human action is a world of force; on the other hand, considering benevolence as the predominant motivation would describe a world of angels. A commercial world, however, has a different motivational force at its base. For Smith, this motivational force is vanity. The absence of the accounts of positive and negative potential of manipulating paper money in Smith's works may imply that only human vanity is (or should be?) necessary to have a functioning, prosperous, and moral society based on commerce.

Notes

Thanks to Tyler Cowen, Dan Houser, David Levy, Leonidas Montes, James Otteson, Eric Schliesser, Todd Seavey, the participants of the 2005 HES meeting, and an anonymous referee.

1 See for example Hume (*Essays*, 355) 'Public stocks, being a kind of paper-credit, have all the disadvantages attending that species of money. They banish gold and silver from the most considerable commerce of the state, reduce them to common circulation, and by that means render all provisions and labour dearer than otherwise they would be.'

2 The possible reasons for this development in the role of the State are outside the scope of this chapter; its presence is simply accepted.

3 'Such members of the society as remain unemployed, either from natural infirmities or misfortunes, and who thereby become a load upon others, are really a load upon the state. This is a disease which must be endured. There is no body, no thing, without diseases. A state should provide retreats of all sorts, for the different conditions of her decayed inhabitants: humanity, good, policy, and christianity, require it' (Steuart [1767] 1966: 73). Or: '59 Whether to provide plentifully for the poor be not feeding the root, the substance whereof will shoot upwards into the branches, and cause the top to flourish?' Berkeley [1735] 1979: Query 59; '158 When the root yieldeth insufficient nourishment, whether men do not top the tree to make the lower branches thrive?' (ibid.: Query 158).

4 'Bankruptcy is, without any question, superior to new excises. It is easier and more expedient. . . . But bankruptcy is too sudden and strikes too impetuously. Worse still, it strikes the people around the prince, the most powerful people, from whom tumult and rebellion are to be feared; it slashes his faith with hideous scars, thus weakening it. Augmentation of the currency had the same effect as bankruptcy, but the harm from it is slower to come and is distributed over everyone as it fails' (Galiani [1751] 1977, 188).

5 '...augmentation of the currency arises from the fact that it has rarely been undertaken in order to satisfy the true needs of a virtuous prince. It has almost always been due to greed or to false counsel of only apparent utility' (Galiani [1751] 1977, 168).

6 See for example Bishop Berkeley ([1735] 1979), who, while disliking gold and silver money (Queries 42–3, 283–7), promotes paper money as an instrument to achieve public happiness (Query 224, 288–9).

7 See, among the examples, the requests to print more money during the French Revolution (Albertone 1992).

8 The tradition to see commercial and monetary activities somehow magical is long. See, for example, Jonson (1987).

9 There is a reference, again quickly dismissive, to Sir Robert Walpole's policy proposal in the student notes to Smith's Lectures on Jurisprudence where Smith claims that 'Sir Robert Walpole endeavoured to shew that the public debt was no inconvenience, tho' it is to be supposed that a man of his abilities saw the contrary himself' (LJ, 515).

10 A 'dictator' is a single decision maker, a person (legal or real) with sovereign decision power. An assembly as well as a monarch may be 'dictator'. Usually, a 'dictator' contrasts a decisional structure based on a plurality of centers. 'Benevolent' means that the 'dictator' is public-spirited, not self-interested. A 'benevolent dictator' will always do only what is best for society, and not what is best for himself.

11 The desire of praiseworthiness is the desire to gain the approbation of the impartial spectator by emulation, once our man within has become impartial. 'Emulation, the anxious desire that we ourselves should excel, is originally founded in our admiration of the excellence of others. Neither can we be satisfied by being merely admired for what other people are admired. We must at least believe ourselves to be admirable for what they are admirable. But in order to attain this satisfaction, we must become the impartial spectators of our own character and conduct. We must endeavour to view them with the eyes of other people, or as other people are likely to view them. When seen in this light, if they appear to us as we wish, we are happy and contented. But it greatly confirms this happiness and contentment when we find that other people, viewing them with those very eyes with which we, in imagination only, were endeavouring to view them, see them precisely in the same light in which we ourselves had seen them. Their approbation necessarily confirms our own self-approbation' (TMS III.2.3, 114).

12 Smith's use of vanity in TMS is not always clear-cut. He usually uses the idea of vanity simply as the desire to attract someone else's attention toward oneself, and to receive approbation. The other, whose attention and approbation one wants, is both the man without as well as the man within. Later in TMS, in particular when he describes different systems of moral philosophy, Smith uses the idea of vanity differently. Smith criticizes Mandeville because he is unable to distinguish between one's desire to be the object of approbation of a real spectator and of the impartial spectator. Here Smith defines vanity as the desire to be approved of even if undeservedly. The vanity to which I am referring in this chapter is the former and not the latter.

13 Smith's reliance on markets is not complete. He is well aware of possible market failure, and he is willing to have government intervene in such situations. See Viner (1991) and Stigler (1971). See also Paganelli (2003), Arnon (1999), Carlson (1999), and West (1997).

14 For an account of the history of free banking in England see White (1995). For a modern version of it see Cowen and Kroszner (1994).

15 Cf. Hume (*Essays*, 363): 'So great dupes are the generality of mankind, that,

notwithstanding such a violent shock to public credit, as a voluntary bankruptcy in ENGLAND would occasion, it would not be long ere credit would again revive in as flourishing a condition as before.... And though men are commonly more governed by what they have seen, than by what they foresee, with whatever certainty; yet promises, protestations, fair appearances, with the allurement of present interest, have such powerful influence as few are able to resist. Mankind are, in all ages, caught by the same baits: the same tricks, played over and over again, still trepan them.'

16 For an excellent account of Smith's aversion for war see Fleischacker (2004). On the role of a standing army in Smith see Montes (2004).

17 'It is much better to keep far on the safe side, and never to stretch the public credit. But, certainly, the limits for such a rich commercial nation as Britain, extended farther than many have imagined' Wallace ([1734] 1969), 50–1.

References

Albertone, Manuela (1992) *Moneta e politica in Francia: dalla Cassa di Sconto agli Assegnati (1776–92)*, Bologna: Il Mulino.

Arnon, Arie (1999) 'Free and Not So Free Banking Theories among the Classical; or, Classical Forerunners of Free Banking and why they have been Neglected', *History of Political Economy* 31 (1): 79–107.

Baroni, Chiara (2002) 'The Man of Credit: an Aristocratic Ethics for the Middle Class?' Manuscript.

Berkeley, George, Bishop of Cloyne ([1735] 1979) 'The Querist', *The Works of George Berkeley, Bishop of Cloyne*, ed. A. A. Luce, London: Nelson.

Carlson, Mathieu (1999) 'Adam Smith's Support for Money and Banking Regulation: a case of inconsistency?' *History of Economic Review* 29: 1–15.

Cowen, Tyler and Kroszner, Randall (1994) *Explorations in the New Monetary Economics*, Oxford and Cambridge, MA: Blackwell.

De Pinto, Isaac ([1774] 1969) *An Essay on Circulation and Credit, in Four Parts, and a Letter on the Jealousy of Commerce; from the French of Monsieur De Pinto; translated, with Annotations, by S. Baggs*, Farnborough: Gregg.

Farrant, Andrew and Paganelli, Maria Pia (2006) 'Are Two Knaves Better Than One? Every Man a Knave: Hume, Buchanan, and Musgrave on Economics and Government', *History of Political Economy, Supplement.* (Forthcoming).

Fleischacker, Samuel (2004) *On Adam Smith's Wealth of Nations: A Philosophical Companion*, Princeton, NJ: Princeton University Press.

Friedman, Milton (1969) *The Optimum Quantity Theory of Money and Other Essays*, Chicago: Aldine.

Galiani, Ferdinando ([1751] 1977) *On Money: a Translation of* Della moneta, Ann Arbor, MI: published for the Department of Economics, University of Michigan.

Gherity, James (1994) 'The Evolution of Adam Smith's Theory of Banking', *History of Political Economy* 26 (3): 423–41.

Humphrey, Thomas M. (1993) 'Nonneutrality of Money in Classical Economic Thought', in *Money, Banking, and Inflation: Essays in the History of Monetary Thought*, Aldershot: Ashgate and Brookfield, VT: Elgar.

—— (2004) 'Classical Deflation Theory', *Economic Quarterly* 90 (1): 11–32.

Jonson, Ben (1987) *The Alchemist*, London and New York: Methuen.

Keynes, John Maynard ([1936] 1997) *The General Theory of Employment, Interest and Money*, New York: Prometheus Books.

Lerner, Ralph (1999) 'Love of Fame and the Constitution of Liberty', in Thomas Angerer, Birgitta Bader-Zaar and Margarete Grandner (eds) *Geschichte und Recht. Festschrift für Gerald Stourzh zum 70. Geburtstag*, Vienna: Böhlau.

Levy, David (1986) 'The Paradox of the Sinking Fund', in James Buchanan, Charles Rowley and Robert Tollison (eds) *Deficits*, Oxford: Blackwell.

Monroe Arthur Eli (1966) *Monetary Theory before Adam Smith*, New York: Kelley.

Montes, Leonidas (2004) *Adam Smith in Context: a Critical Reassessment of some Central Components of his Thought.* New York: Palgrave Macmillan.

Montesquieu Charles de Secondat, Baron de ([1748] 1989) *The Spirit of the Laws.* Cambridge: Cambridge University Press.

Otteson, James (2002) *Adam Smith's Marketplace of Life*, Cambridge: Cambridge University Press.

Paganelli, Maria Pia (2003) '*In Medio Stat Vintus*: an Alternative View of Usuary in Adam Smith's Thinking', *History of Political Economy* 35 (1): 21–48.

—— (2005) 'Adam Smith: Why Decentralized Systems?' *Adam Smith Review* (forthcoming).

Pocock, J. G. A. (1985) *Virtue, Commerce, and History: Essays on Political Thought and History Chiefly in the Eighteenth Century*, Cambridge: Cambridge University Press.

Pribram Karl (1983) *A History of Economic Reasoning*, Baltimore, MD: Johns Hopkins University Press.

Rosenberg, Nathan (1990) 'Adam Smith and the Stock of Moral Capital', *History of Political Economy* 22 (1): 1–17.

Schliesser, Eric (2003) 'The Obituary of the Vain Philosopher: Adam Smith's Reflections on Hume's Life', *Hume Studies* 29 (2): 327–62.

Skaggs, Neil T. (1999) 'Adam Smith on Growth and Credit: Too Weak a Connection?' *Journal of Economic Studies* 26 (6): 481–96.

Smithin, John (2003) *Controversies in Monetary Economics: Revised Edition*, Cheltenham and Northampton, MA: Elgar.

Steuart, Sir James ([1767] 1966) *An Inquiry into the Principles of Political Economy*, Edinburgh and London: Oliver & Boyd.

Stigler, George (1971) 'Smith's Travels on the Ship of State', *History of Political Economy* 3 (2): 265–77.

Vanderlint, Jacob ([1734] 1970) *Money Answers all Things; or, An Essay to make Money sufficiently Plentiful*, Wakefield: SR Publishers and New York: Johnson Reprint.

Vickers, Douglas (1959) *Studies in the Theory of Money, 1690–1776*, New York: Chilton.

Viner, Jacob (1930) 'English Theories of Foreign Trade before Adam Smith', *Journal of Political Economy* 38 (3): 249–301 and 38 (4): 404–57.

—— (1991) *Essays on the Intellectual History of Economics*, Princeton, NJ: Princeton University Press.

Wallace, Robert ([1734] 1969) *Characteristics of the Present Political State of Great Britain*, New York: Kelley.

West, Edwin (1997) 'Adam Smith's support for Money and Banking Regulation: a Case of Inconsistency', *Journal of Money, Credit, and Banking* 29 (1): 127–34.

White, Lawrence (1995) *Free Banking in Britain: Theory, Experience, and Debate, 1800–1845*, London: IEA.

Part IV

Adam Smith and knowledge

13 Adam Smith on progress and knowledge

Craig Smith

Two of the most famous, and critically discussed, aspects of Adam Smith's thought are his 'four stages' theory of social change and his analysis of the role of the division of labor. Over the years much has been written about both of these passages in Smith's work and how they come together in his analysis of the development of commercial society. The purpose of the present chapter is, to a certain extent, to 'rake over old coals' in order to examine the often overlooked role played in these discussions by the concepts of the spontaneous generation of social order, interdependence and, most significantly, the growth of human knowledge. The aim is to demonstrate that Smith's theory of social change is best understood as a process of the development and effective utilization of human skills and knowledge. In other words: new light can be shed on these central aspects of Smith's work by examining the role of knowledge in his analysis.

In what follows, the passages from Smith's work that are examined will be readily familiar to the reader (hence the raking over old coals comment). However, this focus on celebrated passages is entirely deliberate. The purpose of the present chapter is to present an interpretation, which demonstrates that Smith possessed a clear appreciation of the role of knowledge in economic and social phenomena.[1] To this end the chapter will begin by examining Smith's views on the human desire to calm the mind through the acquisition of ordered knowledge as he lays it down in the *History of Astronomy*. It will then follow this by looking at the 'four stages' theory and Smith's analysis of the division of labor in the light of his attitude to the development of human knowledge. The central argument will be that in addition to the noted natural drive to pursue subsistence and the 'propensity' to trade, Smith's analysis of the stages and the division is also shaped by a concern for the role played by the growth and exploitation of human knowledge.

Astronomy

The most obvious indication that Smith was interested in the nature and form of human knowledge is to be found in his writings on the nature and practice of science. In his *History of Astronomy* Smith presents a model of science based on the human propensity to seek after systematized knowledge. For Smith the purpose of science is explanation and the extension of knowledge, but this is not simply for the Baconian utilitarian reason that the knowledge of causes is power. Rather he explains the desire to practice science in terms of the sentiments. Occurrences that disturb the course of our habitual expectations elicit in us a sense of 'surprise' at their having taken place (Astronomy, II.6, 40). This initial surprise gives way to a sense of 'wonder' when we realize that we have nothing in our previous experience that can account for the event (Astronomy, II.12, 46). Wonder is an emotion that strikes up a feeling of 'unease' within us (Astronomy I.7, 36), and the 'imagination feels a real difficulty in passing along two events which follow one another in an uncommon order' (Astronomy, II.10, 43). Wondrous events have this effect upon us, Smith believes, because of the manner in which we form our expectations. Our feelings towards events are shaped by our habitual acceptance of them and our expectation that they will continue to occur in the manner suggested to us by our previous experience. We develop habituated thought patterns or 'passages of thought' which 'by custom become quite smooth and easy' (Astronomy, II.11, 45) and we are shaken from this manner of approaching the world only by events which fail to fit into our established patterns of thought. It is in the reaction to such surprising and wondrous events that we are to find the original impetus to science. This 'psychological need' (Skinner 1974: 169) for the explanation of wondrous events leads us to seek understanding in terms of cause and effect.[2] The desire for explanation is a product of a 'natural disposition to classify', or a 'propensity to categorize or classify' (Becker 1961: 15–16) which is, for Smith, a facet of human nature and one which leads him to regard the human mind as a 'classificatory system' (Brown 1988: 46).

The impulse to explain, to calm the mind through understanding and ordering our thoughts is, for Smith, a manifestation of the fact that 'we are by nature classificatory animals' (Broadie 2001: 195), and it is this which underlines the gradual extension of the corpus of human knowledge. Scientific inquiry does not rest simply with the dispelling of the initial sense of wonder. Once we have explained some part of the causal relationship our interest is piqued and we begin to inquire after other related relationships. As Smith puts it:

> But when law has established order and security, and subsistence ceases to be precarious, the curiosity of mankind is increased, and their fears are diminished. The leisure which they then enjoy renders them the more attentive to the appearances of nature, more observant of her smallest irregularities, and more desirous to know what is the chain which links them all together.
>
> (Astronomy, III.3, 50)

Human curiosity has its origins in a desire to stabilize our expectations and to provide structure to our experience of the world. Our exploitation of the content of that knowledge follows on from the certainty that this structure provides. Thus we begin to form a system of knowledge based on the discrete classification of our experience (Astronomy, II.2, 38). In other words we seek to order the world that we might better understand it, and thus calm our minds. We do not seek understanding simply in order that we might use it to our advantage: on the contrary we have an emotional need for understanding in order that our minds are able to function smoothly. If this is how the human mind operates then the desire to reduce uncertainty and to acquire knowledge becomes a key feature of human behavior. When combined with another key motivation of human behavior, the search for subsistence, we can begin to develop a fresh appreciation of Smith's economic ideas.

The four stages

The theorists of the Scottish Enlightenment base their analysis of social change on the premise that human beings form conventional modes of behavior in reaction to their circumstances. Perhaps naturally the chief focus of human attention is the provision of subsistence. Humans require sustenance and shelter to survive, and as a result these matters become the focus of a great deal of their actions. Food is a product of 'human industry' (WN I.xi.e.28, 206), that is to say, individuals must act in some way to secure it for their consumption. Thus in all societies the provision of subsistence is the 'prior' industry (WN III.i.2, 377), for without it the survival of the species is impossible and thus other activities are equally impossible. In undeveloped, or savage, nations the individuals' first concern is survival. As a result their first efforts are to secure subsistence. The difficulty of securing subsistence leads humanity to focus its attention almost solely upon it. The conventions and forms of human behavior are shaped in great measure by the various devices that they develop to provide for their subsistence. The underlying universality of the human need for subsistence, combined with the similarity of our physical frames, nature and intellect, means that the development of different modes of subsistence is a process that occurs in a similar manner in all human societies. As Smith's student John Millar put it: 'the similarity of his wants, as well as of the faculties by which those wants are supplied, has everywhere produced a remarkable uniformity in the several steps of his progression' (Millar 1990: 3). From this insight, supported and confirmed by the evidence of conjectural history, the Scots develop their stadial theories of social change.

The most clearly defined stadial analysis is that developed by Smith, and mirrored by Millar, which has become known as the 'four stages' theory.[3] Smith divides types of society into four categories based on their reactions to the issue of subsistence. The means of subsistence, he argues, as the primary concern of human activity, necessarily shapes other social institutions that develop in each of these types of society. Smith's four stages – '1st, the Age of Hunters; 2ndly, the Age of Shepherds; 3rdly, the Age of Agriculture; and 4thly, the Age of Commerce' (LJ 14) – are laid down as a general schema of social development which is conceptually applicable to all societies.[4] Thus each stage produces conventional behaviors that are appropriate for the physical conditions and level of security of subsistence which pertain in them.

In each stage a different method for securing subsistence dominates: hunting, herding, agriculture and commercial industry. But each stage also absorbs the stage before: hunting and herding do not cease because agriculture arises, but they cease to be the sole or chief means of securing subsistence. For this reason Smith argues that in a commercial society hunting and fishing persist, but as non-essential activities undertaken for 'pleasure' rather than through 'necessity' (WN I.x.a.3, 117–18). Moreover the 'desire of bettering our condition' (WN II.iii.28, 341) that lies at the heart of Smith's analysis of commercial society in the *Wealth of Nations* appears to grow out of this original impetus to provide for a stable and comfortable existence. Once basic subsistence is secure, human attention moves to ways in which we can improve our situation. By examining the evidence of conjectural history Smith determined that all societies, if left alone to develop, proceeded roughly according to this pattern of change in the mode of subsistence.[5] Change between each of the stages is posited on the discovery of new skills, which prove more productive in securing subsistence than those developed in the past. The 'four stages' theory is as much a theory about the growth of human knowledge as it is about the changing modes of subsistence.

Smith argues that animals multiply in direct proportion to the 'means of their subsistence' (WN I.viii.39, 97): as a result there exists a constant demand for food owing to universal, natural, drives for procreation and survival. As subsistence becomes more secure in each stage the population grows, as larger families may be supported (WN I.viii.40, 98; LJ 14–15). However, population growth itself cannot be the reason behind a change in the stage of the mode of subsistence.[6] It certainly may act as a prompt to that change, but the means depend on the acquisition of the skills and knowledge requisite to pursue the new mode. Thus the change from hunter to shepherd is brought about by the gradual development of the skills necessary for animal husbandry. That is to say that the desire to supply more steadily the means of subsistence for a growing population led to experiments in food production which led in turn to the discovery and refinement of new methods. It is important to stress here that both the desire to provide for subsistence and the incentive provided by population are understood on an individualistic level. It was individuals, whose goal was to secure subsistence for their own families, who carried out experimentation in food production. This means that changes in social structure are the result of adjustments by individuals to their own particular circumstances. If we are to reconstruct the story of the links between the 'four stages' in terms of the rise of knowledge of means of subsistence it would be something like this: hunters are brought into repeated contact with animals and gradually acquire the skills which form the basis of shepherdry; shepherds are brought into contact with the means of subsistence of animals and gradually acquire knowledge of the crops required; their attention is then led to a possible new source of human subsistence and, as they settle geographically, they develop agricultural skills. Once humans have developed settled accommodation the division of labor increases and commercial industry begins to develop.[7]

Smith returns to the central role played by skills and knowledge when he compares colonists with savages: 'The colonists carry out with them a knowledge of agriculture and of other useful arts, superior to what can grow up of its own accord in the course of many centuries among savage and barbarous nations' (WN IV.vii.b.2, 564–5). Thus we see that the key factor here is the possession of knowledge. Colonists draw on the cumulative sum of the experiential knowledge of their mother country to provide for their subsistence. Savages on the other hand have yet to pass through the 'four stages' and acquire the gradual development of knowledge relating to subsistence that it entails.

Government and property

This analysis of social change and of the effect of the mode of subsistence on the nature of society and population is the backdrop to Smith's discussion of the interactive development of property, justice and government in the *Lectures on Jurisprudence.* In terms of the 'four stages' theory it is clear that no abstract conception of property exists in the savage or hunter society. The immediacy of life in such conditions precludes much abstract thought and the mode of subsistence is based around securing from what is wild for immediate needs. As a result of this there is little or no government in hunting societies. As Smith puts it 'Till there be property there can be no government' (LJ 404).

However, government and property do arise, and they do so in the second of Smith's stages, that of shepherds. It is in the age of shepherds that notions of property, subordination and government arise and the development of social institutions starts apace. Experience teaches men to refine the skills necessary for animal husbandry as they learn the benefit in this domestication of animals, as opposed to constant hunting. But shepherdry is discovered and perfected by some before others. These people control increasing numbers of animals, rendering hunting increasingly 'uncertain and precarious' for others (LJ 202). However, this situation was as yet insecure. The shepherd might domesticate and tend his flock, but his claim to them as a result of this could quite easily pass unnoticed by others keen to secure subsistence (LJ 404). Some institution to enforce claims of right was required by shepherds. The origin of that institution was also to be found in this inequality of fortune, for those who could not practice shepherdry and yet saw the stock of wild animals fall would become dependent on those who had mastered the skill. Those that controlled herds and flocks came to occupy superior positions as an unintended consequence of their possession of the knowledge of shepherdry – knowledge which gave them easier access to subsistence through the control of large numbers of animals. However, the control of large numbers of animals is in itself useless because of the physical limits as to how much each individual can consume. As a result the successful shepherd provides for others who have yet to acquire the skill and, consequently, comes to a position of eminence over them and introduces subordination into society for the first time. Dependants develop a habit of obedience and accept their position as clients in order to secure easy access to the means of subsistence. They come, as a result of this process of habit, to accept the validity of the shepherd's claim to his flocks, forming an opinion of his 'right' (LJ 405) to the control of them. They also begin to develop an emotional loyalty to their particular benefactor and his 'heirs' (WN V.i.b.12, 715) that is the foundation of a notion of a nation, or the explicit identification with institutions which express the unity of the community. The first institutions of government arise with the explicit purpose of defending property and are supported by the dependence-led obedience of people to those who have acquired flocks and herds. Thus government and property rights develop as an unintended consequence of the acquisition of the knowledge of shepherdry.

In the age of shepherds the conception of property refers to herds and flocks and the wandering nature of such peoples precludes any definite notion of property in land. But in the age of agriculture property in land develops in reaction to the fixed 'habitations' (LJ 20) of agricultural laborers. For Smith the key step in the development of 'private property in land' (LJ 460) is the development of fixed habitations in cities and towns. In a hunter society social groups are relatively small, each competing for the scarce resources of the hunt. Shepherd societies admit of larger numbers by the greater ease of subsistence, but these numbers do not originally settle in a specific location to practice their arts (LJ 408). They are, however, open to attack by other groups and so, for reasons of mutual defense, erect 'fortified towns' (LJ 409) to which they may take their flocks to avoid attack. The concentration of population in these locales leads to a development of the arts – in particular, agricultural skills – and towns and cities come to develop.

The fact, arising from the conditions which form the conventions of justice and property, that society requires some support for the non-physical claim which is the convention of property implies that the 'first law' (LJ 208, 313) is law determining and governing property. This law exists as convention and custom, and the need to delimit property in an accurate manner, in order to avoid conflicts that would destroy society, leads to the institution of government. Therefore the institution of government arises from the recognition of a common court of appeal for the settlement of property disputes.[8] The conventions of property ownership that arise in a society thus begin to be codified, to become laws, when they are drawn up and made explicit by those appealed to as judges in disputes. This process, the desire for general rules and stability of possession, though it is prompted by a sense of interest arising from a view to utility, is not carried on in any explicit and intended manner. Those who appeal to a judge to decide disagreements over the conventional rules of property do not intend to create the institution of government.[9]

Government develops more 'slowly' (WN IV.vii.b.2, 565) than the arts of subsistence, its attentions being called upon only when disputes arise. In the meantime the advance of knowledge of the arts of subsistence grows. Smith is particularly clear that the chief scene of the advance of knowledge of both government and the arts is in the burgeoning cities where interaction and trade develop productive techniques and institutions (WN III.iii.12, 405). People living in close proximity have more scope for conflict as well as for trade. Thus government develops to more advanced levels in urban areas. However, cities require to trade their produce for that of the country in order to acquire some of the means of subsistence; for this reason Smith spends some time analyzing the relationship between town and country. Local farmers can come to town to trade on market day, but as trade between communities advances immediate exchange becomes unwieldy and the notions of contract and money arise (LJ 91). The desire for certainty in the enforcement of contracts within a given area then becomes the rationale behind the extension of the judicial power of governments. Moreover the need for stability and peace to allow the advance of learning in the commercial arts means that commerce gradually introduces 'order and good government' (WN III.iv.4, 412), reducing the scope for arbitrary uses of authority. Justice springs from a desire for systematized knowledge, a desire to reduce uncertainty. So law, like science, fulfills this function of calming the mind, of leading our habitual thought processes in an ordered manner in line with our expectations. Government and law have 'improved' (LJ 14), just as knowledge of the means of subsistence has, and the stability of expectations provided by law forms a considerable part of this notion of improvement.

The stadial theory is based on the universality of the need for subsistence. As a result Smith is able to trace 'improvement' (WN I.i.1, 13), in its origin, to this concern. The desire to secure subsistence, to cater for the 'three great wants of mankind . . . food, cloaths, and lodging' (LJ 340) is the root of 'the far greater part' (LJ 337) of human art and science. Such a universal concern forms a great part of the concern of each member of a social group: the desire for survival and sustenance being a core aspect of every individual's interest. The concern for subsistence consumes human attention when it is hard to come by. But when subsistence is safely secured mankind's attention is turned to other areas and industries, to other ways of bettering their condition. It appears that progress in 'Opulence and Commerce' is a necessary 'requisite' for intellectual and artistic progress (LRBL, Lecture 23, II.1.115, 137): that some measure of security and ease is required before individuals are able to develop their understanding of the arts. As security and law develop from barbarity, through habitually accepted conventions, and government becomes accepted, so learning and the acquisition of knowledge advance.

Moreover Smith is aware that knowledge can exist in forms that are not immediately explicit. Habit and custom for Smith were forms of experience-based knowledge: knowledge which is non-verbalized yet vital to the success of our actions. As Smith notes: 'And from all those volumes we shall in vain attempt to collect that knowledge of its [agriculture's] various and complicated operations, which is commonly possessed even by the common farmer' (WN I.x.c.23, 143). The basis of such knowledge is indeed experience, but it is individual experience. So when Smith argued that the growth of experience is necessary for 'improvement' he was aware that such experience is experienced by individuals: that though social change is brought about by the growth of cumulative experience, the medium of that progress is the experience of specific individuals.[10]

It was noted above that Smith viewed population size as an indication of progress and also that he considered it to be the driving force behind the advance in modes of subsistence. However, we have also seen that population pressure is not the means for that advance; rather the means lies in the acquisition of new knowledge to support that population. The progress of knowledge on a social or cumulative level is based on the development of experience, thus each stage is based on that before it. Cumulative knowledge is a 'chain' of development that draws upon and refines historical precedent. Social progress, the cumulative sum of human knowledge, requires that knowledge, once gleaned from experience, is preserved and transferred rather than being lost at the death of the individual who held it. This is why the species of man has a progress (through history) greater than that achieved by any specific individual. The whole of Smith's 'four stages' schema is posited on the notion of such an evolutionary, gradualist approach to social change. Smith illustrates the gradual nature of social change by noting that such change is often 'insensible' (WN II.iii.32, 343–4). That is to say that it occurs so slowly that we do not notice it until it has happened. The 'four stages' schema stresses the significance of the development of different modes of subsistence to the form that the institutions of a society are likely to take, while at the same time highlighting the role of the growth of knowledge, understood both as reducing uncertainty and acquiring skill, in Smith's conception of social change.

The division of labor

As we have seen, the use and transferral of knowledge as 'reduced uncertainty' and 'skills' is a key element in Smith's understanding of the nature of social change. This is clearly exemplified by his analysis of the concept of the division of labor. As Smith famously begins the *Wealth of Nations*: 'The greatest improvement in the productive powers of labour, and the greater part of the skill, dexterity, and judgement with which it is any where directed, or applied, seem to have been the effects of the division of labour' (WN I.i.1, 13). It is through his analysis of the division of labor that Smith explains the phenomenon which results in a situation where the most ordinary laborer in a commercial society has more material resources, is better provided for, than the monarch of a 'savage' or undeveloped country (WN I.i.11, 24; LJ 340). But more than this, though Smith's famous example of the productive improvements of the division of labor in the manufacturing of pins (WN I.i.3, 14; LJ 343) graphically illustrates the material benefits of the process, he is also keen to stress the social implications of the division and the wealth that it generates. Smith clearly links the development of the division of labor to civilization. Indeed, he goes so far as to state that civilization itself is dependent on the division of labor; he writes: 'In an uncivilized nation, and where labour is undivided' (LJ 489). This juxtaposition of civilization with the division of labor indicates how central the concept is to Smith's theory of society and social change.

If the division of labor is central to civilization, it is also the result of a process of unintended consequences. As Smith would have it: the division of labor 'is not originally the effect of any human wisdom, which foresees and intends that general opulence to which it gives occasion', rather 'it is the necessary, though very slow and gradual, consequences...' (WN I.ii.1, 25) of the interaction of human nature with the circumstances in which it finds itself: in brief it is a manifestation of the growth of experiential knowledge. Again and again Smith stresses that the social change brought about by the division of labor is not the product of purposive or deliberative human action aimed at securing improvement on a societal level. Smith claims that: '[n]o human prudence is requisite to make this division' (LJ 351), and that this 'division of work is not however the effect of any human policy' (LJ 347).

The social change and wealth generated by the division of labor are not the product of deliberative human action aimed at improving society. A commercial society is not foreseen, nor is it planned; rather it arises gradually because of certain 'natural' forces. The complexity to which it gives rise applies not only to technological and material advance, but also to the increased, and increasing, interdependence that results from the division of labor. As Smith notes: 'without the assistance and co-operation of many thousands, the very meanest person in a civilized country could not be provided, even according to, what we very falsely imagine, the easy and simple manner in which he is commonly accommodated' (WN I.i.11, 23). A division of labor is dependent on an inclination and capacity to trade, and it is here that Smith finds the unconscious spring that allows the development of the division and ultimately of civilization itself. Smith notes the significance of the fact that man is the only animal which trades. 'Nobody,' Smith writes, 'ever saw a dog make a fair and deliberate exchange of one bone for another with another dog' (WN I.ii.2, 26).

Trade is a uniquely human activity. This for Smith indicates a 'disposition' (LJ 351; WN I.ii.3, 27) or a 'propensity' in human nature to 'truck, barter, and exchange one thing for another' (WN I.ii.1, 25). The division of labor is dependent on this facet of human nature: individuals seek to exchange what they have for what they want. This division is the result of a 'regard to his own interest' (WN I.ii.3, 27) on the part of individuals, the initial exchanges being based on a desire to satisfy individual wants, and the eventual decision to specialize resulting from the observation – drawn from experience – that these needs are better provided for as a result of concentration on one productive activity which may then be traded. Individuals stand in need of 'the co-operation and assistance of great multitudes' (WN I.ii.2, 26), and humans come to depend on each other to supply their needs through the medium of trade.

A further important factor is that trade is based on the interaction of individuals seeking to fulfill the short-term goals of securing subsistence and bettering their own condition. Thus experience soon teaches them that the quickest and most efficient means of securing the cooperation and trade of others is to appeal to their self-interest. As Smith famously states: 'It is not from the benevolence of the butcher, the brewer, or the baker, that we expect our dinner, but from their regard to their own interest. We address ourselves, not to their humanity but to their self-love, and never talk to them of our own necessities but of their advantage' (WN I.ii.2, 26–7). The maker of arrows appeals to the self-interest of the hunter. The hunters will no longer be required to produce their own arrows if they can exchange their surplus for those produced by another, and that surplus will grow as a result of the time freed up from arrow making which they can then devote to more hunting. The division of labor is based on the recognition that:

> the certainty of being able to exchange all that surplus part of the produce of his own labour, which is over and above his own consumption, for such parts of the produce of other men's labour as he may have occasion for, encourages every man to apply himself to a particu-

> lar occupation, and to cultivate and bring to perfection whatever talent or genius he may possess for that particular species of business. (WN I.ii.3, 28)[11]

As a result the wider the scope for trade, the wider the scope for specialization; the greater the number of potential trading partners and the more certain the laws governing contract, the greater the incentive to specialize. In scattered communities 'every farmer must be butcher, baker and brewer for his own family' (WN I.iii.1–2, 31; LJ 562); interdependence is not possible because of geographic isolation. Specialization is not possible unless a market of sufficient size is available, unless there are enough potential trading partners. The division of labor advances in proportion to the scope for trade: specialization and interdependence lead to increased contact between people, and through trade to a concomitant increase in population centralization.

Distinct industries or employments develop with this specialization, with the original suggestion of career path being an apparent 'natural' talent for a particular form of labor. However, though this forms the basis of the impetus to specialize in a particular task in the early stages of the division, we see that, as specialization advances, the notion of 'natural' talent begins to take a back seat. What instead comes to matter is the specialized knowledge that individuals acquire from devoting their attention to a particular profession. Smith seeks to make it clear that he is not arguing that differing natural attributes and inherited faculties are the basis of specialization and the benefits which arise from it. Rather that skills and attributes are acquired as a result of the division itself. He says 'The difference of natural talents in different men is, in reality, much less than we are aware of; and the very different genius which appears to distinguish men of different professions, when grown up to maturity, is not upon many occasions so much the cause, as the effect of the division of labour' (WN I.ii.4, 28). He follows this by asserting that: 'The difference between the most dissimilar characters, between a philosopher and a common street porter, for example, seems to arise not so much from nature, as from habit, custom and education' (WN I.ii.4, 28–9). The point that Smith is trying to make is not so much that natural abilities are unimportant, but rather that under a system of specialization the differences brought about by application to a particular field of work are a more decisive factor in explaining the broad variety of different individuals and their respective skills and sums of knowledge.

Having discussed the factors which lie behind the separation of arts and professions, and examined how this is related to the notion of trade, Smith then goes on to examine the division of labor as it develops within the various, now delineated, industries and professions. Smith lays down three reasons why the division of labor produces productive benefits when introduced to the internal operation of a particular productive industry. He attributes this:

> first, to the increase of dexterity in every particular workman; secondly, to the saving of time which is commonly lost in passing from one species of work to another; and lastly, to the invention of a great number of machines which facilitate and abridge labour, and enable one man to do the work of many.
>
> (WN I.i.5, 17; LJ 567)

What is immediately striking about these three explanations, given what we have already seen about the role of specialized knowledge in the separation of arts and professions, is that two of them, the first and the third, refer to benefits which are the result of improved skill and knowledge. The second is categorically different, referring instead to the actual nature of the working environment. The second explanation is also the weakest and least productive of the three. While Smith is right to note this difference between simpler models of production where a craftsman works on each stage of production and the more compartmentalized chain of production under the division of labor, the savings of time attained by the prevention of 'sauntering' (WN I.i.7, 19; LJ 491) surely cannot be considered to be of so great an improving force as the increase of dexterity and the invention and use of machines. Indeed, once the division of labor has first been introduced to an industry it is doubtful as to how great a difference the elimination of time wasting in the change between functions will truly be. On the other hand the role of the other two explanations of the productive powers of the division of labor are not so limited and may fairly be said to be of constant relevance as each industry progresses. It is the increased dexterity of workers and the invention of machines which are the truly progressive elements of the division of labor. Further, the first and third explanations are logically linked together in Smith's argument. The initial explanation for the increase in dexterity is the simplification of the task in hand: 'the division of labour, by reducing every man's business to some one simple operation, and by making this operation the sole employment of his life, necessarily increases very much the dexterity of the workman' (WN I.i.6, 18). By confining an individual's attention to a simple field the division of labor focuses attention and creates a specialist whose skill and knowledge of this operation allow them to perfect it to levels beyond the power of a generalist.[12] What emerges from this is the notion of an occupation as a 'study', perhaps the first definition of the idea of human capital. As Smith puts it: 'Those talents, as they make a part of his fortune, so do they likewise of that of the society to which he belongs. The improved dexterity of a workman may be considered in the same light as a machine or instrument of trade which facilitates and abridges labour' (WN II.i.17, 282).

It is not simply the possession of specialized knowledge that counts, but also the manner in which it is exercised: the skill we have in utilizing our knowledge. For specialization to work, what is required is that specialists are proficient in their own field; that they are able to act in a relatively efficient manner on the objects that are the focus of their attention. Indeed, Smith notes that one of the advantages of such specialization is the scope which it allows for the conduct of experimentation by informed practitioners: a process which is vital to the progress both of knowledge and of wealth. As specialization advances, more people become specialists in the same field, resulting in a situation where, according to Smith, '[m]ore heads are occupied in inventing the most proper machinery for executing the work of each, and it is, therefore, more likely to be invented' (WN I.viii.57, 104). Progress generates population. It also means that, subsistence having been secured, there are a larger number of people who are able to apply their attention to the development of the skills of human life. A more extensive market provides greater scope for the advance of cumulative knowledge and, as a result, greater scope for advance in material production.

The productive benefits of specialization are related to experience and to the acquisition of specialized knowledge: what Hollander (1973: 209) calls the technical progress 'induced' by the division of labor. Smith links this specialization to his third explanation. He argues: 'Men are much more likely to discover easier and readier methods of attaining any object, when the whole attention of their minds is directed towards that single object' (WN I.i.8, 20).[13] This argument is further underlined when Smith admits that some great mechanical innovations are not the result of the experience of workers, but rather are the product of 'philosophers or men of speculation' (WN I.i.9, 21) who specialize in making machines: a further example of the benefits of specialization. The restriction of attention to one field of study, or occupation, naturally increases the scope of the observations that may be made in that field by any one individual.

The process of specialization, however, does have limits and equally gives rise to potentially serious problems. Individuals are restricted by the limits of their mental faculties, they are capable of processing only so much knowledge. As a result the concentration of our attention on one field of study, though efficient, naturally restricts our ability to process knowledge from other fields. It is inevitably the case that we cannot fully comprehend the details of the fields of other specialists, as this information lies outside our experience.[14] One danger of this process is that specialists may acquire tunnel vision, focusing their attention on one field and blinding themselves to the significance of other fields of study. This results in a situation where specialists only acquire experience of other fields second-hand, through the teaching of others or observation.[15] As Smith puts it:

> Let any ordinary person make a fair review of all the knowledge which he possesses concerning any subject that does not fall within the limits of his particular occupation, and he will find that almost every thing he knows has been acquired at second hand, from books, from the literary instructions which he may have received in his youth, or from the occasional conversations which he may have had with men of learning.
>
> (LJ 574)

There is, then, a danger that concentration on a specialist area of study leaves us ill equipped for involvement in other specialist areas: or that our proficiency in one field is bought at the expense of our ability to interact in vital social activities.

Knowledge specialists, as we saw in our examination of the division of labor, must interact for their specialized knowledge to be useful (WN I.ii.5, 30). Moreover specialists become dependent on the knowledge and labor of others to an extent that interaction and trade become vital. We become dependent on the skill and knowledge of others and, as individual fields of experience are focused further and further to reap the benefits of close study, so society becomes increasingly complex, experience increasingly diverse, and interdependence gradually greater and greater. Knowledge is indeed increased in its cumulative sum, but it is also diffused among an ever wider field of specialists. This cumulative growth in knowledge shows us that knowledge itself is a chain of development conducted through the medium of specialists. Specialists build on the work of those who have gone before them. The gradual efforts of individual specialists to exert themselves in their own field benefit the whole of society by increasing the stock of cumulative knowledge. What becomes clear is that specialization reinforces the notion that the knowledge of the whole of a society exceeds that of its discrete members. But specialization also encourages the growth of the sum by focusing attention on individualized fields, leading to a development of proficiency in them which benefits all through trade and interdependence. All of this is posited on the interaction of the individuals: interaction and trade are vital if specialized knowledge is to be gathered or utilized to the benefit of all. If cumulative social knowledge is to mean anything, then there must be social interaction through which to make use of it. In a complex commercial society knowledge must be transferred – indeed, as Smith put it, knowledge must be traded or 'brought into a common stock' (WN I.ii.5, 30).

Just as Smith notes the vital role of the desire to trade, arising from the propensity in human nature to truck and barter, in allowing the development of the division of labor, so, it becomes clear, is trade also vital to the development of the specialist knowledge which underlies the process. However, market relationships differ from other forms of human interaction. As Smith noted, to appeal to the self-love of the butcher, brewer and baker is a more efficient means of securing that which we desire. The truth of these statements becomes even more salient as trade develops and specialization increases. We become dependent on the skills of others to supply our wants, while at the same time they become equally dependent upon us. Such interdependence grows up to a great complexity as the division of labor advances. As Smith famously asked us to observe:

> the accommodation of the most common artificer or day-labourer in a civilized and thriving country, and you will perceive that the number of people of whose industry a part, though but a small part, has been employed in procuring him this accommodation, exceeds all computation. The woollen coat, for example, which covers the day-labourer, as coarse and rough as it may appear, is the produce of the joint labour of a great multitude of workmen.
>
> (WN I.i.11, 22)

The example of the laborer's coat indicates the vast web of interdependence which develops as a result of the division of labor; but it also shows how this complexity supplies our needs in an efficient manner, and in a manner that depends on a market exchange which allows us to depend on the skills of people unknown and unrelated to us. This interdependence in commercial society in turn depends on the stability of expectations provided by known and certain forms of trading behavior: in particular, stable property laws and the observance of contracts. The key to the success of the division of labor is the extent of the market: the implication being that as the division of labor improves products and the division of knowledge extends the cumulative sum of human knowledge, so the market of the greatest possible extent is a desirable situation for mankind. If the basis of Smith's argument in favor of a commercial society is that, as a result of the division of labor, it provides the 'greatest improvement in the productive powers of labour' (WN I.i.1, 13), then there is a clear link between his account of the development of the cumulative sum of human knowledge and the case for a commercial society. His explanatory social theory accounts for the improvements that result from the division of labor in terms of the significance of the enhancement of knowledge through specialization. This occurs when individuals in pursuit of subsistence and in attempting to better their own condition specialize and trade the product of their labor. This, for Smith, is the engine that produces the wealth of commercial nations. If this increased, and increasing, wealth is to be taken as an argument in favor of commercial societies, then a key plank in the justification must be that specialization allows for the enhancement and exploitation of knowledge held by individual specialists through trade.

A difficulty

Further evidence that Smith's analysis is colored by a concern for the role of knowledge is to be found in his discussion of what he views as one of the potential dangers of the advance of commercial society. Smith believed that certain malign unintended consequences may arise from the process of the division of labor and the division of knowledge, and these problems threaten to undercut the process itself by destabilizing society. The division of labor leads, as we have shown, to the fragmentation of knowledge. Specialization necessarily restricts the attention of workmen to one particular field and this field, in the case of many workers, will be a simple operation requiring little thought for its exercise. Smith waxes eloquent on the danger of this phenomenon:

> The man whose whole life is spent in performing a few simple operations . . . has no occasion to exert his understanding, or to exercise his invention in finding out expedients for removing difficulties which never occur. He naturally loses, therefore, the habit of such exertion, and generally becomes as stupid and ignorant as it is possible for a human creature to become. The torpor of his mind renders him, not only incapable of relishing or bearing a part in any rational conversation, but of conceiving any generous, noble, or tender sentiment, and consequently of forming any just judgement concerning many even of the ordinary duties of private life.
>
> (WN V.i.f.50, 782)[16]

There is a very real danger that, as the cumulative sum of human knowledge advances by specialization, the individual sums of knowledge (or the scope of those sums) of a large part of the population may fall to levels below that which they would hold in an less developed society. Smith advances a possible remedy for this apparently necessary evil of the process of specialization: a cure that is itself to be found in yet another division of labor and species of specialization. That is the creation of a specialist group of professional teachers whose job it is to provide a compulsory system of education (WN V.i.f.55–8, 785–6). Education becomes a method of enlightenment and social control, preventing the possibility of disputes that may arise from the susceptibility of a deadened workforce to the forces of religious 'enthusiasm', by socializing them and providing them with a degree of understanding that they would not gain from their everyday employment. Education also has the advantage of increasing the knowledge of individuals, which in turn contributes to the cumulative sum of human knowledge and encourages the possibility of innovation. Smith also describes in detail the nature of his proposed education system, arguing that the levels of education ought to cater to the intended career of the individual, allowing them the opportunity to acquire an appropriate level of skill that might prove useful to them. Smith's discussion of the potential dangers of commercial society and his response to it through a system of education are both conducted in line with the concerns over knowledge that typify his approach to the division of labor.

Conclusion

Throughout the preceding discussion of Smith's work we have observed the interaction of three natural drives: the desire to calm the mind through the acquisition of ordered knowledge, the natural pursuit of subsistence and the 'propensity' to trade. While the last two are part of the usual discussion in connection with the 'four stages' theory and the analysis of the division of labor, the first has often been overlooked or downplayed. It has been the contention of this discussion that the three aspects of Smith's theory come together in his analysis of the interdependence that develops through the 'four stages' and the division of labor. That is to say that Smith's concern with the acquisition and utilization of human knowledge is one of the key aspects of his theoretical approach. For there to be a clear understanding of Smith's central economic ideas the overlooked role of the growth and effective use of human knowledge in his theory must be given more prominence than has, in the past, been the custom.

Notes

1 In more recent times the work of the Austrian school of economics, in particular that of Friedrich Hayek, has shed much light on the significant role played by issues of interdependence, information and knowledge in the operation of economic phenomena. In Hayek's seminal 1945 essay *The Use of Knowledge in Society* he developed the idea that the sum of human knowledge is dispersed amongst the individuals that compose society and that, as a result, we can never hope to centralize all of the knowledge necessary successfully to plan an entire economic system. Hayek's argument highlighted a division of knowledge that is just as significant as the division of labor in the appreciation of the functioning of a commercial society. The aim of this chapter is not to suggest that Smith was a detailed precursor to Hayek on the significance of knowledge to economic analysis, rather it is to make the less sweeping claim that Smith was well aware of the role of knowledge in economic and social change and that an appreciation of this is vital to a proper understanding of his core ideas.

2 Both Smith and Hume are clear that this process, the desire to explain wondrous events in terms of science, is one which arises only after some economic progress has occurred. In simple societies the sense of wonder often invokes a mystical or religious explanation, but when a society materially advances and frees itself from the immediacy of savagery to such a degree as to support intellectual enquiry the reliance on miracles as explanatory devices gives way to rational enquiry. See Reisman (1976: 60–1).

3 Lord Kames provided the earliest Scottish development of the 'four stages' approach in his historical writings, and Ferguson's 'highly idiosyncratic' (Meek 1976: 154) analysis appears to operate with three, rather than four, stages:

savage, barbarous and polished. The origins of the 'four stages' approach have been traced to Grotius (Meek 1976: 14) and the Physiocrats (Meek 1971). However, as Bowles points out, the Scots' explanatory approach prompts us 'to ask historical questions rather than the moral questions of the natural law framework' (Bowles 1985: 197).

4 The 'four stages' analysis is continued throughout the *Wealth of Nations* as a conceptual model for the analysis of social change. Notable passages include the discussion of the development of military forces through the stages (WN V.i.a, 689–708), and the gradual development of judicial systems (WN V.i.b, 708–23).

5 It should be noted that the 'four stages' are not a deterministic model of inevitable development, but rather represent an attempt at explanation through the medium of conjectural history (Broadie 2001: 76; Skinner 1996: 183; Harpham 1983: 768–9). Not all stages must appear consecutively, or if they do all appear they need not do so in the same order, and as a result there is no sense of inevitable stadial development like that found in some Marxist accounts.

6 Heilbroner correctly states that population growth is the force behind the change between stages, but it cannot, by itself, explain the development (Heilbroner 1975: 527). In Meek's terms hunger prompts the search for new knowledge (Meek 1976: 213). Like the mercantilists (Hollander 1973: 58–65), the Scots viewed population growth as an indicator of progress. Danford has argued that Hume's essay *Of the Populousness of Ancient Nations* is a contribution to the debate over the superiority of classical models of freedom to modern 'commercial' freedom. Hume uses population levels to suggest the superiority of the modern approach (Danford 1990: 183–6). Similarly, Spengler argues that Smith regarded a decline in infant mortality as an indicator of economic improvement (Spengler 1983).

7 Hont suggests that the fourth stage differs from those prior to it in that it does not refer to a productive process related directly to the attainment of subsistence (Hont 1987: 254). Rather, trade, which is present in all four stages, comes to represent the chief means of securing subsistence through interdependence. Meek also notes that the change to the fourth stage differs from previous changes, in that it is the development of a factor that has always been present (trade) that is significant, rather than the acquisition of a practical skill of production (Meek 1976: 227).

8 There is an implicit question here as to what extent Smith believed his explanation of the origins of property and government served as a convincing justification of particular forms of government or property.

9 As Ferguson puts it: 'Mankind, in following the present sense of their minds, in striving to remove inconveniences, or to gain apparent and contiguous advantages, arrive at ends which even their imagination could not anticipate, and pass on, like other animals, in the track of their nature, without perceiving its end' (Ferguson 1995: 119). See James Otteson's *Adam Smith's Marketplace of Life* (2002) for a detailed study of the unintended generation of social order in the body of Smith's work.

10 It is for this reason that Hume notes that the growth of the cumulative sum of human knowledge does not lead us all to become geniuses (Hume *Essays*, 210).

11 Though Smith provides little in the way of explanation behind the 'trucking' principle he does make one revealing aside which links it with his conception of sympathy. He argues: 'If we should enquire into the principle in the human mind on which this disposition of trucking is founded, it is clearly the naturall inclination every one has to persuade. Men always endeavour to persuade others to be of their opinion even when the matter is of no consequence to

them' (LJ 352). This desire to persuade is clearly related to Smith's argument in the *Theory of Moral Sentiments* about the human emotional need for the approbation and approval of others. In terms of trade this principle is compounded with the desire for subsistence: with experience teaching men that the surest way to secure the co-operation of others, the surest way to persuade others to assist in the satisfaction of your wants, is to trade – to persuade by bargain and exchange.

12 The suggestions of utility underlie Smith's economic analysis of the division of labor in the *Wealth of Nations* and *Lectures on Jurisprudence*, but he also provides a psychological account of specialization that can be related to those human tendencies that prompt individuals to science. We have already noted that Smith discerned a natural human propensity to seek order in the understanding of the world. From this he drew a notion of the human mind as functioning by classification, and as this classification naturally develops in line with experience, so the differentiation of experience that occurs creates different fields or objects for human study. However, the psychological explanation of the pursuit of specialist knowledge is linked to both utility and sympathy. Smith argues that humans naturally admire the knowledge of specialists (TMS I.i.4.3–4, 20), and moreover they see how specialization has provided these people with a safe route to 'wealth' and 'reputation' (TMS VI.i.4–7, 213). There is a sense in which we pursue specialized knowledge from an emulation of the rich and successful (TMS I.iii.2.5, 55). Inspired by their success we seek to acquire knowledge and express our talents in order not only to secure financial reward, but also to enjoy the acclaim that goes along with expertise (TMS IV.i.8, 181).

13 Smith links this theme to an unintended consequences argument about the motivations of workers: where workers improve a machine in order to reduce the amount of labor required of them (WN I.i.8, 20–1).

14 Smith argues that this phenomenon, and the interdependence which it creates, are a further reason why we 'respect' specialists (TMS VII.iv.24, 336).

15 Rosenberg (1965: 128–9) agrees with this view, and develops it into an argument that a decreasing intelligence in particular laborers, resulting from their concentration of attention on a particular task, need not prevent the continuation of overall technical progress. His view is that the division of labor represents a process of simplification in reaction to complexity, the result of which is that 'the collective intelligence of society grows as a result of the very process' that restricts the breadth of individual knowledge (Rosenberg 1965: 134–5).

16 Or as Ferguson puts it: 'Under the distinction of callings, by which the members of polished society are separated from each other, every individual is supposed to possess his species of talent, or his particular skill, in which the others are confessedly ignorant; and society is made to consist of parts, of which none is animated with the spirit of society itself' (Ferguson 1995: 207).

References

Becker, James F. (1961) 'Adam Smith's Theory of Social Science', *Southern Economic Journal* 28 (1): 13–21.

Bowles, Paul (1985) 'The Origin of Property and the Development of Scottish Historical Science', *Journal of the History of Ideas* 46: 197–209.

Broadie, Alexander (2001) *The Scottish Enlightenment*, Edinburgh: Birlinn.

Brown, Maurice (1988) *Adam Smith's Economics: Its Place in the Development of Economic Thought*, London: Croom Helm.

Danford, John W. (1990) 'Hume's History and the Parameters of Economic Development', in Nicholas Capaldi and Donald W. Livingston (eds) *Liberty in Hume's History of England*, Dordrecht: Kluwer, 155–94.

Ferguson, Adam (1995) [1767] *An Essay on the History of Civil Society*, ed. Fania Oz-Salzberger, Cambridge: Cambridge University Press.

Harpham, Edward J. (1983) 'Liberalism, Civic Humanism, and the Case of Adam Smith', *American Political Science Review* 78 (3): 764–74.

Hayek, F. A. (1945) 'The Use of Knowledge in Society', *American Economic Review* 35 (4): 519–30.

Heilbroner, R. L. (1975) 'The Paradox of Progress: Decline and Decay in the *Wealth of Nations*', in Andrew S. Skinner and Thomas Wilson (eds) *Essays on Adam Smith*, Oxford: Clarendon Press, 524–39.

Hollander, Samuel (1973) *The Economics of Adam Smith*, London: Heinemann.

Hont, Istvan (1987) 'The language of sociability and commerce: Samuel Pufendorf and the theoretical foundations of the "Four Stages Theory"', in Anthony Pagden (ed.) *The Language of Political Theory in Early Modern Europe*, Cambridge: Cambridge University Press, 253–76.

Meek, Ronald L. (1971) 'Smith, Turgot, and the "Four Stages" Theory', *History of Political Economy* 3: 9–27.

—— (1976) *Social Science and the Ignoble Savage*, Cambridge: Cambridge University Press.

Millar, John (1990) [1806] *The Origin of the Distinction of Ranks*, Bristol: Thoemmes Press.

Otteson, James R. (2002) *Adam Smith's Marketplace of Life*, Cambridge: Cambridge University Press.

Reisman, D. A. (1976) *Adam Smith's Sociological Economics*, London: Croom Helm.

Rosenberg, Nathan (1965) 'Adam Smith on the Division of Labour: Two Views or One?' *Economica* 32 (125–8): 127–39.

Skinner, Andrew S. (1974) 'Adam Smith, Science and the Role of the Imagination', in W. B. Todd (ed.) *Hume and the Enlightenment: Essays Presented to Ernest Campbell Mossner*, Edinburgh: Edinburgh University Press, 164–88.

—— (1996) *A System of Social Science: Papers relating to Adam Smith*, 2nd edn., Oxford: Clarendon Press.

Spengler, J. J. (1983) 'Adam Smith on Population Growth and Economic Development', in John Cunningham Wood (ed.) *Adam Smith: Critical Assessments* III, London: Croom Helm, 395–406.

14 Adam Smith's criticism of the doctrine of utility

A theory of the creative present

Estrella Trincado

In the study of distinct visions of the world, the perception of time by different authors is an important differentiating factor. Time frequently has been considered the basis for the continuism/discontinuism classification, but this classification can be more fruitful than is generally assumed.[1] We could imagine various types of continuism; and, in order to cover the whole time arrow, we could talk about a continuism mainly based on the past – on a conservative idea of utility, on the future – on a progressive idea of utility, and, finally, on a non-eidetic present, an eidetic present being human action based on an image or an idea (see Trincado 2003a). Systems derived from utility are goal-oriented, aiming at a *fiction*: in the case of conservatism, the goal is survival, while the progressive system is based on the image of the pleasurable consequences of actions, which shape a perfect future world.[2]

The main objective of this chapter is to show that, unlike most of the theories based on utility, Smith's can be labeled as a *creative present theory* and that we can find a Smithian concept of time as a core element of his 'system'. That is to say, time is a *continuum* linked to a real living present, out of time sequence. Although Smith's motivation as a philosopher should not be confused with the principles he defends in his system, a leitmotif of his work is demonstrating that the search for what has been useful or is supposed to be useful in the future is not the grounds for human action.[3] Actually, Smith's theory is a direct criticism of Hume's idea of utility, something of which Hume was perfectly aware (Raynor 1984). So he reproached Smith in a letter: 'Robertson's Book [*History of Scotland*, 1759] has great Merit; but it was visible that he profited here by the Animosity against me. I suppose the Case was the same with you' (Corr. 44).

Hume's theory, although non-utilitarian if we associate utilitarianism with the human satisfying of some utilitarian foreseeable role, is characteristically based on the idea of utility (as an explanatory function). Conversely, Smith's theory specifically constitutes a criticism of the theory of utility.

I shall apply here the 'present hypothesis' to Smith's philosophy and ethics. I can only get some insights into how it would be applied to theory of law or political economy. Smith describes a philosophical reality based on two different egos: one dependent, unreal and mortal, with reactive principles of movement; the other always present and immortal, where perception and active principles are bound to emerge. It is thanks to this last ego that human beings seek an emotional bond with people in the present and create relationships with present things.

Smithian metaphysics

Smith tried to confront Hume's phenomenalism, in which possibly he became steeped during his first years of study at Oxford University (Scott 1992).[4] In spite of having asked Black and Hutton to burn all his papers, Smith wanted to spare from the flames some philosophical essays dealing with a concept of substance. I shall argue here, the same as Schliesser (2005) and contrary to Griswold (1999: 336–44), that Smith does not 'suspend judgment': clearly he affirms the existence of substance (see Vivenza 2001: 206–9). In some of his statements, Smith seems to approach the idea of an 'overcoming of metaphysics'. Not surprisingly, when he writes about the work on moral philosophy by his friend John Bruce, he says 'It is as free of metaphysics as is possible for any work upon that subject to be. Its fault, in my opinion, is that it is too free of them' (Corr. 296).

Smith asserts the externality and identity of objects: 'though the sensations of heat and cold do not necessarily suggest the presence of any external object, we soon learn from experience that they are commonly excited by some such object' (External Senses 21). 'We consider it, therefore, as what we call a Substance, or as a thing that subsists by itself, and independent of any other thing' (External Senses 8). Besides, nouns instead of adjectives, Smith says, were the first words created, a point made that seems to entail his belief in an intuitive knowledge of substance, previous to touch and sight.[5]

But if there is an intuitive knowledge of substance, objects must not be perceived by 'impressions' (in Hume's terminology, *phantasia* for the Pyrrhonists). There should be a type of perception that is not a plain image. This is 'depth' perception, which Smith was able to discern. 'The tangible world . . . has three dimensions, Length, Breadth and Depth. The visible world . . . has only two, Length and Breadth. It presents to us only a plain or surface . . . (in the same manner as a picture does)' (External Senses 50–2, 150–2). For Smith, it is thanks to movement – in time – that we can perceive the variation of perspective (External Senses 59, 155). If at any point we have perhaps confused flatness with depth, we only need 'time' to situate ourselves in the intuitive position capable of understanding perspective. When the blind man couched for a cataract 'was just beginning to understand the strong and distinct perspective of Nature, the faint and feeble perspective of Painting made no impression upon him' (External Senses 67). See also External Senses 52, 65–7, 151–2, 159–60.[6]

For this reason, we value greater capacity of perception in objects. It is not because it is useful, but because it draws us closer to reality as originally 'we approve of another man's judgement, not as something useful, but as right, as accurate, as agreeable to truth and reality' (TMS I.i.4.4, 61). This greater capacity of perception was shown in the case of the blind mathematician Saunderson, who developed supernormal powers of touch and hearing. His experience encouraged an outburst of philosophical writings about blindness in the eighteenth century, including Diderot's, Berkeley's and Reid's.

Besides, whilst in Hume's theory time and self-existence were called into question by his definition of perception as an unending succession of impressions,[7] according to Smith, the intuition of personal identity is needed even to perceive solidness.[8] Smith comments that in the beginning of the formation of language, human beings must have faced the difficulty that the word 'I' was very special. The verb structure 'I am' does not derive its existence from particular facts, but rather from existence itself (LRBL, Languages, 34, 221). It expresses an internal feeling, which, as shown in TMS, is reflection of gratitude, 'for whatever is the cause of pleasure naturally excites our gratitude' (Astronomy III. 2. 48).[9] In its first stage, this gratitude is inseparable from wonder and the sense of reality (Astronomy III.2, 49). Probably, religious feeling, described as faith put in an ordered world, emerges then. Religious feeling is also the way in which human beings are grateful to whatever is behind this order.[10]

It is true, as Smith intended to confirm 'that our judgements concerning our own conduct have always a reference to the sentiments of some other being' (Corr. 49), in the formation of the ego Smith presupposes the idea of the observer, which is in fact what he wants to explain (TMS III.i.2–5, 109–12; IV.ii). The process of creating the self consists in observing elements external to oneself – other's smile, and rewards – and achieving their acceptance. If the self of this other also has been shaped in a similar way, everything is a reflection of a reflection, pure semblance, a *mask* foreign to the individual himself. As we know, this produces a duplication of the ego, which can draw us into labyrinth-like feelings.[11] This contradiction earned Smith innumerable critics (see the objections by Stewart and Thomas Reid in Thomas Brown lectures, Reeder (1997: 143–4)).

Moreover, Smith recognizes that the imaginary spectator of our own conduct examines it when we are about to act and afterwards, but never when we are acting (TMS III.4.2–4, 157). Consequently, it cannot motivate the action, and to justify the adaptive act in itself we could use the self-deceiving mechanism, related in TMS III.iv.4–6, 157–9.[12] The process of socialization is basic for the adaptive function of the ego (TMS III). This adaptation is mainly based on a Hobbesian fear of death (Cropsey 1957; Pack 1991). We even sympathize with the dead (TMS I.i.1.13, 12) and, in this sense, as Griswold (1999: 89) says, Smithian sympathy is 'egotistical' and self-referencing. Moreover, Smith envisages a non-adaptive present feeling, on which justice is based.

> The revenge of the injured which prompts him to retaliate the injury on the offender is the real source of the punishment of crimes. That which Grotius and other writers commonly allege as the original measure of punishments, viz the consideration of the publick good, will not sufficiently account for the constitution of punishments.
>
> (LJ 104)

The basis for justice, so, is not utility or reason, which are an outline of the future that would use punishment for an imaginary end, but a present feeling (Trincado 2000, 2004). The feeling of indignation precedes the law and the state respects this feeling, it does not create it (Fleischacker 2004: 151). Here Smith clearly tries to refute both Hume and his mentor Hutcheson (LJ 547, LJ (B): 475: 182) and anticipates Nietzsche (1967). Pack and Schliesser (2006) note that in TMS revenge gets replaced by resentment of the injured and the sympathetic observer. So, as in ethics, in his theory of law Smith stresses the idea of the spectator. But the fact that human beings are capable of indignation shows that the concept of sympathy can be distinguished from the 'emotional contagion' or complete identification, which disallows any chance of dissension between persons (Tasset 1995: 101; see also Fleischacker 2004; Griswold 1999: ch. 6; Haakonssen 1981; Vivenza 2001).

In the course of time, Smith became increasingly skeptical of the judgment as of popular opinion (Corr. 48–57) and perceived the influence of a tribunal in moral judgment as different from others´ judgment (TMS III.ii.32, 130). In particular, for Smith, the existence of this tribunal not dependent on imagination seems to imply a momentary psychological break with the idea of death. The man 'sees, with grief and affliction, in how many different features the mortal copy falls short of the immortal original' (TMS VI.iii.25, 247). 'In such cases, this demigod within the breast appears, like the demigods of the poets, though partly of immortal, yet partly too of mortal extraction' (TMS III.ii.32, 131; see also TMS III.v.9, 168; TMS III.ii.12, 121 and TMS III.ii.33, 131). This always-present 'I' that makes depth perception possible would resolve the contradiction of the existence of an impartial spectator who, at the same time, sums up others' judgment and disapproves of all humanity.[13]

The reactive principles of movement

For Smith, pleasure is a positive principle, as it is not the self-satisfaction of the ego, but naturally linked to gratitude (Astronomy III. 2. 48). Although anticipation is, on occasion, a source of pleasure (as is the case for utilitarians), the most pleasurable attitude is the contemplation of the present and people easily empathize with a person who is thankful for the simple pleasures of life (TMS I.ii.5.2, 41–2).

Actually, pleasure is not merely physical. Smith criticizes the Epicurean system's belief that the body is the centre of feeling (TMS VII.ii.1.19–22, 275–8). In the Epicurean system, as uncertainty about the future is painful, abstinence from the search for pleasures allowed man, as in Stoicism, to live tranquilly, without fear, especially of death. But, for Smith, indifference is a requirement neither for tranquility nor for wisdom (TMS VI.iii.21, 246). Epicureanism is based, not on the appropriateness of active sensations, but rather on a reaction to pain–pleasure sensations. Therefore, contradictorily, for Epicureans, individual motions are based on a passive or reactive principle.

For Smith, the first movement at the beginning of life could not be motivated by the contemplation of death or self-preservation, an idea *ex post* to action. It must have rather emerged from the instinctive desire to move that does not depend on past experiences. 'The desire of changing our situation necessarily supposes some idea of externality; or of motion into a place different from that in which we actually are...' (External Senses 86, 167–8). Besides, death instinct cannot be the target of our action, since fear of death is 'the great poison of human happiness' (TMS I.i.1.13, 13). The lack of fear of death makes humans more sensitive (TMS V.ii.11, 208), and they evince a 'character of gaiety, levity, and sprightly freedom' (TMS V.2.6, 203). That is, when people allow themselves to be swayed by the imagination of nothingness, their movements are reactive and evasive, not free.[14]

In this sense, 'the idea of death' implies a break in time where the individual lives in a vacuum 'in the present'. It implies some type of 'not accepting of reality' and this should mean some way of non-existence. So, in such a situation, the only thing the individual can do is try to forget the vacuum by placing a veil over his or her imagination. In fact, 'utility' consists of that image created by the individual. This image 'uses' the present for its self-determination and is unachievable, given that it cannot make itself real. Consequently utility can be defined as *every element of the imagination that sustains us within reality*.

Actually, Smith defines the concept of utility in a way that also obliges us to reconsider his perception of time. The search for utility is love of the system that creates temporary and fictitious hope, but not pleasure. We value the anxiety with which we require that beauty be exact, the ends justifying the means, and ignore the pleasure and pain it produces (TMS IV.i.1–6, 179–80). The feeling of fitness of means to ends is secondary, imaginary and *a posteriori* to action. Moreover, the idea of death can be seen in Smith's theory as a utility to be admired or accepted, something religions have managed to promote. This is a reason why Smith challenged the church as an institution (see Griswold 1999: 10–11). But 'anxious search of utility' wipes out any possibility of a relaxed present, and our own image enslaves us.[15] Only through an understanding of the value of 'Time, the great and universal comforter' (TMS III.iii.32, 151), could self-command dominate passion, enjoying beforehand that tranquillity which we foresee the course of time will restore to us in the end.

Active principles of movement

The imaginary man requires an impulse 'from outside' to act; the 'I' that observes the present acts 'towards the outside' and supposes an identification with ubiquity. It requires, as Ricoeur (1984: 53) says, to be present in the passage. This 'I' does not necessarily imply the existence of Kantian transcendental ego or of innate ideas. A non-eidetic ego can be situated in the observer of memory and of present, out of succession of time. So, it identifies itself with the objects.[16]

Smith's praise for self-command seems to imply belief in the existence of a free, self-restrained 'I', immune to pleasure–pain pulsation (see Montes 2004: 101–14).[17] In Smith's theory, moral sentiments, as self-command, are not totally based on education or custom. 'The principles of the imagination, upon which our sense of beauty depends . . . may easily be altered by habit and education: . . . the sentiments of moral approbation . . . are founded on the strongest . . . passions of human nature; and . . . cannot be entirely perverted' (TMS V.ii.1, 200). The principles of the imagination are contrasted with the sentiments of moral approbation. Morality seems based neither on beauty nor on imagination but on a permanent reality, which cannot be perverted.

For Smith, self-command does not imply negating oneself. The passions, instead of disappearing, 'lie concealed in the breast of the sufferer' (TMS V.ii.11, 208). Self-command is self-actualization of certain principles of justice, which are 'independent of the beauty which it derives from its utility' (TMS VI.iii.4, 238). Besides, the act of self-command that enables us to express 'the highest contempt of death and pain' (TMS V.ii.9, 206), increases the admiration of the spectator. When we see, for example, a man controlling his fear of death for a noble cause, the reduction in his fear facilitates our identifying ourselves with the cause.[18] We admire the person who uses self-command out of gratitude to reality, and if this reality did not exist, our judgment of propriety would be diminished (TMS VI.iii.5, 238–9). See Trincado (2003b).

For this reason, in his work Smith demonstrates active movement principles, which depend to some extent on self-command. The first active principle is *joy*, very closely related with 'the willingness to live' and contrary to the idea of suicide (TMS VII.ii.1.34, 287). Joy requires a feeling of continuity of time that, philosophically, is linked to a real living present, out of time sequence.[19] The confidence in the 'divine plan' allows the wise person to face all types of adversities, including death, 'not only with humble resignation . . . but . . . with alacrity and joy' (TMS VI.ii.3.4, 236).

So the wise person reins in his (or her) self-destructive ideas because he (or she) knows time will cure them. 'Nature, in her sound and healthful state, seems never to prompt us to suicide...' (TMS VII.ii.1.34, 287).[20] Joy is based on gratitude for its own sake and without any justification beyond itself (TMS VII.iii.3.13–14, 325). We submit to divine will because it is right, regardless of the effect on our happiness in the afterlife. For comparison with utilitarian theory, see TMS VII.ii.3.21, 305–6.

Curiosity and *wonder* are also active principles that Smith discusses. Wonder leads men in the direction of novelty and does not seek 'any expectation of advantage from its discoveries' (Astronomy III.3, 51).[21] Non-utilitarian movement is the precise search for something that motivates if, and only if, it is unknown. When led by curiosity, men are not looking for an individual image of utility of the ends.

Curiosity is based on a form of self-love that, as opposed to selfishness, is a morally positive principle, as it is the basis of the capacity to understand: the one who does not believe in himself (or herself) shuts off their intuitive capacity, losing one of the underpinnings of existence, that is, 'attention to life'.[22] 'Those unfortunate persons, whom nature has formed a good deal below the common level, seem sometimes to rate themselves still more below it than they really are. This humility appears sometimes to sink them into idiotism' (TMS VI.iii.49, 260). Besides, for self-love to activate itself it is fundamental that there be a consciousness of reciprocity and that others believe in one's words. 'The man who had the misfortune to imagine that nobody believed a single word he might say, would feel himself the outcast of human society' (TMS VII.iv.26, 336). However, when Smith looks in the mirror, he tries to discern self-love that is neither self-referencing nor dependent but that is grateful or friendly to reality. 'One's own face becomes then the most agreeable object which a looking-glass can represent to us ... whether handsome or ugly, whether old or young, it is the face of a friend always' (Imitative Arts I.17, 186).[23]

Two other principles that Smith sketches are *creation* and *the game*. The solitaire or individualistic game can be harmful, based as it is on an oversized ego and its reactions. 'The over-weening conceit which the greater part of men have of their own abilities' (WN I.x.b, 124) leads them to 'The contempt of risk and the presumptuous hope of success' (WN I.x.b, 126). In Smith's treatment of political economy the active game implies reciprocity, not self-affirmation, and it is tied to creation.[24] For the game to be active, there must be correspondence with the movements of other persons in the present and curiosity about these movements.[25]

The empathizing sympathy

I claim that the unaffected present is the only place where we can experience what I will call 'empathizing sympathy', which is the natural sympathy that Smith defines. This needs some explanation. We can imagine the circumstances of the other person, and even our own, without possessing a critical capability with respect to those circumstances. Nevertheless, when the imaginative process becomes independent of the imaginary ego, and we observe it from the present, our relationship with time opens up. Then, we 'realize' that an independent and active feeling occurs, a feeling of indignation, of compassion, of joy. This is because we seek gratefulness in return from the other person, and not finding it causes surprise. In many cases, this capacity of comprehension is obstructed because, in fact, 'we do not want to understand'. We prefer to maintain our comfortable situation of inactivity or we do not want to recognize a previous error. However, it is possible that a sufficiently moving experience expands our understanding again, and sometimes it can help us make a break with our previous acceptance connections. One familiar case of this sudden shift of mind is Hume's mental crisis (Mossner 1980: 66, 70) or the one suffered by John Stuart Mill (1971).

The Smithian idea of natural 'sympathy' requires a profound belief in the notion of external existence (TMS I.i.1.5, 10) and the possibility of empathetic sympathy. For Hume, we cannot sympathize with the pain without a certain aversion (Corr. 43). For Smith, the pleasure of sympathy comes from the comfort thanks to the agreement of feelings with the motivations of the agent. We like to see that we can sympathize with people's real motives, even when they consist of pain.[26] So, we want to get to know others, not in search of utility, but to feel the reality of things (TMS VII.iv.28, 337).[27] Pleasure in the form of gratitude can be felt equally by the agent and the spectator (TMS VII.iii.1.4, 317).[28]

Some insights into economic growth

We can easily apply this intuitive methodology of 'having realized' to Smithian economics and to his theory of value–cost. When we say a person has discovered how much a thing is really worth we are in effect speaking of its objective value. The person has sewn together for the first time the various relationships of ideas that will lead him to 'realize' the meaning of each one of the minutes of work and experience required to produce an object (WN I.vi.4–9, 65–8). As said above, in many cases the capacity of intuitive understanding is obstructed because really 'we do not want to see'. There is a value that is difficult for people to keep in mind: the passing and harnessing of time, together with the power of saving (WN II.iii.16–20, 337–9). Lastly, the landowner seeks, at least, the same income that is paid to his neighbors for his soil, with alternative uses (WN I.xi.1–9, 160–2). Although it might not cause them any worries, we could calculate the productivity of the appropriation of the land by comparing the status of the lands in private hands with land not privately held (WN III.ii). So, value is an institution defined in terms of institutional effort which commodities can command. It is a function of the sacrifice that the buyer avoids and imposes on others, which is therefore based on externality (WN I.v.1–3, 47–8) and attaches its importance to the spectator also in economics. Ricardo thought that Smith had crossed the line into confusion between incorporated and commanded labor. But, for Smith, the labor incorporated at the moment a commodity is created is already forgotten about. Value–cost requires paying attention to the market, and is 'a certain command ... over all the produce of labour which is *then* in the market' (WN I.v.3, 48). The idea of value comes from the 'labour which we exchange for what is supposed *at the time* ['in the present'] to contain the value of an equal quantity' (WN I.v.2, 47–8). This implies that utility is not an exogenous pleasure that determines its value, but rather an endogenous one that depends on how it compares with other goods in the market. Thus, this makes economics abandon self-contemplation and subjectivity. Demand is not a function of price but the amount of a product that was able to be sold established after price determination (Urrutia 1983: 19).

In Smith's thought, the negation of consequentialism is perfectly compatible with economic action. As 'an augmentation of fortune is the means by which the greater part of men propose and wish to better their condition' (WN II.iii.28, 341), economic growth seems to be the only way of creating hopefulness through the image of wealth.

The positive consequence of the generation of wealth is not that money increases the number of obtainable 'happinesses' but the simple fact of joy itself, the enjoying of feelings such as curiosity and creation in the market, which offer the chance to 'break' habits. 'The progressive state is in reality the cheerful and the hearty state to all the different orders of the society. The stationary is dull; the declining, melancholy' (WN I.viii.43, 99). Smith contrasts cheerfulness with melancholy, that is, curiosity about the future with attachment to past memories. Habits and prejudices, though influential, are obstacles to economic growth (WN IV.v.b.39–40, 539; TMS V.2.13, 209) because, in short, economic growth emerges from creative freedom.[29] That is the reason why in WN Smith absolutely abandoned the LJ's idea that state should 'foment' abundance, choosing instead to concentrate on growth, which the state should 'allow' (WN II.iii.31, 343). Rotwein (1970: 109) affirms that this seems to be a rejection of Hume's position on recognizably universal foundations (see Hayek 1963 and more recently Berry 1997: 68–70).[30]

But Smith maintains both in WN and LJ that the division of labor permits a gradual process arising from an unpredictable creative tendency (LJ 352). However, the feeling of joy that economic growth affords comes from creation about the prideful image of having brought another to one's own side through verbal seduction (WN I.ii.2, 25; see Fleischacker (2004, 90–5) on the butcher/baker's passage), something which is not always morally laudable. 'To perform any thing, or to give any thing, without a reward is always generous and noble, but to barter one thing for another is mean' (LJ 527). Also in LJ 352.[31] The problem is that not only is the state an unconscious image that absorbs the energies of the anxious man: the image that the individual has of himself is unconscious also and forces people into vicious circles. In TMS (VI.ii.1.16–20, 224–6), the real objective of our wanting to improve our condition is the maintenance of social status, a painful fear ratified by the stimulus of the spectator (see Lerner 1999; Otteson 2002). Entrepreneurs 'can never be multiplied so as to hurt the publick, though they may so as to hurt one another' (WN II.v, 7). On occasion, competition hurts the workers when it obliges them to work to exhaustion (WN I.viii.13, 84) or leads them to suffer from 'torpor of mind' (WN V.i.f.50, 782). The ethic of work for work's sake is contrary to the principle of prudence (WN I.viii.44, 100).[32] Nevertheless, continuous growth is necessary to unleash rivalry between bosses for labor.

Conclusion

In this chapter, I have offered a classification of doctrines according to the prevailing perception of time on which different theories are based. By describing the different images that oppress the present, we can free ourselves from them. Smith's theory, in particular, is an attempt to argue a conception of time based on a 'creative present'. This, I believe, clears up some of the confusion displayed by philosophical, ethical and social theories based on the fiction of utility.

Smith describes a type of perception, depth, which is different from perception based on impressions. Depth perception is a form of wonder that can be lost in the socialization process. For this type of perception to occur, it is necessary to recognize the independence and reality of the 'I' and the 'other'. In contrast to the hunt for pleasure, which is a reaction to the pleasure–pain dynamics and requires using imaginative processes, Smith presents active principles that are lived in the present, such as gratitude, joy, curiosity, game playing and creation. The emergence of these active principles depends on self-command. Besides, although imagination is crucial for sympathy, only an observer of present time is capable of putting himself in the place of the other person and maintaining active principles, 'realizing' through an intuitive burst of clarity that leads to an understanding of things.

With respect to economics, Smith also bases his theory on action lived in the present, not reaction. The division of labor is the result of people's natural tendency to be creative and enjoy themselves, and not of individual or societal foresight. The value of goods implies also 'realizing' that there is objective value. Also, the positive consequence of the generation of wealth is not that the amount of 'happinesses' that money provides increases, but rather the chance to 'break' with habit by enjoying the feeling of curiosity and creation.

Notes

1 Wilcox (1987: 4) argues that modern historians generally operate under the assumption of a continuous time line. But in the twentieth century, discontinuity has increasingly preoccupied historians (Eisenstein 1966: 36, 48). The postmodern concept of time is characterized by non-linearity, discontinuity and fragmentation. (see Miller 2001: 2, in particular with regard to Marx's discontinuism; see also Adam 1990 and Kellner 1975).

2 Nevertheless, some doctrines could have no predominance or time bias and gather together all these three time theories.

3 So, Smith is not even a 'contemplative utilitarian', as termed in Campbell (1971), Campbell and Ross (1981) or in Ross (1995: 167). See the criticisms by Fleischacker (2004: 145) and Montes (2004: 51, 114–22). Haakonssen (1981: 135) and Vivenza (2001: 97–104) also labeled Smith a non-utilitarian in moral and legal theory. See also Griswold (1999: 540). For the utilitarian principles in Smith see Levy (1995).

4 Maybe influenced by Hume's psychological state. In his youth, he was diagnosed with 'the disease of the learned'. In his own words: 'I saw that I was not capable of following out any train of thought by one continued stretch of view' (Mossner 1980: 70). See also Mossner (1980: 66) and Livingston (1998).

5 'Do any of our other senses, antecedently to such observation and experience, instinctively suggest to us some conception of the solid and resisting substances which excite their respective sensations...?' (External Senses 75, 164). For Smith, nouns and language seek veracity; it is only a means of expressing intuitive knowledge (Brown 1994).

6 Gestalt theory speaks of perception as something whole. 'Shapes' are perceived in an immediate, intuitive way (Marchán 1996: 239–40).

7 Wright (1983) shows Hume not to be a skeptic, but a skeptical 'realist' (for pro and cons, see Read and Richman 2000). Indeed, in the end, Hume developed a constructive philosophy which, while anti-rationalist, was in no way irrationalist (Tasset 1999).

8 'When he lays his hand upon the table ... he feels it therefore as something external, not only to his hand, but to himself' (External Senses 3–8, 135–6).

9 The person grown up in some solitary place could not think of his own character or of the propriety or merit of his own sentiments and conduct (TMS III.i.3, 111). Sense of merit is made up of direct sympathy with the sentiments of the agent and an indirect sympathy with the gratitude of those who receive the benefit of his actions (TMS II.i.v.2, 74) and, in the case that the agent is the I, this gratitude subsists.

10 Haakonssen (1996: 135–48) points out that Smith is based on Samuel von Cocceji's theory, which asserts that the individual should understand his life to be a personal gift from God.

11 This duplication has been described by Borges, who continually ventured deeper and deeper into his own private phenomenalist labyrinth.

12 Nevertheless, it is not clear that self-deception is part of acting with the impartial spectator (see Gerschlager 2002)

13 Some scholars have considered Smith's impartial spectator to be a collective person (Campbell 1971; Hope 1989: 9). But, then, he would not approve of an action that all humanity would disapprove of.

14 For Smith war is the great teacher of self-command. On self-command and its possible connections to martial virtues in the classical sense, see Montes (2004: 76–86).

15 Then, in the final stage of his life, the *arriviste* understands that wealth and

splendor are 'no more adapted for procuring ease of body or tranquillity of mind than the tweezer-cases of the lover of toys' (TMS IV.i.8, 181).

16 As the observer of the present is ubiquitous, it captures the 'far off' thing from the perspective of the present. This 'I' has something of a 'sixth sense', clearly differentiated, and made up of depth and volume. For example, the depth of a container implies that we feel ourselves to be contained in the object. So the art that most represents the observer is sculpture (feeling it as a voluminous reality). Without depth sense, the object would stay in the area of learned concepts in the mind. See Trincado (2003a) and Huxley (1963).

17 But, curiously, in the Glasgow edition of the TMS there is only one reference to the word 'liberty' (Harpham 2000).

18 According to Griswold (1999: 119) this is due to fear of death being an imaginary pain with which it is more possible to sympathize than if it were a bodily pain.

19 The concept of the 'living present' was analyzed by Husserl and implies direct perceptive contact, a 'now' that retains but also seeks the future. Time is not defined as a succession of moments, but rather it is like the 'third time' of Ricoeur (1984: 27), the identification of the subject as in the following of a narration, with a past, a present and a future.

20 Smith was prompted to write this by Hume's posthumous publication 'On Suicide'. Hume's theory was partially based on stoicism. For stoics, God gave us life for us to 'enjoy' it, and God amuses Himself with our destiny. When we cease to enjoy ourselves, the rule of the gods allows us to stop the game. Gratefulness was limited to giving thanks for being able to leave the labyrinth voluntarily, but this gratefulness was beclouded by the distance between man and his Creator, the former being a dream of the latter. (Remember Borges's stories, which also draw near to stoicism.)

21 Nevertheless, in Astronomy II, Smith also describes wonder in terms of uncertainty about the future and motion of animal spirits. Wonder is a painful sentiment which gives rise to anxious curiosity (Schliesser 2005).

22 For that reason, in Smith's economics, in spite of his believing habit shapes ability, division of labor based on habit alienates workers (WN V.i.f.50, 781–2). Indeed, Smithian liberty holds that the unknown is what motivates human action and not habit.

23 Perhaps Borges's fear of mirrors was due to their making him feel more unreal for lack of self-love: the reflection did not differ from the thing reflected, as its substance did not exist. Here we have another consequence of Borges's phenomenalism and idealism.

24 Theories other than Smith's, as Krishnamurti's, show that creation is 'the miracle of the new'. Human beings can participate in it, but they cannot appropriate it through their ego and concepts (Holroyd 1991: 94–5).

25 Besides, these open movements permit the mechanism of memory to be activated. Elderly people remember clearly moments from their childhood because these memories were recorded from an I which let itself live, which did not look for utility in time lived (Bergson 1911).

26 As Holthoon (1993: 45) says, we feel here the pleasure of understanding nature.

27 Darwall (1998: 264–9) has proposed that we use 'empathy' instead of 'sympathy' when referring to the Smithian imagined change of position.

28 Fontaine (2001: 388) defines Smith's sympathy as a 'complete empathetic identification', but, actually, Smith is only speaking about 'harmony of sentiments'. Raynor (1984) differed from Fointaine's claim. Montes (2004) seems to follow Fontaine, uncovering the etymological meaning of sympathy, but focuses on the sympathetic process.

29 As Griswold says (1999: 349–54), custom can be partially left aside, as human beings are not absolutely influenced by history or convention (see TMS V.ii.1, 200).

30 It could be claimed that it is for that reason that, in spite of the WN containing numerous psychological allusions and much historical material, Smith tends to leave those influences aside in his treatment of political economy. Also, Smith separates WN and TMS theories without making cross-references, although WN was a 'de facto' continuation of the TMS. As Pack (1995: 161) says, neither did Smith's theological grounding affect his work (see also Rothschild 2002). So, for him, an image of God's will is not relevant.

31 So the impartial spectator does not necessarily approve of the causes of economic growth (see also WN II.iii, 42). For a different conclusion, see Young (1997).

32 Smith complains about the mercantile system's 'production for production's sake' (WN IV.viii.48–9, 660).

References

Adam, B. (1990) *Time in Social Theory*, Cambridge: Polity Press.

Bergson, H. (1911) *Matter and Memory*, London: Allen and Unwin.

Berry, C. L. (1997) *Social Theory of the Scottish Enlightenment*, Edinburgh: Edinburgh University Press.

Brown, V. (1994) *Adam Smith's Discourse: Canonicity, Commerce and Conscience*, London and New York: Routledge.

Campbell, T. D. (1971) *Adam Smith's Science of Morals*, London: Allen and Unwin.

—— and Ross, I. S. (1981) 'The Utilitarianism of Adam Smith's Policy Advice', *Journal of the History of Ideas* 42: 73–92.

Cropsey, J. (1957) *Polity and Economy: an Interpretation of the Principles of Adam Smith*, The Hague: Nijhoff.

Darwall, S. (1998) 'Empathy, Sympathy, Care', *Philosophical Analysis*, 89: 221–82.

Eisenstein, E. (1966) 'Clio and Chronos: An Essay on the Making and Breaking of History-Book Time', *History and Theory* 6: 36–64.

Fleischacker, S. (2004) *On Adam Smith's* Wealth of Nations*: A Philosophical Companion*. Princeton, NJ: Princeton University Press.

Fontaine, P. (2001) 'The Changing Place of Empathy in Welfare Economics', *History of Political Economy* 33 (3): 387–409.

Gerschlager, C. (2002) 'Is (Self-)Deception an Indispensable Quality of Exchange? A New Approach to Adam Smith's Concept', in C. Gerschlager (ed.) *Expanding the Economic Concept of Exchange: Deception, Self-deception and Illusions*, Boston, MA and Dordrecht: Kluwer, 27–52.

Griswold, C. L. (1999) *Adam Smith and the Virtues of Enlightenment*, Cambridge: Cambridge University Press.

Haakonssen, K. (1981) *The Science of a Legislator*, Cambridge: Cambridge University Press.

—— (1996) *Natural Law and Moral Philosophy: From Grotius to the Scottish Enlightenment*, Cambridge Cambridge University Press.

Harpham, E. J. (2000) 'The Problem of Liberty in the Thought of Adam Smith', *Journal of the History of Economic Thought* 22 (2): 217–37.

Hayek, F. A. (1963) 'The Legal and Political Philosophy of David Hume', *Il Politico* 28 (4): 691–704.

Holroyd, S. (1991) *Krishnamurti*, Madrid: Colección Esotérika.

Holthoon, F. L. V. (1993) 'Adam Smith and David Hume: With Sympathy', *Utilitas: A Journal of Utilitarian Studies* 5 (1): 35–49.

Hope, V. (1989) *Virtue by Consensus: The Moral Philosophy of Hutcheson, Hume and Adam Smith*, Oxford: Clarendon Press.

Huxley, A. (1963) *The Doors of Perception*, New York: Harper & Row.

Kellner, H. D. (1975) 'Time Out: The Discontinuity of Historical Consciousness', *History and Theory* 14: 275–96.

Lerner, R. (1999) 'Love of Fame and the Constitution of Liberty', in Thomas Angerer, Birgitta Bader-Zaar and Margarete Grandner (eds) *Geschichte und Recht: Festschrift für Gerald Stourzh zum 70. Geburtstag*, Vienna: Bóhlau.

Levy, D. M. (1995) 'The Partial Spectator in *The Wealth of Nations*: A Robust Utilitarianism', *European Journal of the History of Economic Thought* 2: 299–326.

Livingston, D. W. (1998) *Philosophical Melancholy and Delirium: Hume's Pathology of Philosophy*, Chicago: University of Chicago Press.

Marchán, S., (1996) *La estética en la cultura moderna*, Madrid: Alianza.

Mill, J. S. (1971) *The Autobiography*, Oxford: Oxford University Press.

Miller, K. (2001) *Karl Marx's Concept of Time: its Validity for Contemporary Historical Interpretation*, Bentley, WA: Curtin University of Technology.

Montes, L. (2004) *Adam Smith in Context: a Critical Reassessment of some Central Components of His Thought*, New York: Palgrave Macmillan.

Mossner, E. C. (1980) *The Life of David Hume*, Oxford: Clarendon Press.

Nietzsche, F. (1967) *On the Genealogy of Morals*, New York: Vintage Books.

Otteson, J. (2002) *Adam Smith's Marketplace of Life*, Cambridge: Cambridge University Press.

Pack, S. J. (1991) *Capitalism as a Moral System: Adam Smith's Critique of the Free Market Economy*, Aldershot and Brookfield, VT: Elgar.

—— (1995) 'Theological (and Hence Economic) Implications of Adam Smith's "Principles which Lead and Direct Philosophical Enquiries"', *History of Political Economy* 27 (2): 289–307.

—— and Schliesser, E. (2006) 'Smith's Humean Criticism of Hume's Account of the Origin of Justice', *Journal of the History of Philosophy* 44 (1): 47–63.

Raynor, D. R. (1984) 'Hume's Abstract of Adam Smith's "Theory of Moral Sentiments"', *Journal of History of Philosophy* 22: 51–80.

Read, R. and Richman, K. (eds) (2000) *The New Hume Debate*, London and New York: Routledge.

Reeder, J. (ed.) (1997) *On Moral Sentiments: Contemporary Responses to Adam Smith*, Bristol: Thoemmes Press.

Ricoeur, P. (1984) *Time and Narrative* I, Chicago: University of Chicago Press.

Ross, I. S. (1995) *The Life of Adam Smith*, Oxford: Clarendon Press.

Rothschild, E. (2002) *Economic Sentiments: Adam Smith, Condorcet, and the Enlightenment*, Cambridge, MA: Harvard University Press.

Rotwein, E. (ed.) (1970) *David Hume: Writings on Economics*, Madison, WI: University of Wisconsin Press.

Schliesser, E. (2005) 'Wonder in the Face of Scientific Revolutions: Adam Smith on Newton's "Proof" of Copernicanism', *British Journal History of Philosophy* 13 (4): 697–732.

Scott, W. R. (1992) *Francis Hutcheson: His life, Teaching and Position in the History of Philosophy*, Bristol: Thoemmes Press.

Tasset, J. L. (1995) 'Sobre la simpatía en sentido moral: elementos para una crítica de la razón pasional', *Télos: Revista Iberoamericana de Estudios Utilitaristas* 4 (2): 97–128.

—— (1999), *La ética y las pasiones*, La Coruña: Universidade da Coruña.

Trincado, E. (2000) 'El iusnaturalismo no utilitarista de Adam Smith', *Información Comercial Española* 789: 95–9.

—— (2003a) *Crítica a la doctrina de la utilidad y revisión de las teorías de Hume, Smith y Bentham*, Madrid: UCM.

—— (2003b) 'Adam Smith: crítico del utilitarismo', *Télos: Revista Iberoamericana de Estudios Utilitaristas* 12 (1): 43–62.

—— (2004) 'Equity, Utility and Transaction Costs: On the Origin of Judicial Power in Adam Smith', *Storia del Pensiero Económico* 1: 33–51.

Urrutia, J. (1983) *Economía neoclásica: seducción y verdad*, Madrid: Pirámide.

Vivenza, G. (2001) *Adam Smith and Classics: The Classical Heritage in Adam Smith's Thought*, Oxford: Oxford University Press.

Wilcox, D. J. (1987) *The Measures of Times Past: Pre-Newtonian Chronologies and the Rhetoric of Relative Time*, Chicago: University of Chicago Press.

Wright, J. P. (1983) *The Sceptical Realism of David Hume*, Minneapolis, MN: University of Minnesota Press.

Young, J. T. (1997) *Economics as a Moral Science: The Political Economy of Adam Smith*, Cheltenham: Elgar.

15 Adam Smith's benevolent and self-interested conception of philosophy

Eric Schliesser

> [I]deas are not anyhow and at random produced, there being a certain order and connexion between them, like to that of cause and effect; there are also several combinations of them made in a very regular and artificial manner, which seem like so many instruments in the hand of nature that, being hid as it were behind the scenes, have a secret operation in producing those appearances which are seen on the theatre of the world, being themselves discernible only to the curious eye of the philosopher.
>
> (George Berkeley, *Principles of Human Knowledge*, section 64)

The aim of this chapter is to explain Adam Smith's conception of the role of philosophy and, especially, its relationship to common life (as manifested by politics, religion, public opinion, etc.) and natural philosophy (science). I argue that Smith's response to the traditional problem between philosophy and society, the Socratic Problem, by which I mean that rational and free thought can be curtailed by various social demands, and the newer problem of the separate authority of science over philosophy, Newton's Challenge, is best understood in light of his debate with Rousseau's challenge to the worth of commercial society.

In the first section I argue against claims that Smith's conception of science is Baconian (i.e. about utility) and that he denies that philosophy is an end in itself. The second section outlines Smith's response to the modern success of science. Unlike Berkeley or Hume, he does not try to constrain or reinterpret the claims of science; he adopts a theoretical viewpoint in which the results of science are critically examined and potentially endorsed. In the third section, I explain the dual political role of philosophy for Smith: as an adviser to statesmen, philosophy helps design an equitable, institutional framework; within the polity, philosophy can help vaccinate the citizens against the dangers of religion and factionalism.

The final section analyzes Smith's multi-faceted response to Rousseau. I argue that Smith attacks Rousseau's 'abstract philosophy', especially its advocacy of self-sufficiency. Smith's argument with Rousseau proceeds on at least two levels: one concerns the proper understanding of modern republicanism; the other concerns the proper self-understanding of the theoretical viewpoint. My study undermines popular conceptions of Smith's philosophy, namely those that see Smith as a straightforward defender of a marketplace of morals and political economy (e.g. Otteson 2002). Rather, Smith offers an endorsement of commercial life in part as a *means* to philosophy.

Wonder and admiration of the philosophers

In this section, I argue that Smith offers an anti-Baconian thesis about the origin and use of philosophy. (In Smith's time, 'arts', 'sciences', and 'philosophy' can have wider and more synonymous connotations than in ours, see, e.g., 'Astronomy', II.12, 46. For discussion of this issue, see Buckle 1999: 7–8, although this is focused on Hume's usage.) Moreover, while philosophers may believe that they are different from the ordinary bulk of mankind, according to Smith philosophy is just one trade among many. In the first chapter of the first book of WN, Smith prominently includes 'philosophers' as being part of the division of labor (I.i.9, 21–2); shortly thereafter he derides their 'vanity' to think otherwise. (I.ii.4, 29) Thus, he follows Hume in thinking that philosophy takes place *within* society. (See Hanley 2002, and for a different argument Schliesser 2003.) As Smith argues in 'The History of Astronomy' ('Astronomy'), philosophy arises when 'law has established order and security, and subsistence ceases to be precarious, the curiosity of mankind is increased, and their fears diminished. The leisure which they then enjoy renders them more attentive to the appearance of nature' (III.3, 50). Moreover, Smith's invocation of philosophy as one among many trades and his emphasis on the lack of difference between the 'philosopher and common street porter' (WN I.ii.4, 28) signals at the start of WN that his *theorizing* also applies to the 'trade and occupation' of 'speculation' (I.i.9, 21; on this theme, see Levy 1988, 1992; Peart and Levy 2005).

According to Smith, the philosopher's trade is 'not to do any thing, but to observe every thing'. In that capacity, he argues, philosophers 'are often capable of combining together the powers of the most distant and dissimilar objects' (WN I.i.9, 21). Smith's unskeptical reference to 'powers' is Newtonian;[1] it fits with his general tendency to adopt a Newtonian framework. For example, in his essay, 'Of the External Senses', Smith describes planets as 'masses of motion' (12, 137). I argue elsewhere that in one of his main arguments about the adoption of Copernicanism, Smith tacitly accepts Newton's criteria for evaluating the arguments of the prior community of natural philosophers, even though Newton himself was still willing to use arguments that appeal to the old set of norms ('Astronomy', IV.58, 90–1 and IV.67, 98; Schliesser 2005b). Smith is not trying to avoid discussing Newton's action-at-a-distance;[2] he explains how

Newton's theory implies universal, mutual, simultaneous attraction among the planets and the sun ('Astronomy', IV.67–76, 98–104). Smith realizes that the 'Moon may be conceived as constantly falling towards the Earth', and he freely talks about the 'mutual attraction of the Planets' (IV.67–8, 99; on Newton and Smith, see the pioneering efforts by Montes 2003; see also Montes 2006 and Schliesser 2005a, 2005b).

Many have discerned a skeptical stance in Smith's psychological account of theory acceptance (Cremaschi 1989; Pack 1991: 114; Griswold 1999: chapters 4, 8, and epilogue; Rothschild 2002: 138–40, 229). Certainly the examples of Smith's acceptance of invisible forces are compatible with a kind of 'skeptical realism' that has been attributed to Hume (Wright 1983). But, while this cannot be ruled out, there is a very striking and unappreciated example of Smith's rejection of Humean-style skepticism in the 'Astronomy'. In EHU 4.2.16, Hume treats the unknown source of the nourishment of bread as an example of our 'ignorance of natural powers', that is, how 'nature has kept us at a great distance from all her secrets'. Hume interprets Newton's achievements in general as supporting this view. In *The History of England*, he writes, 'While Newton seemed to draw off the veil from some of the mysteries of nature, he shewed at the same time the imperfections of the mechanical philosophy; and *thereby* restored her ultimate secrets to that obscurity, in which they ever did and ever will remain' (VI, 542; emphasis added). Hume treats Newton's refutation of the mechanical philosophy as decisive evidence for the claim that nature will remain unknowable in principle.[3] (In EHU 4.1.12, Hume also *limits* what will be the 'ultimate causes and principles which we shall ever discover in nature', but in context he hedges his bets a bit.) In the 'Astronomy', Smith carefully circumscribes the 'we' implicit in Hume's bread example. Smith discusses the example *only* as an instance of the difference between the 'bulk of mankind' and 'philosophers'. The former 'seldom had the curiosity to inquire' about how bread is 'converted into flesh and bones', while the latter have tried to find the connecting 'chain' that can explain the 'nourishment of the human body'. Smith treats the example not as a confirmation of a kind of fundamental skepticism about possible knowledge of nature, but rather as a *research problem* not unlike the attempts to 'connect the gravity, elasticity, and even the cohesion of natural bodies, with some of their other qualities' (II.11, 44–5; 'Philosophy is the science of connecting principles of nature', II.12, 45.) So the response to the Humean example shows that for Smith there is *some* distinction between the 'bulk of mankind' and 'philosophers'; it manifests itself in a difference in curiosity. This difference is largely the *effect* of the division of labor; it arises from 'habit, custom and education' (WN I.ii.4, 28–9). By contrast, the eminent scholar Sam Fleischacker claims, '[N]or does Smith ever suggest in his writings that there might be a difference between "common life" beliefs and the views of philosophers, as his friend David Hume had done' (Fleischacker 2004: 15). Without endorsing the 'hunt' for 'esoteric doctrines' in Adam Smith (Fleischacker's target in context), this chapter is, thus, an extended criticism of Fleischacker's position.

According to Smith, sometimes philosophers' trade and ingenuity lead to 'improvements in machinery'; presumably this is due to their ability to combine 'together the powers' of distant objects. No doubt it is this harnessing of nature with technological spin-offs that has led some insightful commentators to attribute to Smith a Baconian understanding of philosophy. (See Berry forthcoming, and the broader view defended in Berry 1997: 53–4ff.) But this is misleading. First, only 'some' of the improvements are said to result from men of speculation; 'many' are due to 'the makers of the machines' (WN I.i.9, 21). Moreover, in TMS the tendency to emphasize the usefulness of the 'abstruser sciences' is explained as a post-facto *rhetorical* response to depreciation of those who have 'no taste for such sublime discoveries'. (Hume's treatment of Newton in 'Of the Middle Station of Life' may be Smith's target.) Of course, the sciences may have *some* use: 'The utility of those sciences, either to the individual or to the public, is not very obvious, and to prove it requires a discussion which is not always very easily comprehended' (IV.2.7, 189). But it is not the main point. The Baconian picture does not fit with Smith's account of the origin of science. Contra, for example, Rousseau, who claims that the sciences were 'born in idleness' (*Discourse on the Sciences and Arts*, Part II.39, OC III, 18), Smith insists it is the unpleasant sentiment of

> Wonder . . . and not any expectation of advantage from its discoveries, is the first principle which prompts mankind to the study of philosophy . . . and they pursue this study for its own sake, as an original pleasure or good in itself, without regarding its tendency to procure them the means of other pleasures.
>
> ('Astronomy', III.3, 51)[4]

For Smith, philosophy is originally aimed at calming the imagination: 'Philosophy . . . endeavours to introduce order into this chaos of jarring and discordant appearances, to allay this tumult of the imagination' (II.12, 45–6).

In WN, when Smith discusses 'natural and moral philosophy' (V.i.f.26, 767–70), he emphasizes, echoing the 'Astronomy', how they both originate in wonder and curiosity (V.i.f.24, 767), and that they appeal to the 'beauty of a systematical arrangement' (V.i.f.25, 768; on the importance of beauty and aesthetic considerations in science and philosophy, see also TMS I.i.4.3, 20, and 'Astronomy' IV.13, 62). He notes that theoretical 'men are fond of paradoxes, and of appearing to understand what surpasses the comprehension of ordinary people' (WN IV.ix.38, 678–9; see also 'Astronomy', IV.33, 75). It is 'admiration' that allows us to applaud the 'intellectual virtues' (TMS I.i.4.3, 20; on 'admiration', see also 'Astronomy' 'Intro'.5–7, 34, and IV.5, 56, etc.; WN IV.ix.38, 678–9; see Schliesser 2005b).[5] Given that philosophy is just one of the trades, his account of admiration fits nicely with the psychology of 'professional' ambition in WN, which is articulated in terms of the desire to emulate and eagerness to gain public admiration (V.i.f.4, 759–60; I.x.b.23–5, 123–4).

Thus, WN, TMS, and 'Astronomy' are all consistent in denying the importance of the Baconian approach to the origin and aims of philosophy. It is not 'utility' or love of gain that prompts and sustains theoretical activity. Rather, love of paradox, wonder, admiration, and beauty are far more important motivational pulls. Moreover, speculative activity is an attempt by certain inquisitive people to set themselves apart from ordinary people. Nevertheless, this is just 'vanity'.

Of course, Smith agrees with Hume (cf. 'The Rise and Progress of the Arts and Sciences') that 'in the progress of society', philosophy becomes a specialist trade, itself 'subdivided into a great number of different branches, each of which affords occupation to a peculiar tribe or class of philosophers' (WN I.i.9, 21–2). In fact, it is only after the 'progress of refinement', that is, at a relatively late stage of civilization, that 'philosophy and rhetorick came into fashion'. Then the 'better sort of people . . . send their children to the schools of philosophers and rhetoricians, in order to be instructed in the fashionable sciences' (WN V.i.f.43, 777). The division of labor that enables the growth of opulence creates conditions that stimulate interest in philosophy, which itself must be cultivated; 'for a long time . . . demand for it' was 'small' (V.i.f.43, 777). Once there is a larger demand for philosophy, this enables the division of labor within philosophy, which, in turn, leads occasionally to improvements in machinery that enhance productivity, the division of labor, and a virtuous cycle of opulence (see C. Smith in Chapter 13 above). All of this is conducive to mark philosophy off as a trade among many within society.

Moreover, for Smith, at least certain kinds of (moral) philosophy are responsive to their environment. The 'Introduction' to Book IV of WN seems to imply that the contents of 'systems' of political economy are the result of diffuse social and temporal factors; they somehow represent the state of 'progress of opulence' (IV Introduction 2, 428). Smith leaves oddly unexplained what factors have influenced *his* theory.

Once specialization has taken place among philosophers, one might wonder how is it possible 'to observe every thing' and combine 'together the powers of the most distant and dissimilar objects'? After all, Smith emphasizes at the start of WN that the division of labor causes us to have very partial views of the whole (WN I.1.2, 14; see Levy 1995; Schliesser 2005a). So, how can philosophers be proper philosophers if they participate in the division of labor? This issue only becomes more pressing if one thinks that philosophy merely represents one's 'progress of opulence'. Given Smith's account of philosophy, what claim can it make to comprehensiveness and truth? Because Smith's own ambitions as a *systematic* philosopher were announced in the last paragraph of the first edition of TMS (1759), and reaffirmed in the 'Advertisement' to the last edition (1790; he wishes to 'continue under the obligation of doing' what he can), we may formulate this as a problem about how Smith understands his own theoretical activity.

Moreover, since Socrates, philosophy's relationship to society is not as unproblematic as Smith seems to suggest. It's not only the philosophers' 'vanity' that causes them to think they are different from the ordinary bulk of mankind: even the most free societies, for example classical Athens, can respond negatively to the activities of philosophers. (This is the conceit behind the dialogue in Section XI of Hume's first Enquiry.) Smith knows this. He writes, for example, that 'in Ancient times some philosophers of the "Italian School"' taught their doctrines to pupils only 'under the seal of the most sacred secrecy, that they might avoid the fury of the people, and not incur the imputation of impiety' ('Astronomy' IV.4, 55–6).[6] The 'schools' of the philosophers 'were not supported by the publick. They were for a long time barely tolerated by it' (WN V.i.f.43, 777). In fact, as Smith indicates (recall TMS IV.2.7, 189), one may think that philosophers' emphasis on the usefulness of their activities is precisely the rhetorical response required by society's disapproval (cf. WN V.i.f.43, 778). Smith taught a regular class on rhetoric while he was a professor at Glasgow; he is aware of its power (Ross 1995: 128ff; for important discussion, see Brown 1994, and Fleischacker 2004: 12–15). So, in the next two sections, I explain Smith's attitude, first, to theorizing, and then to political life.

Smith's account of theorizing[7]

The unexpected success of Newtonian natural philosophy threatened the independent authority of philosophy, especially because from the point of view of the reigning mechanical philosophy, philosophy was unable to justify Newton's methods or offer an account of Newton's success on first principles. For the first time, a naturalism motivated by the empirical success of science becomes respectable. Of course, I am not claiming that there were no earlier forms of naturalisms. But, for example, Aristotle's physicalism was motivated by first principles (see *Metaphysics* E.1.1026a27–9). Berkeley and Hume try to re-establish the authority of metaphysics over natural philosophy, by constraining the claims of science or reinterpreting its language. For Berkeley and Hume, scientific theories are very sophisticated tools to make predictions, the interpretation of which is subservient to philosophic considerations. But they cannot do justice to the content and attractiveness of Newton's natural philosophy (see Schliesser 2004, n.d. a, b). As argued above, Smith accepts the Newtonian framework. In this section, I explain Smith's conception of the theoretical viewpoint in response to the success of natural philosophy, and how it connects with common life.

The social and discursive element of science

Smith's moral psychology turns on the idea that people are naturally social animals; from a very early age they are judged by others and once they become aware of this they, in turn, judge the people in their environment and *themselves* (TMS III.i.2–6, 109–13). This is facilitated by the process of sympathy – the mechanism of the imagination by which we have fellow feeling with the passions of others (III.1.2, 109 and I.1.1.5, 10; see Griswold 1999: chapter 2; Otteson 2002: chapters 2–3). Smith thinks people desire praise from others and, more important, they want to understand their own behavior as praiseworthy (III.ii, 113–34). In all professions 'rivalry and emulation will render excellency ... an object of ambition, and frequently occasion the very greatest exertions' (WN V.i.f.4, 759–60). The upshot of Smith's complex developmental account is that all people, including philosophers, routinely desire and seek approval from others and this is the source of our vanity, our ambition, and our morality. Philosophers may be motivated by desire for fame (TMS III.2.8, 117; D'Alembert 1995: 93, also has no doubt about this. For more on love and friendship as reward for virtue, see Cropsey 1957: 51–2; Uyl and Griswold 1996; Brubaker 2003; Schliesser 2003). Smith claims that we behave in ways for which we expect to be applauded or approved of by others (III.i.5, 112). As we grow up, we internalize the values and expectations of our community, or public opinion. We behave as though we are watched and judged by an 'Impartial Spectator'. While emphasizing the importance of imagination, Smith writes '[w]e must, here, as in all other cases, view ourselves ... as according to that in which we naturally appear to others' (TMS II.ii.2.1, 83). Smith is not naïve: He thinks that in general 'we are all naturally disposed to over-rate the excellencies of our own character' (III.2.34, 133). Smith is aware of the dangers of 'self-deceit, this fatal weakness of mankind' (III.4.6, 158; see Gerschlager 2002).

The imagined 'awful and respectable judge' within can help us correct the standards of our community when we desire to be *praiseworthy* (III.2.24–30, 126–8). This desire, based on our natural desire for mutual sympathy and the natural love of virtue, is the crucial step in Smith's theory. (See Hanley (forthcoming) for an excellent treatment.) The source of this desire – that the approval we receive is deserved – Smith locates in the fundamental epistemic *uncertainty* that each of us has about our *own* judgments (TMS III.2.24, III.2.28, 126–7, and 'Astronomy', II.4, 40). Our desire for the right kind of approval originates in our recognition of the fallibility of first-person authority. Smith's philosophy departs from the confidence of the Cartesian ego. One reason for this is the difficulty in applying the correct standard of evaluation to ourselves, and the ease with which our moral sentiments are corrupted (e.g. TMS I.iii.iii, and my treatment of TMS VI.iii.23–6, 247–8, below). Learning to see oneself in a proper light is itself a cultural and intellectual *achievement* for Smith, available to only few of us (TMS III.2.8, 117).

Thus, our imagination is not only the source of our creativity in constructing scientific systems but also the source of our potential impartiality in evaluating them. Smith's account explains how individuals have internalized – through various means of socialization and education – an idealized and correctible version of the values and expectations of the communities they belong to.

If one is a member of a community with fairly exact and clear standards and one's actions accord with those values, the need for overt public approval diminishes because one feels a sense of self-approval and security in one's behavior; one knows, as Smith thought 'possible' of Newton, that one is praiseworthy even in the absence of public praise – the mind is tranquil in its 'independency' (TMS III.2.20, 12; cf. III.3.30–3, 149–52).

Smith believes that success in mathematics and natural philosophy admits 'either of clear demonstration, or very satisfactory proof' (III.2.18, 123; IV.2.7, 189). Once mathematicians and natural philosophers have internalized the criteria and methods of 'clear demonstration, or very satisfactory proof' valued by their disciplines, they need not worry about public opinion because they have already adopted the perspective of the Impartial Spectator. Smith does not think that mathematicians or natural philosophers are better at internalizing norms than others; there are just clear standards in these fields.

But sometimes there are competing standards: for example, in the 'Astronomy', Smith points out that the Copernican system was accepted by 'astronomers only', but that the 'learned in all other sciences, continued to regard it with the same contempt as the vulgar' (IV.36, 77).[8] Smith thinks that 'the coherence, which it bestowed upon the celestial appearances, the simplicity and uniformity which it introduced into the real directions and velocities of the Planets' attracted the astronomers to the Copernican system which 'thus connected together so happily, the most disjointed of those objects that chiefly occupied their thoughts'. Meanwhile, philosophers concerned with local terrestrial motion dreamed up objections against it (IV.38, 77–9). This delayed the adoption of the Copernican hypothesis. So, a focus on different domains of study can lead different groups of experts to embrace different standards of evidence and systems (see Skinner 1996: 44). Smith acknowledges that sometimes the *better* theory *need not* gain such acceptance among non-specialists and the 'vulgar' ('Astronomy' IV.35–8, 76–8), who, for example, exhibit the 'prejudice of mankind' and the 'prejudice of sense, confirmed by education' against Copernicanism. Philosophers are vulnerable to the 'prejudices' of the vulgar; when 'natural', they could even corrupt the thinking of Aristotle, the most 'renowned philosopher' ('Ancient Physics' 10, 116).

Smith does not ignore the situation in which natural philosophers, such as Descartes, Galileo, or Newton, attempt to change or legislate new criteria for a scientific community. He is mindful of the existence of those scientific legislators:

> It is the acute and delicate discernment of the man of taste, who distinguishes the minute, and scarce perceptible difference of beauty and deformity; it is the comprehensive accuracy of the experienced *mathematician*, who unravels, with ease, the most intricate and perplexed proportions; *it is the great leader in science and taste, the man who directs and conducts our own sentiments*, the extent and superior justness of whose talents astonish us with wonder and surprise, who excites our admiration, and seems to deserve our applause: and upon this foundation is grounded the greater part of the praise which is bestowed upon what are called the intellectual virtues.
>
> (TMS I.i.4.3, 20; emphasis added)

Smith ties together the scientific legislator's ability to solve problems, introduce criteria and gain admiration from others. The 'great leader in science' is no mere problem solver or theory constructer; he understands existing norms in a fundamental way. Smith also implies that 'the leader . . . who *directs* and conducts our own sentiments' sets *standards* for others to emulate.[9] Some great scientists do not merely conform to existing values, but introduce new standards. He describes them as 'splendid characters, the men who have performed the most illustrious actions, who have brought about the greatest revolutions, both in situations and opinions of mankind' (TMS VI.iii.28, 250). So, when a natural philosopher contemplates and presents his results, this involves reference to the norms of his community: the Impartial Spectator within anticipates how a scientist's (idealized) audience will judge a new theory, and provides 'self-approbation' (TMS III.2.3, 114) and tranquillity ('Astronomy', IV.13, 61). Of course, when a natural philosopher proposes changes to the standards of a community, then such tranquillity can be expected only if one imagines that the Impartial Spectator will eventually approve of one's improvements; sometimes one's imagination will project such approbation on to posterity (TMS I.iii.1.14, 48–9 and VI.iii.5, 238–9). Moreover, there are two kinds of standards by which one judges one's efforts:

> The one is the idea of exact propriety and perfection, so far as we are each of us capable of comprehending that idea. The other is that degree of approximation to this idea which is commonly attained in the world, and which the greater part of our friends and companions, of our rivals and competitors, may have actually arrived at. We very seldom (I am disposed to think, we never) attempt to judge of ourselves without giving more or less attention to both these different

> standards ... In all the liberal and ingenious arts, in painting, in poetry, in music, in eloquence, in philosophy, the greatest artist feels always the real imperfection of his own best works, and is more sensible than any man how much they fall short of that ideal perfection of which he has some conception, which he imitates as well as he can, but which he despairs of ever equalling ... [Boileau said] no great man was ever completely satisfied with his own works.
>
> (TMS VI.iii.23–6, 247–8)

Hence, on Smith's account the great scientist is satisfied only when he (momentarily) compares his own work to that of his peers, that is, when he directs his attention toward the second standard. The first standard can always inspire critical reflection. Nevertheless, Smith's theory does not say what the source of this 'idea of exact propriety and perfection' is; he merely assumes that *all* individuals, or the sub-cultures they belong to, have access to *some* such notion. (He may have thought the problem was solved in Hume's *Treatise*, 1.2.4.24–5.)[10] But Smith's claim that we sometimes judge our own and other people's efforts by a standard of exact propriety and perfection is not sufficiently appreciated by those who worry where in Smith's moral psychology or epistemology a *critical* stance can be developed.[11] For Smith, 'real imperfection' is present in all of Man's works, so there will always be room for criticism (see also TMS I.i.5.8, 25). This is the source of Smith's commitment to fallibilism.

In fact, the possibility of criticism is crucial to understanding Smith's conception of science and the philosopher's stance toward it. Smith calls attention to how natural philosophy is a discursive practice offering reasons to adopt a theory. ('Of the External Senses', 12, 137; see also Wightman 1975: 61. For the general importance of persuasion in Smith's thought, see Fleischacker 2004, 92–4.) This resembles how Smith treats the moral deliberation of our Impartial Spectator when, say, we attempt to act with self-command and propriety. This is why he often represents it as a 'voice' of 'reason' (TMS III.3.4, 137). Maria Carrasco (2004: 84–9) notes perceptively that Smith distinguishes between our 'natural feelings' and our *cultivated* discipline over these. She has argued that TMS can, thus, be interpreted, despite the language of sentiments and the opposition to rationalism in ethics, as a system of *practical* reason. (See also the important analysis of Montes 2004: chapters 2–4.) Among such *reasons* Smith identifies within natural philosophy are simplicity, distinctness, comprehensibility, lack of reasonable competitors and accounting for the phenomena ('Of the External Senses', 18, 140; 'Astronomy', IV.15, 63–4). Smith often adopts a realist stance. For example, he describes the adoption of Copernicanism in realist terms ('Astronomy' IV.35, 76–7); singles out Newton's ability to calculate the weights and densities of the sun and planets for special praise (IV.75, 103); and is impressed by Newton's amazing prediction that a mutual attraction between Jupiter and Saturn would be strong enough to perturb their orbits when near conjunction (IV.68, 99).

According to Smith, theory acceptance in natural philosophy is not driven merely by arbitrary appeals to the passions and sentiments. (For a similar conclusion, but with a different argument, see Skinner 1996: 41.) Natural philosophy is an ongoing conversation with appeals to the intellectual judgments of the participants. (See Fleischacker 1999 for the important role of judgment in Smith.) There is no inconsistency in considering the reigning scientific theory 'either exactly or very nearly true', as Newton writes in his fourth rule of reasoning, while holding a historically and psychologically sensitive theory about the development and acceptance of scientific theories.

Smith is in awe of the scope and predictive success of Newton's principled, physically plausible, beautiful, consistent, empirically adequate, and coherent theory (TMS III.2.20–2, 124–5). But Newton's account need not be the last word; according to Smith's psychology, informed by his historical research, once people are accustomed to Newton's theory, there is always the possibility that flaws or irregularities will be found in its connecting principles by a suitably sensitive inquirer, or that people's inquisitive ambition and vanity will lead them to discover new phenomena (see also Cropsey 1957: 46). It need not be a finished system with unalterable principles (as Descartes promised), but an important step in an ongoing research project (see Smith's discussion of the 'imperfect notions' in Newton's 'system of the universe' at 'Of the External Senses', 12, 137). Smith's views are very Newtonian. In the *Principia*, Newton expressed the hope that 'the principles set down here will shed some light on either this mode of philosophizing *or some truer one*' ('Author's Preface to the Reader'; emphasis added; see Montes 2006). This, together with the fact that new or better observations can be made, perhaps aided by technological developments,[12] implies that 'Newton's empire' need not last for ever. There will be new reasons for wonder.

So, at first sight it seems that Smith agrees with Aristotle that philosophy starts in wonder and ends in dogmatism.[13] Smith suggests that Aristotle captures a major aim of inquiry of philosophers – they want their minds to be tranquil. Smith teaches that true philosophers will find this goal elusive; the open-ended nature of inquiry means that every theory can be the beginning of a new inquiry. Philosophy is an open-ended enterprise. Smith agrees with Plato (Stein 1988 and forthcoming; for Platonism in Smith, see Griswold 1999 and Schliesser 2003). Philosophy begins in wonder, deepens our understanding, and ends, not in so-called 'Humean despair' (Quine 1969), but in wonder.

Common life and philosophy

Smith emphasizes how far removed from common sense the contents of highly successful scientific theories *can* be: the Copernican hypothesis means that Earth and the planets are traveling with 'a rapidity that almost passes all human comprehension' ('Of the External Senses', 12, 137). Smith distinguishes how different subgroups of the learned and the 'vulgar' can react to theories. (Astronomy, IV.36, 77) Smith agrees that widespread acceptance of scientific theories is possible, but he is also clear that prejudices of common life can prevent better theories from gaining acceptance even among the learned.

Moreover, Smith's narrative in the 'Astronomy' exhibits that the norms of acceptance of a theory in the astronomical community can evolve and diverge from those of the wider public; coherence, predictive power, (etc.) are factors, but in the course of successive 'revolutions' of systems, this list can be expanded. Even before his discussion of Copernicus, Smith shows that criteria of theory acceptance can change. One innovation in astronomy is the demand for a physical explanation of the phenomena. For example, Regiomontanus and Purbach tried to combine Aristotelian physics with Ptolemaic astronomy ('Astronomy', IV.25–6, 69–71); the same occurred when Newton offered a 'physical account' beyond merely aesthetic considerations (IV.67, 97–8).

Simplicity, distinctness, comprehensibility, lack of reasonable competitors, and accounting for the phenomena do not exhaust the reasons for accepting a theory; in the 'Astronomy', Smith writes,

> For, though it is the end of Philosophy, to allay that wonder, which either the unusual or seemingly disjointed appearances of nature excite, yet she never triumphs so much, as when, in order to connect together a few, in themselves, perhaps, inconsiderable objects, she has, if I may so, created another constitution of things, more easily attended to, but more new, more contrary to common opinion and expectation, than any of those appearances themselves.
>
> (IV.33, 75)

Smith is claiming that it is a mark of a successful theory that it is unexpected, even surprising. (See also the comments on Reamur's *History of Insects* in his 'Letter to the *Edinburgh Review*', 9, 249). While Hume had castigated the greedy embrace by philosophers of theories that have 'the air of a paradox', who are, thereby, distancing themselves from the 'unprejudiced notions of mankind' (Treatise, 1.2.1.1), Smith does not criticize these 'triumphs'. Smith is aware that when one is confronted by a beautiful and magnificent system, such as Newton's in his day, even 'the most skeptical cannot avoid feeling' that its principles have a 'degree of firmness and solidity' that make it seem senseless to look for another system ('Astronomy', IV.76, 105). Yet such a theory, almost 'another constitution of things', will almost certainly create a feeling of wonder and surprise, which may induce reflections on its metaphysical or conceptual foundations and perhaps spur on the development of new theories.

Nevertheless, for Smith, satisfying evaluative criteria adopted by a present or future community of inquirers (cf. TMS III.2.20–2, 124–5) can provide one with public reasons to reject the assumptions of everyday life. By contrast, when discussing the relative merits of moral theories, he claims the expert may reject common sense, but the cost (in persecution, disbelief, rejection, satire, etc.) may be high: 'the author who should assign, as the cause of any natural sentiment, some principle which neither had any connexion with it, nor resembled any other principle which had some such connexion, would appear absurd and ridiculous to the most injudicious and unexperienced reader' (TMS VII.ii.4.14, 314–15). The context suggests that Smith can imagine that an account could be dreamed up by a judicious and experienced reader that would explain human behavior in terms that are unfamiliar to people. Yet, such an account would receive a hostile reception. While theories of natural philosophy can create 'another constitution of things ... contrary to common opinion' ('Astronomy', IV.33, 75) this is not the case in moral philosophy. An account of moral life that is phrased in familiar terms can gain approval as long as it has *some* truth. This is why Smith often sounds like a so-called 'common-sense philosopher' when discussing moral philosophy (WN V.f.26, 769; see Fleischacker 2004: 22).

So, on Smith's account what I call the Socratic Problem can arise in natural and moral philosophy. Yet, while moral philosophy must make concessions to the sensibility of common life, natural philosophy can triumph by opposing it. Of course, the conflict between the vulgar and the astronomers over the Copernican hypothesis is, as the trial of Galileo demonstrates, not always without dangers. Yet, *once* one truly understands the arguments and evidential force of Newton's theory (that is, experience the world through it), it, too, must be *felt* to be true; (nearly) 'proven' (recall TMS III.2.18, 123). This is why Smith can speak of empirical events confirming Newton's theory ('Astronomy', IV.72, 101). It can become part of common sense, even if Smith believes that common sense is quite rare; in fact, if common sense were more common, then more people would be able to prevent their vanity from being the foundation of various vices (TMS III.2.4, 115). From the theoretical viewpoint, Newton has made gravity into a 'familiar principle of connection' ('Astronomy', IV.76, 105). For Smith even common sense, and its 'natural prejudice' ('Astronomy', IV.37–8, 77ff. and 'Ancient Physics', 10, 116) can be corrected by discoveries in natural philosophy (cf. TMS III.3.2, 135 and, for a different view, VII.iii.intro.3, 315). As an informed judge, Smith cannot avoid adopting Newton's framework when he evaluates the claims of earlier generations of astronomers and philosophers, especially those of the seventeenth century (e.g. the treatment of Descartes's vortices at TMS VII.ii.4.14, 313 or Descartes's unwillingness to provide a useful, systematic account of how empirical observations can deviate from predictions at 'Astronomy', IV.66, 97). In the same passage, Smith criticizes Descartes's standards that were widely accepted in the seventeenth century, even by Newton prior to writing the *Principia* (although not by Kepler). In effect, Newton showed that one need not rest content with Descartes's criteria.

Nevertheless, Smith does not uncritically adopt Newton's positions. In 'Astronomy' IV.58, 90–1, he criticizes Newton for considering what Smith takes to be a bad argument. And at 'Of the External Senses', 12, 137, Smith tacitly adopts Newton's theoretical framework in talking of 'masses in motion', while making a distinction between those teachings of philosophy 'to which it is scarcely possible to refuse our assent' and those 'imperfect notions' in Newton's 'system of the universe'. In 'Astronomy' IV.58, 90–1, Smith accepts that Newton has given a new and improved set of criteria, even though Newton himself was still willing to use arguments that appeal to the old set of norms. In 'Astronomy', Smith tacitly adopts the stance of an Impartial Spectator when he discusses the impact of Copernicus. He appeals to criteria that Newton introduced into the practice of theorizing about astronomy, criteria that were not accepted by earlier generations of astronomers.

So, the theoretical viewpoint involves a willingness to be persuaded by the reasons and evidence supporting leading theories in natural philosophy. Smith does not try to constrain or reinterpret Newton's theory. Yet, this does not mean he has to be uncritical in his acceptance. Precisely by thinking through and adopting the new norms implicit in Newton's framework, he can offer responsible criticism and suggest revision from within or in light of the idea of perfection. While philosophy cannot rule over science, sophisticated naturalism need not be the end of serious reflection. Moreover, Smith's philosophy teaches the thoughtful inquirer that there is a political dimension to the *origins and reception* of natural and moral philosophy.

Politics and philosophy

In the first few pages of WN, Smith makes a distinction between the opinions of 'men of learning' and those of 'princes' (WN 'Introduction', 8, 11). The latter are said to influence 'public conduct', while the former can probably influence public opinion or the views of princes/statesmen. Theories not only attempt to explain and predict economic behavior, but through the actions of rulers also deliberately or unintentionally influence it. Thus, they run the risk, for example, of becoming self-fulfilling prophecies. Smith may also be signaling a contrast between the opinions of the 'men of learning' and the public conduct of 'princes'.

Theories of political economy may have originated in 'private interests and prejudices of particular orders' of men, although, as always, Smith is careful to phrase it in such a way (he uses 'perhaps') as to allow for other sources of motivation. Moreover, in context, Smith *seems* to be implying that, *once* such theories are around, they can be formulated and proposed with regard to 'the general welfare of the society' (WN 'Introduction', 8, 11).

In fact, it would be *proper* for both 'men of learning' and 'princes' to have this general welfare in mind. For 'The most sublime speculation of the contemplative philosopher can scarce compensate the neglect of the smallest active duty' (TMS VI.2.3.6, 237). In contrast to those who read this as Smith's rejection of the theoretical life (Cropsey, Griswold), I read it as an injunction for philosophers not to ignore their moral obligations nor to reject the theoretical life altogether. In contrast to the 'man of system', who is 'very wise in his own conceit' (TMS VI.ii.2.17, 233), Smith writes approvingly of the 'man whose public spirit is prompted altogether by humanity and benevolence' (TMS VI.ii.2.16, 233; Haakonssen 1981). Given the division of labor, not all philosophers will fit the bill: 'their great abilities, though honourable to themselves, may contribute very little to the good government or happiness of their society' (WN V.i.f.51, 783).

It is a good thing, too, that the (proper) philosopher is motivated by this general welfare (Schliesser 2003). For according to Smith a modern society is composed of three main classes: landowners, workers, and merchants (WN I.vi.17–19, 69–70; I.xi.p.7, 265). Except in new colonies, there is an inherent conflict over resources between the wage-earning laborers and the profit-oriented merchants (I.viii.11, 83, and I.xi.p.8–10, 265–7). Unfortunately, the two 'orders' of society, whose private interest are 'strictly and inseparably connected with the general interest of the society', that is, the landowners and the wage earners, are usually (in the case of the former), if not always (in the case of the latter), unable to 'foresee and understand the consequences of any public regulation' (I.xi.p.8–9, 265–6). Because of this failure, the merchant classes are able to capture the political process and turn it to their advantage (e.g. IV.iii.c.9, 493; I.x.c.61, 157–8). The 'humane and benevolent' political philosopher is required to save society from the narrow interests of the profit-earning class! What is required is an 'extensive view of the general good' (IV.ii.44, 472). Adopting the extensive view is suitable for philosophers, who, after all, 'observe every thing'.

Smith's own activity as a *political* advocate of reform of institutions (Rosenberg 1960; Fleischacker 2004, 242–6; Schliesser 2005a) and educator of princes[14] is not only intelligible but, thus, also necessary in light of the moral psychology implicit in WN. WN's existence as a work of political philosophy, in service of the working poor, presupposes a commitment to a certain kind of public benevolence and humanity. Moreover, while in market relations when we address ourselves to, say, butchers, brewers, or bakers we appeal not to their 'humanity, but to their self-love, and never talk of our own necessities but of their advantages' (I.ii.2, 27, although, 'beggars' *do* depend to a large degree on 'benevolence'), when we design and evaluate our social and political institutions, we appeal to 'equity' (WN I.viii.36, 96, V.ii.k.45, 888–9 and V.ii.k.55, 893), 'humanity', and 'reasonableness' (e.g. WN V.ii.e.6, 842; V.ii.e.19; 846, I.viii.36, 96; I.viii.44, 100, etc.; cf. Smith's outrage at the 'folly and injustice' of European colonists at IV.vii.b.59, 588).

Theoretical advice to princes and legislators about the institutions of society does not exhaust philosophy's role. For Smith argues that a wise legislator must create and enforce various incentives to stimulate mandatory education of the young in philosophy (V.i.9.14, 796 and V.i.f.50–6, 781–6). Presumably, this would teach future citizens the rudiments of mathematics and orderly views of nature. Given the epistemic demands of measuring propriety (TMS I.i.3, 16–19; see Forman-Barzilai, this volume), this may well be required for the proper functioning of morality. While Smith hopes that such education would lend genuine stability to government (V.f.61, 788), he also recommends public 'diversions' (e.g. 'painting, poetry, musick, dancing' and 'all sorts of dramatic representations and exhibitions') to 'amuse' people's minds and make political and religious fanatics the objects of 'ridicule' (WN, V.i.g.15, 796–7). Thus, for Smith, philosophy can play some role in an Enlightenment project against religious enthusiasm (Schliesser 2003) and support public order. Smith is not an optimist about this because he is aware that 'the private' and 'publick morals of the Romans' were superior to those found in the philosophy-rich Greek city-states with their musical education (WN V.i.f.39–40, 776–7; Smith is especially concerned with dangers of fanaticism and factionalism here).

One may think the Socratic Problem is solved when society sees that philosophy serves its needs, and philosophy becomes subservient to society's goals. Yet, it would be strange to attribute this position to Smith because it recapitulates too nicely what he describes as a rhetorical stance against those that depreciate philosophy. In the next section, I argue that, for Smith, concern with the general welfare of society is justified, at least in part, because it unintentionally serves the needs of philosophy. This is clear in light of Smith's response to Rousseau's criticism of the worth of commercial society.

Smith's response to Rousseau

Smith's earliest (1755/56) publication, 'Letter to the Authors of the *Edinburgh Review*' ('Edinburgh Review'), is a review of European intellectual achievements, especially in natural philosophy, with a special emphasis on different national styles. (See Lomonaco 2002 for an important introduction to it.) But the last third of the piece is devoted to Rousseau's *Second Discourse* – then recently published. Smith praises Rousseau's eloquence, but refrains from giving an analysis of his arguments because he claims that is impossible of a work 'which consists almost entirely of rhetoric and description' (12, 251).[15]

In 'Edinburgh Review', Smith includes translations of three lengthy passages of Rousseau's work (13–15, 251–4). In the first of these passages,

Rousseau discusses the 'healthful, humane, and happy' condition of men in their 'rustic habitations'. Rousseau then goes on to describe how from the moment the division of labor was introduced and when one person could see the advantage of having provision for two (or more) people, 'equality disappeared, property was introduced, labour became necessary ... the world beheld slavery and wretchedness begin to grow up and blossom with the harvest (13, 251–2; cf. *Second Discourse*, Part II.19, OC III, 171. Pack 2000: 52 n. 25 points out that Rousseau is more concerned about the physical effects of the division of labor while Smith is more worried about the psychological effects; WN V.i.f.50, 781).

In the second passage, Rousseau describes how, after the development of property and inequality, and the start of commerce more generally, men must only *appear* advantageous to each other. The new needs stimulated by 'insatiable ambition' and secret jealousy cause people to 'often assume masks to each other'. While in the state of nature, man is 'free', civilized man is a 'slave' to nature, and 'above all his fellow creatures'. Rousseau emphasizes the *falseness* of commercial life: 'To be and to appear to be, became two things very different' (14, 252–3; cf. *Second Discourse*, Part II.27, OC III, 174–5).

In the third and longest translated passage, Rousseau contrasts the 'liberty and repose', even beyond the 'ataraxia of the Stoic', of the self-sufficient savage who 'lives in himself' in the state of nature with the never-ending harmful efforts of 'employments' for the 'citizen' in society, who is also engaged in demeaning flattery of his superiors. Civilized man desires 'power and reputation' because he 'lives in the opinion of others', but he ends up with a 'deceitful and frivolous exterior'. Commercial society encourages the discovery and continued importance of 'being vain' (15, 253). Commercial life is, thus, incompatible with true virtue, wisdom, and happiness (15, 254; *Second Discourse*, Part II.57, OC III, 192–3; see Dent 1988: 55ff. for discussion).

Smith leaves unexplained why he chooses these three particular passages. But with the advantage of hindsight, we can see that all three resonate with themes that Smith pursues in his published works later in his life. It is clear, however, that Smith finds Rousseau's description of life in the state of nature one-sided: 'Mr Rousseau, intending to paint savage life as the happiest of any, presents only the indolent side to view.' According to Smith, Rousseau leaves out the 'most dangerous and extravagant adventures' (12, 251; Smith's main criticism of other moral philosophers is precisely that their systems are also 'derived from a partial and imperfect view of nature' (TMS VI.i.1, 265), see Schliesser 2006). While, strictly speaking, this may be accurate, Smith's criticism is a bit unfair. Smith ignores that, for Rousseau, it is the dangers and obstacles that man is exposed to *in* the state of nature that start the chain of events that not only lead men to discover the benefits of technology and comforts of clothing but also create the circumstances that first produce pride in men (*Second Discourse*, Part

II.3–6, OC III, 165–6). There is more Hobbes in Rousseau than Smith *acknowledges.*

Nevertheless, Smith praises Rousseau's rhetorical abilities: 'tho' laboured and studiously elegant . . . [Rousseau's prose is] every where sufficiently nervous, and sometimes even sublime and pathetic' (12, 251).[16] Elsewhere, by contrast, Mandeville's 'eloquence' is described as 'lively and humorous, though coarse and rustic' (TMS, VII.ii.4.6, 308; also VII.ii.4.11, 312: 'The ingenious sophistry of [Mandeville's] reasoning, is . . . covered by the ambiguity of language.') As a way of containing Rousseau's ideas, Smith produces his own rhetorical summary: 'It is by the help of this style, together with a little philosophic chemistry, that the principles and ideas of the profligate Mandeville seem to have the purity and sublimity of the morals of Plato, and to be only the true spirit of a republican carried a little too far' ('Edinburgh Review', 12, 251; see Livingston 1998 on 'philosophic chemistry', although he does not mention Smith). Smith charges that Rousseau is not only somewhat of an extremist in his political convictions (notice that 'little too far'!) but also that, despite contrary appearances ('seem'), Rousseau is at bottom in the same boat as the 'profligate' and scandalous Mandeville – an attempt to convict Rousseau through guilt by association! In an ironic twist, Smith attacks Rousseau's *false* appearances. After all, for Rousseau 'unmasking' was an important activity (Starobinski 1988; see also the second passage that Smith translates from the *Second Discourse* at 'Edinburgh Review', 14, 253).[17]

In Smith's diagnosis, Rousseau and Mandeville share four important features. First, *against* the reaction to Hobbes popular among thinkers such as Grotius, Puffendorf, and Hutcheson, both suppose 'that there is in man no powerful instinct which necessarily determines him to seek society for its own sake'. Second, they suppose the 'same slow progress and gradual developments of all the talents, habits, and arts which fit men to live together in society, and they both describe [it] . . . in the same manner'. (On Mandeville and unintended order explanations see Heath 1998.) Moreover, according to both, 'those laws of justice, which maintain the present inequality amongst mankind, were originally the inventions of the cunning and the powerful, in order to maintain or to acquire an unnatural and unjust superiority over the rest of their fellow-creatures'. Finally, they agree that pity 'is possessed by savages and by the most profligate of the vulgar, in a greater degree of perfection than by those of the most polished and cultivated manners' (11, 250–1).

However, Smith does not gloss over their differences; he recognizes that Rousseau is a fierce critic of Mandeville. Smith singles out the importance, for Rousseau, of pity in producing the virtues. This is perceptive, given how important pity will be in Rousseau's later works (Dent 1988: chapter 4). It is, however, unclear from *Edinburgh Review* where Smith stands.[18] Unfortunately, it would be almost the last time that Smith ever commented on Rousseau in print; in 'Considerations Concerning the First

Formations of Languages', he discusses only Rousseau's views on language (2, 205 of LRBL; see also Lecture 3 of LRBL; Pack 2000: 48; Otteson 2002: 263–5).

I am not the first to observe important similarities between the views of Smith and Rousseau (Force 2003). Smith notes that Mandeville and Rousseau both ascribe the origin of the laws of justice to 'the inventions of the cunning and the powerful' ('Edinburgh Review', 11, 251). Smith's account in WN of the origin of justice makes clear that he, too, thinks that 'Civil government, so far as it is instituted for the security of property, is in reality instituted for the defence of the rich against the poor, or of those who have some property against those who have none at all' (WN V.i.b.12, 715; V.i.b.3, 710; see Schliesser 2005a; Schliesser and Pack 2006). Smith also accepts that there is 'gradual' development of civilizations (e.g. I.xi.g.19, 218) and he agrees that the desire for society is result of socialization (TMS III.i.2–6, 109–13).

Moreover, Smith and Rousseau agree that wealth alone never leads to 'real satisfaction' (TMS IV.1.8, 181; cf. *Second Discourse*, Note IX, 3, OC III, 203). Rousseau and Smith are aware that once our desires are stimulated and cultivated they can become limitless. Throughout TMS, Smith insists that, while we may prefer to be rich in order to be admired (I.iii.2.1, 50ff.), wealth does not lead to happiness, instead 'the chief part of human happiness arises from the consciousness of being beloved' (I.ii.5.1, 41; at III.i.7, 113, Smith adds that we also want to feel that we deserve to be beloved). Rousseau would not disagree with this, but he would claim that the *need* for being beloved only arises once man has moved out of the state of nature; once in society, he 'cannot live but in the opinion of others' ('Edinburgh Review', 15, 253; *Second Discourse*, Part II.57, OC III, 193). So, while Smith can claim that 'what can be added to the happiness of the man who is in health, who is out of debt, and has a clear conscience' (TMS, I.iii.I.7, 45), Rousseau writes, while speaking about a man in a state of nature, 'what kind of misery' can there be 'for a free being, whose heart is at peace, and body in health' (*Second Discourse*, Part I.33, OC III, 152). The mention of debt makes it clear that Smith is only speaking of man as found in a society in which at least *some* commercial relations have already been developed.

In commercial society, genuine freedom, as Rousseau understands it in the *Second Discourse*, that is, independence in the form of 'self-sufficiency', is impossible. It is no surprise, then, that Smith makes no mention of it.[19] Rather, against Rousseau's extremist 'republican' emphasis on self-sufficiency, Smith follows Hume's suggestion of advocating a different form of 'independence': one that emphasizes our mutual *interdependence* (Berry 1989; Schliesser 2003). This is the main point of the context of the oft-quoted beggar/butcher/baker/brewer passage at WN I.ii.2, 25–7: 'In civilized society [Man] stands at all times in need of the cooperation and assistance of great multitudes.'

Thus, from his earliest writings, Smith sees that Rousseau provides a rhetorical challenge to the worth of commercial society. In the name of freedom, Rousseau indicts commercial life for fostering falseness and masking, while suggesting that self-sufficiency is to be preferred over what we may call the 'interdependent independence', which is presupposed and supported by commercial life. In this context, Smith's commendation of Rousseau's dedication to the 'republic of Geneva' as a 'just panegyric' ('Edinburgh Review', 16, 254) takes on new importance. Smith leaves enough ambiguity to leave it undecided if its justness is due to the fact that Rousseau is a 'good citizen' (16, 254), indicating that Smith believes that proper expression of patriotism is an important (prudent) virtue in a philosopher (in light of the Socratic Problem), or that Smith is endorsing Geneva-style republicanism here; the two are not mutually exclusive, of course (cf. Pack 2000: 44).

Following Hume, Smith's response to Rousseau (and Mandeville) involves his well known defense of the morality of the pursuit of self-interest (TMS VII.2.4.12, 312; see Otteson 2002). But it also involves recognition of the political nature of the existence of markets in modern society. (This is not to deny that Smith thinks that *some* barter and exchange can take place in the state of nature; WN I.ii.1, 25.) Smith's insistence in the butcher, brewer, baker passage that even beggars do not chiefly rely on the 'benevolence' of their '*fellow-citizens*' (WN I.ii.2, 27; emphasis added) is not an innocent phrase. Evidently, the beggar and the tradesman do not merely relate to *each other* (Fleischacker 2004: 91) as self-interested, interdependent merchants (WN I.iv.1, 37; Berry 1989: 114ff.) or consumers (WN IV.viii.49, 660). There is also a *political* dimension. Our modern forms of exchange take place in a political context, as the discussion of taxation also suggests: 'Every tax, however, is to the person who pays it a badge, not of slavery, but of liberty' (V.ii.b.3, 825). Our freedom is bound up with our membership in political society.

Smith's moderate political philosophy corrects Rousseau's extremist republicanism (recall 'Edinburgh Review', 12, 251). it is one that rejects freedom based on the slavery of the ancients, the virtues of self-sufficiency, agrarianism, and the public-spiritedness of the citizenry. Instead, Smith's position is that a commitment to the negative virtue of justice (TMS II.ii.3–4, 86), the 'respectable virtues of industry and frugality' (VI.iii.13, 242) together with what Smith calls the virtue of 'inferior prudence' (VI.i.14, 216) are all, together with fuller representation (WN IV.vii.c.77–9, 624–6, and IV.vii.b.50–1, 584–5), that's required in this modern, moderate republicanism (see Fleischacker 2004: 246–9 and, especially, Montes 2003: 58–69). Of course, this presupposes that the public-spirited philosopher can influence the legislator to create the correct institutional framework for the system of 'natural liberty' (Brubaker, Chapter 8 above). Book V of WN is devoted to this project (Rosenberg 1960; Schliesser 2005a).

Of course, Smith disagrees importantly with Rousseau's claims in the translated passages from the *Second Discourse* in at least three further ways. First, Rousseau thinks that tranquillity is available only in the state of nature; he upholds the ideal of a self-sufficient, authentic man. (Rousseau does not use the term 'authentic' but we have seen him criticize (in Smith's translation) the 'false and artificial' appearances of civilized man.) Smith, however, claims that various forms of tranquillity *can* be available in society to prudent men, who through 'continual, though small accumulations' better themselves (TMS VI.i.11–13, 215–16; on tranquillity as a source of happiness, e.g. TMS III.3.30–3, 149–52; III.5.6, 166; I.ii.3.7, 37), and especially mathematicians and (natural) philosophers (III.2.20, 124ff.). Smith believes the former may become tranquil because they live within their means and avoid upheaval. Smith thinks men of theory are tranquil because the norms of their success are not dependent on 'public opinion'; they are not withdrawn from the world, but they can experience the satisfaction of knowing that their success in it is justified. Of course, not everybody in society can achieve tranquillity; in TMS, Smith talks of the 'vain splendour of successful ambition' (VI.i.13, 216) that causes men to elude tranquillity, while in WN 'the mean rapacity . . . of merchants and manufacturers' is singled out for such failure (IV.iii.c.9, 493; Cf. Mirowski 1989: 161).[20]

Second, Smith disagrees with Rousseau that the invention of property inevitably must lead to (vast) inequality; this depends on the institutional framework and policies (WN I.10). For Smith, the invisible hand *can* in the right circumstances be a force for *some* equalization (at least in TMS IV.i.10, 185). Smith is acutely aware of various sorts of market failure (Pack 1991), but he believes that movement towards the system of 'natural liberty' (WN IV.ix.51, 687, and I.x.c59, 157) will be a boon to mankind, especially the working poor.[21]

Third, in the passage leading up to the invocation of the invisible hand in TMS, Smith *appears* to imply that a Rousseauian view, that civilized life is a 'contemptible and trifling . . . deception', is false; this is just an 'abstract and philosophical light' (see also TMS I.iii.3, 52–3). Smith appears to be attacking the philosophers' tendency to look down on our ordinary lives, and it fits nicely with his view that philosophers are themselves part of the division of labor. Moreover, against Rousseau, Smith *seems* to be siding with nature's deception: 'it is well that nature imposes upon us in this manner'.[22] The deception of our imagination is that 'pleasures of wealth and greatness' are 'something grand and beautiful and noble, of which the attainment is well worth all the toil and anxiety which we are so apt to bestow upon it'. Many have seen in this Smith's endorsement of commercial society. But Smith's position is a bit more complicated.

Recall the following fragment from the first of Smith's translated passages:

> from the instant in which one man had occasion for the assistance of another, from the moment that he perceived that it could be advantageous to a single person to have provisions for two, equality disappeared, property was introduced, labour became necessary, and the vast forests of nature were changed into agreeable plains, which must be watered with the sweat of mankind, and in which the world beheld slavery and wretchedness begin to grow up and blossom with the harvest.
>
> (13, 252)

As the editors of TMS point out, following a suggestion by H. B. Acton, this is echoed by Smith:

> We are then charmed with the beauty of that accommodation which reigns in the palaces and oeconomy of the great; and admire how every thing is adapted to promote their ease, to prevent their wants, to gratify their wishes, and to amuse and entertain their most frivolous desires. If we consider the real satisfaction which all these things are capable of affording, by itself and separated from the beauty of that arrangement which is fitted to promote it, it will always appear in the highest degree contemptible and trifling. But we rarely view it in this abstract and philosophical light. We naturally confound it in our imagination with the order, the regular and harmonious movement of the system, the machine or oeconomy by means of which it is produced. The pleasures of wealth and greatness, when considered in this complex view, strike the imagination as something grand and beautiful and noble, of which the attainment is well worth all the toil and anxiety which we are so apt to bestow upon it.
>
> And it is well that nature imposes upon us in this manner. It is this deception which rouses and keeps in continual motion the industry of mankind. It is this which first prompted them to cultivate the ground, to build houses, to found cities and commonwealths, and to invent and improve all the sciences and arts, which ennoble and embellish human life; which have entirely changed the whole face of the globe, have turned the rude forests of nature into agreeable and fertile plains, and made the trackless and barren ocean a new fund of subsistence, and the great high road of communication to the different nations of the earth.
>
> (TMS IV.1.9–10, 183–4)

I quote at length not merely to show that Smith may have echoed a few words (forests are changed into plains) of Rousseau in the lines just before he introduced the invisible hand metaphor in TMS. (Rousseau even mentions an 'invisible hand' in his own Note VI.5, OC III, 200, but the context is very different from the uses Adam Smith gives that famous phrase.) In an important sense, Smith is *agreeing* with Rousseau that from a certain vantage point civilization is a 'contemptible and trifling . . . deception', that is, the product of the vain desires of our imagination. But according to Smith, 'this abstract and philosophic light' is not likely to tempt most of us in a state of health; we are more likely to be overcome by this 'splenetic philosophy . . . in time of sickness or low spirits' (TMS IV.i.9, 183; at III.2.27, 127, Smith also uses the phrase 'splenetic philosophers' and is probably referring to Mandeville, but see Hume's *Treatise* 1.4.7.10).

Somebody with more than a passing familiarity with the *Second Discourse* may be surprised that, on behalf of Smith, I attribute to Rousseau an 'abstract and philosophic' point of view. After all, even in the *Second Discourse,* Rousseau often takes the side of our natural passions against the facile, even vanity-producing (cf. WN I.ii.4, 29), abstract reasoning of philosophers (e.g. Part I.37–8, OC III, 156–7, where Rousseau is discussing Mandeville, and Note XVI1, OC III, 220); such passages read very much like Smith's philosophy. In fact, one such occurrence takes place just before the third long passage that Smith quoted from the *Second Discourse.* But Rousseau goes on to say that the 'attentive reader' will explain why 'Society no longer affords to the eyes of the wise man anything but an assemblage of artificial men and factitious passion which are the product of all these new relationships, and have no true foundation in Nature' (Part II.57, OC III, 192). It would not be strange, thus, that Smith identifies the splenetic and abstract philosophic light, the view that society is a *mere* assemblage of artificial men, with Rousseau's position.[23]

Smith thinks the *rejection* by *most* people of the detached and abstract view is a good thing most of the time. For Smith, this rejection is caused by the way our natures allow ourselves to be deceived by our imagination: it 'rouses and keeps in continual motion the industry of mankind' (TMS IV.i.10, 183).[24] This is why I originally suggested that Smith is disagreeing with Rousseau.

But Smith is speaking from a point of view in which nature's 'deception' can be *identified* and *evaluated.* This is neither 'splenetic philosophy' nor our common point of view. It would be difficult to see how conventional morality could allow for this theoretical point of view because it so clearly suggests that our conventional moral aims are a 'deception' of the 'imagination' (TMS IV.i.9–10, 183). Rather it is the standpoint I have been calling the theoretical viewpoint. Of course, Smith admits it is 'rare' (TMS IV.i.9, 183) and unpopular to adopt the theoretical viewpoint: 'A philosopher is company to a philosopher only; the member of a club, to his own little knot of companions' (TMS I.ii.2.6, 34). Philosophers seek the friendship and admiration of other philosophers: one 'may say with Parmenides, who, upon reading a philosophical discourse before a public assembly at Athens, and observing, that, except Plato, the whole company had left him, continued, notwithstanding, to read on, and said that Plato alone was audience sufficient for him' (VI.iii.31, 253).

Smith endorses nature's deception.[25] For *some* of the unintended achievements of civilization, i.e. the arts and sciences, 'ennoble' our lives (IV.i.10, 183; see also his defense of luxury as producing 'refinement in the arts' at VII.ii.4.12, 313). Smith does not conflate our 'frivolous desires' (IV.i.9, 183) with the noble ones. It is nature's deception that first makes *possible* the noble and finer things in life; our ordinary frivolous and vain desires enable the creation of more noble things! (It is not the only deception that Smith endorses. Pack 2000: 51 calls attention to TMS I.i.1.13, 13, where in a very Hobbesian fashion the fear of death causes 'the great restraint upon the injustice of mankind'. See also Cropsey 1957.) So, not only does Smith think that Rousseau does not give a balanced enough view of the life of the savage by omitting the dangers he faces, but Smith also believes that there are elements of civilization, the arts and sciences, which develop under the rule of law and a host of social institutions (including the division of labor, universities, men of fashion, etc.), that are *worth defending from a theoretical viewpoint*. For our present purposes it is not important to what degree Rousseau rejected this theoretical point of view;[26] Smith is combating Rousseau's *rhetoric*, which seems to reject not merely commercial life, but also its *ennobling by-products*. Smith offers an endorsement of commercial life as a *means to philosophy* (broadly conceived). Of course, this does not prevent an endorsement of commercial life on other grounds (e.g. its role in reducing poverty, the dignity of the poor, or promoting national security).

There is an irony here: Smith's adoption of the theoretical viewpoint is, I think, an instance where the tranquillity of the philosopher does not depend on general public opinion, but on a very narrow public (recall Parmenides and Plato). It is the moment when the philosopher becomes nearly self-sufficient. So, from the point of view of common life, philosophy is just one of many trades, permitting and enabled by the achievement of 'interdependent independence'. But when the philosopher manages 'to observe every thing' – be it the achievements of a Newton or the workings of society – the philosopher will *feel* self-sufficient (cf. the description of how 'independency' is achieved at TMS III.2.20, 12).

Smith's (rare) adoption of this theoretical viewpoint[27] shows that Smith's advocacy of the marketplace of life is by no means straightforward. Smith follows Hume's example; commercial life is justified because it enables a life of philosophy. (See also Schliesser 2003). Strictly speaking, philosophers need not 'do any thing', but their self-interest drives them to public-spiritedness. If the philosopher is prudent, commercial society solves the Socratic Problem. Sometimes Smith, the humane and benevolent philosopher, endorses the deceptions of our imaginations, grounded as they are in ordinary 'frivolous' self-interest, from a point of view more elitist and self-interested.[28]

Notes

I thank Christopher Berry, Doug den Uyl, Abe Stone, Maria Paganelli, Ryan Hanley, Sam Fleischacker, Fonna Forman-Barzilai, James Buchanan, Sandy Peart, David Levy, Larry Mary, Marilyn Friedman, Ali Khan, Steve Viner, and audiences at Washington University for helpful comments on an earlier draft. Moreover, I must acknowledge a debt to Lauren Brubaker and Spencer Pack for innumerable conversations about Smith's conception of philosophy. Leon Montes is to blame for any remaining mistakes in this chapter.

1 See Newton's 'Preface' to *Principia*: 'I consider philosophy ... and write not concerning manual but natural powers and consider chiefly those things which relate to gravity, levity, elastic force, the resistance of fluids, and the like forces, whether attractive or impulsive; and therefore we offer this work as mathematical principles of philosophy, for the whole burden of philosophy seems to consist in this – from the phenomena of motions to investigate the forces of nature, and then from these forces to demonstrate the other phenomena.'

2 Mirowski (1989, 164), while widely read (and entertaining), is highly misleading when suggesting that Smith wanted to divert our attention away from Newton's action-at-a-distance. Not only does Mirowski quote two passages out of context (in which there is no mention of Newton at all), but he also fails to address the passages in which Smith does discuss Newton's principles! One would never know from Mirowski's account that, besides the passages quoted in the text, Smith also writes ('Astronomy', IV.67), 'He [Newton] demonstrated, that, if the Planets were supposed to gravitate towards the Sun, and to one another'.

3 Buckle (2001: 85ff.) reads Hume's remarks as an echo of Newton's famous 'hypotheses non fingo' and, thus, that Hume's (be it instrumental or skeptical realist) position is quite compatible with Newton's. On my reading, Hume is correct to state that by Newton's own lights (and in fact) Newton had 'shewed the imperfections of mechanical philosophy'. But Buckle does not realize that 'Hypothesis non fingo' is a rejection of the norms of evaluation and, especially, criteria of intelligibility promoted by the mechanical philosophy. For Newton one can accept the reality and intelligibility of forces even if one cannot provide an underlying 'physical-mechanical' (to use Kantian terminology) account because Newton rejects the demand for one. But this does not mean that for Newton nature's secrets will therefore remain, in principle, unknowable for ever. (As the queries to the *Opticks* reveal, Newton thinks that it is worth while to speculate about all kinds of potential causal explanations of the phenomena.) Thus, it is far too strong to assert that this means that Newton does not think there is no need to look for further, underlying causes, or that they will remain unavailable on epistemic grounds. (Cf. Strawson 2002: 237 and 247–8.) I thank William Vanderburgh for discussion.

4 This passage is ignored by those, e.g. Cropsey (1957: 7–9) and Griswold (1999), who claim that Smith believed that philosophy is not itself an end. Such a position seems to be suggested by TMS I.i.4.5, 21, but even it ends with: 'The idea of the utility of all qualities of this kind [i.e. the intellectual sentiments], is plainly an after-thought, and not what first recommends them to our approbation.' For useful remarks see Fleischacker (2004: 69).

5 It is sometimes said (see the references to Cropsey and Griswold in the previous note) that Smith neglects the intellectual sentiments in TMS, but as my discussion above and below of TMS I.i.4.3, 20, shows, Smith introduces treatment of these and the theoretical life early into TMS. Given that he diagnoses society's hostility to the theoretical life (see my treatment of 'Astronomy' IV.4,

55–6; WN V.i.f.4; TMS IV.2.7, 189, below), his relative reticence to explore it more fully in a work aimed at a wide public fits his general outlook.

6 Smith remarks in another essay, 'Ancient Physics' (9, 113), that the Pythagoreans were members of 'a sect, which, in the antient world, was never regarded as irreligious'. Smith never makes clear here that the Pythagoreans were the 'Italian school' mentioned in the 'Astronomy'. In context, Smith's wording seems to suggest that in modern times the Pythagoreans were regarded as atheists. (For a similar view, see Hume's treatment of polytheism in chapter IV of *Natural History of Religion.*)

7 The argument of this section leans heavily on Schliesser (2005b), where I give a much more extensive account of the epistemological role of the impartial spectator.

8 The editors of 'Astronomy' take Smith to task for this statement. They ignore the importance of the astronomic engagement with Copernicus to the general philosophic outlook of such luminaries as Stevin, Galileo, Gilbert, and Kepler, who were all unusually early Copernicans by the end of the sixteenth century. For a very provocative book on this topic, see Margolis (2002).

9 According to *OED,* in Smith's time 'direct' can mean to 'guide/lead with advice' or to 'give authoritative instructions'.

10 Hume shows how 'imaginary' standards of perfection can 'naturally' be constructed by individuals. Hume's essay, 'Of the Dignity or the Meanness of Human Nature', contains a discussion of several sources for notions of perfection (cf. *Treatise* 1.2.4.29, for qualifications). See Frasca-Spada (1998: 44–5).

11 Lauren Brubaker called my attention to the importance of this issue for Smith; see Smith's letter No. 40 to Sir Gilbert Elliot (Corr. 49); see Schliesser (2003).

12 Smith does not mention the possible importance of technology as a motor of change in the 'Astronomy'. Yet, his claim that the Eudoxan system of concentric spheres might 'have stood the examination of all ages, and have gone down triumphant to the remotest posterity' had there been 'no other bodies discoverable in heaven' (IV.4, 56) is based on the fact that they did become visible after the invention of the telescope; it also is further evidence for his realist stance toward discoveries of science.

13 The editors of 'Astronomy' point to Plato's *Theaetetus* (155D) and Aristotle's *Metaphysics,* A (982b11–24).

14 Smith practices this too; it is known that in the 1760s he discussed political (especially pertaining to American colonies) and economic matters with Lord Shelburne, who was Secretary of State in Britain, see Rae (1895: chapter XV).

15 It is not clear if Rousseau was made aware of Smith's comments. In *Confessions* VIII, Rousseau writes about the reception of the *Second Discourse* that 'in all of Europe [it] found only a very few readers who understood it, and of those none wished to talk about it' (OC I, 388). Berry (1989, 1992) and Pack (2000) are useful introductory treatments of Smith's relationship to Rousseau. Here I am largely concerned with how Smith may have understood Rousseau, although occasionally I offer a different interpretation of Rousseau. In preparing this chapter, I benefited from reading Berry's (2004) then unpublished review, of Force (2003), and Hanley's (n.d.) very insightful paper on Smith's response to Rousseau. My treatment cannot do justice to Force's complex and provocative arguments.

16 Smith is clearly using 'pathetic' in the traditional sense of 'exciting the passions or affections; moving, stirring, affecting', while by 'nervousness' he probably means something close to 'vigorous, powerful, forcible' (*OED*).

17 During the fallout over the Rousseau–Hume controversy, Smith urged Hume not to attempt to 'unmask' Rousseau 'before the Public', suggesting that Hume

ran the risk 'of disturbing the tranquility of [his] whole life' (Smith's Correspondence, Letter No. 93, 113).

18 Pack (2000, 46–7 and 55) believes that Smith's use of sympathy is a generalization of Rousseau's use of pity; Pack cites TMS I.i.1.5, 10. I read the passage as a warning not to conflate pity and sympathy. For important discussion of Smith's account of sympathy, see Darwall (1998: 264–9) and Levy and Peart (forthcoming).

19 Rousseau's positive views about what is desirable and good for modern man are not clear in the *Second Discourse*. It is unfortunate that we do not have reliable information on how Smith responded to *Emile* or *Social Contract*.

20 Smith appears to think that by nature's *telos* man is a farmer. Under politically stable conditions 'independency' is 'really' available in the countryside for Smith, but it is considered a 'primitive' form of employment even if present in later stages (WN III.i.3, 378). Certain parts of *Emile* read as if Rousseau is advocating rural republicanism. It is true that in WN no examples are given of folks that actually achieve tranquillity; this could tempt one to argue that TMS and WN contradict each other on this point. But as WN III.i.3, 378 and IV.iii.c.9, 493 show, Smith still recognizes it as the aim in life, and nothing he says suggests he has changed his mind on those occupations that do achieve tranquillity.

21 Malthus was the first to note this. This is fast becoming the established view (Pack 1991; Rothschild 2002; Fleischacker 2004). Rousseau's *Discourse on Political Economy* is an unexplored source of Adam Smith's redistributionist strategies.

22 Pack (2000: 49–50) cites Rousseau's Note IX, OC III, 202, to suggest that Rousseau, too, endorses the deception, but the passage expresses the contrary assertion.

23 Of course, Smith never says he has Rousseau in mind here; maybe he is just thinking of Stoicism. I accept Rothschild's (2002), Montes's (2003), and (Fleischacker's 2004: 120) position (against Brown 1994, and many other commentators) that Smith is a subtle critic of Stoicism, but I first learned this in conversation with Lauren Brubaker.

24 It is my impression that for Rousseau the 'voice of nature' can never lie.

25 On may think that this makes Smith's defense of commercial life morally problematic: it may look as if commercial life becomes a deceptive means of satisfying the (elitist) ends of few. This would violate (among other things) the demand for equal recognition identified in Smith's moral theory (see Darwall 2004 and Schliesser 2006). I cannot adequately address this here, but it is worth emphasizing that the deception does not involve commercial life in general, but *only* 'the pleasures of wealth and greatness ... [that] strike the imagination as something grand and beautiful and noble'. The confusion over what is truly grand and beautiful and noble leaves plenty of room for a justification of ordinary commercial activity.

26 In *Observation by Jean-Jacques Rousseau of Geneva on the Answer made to his Discourse*, a response to criticism of the *First Discourse*, Rousseau wrote: 'Science in itself is very good, that is obvious; and one would have to have taken leave of good sense, to maintain the contrary' (7, OC III, 36).

27 Smith *complains* about Johnson's dictionary that it was *not theoretical enough*, and he offers examples of how a 'sufficiently grammatical' dictionary ('Review of Johnson's Dictionary', 1, 232–3 in EPS) would classify and distinguish different words.

28 Of course, this very narrow elitism is compatible with many forms of political, normative, and economic equality, and my argument does not undermine Fleischacker's claims about Smith in those respects.

References

Berry, Christopher J. (1989) 'Adam Smith: commerce, liberty and modernity', in P. Gilmour (ed.) *Philosophers of the Enlightenment*, Edinburgh: Edinburgh University Press.

—— (1992) 'Adam Smith and the Virtues of Commerce', in J. Chapman and W. Galston (eds) *Virtue*, New York: New York University Press.

—— (1997) *Social Theory of the Scottish Enlightenment*, Edinburgh: Edinburgh University Press.

—— (2004) 'Smith under Strain', *European Journal of Political Theory* 3: 455–63.

—— (forthcoming) 'Adam Smith and Science', in Knud Haakonssen (ed.) *Cambridge Companion to Smith*, Cambridge: Cambridge University Press.

Brown, Vivienne (1994) *Adam Smith's Discourse: Canonicity, Commerce, Conscience*, London: Routledge.

Brubaker, Lauren (2003) '"A Particular Turn or Habit of the Imagination": Adam Smith on Love, Friendship, and Philosophy', in Eduardo Velasquez (ed.) *Love and Friendship: Rethinking Politic and Affection in Modern Times*, Lanham, MD: Lexington Books.

Buckle, Stephen. (1999) 'Hume's Biography and Hume's Philosophy: "My Own Life" and *An Enquiry concerning Human Understanding*', *Australasian Journal of Philosophy* 77 (1): 1–25.

—— (2001) *Hume's Enlightenment Tract: the Unity and Purpose of An Enquiry Concerning Human Understanding*, Oxford: Oxford University Press.

Carrasco, Maria Alejandra (2004) 'Adam Smith's Reconstruction of Practical Reason', *The Review of Metaphysics* 58: 81–116.

Cremaschi, Sergio (1989) 'Adam Smith: Skeptical Newtonianism, Disenchanted Republicanism, and the Birth of Social Science', in M. Dascal and O. Gruengard (eds) *Knowledge and Politics: Case Studies in the Relationship between Epistemology and Political Philosophy*, Boulder, CO: Westview Press, 83–110.

Cropsey, Joseph (1957) *Polity and Economy: an Interpretation of the Principles of Adam Smith*, The Hague: Nijhoff.

D'Alembert, Jean le Rond (1995) *Preliminary Discourse to the Encyclopedia of Diderot*, Chicago: University of Chicago Press.

Darwall, Stephen (1998) 'Empathy, Sympathy, and Care', *Philosophical Analysis* 89: 261–82.

—— (2004) 'Equal Dignity in Adam Smith' *Adam Smith Review* 1: 129–34.

Dent, N. J. H. (1988) *Rousseau*, Oxford: Blackwell.

Fleischacker, Samuel (1999) *A Third Concept of Liberty: Judgment and Freedom in Kant and Adam Smith*, Princeton, NJ: Princeton University Press.

—— (2004) *On Adam Smith's* Wealth of Nations*: A Philosophical Companion*, Princeton, NJ: Princeton University Press.

Force, Pierre (2003) *Self-interest before Adam Smith: a Genealogy of Economic Science*, Cambridge: Cambridge University Press.

Frasca-Spada, Marina (1998) *Space and Self in Hume's Treatise*, Cambridge: Cambridge University Press.

Gerschlager, Caroline (2002) 'Is (Self-)Deception an Indispensable Quality of Exchange? A New Approach to Adam Smith's Concept', in C. Gerschlager (ed.) *Expanding the Economic Concept of Exchange: Deception, Self-deception and Illusions*, Boston, MA and Dordrecht: Kluwer, 27–52.

Griswold, Charles L. (1999) *Adam Smith and the Virtues of Enlightenment*, Cambridge: Cambridge University Press.

Haakonssen, Knud (1981) *The Science of the Legislator: the Natural Jurisprudence of David Hume and Adam Smith*, Cambridge: Cambridge University Press.

Hanley, Ryan. (2002) 'Hume's Last Lessons: The Civic Education of "My Own Life"', *Review of Politics* 64: 660 and 682–4.

—— (n.d.) 'Capitalism and Corruption: Rousseau's Diagnosis and Adam Smith's Cure'. Manuscript.

Heath, Eugene (1998) 'Mandeville's Bewitching Engine of Praise', *History of Philosophy Quarterly* 15: 205–26.

Levy, David M. (1988) 'The Market for Fame and Fortune', *History of Political Economy* 20: 615–25

—— (1992) *Economic Ideas of Ordinary People: from Preferences to Trade*, London: Routledge.

—— (1995) 'The Partial Spectator in the *Wealth of Nations*: a Robust Utilitarianism', *European Journal of the History of Economic Thought* 2 (2): 299–326.

—— and Peart, Sandra J. (forthcoming) 'Sympathy and Approbation in Hume and Smith: A Solution to the Other Rational Species Problem', *Economics and Philosophy*.

Livingston, Donald W. (1998) *Philosophical Melancholy and Delirium: Hume's Pathology of Philosophy*, Chicago: University of Chicago Press.

Lomonaco, Jeffrey (2002) 'Adam Smith's Letter to the Authors of the *Edinburgh Review*', *Journal of the History of Ideas* 63: 659–76.

Margolis, Howard (2002) *It Started with Copernicus: How Turning the World Inside Out Led to the Scientific Revolution*, New York: McGraw-Hill.

Millican, Peter (ed.) (2002) *Reading Hume on Human Understanding*, Oxford: Oxford University Press.

Mirowski, Philip (1989) *More Heat than Light: Economics as Social Physics, Physics as Nature's Economics*, Cambridge: Cambridge University Press.

Montes, Leonidas (2003) 'Smith and Newton: some Methodological Issues regarding General Economic Equilibrium Theory', *Cambridge Journal of Economics* 27: 723–47.

—— (2004) *Adam Smith in* Context: *A Critical Reassessment of Some Central Components of His Thought*, London: Palgrave Macmillan.

—— (2006) 'Adam Smith: Real Newtonian and Supposed Father of General Economic Equilibrium Theory', in Sheila Dow and Alistair Dow (eds) *History of Scottish Political Economy*, London: Routledge.

Newton, Isaac, (1999) *The Principia: Mathematical Principles of Natural Philosophy*, trans. I Bernard Cohen and Anne Whitman, Berkeley, CA: University of California Press.

Otteson, James. (2002) *Adam Smith's Marketplace of Life*, Cambridge: Cambridge University Press.

Pack, Spencer. (1991) *Capitalism as a Moral System: Adam Smith's Critique of the Free Market Economy*. Brookfield, VT: Elgar.

—— (2000) 'The Rousseau–Smith Connection: Towards an Understanding of Professor West's "Splenetic Smith"', *History of Economic Ideas* 8 (2): 35–62.

Peart, Sandra and Levy, David M. (2005) *From Equality to Hierarchy: The 'Vanity of the Philosopher' in Post-classical Economics*, Ann Arbor, MI: University of Michigan Press.

Quine, W. V. O. (1969) 'Epistemology Naturalized', in *Ontological Relativity and Other Essays,* New York: Columbia University Press.

Rae, John (1895) *Life of Adam Smith,* London: Macmillan.

Rosenberg, Nathan (1960) 'Some Institutional Aspects of the *Wealth of Nations*', *Journal of Political Economy* 68: 557–70.

Ross, Ian Simpson (1995) *The Life of Adam Smith,* Oxford: Clarendon Press.

Rothschild, Emma (2002) *Economic Sentiments: Adam Smith, Condorcet, and the Enlightenment,* Cambridge, MA: Harvard University Press.

Schliesser, Eric (2003) 'The Obituary of a Vain Philosopher: Adam Smith's Reflections on Hume's Life', *Hume Studies* 29 (2): 327–62.

—— (2004) 'Hume's Missing Shade of Blue, Reconsidered from a Newtonian Perspective', *Scottish Journal for Philosophy* 2 (2): 164–75.

—— (2005a) 'Some Principles of Adam Smith's Newtonian Methods in *Wealth of Nations*', *Research in History and Methodology of Economics* 23A: 35–77.

—— (2005b) 'Realism in the Face of Scientific Revolutions: Adam Smith on Newton's "Proof" of Copernicanism', *British Journal for the History of Philosophy* 13 (4): 697–732.

—— (2006) 'Articulating Practices as Reasons: Adam Smith on the Social Conditions of Possibility of Property', *Adam Smith Review,* 2 (in press).

—— (n.d. a) 'Berkeley's Response to Newton' (under review).

—— (n.d. b) 'Hume's Attack on Newton's Philosophy' (under review).

—— and Pack, Spencer (2006) 'Adam Smith's "Humean" Criticism of Hume's Account of Origin of Justice', *Journal for the History of Philosophy* 44 (1): 47–63.

Skinner, Andrew (1996) *A System of Social Science: Papers relating to Adam Smith,* 2nd edn, Oxford: Clarendon Press.

Skinner, A. S. and Wilson, T. (eds) (1975) *Essays on Adam Smith,* Oxford: Clarendon Press.

Starobinski, Jean (1988) *Jean-Jacques Rousseau: Transparency and Obstruction,* trans. Arthur Goldhammer, intro. Robert J. Morrissey, Chicago: University of Chicago Press.

Stein, Howard (1988) '*Logos,* Logic, and *Logistikē*: Some Philosophical Remarks on Nineteenth Century Transformations of Mathematics', in William Aspray and Philip Kitcher (eds) *Minnesota Studies in the Philosophy of Science XI, History and Philosophy of Modern Mathematics,* Minneapolis, MN: University of Minnesota Press.

—— (forthcoming) 'How does Physics bear upon Metaphysics; and why did Plato hold that Philosophy cannot be written down?'

Strawson, Galen (2002) 'David Hume: Objects and Power', in Millican.

Uyl, D. J. den and Griswold, C. L., Jr (1996) 'Adam Smith on Friendship and Love', *Review of Metaphysics* 49: 609–37.

Wightman, D. (1975) 'Adam Smith and the History of Ideas' in A. S. Skinner and T. Wilson (eds) 1975) *Essays on Adam Smith,* Oxford: Clarendon Press.

Wright, John P. (1983) *The Sceptical Realism of David Hume,* Minneapolis, MN: University of Minnesota Press.

Index